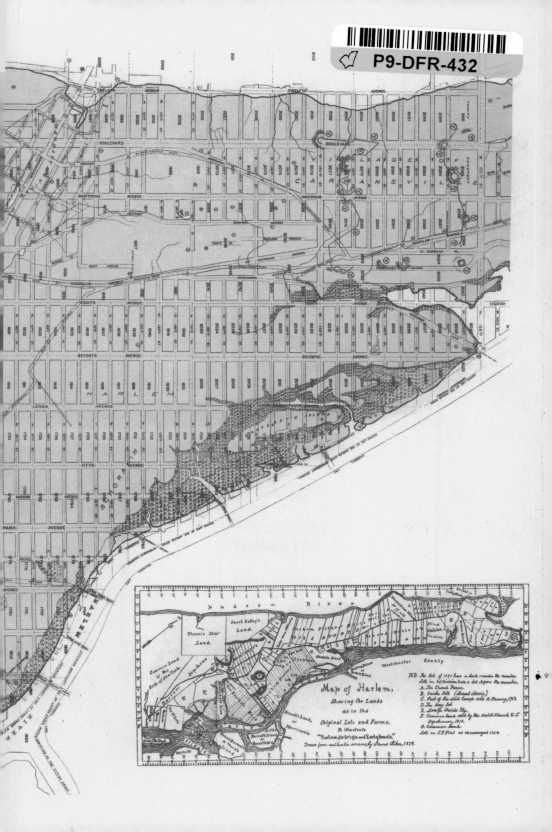

HARLEM

THE FOUR HUNDRED YEAR HISTORY FROM DUTCH VILLAGE TO CAPITAL OF BLACK AMERICA

JONATHAN GILL

Grove Press
New York

Copyright © 2011 by Jonathan Gill

Published simultaneously in Canada
Printed in the United States of America

FIRST EDITION

ISBN-13: 978-0-8021-1910-0

Grove Press
an imprint of Grove/Atlantic, Inc.
841 Broadway
New York, NY 10003

Distributed by Publishers Group West

www.groveatlantic.com

11 12 13   10 9 8 7 6 5 4 3 2 1

For Eveline Ledeboer
Eisch alles, geef alles

CONTENTS

1

UNRIGHTEOUS BEGINNINGS

From Muscoota to Nieuw Haarlem, 1609–1664

The first Harlemites didn't quite know what to make of the strange object that sailed up the river in the late summer of 1609. Was it some sort of gigantic flying fish, or a huge swimming bird? And what of the strange, bearded creatures on board? Where did they come from? What did they want? As the earliest residents of the hilly island they called Manahatta would soon learn, the strange object was the *Half Moon*, a boat belonging to the Dutch East India Company and piloted by the English explorer Henry Hudson. For his part, Hudson seems to have been just as perplexed by the native creatures he saw lining the banks of the waterway they called Mahicanituk, or the River that Flows Both Ways.

Hudson had little time to get to know these people. He was already supposed to be in Asia, and he suspected that the silks and spices of China might lie just upstream. The *Half Moon*, an eighty-five-foot-long, shallow-bottomed boat suitable for ocean travel as well as for exploration of the uncharted North American rivers that might offer a shortcut to the riches of the Orient, had survived the terrors of the Atlantic crossing, but by the time Hudson first glimpsed what would become the city of New York on September 3, 1609, the vessel had wandered far off course. He anchored for several days at what is now Sandy Hook, in the lower New York bay, and sent a party ashore. There Hudson found the same fertile wilderness that he had seen all along the Atlantic coast that summer, with plenty of food and water for the taking. He also found copper-skinned people with black hair and black eyes—the men beardless, the women tall, all ready to trade and quick with laughter and anger. The encounter turned threatening and one member of the landing party was killed by an arrow while racing back to the *Half Moon*. Hudson and his crew of twenty pressed on to China.

By September 11, 1609, when the *Half Moon* entered the mile-wide river, the "great streame" that would eventually bear its captain's name, news of the strange vessel had already reached the indigenous inhabitants of the richly wooded lands just off starboard. Crowds of the natives, including women and children, filled canoes and fearlessly paddled alongside the ship, sensing an opportunity to trade with the crew, offering beans and oysters in return for beads and mirrors. Hudson ordered his men to keep their distance, but the next day he regained his confidence and, as the *Half Moon* reached the shores of the upper part of the island, he decided to anchor. The next morning, just off an inlet at what is now West 125th Street, a crowd of Indians again approached. At the invitation of Hudson, two climbed on board, staying long enough for Hudson to dress them in red jackets and then try to kidnap them. The two visitors broke free and jumped overboard, mocking Hudson and his crew from shore. The first Harlemites learned early on that white men were not to be trusted.

Hudson continued north, encountering numerous native people over the next eleven days, many of them far less suspicious than those downriver. As the mountains lining either side of the waterway grew higher the natives, who quickly fell under the influence of Hudson's wine, seemed ever more willing to swap their corn and pumpkins for trinkets, tools, or textiles. After a hundred miles it became clear that the narrowing river would not lead to Asia, so the captain turned the *Half Moon* around and headed downstream, away from the safety of the upper Hudson Valley and back down the river to more unpredictable territory.

On October 2, as the *Half Moon* passed what is now West 140th Street, the two natives that Hudson had tried to kidnap several weeks earlier led an attack on the ship which, like all East India Company vessels bore a brass tablet fixed to the forecastle reading "Do not fight without cause." Hudson now had cause. One of his crewmen wrote: "two Canoes full of men, with their Bows and Arrowes shot at us after our sterne: in recompense whereof we discharged six Muskets, and killed two or three of them." The natives were not deterred, and they sent another canoe full of men armed with bows and arrows. Hudson's men continued to fire their muskets, aiming their cannons at the Indians on the banks as well. By the time it was all over the blood of nine more native Harlemites stained the river's shores.

The encounters between Henry Hudson and the residents of northern Manhattan in 1609 were but a foretaste of Harlem's future. The clash of words and worlds, the allure of blood and money, the primacy of violence and fashion, the cohabitation of racial hatred and racial curiosity—they have always been part of what uptown means. But from its days as a frontier outpost, to the time when it seemed like the navel of the black universe, to the era when it became the official symbol of poverty in America, Harlem has always been more than a tragedy in the making. Uptown's reputation as the soul of the American century is indisputable. Yet even before the 1920s, when the distinctive beat of Harlem's drummers made the whole world march to a new, syncopated rhythm, Harlem featured one of the largest Jewish communities in the world, counting George Gershwin and Harry Houdini as residents. In the nineteenth century, Harlem represented Manhattan's future, as city planners built trolley, elevated train, and subway lines uptown in hopes of attracting a middle class that could provide the labor for New York's industrial revolution. Before that, John James Audubon, Aaron Burr, and Alexander Hamilton all looked to Harlem for respite from the relentless noise, filth, and danger of downtown Manhattan. In the eighteenth century, George Washington capitalized on his intimate knowledge of the area's topography—he had unsuccessfully wooed Martha's predecessor there years before—to defeat the British in the battle of Harlem Heights, one of the key early conflicts of the Revolutionary War. Peter Minuit's legendary purchase of Manhattan Island in 1626 took place uptown, not far from the fateful first contacts between Henry Hudson and local Indians in 1609. Through it all, Harlem's contending forces of power and protest, intention and improvisation, greed and generosity, and sanctity and suspicion decisively shaped the American character. In that history lies the map of Harlem's even more complex future, though the precise contours of the delicate and yet brutal imperatives of the uptown–downtown relationship, of the changing meanings of race and ethnicity, of the swinging dance of social crisis and economic opportunity have yet to be fixed.

It took millions of years to make Harlem—longer than money, religion, nationality, or race. By the time of Hudson's arrival, Harlem consisted of a broad, arable plain with thickly forested hills along its western boundary, but for countless eons the region had been buried under an enormous inland sea, until about 220 million years ago, when the Appalachian Mountains burst skyward, lifting most of what would become New York City above sea level. Dinosaurs, other reptiles, and mammals roamed northern Manhattan until cycles of warming and cooling entombed the island under a thousand-foot-high glacier moving south along the eastern seaboard. When the ice began receding about twenty thousand years ago, the runoff wore away both the mile-wide estuary that came to be called the Hudson River and the sluggish waterway now known as the Harlem River. As it retreated, the glacial ice also scraped away topsoil and exposed raw bedrock, leaving the soaring cliffs, majestic ridges, and gigantic boulders that still captivate Harlemites. Forests of birch and pine sprung up, followed by fir, spruce, chestnut, oak, maple, and hickory trees. Mastodons, saber-toothed tigers, bison, bear, and beavers attracted humans from across the Hudson River. These original Harlemites, who had been following their prey across the continent since crossing the Bering Strait about thirty-five thousand years ago, tilled the largest, flattest, most fertile spot on the island, a plain that stretched across the upper part of Manhattan. They also took to fishing on both sides of the island as well as in the hundred-foot-wide creek that cut diagonally across that plain and emptied into a marsh on the island's eastern shore.

In the seventeenth century, uptown's native people considered themselves members of the Wappinger band of the Lenni Lenape or Munsee Delaware group, all of whom were technically Algonquins, which is less an ethnic category than a linguistic classification that applies to all Native Americans of the eastern seaboard. Beyond this broad grouping it is hard to say which specific subgroup could be found in Harlem, nor is much known about their daily lives. Most of the information gathered directly from Harlem's Indians in the early seventeenth century was tainted by ignorance or prejudice, and few native informants survived the measles, smallpox, influenza, whooping cough, mumps, typhoid, and bubonic plague brought by the new arrivals. Many also died by the sword. In general the Dutch exhibited almost no interest in Indians beyond ways to make money from them. Where the Spanish and French explorers and settlers who claimed lands to the south and north saw souls waiting to be saved, and languages and customs worth understanding, the Dutch saw gullible rubes with no idea of the value of the beaver, otter, mink, and lynx pelts they plucked effortlessly from the wilderness. The first minister sent by the Dutch found the natives both "uncivil and stupid as garden poles" and "as thievish and treacherous as they are tall." Dutch settlers considered the Delaware language akin to the barking of dogs or the babbling of children. "Even those who can best of all speak with the Indians and get along well in trade," that minister wrote in 1628, "are nevertheless wholly in the dark and bewildered when they hear the Indians speaking with each other by themselves." That may have been deception on the part of the Indians, who in turn found the Dutch as stupid as they were ugly, hairy, smelly, and weak, and who taught the newcomers only enough of their language to gain an advantage in trade. In this respect the Dutch, handicapped by a crippling combination of colonial destiny, tragic incuriosity, and raw greed, had met their match.

It didn't seem that way at first. Harlem's natives had no knowledge of metallurgy, writing, or textiles. The men wore animal-skin breechcloths in the warm weather and the women had knee-length dresses. In the winter everyone wore moccasins with deerskin leggings and robes made from elk, deer, bear, beaver, or fox pelts. They adorned themselves with turkey feathers, painted abstract or animal designs, scarification, tattoos made from the juice of berries, and shell pendants or copper beads. Women greased their long hair with animal fat, while the men shaved with the edges of shells or burned the hair off their heads, except for a braid in back or a strip of hair that came to be known as a "mohawk." They led seminomadic lives, which meant there were few social conflicts based on material possessions. When hostilities did break out, Harlem's Indians put on war paint and adapted stone hunting tools for human adversaries, using bows and arrows, clubs, axes, spears, and knives; there were also special blades for scalping. In battle they proved proud, quick-witted, swift to rise to the defense of their loved ones, and virtually impervious to suffering. Tied to the stake to meet death by fire, Indians would sing boastfully about their bravery even as the flames engulfed them. Unlike the Dutch, these Indians practiced no slavery, although they did take women and children as prisoners of war. Such hostages were treated with respect—the Dutch observed no such graces—but male captives were routinely tortured, usually by the women. The important public roles given Indian women were evidence of their savagery, according to the Dutch, who understood the rationale behind women taking responsibility for agricultural activities, and who had no trouble recognizing the matrilineal descent of political leadership, but who were shocked at the prospect of negotiating military matters with females.

Dutch propaganda seeking to lure settlers to the territory called New Netherland emphasized the economic opportunities of supposedly unoccupied fertile farmlands uptown. In fact, as many as several hundred Indians farmed northern Manhattan. There were three main plots: Schorrakin in what is now central Harlem, Konykast in lower East Harlem, and Muscoota in what is now lower central Harlem, which included a warm-weather village—actually just a group of temporary huts—called Konaande Kongh, or "Place of the Waterfall at the Hill," referring to the waterway that still feeds Central Park's Harlem Meer. Winter camps were more substantial groups of circular or longhouses built with hickory frames and covered with bark. Several families lived in each house, sleeping on leaf and straw mats with fur blankets. Linking everything was a network of footpaths. The main trail from downtown, later transformed into the New England Post Road and then Broadway, came up the east side of the island, veered west into what is now Central Park, and forked at Konaande Kongh, with one branch heading to the East River, where another warm-weather village was set up at what is now East 125th Street. The other path led to the northernmost tip of the island.

The Dutch may have doubted the humanity of the Indians but they admired their mastery of Harlem's natural bounty. After an agricultural festival coinciding with the first full moon in February, Harlem's Indians reinhabited the huts that had been abandoned the year before and burned their fields in order to prepare them for the new season—the Dutch made a tradition out of watching the conflagrations from canoes in the Hudson. In March and April the women sowed corn, followed in May by beans that would grow up symbiotically along the corn stalks. Pumpkins, sunflowers, squash, tobacco, and melons were also in the ground before the arrival of summer. Spring was fishing season, with men using spears, milkweed nets, or lines with bone or stone hooks cast from the eastern and western shores of the island or from dugout canoes made from tulip trees. Harvest took place in September and October, with the corn and beans being combined in enormous ceramic pots to make succotash. They also ground corn into meal for a porridge called *sappaen*. Each autumn apple and plum trees bore fruit, and berries of all sorts were abundant. From December through February, most of the group moved north, to the winter hunting grounds of what is now Westchester County. The men who remained on the island were occupied with trade, repairing or building tools or homes, and also hunting birds and waterfowl with hickory bows and arrows. Deer were herded into the water and killed with stone knives, or forced one by one into narrow, palisaded passages and clubbed to death. Bears and wildcats were stalked in the forest and brought down with spears. Industrious as Harlem's natives were—they rotated plantings or raised certain crops side by side in order to maintain the soil's chemical balance—early-seventeenth-century observers still described upper Manhattan as an untouched paradise of natural fertility. One of Harlem's earliest European settlers described killing 170 blackbirds with a single blast of his shotgun. Nonetheless, on such a small island, game and firewood were easily exhausted, and by the time Europeans arrived most large animals seem to have been hunted to local extinction. The arrival of white men was both timely and tragic.

Because the Dutch were interested primarily in making money, they were baffled by the spirituality that dominated the lives of the first Manhattanites. Far from being a people "proficient in all wickedness and godlessness," serving "nobody but the Devil," as the Dutch believed, Harlem's Indians were committed monotheists, worshipping the god Manitou, who was responsible for animating all material things. This great spirit was generous, according to ancient beliefs, and could be supplicated with offerings that might bring victory in battle, a successful harvest, or a healing experience in a sweat bath. Manitou was also responsible for defeat and death, and funerals were among the most conspicuous of Indian rituals. Dutch accounts noted that while the men grieved in silence, the women wailed, tearing their hair and ripping at their skin. If it was a child being mourned, or a great warrior killed in battle, the women would shave off their hair and burn it, sometimes wearing black makeup to display their sorrow. Corpses were dressed splendidly in a sitting position, surrounded by food and tools for the journey in the hereafter, and placed in leafy graves that were buried under a large hill of dirt and stones. After the burial, there was a festival, and the names of the dead were never spoken again. There would be much silence to come.

Stories of bearded men who came from far away, carrying sticks that could spit thunder and lighting, had long been common among Harlem's inhabitants when Henry Hudson's *Half Moon* arrived. At least three explorers had left their marks in the region, but it wasn't until the dawn of the seventeenth century, with the English founding Jamestown in 1607 and the French settling Quebec in 1608, that Europe committed to the commercial potential of the New World. The English twice sent Hudson on missions to find a Northwest Passage before losing interest, but the Dutch still saw an opening. Hudson's employer on his third try was the Netherlands East India Company, a business founded in 1602 for the purpose of conducting the spice trade with Asia. The company's twenty-one-year charter covered the area from the Strait of Magellan to the Cape of Good Hope, a monopoly that carried with it the right to conquer and settle a quarter of the known world. The venture was enormously profitable almost from the start—by 1607 investors were receiving an annual 75 percent rate of return—so it could afford to take a chance on Hudson, a well-connected adventurer who counted among his friends John Smith, the hero of the Virginia colony. Politics also inspired the Dutch. When the *Half Moon* left Amsterdam, Hudson was representing not only the investors of the East India Company but the pride and anxiety of the Dutch Republic, whose citizens hoped that their presence in the Americas would allow the Netherlands to strike an indirect blow against the Spanish, who had so brutally occupied their country for four decades before recognizing Dutch independence in 1609.

Hudson was mostly good at getting lost. The 1609 voyage, with its bloody encounter at Harlem, was as unsuccessful as his two earlier attempts, at least in terms of finding the Northwest Passage. But his reports of fertile lands occupied by docile and gullible natives spurred the East India Company to invest more heavily in the region. The relative proximity of Hudson's discovery promised even greater opportunities than the Asia trade, leading to a clamor among investors for more vessels to explore the region and set up trading posts and settlements. North America may not have been a shortcut to the spices, dyes, and silks of Asia, but Hudson's reports of dense populations of beaver, otter, marten, muskrat, mink, and fox confirmed that there was plenty of money to be made in meeting the ever-growing demand in Europe for fur hats and cloaks.

Dutch merchants with ties to the East India Company outfitted a ship and sent it to Manhattan within weeks of the return of the *Half Moon* in late 1609, but there was no immediate attempt to capitalize on Hudson's discovery on a larger scale. It wasn't until two years later that a Dutch lawyer turned explorer named Adriaen Block explored Manhattan, buying furs from the Indians and kidnapping two of them for exhibition back in Europe. Two other Dutch adventurers also explored

Manhattan before 1613, when Block returned and glimpsed the village at East 125th Street before heading home to Amsterdam—he produced the first map to identify an island between the Hudson and East rivers and called it Manhattes. Block's map helped inspire the establishment of settlements on the southern tip of the island, though speculation persists that the first groups of fragile huts were actually located uptown.

While the English were putting down roots in Massachusetts and Virginia, the Dutch still considered Manhattan nothing more than a cash machine. That was supposed to change in 1618, when the Dutch instituted a policy of free trade along the northeastern seaboard, which meant that anyone who could afford to outfit a boat, fill it with men, and send it across the ocean was at liberty to do business in the region now called New Netherland. Not many took up the venture, but when hostilities with Spain revived in 1621 the Dutch decided to fight back economically, founding a new business enterprise modeled after the spectacularly successful East India Company. While previous Dutch efforts targeted the region from the Chesapeake Bay to Cape Cod, as well as up the Hudson, Delaware, and Connecticut rivers, the West India Company had a broader mandate: the entire western hemisphere of the known world. Moreover, the West India Company had almost unlimited powers, meaning not just economic activities like the trade in fur, tobacco, sugar, land, and slaves but politics, the military, and religion as well. It was essentially a for-profit nation.

It wasn't until a year later that the first five ships of the West India Company sailed for New Netherland. Agents scouted out business opportunities along the rivers, where they found Indians eager to barter fur and tobacco for tools and textiles. By 1623 there were enough investors to start planning a proper settlement at the mouth of the Hudson River, which was prey to neither the frigid winters of Massachusetts nor the sweltering, malarial summers of Virginia. Moreover, the raw materials that could be exported from New Netherland required no great investment of time and money. Unlike tobacco or rice, fur required little more than the cultivation of relations with expert hunters who were happy to do business.

By 1625 a handful of traders and a few dozen families, mostly French-speaking refugees from Flanders known as Walloons, had made the two-month journey across the ocean, settled at the southern tip of Manhattan, and named it New Amsterdam. They set up log and sod cabins, sided with chestnut bark, covered with thatched roofs, and topped off by the orange, white, and blue flag of the West India Company. The experience of the English in Massachusetts and Virginia made the West India Company aware of the dangers of sending settlers into the wilderness without proper preparation, so the tiny outpost was provided with everything needed to make it through the first harvest: saws, shovels, axes, panes of glass, wheels, plows, and millstones, as well as barley, wheat, and rye that could be cultivated on plots farmed by Indians on the island's northern plains. The company recruited enterprising, motivated workers, including a mason, a carpenter, and a blacksmith, assuring them that the dozens of company boats cruising the coasts of Africa, South America, and the West Indies would now be at the service of New Netherland, for both business and battle.

Money if possible and war if necessary were on the mind of the mustachioed gentleman who, on a summer day in 1626, stepped off a skiff moored in the salt marsh that lined the uptown banks of the Hudson River and sank in the mud. It covered the silver buckles of his boots, soaked his white silk stockings, and reached all the way to the bottom of his velvet breeches; he made sure the pistol and sword strapped to his lace and fur-trimmed waistcoat remained dry. By the time he clambered up the banks, Peter Minuit no longer quite looked the part of the director general of the flagship settlement of the West India Company. But it was the contents of the trunk he brought, not his uniform, that impressed the Indians waiting in a clearing in what is now Inwood Hill Park. As Minuit had previously arranged with Penhowitz, leader of the group of Indians, the Dutch offered sixty guilders' worth of knives, needles, scissors, axes, hoes, pots, blankets, beads, and buttons. In exchange, the West India Company would become the legal owner of the hilly sliver of island conveniently situated between the

fur-rich lands of the Lenape Indians to the north and the mouth of
New York Harbor, the gateway to Europe. It was an oral agreement,
and the exchange lasted only a few minutes, but it remains the founding
event of the city of New York and a central fact of American identity.
It was the first New York real estate deal and it was a steal.

There is no event more enshrined in the mythology of New
York, but little is known about it. The only verifiable account of the
transaction occurs in a letter written by Isaak de Rasières, the settlement's first commissary: "They have bought the island of Manhattes
from the wild men." Later, more expansive sources reveal that Minuit,
a failed diamond cutter and church deacon who only weeks before
had taken over the post of director general of New Netherland, was
at the time congratulated for his business instincts—this was, after all,
a man described by his own preacher as "a slippery fellow, who under
the painted mask of honesty" was "a compound of all iniquity and
wickedness." A trunk filled with sixty guilders' worth—the equivalent
of $2,000 today, not $24—of iron tools and cloth would have been extraordinarily valuable to a people who had no knowledge of the forge
or the loom, but in trade for those twenty-two thousand acres it is still
the ultimate real estate transaction. Four centuries of hindsight offer a
different perspective. It may have been Minuit, not the Indians, who
was duped, since he actually bought Manhattan from the Canarsie
Indians of Brooklyn. Then again, since Manhattan hosted a variety
of native communities, none of them permanent, there was no single
owner, and, even if there were, Indians had no concept of property
ownership as understood by the Europeans. Rather, their territorial
claims sprang from evidence of use as farmland or hunting ground;
no wonder the Indians accepted such a low bid. The officials of the
West India Company were ordered to pursue fair and mutual land
transactions, not "by craft or fraud, lest we call down the wrath of God
upon our unrighteous beginnings." The Indians labored under no such
burden, and when the Weckquaesgeeks of Harlem heard about the
deal between Minuit and the Canarsies, they, too, demanded a piece
of the action and got it. In this way Indians repeatedly sold Manhattan
to the Dutch, as a whole and in pieces, never really giving up title—a

title that they never recognized in the first place—until well into the eighteenth century. The Indians may have considered the concept of land ownership laughable but they were astute enough to master it.

Efforts by the West India Company to attract new immigrants to New Amsterdam made shrewd use of propaganda that contrasted the depleted soil of the Old World with an edenic New World whose stunning fecundity was matched only by the willingness of its native inhabitants to trade it all away for almost nothing. Still, the island that Minuit bought was no paradise, even to Europeans fleeing poverty, plague, political violence, and religious intolerance. Because Manhattan was apparently hunted out, depending on game bought from Indians was untenable and the crops the settlers planted failed to take. Better land was too far away and too vulnerable to Indian attack. But Minuit didn't worry too much about agriculture. Instead, he was determined to make a city out of a trading post that yet lacked a church or a brewery, which meant that it wasn't a place fit for living as far as most Dutch were concerned. The number of pelts sent back to Amsterdam soon doubled, but the ships arriving from Holland bearing necessities such as knives, axes, guns, hoes, wool, kettles, and fishhooks as well as luxuries like rum and gin came more and more infrequently. In 1628 there were no arrivals at all. Almost two decades after the Dutch had staked their claim, there were only 270 people living in New Amsterdam, with perhaps a few dozen traders roughing it up the river at Fort Orange, at what is today Albany. Efforts starting in 1630 to establish agricultural communities outside the safety of downtown failed, and Minuit was recalled to the Netherlands. The string of exceptionally poor leaders that followed didn't do much better. A star-shaped fort began to take shape at the southern tip of the island, but it was a fragile structure made of compacted earth, and the windmill inside for grinding corn and wheat was often in disrepair. The fur trade remained lucrative, but New Amsterdam was still a rough-and-tumble frontier outpost suited mostly to those who had little to lose.

Even as conditions in New Amsterdam stagnated, the West India Company continued to recruit potential investors and settlers. One of the people back in the Netherlands who had from the start followed the reports of the company's ventures in the New World, with its unlimited economic opportunity and religious freedom, was a man named Jesse de Forest, a Walloon wool dyer who had fled religious violence in France and ended up in the Dutch city of Leiden. In 1623, only a few weeks after the formation of the West India Company, de Forest had joined ten other explorers aboard a vessel bound for South America, where he would select a site for a city where he might make his fortune six days a week and spend the seventh giving thanks in a Protestant church. But after an extensive exploration of the Amazon River and the coast of what is now Guyana, a year filled with privation and illness, the group split up without having found a place to settle. Still, half of the men sailed back to Holland to gather their families and return with them. De Forest stayed behind, intent on farther exploring the region. By all accounts he was an extraordinary leader, making peace with and among warring tribes of native people, mapping the region, and scouting out the natural resources—primarily plants for coloring fabrics, a natural occupation for a dyer. But in October of 1624 he fell ill from sunstroke while canoeing and died.

We know about the New World adventures of Jesse de Forest only because of a diary—the manuscript moldered away unread in the British Museum for almost four centuries—kept by his twenty-five-year-old assistant on the voyage, Jean de la Montagne, a French-born Protestant who had studied to become a surgeon in Leiden before signing on with de Forest's expedition. After de la Montagne had seen to the Christian burial of his captain in Guyana he returned to Leiden, where he took up a position at the university's medical school. But Jesse de Forest's dream of founding a homeland in the New World was never far from his mind. De la Montagne rented a room from de Forest's widow and married his daughter, Rachel. In Jesse's sons, Hendrick and Isaack, he found ready partners for another enterprise in a more promising corner of the Dutch empire. A decade after Jesse de Forest's death, Hendrick de Forest applied to the West India Company for about two hundred acres of land uptown and signed on with his brother Isaack and Jean de la Montagne aboard the *Rennselaerwyck,* a ship loaded with settlers, livestock, and all the goods and tools necessary for a new life in the New World. Hendrick de Forest was confident enough to have taken a bride, Gertrude Bornstra, earlier that summer, and it was no doubt with a family of his own in mind that this practical man signed on as a salaried employee who would be able to claim ownership after working the land.

Bad weather and bad behavior—a ship-board brawl resulted in the deaths of a passenger and a drunken steward—meant that it took six months for the *Rennselaerwyck* to make it to the narrows that separate current-day Brooklyn from Staten Island. The captain hoisted the flags of the West India Company and the Netherlands and watched in wonder as more than a dozen whales escorted the ship as it drew close to Manhattan. On March 5, 1637, the *Rennselaerwyck* received the more traditional welcome of a deafening round of fire from cannons mounted at Fort Amsterdam. De la Montagne and his wife settled downtown, but the de Forest brothers didn't remain long in the relative comfort of the fort. The future was uptown, and Hendrick and Isaack took two servants who had also made the journey—a middle-aged wool washer named Willem Fredericks Bout and a sixteen-year-old orphan named Tobias Teunissen—loaded up barges with materials to build a house and barn, tools to farm the land, and guns to protect themselves from Indians, and sailed up the East River.

The two hundred acres that had been granted to Hendrick de Forest lay "between the hills and the kill," or between the cliffs of Morningside Heights and the Harlem Creek. Hendrick had done his homework in selecting the land that the Indians called Muscoota, or "flat place." The fields had long been farmed by Harlem's natives and required only sturdy fences to protect crops from scavenging animals. Hendrick's plot also had ready access to the Indian trails that led uptown and downtown and to the creek that served as a source of fresh water for the corn and tobacco that he planned to raise. There were also salt meadows near the Harlem River that produced the type of hay that the Dutch used to feed their cattle. But before he could accomplish much in the way of building a farmhouse and fencing in the fields, Hendrick was called back to the *Rennselaerwyck*, which had finished its business up the Hudson River and was continuing south to Virginia. Hendrick was still technically mate of the vessel, and so he was obliged to join the voyage. By the end of June the ship had reached Virginia, where the crew did some trading before making ready to return to New Amsterdam. But the southern Atlantic coast was a dangerous place in the summer, with malaria and other diseases claiming the lives of up to half of all European visitors. Hendrick fell ill on the way home and died on July 26, 1637, at the age of thirty-one. Like his father, he had survived perilous journeys across forbidding seas and among hostile natives only to die in bed. Harlem's first European settler—the first to commit to the island's uptown future—was dead and in the ground before the first harvest.

The future of Hendrick's investment was now up for grabs. His twenty-one-year-old brother, Isaack, was too young and inexperienced to take over the building and running of a plantation in the New World. The logical choice was none other than Jean de la Montagne, who was now going by the name Jan, a declaration of his Netherlandish sympathies. Since his arrival in New Amsterdam, he had been struggling to make ends meet, working as a candle maker before practicing medicine. Now de la Montagne moved uptown and began carrying out the dream of his old friend Jesse de Forest. He raised 159 guilders—about the value of two horses, or two pounds of sugar—by selling off Hendrick's personal effects. Then, with the assistance of the de Forest servants and African slaves, as well as several West India Company employees, de la Montagne oversaw the completion of an eighteen- by forty-two-foot farmhouse and barn. While most downtown houses during this period were crude structures made of earth and bark, this first uptown dwelling, with its log and clapboard walls and thatched roof, was intended to make a statement. Inside were three rooms grouped around an elaborate brick chimney that took a downtown mason ten days to install. De la Montagne hired an English carpenter to build a shed for curing tobacco and he completed another barn, located in back of the house and including stables for cows, horses, and sheep as well as a wide threshing floor, a sign that Hendrick de Forest had planted grain in addition to tobacco. The entire compound was surrounded by a stout palisade to protect against attack by wild animals, Indians, and maybe even the British, who had taken the place of the Spanish in the Dutch military imagination. De la Montagne also brought in the 1637 harvest: two hundred pounds of tobacco, which he sold for 135 guilders. That enabled him to stock the plantation for the coming winter with tools, a gun and ammunition, candles, clothing, and rope. He also bought food: meat, salted fish and eels, butter, oil, vinegar, corn, wheat, buckwheat, meal, pepper, and pumpkins. There was even enough money for a sailboat for trips downtown and a flat-bottomed scow for navigating the salt marshes of uptown's eastern shore.

One thing de la Montagne hadn't arranged was the matter of Hendrick de Forest's wife, who was still back in the Netherlands. Dutch widows in the seventeenth century often remarried hastily, especially if the deaths of their husbands left them in economic necessity. Gertrude de Forest now had a potentially valuable plantation—she was one of the few women who owned property on Manhattan—but only if she could find someone to run it. Her transatlantic engagement to a downtown settler named Andries Hudde may have been mutually venial. Since his arrival in New Netherland in 1629, Hudde had worked in a number of positions in the settlement, from money lender to town councillor to surveyor for the West India Company, which gave him an unparalleled knowledge of the topography of Manhattan. Hudde became perhaps the shrewdest, most active player in New Amsterdam's frenzied real estate market during this time, though not the most successful, given the numerous debt proceedings he lost before the town council. Even in the rough-and-tumble atmosphere of New Amsterdam in the seventeenth century Hudde spelled trouble, but Gertrude de Forest read opportunity. By the early summer of 1638 they had reached a long-distance agreement to marry. In order to protect his new claim to the de Forest lands while en route to the wedding back in the Netherlands, Hudde applied for legal title to the two hundred acres in return for 10 percent of its annual proceeds and "a brace of fat capons" to be delivered to the director general each December. Hudde felt so confident about the results of his petition that even before hearing the outcome of his request he had arranged for a Norwegian shipbuilder to begin working the farm. The contract,

recorded in the records of the provincial secretary, would go into effect
as soon as Hudde sent tools and laborers back from the Netherlands.
Hudde then sailed to Amsterdam to claim his bride.

With Hudde away in the Netherlands, Jan de la Montagne saw
an opportunity to recoup some of the money he had spent finishing his
brother-in-law's buildings, fencing in his fields, and bringing in his harvest, work that made him, in his own interpretation, the de facto owner
of the property. Only days after Hudde's departure, de la Montagne
convinced the town council, which helped the director general run the
settlement, to order Hudde to reimburse him 680 guilders for finishing
the farm. When no word had returned from Hudde in the Netherlands by
mid-September, de la Montagne demanded that the Muscoota farm be
sold in order to satisfy the debt. Without waiting for Hudde's return, the
director general and the council ordered the farm sold, and on October
7 the Muscoota bowery was auctioned off for 1,700 guilders, a fraction
of its value, to none other than de la Montagne, who was already living
there. De la Montagne named it Vredendael, or Valley of Peace. Hudde
and Gertrude de Forest didn't learn the news until they arrived in New
Amsterdam in July of 1639. By then it was too late to object.

Isaack de Forest fought for a piece of Hendrick's inheritance
and ended up with a strip of one hundred acres east of the Muscoota
bowery. It was a far less desirable piece of land, Isaack would have to
work for two years before claiming it as his own, and he would still
have to remit 10 percent of the land's annual proceeds after the first
decade. It was a raw deal but Isaack had other consolations. He had
taken a wife to go along with his property, Sara du Trieux, a seventeen-
year-old who was one of the first Europeans born in the New World.
It was no doubt Isaack's father-in-law who, in July of 1641, helped
Isaack pay 300 guilders to English carpenters to construct a thirty- by
eighteen-foot house, a separate twenty- by sixteen-foot kitchen, and
a sixteen-foot-long barn for drying and curing tobacco; even then,
downtown looked to uptown for its stimulants. This farm was fancier
than anything going up on the neighboring lands, with cobblestone
chimneys, clapboard exteriors, extra windows and doors, and a pantry.
But Isaack never took to life uptown. He eventually sold the property

and moved downtown, where he dealt in real estate, lent out money, and trafficked at various times in fur, beer, and flour, as well as holding a variety of official positions from public magistrate to orphan master. He also worked every side of the trade in tobacco—from planter to dealer to inspector—which was by far the business with the biggest potential profits.

Isaack de Forest apparently saw less opportunity in northern Manhattan than did the increasing numbers of investors downtown and across the seas, who believed that was where the future lay. Soon after the de Forest brothers arrived, a Dutchman named Jacobus van Corlaer had bought the two-hundred-acre plot known to the Indians as Konykast—the meaning of the word is unclear—and began building a simple farm. By the summer of 1637 the property he was calling Otterspoor, or Otter Track, was habitable and virtually self-sufficient, with livestock, tools, and a dugout canoe for trips downtown. But van Corlaer didn't last long uptown. The next year, he leased the farm to Claes Cornelissen Swits, a wheelwright who promised to give one-eighth of each year's harvest, plus gifts of butter and livestock, in return for the use of the land, horses, cows, and tools. From the beginning, absentee landlords were crucial to Harlem's economy.

Just to the north of van Corlaer's farm, on a plot the natives called Schorrakin—again, the meaning is lost to us—rose the four-hundred-acre plantation of a Danish sea captain turned merchant named Jochem Pieter Kuyter, who called his property Zegendael, or Valley of Blessings. Like his neighbors, Kuyter didn't spend all of his time on his farm. In addition to dealing in tobacco, he organized the construction of the first proper church in the fort downtown, and eventually he became the conscience of the island, serving on the political council that sought to influence the wrongheaded policies of the West India Company's representatives.

It was with the establishment of these three plantations in the late 1630s that uptown Manhattan began to take on the character of a permanent settlement, with its own particular customs and cultures. The day began before sunrise with the milking of the cows, who were then led out to pasture. Then came a family prayer and a breakfast of

wheat or rye bread and cheese, with buttered cornmeal mush, and milk
or buttermilk for the children and beer for the adults. After another
prayer the children would haul firewood, fetch water, feed chickens, and
collect eggs. Since the education of children took second place to the
work that was necessary for survival, schooling was left to the family
and the church. The men spent most of their days in the fields. In the
spring, they would prepare the fields and then sow wheat, rye, barley,
oats, peas, and beans, as well as tobacco for downtown smokers and
hops for brewing beer. They also planted flax, whose flowers colored
their fields blue before being harvested and spun into linen. Harvest
came in September and October, and every November there was a
livestock market, a custom that lasted until well into the nineteenth
century. There, each family would buy pigs and a cow to be butchered
and preserved for the winter, which was also the time for hunting and
fishing, repairing fences and tools, making trips downtown for supplies,
and conducting business.

Despite the hardships of living on crude and isolated plantations,
settlers considered their situation a vast improvement over the lack
of opportunities back in Holland. Many Dutch customs survived.
The educated landowners and their families and the servants who
shared their living quarters sat down together to a midday meal that
might include chicken, traditional Dutch pea soup, and rye and wheat
bread with butter, as well as local venison and an Indian corn pudding called sampan. The menu suggests that while the Dutch did not
forget their homeland, they found room for Indian ways. Indeed, the
late 1630s saw few conflicts with the locals. Trading with Indians for
corn, beans, pumpkins, and melons was an everyday occurrence, far
more common than making the long trip downtown. Kuyter wrote
that "the farmers pursue their outdoor labor without interruption,
in the woods as well as in the field and dwell safely, with their wives
and children, in their houses, free from any fear of Indians." Bountiful
tobacco harvests even allowed the farms to turn a profit.

The good life was about to end, however, and Harlemites looking
for someone to blame pointed downtown. The West India Company's
inflexible trade policies, combined with good economic times back in

Holland, were making New Netherland an increasingly unattractive business risk. Ships with new settlers from Holland began arriving less frequently. By 1638 there were fewer than a thousand Europeans in the entire settlement, and because of rising tensions with native inhabitants, half of the settlers clung to the fort in case of attack. Although the uptown farms were doing well, not one of the West India Company's five plantations scattered throughout lower Manhattan was functioning, probably because of the poor soil. The village of New Amsterdam, the crown jewel of the Dutch West India's operations, was half the size of Boston and considerably less prosperous, consisting of fewer than a hundred rickety shacks abutting a dilapidated fort that was incapable of providing even basic protection against attack. The fort had no gates, only one of its cannons worked, and only one of its three windmills—a technology that was a matter of national pride for the Dutch—was operational.

Settlers blamed local leaders, whose corruption and incompetence had helped lead the settlement to the edge of ruin. So they had high expectations when, in March of 1638, the West India Company sent a new director general with orders to unleash the vast potential energies of the moribund settlement. Willem Kieft was certainly helped by the recent decision to end the company's monopoly on the fur trade. Anyone could now buy pelts from Indians and sell them in New Amsterdam or even back in Holland, all subject to tax, of course. That attracted a new wave of immigrants, including a blacksmith, a shoemaker, a tailor, a baker, a brewer, a rope maker, a carpenter, and two millers, one for the gristmill and one for the sawmill. At the behest of the company, and assisted by Andries Hudde and Jacobus van Corlaer, Kieft instituted the settlement's first laws, covering everything from public drunkenness to making business contracts. Kieft reorganized the council, reducing it to two members, himself and Jan de la Montagne, now clearly a citizen of some consequence. Kieft had the holes in the fort patched; built a school, a church, and a five-story inn; and put up a fine brick house for himself. He oversaw a network of new roads and canals, lined with gabled stone and brick houses, that made the settlement resemble its namesake across the Atlantic. As a result, by the end of 1639 dozens of new farms had been started. Within a few years the population of New Netherland had doubled.

Kieft achieved these improvements at a heavy cost. His building program was funded by burdensome taxes on both settlers and Indians, but it was his character that so many settlers found most problematic. Back in the Netherlands Kieft was known as a mean-spirited rogue. From his arrival in New Amsterdam he struck residents as disputatious, power hungry, and arrogant, insisting on being addressed as "divinely appointed magistrate." Nor did his focus on morals win him many allies. In the 1630s New Amsterdam was an intoxicating and intoxicated place. Because of the lack of potable water, even babies were given beer to drink "from the moment they are able to lick a spoon," according to one report. Settlers living in fear of Indian attack, epidemics, and food shortage played as hard as they worked, with music, drinking, and dancing lightening their burdens. For all of his efforts to inculcate sobriety among his subjects, Kieft himself developed a serious drinking problem, barricading himself in his quarters in the fort with a bottle at times of public crisis. The first tavern wasn't opened in New Amsterdam until 1641, but drunken brawls were a constant feature of public life. A fight outside the fort in May of 1638, shortly after Kieft's arrival, resulted in the city's first murder. Even though Kieft was given a free hand in meting out punishments—public executions were a form of entertainment—he could no more correct the boisterous spirits of the settlers than he could straighten the crooked streets that still crisscross downtown Manhattan. Kieft's 1638 ordinance outlawing sex between settlers and Indians or Africans is less interesting for its window on Dutch racism than for reminding us that only things that do occur need to be outlawed. Kieft also alienated local religious figures. The monthly days of required fasting and prayer that the church insisted on were a low priority during his administration, though that was less out of immorality than the desire to keep the settlers working. Kieft himself boycotted church services and he persuaded all of his underlings to do the same except Jan de la Montagne, who, after all, was a church official.

Kieft's relations with his subjects were excellent, though, compared to his relations with neighboring Indians. He cracked down on violations of West India Company regulations against the sale of guns or ammunition to the Indians, but the trade was too profitable to stop—Indians were willing to offer as many as twenty beaver pelts for a single musket. Just as unsuccessful was his response to a 1640 incident in which Indians stole some pigs on Staten Island. Kieft, who never led a military expedition against the Indians—he never even spent a night outside the relative safety of Fort Amsterdam—answered with a military campaign that resulted in the death of a number of Raritan Indians, who were immediately avenged in a countercampaign of murder and destruction. Kieft, who had already ordered all settlers to organize themselves into military units, began to feel more confident about going on the offense against Indians. De la Montagne announced, presciently, "A bridge has been built, over which war will soon stalk the land."

The turning point was the 1641 murder of the elderly Harlemite Claes Cornelissen Swits in his wheel workshop, near what is now Second Avenue and East 47th Street, by a Weckquaesgeek Indian who ostensibly came to trade beaver pelts. Kieft called a public assembly to ask advice about a response. He didn't like what he heard. The settlers told him that while retaliation might be just, it was also unwise. Their harvests and livestock were unprotected, and they didn't have enough soldiers to carry out a war. Kieft for once bowed to public opinion and demanded only that the leader of the killer's band apologize or make good the loss. The leader countered that Swits's murder was in retaliation for the 1626 murder by Peter Minuit's servants of the Indian's uncle—he was a boy at the time and witnessed it—and that he wished it were twenty Christians, not one, that had been murdered. Kieft was now in a difficult spot. Anything less than decisive action would be read by Indians, and perhaps some settlers, as weakness. Kieft ignored de la Montagne's pleas for restraint and began planning a raid at Yonkers. It turned out to be unnecessary. Kieft's saber rattling convinced the enemy to sign a peace treaty and deliver up Swits's murderer. De la Montagne was Kieft's closest political ally, and the only other member of the provincial council, but with de la Montagne's knowledge of Indian military thinking and

the state of New Netherland's lack of preparedness, he was often sent
by Kieft on administrative and military missions concerning both the
English and the Indians. His close relationship with Kieft earned
him few friends, though Harlemites appreciated it when he urged
Kieft—who had built a luxurious house for investment purposes at the
Otterspoor—"to give protection to those who are living at a distance."
De la Montagne also had personal reasons for counseling restraint,
since his own lands were so exposed. Nonetheless, de la Montagne
obeyed orders when, in early 1643, Kieft ordered a surprise attack
on a group of several hundred Weckquaesgeeks, including women
and children, who had taken refuge on Manhattan from intratribal
warfare farther up the Hudson Valley. Kieft's strategy was far from
popular. Many prominent settlers, especially those who had valuable
and vulnerable property uptown, advised Kieft to use the weakness
of the Indians' position not to threaten attack but to force them into a
long-term alliance. The ever sensible de la Montagne, sensing Kieft's
desire to solve the problem for good, even suggested simply waiting
for a few more weeks, until the Dutch could mount a better defense
against the retaliation that was sure to follow. Kieft would have none
of it. He ordered his attack, which violated a long-standing West India
Company policy to stay out of conflicts between the natives, and de
la Montagne participated in one of the most gruesome atrocities in
the history of the Dutch colonial empire. One eyewitness recounted,
"Young children, some of them snatched from their mothers, were cut
in pieces before the eyes of their parents, and the pieces were thrown
into the fire or into the water; other babes were bound on planks and
then cut through . . . some were thrown into the river and when their
fathers and mothers sought to save them, the soldiers would not suffer
them to come ashore but caused both young and old to be drowned."

When the soldiers arrived back at the fort the next morning,
bearing the heads of several of their victims, Kieft, who had spent the
night, as usual, in the safety of Fort Amsterdam, embraced the victors
and presided over a primitive version of soccer played by the wives of
the soldiers, who used the heads as the ball, to the delight of the children. De la Montagne himself oversaw the torture and murder of the

remaining prisoners. If blind loyalty to authority or the desire to get ahead had inspired him to violate West India Company policy not to interfere in such conflicts, what could have turned this well-educated, sober, humane physician, a church father who had been schooled by Jesse de Forest in Guyana in the ways of respect and accommodation in dealing with Indians, into a monstrous killer? The Dutch planted seeds of racial, ethnic, and religious tolerance on Manhattan, but the social tensions that have always haunted American society flourished in the same soil.

How could Kieft not have known that the next day eleven Lenape bands from every direction of the compass would put aside their differences and declare war, mustering more than a thousand warriors bearing firearms and powder bought from the Dutch. The few dozen soldiers and poorly armed farmers and merchants that Kieft assembled were no match, and within weeks the Indians had reduced most of New Netherland to ash and bone. No one on Manhattan was safe, and Dutch settlers living outside New Amsterdam, who were otherwise willing to brave the occasional bear that might wander onto their lands, now fled to the relative safety of downtown, which doubled to a population of about one thousand. Those who didn't flee were killed or taken prisoner, their houses burned to the ground, their livestock killed, their grain and hay burned, and their fields destroyed. The properties of de la Montagne, Kuyter, and van Corlaer were protected for a time by their palisades, but eventually these settlers, too, were forced to move downtown and give up their farms and their finances. Harlem, it seemed, had died even before it was born, and the blame fell on Kieft. Within a month, there were two attempts on Kieft's life, one by his own servant, thwarted by de la Montagne himself.

The attacks, counterattacks, reprisals, and revenge missions that constituted Kieft's War cast a shadow over attempts to resettle the uptown plantations. Isaack de Forest leased his farm to John Darnton and de la Montagne rented out Vredendael in return for a percentage of profits, but hostilities flared up again over the summer of 1643 and Kieft ordered all settlers living in outlying areas to retreat to the safety of the fort. At this point, uptown settlers, who stood to lose the legal claim to their properties, were central in the effort to establish a deliberative body to balance the opinions of Kieft and his council. In September of 1643 a group known as the Eight Men, led by Jochem Pieter Kuyter and Isaack de Forest, was elected to resist Kieft's policies. Still, conditions continued to deteriorate. A November 1643 letter to the Netherlands, signed by Kuyter, predicted: "All of us who will yet save our lives must of necessity perish next year of hunger and sorrow unless our God have pity on us."

The insistence of the Eight Men put de la Montagne in a difficult position. His fitness for public office was now questioned, and he successfully brought suit against a fellow settler for slander and assault. De la Montagne knew that Kieft's policies threatened to bankrupt him but he was now working full time for the director general, leading diplomatic and trade expeditions, as well as military attacks that included the torture, mutilation, and beheading of prisoners. It was in response to one of these assaults in early 1644 that Kuyter's farm was burned down—company soldiers stationed in the basement were awakened by Indian gunfire but cowered below until the fire was out. Kuyter's situation was all too typical, as Kieft's war brought on the economic collapse of the settlement, with residents returning to the Netherlands and the West India Company on the verge of bankruptcy. The uptown farms sat ruined, their owners squeezing into huts next to the crumbling and dilapidated fort. A truce was signed in August of 1645, but the articles of peace only ended outright hostilities. With more than a hundred Dutch and sixteen hundred Indians dead, tensions still ran high, and the settlements on northern Manhattan remained empty.

Kieft's recall to Holland and the arrival in May 1647 of a new leader committed to the development of uptown Manhattan seemed promising. Peter Stuyvesant was a thirty-seven-year-old veteran of the West India Company who had lost a leg in battle and kept on fighting, for which the company rewarded him with a silver-tipped prosthesis and the directorship of a settlement in crisis. Trade with the Indians, the economic lifeblood of the settlement, had ceased, and the fabric of the community was disintegrating. The city's seventeen tap houses represented almost a quarter of all the buildings in a city without a printing press or post office; literacy rates were low, and with no settlers left outside of the fort there was no one to send mail to. Relations with the English and French to the north and south, where a more sensible management of trade and Indian policy had made the prosperous New England and Delaware settlements a military threat, were at a low ebb. Stuyvesant, who announced upon his arrival that he would govern the settlement "as a father governs his children," acted swiftly and decisively. He imposed order on the unruly settlement, removing garbage that had piled up for years in the streets, building the city's first permanent pier, instituting a firefighting service, and beginning a road-paving campaign supervised by Jan de la Montagne. He also went to work regulating the social life of the city, instituting strict controls on the sale and consumption of alcohol and restricting the hours when shops could do business. He even closed down the whorehouses, which didn't help his popularity.

The uptown settlers who had a prominent role in the public affairs of New Netherland under Willem Kieft now gained even more influence. Upon Stuyvesant's arrival, Jochem Pieter Kuyter had signed his name to a petition requesting an investigation of the role of Kieft and his allies—including Jan de la Montagne—in the Indian troubles. These citizens also charged that Kieft had illegally put some 400,000 guilders of West India Company money into his own pockets. The commission answering the accusation, which was made up of Stuyvesant and de la Montagne himself, questioned the legitimacy of such an investigation. In May 1647, Kuyter showed up at Kieft's resignation and made a speech that was so frank in its low estimation of the departing director general that Stuyvesant brought charges of slander, sedition, and mutiny. Kuyter was found guilty by Stuyvesant and de la Montagne and sentenced to a 150 guilder fine and a three-year banishment. Kuyter appealed the harsh sentence and in August was sent to Holland to pursue his case. It was, as it happened, the very same boat that carried his alleged victim back home. On September 27, 1647, the vessel ran aground near Wales, sending 86 of its 107 passengers to the bottom of the sea. Kieft directed his last words to his accuser: "I have been unjust towards you; can you forgive me?" Righteous to a fault, Kuyter refused. He tied himself to a fragment of the ship's deck and clung to it all night, until he was washed ashore the next morning. Kieft, friendless to the end, went down with his 400,000 suspiciously earned guilders and a hoard of company documents that historians have mourned ever since as infinitely more valuable. Kuyter made his way to Holland, where he successfully argued his case, and then he came back to Manhattan and settled uptown again, though he kept a close eye on Stuyvesant.

Among the most important changes that Stuyvesant made was a political reorganization of the settlement. A new representative body elected in 1652 and including four Harlemites—William Beeckman, Jacobus van Corlaer, Isaack de Forest, and Kuyter—voiced their concerns about Stuyvesant's policies and pleaded for better protection of settlements on the north end of the island, to little effect. In the early spring of 1654 Kuyter was killed in an Indian attack on Zegendael, and a year later a monthlong conflict known as the Peach War—it started after an Indian woman was killed in the act of stealing peaches from a downtown orchard—caused massive loss of property in the unprotected settlements outside the fort. Indians burned down dozens of farms and destroyed or stole thousands of bushels of grain and five hundred head of cattle. The destruction uptown was particularly distressing, with the murders of Kuyter's widow at Zegendael, Hendrick de Forest's old servant Tobias Teunissen, and Claes Swits's son, who had recently bought the old Isaack de Forest property. Once again, the settlement contracted as settlers abandoned properties uptown, as well as across the Hudson and East rivers, to seek the protection of the city. The population swelled to two thousand, causing severe shortages of food, and making New Amsterdam's already primitive living conditions even worse. By October of 1654 the situation was so bad that Stuyvesant passed a law requiring settlers traveling outside New Amsterdam to obtain permission from him in advance—otherwise, if they were captured by Indians, they would be left to raise their own ransom. In November, Stuyvesant proposed that no more isolated settlements be allowed and ordered that, for now, the uptown farms that had been destroyed remain vacant. When peace eventually took hold, settlers prepared to return, but Stuyvesant still refused to allow it until a properly walled village had been erected there.

De la Montagne was by this time second only to Stuyvesant in his power and authority, with his position on the council bringing in 600 guilders per year plus 200 guilders for expenses, in addition to money he earned as an inspector of cargo for the West India Company and as a real estate speculator. But de la Montagne's position as one of the settlement's most prominent figures didn't last long. Even though he moonlighted as everything from supervisor of the local surgeons and barbers to Harlem's schoolmaster, there were accusations that he owed the West India Company several thousand guilders. Did he have a secret vice? Stuyvesant continued to call on his skills as a military leader and diplomat but tensions began to show. After de la Montagne, who found Stuyvesant's Indian policy too lenient in times of peace and too extreme in times of conflict, made a motion to prevent Stuyvesant from carrying out decisions without first informing the council, Stuyvesant wrote to the directors of the West India Company that de la Montagne was "a bad instrument—a snake harbored in the bosom of the colony." Had de la Montagne changed? Or had he not changed enough?

Either way, de la Montagne got out of town before it was too late. He left his old farm to his son, Jan Jr., already a West India Company official, and moved his family up the river to Fort Orange, where he was to serve as commissary. But his finances were so precarious that he and his wife took in washing in order to buy food and firewood. There, it seems, he died around 1670. This uptown pioneer and key downtown political player—no one, not even Peter Stuyvesant himself, appears as many times in the register of the provincial council—died far from the home he helped to make uptown, in an exile that was only partly self-imposed. This cautious doctor and wily risk taker, this pious Christian and vicious Indian killer, distinguished physician and gentleman farmer who became a political hack and impoverished sycophant, selling his word and his deed to whatever new regime the head office sent over, wasn't the first Harlemite but he was its first improviser, its first survivor.

*   *   *

Eventually, Peter Stuyvesant realized that de la Montagne and the other uptown settlers had been right all along. In order to put an end to the destructive cycles of violence that were preventing New Netherland from being anything more than an insignificant fur trading outpost, he needed to establish a proper village to the north. It was to occupy fifty acres between the Otterspoor and Zegendael, with plots of farmland nearby, between what are now Fifth and Eighth avenues and between what are now West 125th and West 148th streets. The village would serve as an early warning system against attacks by native Indian bands, and perhaps by the English and French as well. In time, the village's grain would help make New Netherland self-sufficient, while its tobacco would help diversify the settlement's export economy. This was also a personal matter, since Stuyvesant, a restless administrator who familiarized himself, peg leg or no, with the entire settlement from the Delaware to Albany, owned property uptown. He knew first-hand that the Indian wars had left northern Manhattan not only empty but without anyone having staked a legitimate claim. Properties there had been so devalued by Indian wars, and their owners so financially burdened by the inability to work the land, that there could be no opposition to the West India Company reclaiming title. Stuyvesant's plan came about on March 4, 1658, when the Common Council of the City of New Amsterdam passed an eight-point ordinance granting privileges to settlers willing to move uptown to a proposed village, to be called Nieuw Haarlem. Stuyvesant's ordinance hoped that "the lovers of agriculture" would see the obvious need "for the further promotion of farming, for the security of this island and the cattle pasturing thereon." The document also envisioned uptown Manhattan as a place for "the further amusement and development of the city of New Amsterdam." For better or worse, for better *and* worse, this founding document enshrined in Harlem a divided economy, one that, because it depended on tourists visiting its taverns and inns—pleasure as business—would depend on the unpredictable downtown cultural whims and economic cycles.

It has been suggested that Stuyvesant chose the name New Harlem because the landscape reminded him of the Dutch city of Haarlem. Others believe that the name was related to a mapmaker named Philips Jansen van Haerlem. Perhaps Stuyvesant called the village New Harlem because it stood in the same geographical relation to New Amsterdam as their namesakes back home. He surely hoped the two settlements would have a similar political and economic relationship. If so, the name was also a reminder of Haarlem's legendary role as a protective buffer for Amsterdam against the Spanish in the 1570s.

Stuyvesant's ordinance promised a great deal. The twenty-five village lots, each of which came with twenty-four to forty-eight-acre plots of farmland, would be exempt from the standard 10 percent tax for fifteen years. Each settler would also receive six acres of salt meadow, although there was no guarantee that it would be located nearby. Stuyvesant further promised military protection consisting of a garrison of twelve to fifteen soldiers, but only upon formal request—this at a time when Harlem was half a day's march from downtown, which meant that an enemy attack would be over by the time help arrived. Stuyvesant also promised to establish a court in the village, with justices to be nominated locally and elected by the director general and his council, once twenty families had settled in. For years, uptowners had been getting by with an initiate, as opposed to a minister, which meant a visit downtown was necessary to get married or to baptize children. Now Stuyvesant promised half the salary of a "good, pious, orthodox minister." He further pledged to have West India Company slaves help turn the rough Indian track leading downtown into a wagon road. He promised to build a cattle market and a ferry "for the better and greater promotion of neighborly correspondence with the English of the North." He also pledged not to let any other villages establish themselves nearby, ensuring that Harlem would have a monopoly on business uptown.

Settlers seem to have been skeptical of Stuyvesant's intentions. Though it was possible for a farm to be self-supporting within a year, especially when farmland was practically being given away, it was no way to get rich quick. It wasn't until sixth months later, on August

14, 1658, that enough "lovers of agriculture" volunteered to join the enterprise, which meant that they would have less than half a growing season. It wasn't for another few weeks that plots for houses were surveyed and streets staked out. There would be two main southwest-northeast paths running parallel about two hundred feet apart from what is now East 111th Street and Fifth Avenue to what is today the Harlem River at East 125th Street. The northernmost street, which ran along Isaack de Forest's old cart path, was called the Great Way. The street to the south was laid out along an old Indian trail and became known as Harlem Lane. The property between was divided by six cross streets, into twenty parcels, from the Harlem River to the Harlem Creek. The village square would be located near what is now East 121st Street, between Third and Lexington avenues.

Once the town had been laid out the festivities commenced: Johannes Verveelen, a newcomer who owned a downtown brewery, served tankards of beer and initiated the toasts. Then the work began. Planting and fencing went forward, but several settlers died of typhoid and the cold weather set in early. Autumn floods washed away a meager harvest. Dropped claims were soon taken up, but it was too late in the year to move uptown. These settlers planned to wait out the harsh winter to occupy their lands, which meant ignoring the requirement that they move in immediately or forfeit ownership, even though Stuyvesant was in no position to bluff. New Harlem grew very slowly.

The half dozen houses that had sprung up along Harlem Lane and Church Lane by the summer of 1659 were more rustic than those downtown, but uptowners exhibited an appreciation for fine things, and there was style and pleasure amid necessity and danger. Harlem's one-story, one-room structures with wood frames, beamed ceilings, thatched roofs, and clapboard sides were becoming less common than more solid houses with separate rooms for living, sleeping, and working, with the attic reserved for storing grain or putting up children or visitors. Most of the new homes had tiled roofs with stepped facades and a gable facing the street, with fieldstone foundations, plastered interior walls painted yellow or green, and Dutch doors that swung on leather hinges. Stuyvesant had brought a glazier with him when he arrived in 1647, so glass windows were common, protected by wooden shutters. The kitchens had brick floors and were dominated by a massive open hearth, surrounded by decorative tiles. Plank floors were covered with sand raked into dainty patterns, and tables were decked with oriental carpets in the Dutch style, all lit by candles or oil lamps. Furniture was fashioned of crudely fitted wood, although wealthier families upholstered their chairs in leather and supplemented ceramic and pewter plates and utensils with glass, marble, or silver. Freshly cut flowers graced the tables of rich and poor alike.

These pioneering Harlemites ate well. Crab, venison, turkey, goose, duck, and partridge were plentiful and cheap, bought from Indians in defiance of the treaty that limited trading to two downtown locations. These transactions were often carried out, interestingly enough, by children, who were among the first settlers to learn the languages of the Indians. The Dutch were passionate gardeners, and villagers began to raise onions, radishes, spinach, beets, carrots, cabbage, parsnips, endive, and dill. In addition to enjoying wild apples, pears, plums, and berries, settlers took advantage of the long summers to cultivate melons, peaches, cherries, and grapes. At the same time, Sunday sermons warned Harlemites about the dangers that this good life posed to their souls. A poem from this time by a downtown settler, Jacob Steendam, hinted at the malevolence of the opportunities of the New World in suggesting that Manhattanites lived amid an "oppressive abundance" that might not last.

The First Esopus War, which started in late 1659 between settlers and Indians upstate, had serious repercussions on Manhattan. Fears that the conflict would spread south sent many of those who had resettled uptown back downtown; it became clear that 1660 would be a crucial year. In March, Harlemites held their first town meeting and instituted a night watch. By August about two dozen families were living uptown, which meant that Peter Stuyvesant was obliged to incorporate the village and institute a court of magistrates. This was a major achievement, since it meant that they could settle minor disputes—civil cases up to 50 guilders and criminal cases as serious as assault—locally, instead of having to travel downtown. There were many court cases right from the start, most concerning petty theft, debt collections, boundary disputes, accusations of improper fencing, and destruction caused by roaming domestic animals. Increasingly, it seemed, the poverty, insecurity, and isolation that characterized the first generation of settlers were becoming things of the past. The new generation reveled in the natural bounty all around them, and they cherished their distance from the stifling involvement of the West India Company in every element of life downtown. But if there is some difficulty in characterizing New Harlem in its earliest years, it is partially because it was such a diverse place. By 1661, when the first census was made, Harlem was home to merchants, a bricklayer, a carpenter, a butcher, a cooper, a shoemaker, a brewer, a mason, and a soap maker, in addition to farmers and soldiers. They came not only from the Low Countries but from France, Denmark, Sweden, and Germany.

The 1661 census tellingly failed to count Harlem's Africans, even though they had a place uptown ever since Jan Rodriguez, a black Portuguese seaman, was stranded in the region in 1613; eventually he settled with the Rockaway Indians, marrying one of them and producing the first biracial Americans. The first African slaves, eleven in total, arrived in New Netherland in 1626, bought from pirates who stole them from Spanish ships. By 1655 Africans were being brought directly from Africa, and by the end of Dutch rule in 1664, 174 men and 132 women had been brought to New Amsterdam as slaves. Reconstructing the lives of Africans in Harlem during this period is problematic. Slavery wasn't practiced in the Netherlands, but it was neither prohibited nor protected by law in the Dutch colonies, nor was racial segregation a social priority—race itself had no legal standing. Under the rule of the West India Company, slaves of African descent and white indentured servants were considered a single social class, subject to the same restrictions with regard to personal freedom and property ownership. Both were allowed to come and go freely, and many bought their own freedom. Slaves belonging to the West India Company were allotted marshy land downtown for their own farms until the late 1630s. At least fourteen deeds in the Dutch period pertain to black landowners leaving property to their children. Free Africans frequently appeared in court as plaintiffs, and at one point a group of blacks traveled to Holland to demand wages equal to that of whites. In wartime, blacks fought on the side of the Dutch with spears and axes, but they were not allowed to carry guns. Nonetheless, free blacks were at liberty to work as they pleased and marry whomever they loved, as long as they converted to Christianity. From 1641 to 1664 the Dutch Reformed Church married twenty-six black couples, all but one of them free. By 1660 there were thirty black property owners in the region, and New Amsterdam boasted the biggest slave market in North America. Many Africans who mounted the auction block downtown ended up building the Harlem Road, settling nearby, and living more like indentured servants than slaves.

The fact that religion could trump race offers some idea of how deeply embedded the church was in the lives of the early Harlemites. The first European residents came from a variety of Christian backgrounds but all worshipped according to the mandatory Reformed faith promulgated with unyielding severity by Peter Stuyvesant. In August of 1660 Harlemites organized their first proper church, with Jan de la Montagne Jr. serving as deacon and Michiel Zyperus, who had arrived from the West Indies with his wife, taking on the role of minister. Zyperus was not officially ordained, but starting in November of 1660 he began leading services, usually in lofts or attics and even in barns.

The official recognition of Harlem, the establishment of the court and the church, and the expiration of the three-year period in which settlers had to either work their lands or give up title all attracted even more settlers. Harlem was now a community, with a sharp distinction between work and play. There were more formal social gatherings, which revolved around drinking and smoking by everyone, including women and sometimes even children. Entertainment at these gatherings might have been provided by an African dancer named Charley, who claimed to be 125 years old. Jasper Danckaerts reported lodging during this time with Resolved Waldron, one of New Harlem's earliest settlers, whose "house was constantly filled with people, all the time drinking." Local hard cider, rum from the islands, and gin from the Netherlands dominated social occasions, and ale was the preferred drink for breakfast, lunch, and dinner, even though fresh water was plentiful. When one uptown brewer was accused in court of producing a less than acceptable product, the magistrates marched across the street to sample the evidence.

Harlemites frowned on dancing but they enjoyed bowling and boating in good weather, and in the winter they skated and went on sleigh rides or played "tick-tack" indoors. Things were less subdued during holidays, when public offices would close for days or even weeks at a time. December 5 was Sinterklaas, the traditional birthday of Amsterdam's patron, Saint Nicholas, and it was celebrated, along with Christmas, New Year's, and Pinkster, with much drinking, drumming, and firing of guns. Stuyvesant banned "pulling the goose," in which riders on horseback would attempt to grasp a live goose suspended from a rope, but the game remained a favorite of Harlemites at Shrovetide. A game called "clubbing the cat," in which a cat was put into a barrel that was nailed shut and hung from a rope—whoever could break the barrel by throwing a club at it and set the cat free won—was also popular. Maypoles were common, not just on May Day but on the wedding nights of neighbors. Such scenes might have serious consequences, especially if the horning, as it was called, got too bawdy. On one occasion, Jan de la Montagne Jr., who became the sheriff and public prosecutor of Harlem, as well the *voorleser,* or parish clerk—which meant that he led prayer, instructed children, kept church records, and ministered to the needy—accused horners of riot. Was de la Montagne simply enforcing the law? Or was he a sober spoilsport intent on making sure that New Harlem distanced itself morally from the raucous ways of New Amsterdam?

Despite such pleasures life wasn't easy or simple. By mid-1661 the church was so overwhelmed by frontier settlers coming to the village to beg for charity that Stuyvesant passed the settlement's first poor law, stating that outlying communities needed to take care of their own poor. In early 1663 Harlemites who still owed money on their lands unsuccessfully begged Stuyvesant to allow them to settle their debts using Indian wampum—white and purple beads made from conch or periwinkle shells and strung into necklaces or belts—a sign that the farms were self-sustaining but not profitable. If hard currency wasn't flowing downstream it was not for the lack of effort. Harlemites worked hard, so hard that they were frequently hauled into court on accusations of working on the Sabbath. The grain and vegetables that they planted in order to turn a settlement dependent on a single cash crop, tobacco—a product now competing with the cheap tobacco from Virginia, with its slavery-backed economies of scale—into a permanent, self-supporting community were much more labor intensive than what the first generation of settlers concentrated on.

Of course, too much time spent outdoors came with risks. Because of ongoing fears of Indians, Harlemites never ventured outside unarmed. After an attack in June 1663 by Indians near Esopus, near the present-day upstate town of Kingston, in which Jan de la Montagne's daughter and granddaughter were captured, Harlemites finally built a proper palisade around the village and welcomed an extra contingent of soldiers from downtown to help man twin seven-pound cannons. Later that month, when settlers learned from Indian allies that warriors were heading south and planning what would become the Second Esopus War, Harlemites did more than follow Stuyvesant's advice to stay indoors, and once again they fled downtown, though many slaves remained in their homes, which were apparently spared during Indian attacks. In late July news came that the Esopus Indians had targeted New Harlem for attack. Many feared the worst, but by the time Stuyvesant sent extra soldiers—a full month later—they were no longer needed. The invasion never took place, and the provincial council soon issued wax passes to allow the Weckquaesgeeks, who were sworn enemies of the Esopus, to fish the Harlem River.

In March of 1664 King Charles II of England gave everything from Maine to Delaware to his brother James, Duke of York, and rumors of a British invasion began circulating. New Amsterdam was guarded by too few soldiers to offer adequate protection from Indians and New Englanders, much less an invasion by foreign armies, and even then Stuyvesant was under constant pressure from the West India Company to reduce that number. In late August three fully armed English men-of-war, plus another vessel carrying troops, drew near

Manhattan. The commander of the force, Richard Nicolls, sent a letter demanding the immediate surrender of New Amsterdam. Stuyvesant tore it to shreds, saying he would rather be carried off the island dead than capitulate. This was not a popular position among the director general's outnumbered and outgunned constituents. There were only about three hundred Dutch soldiers in New Netherland, only half of them armed, and stores of food were so low that settlers might not survive to see the next harvest, much less withstand a blockade or battle with the British, who were supported by French mercenaries and Indian warriors. Moreover, many Dutch settlers felt oppressed by the West India Company, with its greedy meddling and taxation policies, and they believed that the British might be more lenient in this regard. An extended discussion between Stuyvesant and his council ensued in sight of the frigates, which had their cannons trained on the fort. On September 5, almost one hundred of Stuyvesant's most prominent constituents, including Isaack de Forest, presented him with a petition begging him to reconsider. Not all of the resistance to Stuyvesant's approach was so polite. The wife of the Harlemite Nicholaes Meyer came downtown to the fort to excoriate those soldiers who were ready to take on the British. "These lousy dogs want to fight because they have nothing to lose, whereas we have our property here, which we should have to give up," she insisted. Stuyvesant was apparently moved by this argument, and on the next day he surrendered the island, though the articles of capitulation guaranteed religious freedom and property rights, as well as protection against the quartering of soldiers in private houses. New Amsterdam was renamed New York, after the king's brother; Fort Amsterdam became Fort James; the River of the Prince Mauritius became the North River; and New Harlem was renamed Lancaster, after the duke of York's brother.

It all happened "without a blow or a tear," as the old saying went. Only later did it become clear that things were more complicated. In late August of 1664, Isaack de Forest had been on his way back from a business trip when, off the coast of Long Island, he ran into the British invasion force, which had not yet been ordered to approach New Amsterdam. A man-of-war fired on Isaack's boat and captured him, no doubt in order to learn about the state of New Amsterdam's defenses. Upon his release, Isaack went straight to the fort and told Stuyvesant that Nicolls was approaching with a force of as many as eight hundred soldiers, which seems to have convinced Stuyvesant to surrender. Imagine his surprise when he found out that Isaack was wrong. The opposing force was about one-quarter the number expected, something approaching an even fight. Had the British lied to Isaack, hoping he would pass it along to Stuyvesant? Could Isaack not know, after several days among the enemy, their true numbers? There is no way to discover what went on between Nicolls and de Forest. Negotiation, bribe, torture? The likeliest conclusion is that Isaack lied to Stuyvesant in order to ensure a peaceful transition, one that would allow New Amsterdammers and Harlemites to preserve their property. Was he a traitor or a savior? Either way, or both, the village was never widely known as Lancaster or even New Harlem; it became simply Harlem.

2

STRANGE BEDFELLOWS
British Harlem, 1664–1781

In late April 1666, Harlem's constable, Resolved Waldron, went looking for the town council's president, Daniel Tourneur, who had been allowing the hogs that roamed uptown's streets to break through his property's poorly maintained fences and rampage through his neighbors' gardens—no small infraction in a community far from the nearest market. When faced with the accusations Tourneur demonstrated the solidity of his fence by beating Waldron with a piece of it while shouting, "Now, nobody is looking, I'll pay you!" Waldron sued Tourneur before the Mayor's Court that the British had recently established downtown, and he had every reason to expect justice. Although Tourneur had served as magistrate, fire warden, and church deacon, and had been one of the first British appointees uptown, rumor had it that he had come to New Netherland not out of religious or even economic reasons but as a fugitive from justice in France, where he was apparently still wanted for murder. Moreover, the judges had seen him many times in recent years, always as a defendant. Tourneur got off with a warning. What good, the court reasoned, could come from pitting Harlem's two most important politicians, and two of its richest citizens, against each other? Predictably, the judges hadn't seen the last of Tourneur. A few months later he was back in court again, this time accused of sneaking a canoe full of hay into Harlem on the Sabbath. The court fined Tourneur and sent him on his way, but not before he, in turn, raised accusations that another uptown magistrate had been stealing hay from his meadow. Clearly, uptown's most prominent politician had boundary issues, and he wasn't the only one.

Powered by the invigorating energies of the British colonial apparatus, New York flourished in the years after 1664, but Harlem remained mired in the past, and not just when it came to the issue of what to call the village. Despite the change in leadership downtown, uptown the old Dutch council remained in place, and so did the old issues. One of Governor Richard Nicolls's earliest acts was to order the magistrates and constable at Harlem to keep a close eye on alcohol sales to Indians, a practice that continued to put the settlement at risk. Indeed, as New York began a century of rapid growth and urbanization, Harlem remained a sleepy backwater, a remote outpost with no town hall, mill, post office, or regular transportation service to the north or south. One result of this benign neglect was that Netherlandish ways continued to dominate British Harlem. A downtown court ruled in 1674 that documents in Dutch would no longer be accepted, but it remained the lingua franca uptown, and most of Harlem's public officers were drawn from old Dutch families. It was another century before the church uptown hired a minister who could sermonize in English.

Harlemites didn't cling to the old Dutch ways out of simple patriotism. Many Dutch Harlemites had been glad to be rid of the West India Company, which could be at once oppressive and neglectful. Still, while the Dutch were in principle willing to live under the rule of "foreigners," many of whom had lent support to the Dutch struggle against Spain, they had no special love for the British, who after all were longtime economic and political rivals of the Dutch, and whose arrival on Manhattan was viewed with much suspicion. Sheriff Jan de la Montagne Jr. refused to swear allegiance to the British in 1664 but was allowed to remain in his post, though he refused to perform his duties. Dutch Harlemites resented housing English troops, especially during the Anglo-Dutch wars of the 1660s and 1670s, which made Dutch and British citizens official enemies and suspended contacts between Manhattan and the Netherlands. But the thirty-three governors who ruled Manhattan during the long British century from 1664 until the American Revolution for the most part left Harlemites alone, intervening only when the community threatened the growth of New Amsterdam, hence the ban on flour mills and even the sale of bread uptown.

If Harlem was no threat to New Amsterdam, it was because down-town Manhattan, which had always been something of a stepchild in the Dutch colonial family, had its own problems. New Amsterdam's contacts with Europe had always been irregular, and the company had so mismanaged the city that it wasn't even considered a permanent settlement until the 1650s. Boston and Philadelphia, both of which were founded after New Amsterdam, long overshadowed New York. In the city itself, which contained only four hundred houses and fifteen hundred people in the early years of British rule, chaos reigned. Streets were unsafe and unhealthy, with pigs rooting in the waste from tanneries and the filth of outhouses and bedpans. By the end of the seventeenth century, whatever groundwater that remained had been contaminated, bringing epidemics each summer and fall. Political upheaval also made New York City a precarious place to live. This was not only a matter of internal political struggles that so often turned violent but no fewer than six wars during the course of British rule. A refuge became a necessity for anyone who could afford it, and a house in Harlem, just a few hours away by skiff or horseback, was the natural choice.

It wasn't until two full years after the takeover that the British com-missioned a survey of uptown Manhattan that took in everything on the island north of what is now East 74th Street at the East River and West 129th Street on the Hudson River, and Governor Nicolls issued a legal agreement known as a patent that made Manhattan "one Body Politique and Corporate." Harlemites were relieved to find their claims to their lands reestablished—any property not legitimately claimed by individuals went to the village—but they were appalled to learn that they were now obliged to pay taxes and tributes to the duke of York, just like downtowners. Indeed, the newly semi-independent legal sta-tus of Harlem brought few benefits and many responsibilities. Nicolls required the village to provide its own ferry service to downtown, for example. Harlemites, who had already been ignoring the official name, Lancaster, disregarded whatever they found objectionable in Nicolls's patent, and they got away with it. Governor Nicolls reserved the right to confiscate the lands and goods of Harlemites who refused to swear allegiance to the new rulers, and he had the power to confirm or deny the results of uptown elections, but this learned and genteel figure's primary job was to please his own boss, the duke of York, who wasn't terribly occupied with the day-to-day goings-on in the colony named for him and who mostly left the residents of this rural backwater to their own devices. There seem to have been no objections when a handful of Dutch settlers convinced Nicolls to change the official name of the village back to New Harlem.

The old Dutch ways also dominated spiritual life, which meant that the Reformed Protestant Church maintained a religious monopoly uptown. Still, it took curiously long for Harlem to get its own church. Although a congregation had been meeting for years—attendance was in fact mandatory—it was not until after the British occupation that a proper church was built. Even then, the goal was to resist the increasing influence of the Anglican Church and other sects, including French Calvinists, Lutherans, Catholics, Quakers, Sabbatarians, Antisabbatarians, Anabaptists, Jews, and even some freethinkers, according to one accounting. The delay was due less to a lack of commitment than the pittance that was being raised from Sunday collections, donations from wills of the deceased, rent from church-owned land, the sale of common village property, and burial fees. Known as the First Dutch Church, the first house of worship in Harlem was located on a plot on the village square, on the north side of the Great Way, which was renamed Church Lane. A year after construction began in late 1665 the structure still wasn't finished, so more money was raised via a new sale of town land and a special tax to help buy supplies. Even funds reserved for the destitute were raided, which suggests that self-sufficient Harlem harbored few poor people, or that the congregation considered their souls more important than their stomachs. In 1667 pews and seats were numbered and distributed, yet another way to raise money for the construction. Finally the barnlike building, made of wood and topped with a weathervane and diminutive steeple—locals refused to use the church bell for public announcements, preferring the beating of a drum—was ready. The church was a modest structure, with no heating. Churchgoers brought foot stoves along with their Bibles for the service, which lasted all morning every Sunday and on holidays. But it was still a financial burden on the village, so it doubled as a schoolhouse, where the congregation's clerk, Jan de la Montagne Jr., taught reading, writing, catechism, and math. Extra money was also raised by renting out the second-floor attic. But there were still no funds for a preacher. Things looked even more precarious after the structure burned down in the mid-1680s. The congregation soon raised money to build the stone structure called the Second Dutch Church several plots to the east but, even then, New Amsterdam's *domine* would come uptown only once a year to preach a sermon and appoint deacons. Decades after its founding, Harlem was still too small to merit any more attention from downtown.

Even as Harlemites were tending to their spiritual lives, they kept their eyes on their purses. In 1667 Harlem's richest man, Thomas Delavall, a British officer who later served as mayor of New York City, proposed turning the property he had bought in the sale that raised money to build the first church, into a gristmill to be powered by damming the creek that sliced diagonally through Harlem. In fact, he convinced his neighbors to build the mill themselves in return for making the building available as shelter in case of Indian attack, a hint of how fragile life still was. Just as important as the plan for the mill was a British tavern and a ferry located where the village met the Harlem River. The obvious choice of a proprietor was Johannes Verveelen, who had most recently been running the inn at what is now East 123rd Street just west of Pleasant Avenue—certain documents suggest that his real interest was in politics and real estate, and that his African slave Matthys was really in charge of the inn. Between the ferry tolls and the income from the new tavern—he benefited from a one-year tax break on the sale of alcohol, which apparently was intended to compensate for the ban on serving to Indians—Verveelen was soon the third richest man in Harlem. But the fees paid to Verveelen for ferrying passengers, goods, and livestock across the river were considered excessive, and soon merchants and farmers began wading for free through the shallows several miles away at Spuyten Duyvil, at the northern tip of Manhattan. After two years a new ferry was ordered built at Spuyten Duyvil, with none other than Verveelen in charge. This change could not have been good for Harlem, since it meant a decrease in traffic through the village. But the ferry and the tavern at Harlem, taken over by Cornelis Jansen Kortright, thrived, and new and improved complexes were even built at what is now the southeast corner of East 126th Street and First Avenue. By 1684 Kortright had traded up, operating an inn called the Halfway House, at the foot of Harlem Lane, at what is now East 109th Street. This was an even better proposition, since it was located halfway between downtown and the northern tip of the island, and the city government convened there at least once to avoid an epidemic of scarlet fever raging downtown.

Ordinary Harlemites saw these inns as extensions of their homes—many stored a pipe at their favorite tavern. At the same time, they were the most public of places, where different classes, genders, religions, nationalities, political loyalties, and even races met and mixed. The menu consisted mostly of beef stew and terrapin soup, and the entertainment and decor were equally humble. Much smoking of locally grown and cured tobacco was the rule, as was overindulgence in wine, rum, brandy, and locally brewed beer. Also popular was a drink called a "flip"—named so, apparently, because of the shape of the glass—made from sweetened beer or rum warmed up with a poker hot from the fireplace. Harlemites also came to their public houses for auctions, meetings, puppet shows, music, and the public reading of newspapers. Games such as backgammon, chess, and bowls were common, as were cockfighting and gambling. When political conventions and meetings weren't being held in the common room, there were discussions about the public notices posted there, and taverns also functioned as informal stock exchanges. Things were also enlivened by the presence of prisoners who, since there was no jail uptown, often awaited trial in an inn.

The mill and the ferry in Harlem would have been useless without proper transportation. In 1669 the governor formed a commission to put slaves to work improving uptown roads, starting with the fairly impassable Indian track that led from the southern to the northern tip of the island, to be known as the Eastern Post Road downtown and the Kingsbridge Road uptown. It wasn't until the end of 1672 that wagons could travel reliably along the route, and only the following year did a full-time, salaried postman begin leaving downtown on the first Monday of every month bearing letters for Boston, with an initial stop at Harlem. Even then, the route lay across a forbidding wilderness inhabited by bears and panthers as well as Indians who claimed the northernmost part of Manhattan, at least until 1685, when settlers hunting wolves drove out most of the last remaining natives. Harlemites were required by law to donate two work days per year to maintain these roads; the rich could pay a fee to avoid service. Within a few years, travelers could cross from the mainland via the toll span called the King's Bridge, take the Kingsbridge Road south, and then choose whether to take the Post Road down the east side of the island or the Bloomingdale Road, later renamed Broadway, down the west side.

The summer of 1673 brought both welcome and worrying news to the quiet village. Distant events in the Third Anglo-Dutch War returned the island to the Dutch, and they quickly undid the work of almost a decade under the British, starting with officially changing the English place-names back to the Dutch. The British-style political structure of mayor, aldermen, and sheriff was scrapped in favor of the old Dutch system of *burgomaster, schepen,* and *schout.* Oaths of allegiance followed, which caused many a conflict downtown, where British subjects predominated. In Harlem, the Dutch were still in the majority, though there were English landowners among the thirty-two residents who pledged fidelity to the Netherlands. Patriotism clearly played out very differently uptown.

If thirty-two people sounds like a very small community, it is important to remember that only free adult males would have been allowed to take the oath, and most signatories had families, servants, and slaves, so Harlem probably had a hundred or more residents.

Moreover, the fact that five of the signatories were older than age sixty suggests that thanks to British infrastructure such as the ferry and the mill, as well as the fast-diminishing local native Indian population, Harlem was no longer a dangerous frontier outpost. Still, it was not quite a peaceful spot in which to grow old or raise a family. For a time the war meant that Harlem was now once more in a vulnerable spot militarily, and anxieties about a British reinvasion dominated. The church was full the Sunday after the reoccupation, as was the collection basket. There was no party to celebrate the event, but rather a day of prayer, thanksgiving, and fasting, a practice that soon became a monthly ritual. The old routine of night watches, which had proved so ineffective against attacks by Indians from the north, was reinstituted. During the reoccupation, the old Harlem River ferry, near what is now East 125th Street, became a particularly important strategic point. Indeed, one of the reasons that the Dutch reoccupation was successful was that Cornelis Kortright stopped ferry service altogether, preventing British troops from entering Manhattan via the Bronx. Hostilities ended in late 1674, and as a result of negotiations that gave Guyana to the Dutch, the British reoccupied Manhattan, and though the transition was a peaceful one they kept a much closer eye on Harlem, which they had clearly underestimated. But Harlemites had something new to worry about. The danger was that they might be drawn into King Philip's War, which was being waged between Indians and colonists in New England. Strangers were no longer ferried across the Harlem River, all public meetings were banned, and the drum that accompanied public announcements was silenced. Unnerved Harlemites even intercepted and detained almost a dozen canoes filled with Weckquaesgeek women and children bringing grain from their warm-weather encampment in Westchester to the winter home they still maintained on Manhattan.

The community's response to the wars was documented in detail, as were the names and functions of its leaders and the details of business and legal dealings, but it is no simple task to capture the flavor of daily life in British Harlem. Contemporary descriptions, construction and furnishing bills, lawsuits, and personal correspondence all point to a life that wasn't easy. One traveler wrote that the Dutch houses were so dilapidated that in the winter "if you do not keep so close to the fire as to almost burn yourself you cannot keep warm." In October of 1676, with winter closing in, Harlem's town clerk, Hendrick van der Vin, pleaded with the magistrates to be allowed to move his family into the church, so ramshackle was the house that the town provided for him. Still, van der Vin's situation may not have been the rule. The list of effects left by Lubbert Gerritsen, who served in a variety of public functions before his death in 1673, is illustrative of a more comfortable Harlem household in this period. His house contained two beds, two chests, one eight-sided table, two muskets, pewter plates and bowls, iron cooking pans, and a brass candlestick. In the attic, assessors found barrels, axes, wedges, buckets, saws, a cart with extra wheels, and yokes. Gerritsen apparently owned no rug and no stove but there was a mirror, which among the Dutch signaled not vanity but the rigorous moral introspection that the Reformed Protestant faith demanded. Another way to achieve this goal was cleanliness, and legend tells of one homemaker who scrubbed her floor so vigorously that she broke through to the cellar below.

Harlem fed itself but remained dependent on England for glass, stoneware, brick, and ceramics as well as coal, iron, steel, lead, and salt. Farmers customarily wore homemade leather breeches and shoes, and their families wore rough fabrics of homespun wool and flax. Merchants and officials wore velvet or silk trousers over silk stockings and coats with a lace neck cloth and silver or gold buttons, an outfit whose ostentation was completed by a sword and a pistol. But such rigid class distinctions were changing. The local economy was beginning to orient itself toward supplying raw materials such as wheat, lumber, and livestock for England's incipient industrial revolution, which meant that the farmers of Harlem had a chance to become regional economic players again. Most Harlemites worked the small yards attached to their houses and owned garden plots just outside the village, where they planted apple and peach trees amid the wild lilacs and poplars, and they made money from the more labor-intensive agricultural work that took place on distant plots of farmland; indeed, there were bread shortages in the 1690s because the single mill on the Harlem Creek couldn't meet local demand. Even Harlemites with desk jobs owned significant agricultural enterprises, as Lubbert Gerritsen's well-stocked barn shows. He would have overseen two plantings each year, and two harvests, the first consisting of corn, rye, wheat, and flax, followed by turnips, pumpkins, and buckwheat. Men carried out most of the labor in the fields, and women and children helped out at harvest time. Raising livestock was just as important, and the town hired herdsmen to lead dozens of communally owned cattle each morning from the village to common lands at what is now Central Park West and West 96th Street. As late as 1699 the New York Council found that residents of Harlem were "Chiefly Addicted to [. . .] Improvement of Husbandry." Such devotion was a necessity, not a choice. Harlemites had to work year-round to produce and store enough food for their families and salt hay for the cattle to last the long winter.

Much economic activity uptown was made possible by the labor of Africans. Relatively few of the hundreds of Africans, free and enslaved, who lived on Manhattan in the late seventeenth century—more than a third of the island's population—made their homes in Harlem. Still, tiny self-contained, relatively independent black neighborhoods dotted upper Manhattan during this period, with separate markets and establishments for eating, drinking, lodging, and gambling—there was even a Negro burial ground at what is now East 126th Street and Second Avenue. Harlem's blacks lived in their own homes and continued to work with relative freedom from the discrimination and violence encountered in the southern colonies, which was also becoming more common downtown. The first speech of Governor Nicolls, an investor in the Royal African Company, included a description of a runaway slave. His successors introduced restrictions into the lives of slaves, who could no longer make contracts, officially get married, or bear witness in court against free men. After one of Daniel Tourneur's slaves fled into uptown's dense forests in 1669, British officials launched a full-scale police pursuit, complete with hue and cry. Soon thereafter the British passed laws that required slaves to carry passes and prevented them from participating in trade with whites, owning guns, or meeting in public in large numbers. Eventually, the British gave special port privileges to slave ships and introduced even more strict regulation along racial lines. Crimes against slaves were rarely recognized—on at least one instance, a slave child was beaten to death uptown, with no effort on the part of the government to punish the murderer—while crimes by slaves were vigorously prosecuted. A group of Harlemites petitioned the New York Council during this period to protect them from "a band of Negroes, who have run away from their masters at New York and commit depredations on the inhabitants of the said village." By the time a slave market was established on Wall Street in 1711, eighty-four slaves made up almost a quarter of the Out Ward, as northern Manhattan was termed, and half of all families kept slaves.

Slavery was just business for the British—almost everything was, which is why New York became the economic powerhouse that was supposed to have been New Amsterdam's fate. When Governor Thomas Dongan arrived in 1683, he brought with him a mandate from the duke of York to introduce sweeping political changes as a way of squeezing more money out of the colony. By the end of the year Dongan had instituted an elected assembly of representatives and a new court system. He had reorganized New York City into six wards, each electing local officials answerable to a common mayor. The Protestants of the Out Ward looked suspiciously at the Catholic Dongan, but religion wasn't the most important factor. They objected to Dongan's refusal to allow Harlem's elected officials the same independence as those downtown, and they balked at the profoundly un-Netherlandish program of the new administration. Under Dongan's rule, inheritance law favored the eldest-born son, which conflicted with Dutch preferences for Calvinist-capitalist meritocracy. Dongan also restricted the ability of married women to do business or own land, a rule that was unworkable on uptown's family farms.

Even more changes were coming. After the death of Charles II in 1685, the duke of York became King James II and New York became a royal province, as opposed to a proprietary colony. That bureaucratic distinction gave the king the right to void previous charters that covered the island and to dismiss the assembly that had passed them. Harlemites were so worried that the lands granted them under the previous patents were no longer secure that they stopped paying taxes on their lands altogether. In response, Dongan induced the council to pass a resolution reaffirming the political unity of the entire island, an action clearly directed at Harlem and its persistent assertions of independence. Dongan also threatened to seize any lands uptown that had not been specifically and explicitly purchased from Indians. To be sure, Dongan was no friend of the Indians. There were few left on the island who might contest property ownership, much less pose any danger to settlers living in such an exposed situation. Rather, the French were becoming the main security concern, although Harlem was thought to be safer than downtown in case of attack because there was so little to invade.

Harlemites were transforming their community from a village into a town, but events in England continued to determine the course of the community's development. The abdication of the Catholic James II in 1689 and the ascension to the throne of the Protestant King William— events known as the Glorious Revolution—had a profound effect on New York. The governor was overthrown and replaced by a local Prot-estant militia leader named Jacob Leisler who earned his new place with the help of extreme anti-Catholic and anti-aristocrat rhetoric. Leisler was particularly popular uptown, where there were few aristocrats and fewer Catholics. The Committee of Safety that officially promoted Leisler to commander in chief of the province in 1689 included Johannes Vermilyen, a well-connected Dutch Harlemite who also happened to be Jan de la Montagne Jr.'s father-in-law. Leisler, who put Vermilyen on his council, was slow to relinquish power to the new governor sent by the duke of York to straighten things out. After Leisler surrendered the fort in 1691, he was arrested, tried, hung, and beheaded. Vermilyen was found guilty of high treason and awaited execution for seventeen months, until he was pardoned and set free on orders of the king. The new governor even dissolved Harlem's court as a punitive measure.

Ultimately, the Leisler affair and its aftermath did little to inter-rupt the way of life uptown. If downtown New York was filled with the bustle of trade and the din of dozens of languages, with a population that doubled almost every twenty years, Harlem remained a relatively quiet, even stagnant farming village, isolated from the boom times of the slave trade and its related products, such as sugar and rum, and coming to life only in times of war or political upheaval. It wasn't until 1712 that the entire Out Ward was properly surveyed and claimed, and most of uptown Manhattan remained thickly forested for decades to come. A 1731 tax assessment declared it the least valuable of the city's eight wards—less than half of the rural Bowery Ward and about one-twentieth of the busy East Ward. As of 1749 there were only 131 houses in all of the Out Ward out of a total of 1,834 on Manhattan, and the village's streets still weren't properly surveyed and laid out. Harlemites may have supported Leisler, but uptown was no seething cauldron of political dissent—there weren't enough people. Things would be different in the next revolution.

As time went on anti-British sentiment grew uptown, though that was less a matter of national feeling than class tensions. By the mid-1700s rich merchants formed the core of Tory support on Manhattan, and there were few of those uptown. Most of Harlem's established families, including the de la Montagnes, Verveelens, Bogaerts, Delamaters, Bensons, Myers, Kortrights, and Dyckmans, not only supported independence but committed their sons to the fight. If there were Harlemites who were less than confirmed rebels, it was in large part because Harlem was economically insulated from the cost of living increases and unemployment that inspired so many downtown patriots. Until the mid-1700s the Crown wasn't all that interested in America, except when colonists caused trouble, and it was really only in the commercial centers of Boston and New York that colonists consistently came face-to-face with the mother country, mostly in the form of tariffs, duties, and taxes on paper, sugar, ink, glass, and official documents, which affected rural Harlem indirectly. The Provincial Colonial Assembly tried to avoid downtown epidemics in 1752 and again in 1757 by convening at McGown's tavern, located in the pass that cut through the far northern reaches of what is now Central Park. Only half a day's journey away, and therefore not quite yet within commuting distance, McGown's was also the weekly post rider's first stop north—the roads in general had improved so much that the entire round-trip from Philadelphia to Boston now took only a week—so it was as ideally suited for politics as it was for pleasure.

Harlemites saw New York's upper crust, patriot and Tory, only occasionally. But as New York became a hemispheric powerhouse of trade and industry in the mid-1700s, a new generation of prominent citizens began to see Harlem as the perfect spot to show off their wealth, and not just for an afternoon or an evening. They built country homes far from the crime, grime, and disease—smallpox, yellow fever, and measles killed 10 percent of the population in some years—that plagued a city that was growing explosively: between 1732 and 1773 the number of people living downtown grew from 8,600 to 25,000 people, which meant the city was finally bigger than Boston, though still smaller than Philadelphia. Among the earliest of a new type of country estates in Harlem in the eighteenth century was the 1760s-era house of John Maunsell and his wife, near what is now Amsterdam Avenue and 148th Street. Sold soon thereafter amid fears of the turmoil of the coming revolutionary conflict, it served as a tavern before being torn down in the nineteenth century. The only surviving example of such a house was built in 1766 by Roger Morris, a retired English officer whose American wife, Mary Philipse, was the daughter of the Speaker of the New York Colonial Assembly. Morris had made the acquaintance of George Washington when they were allies at the terrible Battle of the Monongahela River in western Pennsylvania, and they became close friends. Philipse's connection with the man who would become the father of his country was more personal: back in the 1750s she had rejected his marriage proposal.

The elegant and practical house that Morris built for Mary Philipse at what is now 65 Jumel Terrace became the envy of the entire colony. The thickly forested property, consisting of more than one hundred acres from the Harlem to the Hudson rivers, had majestic views. If the boast that one could see all thirteen colonies from the second floor was excessive, four of them were indeed within sight, as well as the Long Island Sound and the Atlantic Ocean. Morris, who came from a family of famous architects and designers, commissioned a nineteen-room, 8,500-square-foot manor that was a model of mid-eighteenth-century architectural taste, built in an up-to-the-minute, neo-Palladian style, with a hipped roof, wooden corner quoins, and a two-story front portico with Tuscan columns. The Chinese wall-paper in the drawing room was hand-painted, though the outside of the octagonal back wing was shingled to save money. An icehouse, smokehouse, dairy, garden, and orchard helped make the property self-sufficient, and the yacht that Morris moored on the Harlem River could be used for trips downtown when roads were impassable. The combination of style and function represented the democratic yearnings of the incipient republic as well as its dependence on the traffic in African lives and labor; Morris's slaves lived in the house's attic.

Morris, who served on the king's Provincial Executive Council of New York, had little opportunity to enjoy his new house. Rising anti-British sentiment in the late 1760s convinced him to send his family upstate. His wife, the model for the character of Frances Wharton in James Fenimore Cooper's novel *The Spy*, was eventually accused of treason, one of three such women in the entire Revolutionary War—one of the others was her sister—and her lands were confiscated. Morris himself fled to England, leaving later Harlemites to imagine: if Mary Philipse had married George Washington, she might have become the first lady of the United States instead of a traitor in exile. She responded that had she married Washington, he might have become a royalist fugitive rather than the father of his country.

It was in Harlem that the early course of the Revolutionary War was determined, along with the reputations of more than one founding father, among them Alexander Hamilton, who did more founding and fathering than most of them. A war hero, treasury secretary, preeminent legal mind of his generation, a framer of the Constitution, primary visionary of federalism, abolitionist, publisher, inventor of the modern industrial corporation, George Washington's most trusted colleague, and a pioneering uptowner, Hamilton had an unlikely start in life. He was born in 1755 out of wedlock to a poor, possibly Jewish divorced man and his common-law and possibly part-black wife; convinced of Hamilton's African ancestry, W.E.B. Du Bois called him "our own Hamilton." He came into the world at the edge of empire, on Nevis, one of the leeward islands of the British West Indies, and was raised on nearby St. Croix, where his mother ran a shop and owned five slaves, one of whom took care of the young boy. Orphaned at the age of eleven and deep in debt, Hamilton began working as a clerk for his mother's old business associates David Beekman and Nicholas Cruger, both of whom had originally come from New York and were making a killing in the islands providing everything a planter would need, from tools to food to livestock and slaves. Hamilton hated his job, writing to a friend in a now famous 1769 letter: "To confess my weakness, Ned, my Ambition is so prevalent that I contemn the Grovelling condition of a Clerk or the like, to which my Fortune etc. condemns me, and would willingly risk my life, tho not my character, to exalt my station . . . I wish there was a war." He would get his wish soon enough.

Hamilton received a surprisingly good education and by sixteen was publishing poems in local newspapers. He made his way to New York in early 1773 but was turned away by the pro-independence College of New Jersey. He ended up in downtown Manhattan, at King's College, later known as Columbia University, which had less rigorous admission requirements but a distinctly royalist student body. Hamilton, who was only three years older but already a world wiser than most of his peers, had been at King's College for only two months at the time of the Boston Tea Party, in December of 1773. His patriotic leanings became revolutionary fervor and he began publishing articles and pamphlets in support of the First Continental Congress. Hamilton was too young to be a prime mover of the Revolution, but he was at the vanguard of the next political generation, his patriotic energy matched only by his sense of dignity and propriety. This rootless bastard was inventing what it meant to be an American gentleman.

It took four days for news of the events at Lexington and Concord to reach Harlem. The joy that Harlemites expressed at the information, and their elation at hearing of the looting of the British arsenal downtown shortly afterward, soon turned to worry. If the war came to New York, Harlem's strategic position would once again make it coveted ground for both sides. After the British decided in January 1776 to make lower Manhattan their base of military operations, General George Washington built fortifications uptown, which not only provided an elevated base for controlling the North River via cannon fire but also straddled the land route to the north. By June 1776 Harlem was an armed camp. American soldiers from Connecticut had been moved there from downtown in order to maintain "good order and discipline"—code for avoiding the moral temptations that beckoned in the whirlwind of prewar activity below Wall Street. At the same time, some five thousand rebels were gathering at Kingsbridge, and another three thousand were encamped on the property of Roger Morris. From late July through late August, when General Washington was ordering even more soldiers "to the flat grounds of Haerlem," uptown was busy with revolutionary activity. The Provincial Congress met there, as did the convention drafting a constitution for what would become New York State.

Meanwhile, Alexander Hamilton was drilling daily with a volunteer militia in a downtown churchyard. He was offered the blue and white uniform of a captain in the company of artillery of the province of New York so long as he could find thirty volunteers to follow him. By early summer, Hamilton had more than twice that many. Only nineteen years old, he was put in charge of cannons at one of downtown's forts. He kept a close eye on the British ships that filled the harbor all summer in anticipation of an armed conflict. It was one of the largest invasion forces that England had ever mustered: thirty battleships and three hundred supply ships holding thirty thousand seasoned and equipped British and Hessian soldiers, ten thousand seamen, and twelve hundred cannon. Against this fearsome enemy were arrayed less than half as many American soldiers, most of them untrained and bearing only farm tools. The British crossed over to Brooklyn and met Washington and his forces on August 27 in a disastrous battle that ended at dusk with the bulk of the American army pinned back against the East River, awaiting slaughter the next morning. Washington evacuated virtually his entire army across the river under cover of darkness during the early hours of August 28, a startling maneuver that saved the Revolution—it was in fact Hamilton's idea, or so his descendants claimed. It would have been his last idea had a young Aaron Burr not delivered an order for Hamilton to abandon his position downtown, where the British were executing suspected rebels, and join Washington uptown.

It was raining heavily as the Americans retreated up the west side of Manhattan via the Bloomingdale Road to Washington's fortifications at Harlem Heights. Washington settled into the Roger Morris mansion and waited. His nine thousand soldiers had dug in between what is now West 147th and West 161st streets, on the heights above what was known as the Hollow Way, today's West 125th Street. There, Washington recruited a young man from Connecticut named Nathan Hale to dress up as an itinerant Dutch minister and travel among the British to see what he could learn, a mission that was especially troublesome because spying was then considered ungentlemanly. But Washington was learning fast that good manners would not win the war.

On the morning of September 15, British ships anchored in the East River began bombarding the five thousand Americans stationed at Kip's Bay. Washington, ensconced on the second floor of the Morris mansion, heard the cannon fire, raced to the front portico to see the action, and leaped onto his horse to speed down the Harlem Heights, through McGown's Pass and down the East Side, a four-mile journey taken at a full gallop. Washington found a debacle awaiting him, with five brigades of Americans in full retreat, a scene he later described as "disgraceful and dastardly." The reserved Washington dropped his stern dignity, probably for the first and last time in his life, tearing off his hat and crying out, "Are these the men with whom I am to defend America?" Crossing back over to the West Side of the island and moving up the Bloomingdale Road after the lead of his aide-de-camp Aaron Burr, he returned to the safety of Harlem. It was a bleak moment for Washington, who circumspectly observed that he was "obliged to confess my want of confidence" in his troops. He was hearing reports of so many desertions—some six thousand Connecticut troops had walked away from service in early September, taking weapons and ammunition with them—that he set up a post at King's Bridge to stop them.

Washington didn't despair. He had been trained as a surveyor and cartographer, and he knew how to capitalize on the terrain where most of his army was now dug in—he was intimately familiar with the area from his unsuccessful attempts at wooing Mary Philipse there years before. If the British wished to attack Harlem, they would come down the slope of what is now Morningside Heights and across the Hollow Way, or through the flats surrounding the Harlem Creek and up the rocky precipice of what is now St. Nicholas Park. Either way, Washington could observe them from the Point of Rocks, a now demolished cliff at what is presently West 126th Street and Convent Avenue. The British, who unwisely wrote off Washington's motley army as a mere annoyance, would be totally exposed, while his own troops would remain above, well screened by trees and bushes. Best of all, the British, marching up the east side via the Kingsbridge Road and stopping at the Black Horse tavern, at McGown's Pass, seemed unaware of the extent of Washington's movement up the west side and the solidity of his position.

Still, Washington couldn't sleep after darkness fell. In order to ease his mind he decided to examine the state of his fortifications. As he picked his way through the camp, he saw that most of his exhausted and demoralized men had fallen asleep in the wet meadows. One particular division caught his eye: even after a disastrous day, in the dead of night, in the rain, these men worked with a distinctive alertness, efficiency, commitment, and courage that Washington couldn't ignore. He inquired after their commanding officer and was directed to the red-haired youth who had led them uptown, the last few hours in the dark, lugging their six-pound cannons, and who was now helping to fortify their position. It was Alexander Hamilton, and it would be the decisive encounter in the lives of both men. Washington reached out his hand and met the man who would become his brains, in war and in politics. Hamilton was meeting the man who would make him a man.

While Washington met Hamilton, the enemy was asleep at McGown's Pass, but they were up early the next day, advancing north to confront Washington at Harlem. They hardly expected to be drawn into a fight. The American general Thomas Knowlton, a Bunker Hill hero anxious to redeem the disgraceful conduct of his men the day before, now led a reconnaissance mission with 120 of his Connecticut Rangers, reinforced by Hamilton's cannons on the Heights. The British opened fire at what is now West 106th Street and Riverside Drive and forced Knowlton's men to retreat north through today's Columbia University campus. Knowlton's men fell back as planned, knowing that Washington had flanking forces ready. The British, thinking they were capping off their third victory in a month, engaged with Knowlton's Rangers along their western flank. At eleven in the morning a British bugler, thinking they were about to win the day by overcoming Knowlton's men, sounded the traditional signal of the end of a fox chase, a move meant to humiliate the enemy. It had just the opposite effect on the American soldiers. Washington's troops now descended from Harlem Heights and attacked the British frontally, while the Americans who had mustered at Harlem's church marched along Church Lane to the enemy's eastern flank. They had now pinned down the British from the north, east, and west, and Washington's men forced their adversaries into a bloody retreat through a buckwheat field on what is now the campus of Barnard College. By late afternoon they had been driven back to what is now West 106th Street, where Washington ordered his men to disengage, knowing that English reinforcements would soon arrive. The cowards of Kip's Bay had become the heroes of Harlem. It was a small victory in terms of territory—a "brisk little skirmish," Washington called it—but an important one in other ways: it was the general's first American victory.

The Battle of Harlem Heights was also one of the first examples of American cunning and familiarity with the terrain overcoming brute British force—the Americans had numbered only two thousand, many of them without guns or even shoes, compared to about five thousand well-armed, well-fed, and properly clothed British troops. The Americans counted dozens of casualties, including several high-ranking officers. In contrast, the British lost only fourteen men, none of them of significant rank. Still, this important psychological victory was a turning point in the war. After their earlier humiliations, the Battle of Harlem Heights, which allowed a ragtag band of volunteers to hold on to the northern half of Manhattan, gave them all confidence. "This little advantage," wrote Washington, a man without the capacity to exaggerate, "has inspired our troops prodigiously. They find it only requires resolution and good officers to make an enemy give way." Washington now knew that even a poorly trained and equipped force could hold its own against British regulars, if they used their knowledge of local conditions and acted boldly. In Harlem, for the first time in his career, Washington abandoned his defensive habits and assumed the role of daring tactician, an officer who would humiliate one of the greatest military powers in history.

Washington now believed he could win the war, though the view from his headquarters at the Morris mansion showed him that retaking Manhattan remained a remote possibility. There was little time to reflect. On the night of September 20, a fire destroyed a quarter of New York City—more than a thousand buildings burned down, accounting for the paucity of colonial structures downtown today. Washington watched the conflagration, which some historians believe he actually ordered, from the Morris mansion and then got back to business. The rest of the Continental Army was doing well in terms of supplies, manpower, and strategic position but there was much to worry about in Harlem, where the bulk of the American army and its leadership were surrounded. Washington fortified King's Bridge and hosted two Caughnuaga leaders at the Morris mansion in what was doubtless a strategic bid to send a message to the British, with whom the Indians maintained good relations, that all was well in the rebel camp. He also sent two thousand men down into the Harlem Plains to harvest hay and grain in a nighttime operation that would prevent the loss of a whole year's work by a community whose future was in peril. If Washington was also thinking of provisioning his own men and beasts, it was all aboveboard, for unlike his adversaries he was scrupulous about paying civilians for the use or consumption of their property. He also punished soldiers who abused their hosts. Only a week following the Battle of Harlem Heights, even as he struggled to find enough men to fight the war, Washington prescribed "a little wholesome Severity" for his troops, authorizing courts-martial for those who tried to plunder Harlem.

Two months later the British had learned their lesson, and when they faced Washington again they brought more than enough men to do the job. The Americans had fallen back on the heights just north of what is today Harlem proper, in a chain of fortifications leading from today's West 183rd Street to Fort Washington itself, located at what is now West 192nd Street. It was all part of a race to claim the Hudson River, where any traffic moving north could be exposed to bombardment from the heights. Washington's strategy of making the river impassable by submerging a string of rock-filled boats in a line across the river failed. On October 9, three massive warships made it up the river, and Washington knew he would soon see an attack from the north. He ordered a general retreat to White Plains—his headquarters at the Morris mansion would serve as a base of operations for British and Hessian commanders—though he did leave about two thousand troops at Fort Washington. The two armies finally met again on October 28 at White Plains, where the British routed the Americans and then turned their focus south, to finish off whatever rebels remained on Manhattan. On November 16, 1776, more than fourteen thousand British troops swarmed over the Fort, a victory that gave them control over the whole island. They burned down the village of Harlem the next day, destroying the second church, near what is today East 125th Street and Second Avenue, and razing the mill and farmhouse along the Harlem Creek.

Alexander Hamilton served as Washington's aide-de-camp for the next three years, calm and organized even when facing direct fire or leading bloody assaults on enemy positions. Barely out of his teens, he was soon strategizing and politicking with the general and writing his speeches; Hamilton's influence was so evident that Benjamin Rush, the most prominent doctor in America at the time, noted that Washington was "governed by one of his aides." Such a charismatic figure was bound to clash with his mentor. At first, Hamilton had been swept up in the sheer force of the general's presence. As time went on, however, he revered Washington less. He repeatedly applied for promotion, and

Washington repeatedly refused, since it would have meant losing the benefit of a youth whose "frenzy of valour," as one colleague put it, had already made him one of the greatest figures of his time. By early 1781 Hamilton's frustration was overflowing. To Washington's distress, Hamilton quit, though it seems to have been love and not war that made up his mind. Hamilton had met the woman who would become his great love, Elizabeth Schuyler. No one found it curious that this girl's father would allow his daughter, in whose veins the very bluest of Anglo-Dutch aristocratic blood flowed, to be courted by a poor, illegitimate, possibly black or Jewish orphan—that is how grand Hamilton's reputation had become, even at the age of twenty-one. When Hamilton resigned his position with Washington he was clearly thinking beyond the war, but the call of his adopted country had him back in uniform later that year leading his own company at Yorktown.

After being torched by the British, Harlem came to a standstill, and it remained that way for most of the war. Those few Harlemites who favored the Crown were long gone, having already left in order to avoid the restrictions of martial law and scarcity of goods. Most of the patriots had gone into exile, though some families remained active in the war: Jan Dyckman's grandsons, Sampson, Michael, and William, joined the famed militia known as the Westchester Guides. By 1779 an eyewitness found Harlem totally unoccupied, abandoned by the Americans and destroyed by the British. Redcoats had stripped the woods surrounding Harlem of their trees for firewood and for military construction, and to prevent vegetation that could shield sneak attacks, but by the early 1780s nature had virtually reclaimed the village. The British now found the Harlem Valley perfect for fox hunting, and in September of 1782, seven weeks before the end of hostilities, a horse race was held along Harlem Lane, with "a very neat Saddle and Bridle" offered as first prize. Even in wartime, things never got so bad that downtowners couldn't go uptown for a little fun.

3

SWEET ASYLUM
Founding an American Harlem,
1781–1811

The beginning of the end of the American War of Independence came in October 1781, with the British surrender at Yorktown, Virginia, but it took years for Harlemites to come home. It wasn't until November 21, 1783, four days before the British left downtown, that George Washington crossed over from the Bronx to Manhattan to meet with officers and politicians at Day's tavern, at what is now Eighth Avenue and West 126th Street. Reoccupying the island was first on the agenda, and Washington ordered the army to capture any "offenders" who remained. Peace could be as complicated as war, Washington knew, so he spent a few nights at Harlem, first at the newly opened Blue Bell tavern and then at Leggett's Halfway House, located in the old McGown's tavern, before heading south to New York City. Even then, it took time for the new political realities to sink in uptown. After Washington and his company left, a group of twenty-five loyalists tried to tear down the American flag flying at Leggett's.

The War of Independence had been good for New York. The city, which served as the base of operations for the British, doubled in population, to some thirty thousand people, between 1775 and 1780. Retreating soldiers and fleeing loyalists reduced its size to about twelve thousand inhabitants in 1781, but it soon began growing again, especially when the business of government began in what was then the capital of the new state and the new nation. Trade with the West Indies—importing sugar, rum, and slaves and exporting tobacco and grain—also started up again. By 1790 there were more than thirty-three thousand people below the city's new northern border of Houston Street, and that number more than doubled by the time of the War of 1812. Overcrowding was hardly the only problem. Many of the buildings that didn't burn down in 1776 were still vulnerable because there wasn't enough water available to put out fires. Moreover, poor water quality and deplorable sanitary conditions meant that epidemics continued to ravage New York City. One outbreak of yellow fever claimed the lives of more than 5 percent of the city, with casket makers roaming the streets shouting "Coffins of all sizes!" No wonder not just aristocrats but prosperous downtown businessmen who were supplanting the old hereditary order with a new mercantile upper class wanted to get away, and northern Manhattan was just the place. According to the very first federal census, taken less than a decade after the end of the war, there were only 803 people living in the entire Harlem Division, 189 of whom were slaves. While these may seem like substantial numbers, many of these people lived outside the village proper, and the total number was not even 3 percent of the island's population. The census also characterized 41 people in northern Manhattan as "other," which may have referred to people about whom not enough was known, or to free blacks, persons of mixed race, Indians, or even Jews—among the prominent New Yorkers who owned property uptown was the well-known businessman and proto-Zionist Benjamin Judah.

Matters of both war and government had brought Washington back to Harlem in the fall of 1783, but in the years that followed it was pleasure that the new president was after. Local lore has it that Washington fancied one of the female slaves who worked at the old Stone House Inn, at what is now St. Nicholas Avenue and West 152nd Street. Easier to document is the trip he took in October 1789 with his vice president, John Adams, and their wives through Long Island and the Bronx before ending up with a dinner at Marriner's tavern, at what is now First Avenue and East 126th Street. Washington returned to Harlem the following summer with Vice President Adams and his wife, Abigail, as well as their son, the future president John Quincy

Adams, in addition to Secretary of State Thomas Jefferson, the Secretary of War Henry Knox, and Secretary of the Treasury Alexander Hamilton. Ensconced in a six-horse yellow carriage decorated with mermaids and cupids, they toured the Revolutionary War fortifications at Harlem and imbibed at Marriner's before visiting the old headquarters at the Morris Mansion.

Washington wasn't the only downtowner riding uptown for pleasure. Improved roads meant that Harlem was finally within reach of commuters as well as day trippers. In the years after the Revolutionary War, charges for pleasure excursions were high: one pound, twelve shillings for a full day's excursion in a coach and one pound, eight shillings for a half day, which didn't include a fiddler, food and drink, care of the horses, or the prostitutes who often came along. Trips uptown were not only expensive but hazardous. A 1795 article in the New York *Journal* recounted how passengers were killed when they tried to get out on the steep stretch of road that would later be known as "Breakneck Hill," along what is now St. Nicholas Avenue.

In the years after the war, visitors had a broad choice when it came to lodgings. In addition to Marriner's, Day's tavern, Leggett's Halfway House, and the Blue Bell there were the Crossed Keys and the Black Horse. Many new inns opened in the years after the war, including the Kimmel tavern, the Post Inn, Halsey's tavern, and the Harlem Coffee House. Washington no doubt chose Marriner's because of the patriotic associations of its owner, William Marriner, who had served as a captain during the war, twice venturing into British territory to kidnap high-ranking officers. After the fighting was over he went back into the hospitality business, running a number of taverns, including one at the Morris Mansion, which was renamed the Calumet Inn and described as a "genteel house of entertainment," in the words of the New York *Packet*.

The grandeur of the Morris Mansion, even in its less distinguished phase, still inspired architects and their uptown patrons, more than one of them ex-loyalists who obviously felt at home in Harlem, despite their politics. Cadwallader D. Colden, who was born into a prominent loyalist family and spent the Revolution in England, returned to New York in 1785 and built a country retreat at what would become Seventh Avenue near West 139th Street. Valentine Nutter, a loyalist sympathizer who ran a book and stationery shop downtown, sat out most of the war in Nova Scotia with his two slaves, but after the war he returned to New York and built Nutter Farm, at what is now Lenox Avenue and West 110th Street—he had inherited part of the old de la Montagne property. Perhaps the best-known example of this new generation of uptown mansions was the home of the businessman and chemist John Bradhurst, after whom Harlem's Bradhurst Avenue is named. The property, near what is now West 152nd Street and St. Nicholas Avenue, had belonged to the ex-loyalist officer John Maunsell, whose niece Mary married Bradhurst, bought the land and the house in 1796, and turned it into a grand country estate called Pinehurst.

The most prominent of these new Harlemites was George Washington's former aide-de-camp Alexander Hamilton, who had gone from strength to strength since he fought by the general's side. After becoming a lawyer in 1782, he set up his home and practice on Wall Street. The tireless Hamilton founded the Bank of New York and the New York *Evening Post,* and he invented the modern American corporation in the form of the Society for Establishing Useful Manufacturing, at Paterson Falls, New Jersey. Of course, it is as a public servant that he is best remembered. He published dozens of anonymous Federalist Papers in 1787 and 1788 on the importance of a strong central government, articles that helped ensure the ratification of the U.S. Constitution. As the nation's first secretary of the treasury—at the age of thirty-three—Hamilton dreamed up America's first federal budget, central bank, and tax system and he founded United States Coast Guard and Customs services. As active as he was in politics and business, Hamilton still found time to do pro bono work for St. Mark's Church in the Bowery and for Sailors' Snug Harbor for aged seamen, both of which still exist. Hamilton also helped found New York's oldest high school, Erasmus Hall, and even though his own wife was a slave owner, he was active in publicly confronting America's already disastrous racial situation.

During the Revolutionary War, Hamilton had unsuccessfully urged the use of black soldiers, though this was less a moral position than a pragmatic one, since Washington's army had been decimated by desertions and resignations, and Hamilton did balk at the idea of Negro officers. After the war he founded the Society for Promoting the Manumission of Slaves, started a chain of African Free Schools, and gave free legal representation to runaway or kidnapped slaves. When in 1786 he was elected to the New York State Assembly, among his first acts was a petition to end the slave trade in New York State, and it was partly due to his influence that abolition, albeit gradual, began in the state in 1799. Hamilton's complicated and contradictory position on slavery derived from his curious belief that slavery was morally excusable but economically unnecessary, since America's future depended not on forced labor and agriculture but on immigration, banking, and manufacturing. Such ideas were deeply repugnant to many Americans, but Hamilton never set much store by popular opinion, and he often found himself a party of one.

After the war, Hamilton remained close to Washington, ghostwriting the general's farewell to the troops at Fraunces Tavern and President Washington's seventh and eighth annual addresses to Congress. But as time went on Hamilton became estranged from the other founding fathers, who considered him a vain social climber. They detested the sight of him strutting about New York like a dandy, dressed in the white and tan color scheme of his native tropics. Many also questioned his commitment to representative democracy. No less an authority than Thomas Jefferson warned Washington that Hamilton was "a man whose history, from the moment at which history can stop to notice him, is a tissue of machinations against the liberty of the country which has not only received and given him bread, but heaped honors on his head." Even his Federalist ally John Adams tried to convince Washington that Hamilton was "the most restless, impatient, artful, indefatigable and unprincipled intriguer in the United States, if not the world." Hamilton lost even more friends in the deadlocked presidential election of 1800, which pitted a Federalist ticket of John Adams and Charles Cotesworth Pinckney against the Republicans

Thomas Jefferson and Aaron Burr. Hamilton had no great love for Jefferson but he was terrified at the idea of his old rival Burr in power.

In terms of blood and background, there could be no greater contrast between these two founding fathers. Hamilton was a poor bastard of dubious racial origin, and Burr, born in Newark, New Jersey, in 1756, was the moneyed scion of the finest of colonial stock. This sickly, spoiled boy was also an expert fencer and marksman who excelled in his studies. The times drew many young men into revolutionary activities but Burr, who was short but good-looking and apparently very charming, preferred women to politics. It wasn't until the summer of 1775 that he joined Colonel Benedict Arnold's hopeless expedition to take Canada. Burr distinguished himself by impersonating a priest and delivering a message through 120 miles of savage winter wilderness, and later saving the life of his wounded general by carrying him through the snowdrifts out of the range of British gunfire. In June of 1776 Burr became Washington's secretary but, like Hamilton, he chafed at his subordinate position, quitting after two weeks and returning to the battlefield. By 1779 he felt he had done his duty and resigned his commission, marrying and starting a law practice on Wall Street, just a few doors down from Hamilton. With the end of the war, business was booming, and they set aside differences to do business. Indeed, Burr was equivocal when it came to party allegiance. Though he founded the Tammany Society, an anti-Federalist club that came to dominate local politics, he was known as the "Eel" because he wouldn't commit to party or position. Burr's election to the United States Senate in 1791—his opponent was Hamilton's father-in-law—put an end to the pretension of courtesy between the two men.

Thomas Jefferson called the contest to become the third president the "Revolution of 1800," because it marked the rise of the Republican Party as a permanent force in American politics. Even Hamilton defied his Federalist principles, crossing party lines to support Jefferson, a decision that helped relegate him to the margins of American political life. Something much more personal was also in play. Hamilton was devoted to his wife and family, but he was notorious among the founding fathers for his philandering. In 1797 Hamilton was humiliated by a blackmail attempt—he was convinced it was Burr out to revenge one too many political squabbles—that involved one of his extramarital affairs. Rather than back down, Hamilton came clean and began looking for an exit strategy from public life. He had always loved urban life and New York City in particular, which he had helped turn into a maelstrom of trade, industry, and commerce. Now he began to look elsewhere for refuge.

Hamilton had long regretted his inability to live and entertain in a grand fashion, like Jefferson at Monticello or Burr at Richmond Hill. "If I cannot live in splendour in Town," he wrote, "I can at least live in comfort in the country." Also at work in Hamilton's desire to move to the country was his sense that conditions downtown were worsening. In 1793 Hamilton and his wife had both come down with yellow fever. His sudden embrace of nature and family surely pleased his enemies, especially Jefferson, who had never been able to convince Hamilton, the quintessential New Yorker, of the superiority of rural life. Now, Hamilton began to enjoy fishing and hunting with his sons on visits uptown. It was on one of these jaunts that they came to know the businessman Jacob Schieffelin, whose house in Harlem had a pier where the Hamiltons sometimes docked. Hamilton was impressed by what he saw, and in the summer of 1798 he took a half interest in a farmhouse in Harlem. The weekends that he began spending there with his family inspired him to put down roots. Later that year he hinted in a letter to his wife that he was thinking of buying land in Harlem and building a home for them all. In 1800 he bought from Schieffelin and Samuel Bradhurst thirty-two acres of wooded land, from what is now West 139th to West 146th streets, and from St. Nicholas Terrace to Hamilton Place. Close to the Bloomingdale Road, the property made for easy commutes downtown. It also had the second-best views on the island, next to the nearby Morris Mansion. Just as important, it was close to the scene of Hamilton's first great victory back in 1776.

The passion—he called it "executive energy"—that Hamilton had once put into building a nation now went into building his house, on the south side of what is now West 143rd Street, just east of Amsterdam Avenue. Named after the Hamilton ancestral home in Scotland, the Grange was designed by John McComb Jr., whom Treasury Secretary Hamilton had paid to build lighthouses a decade earlier. Since then, McComb had become the most celebrated architect in the nation, the designer of both Gracie Mansion and New York City Hall and the inventor of Federalist architecture in the years after the Revolution. The Grange was the home of a man with something to prove. The two-and-a-half-story, fifty-by-fifty clapboard house, with front and back porches and piazzas on each side, was at once practical and fanciful. Before it was altered in the late nineteenth century, a broad staircase at street level led to two octagonal drawing rooms for entertaining, trumping the Morris Mansion's single octagonal drawing room. Massive bay windows and mirrored walls made the rooms look bigger than they were. Illusion was also at work in the eight fireplaces, which fed four chimneys, two of which were ornamental. On the second floor were six bedrooms for the family's seven children, while servants and slaves had their quarters in the attic and did much of their work in the basement.

The Grange became Hamilton's obsession, and he became involved in every detail of its construction. He supervised the caulking on the porches, corrected the property's overly loamy soil, and obsessed over an eighteen-foot bed of flowers, instructing workers to arrange three sections of tulips, hyacinths, and lilies into three larger sections, all surrounded by a laurel hedge and climbing wild roses. If nothing else, it was a diversion from the sordid affairs of business and politics. Hamilton wrote to a friend, "A disappointed politician you know, is very apt to take refuge in a Garden."

Much of what we know about Hamilton's obsession with the Grange comes from letters he wrote on a portable mahogany desk, traveling on business in coaches bumping along remote upstate New York lanes or in small inns or modest boardinghouses. For all of his dreams about a peaceful retirement Hamilton, who not only suffered from gout but had frequent pain in his side from an old war wound, had to take to the road and work harder than ever to satisfy what his grandson called his "sylvan longings." He had to be resourceful when it came to raising money to build the Grange, getting a good deal from the general contractor because he had successfully represented his brother in a murder trial. No such economies were available with McComb, who charged Hamilton $2,495.20, an impossible sum even for one of the guiding spirits of the American Revolution. Hamilton more than once failed to qualify for a construction loan, and he had to mortgage the property for $5,000 in order to keep construction moving forward. The completion of the Grange in 1802 demanded a house-warming party, complete with speeches, prayers, and the exhibition of Hamilton's special pride and joy: a grove of thirteen sweet gum trees, raised from seedlings by George Washington at Mount Vernon and representing the thirteen colonies. Eventually, the Grange also became a gathering spot for the best company in New York, though not the political kind. Like his rival Aaron Burr, Hamilton had switched sides too many times and made too many enemies. That still left prominent families like the Bayards, the Birds, the Fishes, the Hosacks, the Kents, the Morrisses, and the Pickerings, who arrived in the evening and were instructed to come down for breakfast at 9 a.m. Hamilton's sister-in-law joked: "The company must wear their nightcaps to arrive in time." They would then eat and socialize until the next evening's formal ball for up to seventy people. But Hamilton didn't move to Harlem to relax. If Mount Vernon and Monticello could be working farms, so could the Grange, though Hamilton admitted that he was as ill prepared to play the role of gentleman farmer "as Jefferson to guide the helm of the United States." Still, Hamilton tried to make the house pay for itself by selling cabbage, strawberries, and asparagus. In the end, the grounds weren't large enough to make money and Hamilton cleared only $18 in two years.

When Hamilton wasn't on the road, he made the two-hour trip to his downtown office five days per week in order to be with his family in the mornings and evenings. The least religious of the founding fathers now recited the Lord's Prayer on family walks, and on Sundays he led a private worship service in the Episcopal manner. Hamilton also now began to spend more time with his children, playing on the Grange's lawn or singing songs with them. In the evening he took to lying on the grass with them until the stars came out. He then put them to sleep and got in bed beside them, often remaining there all night. Few founding fathers did as much founding—or as much fathering.

"Mine is an odd destiny," Hamilton once mused to an old friend. "Tragic" is perhaps a better word. In Harlem, he tried to escape the physical and ideological dangers of downtown, but old troubles haunted him. In late 1801, before the Grange was complete, his son Philip drunkenly insulted one of Aaron Burr's henchmen, Captain George Eacker, in the lobby of a downtown hotel. Eacker returned the insult and upped the ante, claiming that Philip was a "damned rascal," a charge that led to a duel early the next year in New Jersey. Hamilton, who had almost single-handedly shepherded into law a bill outlawing dueling in New York, advised Philip to exercise a gentlemanly maneuver called the *delope*, which involved purposely firing into the air and missing the opponent. Philip shot to kill but was mortally wounded in the encounter. Hamilton went wild with grief on seeing his dying son back in Manhattan and lay next to him in bed for the several days of intense suffering it took before Philip died. The family never recovered, though they were determined to make the Grange a place where, as Hamilton wrote to his wife, "I am always sure to find a sweet asylum from care and pain."

The election of 1800 had also marked the beginning of the end of Aaron Burr's political career. The office of vice president would have been enough for most men, but it wasn't for Burr, and as his term drew to a close he turned his sights to the governorship of New York. Again Hamilton refused to lend the support of the Federalists to a man "of irregular and insatiable ambition" who "ought not be trusted with the reins of government." It was the last straw for Burr, who embarked on a scheme of character assassination that could only end in a duel. Hamilton was aware that Burr had been an expert marksman since he was a boy, but he accepted the challenge and began to prepare for the possibility of his demise. At dawn on Wednesday, July 11, 1804, Hamilton rowed across the Hudson River and met Burr in Weehawken,

New Jersey. It was the same spot where Philip had dueled some two years earlier. Burr had even chosen the very set of guns used in the Eacker duel. When the order to "Present!" came, Hamilton raised his weapon and intentionally shot over Burr's head. Burr, who considered the *delope* cowardly, returned fire directly and shot Hamilton in the gut. The bullet severed his liver and lodged in his spine, but Hamilton remained conscious and was rowed back across the river. When word of the events reached uptown, Hamilton's seventeen-year-old daughter Angelica lost her mind, never to recover. Meanwhile, Elizabeth rushed downtown and watched helplessly as her husband suffered. He died the next day. Hamilton was forty-seven years old when he was buried in the graveyard of Trinity Church.

Letters Hamilton had written to his wife, to be opened in case of his death, explained his decision and bid her farewell, regretting that he "too far sacrificed the interests of my family to public avocations," and explaining that moving to Harlem had been an effort to rectify his error. At the time of Hamilton's death, the Grange was worth $25,000, but its builders were owed money, and he had paid only $2,000 of the $5,000 principle on the 1801 mortgage. Hamilton's political flip-flop during the election of 1800 hadn't left the family totally friendless. In 1805 Archibald Gracie and twenty-eight others bought the house and property for $30,500 and sold it back to Elizabeth for only $15,000. The family remained there until 1813, when they sold it and moved downtown, no longer able to afford the upkeep on such an extensive property. The Hamiltons didn't leave Harlem altogether, though. The Hamilton Free School, the first public school uptown, was chartered just a few years later, on land given by Elizabeth, at what is now Broadway near West 187th Street, and the family owned property uptown as late as the 1890s. Of course, the very names of Hamilton Heights and Hamilton Place keep Alexander Hamilton's memory alive.

Heretical though the thought may be, in one respect Hamilton was lucky to have died when he did. For all his love of the bustle of New York City, Hamilton cherished Harlem's natural beauty and didn't live to see it destroyed. Within a few years of Hamilton's death, his friend Jacob Schieffelin founded Manhattanville, an industrial village just down the Heights from the Grange. Schieffelin, one of the most important figures in Harlem's transformation from suburb to city, was born in 1757 in Philadelphia and grew up in Montreal. A loyalist sympathizer, Schieffelin found himself in 1776 in British-held New York, where he met and fell in love with a young woman named Hannah Lawrence, whose family owned much of West Harlem. A less likely match was hardly possible. Hannah was a Quaker, which meant she was a pacifist and an abolitionist when neither was considered respectable. When it came to bravery, however, she was more than Schieffelin's equal, writing verses critical of occupying English officers and scattering copies on the sidewalk on Broadway in front of Trinity Church, which was a capital offense. The two married in 1780 and settled in downtown New York, where Schieffelin started a drug company. But the venture closest to his heart was an ambitious land deal in the area surrounding his summer home along the Hudson River at what is now West 144th Street.

In 1806 Schieffelin joined with his brothers-in-law John B. Lawrence and James Buckley to establish the industrial hub of Manhattanville, in between the heights of Morningside and Harlem, which had long served as a cattle pasture. Schieffelin, who had acquired extensive holdings in the area, had the land surveyed and laid out a network of roads. Property was offered the following year, and as early as 1807 the *Downtown Advocate* noted, "This flourishing little town, pleasantly situated near the banks of the Hudson, about eight miles from City Hall, to the eye of the [. . .] tourist, appears well worthy of observation." By the next year Schieffelin had a regular ferry running to New Jersey. Manhattanville's success was a threat to the village of Harlem, which had been slow to recover from the destruction of the Revolutionary War years, counting fewer than ninety-one families.

Attracting new settlers uptown, whether to Harlem or to Manhattanville, depended in part on better transportation. Improvements on the Eastern Post Road meant regular stage coaches to Boston and Albany began passing through Harlem again in 1784, and within two

decades the New York City Council authorized the building of another street between the Bloomingdale and Post roads, to be called
the Middle Road. Stages headed to destinations outside Manhattan
also took advantage of improved ferries and bridges across the Harlem
River. The New York City to Albany stage, which passed through Harlem three times a week, now took only three days, and thrice-weekly
service to Boston took only six days. Soon a daily stage was available
to commuters traveling between Marriner's Inn and Wall Street, and
ferries ran downtown along both the Hudson and the Harlem rivers.

Harlem needed more than roads and ferries in order to grow. It
had taken five years for Harlemites to reconstruct the Second Dutch
Church, which the British had destroyed in 1776, and it wasn't until
1823 that Harlem had a church of a different denomination. There
was no proper school or library until 1796, it wasn't until 1804 that
Harlem saw its first fire engine, and the first proper market uptown
came only in 1807. Harlemites remained skeptical of improvements,
often with good reason: they opposed bridges over the Harlem River
because they floated on the surface of the water and limited navigabil-
ity. Yet the time when Harlemites, with a sentimental attachment to
their forested vistas, their quiet nights, their impassable village streets,
their litigious neighbors, and their old-fashioned Dutch customs, could
think of themselves as something other than New Yorkers was drawing to a close.

4

THE FUTURE IS UPTOWN

1811–1863

The young mapmaker hacking his way through uptown Manhattan in 1807 didn't need to worry about hostile Indians or bears, both of whom had been driven off the island long before. His main concern was a barrage of artichokes and cabbages launched by a Harlem housewife who thought he was a vagrant, or just another downtowner bringing "improvements." If she had looked more closely, she would have seen that the twenty-seven-year-old John Randel Jr. wielded not a knife or a pistol but a feather squib and an ink bottle strung from his neck. The city was paying him four dollars per day to make sense of the island's unruly topography and bring New York City into the nineteenth century by channeling Manhattan's explosive growth along a grid of numbered streets. Randel took the long view of the sparsely populated uptown wilderness and saw the following century's urban Harlem. His plan was one of the first fruits of the American Enlightenment, though Randel had to deal with the vegetables, too.

Randel's grid was a decisive factor in making New York City an industrial metropolis of immense wealth and staggering filth, a city intoxicated with opportunity and numb with despair, a boomtown driven by civic vision and political corruption. It was in this period that New York became the biggest city in the country, though that wasn't saying much, since for much of the period its population was still under a hundred thousand. Even so, it was already a troubled place. Despite a local economy that boomed in the years after the War of 1812, nearly 15 percent of all New Yorkers required some form of charity in the winter, and if some New Yorkers lifted themselves out of poverty, they were quickly replaced by needy immigrants arriving from England, Ireland, and Germany.

In the early nineteenth century, New York City was widely acknowledged as the dirtiest city in the nation. Garbage, raw sewage, and waste from slaughterhouses, factories, and stables was simply dumped in the street, where herds of scavenging pigs, goats, and wild dogs roamed free. The death rate was 20 percent higher than that of London or Paris. Yellow fever was often rampant, and that was when scarlet fever, cholera, or tuberculosis weren't ravaging the city. Corpses were buried within city limits, ruining already compromised public wells. Such conditions, and the destruction caused by the fire of 1835, when poor water supplies crippled fire fighters, convinced New York City's leaders to construct a hugely ambitious system to bring water from the upstate Croton watershed, more than forty miles away, to a twenty-million-gallon reservoir on West 42nd Street. Long wary of such enhancements, Harlemites tried to block the system because of the numerous houses that the aqueduct would displace, but they couldn't help but appreciate the fact that the system resulted in some distinctive architecture, starting with the High Bridge, a Romanesque viaduct that carried the water over the Harlem River from the Bronx to Manhattan. But Croton water and the city's increasing focus on improving sanitation services couldn't totally solve problems that were also due to poverty and overcrowding.

In addition to being dirty, New York's streets were also dangerous, especially when the city's notoriously corrupt and barely professional police force was on the job. This wasn't only a matter of the pickpockets and muggers who operated with impunity but of large-scale public violence. In the decades between the War of 1812 and the Civil War, deadly riots downtown targeted abolitionists, Irish immigrants, and even fans of British drama. In contrast there was safe, calm, green, and clean Harlem, which downtown doctors dealing with nervous or exhausted patients frequently prescribed. Long a destination for old-money families escaping the epidemic season, Harlem now became home to new class of New Yorkers getting rich through industry and trade and building country estates amid the farms and forests. They eventually founded the Harlem Yacht Club and the Harlem Symphony Orchestra and they even built a cricket ground next to the Red Horse tavern, at Third Avenue and East 105th Street.

Things were slow to change, and although an established downtown legend held that Harlemites slept twenty hours per day, the old Dutch values of thrift, humility, and hard work still dominated. For most of the early nineteenth century, Harlemites were roused from their beds by the sunrise tolling of the bell in Mount Morris Park. After a long day of work in the fields, markets, stores, or workshops, they retired to their homes or to the local tavern. Despite the reputation that Harlemites had for drinking to excess, nights were quiet. After the bell on Mount Morris Park tolled nine times, the town watchman cleared the streets with a stout wooden rattle. The villagers were up early even on the day of rest, with the church bell ringing at 8:45 a.m. to summon worshippers. Attendance may no longer have been mandatory, but uptown roads were blocked off by chains every Sunday morning to prevent the interruption of services by pleasure-seeking downtowners. But the old Harlem was steadily disappearing. The flat Harlem Valley made the opening of the avenues and streets simple and inexpensive, which made the neighborhood ideal for cheap housing for immigrants working at the factories, shipyards, depots, and lumber and coal yards starting to line the Hudson and Harlem rivers and helping to turn New York City into the capital of capitalism.

What was holding Harlem back was Manhattan's transportation system. None of the three routes leading north out of the city to Harlem was properly paved, much less maintained, so improving what roads already existed clearly wasn't the solution. Rather, city officials decided to divide the island into a dense business district downtown and a roomy residential neighborhood uptown, all contained within a tightly designed, rectilinear grid of avenues and side streets. That was the plan that John Randel Jr. was called on to implement, and over the course of four years he explored the entire island, more than once getting arrested by suspicious policemen. There were those who insisted that providing Harlem with an urban infrastructure was pure folly. Even the 1811 report that accompanied Randel's legendary map found it "improbable that (for centuries to come) the grounds north of the Harlem Flat will be covered with houses." Nonetheless, the commissioners of the report stood behind Randel's design of twelve numbered avenues, with side streets from 14th Street, where the city then ended, all the way up to West 155th Street. There were also two parks planned for uptown: the Harlem Marsh was to be located on seventy acres to be reclaimed from marshy land from Fifth Avenue to the Harlem River, between East 106th to East 109th streets, and Harlem Square was to take up twenty acres between Sixth and Seventh avenues, from West 117th to West 121st streets.

The Randel plan, which recommended a reshaping of Manhattan on a scale almost equal to the changes wrought by glaciers twenty thousand years earlier, was especially unpopular uptown because it swept away the neighborhood's history. In the village of Harlem itself, Randel's vision wiped out the old Indian paths and Dutch village streets because they ran diagonal to the grid. The rigid uniformity of the plan, in which "the scythe of equality," as one critic put it, did away with many of the charms of the old village. That criticism was eventually met by integrating old roads that cut across the grid—Hamilton Place, St. Nicholas Avenue, and Old Broadway—and to counter the plan's aesthetic shortcomings by varying the distance between avenues and the width of streets. Still, the grid usually ignored Harlem's topography. Many valleys, cliffs, and hills were sacrificed, and with them the impressive vistas that had attracted so many visitors and residents in the past. Clement Clarke Moore, now best known for the poem "A Visit from St. Nicholas," told a group of realtors in New York in 1818 that the commissioners of the Randel plan were the kind of men who "would have cut down the seven hills of Rome" to make a buck. Although the 1811 plan rejected downtown's 100-by-25-foot-lot block size in favor of a roomier 200-by-800-foot lot uptown, Randel himself admitted that "buying, selling, and improving real estate" was the goal of the commissioners' plan.

The city was in no hurry to implement the Randel plan uptown. It would be decades before most avenues and side streets were opened, and even this did not always guarantee that the way was passable. Harlemites didn't see their first proper cobblestone street, 129th Street between Third and Eighth avenues, until 1832. The Harlem Creek remained the best place on the island for boys to cast for flounder and perch. Indeed, marshy and swampy areas were not drained and filled in until the end of the nineteenth century, which led to precisely the same health problems that so many downtowners were seeking to escape. The cholera epidemic that killed more than three thousand downtowners in September of 1832 also raged through Manhattanville. There were so many dead that the firehouse at Third Avenue and East 130th Street was used as a morgue. It was an ominous introduction to Harlem's urban future.

The Randel plan took so long to implement in part because history got in the way. In June of 1812 the United States declared war on Great Britain, and once more a key line of defense against attacks on New York City was uptown. By mid-1814 fears that the enemy would try to invade from the north and east led to the construction of fortifications across the island near Harlem's southern border. In a remarkable display of social cohesion, over six weeks in the summer of 1814 the U.S. Army Corps of Engineers led two hundred volunteers, including groups of downtown candle makers, weavers, riverboat pilots, lawyers, butchers, the Sons of Erin, and members of the Asbury African Church, in building a chain of stone forts, blockhouses, entrenchments, and gates. At one point these fortifications, including Blockhouse Number One, which still crowns what is now Central Park's Great Hill, held almost two thousand men, but the war never came to Harlem. The action was primarily in Canada and the southern states. The uptown land rush that followed the end of hostilities in late 1814 created such a demand for building materials that most of the fortifications were dismantled and carted away for use in new housing.

The Harlemites who had most feared the war were the ones with the most to lose. That was certainly the case of the owner of the most gorgeous house on the island, the Roger Morris Mansion. After the Revolutionary War the property came into the hands of John Jacob Astor, the immigrant son of a German butcher who arrived in New

York City in 1784 and made a fortune in the fur trade before realizing that the real money was in real estate. In 1810 Astor sold the house and seventy-five adjoining acres for almost $20,000 to Stephen Jumel, a wine importer from France whose wife became one of Harlem's most memorable characters. Eliza Jumel was probably born in 1775, probably in a Rhode Island whorehouse, and was probably named Elizabeth Bowen. Perhaps it was Eliza Brown. No one will ever know for sure, and she seemed to like it that way. Betsey, as the child was known, was abandoned by her mother and grew up in workhouses or with local families. She grew to be a statuesque, charming, and intelligent lady of ill repute, according to all accounts, with reddish blonde hair and blue eyes that made her the most beautiful woman in Rhode Island. Lazy and ambitious at the same time, in 1794 she made her way to New York City, where she became an actress—this at the time when the stage was only one step removed from the bawdy house—and counted among her intimates Aaron Burr, Alexander Hamilton, and Thomas Jefferson, all of whom suspected her of political espionage.

Eventually Eliza attracted the attention of Jumel, who was rich, handsome, jovial, well connected, and, best of all, unconcerned about her past. They married in 1804 and lived downtown before traveling to France, where they sported among First Empire elites. When they returned to the United States it was to conquer New York. The first step was a splendid house for entertaining, and the old Morris Mansion, which had fallen on hard times, fit the bill. Eliza, who yearned for the life of a society hostess, restored the mansion with an eye toward entertaining downtown's finest. As with Alexander Hamilton, whose Grange was just a few minutes' walk away and whose widow became a close friend, Harlem was a place of new beginnings for Eliza. Her first party was a huge success, covered by both Hamilton's *Evening-Post* and by the *Republican Watch-Tower*. But her fresh start soon soured. Rich and famous men called regularly, but their wives never came along, no doubt because of Eliza's dubious past. There were consolations. Eliza rode out daily in her yellow carriage, accepted the few invitations that came her way, and made shopping trips to Europe, where her spending began to cause financial problems for Jumel, who remained behind in Paris. She convinced him to protect the mansion from creditors by making her the legal owner of all of his property, and for a time the arrangement worked to Jumel's benefit. By the time he returned from France in 1828, she had tripled their net worth to $3 million. If many New Yorkers were still leery of her, Europeans felt right at home in Harlem. She hosted figures such as Talleyrand and Napoleon's older brother Joseph Bonaparte, the Spanish and Neapolitan king, who lived across town at Claremont and who played chess with her every day. After Jumel died in 1832, apparently the victim of a fall from his carriage—some said Eliza pushed him out and watched him bleed to death—she became the wealthiest woman in the United States. Still, something was lacking, until Aaron Burr came back into her life.

Since Burr had known her back in the 1790s, the diminutive, honey-voiced Revolutionary War hero had stained the dignity of the vice presidency by murdering Alexander Hamilton. Acquitted in 1807 of trying to seize the Louisiana Purchase and other western lands on behalf of England and trying to found an empire in Mexico that would be ruled by none other than himself, Burr escaped to Europe rather than face a second trial. After years of wandering, borrowing, and fleeing the law and creditors, he finally returned in disguise to New York in 1812. Burr's new life was marked by new tragedy, as he lost his grandson to malaria and his daughter to a shipwreck. But he made the best of things, indulging in his two favorite pastimes, buying clothing and chasing women. Even though Eliza knew that Burr had long ago been permanently exiled from the nation's pantheon, she couldn't resist the old rascal's brilliant spirit and sugary charms. They were married in 1833 in the front parlor of the mansion in Harlem.

So Burr, who had almost bought the Morris Mansion back in 1803, ended up living there in grand style after all. He commuted to work downtown, still almost a job in and of itself, but his real energies went into gambling away Eliza's fortune. Arguments with Eliza about money, which began during the honeymoon, led to a separation after only two months. Burr had a heart attack and returned to Harlem, where Eliza nursed him back to his old ways, and by mid-1834 he had recovered enough to abscond with $13,000—he even sold her carriage and horses to pay off his debts. Eliza sued for divorce, using Alexander Hamilton Jr. as a lawyer, which hit Burr where it hurt. Burr countersued, charging Eliza with having a lover but, as Eliza and her lawyer knew, no judge in the land would see the randiest of all of the founding fathers, even at the age of seventy-eight, as the victim of infidelity. These matters were all over the newspapers, and jokes, poems, and songs about the stormy marriage up in Harlem were popular. Burr had nowhere to hide. Mothers on the street who spotted the sick, desperately poor old man pointed him out to their children as an example of the wages of sin, but he was unrepentant. Shortly before his death on September 14, 1836, the very day his divorce from Eliza was made official, Burr insisted, "I offer no apologies, no explanations." It was a fitting coda for a skirt-chasing visionary who was on principle unprincipled, coming as close to wearing treason's noose as he did to becoming president.

Eliza was an efficient mourner. She made several extended jaunts to Europe, where she advertised herself as the "Ex-Vice Queen of America." But by 1839 she was withdrawing into the house at Harlem, venturing out only for morning rides or regular visits to the nearby Chapel of the Intercession, built at 152nd Street and Tenth Avenue as a branch of downtown's venerable Trinity Church, or to her few friends in the neighborhood. Eliza became more and more eccentric, dressing in yellow satin and purple velvet, hiring musicians to play for her during breakfast and then waiting for guests who never arrived. One legend has her hosting Charles Dickens, who apparently used her as the model for the character Miss Havisham in *Great Expectations*. She indulged in ever more fanciful stories of her life that included romances with George Washington, Thomas Jefferson, and Benjamin Franklin. She was known as a notorious penny pincher who once used a shotgun to convince her plumber to reduce his fees. Then again, Harlemites knew that the astronomical twenty dollars she spent each day at one point at Valentine Johnson's butcher shop at Amsterdam Avenue and West 158th Street was going to feed the dozens of poor locals she invited to eat in the basement kitchen and stay indefinitely

in her barn, though she required them to march with fake rifles while
she supervised on horseback. No one came to see her anymore, but her
Irish servants made sure Eliza was dressed for company each morning, especially on Sundays, when she would adorn her black dress
with a single white ostrich feather, issue invitations to tea, and make
a grand entrance down the stairs. She finally died in 1865, dressed
in pink with a ribboned lace sleeping cap, as ready to meet death as
she had been to meet life. She was buried in Trinity Cemetery and
rests there still—except when she doesn't, apparently. Generations of
schoolchildren visiting the mansion, which was eventually donated to
the city and turned into a museum, have reported seeing Eliza's ghost
wandering the halls.

When Eliza Jumel first saw Harlem in the 1790s, the sleepy backwater
had only two churches and a single school serving fewer than one hundred families, none of whose homes had gas or sewer service. There
were no residents willing to serve as village trustee and the town had
no proper borders—even its legal status was unclear. By the time of
Eliza's death, Harlem was being swept along in the surge of downtown's growth. In the eighteenth century Charleston, South Carolina,
had been the most significant destination for imports to the United
States, and Philadelphia was the country's export capital. In the early
nineteenth century, New York City surpassed them both, becoming
the nation's center of international commerce and industry precisely
because of its port, which was ideally situated to capitalize on a transatlantic shipping boom and ever more open trade with Asia. The city's
population surpassed two hundred thousand in the late 1820s, and the
number of people living downtown tripled by the early 1850s; such
growth was supported by a network of canals that linked New York
City with Albany and Buffalo and eventually the Midwest and Canada.
Canals proved such a powerful engine of economic growth that Harlem
even tried to get one of its own to link the Hudson and Harlem rivers.
In 1827 the Harlem Canal Company began a three-mile-long canal
parallel to Benson's Creek, as Harlem Creek was sometimes known,

complete with locks to raise and lower vessels, that would be not only a trade route but a sixty-foot-wide thing of beauty, flanked by broad roads and forty waterside estates. The start of work at the Hudson River was announced with a fanfare of trumpets, but after four years of work the canal had not yet reached Fifth Avenue. The company went under and the canal was filled in. Work started again under the initiative of the Scottish immigrant Archibald Watt, but his dreams of cashing in on the mania for water-based transportation went nowhere.

Meanwhile, more old-fashioned means of transportation sufficed. The first scheduled ferry service between Harlem and New Jersey had begun in 1808, and soon passengers could travel from 125th Street downtown along the East or Hudson rivers in side-wheel steamboats in two hours or less. But ferries became less popular once bridges were built that linked roads between Harlem and the mainland. One-horse coaches or omnibuses began running from Wall Street or Bond Street via Second, Third, Fourth, Fifth, Eighth, and Tenth avenues. The ride was anything but comfortable. The six-passenger vehicles were cramped and filthy, with mice nesting in the straw that covered the floor. Nor was a ride in these coaches, at 25 cents, inexpensive.

A crucial change, and some say the decisive point in Harlem's history, came in 1837, when the New York and Harlem Railroad completed the country's first horse-drawn railway along Fourth Avenue from Chambers Street to the Harlem River. The line was successful from the start because it finally made daily commuting from Harlem a practical option for downtown's shopkeepers, clerks, and civil servants. The cars, painted on the outside with lively advertisements, were half the cost of the old coaches and considerably more comfortable. They also ran on more predictable schedules, every half hour in some cases, and could reach speeds of up to twenty miles per hour, though there were plenty of delays, immortalized in a children's rhyme from the period.

> *The Harlem Road is a smashing line*
> *It starts at four and stops at nine*
> *And if you want to go to town*
> *The quickest way is to foot it down.*

The Fourth Avenue line was largely the work of Charles Henry Hall, who made a fortune as a downtown lawyer and land speculator before moving, in 1829, into a mansion near West 131st Street and Fifth Avenue. A founder of St. Andrew's Episcopal Church, Hall more than any other figure was responsible for bringing Harlem into the nineteenth century, getting into both uptown's politics and its real estate, which were almost the same thing. He was behind the mapping out and opening of streets all over Harlem, and he brought in water, gas, and sewer lines. Now largely forgotten, it was Hall who took advantage of the land boom caused by the arrival of the New York and Harlem Railroad and transformed what the city's Board of Aldermen called "a third or fourth-rate country village" into a city unto itself. As always, Harlemites were ambivalent about such changes. When Robert Macomb Jr.'s bridge over the Harlem River blocked water traffic and threatened to put an end to the best bass fishing in New York, locals destroyed the span, an action that was eventually upheld in court.

The infrastructure, housing, and industry that turned Harlem into an urban community created divisions between rich and poor—especially after the arrival of destitute immigrants from Ireland—that still survive. The area east of the New York and Harlem Railroad tracks along Fourth Avenue came to be dominated by the cramped shacks of the poor, while West Harlem attracted comfortable row houses and freestanding mansions with spacious gardens. Competing visions of Harlem's future meant that there were still attempts to make money from farming. James Roosevelt, the great-grandfather of President Franklin D. Roosevelt, bought most of the land from East 110th to East 125th streets east of Fifth Avenue for farmland, but the effort failed and he sold off the property in 1825. Each wave of new immigrants would work small plots for another century, but it was clear that large-scale agriculture had no significant place in Harlem's future. An 1851 survey for a Hudson River railroad saw that Harlem's days as a "rural and retired spot" were numbered, and that it would "soon be but a part of the city" and "quite a manufacturing place."

Meanwhile, the village of Manhattanville was growing fast because of its excellent transportation links to downtown. Jacob Schieffelin's children were, like their father, important boosters of uptown's urban future. While Charles Henry Hall was pushing for a rail line to run up the east side, Schieffelin's sons were pushing for a west side line to be called the Hudson River Rail Road. The years after the War of 1812 saw improvements to the shoreline, including the construction of piers north of West 125th for loading and unloading grain, hay, milk, meat, coal, lumber, and many other raw materials as well as finished goods. Manhattanville came to resemble a tiny New England mill town, with eighty homes housing five hundred residents, most of whom worked in local tanneries, bottlers, a foundry and a fabric mill, breweries, stables, a hotel, rooming houses, and taverns. Manhattanville's founders took their places among the city's most prominent citizens. John B. Lawrence's son, Cornelius Van Wyck Lawrence, moved to Harlem in 1812 and got involved in Tammany politics, serving in Congress in the 1830s and eventually becoming the city's first popularly elected mayor. He was succeeded in office by another Harlemite, Aaron Clark, who had made a fortune as the so-called King of the Lotteries. During his two terms in City Hall, Clark was best known for an anti-Tammany campaign to curb the immigration that was helping to make downtown such a disaster. The best-known Harlemite to become mayor, Daniel Tiemann, knew that because immigrants were already creating the city's industrial future, anti-Tammany forces would have to find something else to focus on. Tiemann built a paint and dye factory in Manhattanville in 1839 taking advantage of the port to unload Caribbean logwood (for black dyes), South American lime wood (for purple), and Virginian oak bark (for yellow). He built a home on West 127th Street before running for mayor in 1857 and defeating the Tammany candidate, Fernando Wood, by promising to fight corruption in the police and civil service sectors.

Roads, ferries, bridges, and railway lines at Manhattanville and the village of Harlem would have gone nowhere without attracting 'the working and laboring classes wishing to settle themselves in

New York at moderate rents," according to the *New York Evening-Post.*
Four-story wooden row houses, built quickly and cheaply, had started
popping up for rent in the 1820s and '30s. Such housing dominated
a new village called Carmansville, founded in the 1840s by Richard Francis Carman, a downtown cardboard-box maker who sensed
enormous economic opportunity in the coming of the Hudson River
Rail Road. Located from West 142nd to West 158th streets along the
Bloomingdale Road, Carmansville boasted its own hotel, churches,
police station, and a railroad depot at West 152nd Street.

Despite increasing numbers of residents, Carmansville, Manhattanville, and the town of Harlem itself, were still dependent on
visitors. In the years after the War of 1812, no trip to New York was
complete without a look at Harlem. What was left of the area's fast-
vanishing natural beauty in the 1840s attracted Edgar Allan Poe, who
appreciated the respite from the "insufferably dirty" downtown, with
its dubious "spirit of Improvement." Many downtown newspapers
carried advertisements for excursions to Harlem to ride horses on
Third Avenue or on Harlem Lane, or to watch them at the trotting
course at the Red House tavern, at First Avenue and East 106th Street.
Particularly popular were day trips to a curiosity called the Harlem
Jet, a 115-foot-high artificial geyser in the Harlem River formed by an
opening in the underwater pipes through which Croton water passed.
The jet was closed upon the completion of the aqueduct along the
1,450-foot-long, 114-foot-high High Bridge, which also became a tourist attraction.

Sundays, when most visitors arrived uptown, were a moral battle-
ground. The most prominent church in Harlem in the decades before
the Civil War was the Third Reformed Dutch Church, a brick structure
with a towering spire constructed in 1825 near East 121st Street and
Third Avenue. Harlem was getting too big and too diverse for a single
church, however. Starting in 1823, Episcopalians could worship in
Manhattanville at St. Mary's Protestant Episcopal Church, a mission
institution run by St. Michael's Protestant Episcopal Church up the
hill in Bloomingdale. Unlike most churches in New York, St. Mary's, a
utilitarian clapboard structure, welcomed everyone from servants and

farmhands to the local aristocracy, regardless of race, and the church started New York's first free, mixed-race, nondenominational school. It was an initiative of the Reverend William Richmond, who was also behind the decision to stop charging annual rental fees for pews, making St. Mary's the first free Episcopal church in the United States. He also pioneered spiritual guidance to the inmates of insane asylums as part of a broad humanitarian program that included ministering to victims of the 1832 cholera epidemic. During times of financial crisis Richmond even helped ease local unemployment by arranging to have jobless Harlemites pave their own streets.

Methodist, Presbyterian, Baptist, and Congregationalist churches were flourishing, but the large number of Irish immigrants arriving uptown in the wake of the devastating potato blight that struck Ireland in 1845 made Catholicism the fastest-growing denomination. Land once belonging to the tobacco magnate Pierre Lorillard, at Broadway near West 131st Street, became the Academy of the Holy Infancy, a peaceful enclave that was intended by its founders, a French sect called the Catholic Brothers of the Christian Schools, to redirect the minds of students away from "the hum and bustle of the busy world." Nearby, the Ladies of the Sacred Heart erected a residence—hence the later name Convent Avenue—whose rustic setting was considered ideal for the contemplative life for "young ladies of the highest class." They seem to have avoided their working-class neighbors at the Roman Catholic Church of the Annunciation, which was founded in 1854 on West 131st Street between Broadway and Amsterdam and welcomed the Irish immigrants building the Hudson River Rail Road.

Although the state started funding public schools in 1812, the city educational system came into being only with the creation of the Board of Education in 1856. Until then, private schools dominated. The Manhattanville Boarding School and Scientific Academy opened in 1813 and featured an unusual mix of academic and practical subjects, including Greek, Latin, French, English, math, navigation, drawing, and painting. Girls of a certain class studied at Miss Pickersill's School, a private institution at 125th Street and Fifth Avenue, and starting in 1827 the children of local laborers attended the Manhattanville Free

School on West 129th Street, which, in 1854, was absorbed by the newly
built Public School 43 down the street. By 1856 Carmansville had its
own school, P.S. 46, at West 156th Street near the Hudson River. Education for black people was a different matter. Racial segregation and
discrimination in education was the rule in Harlem, as elsewhere in
the city. There were exceptions: a private school at Lenox Avenue and
West 128th Street welcomed black students, and a public school on East
125th Street near Second Avenue admitted its first African-American,
a twelve-year-old girl, at the insistence of her father, who worked as a
cook for a local family. Such conflicts weren't new to Harlem, where
white and black, rich and poor, immigrant and native-born had always
clashed over money, land, politics, religion, or simply the right to be
left alone. Urbanization was changing the scale and the very nature of
such conflicts in Harlem, but there were a few holdouts.

The most prominent figure opposing the urbanization of Harlem was
John James Audubon, one of the most accomplished naturalists of his
time and one of the most popular artists of any time. Audubon's motto
was *Le temps decouvrira la verité* ("time will reveal the truth") but as with
so many Harlemites his origins remain obscure. Throughout his adult
life, Audubon kept alive speculation he was the missing son of Marie
Antoinette and King Louis XVI. In fact, this man devoted to discovering
"the dark and hitherto misunderstood Histories" of the animal kingdom
seems to have been born out of wedlock on a sugar plantation on Santo
Domingo in 1785 to a French chambermaid who soon died from illness
and a French officer and merchant with a wife back home. In the late
1780s the rising tide of slave unrest convinced the boy's father to return
to France. There the boy was welcomed into the Audubon family estate
near Nantes, where he tirelessly collected plants, rocks, and the eggs
and nests of birds. At the age of eighteen he sailed for New York and
settled near Philadelphia, where he taught himself to paint and started
a family. From the start, Audubon's art had a scientific twist. He carried
out the first experiments in bird banding and he began learning about
taxidermy in order to pose the animals he was painting.

Audubon struggled to support his family as a clerk and merchant, and it wasn't until he was thrown into debtor's prison that he finally gave up the business life. He worked as a freelance taxidermist, commercial artist, and art teacher in New Orleans and Cincinnati and became obsessed with producing a strange hybrid of art and science, work that would combine life-sized images of birds in their natural habitats with accompanying "bird biographies." After a decade of painting in the American wilderness and fund-raising in Europe, where he was more appreciated than he was at home, Audubon finally published the rara avis called *Birds of America*. His years of close observation of birds in their habitats and experimentation with ways of reproducing natural poses, including the invention of the wire support structure that taxidermists still use, produced a dramatic tension between scientific realism and artistic storytelling. In visually demonstrating how character is best revealed in the depiction of everyday action, *Birds of America* became one of the greatest artistic achievements that America had yet produced, and the most American as well. But Audubon wasn't finished yet, and he staged his next act uptown.

Audubon's next project was a massive work with the atrocious title *Viviparous Quadrupeds of America*. Reduced to hunting rodents at dawn downtown, Audubon admitted that he was coming to hate "that crazy city," and he began looking for a place in the country. In 1841 he found a forty-two-acre plot west of the Bloomingdale Road at West 155th Street, with a thousand feet of Hudson River waterfront packed so tightly with chestnut, elm, pine, tulip, and oak trees that there was almost no room to build. Audubon's son John supervised the construction of a simple, wooden-shingled house with pens for chickens, geese, turkey, and pigs, and stables for horses, as well as fenced-in areas for deer and even elk and room to keep foxes, wolves, and badgers. Audubon had long called his wife "Minnie" and he honored that long-suffering woman by naming their new home Minniesland. It was not only a laboratory and studio but a refuge from urban life. He wrote to a friend, "How I wonder that men can consent to swelter and fret their lives away amid those hot bricks and pestilent vapors, when the woods and fields are all so near." Audubon enjoyed as much nature as Harlem still offered on his morning walks through the property. He could see eagles, deer, and muskrats from the high porch facing the river. Of course, Minniesland wasn't quite as remote as Audubon made it seem. Rapidly expanding Carmansville and Manhattanville were a short walk away, and downtown was less than an hour away on any number of railway lines. Two Harlems, rich and poor, rustic and industrial, still existed side by side, but not for long.

Like Hamilton, Audubon lavished so much attention on his home uptown that he was forced to spend much of his time away in order to pay for it. A working farm, a bustling menagerie, a zoological laboratory, and an artist's workshop, Minniesland was also a crowded and chaotic home, with pets, children, servants, and visitors, among them Samuel F. B. Morse, who experimented with telegraph transmissions there. But Audubon soon ventured west to gather material for *Quadrupeds*, though he wrote from Missouri, where he was traveling with pioneers, hunters, trappers, and Indians, to wonder what was happening back in Harlem. Was John Jr. fishing the Hudson for shad? How was work proceeding on the new dock? Had the potatoes been planted?

Audubon returned intending to get back to work on *Quadrupeds*, but he had changed. His collaborators began to complain that he was doing no work at all, or at best poor work, and that his ignorance about natural history and his lack of curiosity about the work of others was impeding him. There were even accusations that he was simply inventing new species when nature wouldn't oblige. Eyeglasses would have helped his deteriorating vision but his vanity forbade them. His hair was turning white, his teeth were falling out, and he was losing his memory. The first book of *Quadrupeds* was finally issued in 1845, but the next year Audubon stopped work on the following volume, unable to see his own work. What was probably Alzheimer's disease rendered him incapable of reading and understanding the texts that were to accompany his images. By 1847 he was completely blind. One visitor recounted, "The outlines of his countenance and his form are there, but his noble mind is all in ruins." Perhaps it was just as well that Audubon never learned that the New York Central Railroad was planning to run its tracks through his property, with a station practically in his front yard. He finally died in his sleep in 1851 at the age of sixty-six after muttering, "We'll get the ducks!" He was buried just up the hill, at Trinity Cemetery.

The Audubons stayed on at Minniesland, struggling to complete *Viviparous Quadrupeds of America*. They tried to bring in some money by starting a school in 1857. Among the students was George Bird Grinnell, who went on to become a pioneering conservationist, editing *Forest and Stream* magazine, founding the Audubon Society, and guiding Theodore Roosevelt's thinking about the national parks system. But Lucy Audubon was eventually forced to sell her husband's own copy of *Birds of America*, and Minniesland was divided and sold to meet debts, though the main house survived, hemmed in by railroad tracks on one side and Riverside Drive on the other, until its demolition in the early 1930s.

Even the most passionate boosters of Harlem's urban, industrial future saw the need for parks. The site in the Harlem Valley that the Randel plan identified for Harlem's first park was abandoned in the 1830s because extending Fifth Avenue uptown would have required blasting through the seventy-foot-high Snake Hill at 121st Street. Instead, the city turned the entire area around Fifth Avenue, from 120th to 124th streets, into Mount Morris Square. These twenty acres, named after the family that seems to have once operated a racetrack there, opened to the public in 1840, though the site remained fairly wild for another two decades, with one important exception. Mount Morris Park would eventually blossom into "the most charming, delightful and picturesque park in the city," according to a contemporary guide published by New York City realtors, but for the time being visitors could marvel at the wonder of firefighting technology mounted at the top of the hill. Fire was still one of New York City's most pressing problems, and it was getting worse all the time, due to the increasing concentration of wooden buildings, widespread use of gas lighting starting in the 1820s on streetlamps and in homes, and a paucity of water sources with which to fight fires. The drummers and bell ringers who had been raising the alarm for two centuries were no longer sufficient. In 1856 the city built a forty-seven-foot-tall octagonal fire tower with Doric columns, supported by a then futuristic post-and-link steel cage that would decades later be used in the first skyscrapers. It was staffed by watchmen who rang bells and used lamps and flags to alert firefighters, a system that remained in place for decades, until tall buildings and street-level call boxes made the tower obsolete. Still, Harlemites were loath to see the tower abandoned, and for years after that the bell was rung twice a day, at noon and nine p.m. on weekdays, and at nine in the morning and nine at night on Sundays. It was the sound of a way of life rapidly disappearing.

Of course, the park with the most significance to Harlemites wasn't quite in Harlem at all. Daniel Tiemann liked to think Central Park was his creation, but the credit belongs to Ambrose Kingsland, who worked in the dry goods, whale oil, and shipping businesses before becoming mayor and building a massive home in 1851 at what is now West 161st Street and Fort Washington Avenue. Kingsland's single term is remembered for his battles with a city council known as the "Forty Thieves," but he was also responsible for the first official proposal in 1851 for a green, open space to serve as the "lungs of the city." Two years later a bill was passed providing for the acquisition of 778 acres, from West 59th Street to West 106th Street, from Fifth to Eighth avenues, to be acquired for $7,800 per acre. Within five years of the start of construction the land around it doubled in value, and when the city decided, in 1859, to add sixty-five acres from West 106th Street to West 110th Street it had to pay $20,000 per acre. Though the park's construction promised thousands of jobs, the idea wasn't universally popular uptown. Hundreds of houses and shacks, including the black community of Seneca Village, were condemned, and many Harlemites who lived above 125th Street resented being taxed for such a distant amenity.

The coming of Central Park inspired yet another wave of arrivals uptown, many of them wealthy and prominent figures who could afford the very latest in architectural style, which was moving away from the Federal and neoclassical style typified by the Morris-Jumel Mansion and the Hamilton Grange and toward the Gothic eclecticism on display in William Wheelock's mansion at 661 West 158th Street. Also popular were Italianate and Greek Revival houses like that of the home of Shepherd Knapp, known as the "Merchant Prince," at West 162nd Street and Riverside Drive. The Craigmoor, built near Amsterdam Avenue and West 138th Street, was the home of Daniel Devlin, an Irish immigrant who made a fortune introducing "off-the-rack" clothing to New York before serving as city treasurer. A visitor to Harlem in 1855 found that such grand estates were "starting up like mushrooms on spots which five years ago were part of the dense and tangled forest." In fact the great estates, old and new, were becoming a thing of the past. Harlem no longer offered refuge from downtown-style problems, and better roads, ferries, bridges, and trains made more isolated properties outside of Manhattan more accessible. The implementation of Randel's street grid, the construction of the Croton Aqueduct, and the arrival of train lines uptown also impeded the construction of grand manors, largely because there was too much money to be made in subdividing property into individual building lots. John Jacob Astor, who had gotten into uptown real estate before the War of 1812, when he owned the Morris Mansion, bought much of the Harlem Flats above 125th Street in order to split up the property and sell it off.

One reason rich downtowners were selling their uptown properties or passing by Harlem altogether was the expansion of the local African-American community. Most were scattered among the Irish in the shacks and shanties that dotted Harlem. But the community of black farmers living near what is now East 130th Street and Park Avenue in the 1830s was growing fast. In 1843 Harlem's all-white First Baptist Church, later known as the Mount Morris Baptist Church, founded the Bethel Chapel for blacks at East 121st Street near Second Avenue. Around the same time, the "Mother Zion" AME Zion Church started a mission called Little Zion for about sixty black worshippers on East 117th Street. In the 1850s there was even a school devoted to black children. But it would be a mistake to overestimate the freedoms that black Manhattanites enjoyed in this period. Although the trans-atlantic slave trade was abolished by 1808, New York State, whose banking, insurance, and garment industries were deeply implicated in southern slavery, decided only in 1818 on the abolition of its own slaves, and then only starting in 1827. Until 1841, when slavery was finally outlawed in New York, most wealthy uptown families, even those with abolitionist leanings, owned slaves, most of whom worked as domestics. And even after that, property requirements meant that suffrage was denied to most blacks.

In the seventeenth and eighteenth centuries, escaped slaves found refuge in uptown's dense forests, and by the early nineteenth century Harlem was a center of abolitionist activity. Jacob Schieffelin's wife, Hannah Lawrence Schieffelin, a longtime abolitionist, was a driving force behind the 1823 founding of St. Mary's Protestant Episcopal Church in Manhattanville, which welcomed worshippers without regard to race. A nearby Friends Meeting House run by Quakers was also devoted to the cause of abolition, and a Negro named Cato Alexander ran a saloon on the way to Harlem that doubled as a station on the Underground Railroad. The work of abolitionists became more complicated after the passage of the Fugitive Slave Law of 1850, which protected the "blackbirders" who received up to $70 for each escaped slave they captured, and the 1857 *Dred Scott* decision by the United States Supreme Court held that blacks were not American citizens and therefore not entitled to most constitutional protections. And as the conflict between the North and the South began to seem inevitable, many New Yorkers began to rethink the whole question. Southern cotton was so important to the garment industry, uptown and downtown, that Mayor Fernando Wood was actually in favor of New York City seceding from the Union.

Simmering tensions between Republicans and Democrats, rich and poor, native-born and immigrant, and white and black came to a boil in riots that engulfed Manhattan for almost a week in the summer of 1863. The ostensible reason for the trouble was the federal government's desperate search for cannon fodder. In the first few months of the Civil War, more than sixty thousand men, about one in ten New

Yorkers, volunteered for military service. Still, the war effort required much more manpower, and New York City "owed" the federal government almost twenty thousand soldiers by March 1863. The Conscription Act passed shortly thereafter targeted all male citizens from twenty to forty-five years old if single (up to thirty-five if married), though draftees were able to buy a substitute and therefore avoid service, or just pay $300 for an exemption. That enraged Democrats, who saw the conflict as "a poor man's fight but a rich man's war," and they blamed the Republicans. But their rage was aimed at New York's African-Americans. After all, wasn't it their war? Wouldn't emancipation and victory result in southern blacks flooding north, taking jobs, and driving down wages? The final irony was that New York's blacks weren't even subject to the draft, because they weren't quite citizens. Of course, poor white and black New Yorkers had more in common than they thought: property requirements kept most white men from voting in state elections, while Jews and Catholics knew they would fail tests of their loyalty to a secular government as the ultimate authority, and women could not vote under any circumstances.

The draft began on Saturday, July 11, 1863, in relative quiet, but two days later, starting at 6:30 a.m., tens of thousands of New Yorkers, including women and children, roamed the streets, lynching dozens of blacks and their white sympathizers and then desecrating their bodies. The most heinous incident was an attack on the Colored Orphan Asylum, on Fifth Avenue near 43rd Street. "Burn the niggers' nest!" the rioters bellowed as they approached the institution. The staff was able to lead 230 children to safety before the crowd swarmed over the building, murdering a girl they found hiding under a bed, setting fire to the building, attacking any firefighters who tried to put out the flames, and tearing up the grounds.

Harlem's significant black presence, its white population strongly in favor of abolition, lots of disgruntled immigrants fired up by Democratic propaganda, and many wealthy families who had been able to buy their way out of the draft made the neighborhood the object of special rage. There the rioters were mostly working-class Irishmen, with whom black New Yorkers already had a long and troubled history, often clashing in the decades before the Civil War over competition for jobs and housing. Their protest against the draft took a mischievous form at first. Mostly it was just men and boys, albeit armed, raising drunken hell by shaking down Harlem shopkeepers for alcohol or money to buy it. On the first day of the riots, "Colonel" Jacob Long, an alderman and the president of the Harlem Gas Company, was accosted on the street by a mob led by a firefighter. Long gave them two dollars as drinking money and they left him alone.

Things turned uglier as the riots entered their second day. Rioters destroyed eight homes and tried to torch the bridges across the Harlem River, but they were prevented by a fortuitous rainstorm. One of Jacob Long's employees, Martin Hart, led an attack on Washington Hall, at Third Avenue and East 126th Street, no doubt a target because it sponsored meetings of the pro union, pro draft Loyal Citizens of the city's Twelfth Ward, which included Harlem. The army had orders "to attack and stop those who have commenced their infernal rascality in Yorkville and Harlem," but it was too late. The crowd had burned Washington Hall to the ground. Just a few hours later, a doctor named Thomas Fitzgerald and a laborer named Thomas Cumiskie led a torch-carrying mob to threaten the home of Edgar Ketchum, an abolitionist and tax collector. Mobs also reduced a temperance club to ashes. The next night, the cottages of blacks living at East 130th Street along the Harlem River went up in flames. Still the *New York Times* didn't get the message. "Small bands of the rioters," the newspaper reported, "composed in great part of boys, have amused themselves by prowling about the streets shouting, singing, and drinking, and a great many threats have been made."

In the end, the five-day Draft Riots claimed the lives of more than a hundred people, over eighty of them black, and left 128 injured and some three thousand blacks homeless—many took refuge along the banks of the Harlem River and stayed. More than four hundred people were jailed (though only nineteen were convicted of crimes) and hundreds of buildings were destroyed or damaged. Estimates of property damage went as high as $5 million. Armed masses had battled their elected government and almost captured the biggest city in the country. Antiblack violence had never been rare in New York City, but the events of the summer of 1863 were unique, lingering in the collective memory of New York's African-American population and inspiring them to search for a neighborhood to call their own. The Draft Riots also revealed that Harlem was not immune to the more general social unrest of the nineteenth century, not just racial conflict but the labor troubles, poverty, crime, and corruption that seemed inevitable in a rapidly industrializing city dominated by foreigners—in the 1860s, more than two-thirds of all New Yorkers had been born overseas, compared to fewer than 10 percent in 1820, and hundreds of thousands more were arriving each year, compared to only four thousand or so in 1820. In exposing such social tensions, the Draft Riots were perhaps the most significant social incident in the history of the city, and a harbinger of what was to come, in Harlem and all of New York.

5

THE FLASH AGE
1863–1898

The decades after the Civil War are often referred to in New York as the "Flash Age," so swift and gaudy was the city's growth—the invention of the photographic lighting technique that first captured Manhattan for posterity may also have inspired the phrase—but for a time it seemed like uptown would be left behind. Harlem's unofficial mascot during this period was a goat rooting for food on a barren, rocky hill. That didn't quite capture the complexity of this rapidly changing neighborhood. Luxurious homes were still for rent, for those downtowners escaping the poverty, crime, social unrest, and epidemics that still reigned below 14th Street. Home to fewer than twenty thousand people at the start of the Civil War, Harlem was still the choicest spot on the island for horse racing, yachting, cricket, sleighing, swimming, and skating or simply glorying in the beautiful vistas and virgin forests that remained. At the same time, residential, commercial, and industrial development meant Harlem was coming into its own as an urban neighborhood, if not a metropolis in its own right. An economic boom that began in 1868 meant rising real estate prices, with property values sometimes doubling or even tripling in value overnight as rich, ambitious, well-educated immigrants from central Europe—many of them Jewish—strove to outdo one another's country estates and fancy row houses. German immigration to the United States is largely neglected by historians, but it played a major role not just in the development of Harlem but in the shaping of nineteenth-century America. Between the end of the War of 1812 and the start of World War I a century later almost six million Germans arrived, far more than the number of Irish who arrived in the same period. Beyond their mere numbers, the social impact that Germans had on life uptown would remain decisive for decades.

The Reverend S. H. Tyng's prediction in 1869, at the laying of the cornerstone of Trinity Church, at Fifth Avenue and 125th Street, that the neighborhood was "destined to be, twenty years hence, the centre of the wealth, intelligence, and refinement of this metropolis" didn't quite come true. After the waves of German and Irish immigrants in the 1840s and 1850s came a new generation of southern Italian and eastern European Jewish newcomers, most of them poor, uneducated, and unskilled. They were not considered white in the racial taxonomy of the day. Whatever troubles they had in the old country, they arrived ready to compete for jobs and housing. A postwar economic boom, boosted by inexpensive immigrant labor, cheap raw materials brought via canal from the Midwest, and an exploding domestic market for manufactured goods, transformed downtown and turned Harlem's shorelines into ever denser industrial zones. The Hudson River attracted meatpacking plants, coal yards, gasworks, an ink factory, a ribbon maker, ironworks, breweries, bottling plants, and dairies—the milky white glazed facade of Sheffield Farms Pure Milk Bottlers, on West 125th Street between Broadway and Riverside Drive, still reminds Harlemites of Manhattanville's industrial past. The banks of the Harlem River sprouted stockyards, tar dumps, garbage transfer stations, gasworks, rubber factories, masonry and lumber yards, flour mills, icehouses, ironworks, plumbing supply houses, and elevator and dumbwaiter manufacturers.

Even as the future beckoned, Harlemites were not quite done with their past. The shocking unrest of the 1863 Draft Riots echoed in 1870 when immigrant stonecutters at Westervelt's Yard on East 129th Street near Third Avenue rioted, and the next year uptown Protestants and Catholics battled each other in the streets on the two hundredth anniversary of the Protestant William of Orange's ascendance over the Catholic King James II. Despite such conflicts, two years later the *New York Times* was celebrating uptown Manhattan as "one of the most densely populated and prosperous wards in the City," with almost fifty thousand people, a police precinct, a public library, and four newspapers. But by the end of 1873 such predictions seemed hopelessly naive. A nationwide financial panic descended, stifling Harlem's real estate boom and delaying plans for the roads, bridges, railway lines, schools, parks, and courthouses that had made government so profitable for the corrupt politicians of the Tweed Ring. Fears that Harlem might not be able to go it alone were no doubt one reason that the city was finally able to annex all of Manhattan up to 155th Street. After more than two centuries, uptown and downtown at last became one political unit, but many Harlemites remained wary of downtowners bearing gifts.

Harlem was home to the most prominent members of the Tweed Ring, which as a subset of the Democratic dynasty founded by Aaron Burr in 1779 as Tammany Hall, was the first American political machine and would become the voice and muscle of the Democratic Party in New York City as well as a synonym for municipal corruption. They earned much of their money there as well—nothing whetted the appetites of corrupt politicians in nineteenth-century New York like civic improvement. The Tweed Ring succeeded because it attracted the votes of the city's swiftly expanding working-class immigrant population; the number of Irish immigrants in Harlem alone doubled from six thousand in 1855 to twelve thousand in 1875. In return for their votes, Tammany offered government jobs, some of which existed only on paper, and all of which kicked back a percentage to the organization. This strategy was the brainchild of William "Boss" Tweed, who was born downtown in 1823 and grew up in the rough-and-tumble atmosphere of the East Side, as lower Manhattan east of Broadway was then known. Tweed parlayed control of the local volunteer firehouse into a seat in 1860 on the ravenously corrupt, Tammany-controlled Board of Aldermen: the so-called Forty Thieves. A huge man, vulgar, sociable, and endlessly resourceful, exercising power with a feudal brutality, Tweed soon controlled all three branches of the city government and much of the state government as well, making or breaking laws at will and using the courts to punish his enemies and reward his friends. He extorted money from restaurants through corrupt health inspectors and determined the editorial policies of newspapers by buying large blocks of advertising that became addictive to the publishers. A Tweed-owned printing company even overcharged the city for printing public reports of the officials investigating city corruption.

Tweed realized early that some of the most tempting opportunities for plunder were in Harlem. Gas lighting had been used downtown since the 1820s, but it wasn't until the supposedly civic-minded efforts of Tweed, a director of the Harlem Gas and Light Company, that it came uptown. When Harlem Hall was turned into a church, he paid five dollars for each of the building's three hundred benches and sold them to the city for use in the armories for $600 each. He pocketed half the funds devoted to modernizing the waterfront on both the Hudson and the Harlem rivers. Tweed and his ring, who controlled the Brooklyn Bridge Company, also profited from replacing spans over the Harlem River at Third and Park avenues.

The most infamous monument to Tammany plunder was the building still known as the Tweed Courthouse, a $250,000 project that cost the city more than $13 million, almost twice as much as the federal government paid for the entire state of Alaska. It was such a moneymaker that Tweed tried to repeat the experience uptown. In 1869 he paid more than $60,000 for five lots at East 129th Street and Fourth Avenue, including a building called National Hall. The next year he leased the property to the city, had it renovated at public expense, and installed two Harlem judges, Josiah Porter and John McQuade, as courthouse commissioners. But the building's boiler exploded in 1873, killing several people—it turns out that a Tammany crony with no experience was in charge of maintenance. After the building was declared unsafe, Tweed got the city to buy land for a new courthouse, to be built from scratch at West 128th Street near Sixth Avenue. The $300,000 that the state contributed disappeared, no doubt into Tweed's pocket, and construction stopped. It wasn't until 1893, long after Tweed's heyday, that the city completed the Harlem

Courthouse, a magnificent Gothic–Romanesque Revival structure that still stands at 121st Street and Sylvan Place.

Tweed also got in on the campaign of road building that was so crucial to Harlem's urbanization. Most roads that had been officially laid out and opened were still not much more than dirt paths. Such improvements were supposedly the responsibility of the commissioners of Central Park, who had been empowered by the state to assume control of the roads above 110th Street, but Tweed used his role as chair of the Board of Aldermen to influence the rewarding of road and sewer contracts. By the time Tweed had consolidated his power toward the end of the Civil War, he could use his new position as deputy street commissioner to take his share of the $5,000 it typically cost to pave each city block. The benefits to residents couldn't be denied, but Tweed benefited most of all. One uptown property owner who was assessed $812.94 for the paving of his twenty-five-foot frontage along Third Avenue calculated that the ring made 21 cents profit on every stone laid. Even after completion, road maintenance remained a profitable business: the Tammany soldier charged with maintaining Harlem Lane took home a then astronomical $30,000 a year.

All of Tweed's road building couldn't make up for a mass transit system—if it could be called a system—that was totally inadequate to the changing needs of the fast-growing city. In the years after the Civil War more than a dozen horse-drawn railway lines made street life perilous. In just one month in the spring of 1873, five people were injured and one was killed in accidents along the Fourth Avenue railway alone. In some respects, this was the price of success. Harlemites had been commuting downtown in large numbers since 1837, but by 1867 the New York *Evening-Post* was complaining that delays due to poor maintenance—travel time could be twice as long as the six ferry lines making the forty-minute trip downtown—meant that "the upper part of the island is made almost useless to persons engaged in daily business of any kind in the city." Tweed, who already owned a major interest in the Erie Railroad, saw yet another opportunity and took over the line that ran along Amsterdam Avenue to Manhattan Street, near the Manhattanville ferry, and then on to West 186th Street. Then, in the early 1870s, he tried to push through a $10 million narrow-gauge railroad line to replace the horse-drawn railway on Fourth Avenue. He ran into local opposition when it came to construction, and not just on the grounds of good government. Blasting through the rocky path of the Fourth Avenue line posed a serious danger to neighbors, who had to flee from flying debris and who suffered so much from construction noise that apothecaries ran out of headache remedies. All along, Tweed knew that one easy solution to Harlem's mass transit problems lay neither on land nor water but in the air. Elevated trains were fast, predictable, and cheap: five cents during rush hour, compared to five dollars for a private carriage, and ten cents for horse-drawn railways or omnibuses. In the early 1870s, Tweed was behind a $7 million proposal to put up a part-elevated line from the Battery to Harlem along Third Avenue. As always, delays could be profitable, too, and it wasn't until almost a decade later that elevated trains along the major avenues reached Harlem. The most famous was the line that traced a sharp S-curve a hundred feet above West 110th Street as the route veered east from Ninth Avenue to Eighth Avenue, a stretch known as Suicide Curve because it was the preferred place for New Yorkers bent on self-destruction after the Central Park reservoir was fenced off.

Tweed and his ring were also in on the housing boom that led to the last remaining large parcels of land being drained, filled in, subdivided, and auctioned off in a frenzy of speculation. At the first such sale, in 1869, prices ranged from $2,500 for a lot on East 134th Street near Fifth Avenue to a stunning $10,000 for land at the northeast corner of Fifth Avenue and East 110th Street, so powerful a draw was the coming of Central Park. Tweed and his coconspirators snapped up some of the choicest lots and had the city pave and open streets. He convinced the state to lay out Seventh Avenue from West 110th Street to the Harlem River as a broad, tree-lined thoroughfare. He had elm trees planted along the wide expanses of Sixth Avenue, soon to be renamed Lenox Avenue after the philanthropist James Lenox, and put in gas and sewer lines, taking a cut at every stage of construction and maintenance. Then there were the kickbacks from real estate auctioneers, contractors, and land agents—there were twenty-four real estate brokers uptown during this period—who helped build Harlem mansions for Tweed, who was the city's third largest landowner, and his friends. Any property they didn't use for their own homes was sold as prices for the housing that rose on the former farmlands skyrocketed.

The ring's number cruncher, city controller Richard "Slippery Dick" Connolly, never earned an official salary of more than a few thousand dollars per year, but his mastery of the city's byzantine system of accounting made him a millionaire. A chillingly obsequious glad-hander, a sweaty, corpulent presence at baptisms, weddings, and funerals, Connolly took 10 percent of everything he touched, from unnecessary bond issues to the salaries of his 131 clerks, most of whom never showed up for work. In 1871 Connolly built a $300,000 mansion at the corner of Fifth Avenue and East 130th Street, not only figuring out a way for the city to pay for it but even making money on the project through kickbacks from workers such as Andrew Garvey, a Tammany grand marshal known as the "Prince of Plasters," who was paid $40,000 for superficial work on the house. Just as ingenious was the scheme by which Henry Genet, the Prince Hal of Harlem to Tweed's Falstaff, ended up in Harlem. New Yorkers were surprised when Genet stepped down from the State Senate Railroad Committee, which brought him $100,000 under the table per year, and became a lowly, $3,000-a-year building inspector. Genet knew the position offered almost unlimited opportunities for bribes and kickbacks. Funds siphoned off from the Harlem Courthouse budget paid for Genet's fanciful four-story castle, built in 1871 at Fifth Avenue and West 126th Street.

Things were about to change. It seems obvious in hindsight that the process by which the Tweed Ring shaped Harlem was tragically corrupt. But many New Yorkers saw fraudulence as the price of progress. The diarist George Washington Plunkitt, himself a Harlem property owner hired by Tammany on uptown road and bridge maintenance schemes, famously characterized Tweed's approach as "honest graft." There was little opposition to Tweed in his heyday, certainly not uptown, where the poor Irish got the construction jobs and the rich real estate investors got the profits from property values that had increased as a result of the transportation lines, street openings, and parks. The *Real Estate Record and Builder's Guide* insisted that Harlem had been transformed into "the highest style of Tammany Art." But Tweed and his cronies were not able to operate totally unfettered for long.

Like so many of his uptown neighbors Thomas Nast, the most popular American illustrator and artist of the period, whose Harlem studio was the birthplace of American political cartooning, was born in Germany and came to the United States because of politics. Nast's father's outspoken opposition to the government forced the family to flee in 1846, when Nast was six. The family settled downtown and the chubby boy with the German accent began haunting the very neighborhood firehouse where Boss Tweed was getting his start. Beginning in 1855, Nast made his living as an illustrator in popular periodicals, drawing everything from scenes out of Shakespeare and Dickens to commentaries on urban poverty, vice, and corruption among city milk inspectors. He joined the newly formed Republican Party, which had been created by dissenters from the proslavery stance of the Whigs, and attended John Brown's funeral in 1859. He even met President Lincoln, who called him "our best recruiting sergeant" after the Civil War began. Nast witnessed the attack on the Colored Orphan Asylum during the Draft Riots and, like the orphans, moved uptown shortly afterward, settling into a house at Fifth Avenue near 125th Street. There, Nast, who was only twenty-four years old, worked in a backyard studio that shielded him from the din created by his family, which now included three children, and began focusing on the circle of men who were turning New York City into their own private business. Adopting a sharper, edgier line than he had used before, he transformed the Tammany mascot, the Tiger, into a symbol of rapacity and corruption, an image that was so powerful that Boss Tweed lamented, "I don't care so much what the papers write about me. My constituents can't read; but damn it, they can see pictures!" Tweed should have known better than to try bribing Nast. Still, one Sunday a representative of the Broadway Bank, which had been set up solely for the ring's business, was sent up to Harlem to offer Nast $200,000 to lay off. Nast jokingly made a counteroffer of $500,000 and was perplexed about what to do when it was accepted. The bribe attempt convinced Nast, described by one newspaper as "the most cordially hated man in New York—hated by men whose friendship would be a dishonour," to break the ring. Tweed accused the artist of having arrived in the United States as a fugitive from conscription, despite the fact that Nast was still a child when he left Germany. Tweed then moved on to death threats, arranging for the transfer of the Harlem police captain assigned to protect Nast. But Nast was soon the least of his problems. By late 1871 Nast had made Tweed's excesses public knowledge, and the ring's influence over the press, the courts, and the banks eventually became impossible to maintain. Even Harlemites, who had benefited so much from Tweed's efforts, had had enough. An anti-Tammany meeting at Lincoln Hall, at East 125th Street near Third Avenue, sponsored by the Taxpayers and Citizens Association of the Twelfth Ward, demanded reform of a system that had become "fearfully corrupt and debased." A full slate of prominent Harlemites, including former mayor Daniel Tiemann, demanded the resignation and prosecution of the ring's members; "Harlem Aroused" was the headline in the next day's *Times*.

On election day of 1871, readers opened *Harper's Weekly* to what became Nast's most famous image: a double-page spread of "The Tammany Tiger Loose" in the Roman Colosseum mauling the prostrate body of the Republic while Tweed, Connolly, and the rest of the ring look on. Amazingly, Tweed was reelected as state senator that day. His friends weren't so lucky. Connolly was arrested on corruption charges and after raising bail he fled the country with $6 million. Henry Genet lost his State Senate seat to Daniel Tiemann and was ultimately charged and convicted of fraud in connection with the Harlem Courthouse scheme and sentenced to six months in prison. Tweed was also eventually charged and found guilty of more than two hundred counts of fraud and sentenced to a $12,750 fine and twelve years in prison. Still a figure of some influence, he managed to have both punishments reduced on appeal. He was even free to leave his downtown jail cell, taking his coachman and footman as companions on leisurely rides through the city and dining at home, surrounded by servants. In 1875, facing a civil suit, Tweed fled to Spain. He was tried in absentia the next year, found guilty, and ordered to pay $6 million.

The end came only after one of Nast's allegorical images of Tweed as father of state abusing his public, portrayed as his children, made its way across the Atlantic. Someone connected the image with the man, thinking he was wanted for child abuse. Boss Tweed, who once seemed to control everyone in New York from the local bricklayer and priest to the mayor and governor, who presided over the theft of some $80 million in public funds, was extradited to the United States, where he died behind bars in 1878.

Nast had already moved on. In the summer of 1871 he had taken his family to Morristown, New Jersey, to escape an epidemic of malaria, caused in part by the industrial waste that factories in the Harlem Flats discharged directly onto the ground, where it mixed with raw sewage from outhouses to form a toxic brew—so much for "Tammany Art." He commuted to Harlem every day before relocating permanently to New Jersey the next year, though he held on to his Fifth Avenue property for more than a decade. Nast, who not only captured but directed the national mood in the decades after the Civil War in more than three thousand published images that attacked racism, nationalism, religious intolerance, war, imperialism, and political corruption, who invented the symbol of the Republican elephant as well as the popular image of Santa Claus, eventually fell on hard times. He was rescued by President Theodore Roosevelt, who claimed that he had learned everything he knew about politics from Nast's pictures and who made him the American consul at Guayaquil, Ecuador, although he contracted yellow fever there and died in 1902.

Harlemites rejoiced at the downfall of Boss Tweed and his ring. Indeed, the early 1870s brought plenty of good news to Harlem. By the summer of 1873 four hundred buildings were under construction and the *New York Times* commented, "Houses are being built in every part of Harlem, and handsome houses, too, with every modern convenience that taste can apply or necessity demand." But the financial panic that struck that year caused a depression that drove down prices by as much as 80 percent. Although the population of the Twelfth Ward

was more than sixty thousand and growing steadily, when the Third
Avenue and Eighth Avenue elevated trains were finally completed they
ran above empty fields, only occasionally passing a private house in
the distance. A much-reproduced photograph from the period shows
new Federal-style row houses on West 133rd Street between Fifth and
Sixth avenues standing incongruously on barren wasteland. But the
economic slowdown didn't last long. By the centennial of the Battle
of Harlem Heights in 1876 builders had begun returning. In 1879
Oswald Ottendorfer, the president and editor of the *New Yorker Staats-
Zeitung* and one of the most prominent German immigrants in the city,
turned his modest 1850 house on West 136th Street near Broadway
into the most fabulous property in Harlem, a huge and ostentatious
pagoda and a Moorish pavilion with a Jewish star in the dome in
the garden. The period saw a number of these quixotic architectural
visions, among them the 1887 house of the German-born diamond
broker, theosophist, and pornographer Emil August Neresheimer, at
Lenox Avenue and West 119th Street, and the thirty-room limestone
and granite mansion built in 1888 in the popular Romanesque Revival
style by James Anthony Bailey, of Barnum & Bailey circus fame, at 10
St. Nicholas Place. Bailey's eccentricity didn't limit itself to architecture: each spring he would take his taxidermy collection to air out on
the front lawn, to the delight of the local children.

Such houses were becoming anomalies. The era of the grand
mansions was ending, partly because of a lack of buildable lots and
the astronomical prices of those that remained, and partly because
there was so much money to be made in other kinds of housing as
the middle classes continued their exodus from downtown. Soon,
block after block saw the construction of bay-windowed and corniced
row houses in Italianate, Greek Revival, Gothic, or Second Empire
styles. A step down in status from the freestanding mansions, these
structures, often built on speculation, were profitable in part because
they were cheaper to develop. Several fit into a single lot, and common walls and exterior ornamentation limited to the front facade
drove down costs. The finest examples of such architecture, and the
lifestyle that went along with it, were on display in the Mount Morris

Park neighborhood, which was within walking distance of the first elegant shops in Harlem that went up along Third Avenue at East 117th Street. This area was home to many politicians, such as Mayor Thomas Gilroy and New York's postmaster Charles Dayton. The neighborhoods near Morningside, Riverside, and Central parks, the stretch of West 122nd Street between Mount Morris Park West and Lenox Avenue known as Doctor's Row, and the area that came to be known as Hamilton Heights were also popular among the builders of fancy row houses and brownstones, which might sell for as much as $40,000. More affordable were the three-story brick row houses of Astor Row, which were built as rental properties in 1883 on West 130th Street near Sixth Avenue. These single-family homes rented for as little as $300 per year, compared to $1,200 a year for row houses with gardens, which meant that they were within reach for laborers or clerks who might make between two and three dollars a day in the decades after the Civil War. The wooden row houses of Sylvan Terrace, once the carriage path to the Morris-Jumel Mansion, were built expressly for such middle-class families. In 1889 the *Harlem Local Reporter* quoted one resident as saying, "When I see the prices that real estate is now bringing in Harlem, it makes me feel that I was a fool for not making . . . investments years ago when property was so cheap." The newspaper was of course a constant booster of development, crowing the next year that Harlem was "a continuous swim of development and prosperity," and a "wilderness of brownstone, brick and mortar."

Although architectural historians prize the row houses of Astor Row, Sylvan Terrace, Sylvan Court, and Hamilton Terrace, the best-loved homes in Harlem are the King Model Houses, later known as Striver's Row, 146 row houses and three apartment buildings on the old Watt-Pinckney lands, on West 138th and West 139th streets between Seventh and Eighth avenues. This experiment in urban planning began with David H. King Jr.'s purchase of the land from the Equitable Life Assurance Society in 1890 for the purposes of constructing a middle-income development. King, who had built the old *New York Times* building on Park Row and designed the base of the

Statue of Liberty, recruited his friend the notorious architect Stanford White to conceive of an overall vision. The diversity of styles that resulted—neo-Renaissance, neo-Georgian, colonial, neoclassical, and Federal—was far greater than the sum of its parts. The development was as practical as it was elegant, starting with use of open space, in the form of not only gracious lanes graced by fountains but a service alley, unique on Manhattan, that still runs in back of the houses. King also insisted that the dwellings have indoor plumbing, still unusual uptown.

The King Model Houses were an aesthetic triumph but a financial disaster. The financial viability of new row house construction was becoming uncertain even before there was yet another slowdown in the housing market that began in 1893, and at first only nine units attracted residents. There were still plenty of "genteel persons of moderate means," as advertisements for the King Model Houses put it, able to afford to rent for $1,700 per year or buy for $11,000. But they didn't want to live in single-family houses anymore. Instead, uptown developers had started meeting the demand for upper-middle-class housing by building large apartment buildings, only recently made practical because of refinements in the design of the electric elevator. The first such structure in Harlem was a co-op built in 1883 at 10 East 130th Street. With two apartments per story and two elevators—one for residents, one for service—this building was intended to rid Harlemites of a certain class of the notion that living in multiple-family dwellings was beneath them. In fact, grand apartment houses succeeded because they weren't only for the rich. Upper-middle-class families like those of the novelist Nathanael West, the publisher Bennett Cerf, the composer Howard Dietz, and the economist Merryle Stanley Rukeyser might pay under $1,000 per year for ten or more rooms and two or more bathrooms. The Mount Morris Bank at East 125th Street and Park Avenue, built by the famed uptown architects Lamb and Rich in 1884, featured apartments on the upper floors—apparently, the right kind of real estate was a surer bet than the financial institution offering the mortgage.

The most conspicuous developer of apartment houses in this period was a German-Jewish immigrant named Oscar Hammerstein, who arrived in America almost penniless and turned himself into one of the most distinctive figures of the era, the inventor of both 125th Street and Times Square as entertainment districts, and the founder of one of the most distinguished dynasties in American show business. Hammerstein was born into a wealthy Jewish family in Germany in 1847 and ran away after his father, a stockbroker and building contractor, beat him for going ice skating instead of practicing his violin. The sixteen-year-old boy ended up in New York, where he found work sweeping floors in a cigar factory. As inventive as he was ambitious, Hammerstein was soon not only rolling cigars but supplementing his income by thinking up new gadgets for the industry, which brought him enough money by the early 1880s to start investing in uptown real estate. He entered the business at the right moment. Prices held back by the depression of the mid-1870s had rebounded, especially in the villages of Harlem, Manhattanville, and Carmansville. The rest of uptown Manhattan was still largely unsettled, with only a few hundred buildings in total and scavengers, both human and goat, still roaming free. But that era was ending, as the old estates continued to be divided and auctioned off to real estate speculators like Hammerstein and William De Forest, an interior designer and silk importer who was also a descendant of the very first Harlem settlers. Prices ranged from $500 to $36,000 per acre, depending on the condition of the land—farmland commanded more than swampy ground or a rocky outcropping—and access to public transportation. The lands belonging to Alexander Hamilton's descendants were sold off to make way for the Eighth Avenue and Ninth Avenue elevated lines. The Grange itself was doomed for demolition before it was donated to St. Luke's Episcopal Church and pulled, dragged, and rolled three hundred feet to the south and squeezed into the lot just north of where the new St. Luke's was being built at Convent Avenue and West 141st Street.

Hammerstein got his start in real estate by buying and selling private homes. He bought his own row house on West 115th Street in 1887 and the next year moved into a fantastical mansion he called "my Moorish Castle" at 44 West 120th Street. He also started building apartment houses, the best known of which was the curiously named Kaiser Wilhelm. The chief visionary of a unified Germany, Wilhelm I was also responsible for the 1848 counterrevolution that sent so many Germans to America, which may help explain why Hammerstein's pride and joy on Seventh Avenue got off to a slow start. When the blizzard of 1888 blew into town, Hammerstein was seen in a top hat shoveling the snow off the roof of the building, whose construction had been halted after he ran out of money.

Hammerstein's claim that he invented the top hat—"I even sleep in it!" he boasted—sent a clear message about the kind of head covering he wasn't wearing: the skullcap traditionally worn by the Hebrews, as they were then somewhat derisively known. The fabled figure of the New York Jew has deep roots in Manhattan, reaching all the way back to the arrival of a group of "Oriental Israelites who fled coastal Braszil after the Dutch lost the territory to the Portugese." Such Sephardim dominated New York's Jewish community for the next two centuries. After that, Ashkenazic Jews from Germany began to dominate. Their good education, modern outlook, and intense desire to become Americans—most had long ago given up the skullcap—all helped account for the rapid rise to wealth and prominence by families with names such as Guggenheim, Lehman, Seligman, Schiff, Warburg, Sulzberger, and Adler. The first Jewish community uptown dates to 1869, when a handful of German Jews of relatively modest means moved from the Lower East Side. A jeweler named Isaac Reiser and two brothers, Samuel and Gershon Boehm, who ran a downtown liquor store, settled near East 125th Street and Third Avenue. Meanwhile, Marcus Marks, who owned an East Broadway haberdashery, and Israel Stone, who was also in the garment trade, moved to the neighborhood of East 110th Street and Third Avenue. Together, they started holding weekly services in a rented space above the Harlem Savings Bank, at East 124th Street and Third Avenue, an activity that led to the 1873 founding of the first uptown synagogue, Congregation Hand-in-Hand. There were only a dozen members at first—barely above the minimum of ten demanded by Jewish law—and no rabbi or cantor. But Hand-in-Hand grew rapidly, especially among Jews interested in modernizing the religion. The synagogue defied the ancient practice of separating male and female worshippers and in 1877 the members installed an organ. The changes were too much for those who clung to the old ways, but Hand-in-Hand survived a split in its ranks and even continued growing, moving into the larger quarters of Grace Episcopal Church. Nonetheless, Hand-in-Hand had no proper rabbi until the arrival of a young Englishman named Maurice H. Harris, who came to the United States in 1878 at the age of nineteen and began studying at Columbia University and the seminary of Temple Emmanu-El. By the mid-1880s Harris was moving the congregation toward even more liberal worship traditions. He held services in English instead of Hebrew, and in 1887 he organized a costumed benefit ball for two thousand people at the Harlem Casino to celebrate Hanukkah. Harris's vision was controversial but ultimately successful, and in 1888 he convinced the synagogue's trustees to buy the Church of the Holy Trinity, at Fifth Avenue and 125th Street, for the very substantial sum of $140,000—an indication of the financial health of Harlem's Jews—and to rechristen themselves Temple Israel of Harlem.

Of course, Harlem didn't turn Jewish overnight. The years after the Civil War saw the arrival of Episcopalian, Methodist Episcopal, Presbyterian, Lutheran, Seventh Day Adventist, Congregationalist, Unitarian, and Mormon houses of worship. The old Reformed Low Dutch Church of Harlem, the first and the only church in Harlem until 1823, flourished at Lenox Avenue and West 123rd Street and even spawned two more affiliates, the Elmendorf Reformed Church, located at 171 East 121st Street, and the Fort Washington Collegiate Church, whose first pastor was Abraham John Muste, a founder of modern pacifism. Irish immigrants built half a dozen Catholic churches and sent their children to parochial schools. The most distinctive of Harlem's Catholic institutions was Manhattanville College of the Sacred Heart, at Broadway and West 135th Street, which was Harlem's first college campus. After fire destroyed its distinctive, octagonal Gothic Revival building at the top of Convent Hill in 1888, the college moved into Oswald Ottendorfer's fabulous and quirky estate across the street.

Harlem's upwardly mobile German Jews showed off their children's status as Americans by sending them to local public schools like East Harlem's P.S. 72 and West Harlem's P.S. 43, also known as the Manhattanville Free School. More prosperous German-Jewish families sent their children to Grammar School 68, known as the "Silk Stocking School," where the curriculum was weighted heavily toward training students for the business world. That meant attention to penmanship and deportment, not to mention clean fingernails and properly shined shoes. Co-education was still controversial. The *New York Times*, which was owned by the German-Jewish Sulzberger family, found in 1883 that "the sinful pleasures of co-education," had "thoroughly undomesticated" Harlem girls by introducing them to "Latin, Greek, mathematics, and other studies to which the advocates of co-education would brutally expose our daughters and sisters."

No matter how proper their handwriting and hygiene, Harlem's German-Jewish children were subject to anti-Semitism that made them largely unwelcome at private schools including the Harlem Kindergarten and Preparatory School and the Lenox Institute. Nor were their sisters welcome at the all-girl schools dedicated to training students in how to get a husband, for example, Madame De Valencia's "Protestant French and English Institute for Young Ladies," which opened in the early 1880s and offered rigorous instruction in manners.

Harlem's German Jews may not yet have been considered fully American, but they occupied a place one step above the Irish immigrants moving into the neighborhood. Indeed, while uptown's German Jews filled up lower and central Harlem's relatively comfortable single-family row houses, the Irish were condemned to a new kind of housing called the tenement, an infamous architectural development in which a third of all New Yorkers still live. The first tenement went up downtown in 1833, and factory and brewery workers in Manhattanville and East Harlem lived in three- and four-story, multifamily buildings in the years before the Civil War, but it was not until the 1870s that tenements began to dominate the uptown landscape.

Uptown developers like Oscar Hammerstein had been looking for ways to cram as many row house units as possible into a single building lot, squeezing five single-family structures into four and then into three building lots—the average width of these houses shrank from twenty-five to seventeen feet in this period. But there was only so much that could be done to bring down the cost of row houses and brownstones, and the tenement was the best alternative. With the financial recovery of the late 1870s, and the arrival of the Third Avenue elevated line in 1879, tenements began to rise in numbers on swamplands in the Harlem Flats and in East Harlem. These were not only the most level lands to build on but among Manhattan's cheapest, with odors from gigantic tanks that supplied gas to streetlights, businesses, and homes, and smells and refuse from industry and dozens of horse stables. Because these nearly identical structures were built from prefabricated elements of wood, plaster, sheet metal, and glass, many manufactured right in East Harlem, they could be put up more quickly and cheaply than the brownstones, apartment buildings, or freestanding houses of Harlem's middle and upper classes. Landlords found they could also construct flimsy additions in the rear lots of tenements, packing in working-class families grateful to have a roof over their heads.

Tenements were unpopular among those who prized Harlem's beauties, natural and man-made. Frederick Law Olmsted, the designer of Central Park, wrote in the New York *Daily Tribune* in 1879: "The elevated roads and the uptown movement lead as yet to nothing better, for even at [. . .] Harlem and Manhattanville, five or six miles away from the centre of population, there are new houses of the ridiculous jammed-up pattern, as dark and noisome [. . .] as if they were parts of a besieged fortress." Class concerns were often behind the criticism of the way Harlem was developing, especially when it came to those uptowners who were so destitute that even the dangerously overcrowded tenements looked good. Harlem's poorest lived in wretched, improvised shacks constructed from wooden crates cast off by factories in Manhattanville and East Harlem. A health inspector caught the spirit of these shantytowns: "Men, women, and children, dogs, cows, pigs, goats, geese, ducks, and chickens are almost promiscuously mixed together. The street is rank with filth and stench, and the consequence is that mortality holds high carnival there."

The city's most influential architectural critic, Montgomery Schuyler, observed in the *Real Estate Record and Builders Guide* in 1883 that large swathes of Harlem still had "the character of a frontier town." But its increasingly metropolitan character also meant social problems more associated with downtown's immigrant neighborhoods. Juveniles were a particular source of concern. Among the twenty-five thousand homeless children that the social reformer Charles Loring Brace counted in Manhattan in 1876 were two newsboys who spent the winter in an iron pipe under the Harlem Bridge. The Sheltering Arms Asylum, at West 129th Street and Tenth Avenue, was dedicated to caring for such "children in the midst"—the homeless, neglected, abandoned, or orphaned, most of whom were unwelcome at the city's other hospitals, homes, and asylums. Sheltering Arms welcomed children regardless of race, but most Negro youngsters in need were steered to the Colored Orphan Asylum, which had settled into the Hickson Fields Mansion, a neoclassical villa near Broadway and West 151st Street, and then into its own building at Tenth Avenue and West 143rd Street.

Harlem had long attracted such moral infrastructure because New Yorkers wanted their most vulnerable populations out of sight and therefore out of mind. The Bloomingdale Asylum for the Insane, the Leake and Watts Orphan Asylum, and the New York Institution for the Instruction of the Deaf and Dumb all dated to before the Civil War. Now came North General Hospital and the Manhattan Dispensary, which welcomed New Yorkers too poor to pay for a private doctor. Another hospital dating from this period was Harlem Hospital, which was no one's first choice: it opened in 1887 as a branch of Bellevue and was used mostly for emergency cases, or for patients waiting for beds at facilities on Randall's or Ward's islands. A decade after its founding, the Harlem Board of Commerce heard horror stories about Harlem Hospital's overcrowding, filth, vermin, and, worst of all in some minds, mixed-race wards.

There was a sharp contrast between Harlem's moral infrastructure and the worldly pursuits of the Flash Age, when getting so often trumped giving. Most Harlemites around the turn of the century did their shopping at local open-air pushcart markets and tiny dry goods stores. But fancy shops now began to line Third Avenue, and 125th Street also began to boast stores with stylish arcade storefronts made for conspicuous consumption. Among the earliest businesses that helped make shopping into a spectator sport was Blumstein's department store. Founded downtown in 1886 by the German-Jewish immigrant Louis Blumstein, the store moved to 230 West 125th Street two years later. At a time when signs reading *Keine Juden, und Keine Hunde* ("No Jews, and No Dogs") could be seen in shop windows, Blumstein's became a favorite of uptown's German Jews. Soon there was competition in the form of Koch's, founded by Henry C. F. Koch, another German immigrant convinced that the future was uptown. He built the largest store Harlem had ever seen, a six-story dry goods emporium at 132 West 125th Street that was devoted to the latest ladies' fashions in silk, lace, feathers, and camel's hair—there was a while-you-wait hat-trimming service, a department devoted solely to ribbons, and even a mock-up of a bridal chamber.

Koch became one of the most prominent and hardworking businessmen in Harlem, moving his family into a Lenox Avenue row house and helping to found the Harlem Board of Commerce. Like so many successful Germans uptown, he took his pleasures very seriously, especially when it came to the horse trotting and racing that took place along Harlem Lane, and later along the Harlem Speedway, a ninety-five-foot-wide route along the Harlem River from West 155th Street to the northern tip of Manhattan. Such events were less about the horses than about being seen by the right people. General Ulysses S. Grant's first visit to New York City after the conclusion of the Civil

War included watching harness racing on Harlem Lane, and such figures as Commodore Vanderbilt, August Belmont, and Henry Ward Beecher all sponsored entrants. Watching and being watched wasn't only for the very wealthy; the front yards and porches of homes along Harlem Lane were full of spectators, and taverns and hotels sprang up along the route. Meanwhile, Riverside Drive was becoming so crowded that a local group tried to have the city install separate paths for pedestrians, riders, and carriages.

Many yacht owners watched the horse racing action while anchored in Montagne's Creek, which was still navigable as far west as Third Avenue. Despite the growth of industry, Harlem's waterfronts were also favorite leisure-time spots for locals and visitors in the years before the turn of the century. The blasting out of the treacherously shallow passage at Hell Gate attracted tourists, and the High Bridge remained a popular attraction, with visitors taking the Hudson River Railroad line to the Carmansville station and then walking across town to see the span. A member of one of Harlem's royal families, Archibald Watt, served as commodore of the American Yacht Club and built a $700,000 steam yacht named *American*, which he launched at the foot of East 118th Street. Those who were caught up in the health and fitness craze that swept the nation in the decades after the Civil War enjoyed the public bathhouse on the Hudson River near Manhattanville, where 25 cents bought a swim in the river and a place to change. A covered wharf in the Hudson River at West 129th Street hosted lectures, dances, and concerts, and before the turn of the century the city opened Free Bath #9, a swimming area at West 134th Street. The Harlem River was also a popular spot for rowing and swimming. The poet Walt Whitman used to watch that "peculiar and pretty carnival—at its height a hundred lads or young men, very democratic, but all decent behaving."

The many public parks that opened during the Flash Age were seen by city officials as nothing less than a necessity in a neighborhood that was urbanizing so quickly. Mount Morris Park, Morningside Park, Riverside Park, High Bridge Park, Colonial Park, Fort Washington Park, St. Nicholas Park, and Thomas Jefferson Park were all opened during this period, though they were all overshadowed by Central Park, finished in 1876. It quickly became the most famed and beloved of uptown's green spaces, a carefully constructed natural landscape where those who could afford a horse and carriage might meet their own servants out for a stroll. In the winter, Harlemites on ice skates could follow Montagne's Creek as it emptied into what is now the Harlem Meer, and before the turn of the century a giant ice slide was set up for tobogganing near Sixth Avenue and Central Park North.

The empty field at the corner of Sixth Avenue and West 116th Street saw more organized entertainments. In the summer of 1880 visitors paid prices ranging from 50 cents general admission to a six-seat box for $12 in a ten-thousand-seat bullfighting ring. But nothing drew crowds like the Polo Grounds, two athletic fields located just north of Central Park, between Fifth and Sixth avenues, on property owned by James Gordon Bennett of the New York *Herald*. An obsessive polo fan, Bennett lent his fields to the Manhattan Polo Association in the 1870s. The sport never quite caught on, though the name did. In contrast, upper-class Harlemites had been playing cricket since before the Civil War, and the game had become baseball. The Polo Grounds was the place to see the new sport. More than fifteen thousand people, including ex-president Ulysses S. Grant, came to watch the first National League baseball game in 1883, and the next year the Polo Grounds hosted the first World Series, between the Providence Grays of the National League and the New York Metropolitans of the American League. The original Polo Grounds was replaced by a new stadium in the late 1880s and renamed Manhattan Field, but the new name never stuck. Soon there was competition from Brotherhood Park, a stadium erected in the late 1890 on a plateau at West 155th Street between Eighth Avenue and the Harlem River Drive. The neighborhood was called Coogan's Bluff, after James J. Coogan, a Bowery upholsterer and furniture dealer who became a Tammany politician and a major real estate player. Eventually, this stadium, which was also named the Polo Grounds, was home to the Players League New York Giants and then to the National League Giants, who played there for the next seven decades.

*   *   *

Harlem had sports, stores, restaurants, and parks, and tens of thousands of people took streetcars uptown each Sunday to enjoy them. Still, there was not much to do at night, at least according to Oscar Hammerstein's publicity machine. The Mount Morris Theatre was built in the early 1880s on East 129th Street by the Third Avenue Railroad Company, but it was housed on the third floor, and audiences who came to see productions such as Robert G. Morris's *The Irish-American,* an immigrant romance with not one but two mustache-twirling villains, complained about smells from stables on the ground floor. At the same time, amateur music and theater companies such as the Harlem Theatre Comique, the Harlem Philharmonic Society, the Harlem Mendelssohn Union, and the Harlem Mannerchor regularly held events in rented halls. In addition, starting in the early 1880s, Sulzer's Harlem River Park Casino, a German-style beer hall at Second Avenue and East 126th Street, was as a veritable entertainment complex, with a bowling alley, slot machines, rifle range, and a demonstration space for purveyors of patent medicines. Sulzer's soon inspired an imitator, the Harlem Casino, at Seventh Avenue and West 124th Street, which had its own house orchestra and outdoor amusement gardens that could hold ten thousand people. It became a favored place for political gatherings, and it even hosted the annual Purim balls of local synagogues. It was only in 1889 that Harlem got its own proper theater in the form of the West End Theatre at West 124th Street and Seventh Avenue. It was quite an event. "All the women and children of Harlem seemed to have turned out" to see the child stage star Tommy Russell, dressed as Little Lord Fauntleroy, lay the cornerstone of the theater, the *Times* reported. But it was only when Oscar Hammerstein got out of real estate and into show business that Harlem became synonymous with entertainment.

Hammerstein's real estate ventures had been financially successful but he knew that something else was holding back the neighborhood. His answer was the Harlem Opera House, squeezed into the lot at 207 West 125th Street. It may not have been the first theater uptown but it was the biggest, and not only in Harlem but in all of New York, with room for more than one thousand people on opening night in 1889. It almost didn't get built at all. Construction started just a year after Hammerstein's financial troubles with the Kaiser Wilhelm, and problems with the excavation of the site forced Hammerstein to sell his *Tobacco Journal* and borrow $10,000 from his brother-in-law just to keep on with construction. When the theater was finished, it was discovered that there was no box office, not surprising for a man who rarely carried cash. Hammerstein made sure to get the rest right. On that first night the audience marveled at the 130-foot-long frescoed entry to the theater itself, which was all mirror and marble, gold, rose, and bright blue. Hammerstein's devotion to high culture meant that the Harlem Opera House eschewed vaudeville, which had been packing in New York audiences for almost a decade. Instead, a bust of Richard Wagner presided, and the stage curtain was painted with an illustration of Queen Elizabeth listening to Shakespeare read. Nonetheless, Hammerstein had a broad vision of what uptown the-atergoers wanted, and he produced both popular and genteel drama and opera in English translation, an experiment that proved attrac-tive to audiences who were willing to pay up to $2.50 for a ticket. He hired the best downtown performers he could find, including Edwin Booth, Georgie Drew Barrymore, Fanny Davenport, and Joseph Jef-ferson, and paid them a fixed fee plus a percentage of the door, often making up any losses from his own pocket. The first season ended in the red, and the second season began in May of 1890 with police preventing the curtain from going up because the building didn't have the proper city licenses—they even arrested Hammerstein himself. In June things got so bad that Hammerstein had to raise cash by liq-uidating much of his uptown real estate, which by this time included thirty private homes and two dozen apartment buildings. The show eventually went on, and later that season Hammerstein brought in performances of *Ernani, Faust, Mignon, The Bohemian Girl, Carmen,* and Charles Hoyt's *A Trip to Chinatown.* The crowds came, but the critics were less pleased. "Lord deliver us from such music!" complained the *Musical Courier.*

When Hammerstein realized that competition with the downtown's Metropolitan Opera House, which even then fancied itself the only legitimate opera house in New York, was keeping his seats empty, he brought in star Met performers for productions of *Norma, Les Huguenots,* and *Il Trovatore.* Hammerstein's "song of defiance" was a sellout and more. As Hammerstein sat at stage right on a kitchen chair and watched these performances, he had a new idea. Uptown opera clearly had potential, convincing many downtowners to make the trip to Harlem for the evening, but in order to attract bigger crowds he needed a venue to offer something more popular. Within days Hammerstein had sold off most of his remaining real estate and put the money into creating a new theater. The 1,800-seat Columbus Theatre, strategically located five blocks away, at the other end of Hammerstein's planned entertainment district, opened its doors at 114 East 125th Street in October 1890. It was even more successful, with cheaper ticket prices, easy access to the East Side elevated train lines, and programming that ranged from Shakespeare and grand opera to more popular fare, including vaudeville, minstrelsy, musical comedies, and variety shows—it was Hammerstein's son Willie who invented the pie-in-the-face gag and booked novelty acts like an armless sharpshooter, a team of Australian lumberjacks, and a belly dancer who performed while holding a chair between her teeth.

Successes in the tobacco industry, real estate, and theater had made Oscar Hammerstein one of the most famous men in America. Much loved and feared, dictatorial, mercurial, lavish with money, and always hungry for publicity, he wasn't above brawling with business competitors on 125th Street, initiating endless lawsuits, or booing his own singers. Once the Harlem Opera House and the Columbus were both in the black, this restless genius—in 1895 alone he received thirty-eight patents, most having to do with the acoustics of theater architecture—became determined to turn Times Square, then known as Longacre Square, into an entertainment district. But his new ventures got off to a slow start and Hammerstein had to sell the Harlem Opera House in 1897. Soon he was totally broke, losing his home on West 120th Street and all of his theaters, downtown and uptown. Both the Harlem Opera House and the Columbus were taken over by the vaudeville pioneer F. F. Proctor, who renamed the latter Proctor's 125th Street Theater—the giant "P" on its marquee was visible from one side of the island to the other. By the next year it was being run as a vaudeville and burlesque house featuring the young George M. Cohan and his siblings. But Hammerstein, who played a central role in the shift in American popular culture from German operetta to Jewish vaudeville, was far from finished. His constant tinkering in the cigar business had resulted in an invention that made tobacco stems usable in filling cigars, and flush with income from the sale of the rights to this device Hammerstein built no fewer than seven theaters in Times Square before taking a $1.2 million payoff from the Metropolitan Opera House to do business elsewhere. Ever resourceful, Hammerstein built theaters in Philadelphia and then London before his death in 1919. Among the mourners at Temple Israel who gathered around the bronze coffin holding this indifatiguable producer, composer, editor, inventor, and builder were, according to a United Press dispatch, "a weeping colored cook, and a ragged, whimpering stick boy, servants of the impresario who sat alongside richly gowned actresses from the leading New York theaters." It was an appropriate audience for a man who strove to fulfill the vision of Harlem's founding charter as a self-sustaining neighborhood thriving on a balance of work and pleasure, business and culture, everyday life and the fantasy of something better.

Oscar Hammerstein longed to make the kind of impact in politics that he had made in real estate and entertainment. One Sunday in 1894 he gave over the entire Harlem Opera House to a Tammany fund-raiser to benefit the poor and jobless. But the Democrats who inherited the spoils of the Tweed Ring never quite offered real power to this older generation of German Jews, not even to "Oscar the Immortal." Many German-Jewish Harlemites were, like their gentile counterparts, from upper-middle-class families with intellectual and left-wing associations. American politics played by different rules. The economically

and racially progressive platform of the Republicans was a natural
for New York's German Jews, who were among the earliest founders
of the Harlem Republican Club in 1888. But the Democratic party
was still the only game in town. So it was understandable that the
first uptown Democratic club would include a dozen German Jews as
founding members, including Daniel Hays and Cyrus Sulzberger, the
original publishers of the *American Hebrew*—their names also graced
the masthead of the staunchly Democratic *New York Times*. But they
could get only so far in Democratic politics due to an anti-Semitism
that was no less objectionable because it was genteel.

Nominally gentile clubs like the Harlem Young Men's Christian
Association, which was founded in 1868, by definition wrestled with
the question of admitting Jews to its library, gymnasium, parlor, and
lecture hall. The stakes were higher at the Harlem Club, a highbrow
social society founded in 1879 in a clapboard mansion at Fifth Avenue
near West 127th Street. A decade later, the club hired the distinguished
architectural firm of Lamb and Rich to build a massive sandstone and
terra-cotta mansion in a mixed Romanesque Revival and Byzantine
style at West 123rd Street and Lenox Avenue. There, more than seven
hundred members, among them E. W. Townsend, the author of the
popular *Chimmie Fadden* series of Irish-dialect novels, enjoyed their
own bowling alley, library, dining room, and billiards and cards rooms.
There were even bachelor apartments next door, on the top two floors
of the old Harlem Free Library, which had been subsumed by Andrew
Carnegie's quest to start a municipal library system, starting with a
number of distinguished new buildings by the famed architectural team
of McKim, Mead, and White. The prominent Republican lawyer and
diplomat Benjamin Peixotto was a member of the Harlem Club, but
that was an exception. The pioneering uptown journalist, lawyer, and
Democratic politician Jacob Cantor was turned away in 1889. That
may have been in part because of politics, but either way the members
eventually chose to close the doors rather than open their minds.

Cantor's unsuccessful effort to join the Harlem Club was a sign of
the political challenges and opportunities that the new century would
bring. The fall of the Tweed Ring in the early 1870s only temporarily

interrupted Tammany Hall's domination of city politics. The boss of Tammany Hall in the waning years of the Flash Age, the Harlemite Richard Croker, often called the last absolute monarch of the city, solved the problem by making sure that Tammany Hall stayed true to its calling: rewarding the votes of the newest New Yorkers with jobs and sometimes even cash. Croker was born in Ireland in either 1841 or 1843 and immigrated to America with his family as a child. When he wasn't boxing, swimming, or leading the local gang, he was tending horses at the Harlem Car Company. At the age of sixteen he quit school to become a machinist in the New York Central Railroad's uptown locomotive shop, where he worked for five years, making extra money as a Tammany ward heeler and a multiple voter—one election day he "repeated" seventeen times.

By the late 1860s the *Times* was calling the bearded and brawny Croker "a rowdy and election bully of well-established fame." He had held just about every sort of no-show job the Tweed Ring could offer, from municipal court guard to engineer at a steam plant, and he made himself indispensable to the new boss of Tammany, ex-congressman "Honest John" Kelly, who like so many Tammany figures owned property uptown. Croker served as city marshal and fire commissioner before becoming city coroner, at the time an elected position that paid the princely sum of $15,000. That was still nothing compared to the amount of money he was making on the side. Like so many of his cronies, Croker celebrated his financial move up in the world by moving uptown, to 26 Mount Morris Park West.

After the death of Kelly in 1886, Croker became known as the "Chief of the Chiefs." He revitalized local Democratic politics, putting four mayors in office, two of whom, Thomas Gilroy and Robert Van Wyck, came from Harlem. Croker outranked them all because of his position as Tammany's Finance Committee chairman, which by tradition kept no written records. Under Croker, it cost $300 to become a police officer, $1,600 to make it to sergeant, and $10,000 to become captain, and there were waiting lists for all three ranks, since the money could easily be recouped through shakedowns and bribery once on the job, especially in vice districts. Croker became even more powerful than Tweed in his day, and by 1890 he was basically running the city, taking a piece of every significant deal, public and private, with the power to hire and fire any one of some ninety thousand municipal workers. A new burst of Tweed-style infrastructure followed, including the completion of uptown parks, the building of new bridges connecting Harlem with the Bronx, and the long-awaited completion of the Harlem ship canal—a mastodon tusk was unearthed during construction—at the northern tip of Manhattan, which accelerated the industrial development of East Harlem's waterfront.

Croker also benefited from gambling and prostitution. Sometimes the money rolled in so fast that he had to use his young daughter as bagman. But he never forgot where his power came from. The *Harlem Local Reporter* noted days before Christmas 1893 that Tammany politicians had set up "people's restaurants" where those hit by the terrible winter that year could eat in a warm place for 5 cents. Such measures couldn't insulate Tammany Hall from the city's growing political reform movement. After the financial crisis of 1893 Croker retired from public life, sold his house on Mount Morris Park, and took off for Europe, ostensibly to lose weight at a rest cure but in reality to avoid the scrutiny of municipal corruption during his reign.

By 1897 Croker was no longer in immediate danger of investigation, and he returned to New York in what was billed by one journalist as "the Return from Elba." But reformers posed more of a threat than ever at the ballot box, and Croker took up the fight using the slogan "To Hell with Reform!" He successfully backed Judge Robert Van Wyck, himself a Harlemite, for mayor against Columbia University's president Seth Low, former state legislature and good government proponent Theodore Roosevelt, and the Harlem economist Henry George, whose 1880 antimonopoly tract *Progress and Poverty* was already a classic. Croker had won the battle but he couldn't avoid corruption investigations forever. He got a public relations boost from a celebratory biography written by Alfred Henry Lewis, a journalist for the Hearst organization whose stint as a wandering cowboy in the Southwest inspired him to invent the genre of the western and paid for a house on West 148th Street. Nonetheless, Croker quit Tammany Hall in 1902.

A lion among Tammany tigers, Croker spent the last two decades of his life dividing his time between Florida and Ireland, where he had a fake coat of arms made up to grace his stationery and his carriage.

The ever wily leaders of Tammany staved off reform and maintained power, at first by reaching out to the uptown German-Jewish establishment, which was frustrated by the perpetual irrelevance of the Republican Party in New York. The 1894 benefit at Oscar Hammerstein's Harlem Opera House had been Croker's idea, and even though more than 60 percent of all New Yorkers were Irish-born, Croker reached out to Harlem's eastern and southern European immigrants. As if answering Henry George's speculation about the political empowerment of minorities—what will happen, this confirmed progressive wondered, when "our human garbage can vote?"—Croker had been among the first to see Harlem's racial future, pioneering what seemed like a crazy idea at the time: black Democrats. Believing he might lure blacks away from the party of Lincoln, Croker founded the United Colored Democracy and installed its first leader, Edward E. Lee.

The consolidation of the city in 1898 changed forever the way Harlemites thought about their future. Not long before, the *Harlem Local Reporter* observed that "a great city" was developing north of Central Park. *Harlem Monthly Magazine* predicted that "the centre of fashion, wealth, culture, and intelligence must, in the near future, be found in the ancient and honorable village." Boosterism trumped reality in these publications, and Harlem greeted the new century as an economically dependent and culturally provincial village with all of the social problems of a big city. Not only were the tenement districts and industrialized areas unsafe and polluted, but even quiet brownstone neighborhoods were becoming dodgy. The blocks around Sylvan Place were, ironically, "a lurking-place for dangerous characters," according to the *New York Times*.

Hints of the old Harlem remained, its "well-bred seclusion" making it the preferred "rural retreat of the aristocratic New Yorker," as *Harper's Monthly* put it. German was still a mainstay of the public school curriculum, and German clubs such as the Harlem Independent Schuetzen Corps, a riflery club located at 2258 Second Avenue, remained active into the new century, but an era was ending. "Gone are the comfortable *Weinstuben* where one could smoke his pipe and peacefully drink his glass of Rhine wine," one Harlemite wrote. Another veteran of the old German Harlem mourned, "It used to be so pleasant to pass a Harlem street on a summer evening. The young ladies were accompanying their *lieder* with the twanging of the soft zither, and the stirring robust melodies from the Lutheran churches used to fill the air on a Sunday." But the Democratic machine was unstoppable, "Tammany Art" having made uptown Manhattan all but unrecognizable to the old-timers who remembered when the neighborhood was a rural oasis, an alternative to everything that was urban and modern. Shortly before the turn of the century, the *Local Reporter* quoted an uptown billy goat complaining that "browsing days are over, and I can hardly find a blade of fresh grass." But it wasn't urbanization that troubled newspaper editors so much as the arrival of eastern European Jews and southern Italians hoping to trade the intolerance and poverty of the old world for the religious freedom and economic opportunity of the new. As top hats gave way to skullcaps a whole new Harlem was being born.

6

NOSTRA HARLEM,
UNDZERE HARLEM
The Age of Immigration

What the Fourth Avenue horse-drawn railway line was to the nineteenth century, underground transportation was to the twentieth. Southern Italian and eastern European Jewish immigrants, blacks from the deep South and the West Indies, and Latinos from the Spanish Caribbean all took the subway uptown and shouldered aside both Harlem's Irish underclass and its German upper class, helping to make the newly consolidated city into the country's biggest urban center and its undisputed center of finance, industry, the media, sports, arts, and entertainment. The benefits of underground rapid transportation had long been obvious to the *Harlem Local Reporter,* which carried on a "Fifteen Minutes to Harlem" campaign in its pages. New York City's police chief had a different perspective: "This subway is going to absolutely preclude the possibility of riots in New York. If a riot should break out at any time now we could clear the road and send out a trainload of a thousand men, dropping off as many of them at every station as necessary, and have an armed force in Harlem in 15 minutes." Mayor George McClellan had something a little more lighthearted in mind when, on October 27, 1904, he boarded a brand-new train at City Hall Station and ratcheted the Tiffany-made silver throttle up to maximum. McClellan was supposed to stop at West 125th Street but he was having so much fun that he surprised everyone and drove the train all the way to West 145th Street. In the thirty-one minutes that it took to travel nine miles, Harlem crossed the threshold into the modern world.

As the city entered a new century and a new era, ashes of the Flash Age still smoldered. The old German establishment enjoyed old-fashioned operetta by the uptown composer Sigmund Romberg at the Pabst Concert Hall on West 125th Street between Seventh and Eighth avenues. They still dined next door, at A. H. Meyer's Pabst Harlem Restaurant, reputedly the biggest restaurant in the world, with room for fourteen hundred dinner guests who were urged on by paid actors disguised as patrons to raise a glass of beer and toast the brewer. Down the street, a roof garden called the Metropolis featured pig knuckles and beer. Most of Harlem's thirty thousand southern Italian and hundred thousand eastern European Jewish immigrants were priced out of uptown's fancy restaurants and theaters, but that wasn't enough for uptowners striving to maintain the old order. Around 1908 the Harlem Property Owners Protective Association began an effort to stop a decline in housing prices supposedly due to those newcomers.

While tenements rose by the thousands, Harlem's mansions continued to attract the newest members of Manhattan's commercial aristocracy. John McLouglin, who was the first American businessman to take toys seriously and who also invented the first board games, bought Tammany Hall kingpin Henry Genet's mansion at Fifth Avenue and West 126th Street from Carl Schurz. Far more typical were the fancy apartment buildings that were popping up, the most desirable of which was the eight-story Graham Court, built by William Waldorf Astor in 1901 at Seventh Avenue and West 116th Street. Such buildings were in demand as much because of what they showed off as for what they kept out of sight. Graham Court's residents, all of whom were rich and white, entered the building through a gracious arch that led into a grand inner courtyard built over an underground stable. Domestic servants were housed in the attic. The kind of parents who made homes for themselves at Graham Court might have sent their daughters to the nearby Manhattanville College of the Sacred Heart, whose students included Rose Fitzgerald, who later married Joseph Kennedy, and the actress Tallulah Bankhead, who remembered it as the "favorite among all the schools I was thrown out of." Affluent Harlemites also set the social tone, especially when it came to leisure time. Cricket, baseball, and horse racing had long been signs of wealth, and bicycling became especially popular after the 1886 founding of the Harlem Wheelmen. By 1909, when crowds lined the shore of the Hudson River to celebrate the three hundredth anniversary of the Dutch arrival on Manhattan, swimmers who preferred not to mix with the rascals and rogues being bred in the tenements could enjoy the private bathing beach at West 149th Street.

Even as Harlemites were swept up in the national craze for fitness, they frequented the Ohlkert Candy Shop, Eichelberger's bakery, which specialized in cheesecake baked especially for Sunday morning shoppers, and Horton's Ice Cream Parlor, which sold some seventy thousand quarts of ice cream each day, mostly to restaurants and hotels but also to customers who sat at mahogany tables amid crystal chandeliers, mirrored silver fixtures, and a marble and mahogany fountain. These businesses also catered to well-heeled visitors, who had their choice of fancy hotels, such as the five-story Hotel Winthrop, built in 1888 at Seventh Avenue and West 124th Street. Entertainers at Hammerstein's Columbus Theatre stayed at the Hotel Peteler, at East 124th Street and Lexington Avenue. Businessmen and tourists favored the Balmoral Hotel, at Lenox Avenue and West 113th Street, which ferried guests to and from the 116th Street elevated lines via horse-drawn coaches. The fanciest hotel uptown was the Hotel Theresa, which opened in 1913 on the site of the old Hotel Winthrop and, at thirteen stories, still towers over the southwest corner of West 125th Street. Named for the first wife of the man who built it, a German immigrant named Gustavus Sidenburg who had made money in lace goods, the white-brick Theresa stood astride two eras. It was one of the first modernist buildings uptown, though it had a distinctly old-fashioned racial policy: whites only. But that way of life was slowly coming to an end. Within a few years a *New York Times* reporter was musing that "ancient Manhattanville is witnessing so radical a transformation that within a few years evidence of old-time quaintness in that curious section of Harlem will be eliminated." Changes in demographics inspired a "Buy in Harlem" campaign aimed at white, native-born Americans in 1914, and the next year a *Times* article asked "Is Manhattanville Section of Harlem Doomed?" The answer was yes, and not only Manhattanville but all of Harlem, because no uptown neighborhood had ever stood still for long. The new breed of immigrants from Italy and eastern Europe making New York City into the capital of the twentieth century were again remaking Harlem.

Eastern European Jews and their southern Italian neighbors may have come from different worlds but they all came from the same Old Country. Poverty, famine, unemployment, disease, intolerance, and overpopulation had for centuries characterized their lives. But it was only in the late nineteenth century when things got so bad—or the rumors about the way things were across the ocean got so much better—that the era of mass immigration began. While Italians from the *mezzogiorno,* where shoes were a rarity and *acque sale,* a soup made of water, salt, olive oil, and old bread, often constituted the day's single meal, came to America for economic reasons, two and a half million eastern European Jews had other motives. Many of them were effectively refugees, running for their lives from forced resettlement, mass detention as suspected political dissidents, compulsory military service, and anti-Semitic discrimination and terror. Russian pogroms in 1859 and 1871 were dwarfed by attacks that followed the assassination of Czar Alexander II in St. Petersburg in 1881 and haunted eastern Europe for decades.

Falling ticket prices for ocean passage to the United States in the 1880s made the decision to leave easier, though the typical charge of $34 was nonetheless an enormous amount for many immigrants, and hidden charges even for a spot on the floor in steerage meant that most immigrants gave up the last of their savings even before they got on board. Many Italians sailed on tickets subsidized by *padroni* who kept them in virtual slavery for the years that it took to pay back the debt. The three-week crossing of the Atlantic was a crowded, filthy, and storm-tossed ordeal for these passengers, most of whom could not swim and had never seen the ocean. Moreover, many religious Jews on board fasted rather than eat something that wasn't kosher.

Things often got worse at the end of the journey, when they arrived at Castle Garden, an old music hall that served as the city's point of entry from 1855 until the 1892 opening of Ellis Island, a modern facility that was nonetheless known among Italians as *l'Isola delle Lacrime* and Jews as *Trer Indz'l,* or "island of tears." News of the pogroms, as well as the Dreyfus case in France, quickly made its way uptown, but many of Harlem's German Jews favored turning away the immigrants and widely supported popular legislation intended to exclude "lunatics, idiots, persons likely to become public charges" and to give enormous discretion to Ellis Island's notoriously unenlightened officials. Humiliating regulations also barred illiterates, those with physical defects, and unaccompanied children. With the Haymarket riot of 1886 still fresh in the memory of so many Americans who considered "Jewish" and "Italian" synonymous with "socialist" and "anarchist," President Roosevelt ordered officials to turn back anyone exhibiting "a low moral tendency" or an "unsavory reputation." Still, hundreds of thousands of Jews from Russia, Poland, Romania, and Austro-Hungary as well as Italians from south of Rome—entire villages were emptied out, not only of inhabitants but, in some cases, the priest and the holy objects in the church as well—continued to pour into the United States, inspiring the joke that Ellis Island was like the Day of Judgment, only more crowded.

Two-thirds of all immigrants were headed for the East Side, which by the turn of the century was a hive of hats and beards, black shawls and Roman Catholic amulets. Italian immigrants said they wanted nothing more out of America than "peace and onions." They got a good deal more. The downtown immigrant neighborhoods, a "gray, stone world of tall tenements, where even on the loveliest spring day there was not a blade of grass," as the Yiddish playwright and actor Leon Kobrin described it, suffered from many of the same problems that marked the old country, plus a few new ones. No wonder so many recently arrived Jews and Italians yearned for Harlem's wide, leafy boulevards and spacious, clean parks.

*   *   *

The famed cantor Joseph Rosenblatt remembered not one but two
Jewish Harlems at the turn of the century, a division that was conveniently symbolized by the imposing streetcar viaduct built in the
1890s along Fourth Avenue. West Harlem meant the fancy mansions,
brownstones, row houses, and apartment buildings of the established
German-Jewish families. This was the world that produced so many
of the uptowners pointing the nation in new directions in politics,
publishing, industry, business, fashion, sports, religion, education, and
especially in arts and entertainment. West Harlem spawned the composer Richard Rodgers and both of his writing partners, Lorenz Hart
and Oscar Hammerstein II, who rewrote the genetic code of American
music, forging from the raw material of nineteenth-century operetta
and vaudeville the genre that would come to be known as the Broadway
musical. Their boyhoods reveal as much about the old Harlem in the
twilight of the nineteenth century as they do about the new Harlem
at the dawn of the twentieth century.

Lorenz Hart was born downtown in 1895 to the former Max
Hertz, a German immigrant and descendant of Heinrich Heine,
though he is best remembered today for discovering the first jazz
group, the Original Dixieland Jass Band. In his own day Max Hart,
as he rechristened himself, was an important real estate developer
and Oscar Hammerstein's best friend, a corpulent bon vivant who
threw Rabelaisian, celebrity-packed parties that featured everything
from readings of erotic poetry to raucous political discussions. Hart
was "an ardent Tammanyite," according to the *New York Times*—how
else to get things done?—but he was scorned behind his back for his
vulgarities, such as urinating out windows when a trip to the bathroom
proved to be too much trouble, or talking to tenants in Yiddish. Not
surprisingly, he never gained acceptance among New York's power
brokers. Nonetheless, Hart gave his second son the middle name Van
Wyck, after the Democratic candidate in the 1897 mayoral race, and
he moved his family into a three-story house at 59 West 119th Street,
a neighborhood favored by politicians. There, the family's half-blind

Jamaican maid, Mary Campbell—she became something of a celebrity herself after she was immortalized in the beloved 1936 play *You Can't Take It with You*—ran a proper German-Jewish kitchen, with chicken on Sunday, sweetbreads on Monday, pot roast on Tuesday, and sausage on Wednesday. Among those who came to eat were such famed stars of the German stage as a Greta Meyer, Christian Raab, and Gustave Hamburg. The young Larry Hart, as he was known to his friends, began taking in German-language productions downtown and Broadway shows, especially at the Manhattan Opera House and other Hammerstein venues, where he got in for free. Hart also saw local burlesque and vaudeville with a friend from the neighborhood, Morrie Ryskind, who later collaborated with the Gershwins on Broadway and with the Marx Brothers in Hollywood. Other favorite spots were the Star Theatre and Hurtig and Seamon's Music Hall, which opened as a burlesque venue shortly after the turn of the century next to the Harlem Opera House. Hart got his own stage experience at the upstate New York summer camps that were breeding grounds for so many German-Jewish strivers around the turn of the century and he attended the progressive Weingart Institute before enrolling in the all but obligatory DeWitt Clinton High School. As Hart grew up, though, school appealed less and less and he dropped out of Columbia University.

The life of this little rich boy, and the history of American music, changed for good on a Sunday afternoon in 1919, when Hart opened his front door to a sixteen-year-old Columbia student named Richard Rodgers who was looking for a writing partner. The Rodgers family was of poor eastern European stock, but they had somehow made the leap across the barrier that separated the two Harlems. Sometime before Richard's birth in 1902, the family moved from 146 East 115th Street to 3 West 120th Street, a four-story brownstone with ground-floor space for Rodgers's father's medical practice and a flight of stone stairs to the first floor, perfect for stoop ball. Like Larry Hart, Rodgers got a progressive education, attending P.S. 81, also known as the Model School, on West 119th Street near Seventh Avenue—the publisher Bennett Cerf was a classmate—and then P.S. 10, two blocks to the south. His musical education was fairly informal. The family's Saturday

outings along 125th Street focused on Viennese-style operettas, and his
mother liked to buy the sheet music for songs such as "Harlem Square
Polka" and "My Pretty Harlem Belle" sold in theater lobbies. Like so
many uptown Jews, the Rodgers family left for the Upper West Side
in the years before World War I, but Rodgers was soon back uptown,
at Townsend Harris Hall, a three-year feeder school for City College.
But Rodgers ended up at Columbia, not so much for the education
as for the opportunity to work on the college's famed Varsity Show,
which was then as professional as any Broadway production. When
Rodgers learned that Hart wasn't on Morningside Heights anymore,
he went down the hill to find him and strike up a partnership. Eventually, in songs such as "The Lady Is a Tramp," "My Funny Valentine,"
"Bewitched, Bothered, and Bewildered," and "Isn't It Romantic," the
pair perfected the elegant yet informal tone, the cynical yet romantic
attitude that is surely one of the hallmarks of Harlem style.

Later, when Hart's drinking began to get in the way of work,
Rodgers teamed up with another Harlem boy, and not just any Harlem
boy but the grandson of Oscar the Immortal himself. Born in 1895
on East 116th Street, Oscar Hammerstein II was still a child when
the family moved into adjoining apartments in a 112th Street row
house. Until 1901, when the family joined the exodus to the Upper
West Side, Hammerstein played in Mount Morris Park every day and
made regular trips to the Harlem Opera House and the Columbus
Theatre. He began writing lyrics as a child and eventually teamed up
with Florenz Ziegfeld and Jerome Kern on *Showboat* before he got the
call from Richard Rodgers, whom he knew from the Columbia Varsity
shows. Rodgers and Hammerstein picked up right where they had left
off, and together they opened a whole new chapter of Broadway history in which the melancholy modernity of Rodgers and Hart's *Babes
in Arms* and *Pal Joey* gave way to the old-fashioned yet globe-hopping
sentimentality of Rodgers and Hammerstein's *Oklahoma, South Pacific,
The King and I,* and *The Sound of Music.* No matter how exotic the locale,
Harlem was always audible, and still is.

*   *   *

A huge distance separated the genteel West Harlem neighborhood of Rodgers, Hart, and Hammerstein and the squalid tenement districts of Little Russia and Little Italy, which were as "lousy and congested as our East Side, with the same absence of light and air," according to the *Jewish Daily Forward*. For many among the old guard, it was still too close for comfort. Whom did the *Harlem Local Reporter* have in mind when it complained about the threats that "foreigners" posed to the good life uptown? The newspaper seems to have been warning about Harlem's Italian community, which dates from the early 1870s, when a handful of newcomers, made to feel distinctly unwelcome at local Irish Catholic churches, built Saint Cecilia at 125 East 105th Street. But it wasn't until 1878, when immigrants from the town of Polla, near Salerno, settled on East 115th Street, that the story of uptown's Italians really got under way. West Harlem was booming, but across town newly arrived Italians were lucky to pick up day work at local factories. The rest scavenged to survive. One contemporary observer wrote, "Here can be found the refuse of Italy making a poor living from Harlem ashbarrels." Still, more Italians kept arriving, recruited as strike breakers on the First Avenue trolley line and housed in a shantytown made of cast-off scrap metal and lumber near the East River at East 106th Street. Eventually, Italians began occupying the endless rows of tenements blanketing East Harlem, and by the end of the 1880s about four thousand lived in the neighborhood surrounding Third Avenue from East 104th Street all the way up to East 110th Street and beyond. By the turn of the century Harlem's Little Italy— downtown's neighborhood got that name only decades later—boasted an Italian population that was not only three times as large as that of the East Side but larger than Sicily as well. Block after block of East Harlem from East 110th to East 130th streets east of Third Avenue was "as thoroughly Italian as Rome, Naples, Palermo, or Messina," according to one contemporary account. By 1910, when there were only about ten thousand Italians downtown, some fifty-nine thousand Italians called East Harlem home, and another thirteen thousand or so had settled in other parts of Harlem, numbers that would double within a decade.

The story of one East Harlem *ragazzo* who grew up to become an eminent educator and advocate for all of Harlem's immigrants powerfully communicates the inspiring and sobering realities behind such statistics and illustrates many of the differences between Little Russia and Little Italy. Leonardo Coviello was born in 1887 in the impoverished southern Italian town of Avigliano and said good-bye at the age of three to his father, who had been seduced by stories about the ease of getting work in *L'America*. They didn't see each other again until 1896, when the boy made the journey across the Atlantic with his mother, his two siblings, and his grandmother. He learned his first English word, "yes," on the ferry from Ellis Island and he never lost that sense of optimism. The family settled into a building on East 112th Street between First Avenue and the Harlem River, a block filled with *paesani* from Avigliano. Italy had been a united country with a single language only since 1871, and immigrants from different regions could barely understand one another's dialects, so longtime neighbors from the old country stuck together in the New World. Northern Italians settled in lower East Harlem, with the Genovese on East 106th Street and the Piacenzanese on East 104th and East 105th streets. Southern Italians dominated the rest of the neighborhood, with Neapolitans on East 105th and East 106th streets, Sicilians on East 104th and East 107th streets, and Calabrians on East 108th and East 109th streets. Such settlement patterns caused as much social conflict as they did social stability, especially when it came to competition for work, or the operation of each region's criminal element.

The making of the uptown ghettos wasn't only a matter of flesh and blood but of brick and mortar. In response to the demands of religious reformers and progressive architects, the city had recently embraced systematic sanitary inspections of tenements and laws mandating fire escapes in new buildings. Official regulations began restricting the size of the "footprint" of tenements to 65 percent of the plot, required at least twenty-five feet between buildings, and forced landlords to provide at least six hundred cubic feet of space for each resident.

But it was a police reporter turned journalist named Jacob Riis and his legendary 1890 book *How the Other Half Lives* that made the city's housing problems a matter of public debate. The "vile tenements," as the *Local Reporter* put it, in which three-fourths of all New Yorkers lived, were finally recognized as a major public health problem, though families like the Coviellos didn't complain. A shared toilet in the hall was more plumbing than they had back in the old country. Partly in response to Riis's book, regulations for newly constructed tenements now mandated private bathrooms with toilets, hot and cold running water, a window in every room, fireproof construction, hall lights, and a superintendent to maintain it all. That still left thousands of "old law" tenements breeding trouble. Rising rents forced Jewish and Italian families to squeeze as many as possible into their apartments. With up to fifteen people, most of them lodgers, occupying each four-room unit, buildings designed to house fifty people sometimes contained as many as three hundred. Some blocks contained more than fourteen hundred residents, when they should have had around twenty-three thousand. Such overcrowding inevitably incubated all kinds of problems. Once upon a time, Harlem had been a refuge from the epidemics that raged downtown, but since diphtheria hit the immigrant blocks of East Harlem, in 1880, the neighborhood had some of the city's most alarming rates of infectious disease, particularly tuberculosis.

The popular image of East Harlem during the tenement years is of a squalorous, defeated neighborhood, with garbage and horse manure piled everywhere and coal dust coating every surface. That is not a fully accurate description of the world that Italians and Jews made uptown. Despite the poverty, the homes of Italians in particular were famed among social workers for their cleanliness and coziness. Even the most modest tenement of the most rude and materialistic *cafono*, or country bumpkin, was graced by window boxes filled with tomato plants and geraniums, and the tenants grew vegetables and raised goats for milk and meat in vacant lots. Of course, making it in what Jews called the Goldene Medina, or the "golden city," would take more than pretty flowers. Immigrants arrived with the hope that public education would offer their children a different future, especially since the city was in the middle of a surge of construction that brought to Harlem more than two dozen new schools, many of them grand, dignified edifices in an appropriately neo-Italianate architectural style. The best known of these schools was the massive Wadleigh High School, named for Lydia F. Wadleigh, a nineteenth-century proponent of female education. Built in 1901 for an unheard-of $900,000, the school was designed to hold about twenty-five hundred students, and had eighty classrooms, three gyms, and a huge auditorium. Wadleigh, like most of the new schools, was located in West Harlem, far from the antiquated and overcrowded schools that most of the children of East Harlem's immigrants attended. It is no surprise, then, that Leonardo Coviello's parents sent him to a private school run by the Female Guardian Society of America, a philanthropy working to make good American Protestants out of East Harlem's newest arrivals. Despite broader ends that were considered progressive at the time, old-fashioned rote learning and corporal punishment were the means at the Soup School, as it was known, because soup was served for lunch every day. It was there that Leonardo Coviello was renamed Leonard Covello.

Covello's father was furious that a school so backward that it sent students home with oatmeal for breakfast—fodder for swine back in the old country—renamed his son, but he was different from his neighbors. He earned the handsome sum of $8 per week at a bowling alley and café downtown at a time when rates of unemployment among the Jews and Italians of East Harlem were a third higher than the city average, and when those who worked earned the pittance paid to the unskilled. Many were so poor that they wore shoes only in the winter. As time went on and Tammany Hall began to reach out beyond its Irish base, there was work building and maintaining streetcar and subway lines. Jobs in sweatshops, local lumberyards, coal yards, slaughterhouses, factories, junkyards, stockyards, docks, breweries, or masonry yards opened up, but these were often scab labor positions, intermittent and dangerous. Those who managed to save up enough money often went into business for themselves, with Jews opening clothing, hardware, and jewelry stores and Italians going into the coal or ice business or opening bakeries, flower shops, green groceries, barbershops, or shoe shine stands. Women worked in factories in the garment, tobacco, candy, artificial flower, and cardboard industries, or did piecework at home. Italian children made money by collecting horse manure from the streets and selling it to housewives, who used it as window box fertilizer.

Like his father, Covello was determined to do better, which meant going to college and moving into one of the posh row houses of Doctors and Lawyers Row, as East 116th Street was known. He started out at the age of twelve as a delivery boy for Griffin's Bakery, at Fifth Avenue and East 112th Street, which paid $1.75 for six mornings a week, a substantial contribution during a time when milk was 6 cents a quart and meat cost 12 cents a pound. A model student, he got a scholarship—tuition plus $25 per month expenses—to attend Columbia University, which was visible but out of reach to most East Harlemites. The Harts and the Hammersteins sent their sons to Columbia, but the new generation of eastern and southern European immigrants found the Ivy League not only too expensive but distinctly inhospitable. Neither problem held back Covello, who somehow found time to teach at the East 116th Street branch of the YMCA. Even as a teenager Covello was passionately devoted to helping immigrants integrate themselves into American culture, and after graduating from Columbia in 1911 he remained on Morningside Heights to work on a graduate degree in French but looked forward to meetings of the youth group he ran on Friday nights at the Jefferson Park Italian Methodist Church.

Matters of religion also set Covello apart from his neighbors, who looked warily at the missionaries for whom Protestantism and Americanization were one and the same. Most of East Harlem's Catholics stuck with the religion of their ancestors, worshiping at dozens of newly built Italian Catholic churches. The most beloved was the Church of Our Lady of Mount Carmel, which was started by that same group of immigrants from Polla who had settled uptown in the late 1870s. The church was named for the saint whose life-size statue had for centuries shielded her devotees from poverty and illness and redeemed their lives from sin. This likeness of the Madonna, considered by worshippers to be a living being, had also made the trip to America, but she didn't have a permanent home until the mid-1880s, when her parishioners built a church on East 115th Street, though uptown's Irish and German Catholic religious establishment insisted that the Italians hold separate services in the basement. The church also brought the traditional annual pageant held to honor her to East Harlem, where it became a full-fledged neighborhood celebration, a firework-filled, all-day holy drama that soon overshadowed similar local celebrations devoted to San Gennaro and Saint Cecilia. Starting in early July, the entire neighborhood, from stoop to roof, was festooned with flags, banners, and colored streamers, and celebrants began arriving from across the country. As the church bell rang on July 16, Mass began, the first of a series that would last continuously for the next twenty-four hours. The flash and bang of firecrackers and guns fired into the air competed with bands that had been playing nearly nonstop for several days and wouldn't get much rest for a few days more. Lining the procession route were stands selling religious figurines, pamphlets, and medals as well as tomato pie, sausage, pasta, beans, corn, candy, pastry, cake, ice cream, and lots of beer and wine. The climax of the event came when the Madonna, crowned in gold and jewels and mounted on a high dais decorated with ribbons and flowers and obscured by clouds of incense, was carried out of the church and into the streets by members of the church's all-male Holy Name Society—it was Italian Harlem's highest honor. The Madonna's platform, which held a container that quickly filled up with jewelry and cash, was surrounded on all sides by girls dressed in white, followed by men organized by place of origin in the old country, neighborhood in East Harlem, profession, social club, and various church associations. Next came the women, singing, chanting, weeping, laughing, shouting, wailing, and screaming, swept up and away by a passionate reverence and gratitude toward the figure who watched over them in this strange land. Many recipients of her favors offered candles, manufactured at the candle factory a few blocks away in the shape of body parts that needed healing, from eyes and livers to whole limbs. Finally came the shoeless pilgrims, some of whom walked barefoot all the way from downtown. Some devotees crawled the last few blocks of the procession.

Such devotion led local Irish and German priests to try to shut down the *festa,* to no avail. It even shocked the Jews, Irish, and blacks from the neighborhood who also lined the route of the procession every year. But that kind of social harmony was rare. A 1903 strike by the mostly Italian Rockmen's and Excavator's Union for an eight-hour, two-dollar day turned into a monthlong work stoppage that attracted African-Americans willing to take their jobs building the city's new subway system, even if it meant defending themselves against the violent attacks of Italian union members—just a generation after the *padroni* had brought Italians uptown to break the strikes of Irish union members. In fact, Italian immigrants were for the most part not only made to feel unwelcome in Catholic churches but kept out of the Irish-dominated construction industry and banned from Irish political clubs. The Italian children who went to P.S. 29, on East 125th Street, had to fight their way north through Irish territory every morning just to get to school. Such prejudice cut both ways. The Irish children of East Harlem who lived between Fourth and Second avenues had to brave a gauntlet of Italian kids in order to swim in the Harlem River at East 114th Street. Relations between Italians and the much larger Jewish community were similarly tense. Most Italians bought their olive oil, cheese, wine, salami, pasta, fruit, and fish from Italian peddlers who crammed the streets, but dry goods came from Jewish-owned stores, making for conflicts over prices and credit that played into ancient forms of anti-Semitism. Belief was at stake as well, with many Italians accusing the inhabitants of Harlem's Little Russia of being Christ killers, though Italian children in East Harlem planning mischief also took to speaking Yiddish in front of their parents.

Even if those kinds of conflicts escalated into nothing more than bloody noses, they could have devastating psychological effects on immigrants caught between the religious traditions of their parents and the imperatives of American modernity. Such encounters decisively shaped the supreme literary chronicler of Jewish New York, Henry Roth, who escaped East Harlem to write *Call It Sleep,* no mere exemplar of immigrant fiction but a full-fledged masterpiece of literary modernism. Born in 1906 in what is now Ukraine, Roth and his mother followed his father to America the next year, living in Brooklyn and on the Lower East Side before moving uptown in 1914. At first the family lived on a Jewish block on East 114th Street, but they soon relocated to hostile Irish territory at 108 East 119th Street. Roth's father worked as a conductor on the Madison Avenue trolley line before opening his own deli on 116th Street, so he brought home more money than his neighbors who worked in local sweatshops, most of which were owned by German Jews. Conditions in these establishments were so atrocious that many East Harlemites did their work at home, where an extended family, including children, might finish enough pairs of trousers at 75 cents per dozen to make $15 per week, though that meant twelve-hour days, six days per week, and the work was often only seasonal. Other Jewish Harlemites, kept out of construction by the Irish, made cigars or sold penny peaches or hats, though a 1915 campaign against street peddlers on 125th Street—combined with a "Buy in Harlem" promotion that would presumably benefit store owners who identified with the Harlem of old—made that an unstable source of income. Then there were the *luftmenschen*, literally "air people," jobless *schlemiels* who seemed to survive off the air itself and who made up as many as one-third of all Jewish Harlemites. These were the characters who populated the stories of Jewish Harlem's poet laureate Solomon Libin, a Russian-born hat maker whose Yiddish sketches of life in the uptown tenements came to the attention of Abraham Cahan, the publisher of downtown's *Jewish Daily Forward*. Through Cahan's support, Libin began publishing in the city's major Yiddish newspapers, including the *Arbeiterzeitung*, the *Warheit*, the *Zukunft*, and the *Vorwarts*, alongside the work of the popular Jewish writer Sholem Aleichem, who lived for a time at 110 Lenox Avenue, a world away from the urban shtetl to the east. Instead of drawing inspiration from the old country, Libin focused on his neighbors, specializing in fashionably realist portraits of *dos klayne menshele*, or "the little man." One story, "The New Law," ironically charts the disastrous impact that labor regulations reducing the length of the workweek have on a poor family. Another, "She

Got Her Prize," was a farce about a woman who mistakenly sells her husband's only suit to the ragman.

Henry Roth would surely have recognized Libin's characters from his own experience, but he got glimpses of another Harlem while working as a delivery boy for Park and Tilford, the classy downtown grocery store with a branch at Lenox Avenue and West 126th Street. He also took tickets and hustled soda pop at the fourth Polo Grounds, a horseshoe-shaped, Greco-Roman amphitheater built after the third Polo Grounds burned down in 1911. The new stadium became famous not only because it was where the term "hot dog" seems to have been invented in 1901—Chicago also claims that uncertain honor—but because the center field fence was a jaw-dropping 483 feet away, making a home run there a near impossibility.

After finishing the school day at P.S. 103 and later at P.S. 24, Roth was sent for Hebrew lessons at his local Talmud Torah, where he was praised by his teacher as a prodigy with the makings of a great rabbi. That meant something different in the orthodox shuls of East Harlem than it did in the grand Reform temples of West Harlem. Since 1891, which saw the start of the first uptown congregation for eastern European Jews, Nachlath Zvi, the religious life of immigrants from eastern Europe was dominated by small, ramshackle synagogues that clung to the old ways and instructed young boys according to ancient traditions that scorned assimilation. The most prominent Hebrew linguist in America, Moses Reicherson, a native of Vilnius who had published numerous books of grammar and collections of fables as well as a twenty-four-volume biblical commentary before coming to the United States and settling on East 106th Street, survived only by running a small Harlem Hebrew school.

While Harlem's eastern European Jews often considered the imperatives of the faith an all-or-nothing issue, many of the German-Jewish residents who remained in West Harlem approached religious law with a guilt-free flexibility. Max Hart demanded that his sons fast on Yom Kippur, the Jewish day of repentance, though he installed himself in a window seat at Pomerantz's delicatessen with a blonde companion and indulged in a sandwich. The family of Richard Rodgers

rarely worshipped formally and eventually stopped going to synagogue altogether. Rodgers was even "baptized" in a Reform ceremony,
and starting in 1912 he attended "Sunday school" at Temple Israel,
at Lenox Avenue and West 120th Street, the most prominent and
respected of the German-Jewish synagogues in Harlem, counting as
members Louis Blumstein, city Municipal Services Commission head
Daniel P. Hays, and the lawyer Myron Sulzberger, whose son Arthur
was born in Harlem and went on to become the publisher of the *New
York Times.* German Jews looking for more tradition gravitated toward
Congregation Ohab Zedek, which left the Lower East Side and built
a gorgeous Gothic-Tudor structure at West 116th Street and Fifth
Avenue in 1906. Ohab Zedek refused to install an organ and rejected
mixed seating, decisions that attracted the most famous cantor in the
world, Joseph Rosenblatt. His performances of secular material at
venues ranging from Carnegie Hall to vaudeville houses across the
country—always in his black skullcap—made him so well known that
it is said letters addressed to "Yossele Rosenblatt, America" reached
him at his Harlem home.

Just across the street from Ohab Zedek but a world away spiritu-
ally was the Institutional Synagogue, founded in 1919 not merely as
a place to pray and study but as a community center for Jewish life,
with reading groups, drama clubs, and even sports, hence the synagogue's nickname "the shul with a pool." A middle course between
the assimilationist tendencies of Temple Israel and the archaic literal-
ism that prevailed at Henry Roth's tiny, traditional shul, between the
dangerous freedoms of assimilation on the one hand and the rigid
formalities of orthodox observance on the other, was the goal of Congregation Ansche Chesed, whose mostly German membership arrived
from downtown around the turn of the century and in 1907 built a
magnificent neoclassical structure at West 114th Street and Seventh
Avenue. There they all but invented the Conservative movement in
Judaism, which accepted an organ and choir, welcomed the use of
English, and allowed families to worship together in mixed pews,
even as they clung to age-old traditions regarding kosher laws and
the observance of the Sabbath. Among the members were the Zion-

ist poet Jessie Sampter and the scholar Henrietta Szold, who ran the Harlem Zionist study group for women that later became Hadassah, the largest Jewish organization in the world. But even the most progressive of these synagogues could prove all but irrelevant to the realities of life. When, in 1902, Harlem's kosher butchers suddenly raised prices by 50 percent, none of these synagogues did much to help. Instead, it was the Ladies Auxiliary of the Workmen's Circle, a Jewish socialist cultural and fraternal order geared to labor issues, that organized a boycott. As many as twenty thousand Jewish women not only refused to buy meat but patrolled the streets "armed with sticks, vocabularies and well-sharpened nails," according to the New York *Daily Tribune,* and they forcibly confronted anyone who broke the boycott. One woman was arrested after hitting a policeman in the face with a slice of raw beef liver. Others lay down on trolley tracks to prevent deliveries, broke into butcher shops, and burned meat on the streets. It was only after the women stormed synagogues during readings of the Torah that Harlem's rabbis got on board, after which beef wholesalers began lowering prices, though the conflict only came to an end a decade later when the Harlem and Bronx Live Poultry Association pleaded guilty to conspiring to fix prices, especially during the Jewish holidays.

Parsing the subtleties of Jewish sectarianism held no interest for Henry Roth, who early on declared himself an atheist. He read at the Mount Morris Park branch of the New York Public Library or hung out with his best friend, Frank Hussey, the son of an Irish undertaker on 129th Street, who went on to win a gold medal in track and field at the 1924 Olympics. Like so many bright, assimilated Jewish boys of the time—including Lionel Trilling and Nathanael West—Roth went to DeWitt Clinton High School, but when the time came for college his choices were limited. The Columbia that Rodgers, Hart, and Hammerstein II attended was beginning to institute geographic quotas as a way of keeping out undesirables: rejecting applicants from East Harlem and the Lower East Side was all it took to make sure Jews and Italians didn't sully the ranks of the Ivy League. Roth went instead to City College, which was the next best thing, maybe even better. In 1907 CCNY had moved from its downtown campus to the grounds of the old Convent and Academy of the Sacred Heart and hired George B. Post to erect five neo–English Gothic buildings clad in terra-cotta and stone. Post's family had owned the Claremont mansion on Morningside Heights, so he knew uptown well, and he was determined to thumb his nose at the cold, Beaux Arts style of the Columbia campus. He found it difficult to convince his Italian stonemasons of the merits of the raw, discolored schist, which was taken from the excavation of the IRT subway just a block to the east, that jacketed the campus. Nonetheless, he was able to achieve a precision naturalness that perfectly captured what Harlem style was beginning to mean. Within a few years of the opening of the new campus, more than 90 percent of the students were Jewish, attracting Jewish benefactors such as Adolph Lewisohn, who donated the Greek amphitheater that bore his name and hosted athletic events—Lou Gehrig and Hank Greenberg both played high school baseball there—as well as free summertime open-air concerts by the New York Philharmonic and the Metropolitan Opera.

City College may have been dominated by Jews, but anti-Semitism was still a fact of life there. An unspoken rule meant that Jewish faculty members didn't get tenure—the math department refused to hire a Jew until the 1940s—and, just a few years before Roth attended, one of the college's fraternities was suspended. "The Hebraic element is greatly in excess," the national organization argued. That only made the achievement of professor Morris Raphael Cohen all the more impressive. Harlem's preeminent philosopher was born in Russia in 1880, a distinctly unimpressive child who earned the nickname *kalyleh*, or half-wit. The family came to America in 1892, preferring to eat nothing during the voyage over rather than risk contact with nonkosher food, and settled on the Lower East Side, where Cohen received a traditional Jewish education, though he also worked in the pool hall where his father had a seltzer booth. City College turned Cohen into an philosopher, but he couldn't deny the influence of Harvard, where he studied with William James and roomed with Felix Frankfurter. After graduation, Cohen found that teaching positions in the Ivy League weren't open to Jews, so he moved to 493 West 135th Street, joined the faculty at City College, and became the school's best-loved teacher. But this free, publicly funded passport to achievement remained out of reach to most immigrant children, not so much because of the lack of academic preparation as because most Jews and Italians in Harlem needed the wages of everyone in the family, even children.

As the best and brightest of West Harlem left for the Upper West Side, the outer boroughs, or the suburbs, uptown remained the destination of choice for yet another generation of Italian and eastern European strivers. The sense of opportunity as well as the sheer misery of uptown's immigrant blocks, the poverty, overcrowding, prejudice, crime, and disease, was passed on to another generation. Things could go on like that for only so long before East Harlemites turned to less respectable ways to make a living. Children were among the first to appreciate the opportunities for fun and profit the streets offered, and juvenile delinquency was one of the neighborhood's most pressing problems. It wasn't only a matter of petty thefts by street urchins. Around the turn of the century, Harlem's homicide rate was the highest in the city. Much of it was due to organized crime, which offered alternatives to crushing poverty in the form of drug dealing, robbery, gambling, prostitution, extortion, and blackmail, all with the help of the police.

Surprisingly enough, the founding father of Italian organized crime uptown was a woman. Sometime before the turn of the century, Pasquarella Spinelli, an outspoken, auburn-haired Neapolitan, turned her horse stable at 334 East 107th Street into a training school for thugs, where she taught how to steal, rob, pickpocket, safecrack, and even murder. Pasquarella's operations began to attract the attentions of a gangster named Don Giosuele Galluci, who operated from a café at 318 East 109th Street. It was also a gambling house, and Don Giosuele claimed 5 percent of the take, while loaning out fresh funds to patrons at 20 percent interest, and extorting one dollar of protection money each week from the vulnerable immigrant owners of fruit and vegetable stands. Don Giosuele's operation, called the Black Hand, was clearly not going to be able to thrive if Pasquarella remained active. His henchmen gang-raped her daughter as a warning. Pasquarella publicly swore revenge but was shot and killed by Don Giosuele's men. Don Giosuele became known among cops as "the mayor of Little Italy," running everything from legitimate businesses like bakeries, shoeshine stands, ice and wood dealers, and real estate offices to less respectable ventures. But Pasquarella's men eventually struck back, killing him and his young son at a café at 336 East 109th Street.

The Black Hand was taken over by two graduates of Pasquarella's academy, Vincent and Ciro Terranova, natives of Corleone, Sicily, who had come to East Harlem sometime before the turn of the century. They used what they learned from Pasquarella to turn the Black Hand into a precision criminal organization called the 107th Street gang. They pioneered the concept of the large-scale drug deal (mostly co-caine), turned gambling on the numbers from a neighborhood hobby into a profitable business, built links with politicians and police who would look the other way, and worked with unions who could extort no-show jobs out of local businesses.

Ciro Terranova could not have become New York City's first Italian organized crime kingpin without the help of a counterfeiter named Ignazio Saietta, another native of Corleone who married Ter-ranova's sister, creating the first major blood alliance in the history of the American mafia. The dapper and dashing Terranova and the private and silent Saietta, known as Lupo the Wolf, who was friendly with the opera singer Enrico Caruso, set up an extortion business near the fruit and vegetable market located from East 101st to East 104th Streets and camouflaged their activity by cornering the emerging market on artichokes from California, which they bought for six dollars a crate and sold for nine dollars a crate. While Terranova provided cover as the so-called Artichoke King, Lupo the Wolf brought in Terranova's half brother Giuseppe "The Clutch Hand" Morello, who opened a murder stable at 323 East 107th Street and killed as many as sixty people there in the years before World War I. He was eventually made

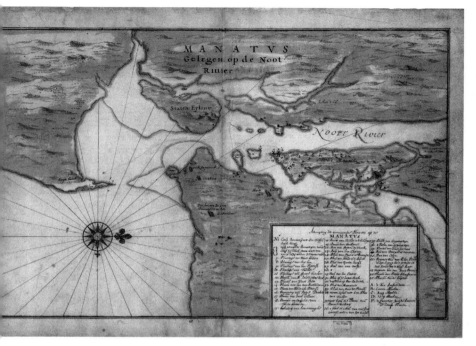

One of the earliest representations of Manhattan, the Manatus map of 1639, was probably drawn not as a topographic document, but as a promotional device to attract settlers to Nieuw Nederland.

The skeletons of a Native American child and a woman with an arrowhead embedded in one of her ribs are evidence that uptown Manhattan was settled—and embattled—long before the arrival of Europeans

All that remains of Harlem's first real settler, the farmer, surgeon, deacon, and politician Jan de la Montagne, is his signature.

Pieter Stuyvesant is less well remembered for authorizing the establishment of "Nieuw Haarlem," where he owned property, than for his efforts to tame his rowdy subjects, to contend with financial crisis, and to negotiate with hostile Native Americans.

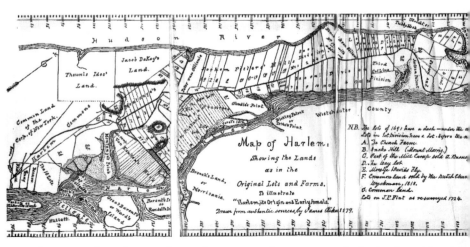

This map of Harlem in the mid-seventeenth century includes both residential plots and the corresponding gardens that were essential for the isolated community at the time.

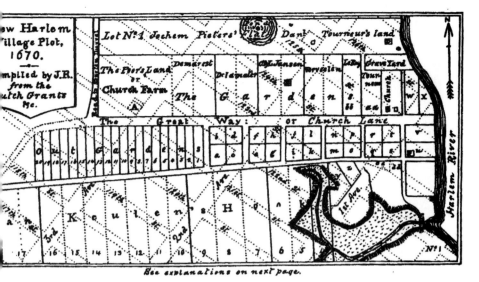

By the end of the seventeenth century, most of Harlem had been surveyed and claimed for farmland, though in practice, much of uptown Manhattan would remain untouched for generations to come.

One of the oldest houses on Manhattan, the Morris-Jumel mansion was built in 1766 and served as General George Washington's headquarters during the early months of the American War of Independence. Later it was home to Aaron Burr and his wife, the courtesan turned socialite, Eliza Jumel.

VIEW of HARLAEM from MORISANIA in the PROVINCE of NEW YORK Septemʳ 1765.

In 1765, more than a century after its founding, "Harlaem" was less a village than a group of rude country houses arranged around a simple church, without even a proper pier, much less sidewalks or other urban amenities.

The Battle of Harlem Heights was a minor military victory but an important psychological boost to General George Washington's struggling troops.

Alexander Hamilton hoped to make his Harlem mansion into a working farm that would support him and his family after he retired from politics.

HARLEM PLAINS 1814.

In the early-nineteenth century, Harlem became a refuge for those fleeing the dirt, disease, and danger of downtown Manhattan.

Eliza Jumel was one of Harlem's quintessential improvisers, making the leap from courtesan—and alleged lover of more than one Founding Father—to the richest woman in the United States and the wife of Aaron Burr.

John James Audubon, seen here at right in a painting by his son, Victor G. Audubon, fled downtown Manhattan in 1841 and built a country estate and menagerie he named Minniesland, after his wife.

FAST TROTTERS ON HARLEM LANE N.Y.

In the mid-nineteenth century, Harlem Lane, which ran along what is now St. Nicholas Avenue, became a haunt of wealthy downtown equestrians.

LENOX AVENUE NORTH FROM ONE HUNDRED AND TENTH STREET AND CENTRAL PARK, 1869. THIS REGION IS NOW ENTIRELY COVERED WITH LARGE APARTMENT HOUSES.

Although the village of Harlem grew quickly in the mid-nineteenth century, as did the hamlets of Manhattanville and Carmansville, most of Harlem remained undeveloped, as this photograph from 1869 shows.

Jacob Cantor served as president of the New York State Senate, Manhattan Borough president, and in the United States Congress, but his religion remained a problem in Harlem, where the establishment was slow to welcome those of "the Hebrew persuasion."

JACOB AARON CANTOR

JOURNALIST. LAWYER AND LEGISLATOR

STATE ASSEMBLYMAN (1885–87). STATE SENATOR (1887–)

WHO STOLE THE PEOPLE'S MONEY? — DO TELL .N.Y.TIMES.   'T.WAS HIM.

It was from his backyard studio in Harlem that cartoonist Thomas Nast brought down the famously corrupt Tweed Ring, including from left William "Boss" Tweed, Peter Sweeney, Richard Connolly, and Oakey Hall, all of whom owned property uptown.

The rowhouses that suddenly appeared in the middle of empty fields on the north side of West 133rd Street between Fifth and Sixth Avenues in the early 1880s were typical of the speculative real estate development that dominated Harlem in the decades after the Civil War.

HEBREW ORPHAN ASYLUM,
AMSTERDAM AVE.,
NEW YORK.

By the early-twentieth century, poor Jewish immigrants from Eastern Europe flooding into Harlem were served by a variety of sanitariums, asylums, and orphanages, most notably the magnificent Hebrew Orphan Asylum on Amsterdam Avenue at West 137th Street.

By the turn of the century, Manhattanville's location on the Hudson River made it ideally suited for both industry and recreation.

RICHARD CROKER
REAL ESTATE DEALER, POLITICIAN AND TURFMAN
ALDERMAN (1870). TAMMANY HALL LEADER, SINCE 1885

OSCAR HAMMERSTEIN
PLAYWRIGHT AND COMPOSER. FOUNDER HAMMERSTEIN'S
OLYMPIA. HARLEM OPERA HOUSE AND COLUMBUS THEATRE

Though less well known than Boss Tweed, Tammany Hall kingpin and longtime Harlemite Richard Croker wielded power even more profitably, despite growing opposition from the forces of reform.

Oscar Hammerstein was a German-Jewish immigrant who went from cigar roller to real estate tycoon to entertainment mogul, in the process turning 125th Street into a major entertainment district in the 1890s.

Oscar Hammerstein's first foray into the entertainment business was the lavish Harlem Opera House, built on West 125th Street between Seventh and Eighth Avenues in 1889.

East Harlem's Italian neighborhood, pictured here in 1890, was New York's Little Italy from the 1880s to the 1930s, far larger and more crowded than the Italian neighborhood downtown.

Around the turn of the century, boat parades along the Harlem River were a popular form of weekend entertainment for Harlemites of a certain class.

Harlem at the turn of the century was a place of contrasts, with everything from palatial mansions and modern apartment buildings to shockingly dilapidated shacks occupied by immigrants from eastern and southern Europe.

Polo was apparently never on the bill at any of the four facilities known as the Polo Grounds—the one pictured here at West 155th Street and Eighth Avenue was the last—although almost every other sport was, from baseball to bull-fighting.

Uptown hoodlums "Lefty Louie" Rosenberg and "Gyp the Blood" Horowitz became folk heroes after police paid them to murder Harlem gambling king-pin Herman Rosenthal.

In blending Jewish and black musical legacies to arrive at an all-American style that still defines the Broadway and jazz standard traditions, George Gershwin took inspiration from the sounds he remembered from his Harlem boyhood.

Growing up near East Harlem's raucous entertainment district, the comedy quartet known as the Marx Brothers—pictured here near their childhood home are Groucho and Harpo—moved from the vaudeville stage to Hollywood.

By age thirty, Harry Houdini's success as a magician and escape artist allowed him to move to 278 West 113th Street, in the heart of Harlem's poshest Jewish neighborhood.

MRS. HATTIE McINTOSH   GEO. W. WALKER   ADA OVERTON WALKER   BERT A. WILLIAMS   MRS. LOTTIE WILLIAMS

Bert Williams and George Walker came to fame in blackface, a genre popular among both white and black entertainers and audiences well into the twentieth century.

Even well-educated, racially progressive entertainers like Bob Cole and James Weldon Johnson—here identified as Billy Johnson—answered the lucrative demand among both black and white music lovers for "coon songs."

The 1917 Silent Protest Parade, Negro New York's response to a recent race riot in East St. Louis, was the brainchild of James Weldon Johnson (second row, far right) and W. E. B. Du Bois (second row, second from right).

the "Boss of All Bosses" before being murdered at his headquarters at 362 East 116th Street.

The Italian mobster is a central figure in the pantheon of modern American antiheroes, and the uptown Italians idealized their gangsters as neighborhood heroes who kept things safe, with colorful and popular brutes with such names as Joe Stretch, Joe the Heat, Pop Bullets, the Dwarf, or the Count. But even as these gangsters came to the protection of mothers and children, they were targeting their husbands, brothers, sons, and fathers. After Luigi de Laura, a Calabrian mason who lived on East 109th Street, was unable to come up with the $100 he had promised to leave under a trash can on First Avenue, mobsters cut off his son's left hand. They had their money the next day.

After Lupo the Wolf and Giuseppe Morello were put away in 1909 for counterfeiting, Ciro Terranova maintained their power by murdering rivals, putting business before ancient ethnic rivalries, and even going so far as to reach out to the Neapolitans. Still, relations between immigrants from Naples and Sicily remained combustible. After a shooting party that broke out at Third Avenue and East 114th Street in 1912 and left five dead, it was war, and for the next five years East Harlem's street corners, barbershops, cafés, and wine cellars ran with the blood of both the Sicilian mafia and the Neapolitan *camorra*. Eventually the Sicilians won out, and Ciro Terranova became the undisputed crime kingpin of East Harlem, with his headquarters at 352 East 116th Street. He found that maintaining power could be more difficult than seizing it, especially after Vincent was shot and killed by a passing car at the corner of Second Avenue and East 116th Street. The arrival of downtown gangs made everything more complicated and bloody.

With legitimate work hard to find, organized crime became too glamorous and too profitable for Harlem's other racial and ethnic groups to pass up. Eastern European Jews in particular were gaining a bad reputation, despite dubious claims by Jewish organizations that Jewish

criminals confined themselves to nonviolent offenses like pickpocket-
ing, burglary, or fencing stolen goods. City investigations around the
turn of the century identified a growing criminal mentality among New
York's Jews, along with rising rates of arson, extortion, prostitution,
and corruption. Even as Harlemites cheered on their own Benny "The
Great Bennah" Leonard, one of the most feared lightweight prizefighters in the world, Jewish strongmen known as *shtarkers* used physical
intimidation and worse in conflicts involving everything from labor
unions to kosher certification. Jews in trouble with the law became
a staple of the city's more sensationalistic newspapers. The police
commissioner claimed in 1908 that half the city's criminal class were
Jews, who were by nature "firebugs, burglars, pickpockets, and highway
robbers—when they have the courage." Whatever the accuracy of the
claim, in the years before World War I, downtown Jewish gangsters
were leaving East Harlem to the Italian mobsters and shifting their
operations to West Harlem, transforming West 116th Street between
Lenox and Eighth avenues into a full-fledged vice district, with dozens
of places to go for gambling, prostitution, and drugs.

The event that fixed the public association between uptown Jews
and crime was the 1912 murder of a Tammany soldier from Harlem
named Herman "Beansie" Rosenthal, shot by a gang of thugs just before
he was set to testify against a corrupt policeman in a case that promised
to damage cops, gangsters, and politicians alike. It had all started back
on Christmas Day of 1910, when a massive explosion interrupted a
dance sponsored by the Wilner Verein, a social club for Lithuanian
Jews, at the Lenox Dancing Academy, at 102 West 116th Street. The
gangsters who came streaming out of the gambling halls and social
clubs that lined the block suspected it was Beansie Rosenthal sending
a signal to his competitors not to interfere with the pool room and
gambling hall he ran just a few doors away.

Rosenthal's enemies seemed to have gotten the message, and
soon he was running half a dozen gambling joints in the neighborhood. But the next year cops rounded up 150 gamblers in Rosenthal's
Mauretiana Club. Apparently, he hadn't been responding properly
to the shakedowns of Charles Becker, a bouncer turned cop whose

brutally profitable methods had once attracted the attention of the novelist Stephen Crane writing in the New York *Journal*. Becker ran a new antigambling squad, which meant that he could take 20 percent of all the deals he learned about—as much as $10,000 a month, too much money for a cop on a $2,250 annual salary to keep and keep alive. After another one of Rosenthal's Harlem operations was closed in a raid supervised by Becker, Rosenthal walked into the Manhattan district attorney's office and told them everything he knew. Becker could quash indictments before they were issued but he had no such power over the press.

When word got out that Rosenthal was going public with their arrangements in the New York *World*, Becker paid an alopecic bagman named Jacob "Bald Jack Rose" Rosenzweig $2,000 to make Rosenthal disappear. Bald Jack, who ran an opium den on the side, reached out to an uptown gangster named "Big Yid" Zelig, known among Jews as the "Great Emancipator" because he had stood up to Italian gangs, charging $10 for a face slashing, $35 for a nonlethal shooting, and $100 for murder. Sprung from jail and put in charge of the Rosenthal job, Zelig in turn recruited gunmen from the Lenox Avenue gang: an opium addict named "Whitey Lewis" Seidenheimer, a pickpocket turned murderer named "Lefty Louis" Rosenzweig, and "Gyp the Blood" Horowitz, a brute who could crack a man's spine with his bare hands, though he preferred bombs; "I likes to hear da noise," he used to say. A gangland strongman named "Dago Frank" Cirofici was also brought in, a most unusual instance of Jewish-Italian cooperation.

On the evening of July 16, 1912, Lefty Louis borrowed a gray Packard that had been rented by Bald Jack and gathered the rest of the team. They made their way after midnight down to Times Square, where they shot and killed Rosenthal point-blank and sped back uptown to get paid. It wasn't until two weeks after Rosenthal's funeral that a tip led cops to the West 138th Street apartment where Dago Frank was hiding out with his girlfriend in a haze of opium smoke. Soon the entire operation, detailed day after day on the front page of the *New York Times*, was exposed and the murderers were apprehended. Big Yid Zelig turned state's witness but he was rubbed out before he could testify. Eventually Becker, Lefty Louis, Gyp the Blood, Whitey Lewis, and Dago Frank were convicted and electrocuted, an event that left Harlem's Jews with mixed feelings. Like their Italian neighbors, uptown Jews despised criminality on ethical grounds as well as for the reputation it gave all of them—"We are all in trouble today," remarked the Jewish owner of a local ballroom upon hearing of Lefty Louis's fate—even as they admired neighborhood boys who stood up to the notoriously corrupt police.

Harlemites had similarly complicated attitudes toward the ring of Jewish arsonists operating in this period. It has been estimated that in the late nineteenth century, a quarter of all arson cases covered by the *New York Times* were committed by Jews. Arson was known as "Jewish lightning," and the subject even became a popular joke: "What's the only thing a Jew hates more than pork? Asbestos." By the turn of the century Jews were said to be behind almost half of all arson cases. The most notorious of them all was Isidore Stein, known as "Izzy the Painter" because he posed as a house painter when buying the kerosene he used to start fires. Over the five years that followed his arrival in New York in 1907, more than a thousand customers came to him for his services. He was so well known as the head of the local "arson trust" that all he had to do was show up on an uptown street corner and wait for clients. Izzy the Painter ran a complicated business, with all of the details worked out far in advance, from informants in the police and fire departments to scouts in the insurance companies, from the precise split of the payoff to alibis for everyone involved. He charged "clients" five dollars, plus 10 percent of the insurance settlement, never asking extra for calling in the alarm himself. Izzy the Painter's arrest, conviction, and imprisonment in 1912 halved the number of fires in Manhattan and the Bronx, while the conviction of Beansie Rosenthal's murderers all but ended the cooperation between police and Jewish gangsters that had been so mutually profitable. But Harlem continued to incubate Jewish criminals, who called the New York City prison known as the Tombs their "city college"—among its most famous alumni was the one-man crime wave named Arthur Flegenheimer, who got his start with Arnold Rothstein, and eventually changed his name to Dutch

Schultz to honor a legendary German mobster. As characters like Schultz challenged their Italian neighbors for the criminal supremacy of New York, it became clear that the ambition that Jewish and Italian parents instilled in their children had led many of them straight to the criminal underworld. What was to be done?

The religious establishment—Jewish, Protestant, and Catholic—was determined to intervene in the social crisis that was simmering in East Harlem, where by the turn of the century population density surpassed even that of the East Side. This took the form of ostentatious support of the temples, churches, and charities that helped the poor, the elderly, the homeless, the ill, and the orphaned. Ministers, priests, and rabbis raised money from congregants and philanthropists to start programs offering language classes, job training, civics lessons, and even advice on American-style hygiene. The railroad tycoon and financier Jacob Schiff, who gave up strict religious observance when he left Germany but who remained devoted to Jewish causes, took a strong interest in settlement houses, health clinics, the YMHA, free loan societies, and the Montefiore Home for Chronic Invalids at Broadway and 138th Street, where he spent each Sunday morning visiting patients. An uptown native named Belle Moskowitz, who later came to prominence as Governor Al Smith's right-hand woman, got her start organizing antivice campaigns in Jewish neighborhoods. Courses in Americanization were pioneered by Julia Richman, a Harlem-bred German Jew who became New York City's first Jewish high school principal. A broader social agenda characterized the Harlem branch of the Workmen's Circle, which in addition to organizing women against unfair kosher meat prices offered mutual aid and benefits to members: everything from sickness and death benefits to schools, clubs, summer camps, and publications. The Hebrew Orphan Asylum, a redbrick neo-Gothic building that took up the entire block from West 136th to West 138th streets along Amsterdam Avenue, accommodated six hundred children, many of whom lived there for their entire childhoods. The asylum's strict regimen included lots of discipline—corporal punishment was liberally applied—and secular and religious education. The bakery and cobbler's workshop were clearly meant to offer the children, among them the writer Art Buchwald, a future in the form of a trade, but the asylum was considered a progressive institution for its time, with sports fields and a gymnasium and a medical staff administering regular checkups and smallpox inspections. Somewhat less broad-minded were the efforts of the Hebrew Emigrant Society to resettle eastern European Jewish immigrants in upstate New York or New Jersey, where their attachment to the old ways might no longer embarrass the rest of the tribe.

Many Italian immigrants also found themselves struggling to become more American. The only figure to rival the gangster in East Harlem for authority and glamor was the local priest, but the Italian adherence to Roman Catholicism was weakening in the face of attempts by missionaries offering everything from food and clothing to Bible study, summer camp, arts education, day care, job training, language classes, hygiene instruction, and health care. The earliest such effort aimed at Italian Americans uptown seems to have been the Home Garden, later known as Haarlem House and LaGuardia Memorial House. This Protestant mission was founded in 1890 and "dedicated to the welfare of the street arab," as street urchins were then called, and it helped keep generations of Italian youngsters, including Leonard Covello, off the streets. Less religious in orientation was the Union Settlement, which offered tutoring, athletics, music, and drama—the actor Burt Lancaster, who was born and raised on East 106th Street, took classes there.

The best known of all of these efforts was the American Parish of East Harlem, which served as the crucible in which the political conscience of Norman Thomas, that giant of American left-wing politics, was refined. Like so many uptown social workers, missionaries, and settlement house employees, Thomas had very little in common with his neighbors. Born in 1884 in Ohio to a well-educated family of Presbyterian ministers, he graduated from Princeton and in 1905 he took a $2,500 per year job bringing the "social gospel" to the East Harlem Presbyterian Church, the Italian Church of the Ascension, the Italian Presbyterian Church of the Holy Trinity, and the Friend-ship Neighborhood House. Over the next seven years he transformed the American Parish into a model of urban outreach. Thomas, who lived with his wife and five children in the neighborhood, came into contact with many of the different kinds of people who lived in his neighborhood, not only the southern Italians but poor Slovaks, Swedes, Hungarians, and even newcomers from Ireland and Germany. Thomas, who spoke Italian, would spend much of his time buying coal for neighbors who would otherwise go cold, begging landlords to delay the eviction of poor families, or even paying their rent out of his own pocket. He intervened with doctors or merchants or undertakers when his parishioners were late with payments and started clubs for sports, crafts, and the arts; classes in cooking and public speaking; and discus-sion groups that focused on everything from politics to entertainment. He welcomed all of the local children to play basketball or punch ball, although one of the local Catholic priests counseled avoiding Thomas's drinking fountain on spiritual grounds. Thirst prevailed, and many of these children also showed up at Thomas's annual Christmas party, where every child, regardless of religion or race, received a gift. Their mothers were also the beneficiaries of Thomas's mission, going along on day trips out of the neighborhood that he organized especially for a population that was otherwise housebound. Thomas brought in and trained social workers, and he even invited the American Federation of Labor to organize Italians, Hungarians, and Slovaks who worked at the Washburn Wire Mills, though the unions declined to organize what it considered a lower class of white people.

Thomas's greatest achievements were the things that didn't hap-pen. He wasn't above buying guns and throwing them in the Harlem River, though he spent more time trying to convince local boys to find peaceful solutions to conflicts among themselves. It wasn't always so easy in a neighborhood in which even different Italian-American Pres-byterian Bible study groups brawled after basketball games. Thomas's favorite story was of a parishioner who robbed a man of seven dollars on Christmas. The victim pleaded and prayed for the stickup man to give back the money, which he was going to use to buy holiday gifts.

The stickup man relented, leading the victim to exclaim "God bless you!" Later that day, when the thief stuck up another victim in Mount Morris Park for almost a hundred dollars, he told himself that God had rewarded him for his earlier good deed. It was proof, Thomas recalled, of the power of prayer. Thomas's almost superhuman energy, driven by an endless supply of optimism and harnessed to projects that were simple, accessible, and effective, made him a much-loved figure. But Harlemites in the age of immigration did not survive by faith alone, even when it came in the form of Norman Thomas carrying a food basket.

Musical theater had long been religion for many Harlemites, and seismic changes in the American entertainment world, many of which started uptown, helped make converts among the new immigrants. As a new generation of performers made the leap from vaudeville, genteel drama, and operetta to burlesque, film, and the musical, established venues like Hurtig and Seamon's and newer theaters like the Orpheum Music Hall featured everything from tear-jerking melodrama to the "Hebrew dialect artists Gilbert and Trixedo" to Yiddish versions of the classics. The legendary Yiddish drama company of Jacob Adler, father of theater giant Stella Adler, played in Shakespeare's *Merchant of Venice* at Proctor's in 1905. He returned to Harlem the next year, to the four-year-old West End Theatre, built by the vaudeville team of Joe Weber and Lew Fields at 360 West 125th Street, to play in a Yiddish-language version of *King Lear. Vartaitcht un varbessert!*, in other words, "translated and improved!," advertisements for such productions shouted.

Oscar Hammerstein's Columbus Theatre managed to offer something for everyone. It was there, in 1908, that a thirty-four-year-old Harry Houdini, born Ehrich Weiss in Hungary, escaped from the bonds of a "Weed Chain Automobile Tire Grip." After years of playing the fly-by-night freak companies, medicine shows, and dime museums, displaying his talents in hypnotism, magic, psychic displays, puppeteering, and gymnastics, Houdini had become a headliner on the famed Orpheum circuit of vaudeville theaters. Billed as the "King of Handcuffs," he was earning enough money to buy the twenty-six-room mansion at 278 West 113th Street in 1904. The house had been built in 1896 and then sat empty, part of the wave of speculative building. With the opening of the subway just months away, Houdini saw an opportunity, and he installed his wife, mother, sister, and two brothers, one of whom set up his radiology practice in the house, as well as a fox terrier who could also escape from a straitjacket and handcuffs. It was in this house, with a library containing the finest collection of magic books in the world, as well as a laboratory and a workshop, that Houdini devised and rehearsed the escapes that made him world famous.

Houdini was popular enough to fill a new generation of uptown theaters that were actually larger than their downtown competitors, because property in Harlem was cheaper. The Gotham Theatre was built in 1903 at 165 East 125th Street, followed two years later by the Alhambra at Seventh Avenue and 126th Street. At the other end of Harlem was Thomas Lamb's twenty-four-hundred-seat Audubon Theatre, built in 1912 at Broadway and West 165th Street by William Fox, a Hungarian-Jewish immigrant who also ran the Star, at Lexington Avenue and East 107th Street, and who later founded the movie studio Twentieth Century Fox—the Audubon's facade was decorated with foxes that honored its owner. Just a year later Lamb designed the Regent Theatre, which opened in 1913 at Seventh Avenue and West 116th Street. The exterior of the Regent was inspired by the architecture of the Venetian palazzo, but the interior incongruously featured a mural showing the Spanish king Ferdinand and his queen Isabel taking over Granada from the Jews and Moors. Was it a subtle protest against recent demographic changes in the neighborhood?

Many of the new theaters were built to accommodate the moving pictures that were starting to change the way Americans spent their leisure time. By 1907, just a few years after film became commercially viable, nickelodeons were crammed five to a block along 125th Street, many of them run in tandem with penny arcades and vaudeville stages. Limited to 199 seats or fewer because of licensing laws, these venues managed to compete with the bigger theaters by offering dozens of showings per day. The Regent's 25-cent admission charge bought admission to six vaudeville acts, a two-reel comic film, and a five-reel movie drama, but the theater, which had eighteen hundred seats and room for a full orchestra that could play along with the film, didn't make money until it was taken over by Samuel "Roxy" Rothafel. There was also a surge of construction of movie houses around this time and soon Harlemites could see films at the Orient, at Lenox Avenue and West 125th Street, which had both an organ and a sound effects department, and which undercut the Regent by charging children 5 cents and adults 10 cents to see a newsreel; a comedy short featuring Charlie Chaplin, Fatty Arbuckle, or the Keystone Kops; a travel film; a serial offering; and a feature such as *The Haunted Pyjama* or *The Woman God Forgot*. The fast-food restaurant currently operating at Broadway near West 147th Street got its start in 1913 as the Bunny Theatre; still visible on the facade are the ornamental rabbits installed in homage to the silent film star John Bunny. Some of the films were made right in the neighborhood, at the old Harlem Casino, which William Randolph Hearst turned into the Cosmopolitan Pictures studio at a time when Hollywood was still a desert.

The most successful uptown pioneer in the vaudeville and penny arcade business was Marcus Loew, who grew up on the Lower East Side, the son of German immigrants. He became a fur salesman and then a player in uptown real estate, managing properties for his neighbor, the comedian David Warfield. Loew moved into nickelodeons, running theaters that featured "peek machines" showing shorts with titles like *In My Heaven* and *Her Beauty Secret* that appealed to working-class and immigrant Harlemites, who might not be able to afford a ticket to a proper show. Eventually, Loew went into the movie business full-time, where he competed against Adolph Zukor, who had also started out in the fur business and who also found nickelodeons more profitable.

Despite the popularity of the movies, live musical entertainment remained the big draw. Few entertainers moved Harlem audiences in the years after the turn of the century like the legendary Jewish entertainer Sophie Tucker, who was born Sophia Kalish somewhere between Poland and Russia in 1884. At the age of eighteen she came to New York and got her first gig at the People's Vaudeville, a theater at West 116th Street and Lenox Avenue with only three hundred seats and an entrance lit by flaming torches. Eventually she changed her name and sometimes her race, too, at least onstage. White Harlemites may not have had much to do with the small but quickly growing Negro population uptown in the years after the turn of the century, but they were obsessed with representations of blacks onstage, whether by whites or blacks. Larry Hart played in summer camp minstrel shows, as did Oscar Hammerstein II, who also regularly entertained his family with a minstrel-style performance of something called "Little Boy Black," a homemade melodrama about a Negro child who meets an untimely death.

However embarrassing such antics may seem a century later, it is important to remember how deeply rooted in American culture this play with race was. The earliest documented instance of a blackface performance uptown seems to have been in 1907 by Nat Haines at Keith and Proctor's 125th Street Theatre, and within a few years many of the most popular performers of the day, white and black, uptown and downtown, were performing in blackface, and not just for white audiences, though there were limits. Tucker used to end her blackface performances by taking off her gloves in order to prove to the audience that she was not black. The act became popular, but it was as a Jewish blues shouter that she hit it big in 1909 with Ziegfeld's Follies and on recordings with tunes such as "Some of These Days" and "My Yiddishe Mama." Fanny Brice, born Fania Borach on the Lower East Side in 1891 and raised partly in Harlem, was another Jewish performer for whom blackface was a way of becoming white. She got her start as a teen after she won an amateur contest and began performing on Harlem chorus lines, which paid $18 per week, a huge sum in the years before World War I. Brice, who lived on West 128th Street and then on West 118th Street, was purposely not taught Yiddish as a child, and she tried to avoid Jewish roles, but she looked too Jewish to do anything else, audiences thought. Even a nose job failed to help. Indeed, it was with her rendition of Irving Berlin's Yiddish parody of Strauss's *Salome* dance that she broke through to a wider public, though it was her blackface version of "Lovie Joe," by the black songwriters Will Marion Cook and Joe Jordan, that made her a star.

That kind of racial interchange had a formative effect on two Harlem street urchins named Jacob and Israel Gershowitz, who haunted the 125th Street theaters long before their music and lyrics became the soundtrack of the century. George and Ira Gershwin, as their public school teacher rebaptized them, were born in 1896 and 1898, respectively, to Russian immigrants. Their father worked any kind of job he could get, including shoe factory foreman, stationery store owner, and owner of a chain of restaurants, and the family moved no fewer than twenty-eight times as the boys were growing up, which was less a matter of upward class mobility that plain economic instability. Ira was an excellent student, eventually entering the prestigious Townsend Harris High School, where he knew E. Y. "Yip" Harburg, but George played the bad boy, constantly in trouble for misbehaving when he attended school at all. The rest of the time he was just another street urchin, exploring Harlem on roller skates until the day shortly after the turn of the century when he stopped in front of a 125th Street arcade, transfixed by the tune that floated out through the front door. From the moment when he heard that mechanical keyboard perform Anton Rubenstein's 1890 composition "Melody in F," George was hooked. He taught himself piano until the family moved to 108 West 111th Street, where he began to study classical music. His first composition was "Ragging the Traumerei," an uptown version of a work by Robert Schumann. Eventually, George dropped out of high school and took a job as a piano pounder and song plugger on the stretch of West 28th Street known as Tin Pan Alley, then the nerve center of the American music business. Still a teen, Gershwin made a reputation for himself among uptown pianists, black and white. This Jewish child of the East Harlem tenements came to know West Harlem, too, entertaining guests at the West 112th Street salon of the socialites Lou and Herman Paley and later writing an opera called *135th Street*. It was in 1918, in the tenement at 520 West 144th, that he wrote "Swanee," apparently composed in fifteen minutes while Pop Gershwin was absorbed in a card game in the next room. When the song—or was it the card game?—was finished George convinced his father to accompany him on an improvised Jew's harp (a comb threaded with tissue paper) for the song's premiere. Al Jolson, who heard it when George performed it for him at Bessie Bloodgood's Harlem whorehouse, put the song, with lyrics by Irving Caesar, in his show *Sinbad*. A plantation tune by a Jew in a show about an Arab folk hero was the way they did things in Harlem even then, and it was George's first hit, selling two million copies.

An early start in show business wasn't anything unusual among Harlem's Jewish entertainers. Among the child performers to make it big in the years after the turn of the century were five poor German-Jewish boys named Marx who grew up at 239 East 114th Street, then a poor Italian block. The oldest son, Leonard, used to pretend he was Italian in order to avoid fights, developing the signature accent he used to play "Chico." Julius, the third-born son, known as "Groucho," took to playing the role of a gentile German in the neighborhood, while Adolph would be known as Harpo. Around 1905 Groucho, who left P.S. 86 after the sixth grade, began performing seriously, as a boy soprano with the Leroy Trio, and soon he was working with a variety of groups, including with Gus Edwards' Postal Telegraph Boys, which performed uptown at the Alhambra Theatre in 1906. Within a decade the Marx brothers were on Broadway—by then Groucho was wearing his notorious greasepaint mustache—with the fourth son, Milton, going by "Gummo," and the fifth son, Herbert, taking on the role of "Zeppo," names they kept when they made a string of films that are some of the most venerated works of American cinema from the era, and no doubt among the funniest.

For a time, the Marx Brothers had serious competition from another Jewish child star who also made the transition from the vaudeville stage to the silver screen and then television. Milton Berle was born Milton Berlinger in 1908 at 68 West 118th Street and first appeared on stage at the age of five, when he took home first prize in a Charlie Chaplin look-alike competition. He traveled the vaudeville circuit before getting hired by the Mount Morris Theatre, at 116th Street and Fifth Avenue—he actually had to sing from a side box in the audience because of rules preventing children under the age of sixteen from performing. His career didn't take off, though, until he got a job acting in *The Perils of Pauline*, which was being filmed in Fort Lee, New Jersey, just a short ride away on the ferry from Manhattanville.

A very different kind of stagecraft appealed to one of the last Jews to call himself a native son of Harlem: the dramatist Arthur Miller, whose mother was raised uptown and whose Polish father came to the United States as a child and ended up on the Lower East Side, where he built up one of the biggest manufacturers of women's wear in the country before moving uptown. Miller was born in 1915 into a Jewish community that still numbered almost two hundred thousand. He grew up on the top floor of a row house at 45 West 110th Street, a popular building for the last generation of Harlem's Jewish strivers. Miller remembered that each morning the Franklins, Minervas, Stearns-Knights, Pierce-Arrows, Locomobiles, Marmons, and Hispano-Suizas, some with a chauffeur and a footman, would line up at the sidewalk to take all of the fathers to work. The Millers lived in a luxurious apartment, with a formal dining room that was at first used only for company, and later for homework, once he started at P.S. 24, where his mother had also gone. But Jewish life in West Harlem could still resemble the East Side existence that so many eastern European Jews were fleeing. There was plumbing in the most rudimentary tenements in Harlem, but even tony buildings on the Golden Edge did not yet have hot water, hence the public campaign in the years before World War I to install bathtubs in public schools. Until then, families like the Millers made use of bathhouses such as the nearby St. Nicholas Baths, at 27 Lenox Avenue, which Pop Gershwin bought in 1916, and where Ira Gershwin manned the front desk while he did his City College homework. The Millers heated water for laundry in huge tin tubs on the stove, and milk and ice were delivered by a horse-drawn wagon. Although Jewish Harlem was dwindling fast, food shopping still involved selecting pickles from a barrel; watching the vegetable grocer grind fresh horseradish to be served with carp, whitefish, and pike bought live from the fishmonger; or selecting live chickens from the kosher poultry man.

The meals that graced the family dinner table were pure Old World: brisket, gefilte fish, and *tsimmes.* But the Millers resembled many of their neighbors in their ambivalent efforts to distance themselves from the religious traditions of the Old World and simply become good Americans. Miller himself spoke no Yiddish at all, unlike both of his grandfathers, who prayed at an old-fashioned orthodox shul that was segregated by gender. His brother's bar mitzvah speech was given in Hebrew, English, and German, and the High Holidays meant little more than a relaxing ten-day jaunt to Atlantic City. But the family never celebrated birthdays, a holdover from the orthodox Jewish practice of banning "pagan" celebrations. There was still plenty of fun. Miller and his friends would play on the street—stoopball, marbles, punch ball, and a New York version of tag called ringalevio—chase each other across the rooftops, and ice-skate in Central Park, but only when a red ball hung from the flagpole next to the boathouse on the Harlem Meer meant the ice was safe. There were also excursions farther from home. After he learned to ride a bicycle, Miller explored the Italian territory east of Madison Avenue. He even ventured into the neighborhoods north of 125th Street that Negroes were beginning to call their own. He saw drama such as Erskine Caldwell's *Tobacco Road,* which played at Lenox Avenue's Schubert Theatre, as well as black and Jewish vaudeville stars Bojangles Robinson and Eddie Cantor and others on 125th Street. The 1929 stock market crash bankrupted Miller's father, and the family moved to Brooklyn. Miller did briefly attend City College but he lacked the fervor of his peers, who studied so hard that there were no seats available in the library even late at night.

For those City College undergraduates burning the midnight oil, Harlem was a step up, but it could also be a step out. The *Jewish Daily Forward* regularly published a "Gallery of Missing Husbands," which carried announcements like this: "Sarah Solomon is looking for her husband who is now uptown." We have no way of knowing why Mr. Solomon left his wife, but it may well be that he was leaving a place more than a person. Moving uptown no longer always meant moving up in the world, but Harlem still offered newcomers a certain freedom: from religion, from poverty, even from an unhappy marriage. Mr. Solomon might have been lost in the haze of an opium den, or he might have been studying in the City College library. He might have become rich in the Wild West atmosphere of the Jewish underworld, or he might have made a legitimate fortune in the booming real estate market. He might be living in a squalid East Harlem tenement rolling cigars or he might be smoking them in his fancy Mount Morris Park town house. Uptown, he could do it all, but not for long.

Harlem was reinventing itself yet again, as those eastern European Jews who could afford it, and some southern Italians as well, began to look for opportunities elsewhere, especially as "their" neighborhoods—were they not the undesirable interlopers just a few years earlier?—attracted blacks, Latinos, and West Indians. It didn't happen overnight. During the World War I era there were more than eighty synagogues uptown, including two Negro congregations, and more were on the way. No fewer than twelve Harlemites made their living as *shochetim*, or kosher inspectors, and nine *mohels* performed ritual circumcisions. After the war, Henry Ford's notoriously and hysterically anti-Semitic Dearborn *Independent* identified seven distinct Jewish neighborhoods in East Harlem alone and another handful in central and western Harlem, the latter serving as "the residential goals of the prosperous Jews of New York." In fact, most of Harlem's Jews, German and eastern European, had set their sights elsewhere. As early as 1902 the *Forvertz* had been predicting that Harlem wouldn't remain Jewish for long; even then there were Jewish businesses failing because of dwindling clientele, and some synagogues had trouble putting together a minyan, or the minimum of ten Jewish men needed for prayer services. Soon almost all of them were gone, along with their synagogues, to "better" neighborhoods on the Upper West Side, or in Washington Heights, Brooklyn, or the Bronx. In the 1920s the number of Jews in

Harlem fell from almost two hundred thousand to five thousand, and by the end of the Depression virtually all had left.

Why were Jews so quick to leave East Harlem while many of the neighborhood's Italians refused to budge? When they arrived uptown, Jews were running less toward something than away from something. George Gershwin, who eventually decamped with his brother to adjoining penthouse apartments on lower Riverside Drive—he was a favorite performer at the free summertime concerts at Lewisohn Stadium before he died at the age of thirty-eight in California after surgery to remove a brain tumor—told his biographer, "I am a man without traditions." This was, after all, a member of a tribe that often defined itself through sheer assertion. A City College student once asked the philosophy professor Morris Cohen, "How do I know I exist?" to which Cohen replied, "Who's asking?" No wonder so many Jews seemed to assimilate so effortlessly, and to leave uptown so quickly, especially East Harlem, which was facing what they called the "New Spanish Inquisition" in the form of arriving Puerto Ricans. In contrast, Italians, like the Irish before them, were economic migrants who chose Harlem over Toronto or Buenos Aires or Melbourne. They went where they could find work and other Italians, and having found both they were slower to give up what they called Bella Harlem, Nostra Harlem—"Beautiful Harlem, Our Harlem." Indeed, Italian Harlem would expand up to East 125th Street and down to East 96th Street, its 150,000 residents eventually overtaking the neighborhood's Jewish population. The opening of Jefferson Park in 1902 seemed like a sign from the city, while the higher authority who elevated the Madonna of Mount Carmel to the official status of miracle worker in 1904 made her one of only three official sanctuaries of the Virgin Mary in all of the Americas. East Harlemites considered her another immigrant who made good. Whatever their traditions, or lack of them, Harlem had made them all American, just in time for a war that would change the neighborhood once again and, many thought, for good.

7

"TO RACE WITH THE WORLD"
The New Negro and
the Harlem Renaissance

When did the Harlem Renaissance start? Was it in the years after the turn of the century, when blacks fleeing the poverty and racism of the American South and the West Indies arrived uptown and began buying their own homes and starting their own grocery stores, laundries, cigar shops, newsstands, bookstores, florists, funeral homes, newspapers, churches, orchestras, nightclubs, and even an all-black cricket club? Or was the New Negro Movement, as it was then known, inaugurated during the run-up to World War I, when radicals opposed to America's entry into the conflict mounted stepladders and soapboxes at the corner of Seventh Avenue and West 125th Street to recruit the man and woman on the street to the cause? Perhaps it was during the war itself, when economic prosperity helped create a new black middle-class that no longer took its political cues from Booker T. Washington's Calvinist ethic of capitalist thrift, in which Negroes were to work within the system and uplift the race incrementally; instead, they looked to W.E.B. Du Bois's insistence on taking racism and segregation as challenges to be countered by lawsuits if possible and civil disobedience if necessary. Or does the Harlem Renaissance date from after the end of the war, when black soldiers returned to Harlem, now being called the Negro Mecca, and rode a rising tide of racial pride to claim for themselves the freedoms they had delivered to Europe, a sea change marked by the 1919 publication of the poet

Claude McKay's militant anthem of postwar black disillusionment "If We Must Die"? Should we look to the act of Prohibition that went into effect in 1920, which made a new generation of uptown nightclubs a sure investment and helped turn the bittersweet harmonies and ironic rhythms of ragtime into a joyously syncopated new music known as jazz? Or does the impossibility of finding the precise moment when Jim Crow and Lady Liberty conceived the New Negro and set off a burst in creativity in everything from art to politics to business to religion suggest there never was any such thing as a Harlem Renaissance?

Historians have traditionally dated Harlem's identity as a black community to 1904, when a speculative construction boom, inspired by the coming of the subway, supposedly led greedy speculators to tear down the dilapidated shacks belonging to Irish, Italian, and Jewish squatters and put up block after block of overpriced row houses and tenements that failed to attract tenants. The story then goes that a nationwide financial crisis from 1904 to 1907 was taken for an opportunity by a black realtor named Philip Payton, whose idea of filling empty apartments with Negroes was as financially successful as it was racially progressive. In fact, the growth of black Harlem was not the result of the sudden intervention of a single race hero, but a slow and steady process that took centuries and isn't over yet.

Starting with the arrival of eleven Africans in chains in New Amsterdam in 1626, the search for freedom by Manhattan's blacks was inextricably linked to real estate. Under the Dutch and the British, official restrictions imposed on both free and enslaved blacks regarding suffrage, education, and public accommodation didn't apply to housing, so they were free to live where they pleased, though that was no guarantee of safety from the kind of racist terror more often associated with the deep South. Such considerations led black Manhattanites to settle together at the city's periphery, which kept moving north: from the Five Points district of the old East Side to the area around Thompson Street in Greenwich Village. The Draft Riots of 1863 exposed the vulnerability of even all-black neighborhoods and kept Manhattan's African-Americans on the move. By the end of the nineteenth century twenty-thousand African-Americans were living in what is today Chelsea and Hell's Kitchen, an area known as the Tenderloin, a vice district that offered the tastiest morsels for policemen who knew how to profit from prostitution and gambling. Around five thousand African-Americans also lived in the area now taken up by Lincoln Center but then known as the Jungles or San Juan Hill. Between them was West 53rd Street, with businesses, churches, hotels, nightclubs, and fraternal organizations that catered to an exclusively— and exclusive—black population. It was the black Fifth Avenue, the black bohemia, and the black Broadway, all on one street, but not for long. Booker T. Washington, who realized that even though property requirements for suffrage had been abolished two decades earlier home ownership remained key to racial uplift, came to Harlem as early as 1893 to speak before the Lenox Avenue Unitarian Church. He returned the next year, addressing a crowd of thousands at the Harlem Casino about taking advantage of the recent burst of speculative housing begun in response to plans for a metropolitan subway system. He urged his audience, "Stop staying here and there and everywhere and begin to live somewhere." It wasn't ideology or even economics, however, that conspired to keep black Manhattanites northward-bound.

A turning point came in the Tenderloin in 1900, when a white cop wearing plain clothes propositioned a Negro woman. Her boyfriend, who was also black, overreacted, stabbing and killing the officer. Soon, more than three thousand whites, most of them Irish, and some of them police in uniform, were trawling midtown looking for trouble, which they defined as anyone—including women and children—who was black. It seemed like the Draft Riots all over again. By the time the riot of 1900 was over, seventy blacks had been attacked by roving mobs, among them the writer Paul Laurence Dunbar and the entertainer George Walker. The actor Ernest Hogan escaped with his life only by taking refuge for the night in an empty theater. Many white New Yorkers expressed shock at these events. Most blacks, aware that there had been more than fifteen hundred lynchings in the United States in the preceding decade, were anything but surprised, even after they learned that not a single police officer was indicted, much less convicted. The writer and diplomat James Weldon Johnson concluded,

"The riot of 1900 woke Negro New York and stirred the old fighting spirit." That old spirit would certainly have remained dormant had it not occupied the bodies of both southern Negroes and West Indians joining the great migration to the cities of the North in decades to come, for whom the solos of Louis Armstrong were like Gabriel's trumpet calling the faithful home to redemption on Judgment Day. This was especially true in Harlem, where the struggle for everything from social and economic justice to real estate was at its most intense, and where blackness itself—its history, its significance, even its existence—was being redefined.

The new arrivals were hardly pioneers. There had been a significant and continuous uptown black presence, free and enslaved, since the 1630s. Some owned property, practicing their trades in peace and profit, and by 1703 a census of northern Manhattan counted thirty-three black men, thirteen black women, and twenty-six black children. There was even a burial ground for Harlem's Negroes, no doubt due to both racism and the desire for self-determination. The first federal census of 1790 counted more than 115 slaves uptown—26 lived in their own houses, some of them with large extended families—and 44 nonwhite free persons, which together made up more than one-third of all uptowners. Still, equality remained elusive even after the abolition of slavery in New York State in 1827, when blacks were in danger from bounty hunters searching for escaped southern slaves. In 1837 a Negro gardener from Harlem named George Thompson was captured and taken south. Such events helped convince legislators in 1840 to protect Negroes accused of having escaped slavery. By then, Harlem's tiny Quaker community had started the Association for the Benefit of Colored Orphans at West 128th Street and Sixth Avenue, and uptowners, black and white, began broadening their horizons. The black abolitionist Lucy Nicholls and her husband, Peter Nicholls Sr., became forceful advocates of black male suffrage. These efforts weren't immediately successful, since race wasn't the only issue. Most blacks who had settled into shantytowns along the shore of the Harlem River in the East 130s after the Draft Riots didn't meet a $250 minimum property requirement for suffrage, though their white neighbors didn't either.

After the Civil War, many blacks worked as live-in servants for white families, especially in the German-Jewish neighborhoods west of Mount Morris Park. In the 1880s there was a real estate agent who specialized in houses and apartments for Negroes along Second and Third avenues below East 125th Street, then Manhattan's second biggest Negro neighborhood. It was there, where blacks were increasingly displacing Jews, Italians, and Irish, that a bizarre incident laid bare how vexed relations between uptown's minority groups could be. In 1887 a judge awarded custody of a missing five-year-old child being claimed by a downtown Jewish family as Yetta Brodsky to the uptown African-American family raising her as Nellie Lee. The decision caused "great joy among the colored folk in Harlem," according to one account of the trial. The rules of the all-American skin game were getting complicated.

Jacob Riis's *How the Other Half Lives* jump-started the tenement reform movement, but it also made a contribution to the history of black Manhattan by identifying a colony of blacks in East Harlem that was "clean and orderly" compared to the filth and squalor of Greenwich Village's Negro community. Less than a decade after Booker T. Washington's visits to Harlem in 1893 and 1894, there were all-black buildings on West 125th Street, while West 130th Street between Broadway and Amsterdam Avenue was being called Darktown, and West 146th Street was known as "Nigger Row." Newspaper advertisements from the period trumpeted "Desirable Properties for Colored People," and landlords hung signs outside their buildings seeking "Colored Tenants"—this at a time when the old German-Jewish elite hoped to hold the neighborhood against what even the reformer Riis called "the lower grades of foreign white people." As the turn of the century approached, middle- and upper-class blacks looking for respectable neighborhoods settled on West 134th Street. An article in the *New York Times* devoted to "Wealthy Negroes" called attention to a well-to-do black minister who lived in Harlem and boasted of having white servants. As with Jews and Italians arriving from both downtown and the old country, this more respectable class of blacks was attracted by talk of safe, clean, wide-open avenues and parks, new schools, and modern housing with heat and hot water and private tiled bathrooms, at a time when such amenities were rare even for whites. The image and the reality were quite different.

A popular song from 1899 called "You Can Take Your Trunk and Go to Harlem" has a Negro wife ordering her husband out and uptown, but by that time the area was already less a place of exile than a Promised Land for blacks with money, since the informal racial boundaries that kept them out of most downtown neighborhoods weren't yet being enforced uptown. Starting in the late 1890s, the black-owned and -operated New York *Age* carried advertisements for luxury apartments—with closets, heated hallways, kitchen ranges, walnut mantelpieces, and marble fireplaces—in the Sumner and the Garrison, on Broadway between West 125th and West 126th streets, blacks-only buildings named after white abolitionists. By the turn of the century tens of thousands of Negroes made their homes uptown. It wasn't all that they dreamed of. Whether they lived in houses, brownstones, luxury apartments, or tenements they paid more than whites did: the average three- or four-room flat in Harlem cost a black tenant up to $23 a month, while whites could get the same for $15 or less. This meant there was plenty of room for an African-American realtor looking to do some good for himself and for his people.

Was that man Philip Payton, the "Father of Colored Harlem," as he is often called? Yes and no. Born in 1876 in Massachusetts, Payton moved to New York City in 1899 and despite a college degree was unable to find anything but menial labor. He took the advice of Booker T. Washington to "Cast down your bucket where you are" and worked as a barber and a handyman before getting a job as a janitor in a real estate office. There he picked up enough clues about the business to open his own brokerage. His plan was to approach white landlords in Harlem and fill their buildings with Negroes able and willing—or forced—to pay higher rents uptown. Harlem landlords actually preferred black tenants as more reliable than Irish Catholics or eastern European Jews. Moreover, Payton would manage the buildings, capitalizing on the notion held by white landlords that a Negro could better manage Negro tenants. Payton's first venture, on East 135th

Street between Fifth and Sixth avenues, was a failure. He was actually evicted from his home and office for missing his own rent payments. Payton regrouped and in late 1901 he saw another opportunity. Two white landlords on West 134th Street had become embroiled in an ugly business dispute and one decided to take revenge on the other by filling his buildings with black tenants, which he hoped would make his adversary's building unrentable to whites. Payton was clearly the man for the job, and soon he was bringing in black tenants in nearby buildings and blocks as well.

Yet it was racial passion, not cool calculation, that redrew the color line in Harlem. On Christmas Day 1901, on West 130th Street between Broadway and Amsterdam Avenue, a gang of Irish boys attacked a drunk black man, who was defended by three local white men. After three apparently drunk black Harlemites, all residents of West 130th Street, mistook the three rescuers for assailants, it didn't take long for a crowd to gather and divide along racial lines. Within minutes the street was in pandemonium, with whites and blacks going after each other with rocks, clubs, razors, and pistols. One wounded black man tried to escape the police by taking refuge in the drugstore of B. B. Myers, at West 130th Street and Broadway, but he was followed by a mob that trashed the store. One of the men that police identified as an instigator was cornered on the roof of 611 West 130th Street, where he tried to ward off the blows of their nightsticks with his now empty pistol but was soon made "as submissive as a lamb," according to one newspaper's version of events. Nonetheless, the Upper West Side and the Bronx started looking better and better to many Harlem whites.

The aftermath of these incidents helped teach Payton that race made real estate different from other businesses. He incorporated a company called Afro-American Realty and began taking out ads seeking to attract investors interested in "trying to solve the so-called 'Race Problem.'" Among the ten investors who helped come up with a total of $500,000 in start-up capital were such black movers and shakers as New York *Age* publisher Fred R. Moore, the Reverend William H. Brooks, the construction and housecleaning magnate James C. Garner, the attorney Wilford H. Smith, the politician Charles W. Anderson, and the mortician James C. Thomas. With that kind of backing, Payton started filling even more white buildings with blacks, charging them as much as $30 per month for a four-room apartment in a tenement, plus a 10 percent management fee, about five dollars more per month than the whites had been paying. As in centuries past, change came to Harlem less through goodwill than good business instincts and an even better publicity campaign.

By the end of 1904 Payton owned four tenements outright and was managing a dozen buildings, despite a downturn in the economy. Payton's message to landlords—"Rent Colored!"—was clearly working, due partly to his groundbreaking use of billboards and subway advertising. History stayed on Payton's side. A murder in late December 1905 at 31 West 133rd Street, just down the street from his office, convinced the few whites who still lived on the block to leave. By then Payton had become a member of New York's nascent black aristocracy. With his light skin color, distinguished bearing, and beautiful home on West 131st Street, he certainly looked and played the part, but he stayed focused on business, especially when it came to those who opposed him. When a white real estate concern, Hudson Realty, bought three of Payton's buildings—40, 42, and 44 West 135th Street—and threw out the tenants, all of whom were black, Payton bought buildings on either side and evicted the white tenants. Hudson Realty quickly capitulated. Afro-American Realty was soon worth more than $1 million and collecting more than $100,000 in rent each year.

Payton's success didn't last. The recession that had started in 1904 eventually left him unable to fill empty apartments and by 1908 the business failed. But Payton was no mere victim of national economic trends. Investors charged him with having defrauded them and old allies refused to bail him out. His business practices had soured many of his old supporters, who failed to see how making money off African-Americans desperate for a better way of life could be considered uplift. Payton denied any wrongdoing in his effort to transmute "race prejudice into dollars and cents" and argued that he was forced to charge more because banks charged him higher interest rates for working exclusively with black tenants. Eventually, Payton retreated to West 134th Street, where he maintained a modest but profitable real estate brokerage until his death in 1917.

Payton was not the only black realtor working uptown in the years between the turn of the century and World War I. John Nail, the scion of one of the most distinguished of Brooklyn's colored families—his sister married James Weldon Johnson—actually worked for Afro-American Realty until 1907, when he and another employee, a South Carolina native named Henry C. Parker, left Payton's sinking ship and started their own brokerage. Nail and Parker dominated uptown real estate for more than two decades, advertising in the *Messenger* that they collected more than $1 million in rent each year. They also paved the way for more than two dozen other black real estate and rental agents—more than the number of black doctors or lawyers at the time—who helped settle waves of Negroes arriving from the West Indies and the American South. It was in no small measure due to these realtors, most of whose names are lost to history, that by 1915 fifty thousand of Manhattan's sixty thousand Negroes called more than a thousand buildings in central Harlem home, though this community was still dwarfed by the seventy-five thousand native-born whites and 375,000 immigrants who lived uptown. As an Urban League study put it: "Those of the race who desire to live in grand style, with elevator, telephone and bellboy service, can now realize their cherished ambition."

John Nail and Henry Parker's most significant deal involved St. Philip's Colored Presbyterian Episcopal Church, the most venerable black Episcopal organization in the city and the first in a long line of downtown Negro churches to move to Harlem. It was certainly not the first black religious institution in the neighborhood. That distinction belonged to the Harlem African Methodist Episcopalian (AME) Zion Church, also known as Little Zion, which was founded in the 1830s in East Harlem by downtown's venerable "Mother" AME Zion Church to serve the black farmers who made their homes nearby. The years after the Civil War saw the opening of St. Luke's AME Church on West

153rd Street, but it was not until 1891 that the next black church was organized uptown: the Mount Gilead Baptist Church, which was led by the Reverend L. B. Twisby, known as the "Roaring Lion of Harlem." The turn of the century brought the Mercy Street Baptist Church, later known as the Metropolitan Baptist Church, the Mount Olivet Baptist Church, and St. Thomas the Apostle Church, all of which had hundreds of members and elegant facilities to match. More typical were the storefront missions serving the expanding population of Baptist or Methodist blacks working as servants for white families. The best known of these storefront missions was perhaps the Reverend Frederick Asbury Cullen's Salem Memorial Mission, which started with only three people in a Harlem cellar but soon became the Salem Methodist Church, taking over the all-white Calvary Methodist Episcopal Church, then the largest Protestant institution in the city. Baptisms in the Harlem River soon became a common sight.

None of these institutions surpassed St. Philip's Episcopal Church when it came to class. Organized downtown in 1809 by black congregants of Trinity Church and St. Paul's Chapel and led by Peter Williams Jr., the city's first Negro Episcopal preacher and an important abolitionist, St. Philip's became the first black church in New York City to have members bid for pews, a sign of wealth and prestige. After the riot of 1900, the St. Philip's rector, Hutchens C. Bishop, a calm but wily Baltimorean, began investing in uptown real estate, often passing for white in order to complete the transactions. Such tactics weren't always successful, as Harlem's old guard, which had long tried to keep out southern Italian and eastern European Jewish immigrants, now began turning its focus to race. When Bishop tried to buy the Church of the Redeemer on West 137th Street in 1909 his generous offer of $50,000 was rejected. Bishop didn't give up. A year later he engaged Nail and Parker in a record-breaking million-dollar deal involving ten buildings on West 135th Street, between Lenox and Seventh avenues. The sign reading "These houses will be rented only to WHITE people" was replaced by one that advertised "For Rent, Apply to Nail & Parker." Bishop used the rental income to buy land at 210 West 134th Street, where New York's first black architect, Vertner Woodson Tandy, teamed up with George W. Foster Jr. to build a striking brick Gothic structure that quickly became the most prestigious and richest black church in the city. Many black churches followed St. Philip's, taking over white churches and synagogues being sold by congregations moving out of Harlem, transactions that often required some guile. Mother AME Zion Church used a white intermediary to buy the Church of the Redeemer in 1914. That same year St. James Presbyterian Church also came to West 137th Street—when the Reverend D. William Lloyd Imes asked the Presbytery for more than half of the $83,000 it would cost to build a proper building, they demanded that white architects design the Georgian-classical structure. St. James quickly became one of the fanciest houses of worship uptown, hosting the wedding of the daughter of Madame C. J. Walker, Harlem's "Mahogany Millionaire."

Other black churches were more circumspect when it came to relocating uptown. Adam Clayton Powell Sr. caught what his son called "the Harlem vision" only in 1911, and he didn't move the Abyssinian Baptist Church until more than a decade later. It wasn't until 1926 that St. Mark's Methodist Episcopal Church left West 53rd Street and built a new home on West 138th Street. Nonetheless, by the end of the decade, there were more than 140 established churches in Harlem, in addition to dozens of basement and storefront operations, and more were opening every year. The racial landscape had changed so radically that, even as it became impossible for white churches to stay open because of the flight of so many of their congregants, some Harlem churches held five Sunday services. Even the old Collegiate Reformed Church, descended from the original Second Dutch Reformed Church, sold out to the black Ephesus Seventh Day Adventist Church.

By 1914, 40 percent of Harlem's private houses and 10 percent of its tenements were owned by blacks, according to John Royall, a prominent uptown realtor. More reliable figures published by the NAACP's *Crisis* magazine several years later estimated that Negroes owned $20 million of real estate uptown. None of it was as simple as Booker T. Washington's advice to "Get some property." If blacks acquired property around the turn of the century in spite of the white opposition, in the years before World War I whites were increasingly desperate to profit from the now inevitable development of a black community uptown. Long after the 1860s, when streetcars were desegregated, real estate developers tried to keep parts of Harlem white by building luxurious houses and apartment buildings that few African-Americans could afford. In 1889 the *New York Times* published an article called "Prejudices of Landlords" attacking a system in which colored people "are kept within narrow limits" in order to charge them rents that were up to 50 percent higher than those whites paid. One landlord claimed, "After a house has been occupied by colored people no white family will ever live in it—except some desperately poor and ignorant immigrant family." Both black and white landlords used the "Negro scare racket," threatening to bring blacks into buildings if white tenants didn't pay higher rents. This kind of racism wasn't always the rule. In 1886 a huge Independence Day celebration run by the Harlem branch of the Grand Army of the Republic, a Civil War veterans organization that included several prominent Jews, invited "all Harlemites, white or black, Democratic or Republican, naturalized or native-born." Those views seemed to have less currency as blacks became a significant political, cultural, and economic force. Starting in the mid-1890s white landlords whose appeals to "civic responsibility" went unheard used agreements known as covenants to prohibit white owners or buyers of white-occupied real estate from selling to "any negro, quadroon, or octoroon," diction that suggests how deeply racial obsessions associated with the South ran in the North. These agreements, which were legally binding—anyone who broke them could be sued by fellow signatories—resulted in what were known as covenant blocks, which remained white even as blacks moved in and dominated nearby streets.

The arrival of the subway and the expiration of many racial housing covenants in 1904 doomed block-by-block resistance to the arrival of African-Americans. In 1905 the New York *Herald* was alarmed to report that West 133rd to West 135th streets between Lenox and Seventh avenues had been "captured for occupancy by a Negro population," and that property values in parts of Harlem had fallen by up to

20 percent. That same year the New York *Indicator,* a journal devoted to real estate interests, opined, "Their presence is undesirable among us . . . They should not only be disenfranchised, but also segregated in some colony in the outskirts of the city, where their transportation and other problems will not inflict injustice and disgust on worthy citizens." In 1906 the New York *Herald,* reporting on a furor over thirty-five white families being evicted and replaced with black families, joylessly predicted that "the establishment of the Negroes in 135th Street is only the nucleus of a Negro settlement that will extend over a wide area of Harlem within the next few years."

Encouraged by such press, white Harlemites began new efforts to oppose black arrivals. Organizations such as the Save Harlem Committee, Anglo-Saxon Realty, and the Protective Association for 130th to 132nd Streets all fought to keep Harlem white. They were joined, starting in 1908, by the efforts of the infamous Harlem Property Owners Improvement Association, an updated version of the groups that had targeted immigrants before the turn of the century. Led by John G. Taylor, who had made his money investing in black saloons in the Tenderloin before settling at 213 West 136th Street, a block that like so many others in central Harlem was turning color, the association raised $100,000 to buy properties that were in danger of being sold to Negroes. He used moral suasion to prevent other deals, opposing policy changes that allowed Negroes to use the New York Public Library branch at 103 West 135th Street, approving of mass evictions of blacks, working for the resegregation of the Sixth Avenue and Ninth Avenue elevated trains, hiring detectives to investigate new arrivals, and advocating a twenty-four-foot-high fence along West 136th Street to keep blacks from moving north. Taylor's group didn't accomplished much at first. One Harlem newspaper in 1910 noted, "Although organizations to prevent the settling of colored citizens in certain sections of Harlem mushroom overnight, the colored invasion goes merrily along." But later that year Taylor got the signatures of 121 out of 142 property owners on West 136th Street between Lenox and Seventh avenues after the black owner of 121 West 136th Street rented out apartments in the building to Negroes. In 1911 Taylor was advertising under the headline "Harlem Redeemed" and offering discounts to white renters. Before the year was out he controlled more than two hundred homes in all-white neighborhoods uptown. Taylor boasted two thousand supporters by 1912, when he campaigned for William Howard Taft's bid for the presidency under the slogan "Save Your Property." Two years later he was still going strong, attracting some five hundred people to a meeting at Harlem's all-white YMCA. That gathering led to the formation of the Property Owners Improvement Association of Harlem, which insisted that the arrival of thirty-five thousand blacks in Harlem since 1903 had reduced the assessed value of twenty-two square blocks in central Harlem from $400 million to $260 million. The group, which included Eduin van der Horst Koch, of the well-known Koch's department store on West 125th Street, successfully evicted blacks from 312 West 133rd Street and prevented a black movie theater from opening on Lenox Avenue between West 129th and West 130th streets, an effort that led to the resegregation of most uptown theaters. Many had never given up on enforcing the color line. What is today the Apollo Theater got its start as Hurtig and Seamon's Music Hall shortly after the turn of the century, a burlesque house that was not open to Negro audiences—the nightclub in the basement, Joe Ward's Swanee Club, where Jimmy Durante was the house pianist, made its racial policy clear on a placard placed in the entryway: "No Niggers!" New owners ended the theater's all-white policy before World War I, though they let in blacks only through a back door on West 126th Street, and for years to come they had to sit in an upper mezzanine.

The New York *Age* celebrated the exploits of black real estate magnates, but white papers favored Taylor and his allies. Even the supposedly progressive *New York Times* trumpeted the formation of one group allied with Taylor with the headline "Invasion of Negroes Cuts Harlem Values." Taylor's kind also had their own press organs. One was *Harlem Magazine,* organized around 1910 by the all-white Harlem Board of Commerce, which had long worked to keep immigrants out of uptown's fancier neighborhoods. There was also the *Harlem Home News,* which uncritically quoted Taylor calling blacks "the common enemy" and promising to pay for their relocation to colonies outside of the city. "Wake up and get busy," the newspaper warned in the aftermath of Nail and Parker's St. Philip's deal on West 135th Street, "before it is too late to repel the black hordes that stand ready to destroy the homes and scatter the fortunes of the whites living and doing business in the very heart of Harlem ... The Negro invasion must be fought until it is permanently checked, or the invaders will slowly but surely drive the whites out of Harlem." The rhetoric became more extreme. Eventually, the *Harlem Home News* scared readers with talk of "the black plague" and quoted at length from a speech at a 1912 meeting of the Harlem Board of Commerce that sounded like it was drawn from a Ku Klux Klan meeting. "The Negroes are Negroes and that's all there is to it," insisted one resident of West 130th Street, leading the crowd to roar: "Drive them out and send them to the slums where they belong."

Ultimately, the conversion of Harlem into a black neighborhood in the years before World War I was something that no one man could achieve or prevent. Rather, it was the oddly beneficial mix of economics and prejudice that changed things. Race relations in New York, as in the rest of the United States, had deteriorated sharply in the 1890s. Ever stricter racial segregation meant that vacancy rates in black neighborhoods elsewhere in Manhattan dropped to the extraordinarily low rate of 3 percent by 1914, and many uptown landlords, black and white, couldn't resist meeting demand, for a price. Blacks, who were increasingly shut out of neighborhoods downtown, paid it.

The death of the old Harlem meant the birth of several new ones. The gourmet food store Park and Tilford shut down, as did fancy 125th Street shops like Horton's Ice Cream, rather than serve blacks, even as more and more could afford such luxuries. A survey of black Harlem by *Outlook* magazine in 1914 counted twenty-eight doctors and dentists, twenty-five nurses, four pharmacists, and fifteen lawyers, in addition to restaurant and hotel owners and self-employed black photographers, printers, undertakers, and barbers. By the end of World War I Harlem was the biggest black community in the world, though whites were still in the majority. A decade later the neighborhood was solidly black, with two hundred thousand Negroes living from the Golden Edge of West 110th Street to Coogan's Bluff. Paul Robeson's wife, Essie, could even claim "only Negroes *belong* in Harlem," though as late as 1932 the old guard still hadn't made peace with the new racial reality. In that year *Harlem Magazine* changed its name to *Uptown New York*—the very word "Harlem" now signified "Negro"—and a year later it editorialized: "How our old Dutch burghers would writhe if they could be reincarnated for just long enough to grasp the modern idea of what was once their cherished 'Nieuw Haarlem.'"

Economics and art advanced together during the early years of the Harlem Renaissance. Black societies and clubs held occasional concerts, dances, balls, and picnics uptown well before the turn of the century, but the first documented formal stage appearance by an African-American in Harlem, seventy years after the birth of downtown's African Grove Theatre, was nothing to celebrate. In 1895 a young African-American actor named Henry S. Arnold was performing in *On the Mississippi* at Oscar Hammerstein's Columbus Theatre when his straw skirt caught fire, probably from the gas footlights. A fireman felled him with an iron bar and managed to smother the flames, but the boy later died in the hospital. It was not a very promising beginning for the street that would one day symbolize the soul of modern American culture. In fact, the proper start of Harlem's constitutive role in the cultural revolution known as the New Negro movement came more than a decade later, in 1908, when a group of musicians from the Tenderloin's black bohemia chose the uptown West End Theatre as the site for a concert to benefit the now largely forgotten entertainer Ernest Hogan. It is difficult to understand Hogan's popularity a century after his heyday not simply because he made no recordings but because he was a primary exponent of a decades-old genre known as the "coon song," in which a "country coon" named Jim Crow and a black dandy called Zip Coon engaged in a playful musical contest. The decision to hold the benefit for Hogan uptown, and at the West End Theatre no less, which had recently been presenting plays in Yiddish, was a heroic leap of the racial imagination, especially when we recall that, although thousands of blacks lived uptown in

1908, their culture—their theaters, clubs, restaurants, schools, and churches—was for the most part still downtown.

Hogan, who was born in Kentucky before the Civil War and got his start in show business performing coon songs on the blackface minstrel show circuit, became a bona fide national celebrity with his 1896 song "All Coons Look Alike to Me (A Darkey Misunderstanding)." "The Unbleached American," as Hogan was billed, was now working in the United States and abroad with every major Negro stage talent. Even greater things were to come. After barely surviving the riot of 1900, Hogan founded the Memphis Students, a pioneering ragtime orchestra that was the breeding ground for virtually every black musician of note working in New York City in the pre–World War I years. The Memphis Students may not have improvised much, but they seem to have been the first musicians, black or white, to perform jazz, then known as syncopated music because of its whimsical, off-the-beat rhythmic emphasis, half gallop, half hiccup. Unfortunately, the Memphis Students didn't provide steady work for Hogan, and in 1907 he fell ill with a terminal case of tuberculosis.

The 1908 benefit to pay for Hogan's treatment attracted the best-known black musicians in the country. It was a historic moment: the first time that the city's black cultural elite purposefully identified with Harlem. The benefit was a huge success, and a month later the participants gathered again in Harlem, as the Frogs, and began planning a debut at Harlem's Manhattan Casino, to be called "The Frolic of the Frogs." Despite the lighthearted tone, the Frogs were serious in their aim: to improve Negro entertainment and to "elevate the race generally." That was easier said than done. The state refused to incorporate the group, with the presiding judge noting, "I hesitate to cement the connection between the sublime and the grotesque," which was precisely their plan. The decision was eventually overturned and the group bought a building at 111 West 132nd Street to serve as clubhouse.

The Frogs' agenda was set by the club's librarian, James Reese Europe, a tall, dignified, classically trained pianist, violinist, and composer who more than any other figure was responsible for distilling from the vulgar crucible of minstrelsy and vaudeville a black musical culture that prized modern, cosmopolitan elegance and a swinging sense of American wit—a new sound for a new century's New Negroes. Born in 1880 in Alabama and raised in Washington, D.C., Europe was the son of an ex-slave who became a Republican civil servant. In 1902 Europe came to New York and began performing in white clubs, though most of his time was spent among the black bohemians who made the Marshall and Maceo hotels on West 53rd Street the nerve center of Negro culture in New York.

Europe arrived just as African-American musical entertainment was in transition. Around the turn of the century, many black musicians had begun distancing themselves from blackface and coon-song traditions. Despite Hogan's popularity, these pioneers of early jazz rejected the popular but demeaning stereotypes in which both black and white minstrels and vaudevillians trafficked. In their place, in a new generation of saloons and nightclubs, came an elegant and eclectic piano style known as ragtime, derived from classical traditions, popular waltzes and marches, quadrilles, Irish banjo jigs, country dances, *habaneras*, Afro-Caribbean chants, and ring shouts from Georgia and the Carolinas; the name described the way ragtime pianists "ragged" time by playing right-hand syncopated passages against the marchlike regularity of the supporting left-hand part. One of the very first published examples of the genre was "Harlem Rag," composed in 1896 by Tom Turpin and Joseph Stern, but ragtime was considered an import from St. Louis, where its foremost exponent, Scott Joplin, lived. Born in 1868 in Texas to former slaves, Joplin was a child prodigy who left home at fourteen for the life of an itinerant musician. After the success of his 1899 tune "The Maple Leaf Rag," Joplin ended up in New York City, settling into 163 West 131st Street, which his wife ran as a boardinghouse. Joplin worked in the basement on his opera *Treemonisha*, which he eventually brought to the Lafayette Theatre. Frustrated and angered by its poor reception, Joplin was institutionalized at the mental hospital on Ward's Island, where he died in 1917, not yet fifty years old. By then Joplin's music was a fixture of uptown's nightclubs, cafés, and hotels, where it cross-fertilized with James Reese Europe's early syncopated experiments and the "Charleston," which the pianist James P. Johnson

created to accompany the boisterous lunchtime dances of South Carolina stevedores working the docks near San Juan Hill. The new music's
lowly origins and its connections with such shockingly modern vices
as public dancing and smoking by women—cigarettes today, suffrage
tomorrow, many people worried—made for much intergenerational
conflict uptown in these years. Since few Negroes were able, by law,
custom, or finance, to study at classical conservatories, being a black
musician meant playing music associated with bars and whorehouses.
Indeed, in the years before World War I, James Reese Europe preferred to dignify his art with the term "syncopated music" rather than
"ragtime," while the pianist Eubie Blake's mother forbade him to play
ragtime when he was a child because of its unseemly associations.

In unshackling African-American music from its supposedly
backward and sinful origins, by transforming black vaudeville, coon
songs, and blackface minstrelsy into jazz, and by relocating the center of African-American culture from midtown to uptown, Europe
counted on the help of a generation of musicians who arrived as part
of the great migration north. Among the most prominent was Bob Cole,
who was born in Georgia in 1868 and arrived at the age of twenty-
five in New York City, where he performed with minstrel troupes
and also wrote coon songs. After appearing in Broadway's first black
show—here the epistemology of race fails us, since the show, called
Oriental America, included opera arias by Verdi and Berlioz—Cole
organized the 1897 *A Trip to Coontown,* which was the first New York
show written, directed, produced, and performed entirely by blacks.
The show was also significant because it departed from the tradition
of black shows as a loose collection of dramatic scenes, comic sketches,
and musical interludes, all punctuated by tap dancing and juggling.
Cole invented a new kind of musical theater, with a single plot line
artistically integrating text, music, and dance, which owed more to
operetta than to minstrelsy.

A Trip to Coontown represented everything that two musical brothers from Florida had been waiting for. James Weldon Johnson and
James Rosamond Johnson were born in 1871 and 1873, respectively,
into a distinguished Jacksonville family that had fallen on hard times,

though not so hard as to prevent the visits of Frederick Douglass and T. Thomas Fortune, among other prominent race heroes. After graduating first in his class at Atlanta University, James Weldon returned to Jacksonville to run his old primary school, even while he became the first Negro in Florida to pass the bar exam. In 1897 he started a law practice, but the world of literature and entertainment attracted him. His Negro dialect poems were set to music by his brother, James Rosamond, a prodigy who studied classical music before becoming Bob Cole's partner on stage. By 1902 the "Ebony Offenbachs" were collaborating with Cole in New York City on hits such as "Congo Love Song" and "Under the Bamboo Tree," songs that, despite their titles, rejected coon song traditions in favor of dignified love tunes that attempted to "clean up the caricature," as James Rosamond Johnson later put it. These songs were popular and influential; T. S. Eliot quoted "Under the Bamboo Tree" in that revered monument to European high culture *The Waste Land.*

Despite his success in show business, James Weldon Johnson announced that he was retiring from the entertainment world and getting into politics. It came as no surprise to those who knew him. Since coming to New York he had befriended Charles Anderson, the head of the Colored Republican Club of New York City and an intimate of Booker T. Washington. Johnson also became close with Theodore Roosevelt, who as president sent him to diplomatic postings in Venezuela and Nicaragua, jobs that took him away from the black Harlem that he had helped to midwife. Nor was Bob Cole to see the flowering of the Negro renaissance. After buying a home on West 136th Street, which made him the first Negro to settle in the neighborhood, he contracted syphilis and died in 1911. James Rosamond Johnson went on to become the first Negro to conduct white musicians before a white audience in New York, all the while remaining a fixture of Harlem's new black aristocracy.

A focal point of the crowd of black bohemians who made the move to Harlem was the team of Bert Williams and George Walker, who for more than a decade helped set the pace for American entertainers, black, white, and everything in between. Williams was born in 1874 in the Bahamas and grew up in New York City, where as a child he performed with the young Walter Winchell and Eddie Cantor. While studying engineering in California, he worked in minstrel shows, where in 1893 he met Walker, a twenty-year-old singer from Kansas. Their big break came the next year, when they were called upon to fill in for "real" Africans from Dahomey who missed their scheduled performance at San Francisco's Mid-winter Exposition. The act made Williams and Walker a sensation on the blackface circuit, and by the time they brought their "Two Real Coons" act to New York in 1896, they were ready to take on more ambitious material. Their show *Bandana Land* introduced the song "Nobody," which became Williams's biggest hit, perhaps because of the way it bridged two cultural eras: it was at once a riff on the old sorrow song "Nobody Knows the Trouble I've Seen" and a modernist monument to social alienation. Walker's death in 1911 couldn't stop the ever adaptable Williams, whom no less an authority than W. C. Fields called "the funniest man I ever saw, and the saddest." Williams became president of the Frogs before joining Ziegfeld's Follies, a milestone for a black entertainer, but he never broke through on film or in recordings before his death in 1922 at the age of forty-nine. New Negroes who disdained Williams's blackface act mourned him as the first black performer in the history of American entertainment to appeal widely to whites, even as Harlem claimed him for its own. Booker T. Washington admitted, "He has done more for our race than I have. He has smiled his way into people's hearts; I have been obliged to fight my way."

No one in the years before World War I wrestled more earnestly with the thankless yet lucrative challenge of representing the race onstage than Will Marion Cook, who was born in Washington, D.C., in 1869 and studied violin at Oberlin and at the University of Berlin, an education that was paid for with funds raised by Frederick Douglass himself. But Cook quit his classical career after he couldn't convince his promoter to stop calling him "the Greatest Negro Violinist." Cook wrote many songs in the coon tradition, which he valued as racially authentic, but like most of his peers he was ready for something more challenging. In 1898 he teamed up with Williams and Walker and Paul Laurence Dunbar to write *Clorindy, or The Origin of the Cakewalk*, a retelling of the duo's breakthrough. This sixty-minute turning point in American musical theater was a modest endeavor, but apparently it was the first time that professional American actors sang and danced at the same time. The show, which starred Ernest Hogan, became hugely popular, though Cook's mother saw it and shrieked, "I've sent you all over the world to study and become a great musician and you return such a nigger!" Cook ignored her and became a central early figure of the New Negro movement even before it had a name, stepping into the gap left by the deaths of Ernest Hogan, Bob Cole, and George Walker.

Like so many of those associated with midtown's black bohemia, Cook increasingly found work uptown. In 1913 he helped found a Harlem theater company where he often worked with his wife, Abbie Mitchell, a half black, half Jewish native of the East Side who had appeared in *Clorindy* at the age of fourteen. But Cook knew that his race was the reason why his talents weren't being properly recognized. Ironically, it was in Europe, as the conductor of two of the pioneering jazz ensembles, the Memphis Students and then the Southern Syncopated Orchestra, that the embittered Cook finally got some of the respect he deserved. America still wasn't ready for black Harlem.

The indignities that prevented Will Marion Cook from assuming a central role in the musical life of his country inspired James Reese Europe to keep struggling, more and more frequently uptown. It was Europe's music coming from a Harlem saloon in 1905 that mesmerized the young George Gershwin. But Europe had ambitions beyond nightclub gigs. After helping form the Memphis Students and the Frogs, he moved from the Marshall Hotel to 67 West 131st Street, where he began to ponder the role of the Negro artist in the new century. Europe had long rebelled at the working conditions of black musicians. Black composers typically received one-tenth of the royalties that white composers did, and though the standard fee of $50 per week for black performers was good money—five times what black domestics made—it was still far less than what comparable white entertainers were making. Local 310 of the American Federation of Musicians didn't accept blacks, Harlem's New Amsterdam Musical Association refused to book ragtime, and uptown's Colored Vaudeville Benevolent Association had little to offer black musicians trying to uplift the race. Europe, a black Republican and acolyte of Booker T. Washington's gospel of hard work and self-sufficiency, filled the gap by founding the Clef Club, a union, booking agency, and social group that helped demolish the barrier between popular and concert music in the United States and therefore had a central role in making black music the popular music of all Americans.

The Clef Club was headquartered on West 53rd Street but debuted uptown in 1910 with a mixed-race benefit concert at the newly built Manhattan Casino on West 155th Street. "On with the dance," one advertisement exhorted, "and let joy be unconfined." With fourteen pianos, forty-seven mandolins, and two church choirs, all arrayed onstage in a huge C-clef-shaped semicircle centering on an ivory-clad Europe, the Clef Club orchestra didn't quite play jazz. But Europe soon concocted the mix of instrumental voices that would characterize the big band jazz sound. He was the first musician to use the saxophone as something more than a novelty instrument, and he was the first to substitute trombones for bassoons and clarinets for oboes, which lent his ensembles the full-throated, expressive timbres—sometimes sweet, sometimes hot—soon to be associated with jazz. It was a Clef Club member, Buddy Gilmore, who invented the notion of playing with a full drum kit, which helped move percussion out of the limited role of timekeeper and into a more interpretive function, again one of the signal characteristics of jazz. All the musicians could read music. Eubie Blake remembered, "They could read a moving snake, and if a fly lit on that paper, he got played." There were no improvised solos, but Europe's band members never played from sheet music either. The cognitive dissonance of black musicians mastering musical notation, Europe believed, would have put an end to the club's popularity with white audiences, who preferred their black music to appear spontaneous. Europe's material ranged widely, from classics and show tunes to spirituals and minstrel-style numbers, as well as ragtime versions of waltzes and gypsy tunes, and even the very first blues, W. C. Handy's "Memphis Blues," in the process raising the artistic stakes not just for black music but for American entertainment in general.

The talent so abundantly on display at the Clef Club concerts belied the difficulty Europe had in finding well-trained musicians. Many of the club's instrumentalists were self-taught and worked regular jobs, and he recruited his singers from the choirs of St. Philip's and St. Mark's. In order to guarantee a future for his music, Europe founded the Music School Settlement for Colored People, which was located at Sixth Avenue and West 130th Street and quickly attracted more than two thousand pupils who paid 25 cents per lesson, or nothing at all if they couldn't afford it. The school promoted the notion that music was "a universal language and that through it the Negro and the White man can be brought to have mutual understanding." Still, Europe insisted that blacks run the school, starting with James Rosamond Johnson as director. It was his way of balancing the twin imperatives of race and art, and it would haunt jazz once it left the protective nest of uptown Manhattan.

One reason for the Clef Club's success was the artistic vacuum left by the deaths of an older generation of entertainers and the attractions that Broadway held for a younger generation. The entertainment business uptown was also changing, with a handful of black-owned or black-oriented theaters and nightclubs opening, their repertoire passionately promoted by two newly hired full-time theater critics uptown, the *Amsterdam News*'s Romeo Daugherty and the New York *Age*'s Lester Walton. The benefits of a new generation of black entertainers performing for black audiences were soon obvious. Minstrel or coon imagery was dying out at the same time that what James Weldon Johnson famously called "the term of exile" from Broadway, when racial segregation on and off stage effectively shut out serious entertainers, was ending. Ironically, the arrival of black talent on Broadway marked the start of a new golden age of Harlem stagecraft. Within a few years, Seventh Avenue was being called the black Broadway, even though a number of established theaters, especially film palaces such as the Regent Theatre, which opened in 1915 at the corner of Seventh Avenue and 116th Street, were still segregated or open only to whites. Black musicians were to be found only in the orchestra pit of the newer Roosevelt Theatre, a three-thousand-seat venue built by Leo Brecher on Seventh Avenue, as well as in Brecher's comparably sized Douglas Theatre, at 142nd Street and Lenox Avenue. Things were more progressive at the West End Theatre, the Manhattan Casino, and the Palace Casino, on East 135th Street between Fifth and Madison avenues, where "nigger dances" like the Cakewalk, the Eagle Rock, the Grizzly Bear, the Hump-back Rag, the Shiver, and Ballin' the Jack were the rage. Black Harlemites could also sit where they liked at the Crescent Theatre, at 36 West 135th Street, which since 1909 had been featuring high-class entertainment, meaning legitimate drama, music, and film. A few doors down from the Crescent was the legendary Lincoln Theatre, which also opened in 1909. It started out as a movie theater but the owners soon switched to blackface and vaudeville acts, and in 1914 the management invited a thirty-two-year-old New Yorker named Anita Bush to join Bert Williams and George Walker in starting a house theater troupe. After the Lincoln was demolished in 1915 and replaced by a thousand-seat venue with links to the Theatre Owners Booking Association (performers joked that TOBA stood for "Tough on Black Asses"), Bush took her company to the two-thousand-seat Lafayette Theatre, changed the name of the company to Lafayette Players, and turned it into the most important black drama company in the United States. Much of the credit must also go to the *Age*'s Lester Walton, who never let conflicts of interest get in the way of a cultural revolution. As manager of the Lafayette he turned J. Leubrie Hill and Will Vodery's show *Darktown Follies* into one of the first must-see events for whites who wanted to go uptown to hear tunes like "The Night Time Is the Right Time," "Rock Me in the Cradle of Love," and "At the Ball."

The Clef Club made most of its money not from long-term engagements at theaters like the Lafayette but from "gigs"—apparently a coinage of James Reese Europe—in the form of private parties and society events in the New York area for the likes of the Goulds, Astors, and Vanderbilts. There were also performances as far afield as Philadelphia, White Sulfur Springs, Palm Beach, and New Haven, where the teenaged Cole Porter heard them at a Yale fraternity party. Europe also made sure his men got work in the nightclubs and saloons that were moving from midtown to Harlem. By 1914 the New York *Age* claimed that Harlem was "infested" with saloons, and the next year the Urban League counted more than one hundred places in Negro Harlem to drink, dance, and listen to music. The first black nightclub was Leroy's Cafe, located in the basement of 2220 Fifth Avenue, at 135th Street. It had been opened in 1910 by Leroy Wilkins, who strictly opposed all forms of racial integration, admitting only blacks in black tie. The bandstand at Leroy's, which soon moved to Seventh Avenue and West 134th Street, was occupied for a time by Jelly Roll Morton, a former pimp from New Orleans whose getup, including a derby, silk shirt, and diamond-and-gold-studded teeth, perfectly matched his flashy piano style. Another favorite at Leroy's was an eccentric, half black, half Jewish native of Newark, New Jersey—he spoke Yiddish and claimed to have worked as a cantor—named Willie "The Lion" Smith, who seems to have invented the roiling, headlong style of keyboard virtuosity that became known as Harlem stride. It was a lucrative gig, paying $20 a week, plus tips, for performances that lasted from 9 p.m. until dawn. There were few other places to catch the attention of the black aristocracy. Initially the response of nightclub stages that were too small to accommodate a large ensemble, Harlem stride outgrew the solo piano traditions of ragtime by voraciously assimilating the influence of mazurkas, waltzes, marches, cotillions, and even hymns. With his vigorous left hand pumping out rhythms that would lope up and down the keyboard, and his sophisticated yet loose right hand pulling off orchestral chords that spanned tenths, the stride pianist's elegant and extravagant genre matched the speech and dress that were beginning to characterize a new kind of Harlem style. Most "ticklers" had little formal training, but they put on great shows, especially when competing against one another in what were known as cutting contests, an updated version of the ancient West African cultural custom of improvised competition. The venues that presented the ticklers were all in the West 130s—125th Street wouldn't become the focus of black Harlem until well after World War I. Aficionados recommended Edmund's Cellar, which opened at Fifth Avenue and 132nd Street and was known as the Bucket of Blood, because the crowd was so violent. A world away in terms of class was John W. Connor's Royal Café, at 71 West 135th Street, which attracted wealthy black Harlemites to its afternoon "ragtime teas." Another popular spot was Kid Banks's Club, which relocated from the Tenderloin to 29 West 133rd Street.

The very best place to see black music uptown in the years before World War I was the nightclub run by Leroy Wilkins's younger brother, Barron, an obese, kindhearted Tammany Hall fixture who had run a West 35th Street nightclub called the Little Savoy, an elegant venue that featured black talent and white patrons, before relocating to a basement space near Seventh Avenue and West 134th Street. The scene at Barron Wilkins's club, documented by modernist painter Charles Demuth in 1917, was as varied as the American experience itself. In addition to stride ticklers and ragtime ensembles—including one of the earliest public appearances by Duke Ellington's first ensemble, the Washingtonians—Wilkins featured tango teas and dances. An all-American racism also prevailed at the front door. Like all of the fancy hot spots uptown in the years before the war, Wilkins demanded that his doormen master the intricacies of class and race, parsing the pennies and pigment of its patrons. The club was open only to formally dressed whites, white celebrities like Al Jolson and Lucille LeSueur (later known as Joan Crawford), and light-skinned Negroes in black-tie formal dress and with the money to match. Exceptions were also made for dark-skinned black celebrities such as the Texas-born boxer Jack Johnson, whose successes in the ring against both black and white opponents made him one of Harlem's most beloved figures in the years before World War I.

In this ferment of talent, James Reese Europe reigned supreme. Between concerts, society dances, and nightclub dates, his Clef Club was bringing in more than $100,000 per year. Europe was in such demand that he booked himself into two or three events each evening, leaving much of the conducting to trusted colleagues such as the pianist Eubie Blake and the singer Noble Sissle. Europe even started a new organization, the Tempo Club, where he could more easily indulge his taste for innovations such as conducting an orchestra as accompaniment to a film.

Europe's continued success was also due to his brilliant decision in 1913 to enter into a partnership with a lean, rich, white dance team named Vernon and Irene Castle, whom he had met at a ball in Newport, Rhode Island. Irene Castle, who daringly bobbed her hair and shockingly displayed her slim figure without the benefit of whalebone petticoats and corsets, was so impressed with Europe's music that she put him in charge of the team's orchestra at private engagements and concerts. It was a natural match. The Castles and Europe combined British refinement and American energy in their tangos, polkas, waltzes, and marches. They also translated vernacular black dancing for the white upper crust, popularizing once-naughty dances like the Black Bottom, the Texas Tommy, and the Turkey Trot. The whirlwind tour of thirty cities that the Castles and Europe undertook in 1914 introduced the world to a new dance called the Fox Trot, which Europe had invented by slowing down W. C. Handy's "Memphis Blues" and combining it with a dance he'd seen as a child in Washington, D.C., called the Get Over Sal. It quickly became the most popular dance in America and helped Europe and the Castles turn public social dancing from a lowbrow habit associated with the immoral ways of the wrong race—it was illegal in some parts of the United States—into a national craze. This seismic shift met objections from both sides of the racial divide. The *Harlem Home News* deplored this "'nigger' dance [. . .] in which hugging and squeezing and suggestive motions play a prominent part," while the New York *Age* featured Adam Clayton Powell protesting, "The Negro race is dancing itself to death." The relation between the Castles and Europe was short-lived. A year after the start of World War I, the British-born Vernon Castle, whom Europe called "my one real and true friend," signed on as a combat pilot for the Royal Air Corps, flying more than a hundred missions before dying in a training exercise.

*   *   *

Europe couldn't resist a challenge, but when in the summer of 1916, almost a year before the United States entered World War I, he received an offer to run the regimental band of the Fifteenth New York Infantry, an all-black division of New York State's racially segregated National Guard unit, he was torn. The formation of a Negro unit had been authorized on the condition that it be led by white officers, and Europe wasn't one to take orders from anyone, black or white. The war in Europe was inspiring a variety of responses among uptowners. Many protested the prospect of America's involvement in the European crisis. Speaking from the pulpit of the Abyssinian Baptist Church, Adam Clayton Powell declared his patriotism but demanded in return that the government take some action on racial discrimination, not just in the military overseas but back home as well: "It is infinitely more disgraceful and outrageous to hang and burn colored men and boys and women without a trial in times of peace than it is for the Germans in times of war to blow up ships loaded with mules and molasses." The most influential voice in the uptown antiwar movement belonged to Norman Thomas, who was troubled by masses of industrial workers losing their jobs because of disruptions to international trade caused by the outbreak of the conflict. Realizing that East Harlemites were increasingly left to choose between "booze and beatitudes," as one observer put it, Thomas resigned from the church to focus on his socialist and pacifist activities.

James Reese Europe's decision to join up was just as principled. From his office in a Harlem beauty parlor he began signing up not just foot soldiers but musicians, singers, dancers, and even comedians, telling them that joining was part duty and part opportunity, since he planned on taking the band on tour when the war was over. Europe held meetings, rallies, and concerts, and by the end of the summer he had more than two thousand soldiers under his command, many of them entertainers drawn from the Clef Club and Tempo Club. Europe signed up local celebrities including James Rosamond Johnson and Bojangles Robinson, but most of the recruits were anonymous, middle-class Harlemites who worked as doormen, waiters, bellhops, clerks, messengers, janitors, or porters. For many of them, Europe's latest gig was a ticket to fame, musical and otherwise. Among Europe's recruits was a twenty-nine-year-old artist from Pennsylvania named Horace Pippin, whose painting *The End of War: Starting Home* would become a key image of the era.

By the fall of 1917 Europe had begun the difficult task of training his men. Unlike white units, Europe's men had no uniforms or weapons, so they paraded before adoring crowds up and down the avenues in street clothes, with broom handles on their shoulders. Often they drilled in dance halls or empty lots, or even in the cellar of the Lafayette Theatre. Despite such challenges, Europe's recruits finished basic training and sailed to France. On their first day, they performed "The Marseillaise," but French soldiers were slow to recognize their own national anthem, so new were the sounds coming from the instruments of Europe's men. Europeans traveling to the United States before World War I had heard early versions of jazz, but this was the first time that authentic African-American music had been heard across the Atlantic. The concerts that followed—unsegregated, except when sponsored by Americans—met with wild enthusiasm, especially Europe's versions of tunes such as "Memphis Blues," "Way Down Upon the Swanee River," and "Joan of Arc," which vocalist Noble Sissle sang in French. Even "The Star-Spangled Banner" got a jazz treatment.

Despite such expressions of patriotism, Europe's men encountered the same sort of racist treatment they were so used to back home, but not from their allies. While the French army gladly put African-Americans in the trenches alongside French troops so covered with mud that race wasn't visible anyway, the American command wouldn't allow blacks to fight alongside white Americans. American commanders tried to convince the French to order their officers not to shake hands with black soldiers, talk to them socially, eat with them, or let them become familiar with French women; the fear was that equal treatment might spoil Negroes, making them ungovernable once back in the United States. The newly christened 369th Colored Infantry Regiment was enlisted in the Rhine offensive, where they charged again and again into no-man's-land, bravely engaging in hand-to-hand combat. Europe himself even put down his baton and with "complete contempt for danger," according to French observers, took up a machine-gun position, becoming the war's first African-American combat officer. Europe was gassed in June of 1918, but he was soon back despite pleas from the Harlem Hellfighters, as they were known, to take a medical discharge. He responded: "My country calls me and I must answer; and if I live to come back, I will startle the world with my music."

The Harlem Hellfighters weren't the only American blacks in uniform. More than a third of all World War I draftees were black. Nor was Europe the only black bandleader in uniform. Will Vodery, a Philadelphia native who had worked with Europe in Harlem before the war, led the 807th Infantry band. Europe's colleague from the Clef Club, Tim Brynn, led the 350th Infantry Field Artillery band, known as the Black Devils, which included Willie "The Lion" Smith. But the Hellfighters were the most famous Negroes in Europe, and not just because of their music. Their 191 days in the trenches—they never once retreated and never allowed the capture of one of their own—was longer than any other American unit, white or black. Such behavior earned 171 of them the Croix de Guerre, the highest French military honor, as well as a regimental Croix de Guerre and Legion of Honor. When the Hellfighters finally returned home they would be primed to make demands.

While the Harlem Hellfighters were busy saving civilization, back home the war was more controversial than ever. Despite the pride that Harlemites took in the accomplishments of the Hellfighters as news of their valor and artistry reached home, many still insisted that black Americans had no obligation to face German guns on behalf of a government that denied them basic rights at home. Nonetheless, they were helpless to accomplish much in New York because of the continuing political dominance of the Democratic Party, which had a long and deplorable record on racial issues. Tammany Hall had strongly supported slavery for decades before opposing Lincoln and the Civil War and proposing that the city secede from the Union. After emancipation, Tammany Hall opposed black suffrage, supported property requirements that prevented all but a handful of Negroes from voting, and embraced Jim Crow attitudes that made the city even more hostile to blacks in 1900 than it had been a century earlier. Then there was the matter of the Democrat in the White House, President Woodrow Wilson, a racist who won the presidency in part because black voters believed his promises to keep America out of World War I and to fight for racial freedom at home. No wonder dozens of new black political clubs sprang up starting in the late nineteenth century, and not only among Democrats. The Republican Party, which had come to power with Lincoln and promulgated Booker T. Washington's strategy of compromise and conciliation, may have wielded power at the national level but the party had little local power. Most of the city's black Republicans may as well not have exercised their right to vote, because they were effectively frozen out of the political process. But a thaw was coming.

The first African-American to have a substantial impact on New York City politics was Charles Anderson, an acolyte of Booker T. Washington who came to New York from the Midwest at the age of twenty in 1886. Just five years later he was being called the "Colored Demosthenes" and being invited by the Harlem Republican Club to speak at Urbach's Hall. Anderson's leadership of the New York County Young Men's Colored Republicans Club led to a low-level posting at the local offices of the Internal Revenue Service. He worked his way up to collector of the IRS's Wall Street district, where he focused on putting blacks in patronage positions as clerks, messengers, inspectors, and examiners. He was even behind the appointment of New York's first Negro cop, Samuel Battle. But Anderson's signal achievement was convincing Booker T. Washington to put James Weldon Johnson, out of a job after President Wilson dismantled Roosevelt's network of ambassadors and consuls, on the editorial page of the most important black publication of the era.

The New York *Age* was founded in 1882 as the *Globe* by an ex-slave from Florida named Timothy Thomas Fortune, who is sorely neglected by historians. In addition to serving as Booker T. Washington's ghost writer, Fortune was a pioneering political activist who ran the first black newspaper to make a national readership for itself. He even invented the term "Afro-American" as a more respectful alternative to "Negro." By the time Johnson came to the *Age*, Washington had replaced Fortune, whose alcoholism was getting in the way of his work, with another acolyte, Fred Moore, who came from Washington, D.C., to New York in 1888. Inspired by Philip Payton's success, Moore started the Afro-American Investment and Building Company, but he put most of his energy into the *Age*, which was located at 228-30 West 135th Street, next to Moore's own home, in the heart of what Moore hoped would become the capital of black America. Moore used the paper to promulgate Washington's belief that economic development should be the chief means of racial uplift, but the *Age* was a quirky publication. Even as white Harlemites sought to halt the "invasion" of blacks, the *Age* was urging, in a 1910 article called "Dragging Down the Race," that blacks with questionable morals and manners be "driven out by whatever means necessary." It was only under Johnson's influence that the *Age* found a more relevant focus: the advocacy of forceful measures to counter segregation, poverty, and racist violence. Of course, Johnson wasn't alone in exploring what it meant to be a New Negro. The *Amsterdam News*, founded with ten dollars in 1909 in San Juan Hill by James H. Anderson, relocated to Harlem the next year and imitated both the four-page format of the *Age* and its debt to Booker T. Washington's Republicanism, spicing things up with plenty of gossip and social news. Starting in 1914 this golden age of Harlem journalism even supported a third weekly, the New York *News*, though competition with national black publications including the Pittsburgh *Courier*, the Chicago *Defender*, and the Baltimore *Afro-American* limited its success.

Charles Anderson's mission as Booker T. Washington's man uptown climaxed in 1917, when he backed the fifty-seven-year-old Edward Austin Johnson, a Republican lawyer and real estate investor originally from North Carolina, in his successful bid to become Harlem's first black representative in Albany. There Johnson was responsible for the 1918 law that extended the standard of "equal accommodation" to all businesses serving the public, from theaters to restaurants to hotels to pool halls, ending at least in legal principle most racial segregation in New York State. The next year Anderson helped elect New York City's first black alderman, a dentist from North Carolina named Charles H. Roberts, which opened the way for a slew of Republican Negro politicians. These successes were only symbolic, however, because white Republicans still took the black vote for granted. Things didn't change politically for Negroes in New York City until they finally stopped voting Republican.

After black refugees from Republican politics began convincing their neighbors to put their weight behind a Democratic mayoral candidate in the election of 1898, Tammany Hall called on the Saint Kitts native W. I. R. Richardson to form United Colored Democracy, an all-black club whose leadership was hand-picked by Richard Croker. The Democrats, like the Republicans, did little at first for their black constituents beyond a few patronage jobs. There were still only a few hundred black Democrats in New York City a decade later, and they were all locked into the separate and unequal wing of the party. Things only began to look different in 1912, when United Colored Democracy moved uptown, to West 136th Street, and under the leadership of a Mississippian named Ferdinand Q. Morton began recruiting arrivals from the American South and the West Indies. Morton, who suffered from the taint of his association with the party of the reviled Woodrow Wilson, focused his efforts locally, grooming the physician Eugene Roberts—the brother of New York City's first black alderman—to take charge of all patronage positions uptown. Morton made black Democrats a force to be reckoned with, and their support in 1921 for the Democratic candidate for mayor, John Hylan, bought them significant returns. Hylan, who spent much time walking uptown's streets, became the first mayor to keep records on black voters and issues.

The wild card was held by the Italians, who had long been unfairly accused of lacking the democratic instinct. At the turn of the century East Harlem politics included a heady brew of Republican, socialist, anarchist, syndicalist, and communist parties. What they were not,

in any great numbers, were Democrats, at least not until the party
began making overtures to immigrants. The key figure here was an
East Harlemite named Salvatore Cotillo, who was born in Naples in
1886 and whose family came to the United States in 1895, settling on
East 113th Street. Cotillo's father became a well-known caterer and
opened a popular pastry shop. Cotillo attended P.S. 83, but his passion
was baseball, and he cleaned seats at the Polo Grounds in exchange
for free tickets to the games. School won out in the end and Cotillo
followed college with a law degree before throwing himself into local
Democratic politics. He was elected to the state legislature at the age
of twenty-seven, where his advocacy of gun control, female suffrage,
school lunch programs, an end to the death penalty, and after-hours
naturalization ceremonies for immigrants endeared him even to the
dwindling community of Irish Harlemites who lined up to see him
when he held court at Kullman's bakery, at Third Avenue and East
115th Street. It was all good news for Tammany Hall, which was still
unable to attract many New Negroes. Indeed, Democrats divided the
black belt of central Harlem into two political districts in order to split
the black vote come election day, a situation that allowed Harlem's
Irish, Jewish, and Italian voters to hold on to a power that was far out
of proportion to their numbers.

One reason that mainstream politics grew so fitfully was the rise of a
vital generation of black Harlemites wary of entangling alliances with
any established party. W.E.B. Du Bois was most independent of them
all, and the least predictable. Born in 1868 into a working-class family in racially segregated Great Barrington, Massachusetts, Du Bois
experienced little of the humiliation and terror that characterized
the African-American experience—this was, after all, the heady early
period of Reconstruction, which promised to make racism ancient
history. Only fifteen when he began writing for T. Thomas Fortune,
he got a scholarship from his local church to attend the all-black Fisk
University, where he learned that race was not a biological category
but a social one. Du Bois claimed that Fisk turned him into a Negro,

but it is more accurate to say that there he became a New Negro and, indeed, that was the title of one of his undergraduate essays, long before anyone dreamed of a renaissance in Harlem. By the time he graduated, Du Bois was a mustachioed dandy who was as serious about philosophy as he was about the ladies. After attending Harvard—he was one of only two black students out of a student body of more than one thousand—and the University of Berlin, he applied to Booker T. Washington for a job. The "Wizard of Tuskegee" balked at hiring the budding young race radical. Du Bois, who ended up teaching at Atlanta University while he worked toward becoming Harvard's first black Ph.D., decided that race was not just any social construct, but a uniquely powerful cultural determinant. He famously told a gathering of international race leaders in London in 1900: "The problem of the twentieth century is the problem of the color line," an assertion that blossomed in 1903 into the groundbreaking *Souls of Black Folk*. Despite Washington's instructions to the black press to ignore it, *Souls* became Du Bois's best-known—and best—work. It was at once an attack on Washington's accommodationist strategy, an angry rejection of the Supreme Court's 1896 *Plessy v. Ferguson* decision legalizing racial segregation, and an exploration of "double consciousness," a psychological state that Du Bois believed defined the African-American experience. For better or worse, Du Bois argued, Negroes possessed constitutionally conflicted characters whose efforts "to race with the world" were bound to be complicated.

The success of *Souls* charted a way out of the inferno of Jim Crow and into a new racial era led by an elite "Talented Tenth" of the race, as well as helping to inspire the founding of the National Association of the Advancement of Colored People. The fact that an organization dedicated to securing social justice for African-Americans was dominated by white philanthropists and located in a white neighborhood in midtown didn't bother Du Bois, or anyone else, it seems. In the summer of 1910, Du Bois moved to New York City to join the NAACP, but it would be another decade before he would move to Harlem, late in the day for someone who had pioneered the New Negro movement. Then again the light-skinned Du Bois seems to have found himself most comfortable when straddling the color line. Nor did he shy away from mixing scholarship and advocacy. One of his first acts at the NAACP was to found *The Crisis: A Record of the Darker Races,* a monthly magazine whose message of interracial cooperation and uplift, backed by a forceful confrontation with racial discrimination, made it holier than scripture in many Negro households.

Another organization founded around this time by rich white liberals was the Urban League, which vied with the NAACP for both the dollars of white philanthropists and the pennies of poor Negroes. Among the founders of the Urban League was William Jay Schieffelin, whose family had roots in Harlem going back a century, but as with the NAACP it would be years before the organization opened an uptown office. The Urban League's racial agenda, on display each month in its journal, *Opportunity*—its motto was "Not Alms, but Opportunity"—borrowed much from the self-help gospel of Booker T. Washington, but it was far too timid for the likes of Du Bois. In fact, from the start the organization devoted considerable resources to changing the lives of Harlem's sixty thousand Negroes, informing authorities about trash in the streets or problems with fire escapes, working for more playgrounds, clubs, and community centers, and even supporting the Empire Friendly Shelter, a "rescue home for unfortunate colored girls and women."

Du Bois compared the Urban League's immediate impact on Harlem with the NAACP's slow-moving program of litigation at the national level and began casting about for a new ideological home. For a brief period, Du Bois joined ranks with the Socialist Party, but he quickly found himself feeling marginalized and betrayed by the socialists' refusal to recognize racism as a priority. Du Bois took consolation in culture, marking the fiftieth anniversary of the Emancipation Proclamation by producing a three-hour, 1,200-performer theatrical pageant called *The Star of Ethiopia,* with music by James Reese Europe. The presidential election of 1912 that put Wilson in the White House brought Du Bois back to earth. He maintained no romantic notions about the Republicans. Although raised to be faithful to the party that freed the slaves, Du Bois never forgot the way the Republicans turned their backs on Reconstruction, nor did he forgive them for continuing to treat Negroes as something less than full political agents. But many considered Du Bois's support for the Democrat Wilson naïveté at best and race treason at worst.

Few Harlemites felt more betrayed by Du Bois than a slight, genteel Floridian named A. Philip Randolph, a black Bolshevik who went on to become a giant of American labor and the brains of the civil rights movement. Almost as soon as he could think for himself, Randolph distanced himself from both the AME Church and the Republican politics of his father in favor of Du Boisian integration. A trip to New York City in 1909, where the twenty-year-old Randolph saw Bob Cole and James Rosamond Johnson perform, convinced him to become an entertainer, but two years later he was working as a switchboard operator at a building for whites on West 148th Street. Events in Europe and at home were energizing political movements of every stripe, and Randolph was caught up in the ferment, taking classes at City College, where students were increasingly forsaking Morris Raphael Cohen for Karl Marx—just as Du Bois was moving the other way. The campaign flyers that Randolph distributed in 1913 for John M. Royall, the black Republican real estate man who ran for alderman as an independent after the Republicans nominated a white candidate in the increasingly black district, read: "The black man first, the black man last, the black man all the time." But Randolph was never simply a race man. The next year, he began working for the Brotherhood of Labor, a 135th Street employment agency that also acted as an advocacy group for black unions. He also befriended a twenty-five-year-old acid-tongued gambler and womanizer from South Carolina named Chandler Owen, who lived at the old North End Hotel, which had been renamed the Olga Hotel, at Lenox Avenue and West 137th Street. Fired from job after job for speechifying on the boss's time about working conditions, Harlem's own Lenin and Trotsky, as Randolph and Owen became known, began spending all their time reading, talking, and listening to stepladder orators, who were unconstrained by the demands of party politics and beholden to nothing but their ideological passions.

Randolph's and Owen's favorite street corner preacher was Hubert Harrison, who was born on Saint Croix in 1883 and arrived at the age of sixteen in New York, where he gave up liberal democracy for socialism. Though Harrison never graduated from college, he became Harlem's favorite intellectual, a self-styled polymath who worked as a telephone switchboard operator, hotel bellhop, and postal clerk. Eventually he talked his way into jobs as assistant editor for the *Masses*, spokesman and organizer for the Socialist Party, and a staffer for the International Workers of the World, in addition to writing for both socialist publications and mainstream periodicals—the novelist Henry Miller was one of his biggest admirers. Harrison also wrote many books, most of which were on sale only in corner stores and barbershops. But it was on "the Campus," as the corner of Lenox Avenue and West 135th Street was known—the white *Harlem Magazine* preferred to refer to it as "Harlem's 'bug house' corner"—that Harrison had his greatest influence, lecturing passersby on everything from race and evolution to birth control, comparative religion, and colonialism. In June 1917 Harrison attracted more than two thousand people to the Bethel AME Church for the inaugural meeting of the Liberty League, an organization that recommended Negroes stop looking at their race as a problem but as a solution. The mouthpiece of this early form of black nationalism was the New York *Voice*, a "newspaper for the New Negro," as Harrison put it. Its very first issue argued against American entry into World War I on the grounds that the United States had no business making the world safe for democracy if conditions back home were unsafe for blacks. Although such positions weren't uncommon uptown, the *Voice* was unable to challenge the *Age* or the *Amsterdam News* because of Harrison's fire-breathing denunciation of what he called "Jim Crow Jesus." His contempt for everyone from Adam Clayton Powell to Booker T. Washington to W.E.B. Du Bois and the NAACP, which he called the "National Association for the Advancement of Certain People," made sure Harrison remained somehow both popular and marginal.

Harrison was part of a wave of immigration from the West Indies and the Spanish-speaking Caribbean to the United States that changed the landscape of Harlem once again, much in the manner of Jews and

Italians a generation earlier. But where turn-of-the-century immigrants from eastern Europe and southern Italy made the biggest impact in the fields of business and entertainment, West Indian New Negroes were obsessed with politics, considering themselves the shock troops of a war of self-defense against American racism. Harlemites looked for guidance to figures such as the Surinamer Otto Huiswood, the only Negro present at the creation of the American Communist Party, and the Jamaican black Bolshevik W. A. Domingo. Another prominent race radical was Grace Campbell, a half-Jamaican socialist who worked with the African Blood Brotherhood, one of whose members, the Barbadian Richard Moore, ran the Pioneer Cooperative Society, a food store specializing in Caribbean goods. A serious stutter made the founder and leader of the African Blood Brotherhood, Cyril Briggs, who came from Nevis to Harlem at the age of eighteen, less suited to stepladder preaching than to journalism; Briggs's interest in black self-determination for a time blended easily with the *Amsterdam News*'s gospel of capitalist uplift. The magazine that Briggs founded, the *Crusader,* had a more extreme point of view, one that bid farewell to the "old Negro," with his "crawling and pleading." Finally, there was J. A. Rogers, a Jamaican socialist who arrived in Harlem near the end of World War I and saw everything through the lens of race, insisting that even Beethoven and Pushkin were black.

Southern Negroes and West Indians weren't the only new arrivals remaking Harlem. Even before the great migration made the neighborhood synonymous with black America, entire blocks in East Harlem already resembled a Spanish-language version of the Negro mecca. Of course, the fact that uptown Hispanics were white, black, and everything in between—among these *Nuevo* Negroes was Sammy Davis Jr., born uptown in 1925 to an African-American father and a Cuban mother—confounded census takers. Eventually, Latinos had their own Harlem Renaissance, complete with their own radical politics, newspapers, literature, soul food, dance music, rent parties, policy gambling, blackface theater, and big bands battling it out, using as weapons Puerto Rican *bombas;* Cuban rumbas, *son,* and *plenas;* and Dominican merengue.

Even in the 1920s Hispanic Harlem had deep roots. Adventurers from Spain had long passed through the region in search of the Pacific, but it was money that brought sugar, fruit, and molasses traders from the Spanish-speaking Caribbean to New York in the eighteenth century. Politics also played a part. Some arrivals had fled the revolution that, starting in 1791, turned Santo Domingo into Haiti. Others came in the nineteenth century to spread the word about independence movements in Cuba and Puerto Rico. In 1890 the Cuban Revolutionary Party formed the Dos Antillas (Two Islands) Club for East Harlem's Cubans and Puerto Ricans—among the organizers of the effort shipping weapons and medical supplies to support the independence movement was the famed black German–Puerto Rican bibliophile Arturo Schomburg—which seems to be the earliest evidence of a formal Latin American community uptown. The Spanish American War of 1898 resulted in the reorientation of the Spanish-speaking Caribbean toward the United States, whose huge sugar, tobacco, and fruit companies were disrupting long-standing plantation economies and dislocating tens of thousands of peasants. The war was nominally about Cuban independence, but the treaty that ended the conflict had broad consequences. The United States soon dominated the ostensibly independent Cuba culturally, politically, and economically; in addition to colonizing Puerto Rico as well as the Philippines; and the entire Caribbean soon became a market for American exports and provided American industry with cheap agricultural goods, especially sugar.

The sudden upswing in travel between islands brought together whites, native islanders, and blacks, which ironically produced the kind of racial mixing that was at the time outlawed in much of the United States. The boldest or the most desperate of these migrants, enticed by the possibilities of better economic opportunities, left for New York and settled uptown, which was safer, greener, and less crowded than downtown. By 1913 the *New York Times* was reporting a colony of Latin Americans on Striver's Row, where blacks were still banned, and three years later fifty Puerto Rican families had settled along Park Avenue between East 110th and East 117th streets.

The 1917 legislation that made Puerto Ricans citizens of the United States also made the islanders eligible for service in World War I. The first mass migration of Puerto Ricans to the United States came in the form of some eighteen thousand draftees, although there were volunteers as well. Among them was a group of clarinetists and flutists, most of them mere teenagers with no knowledge of English, who answered when James Reese Europe came to Puerto Rico to recruit for his military band. Upon their return from the European theater of war, they found their place in the theaters of Harlem, where they became the pioneers of Latin music in America. By then there were more than seven thousand Puerto Ricans in New York City and, as the American economy entered its postwar boom, even more began arriving, attracted by the factories of East Harlem and the shipbuilding works at the Brooklyn Navy Yard. By the mid-1920s as many as forty thousand Spanish speakers, about 90 percent of them Puerto Rican, had arrived in East Harlem, spreading from the northeast corner of Central Park to Madison, Park, and then Lexington avenues. They were increasingly joined by arrivals from the Dominican Republic whose journey to the United States was expedited by the U.S. occupation of the island from 1916 to 1924. By the end of the decade, following the 1928 hurricane that devastated the islands, New York City's Puerto Rican population was forty-five thousand strong and centered in East Harlem. There they lived in tense proximity to the neighborhood's Irish, Jewish, and Italian immigrants, who had started resorting to thuggish tactics, including hiring gangsters to intimidate Puerto Ricans into keeping out of certain uptown neighborhoods and businesses. What Harlem's Latinos soon learned from their West Indian neighbors was that ambition could trump prejudice. The only thing both groups needed was a leader.

The most significant islander to make uptown home, and perhaps the most famous, best-loved, and influential Harlemite of them all, was Marcus Garvey, whose image still proudly watches over myriad barbershops, shoe-shine stands, laundromats, and newspaper kiosks. Born in 1887 in Jamaica, Garvey was known among his schoolmates as "Ugly Mug" because of his dark skin color. He left school at the age of fourteen, still a poor reader and writer, but he was able to get work in print shops. Booker T. Washington's *Up from Slavery* and a meeting with the Egyptian nationalist Duse Mohamed Ali inspired Garvey to form the Universal Negro Improvement Society and the African Communities League, organizations that advocated "civilizing the backward tribes of Africa." Garvey came to the United States in early 1916 at the invitation of Booker T. Washington but soon recognized that he had little in common with Washington's politics of compromise and conciliation. Garvey ended up where every Negro, it sometimes seemed, with something to say ended up: amid the strollers, strutters, and shouters on the corner of Lenox Avenue and West 135th Street. One April night in 1916, A. Philip Randolph was just finishing a speech when a voice from the crowd shouted: "There's a young man here from Jamaica who wants to be presented to this group! He wants to talk about a movement to develop a back to Africa sentiment in America."

Garvey was a "little sawed-off, hammered-down black man," Randolph recalled, but a terrifyingly effective public speaker, with a regal bearing and a booming voice. That evening, however, the crowd was unimpressed. The average Negro Harlemite wasn't quite ready for Garvey's race-obsessed brand of black self-determination, which emphasized the supposedly inborn nobility of the Negro race and the importance of returning to Africa. While repatriation had been supported by figures as varied as Thomas Jefferson, James Madison, Andrew Jackson, and Henry Clay—more than ten thousand American Negroes had returned to West Africa in the years before the Civil War—most black New Yorkers had always opposed the idea. Garvey didn't give up, and soon he was appearing on his own soapbox every night during the week and at Lafayette Hall on Sunday nights. The *Crisis* noted Garvey's growing prominence, but that was the extent of interest that W.E.B. Du Bois was willing to show. Garvey was shocked by Du Bois's lack of interest in a political agenda that put race first. Eventually the two became bitter enemies, with Garvey calling

Du Bois "the white man's nigger," and Du Bois remarking on Garvey's political resemblance to an embarrassing blackface minstrel routine.

In the meantime, uptown's black radicals were taking a giant step forward. Randolph and Owen had been editing the *Hotel Messenger,* the publication of the Headwaiters and Sidewaiters Society of Greater New York, which gave Randolph and Owen office space and money and then left them alone, at least until the newspaper began denouncing not only colonialism and the war but corruption in the union itself. Randolph and Owen were fired, but they took the office furniture to 513 Lenox Avenue and came out with their own newspaper, the *Messenger,* which focused on news and opinion pieces about race, labor, and radical politics—this was, after all, only a few weeks after the Russian revolution—as well as poetry, theater and music reviews, and even art. Randolph and Owen's newspaper became one of the main organs for the cultural revolution that would soon be known as the New Negro movement. But even after counting revenue from advertisements placed by socialist groups, and cash infusions from the beauty parlor owned by Randolph's wife, the "only radical magazine published by Negroes" still lost money. The most prominent black labor activists in the country couldn't even pay their own staff.

The contentious variety of racial viewpoints and programs that prevailed uptown meant that nothing much changed until W.E.B. Du Bois started paying closer attention to James Weldon Johnson's essays on the editorial page of the New York *Age.* Du Bois had never thought much of the newspaper, which was the mouthpiece of his nemesis Booker T. Washington. For his part, Johnson, an old-fashioned black conservative who had loyally served Republican administrations and who despised socialism and labor activism in general, hadn't much use for Du Bois. But Johnson recognized Du Bois's offer to make him the NAACP's field secretary, in charge of the search of new members and new money, as nothing less than a crusade to "awaken black America," as Johnson later put it.

Within three years, Johnson increased membership tenfold, to about a hundred thousand, and opened more than two hundred local offices, most of them in the South. He broke the organization's addiction to white benefactors and helped reorient its agenda from the legal struggle for civil rights and antilynching campaigns to the "right to contend for rights," a more activist line of thinking that echoed Du Bois's own turn away from analysis and toward action. Johnson's greatest achievement at the NAACP may have been organizing a public response to the worst antiblack violence since the Draft Riots of 1863. Racial terror had been on the rise in the United States ever since the late nineteenth century, when lynchings seemed to have become, in the words of the writer George Schuyler, a national sport. More than one hundred blacks on average were lynched each year in the 1890s, a number that actually rose after the turn of the century. The year 1917 was particularly bad, with racist terror in Waco, Memphis, and East St. Louis, where in July a riot—today we would call it ethnic cleansing—broke out that left two hundred blacks dead and six thousand homeless, shocking many Americans, black and white. Working with the NAACP's Harlem branch, at 224 West 135th Street, Johnson dreamed up a public demonstration to show the world what American Negroes thought of such events. The Silent Protest Parade, as it was known, took place on July 28, 1917, and began with hundreds of black women and children dressed in white striding wordlessly down Fifth Avenue from 59th Street to 23rd Street while drummers kept up a quiet but insistent beat. Next came thousands of men dressed in black and carrying a banner that read "Bring Democracy to America Before You Take It to Europe" and featured an image of an African-American kneeling before President Wilson. Police tore the banner away from marchers and confiscated it, but this march into America's racial future couldn't be stopped, not by a lynch mob's rope, not by a cop's nightstick, not even by a judge's gavel—leave it to Johnson, a veteran of Broadway, to create a spectacle to match the drama of the historical moment.

The Silent Protest Parade was a crucial event in the history of black Harlem because it united for the first time the entire range of

Negro political opinion. A more lasting racial consensus remained elusive. In June 1918, the editors of the most prominent black newspapers
in the country were called to Washington, D.C., by the War Department
in an effort to raise support for the war. The editors agreed. Most of
the major publications already considered a prowar stance a matter of
patriotism. Still, they took the opportunity to extract promises from
the government to address conditions at home, especially lynching and
segregation. Marcus Garvey had no patience for the promises of white
men, and the next month he convinced New York State to incorporate
the New York City branch of the UNIA as a "benevolent and social
organization." Garvey's time had finally come. He quickly attracted
almost a thousand members in Harlem, and within a few months he
had doubled and then tripled membership rolls, or so he bragged. Just
as unreliable was his claim a year later of two million members and
offices in thirty locations in the United States, Africa, Latin America,
and the West Indies. Nonetheless, the UNIA soon outgrew Lafayette
Hall. Garvey moved meetings to the Palace Casino, at Fifth Avenue
and 135th Street, but that, too, couldn't accommodate the growing
crowds, so Garvey began speaking at even larger venues, such as the
Crescent Theatre. Garvey's personality was almost enough to guarantee the success of the UNIA, since the more trouble he ran into with
the authorities, the more supporters he attracted. The rest was due to
Garvey's newspaper, *Negro World,* whose sixteen pages—four times as
long as the other Harlem weeklies—showed off the work of the best
black writers in the country, all of whom focused on building a single,
unified community of Africans worldwide. There were even sections
in French and Spanish.

However much Garvey liked to take credit for this surge in
political activity by black Harlemites, demographics was the decisive factor. The drop in immigration to the United States during
the war—1.2 million people arrived in 1914, compared to fewer than
111,000 in 1918—coincided with the participation of four million
Americans in the war effort, adding up to a huge demand for labor
and rising wages in the industrial North. More than 2 million blacks
left the South, where a boll weevil infestation from 1913 to 1915, and

widespread flooding in 1915 and 1916, had made an already dire situation, characterized by chronic underemployment and discrimination,
even more desperate. These sharecroppers bet it all on the cities to
the north. Whether they won is still in question.

Negroes wanted to go to Harlem the way the dead want to go to heaven,
the old saying went, but even before World War I black Harlem was in
trouble. To be sure, there were migration success stories like that of Pig
Foot Mary, who arrived in New York City after the turn of the century
and set up a business selling chitlins out of a baby stroller, eventually
becoming one of the wealthiest women in the United States. But many
female migrants ended up in situations that were less than respectable:
on chorus lines, as taxi dancers, or as prostitutes. Even those women
who got jobs as domestics were little more than virtual slaves to the
agents who had brought them north. The economic realities faced by
men were often no better. No wonder Booker T. Washington urged
southern blacks to stay where they were. The New York *Age* was warning its southern readers as early as 1907 that employment in New York
City was "severely limited," although that might have been part of the
journal's efforts to keep out unskilled, uneducated southern blacks.
Washington even tried to organize a movement to move Negroes from
the northern cities back to the South, to no avail. While blacks in the
South were lucky to make a dollar a day, there were plenty of jobs
in New York City that paid three dollars per day or more before the
war. Consolidated Edison hired blacks to bring electricity uptown, a
job that came with the dubious perk of working with Thomas Edison
himself, who openly called them "niggers." From 1917 to 1919 more
than seventy thousand southern blacks arrived, having scraped together
eight dollars' passage north, a scenario powerfully documented by
George and Ira Gershwin in *Porgy and Bess*'s "There's a Boat That's
Leavin' Soon for New York." Eventually, employment and recruiting
agents, some of whom were members of the clergy, emptied whole
towns and took as much as two months' wages in return, with promises
of free transportation by rail, employment, and good schools. Things

got so bad that some southern communities banned labor recruiters altogether. Yet still the migrants came north.

Before his death, Booker T. Washington agreed with W.E.B. Du Bois on one thing: it was the bottom of the black barrel that was coming north. Those children who had attended the appallingly bad segregated schools of the South struggled with the most basic lessons. Up to a quarter of students who arrived for their first day of high school were still reading at a grammar school level, which resulted in these students being labeled mentally unsound. Remedial efforts failed, because three-quarters of all children changed schools every year as their parents tried to stay one step ahead of the landlord. After the school day was over things got worse, as children came home to empty apartments. Even in the supposedly flush times of the 1920s, mothers and fathers both had to work to pay the bills, and a generation of unsupervised youth resulted in a quadrupling between 1914 and 1930 of crimes committed by young, black Harlemites. This was the other side of the Harlem Renaissance.

Life in Latino East Harlem closely resembled that of Negro Harlem. Whereas Spanish-speaking businessmen and political exiles who arrived around the turn of the century were skilled, educated whites, the immigrant wave of the World War I era consisted largely of mixed-race families led by frequently uneducated and unskilled parents, and during the 1920s four thousand more were arriving each year, paying $50 for the four-day journey from San Juan to La Ciudad del Dollar. The mass immigration of Puerto Ricans and Cubans came well before New York City began losing the industrial base that offered steady work to unskilled immigrants swarming into the city from the islands to take advantage of a significant wage differential. In the mid-1920s the average weekly salary on the islands was about $13 per week, compared to the $19 per week earned by East Harlem's dockworkers, construction workers, hotel clerks, porters, elevator operators, waiters, salesmen, carpenters, building superintendents, janitors, butchers, laundry workers, and shoemakers. Among the biggest employers of Latinos was the uptown cigar-making industry, which consisted of hundreds of large and small operations. Many of these workers had followed in their fathers' footsteps, beginning their work as apprentices back in Puerto Rico, learning to select and strip tobacco leaves and then pack and roll up to two hundred cigars per day. That kind of productivity could earn a *tabaquero* up to $10 per day, which put them in the same economic class as Latino East Harlem's 150 Spanish-speaking doctors, lawyers, dentists, and accountants. Puerto Ricans also started their own small businesses in the neighborhood. One survey counted twenty-five bodegas, twenty-five barbershops, and three pharmacies owned by Puerto Ricans, in addition to a handful of funeral parlors, candy stores, taverns, and tailor shops. The first Latino restaurant in East Harlem, La Luz, which was owned by a Sephardic Jew from Puerto Rico, opened before World War I, and by the mid-1920s there were forty Puerto Rican–owned diners and cafés serving up codfish fritters, spare ribs, chicken with rice and beans, and the mashed plantain dish known as *mofongo*.

As in Jewish and Italian East Harlem, uptown's Puerto Rican women tended to get unofficial work, mostly doing piecework in the garment industry, which them paid 13 cents to hem a dozen hand-kerchiefs or 25 cents to sew a dozen collars onto blouses, although union garment factories in East Harlem were becoming more com-mon. Another way for women to make money was child care, which paid $3 per week. Signs in apartment windows reading *Se Cuidan Ninos,* or "We babysit children," were common. Other women worked the streets, peddling a variety of food, including the sweet, crushed ice concoctions known as *piraguas.*

Ultimately, Latinos in East Harlem between the wars were mar-ginally better off than their Negro neighbors, though worse off than white New Yorkers, having traded in the hunger, lack of economic opportunity, and high infant mortality rates of the islands for the asthma and tuberculosis caused by ghetto life and factory work. Poor-quality housing also accounted for many of these problems. During this period, a fifth of all buildings in East Harlem were officially classified as substandard. Because Puerto Ricans experienced only marginally less discrimination in housing than their Negro neighbors, many had no choice but to live in the tenements of East Harlem, where rents were even higher than in already overpriced central Harlem. As many as half of all East Harlemites took in lodgers, so that fifteen people in a single apartment wasn't uncommon, and with a shared toilet in the hall or in an outhouse in the rear yard it was far from comfortable. Such conditions created enormous social instability in Negro Harlem, but not in Puerto Rican Harlem, where families were larger and differently structured. Unlike southern Negroes during the great migration north, men and women came from Puerto Rico in almost equal numbers, often in couples, and, because the Catholic church played such an important role in the life of Latino East Harlem, more than half of all Puerto Rican households were organized around a married couple, compared to about a third of Negro homes.

The political establishment was slow to help Puerto Ricans, who were United States citizens but couldn't vote in New York. Language was one impediment. Another was the failure of Puerto Ricans and Cubans to develop the kind of institutions, legal and illegal, that provided political access for so many immigrant groups. This is not to say that they were apolitical. Many of the earliest immigrants from the Spanish Caribbean were political refugees from anticolonial movements, or they had spent their childhoods listening to readings from novels or newspapers, including radical publications, as they rolled cigars, a practice that survived uptown, with each *tabaquero* kicking in 10 cents per week to pay the reader, so they arrived radicalized. It was hardly surprising, then, to see the rise of a Spanish-language speakers' corner at Fifth Avenue and 110th Street, as well as political meetings and rallies by communists, socialists, and nationalists at the nearby Park Palace. But as in Negro Harlem, radical politics was primarily a matter of the printing press, not the ballot box. The town of Cayey, Puerto Rico, produced two of East Harlem's most prominent radical journalists. Jesús Colón, who came to the United States in 1917 at the age of sixteen as a stowaway in the linen closet of the S.S. *Carolina,* helped found the first Communist Party branch in East Harlem, El Centro Obrero, which sponsored the party newspaper *La Vida Obrera* and published *La Voz.* He often crossed paths with another *jíbaro,* or highlands peasant, Bernardo Vega, who had founded Puerto Rico's Socialist Party before coming to

East Harlem, where he worked as a cigar maker by day and fought colonialism and capitalism by night. He founded the Liga Puertorriqueña
e Hispaña, one of the city's most important movements struggling for
Puerto Rican independence, and helped start the neighborhood's first
Spanish-language newspaper, *El Gráfico*.

The return of the Harlem Hellfighters from Europe helped Harlemites
of every stripe forget their woes for a while. Indeed, the February 17,
1919, parade that honored the Hellfighters is enshrined in Harlem
history as one of the proudest moments of the African-American experience and another candidate for the start of the Harlem Renaissance. However divided uptowners may have been about sending their
sons off to Europe, they welcomed them home in style, and on that
cold, sunny day the more than twelve hundred surviving members
of the 369th Infantry Regiment marched up Fifth Avenue, their band
performing the military music that had so enthralled French audiences. First came the mounted police, then the unit's officers, then the
police band, and finally the Hellfighters themselves in their threadbare
uniforms. After the flag bearers and almost two hundred wounded
soldiers came James Reese Europe—suffering from pneumonia—and
"the proudest band of blowers and pounders that ever reeled off a
marching melody," the New York *World* reported. The Hellfighters
were as well known for their music as for their valor in combat, but
their playing was virtually inaudible over the cheering of hundreds of
thousands of spectators, including the black children who were given
permission by the city to skip school. When the Hellfighters reached
the reviewing stand at West 130th Street, then the southern border of
black Harlem, the band, which had been slowly stepping up what one
observer called the "peppery tang" of the music's temperature, broke
into a jazzy rendition of "Here Comes My Daddy." It was a triumph
not just for Europe and his men but for Harlem and all of America.
Things would surely now be different, racially speaking.
       By the time Europe got back home and moved into an apartment
at 67 West 133rd Street, American popular culture had undergone

a sea change. Jazz was suddenly the dominant popular music of the United States, and Europe led eighty-five of his men on a wildly successful nationwide tour. The first African-American bandleader to sign a contract with a recording label, Europe brought the band into the studio and committed to posterity "On Patrol in No Man's Land," a tune he had written in the trenches with Noble Sissle, and whose battlefield special effects anticipated Jimi Hendrix's "Machine Gun" by half a century. The leader of syncopated ragtime orchestras and military ensembles now headed up the very first jazz big band. But the night before a May 10 concert scheduled for the steps of the Boston State House, Europe was in his dressing room chatting with the singer Roland Hayes when he was confronted by Herbert Wright, a diminutive orphan whom Europe had taken under his wing and turned into a drummer. Wright accused Europe of playing favorites, pulled out a knife, and stabbed him in the neck. A decorated war hero who had faced down German attack and American racial insult with equal equanimity, Europe remained professional, instructing Noble Sissle: "Don't forget to have the band down at the State House at nine in the morning." They were among his last words. Europe died the next day. The *New York Times,* which usually ignored Europe's activities when he was alive, put the news of his murder on the front page, while the New York *Herald* reported that "'Little Africa' went into mourning." Funeral arrangements were complicated—in addition to a wife, Europe left behind a mistress with a young son—but dignity prevailed at the viewing at Paris Undertakers on 131st Street, during a silent parade of Europe's orchestra through black Harlem, and at a public funeral at St. Mark's Episcopal Methodist Church in midtown, the first such event for a Negro in the city's history. As much a cultural strategist as an artist, Europe had made black music synonymous with American music, even as he became a central force in the struggle for racial equality, all before he turned forty. What would the Harlem Renaissance do without him?

Efforts by A. Philip Randolph and Chandler Owen to spread the notion among Harlem's poorest that the patriotism of African-Americans should be predicated on improvements in race relations had caught the attention of the authorities, who arrested the pair under a federal law targeting anyone who interfered with the orderly conscription of soldiers. The charges were dismissed when the judge saw how young and harmless they looked. In fact they were almost thirty and far from harmless. Still, Randolph and Owen were drafted, with Owen called up immediately and stationed at a camp in the South, where he remained for the rest of the war, but Randolph wasn't called up until the day before the armistice. The federal government did revoke the second-class postal privileges of the *Messenger*, which the U.S. attorney general called "the most able and dangerous of the Negro publications." Ironically, the *Messenger* wasn't a danger only to white warmongers. The newspaper had labeled W.E.B. Du Bois, who had continued to stand by Wilson—his articles in the *Crisis* had counseled Negroes to "close ranks," to set aside their grievances about racism and stand united with the rest of the country in the battle for civilization—a hypocrite, a sellout, and a race traitor. The newspaper lashed out at "handkerchief-head, hat-in-hand, sycophant, lick-spittling Negroes" such as Fred Moore and Charles Anderson. They even published a mean-spirited drawing that showed "The New Crowd Negro Making America Safe for Himself."

Du Bois stayed his own course, which continued to change. After working to help pass New York State's female suffrage bill, Du Bois toured postwar France on a fact-finding mission for the NAACP and was disturbed by what he saw, especially the treatment that African-American soldiers continued to receive from their own countrymen overseas. He returned, much radicalized, to New York in April 1919 and in an editorial in the *Crisis* wrote the fateful words: "We return from fighting. We return fighting." The next month the magazine, whose circulation was topping a hundred thousand, featured a Du Bois editorial that read: "Make way for Democracy! We saved it in France, and by the Great Jehovah, we will save it in the United States of America, or know the reason why."

*   *   *

As much as Du Bois was determined to lead Harlem and all of black America into a different future, it was yet another countryman of Marcus Garvey, and a poet at that, who fired the first shot. Claude McKay was born in 1889 in Jamaica and got a good education before joining the Jamaican police force. He published two volumes of dialect verse that celebrated the experiences of the Jamaican peasant classes. Then in 1912 Booker T. Washington invited him to Tuskegee to study agronomy. Once in the United States, McKay's naive fantasy of life in the land of opportunity met the horrifying realities of Jim Crow. He read Du Bois's *Souls of Black Folk,* which shook him "like an earthquake," McKay later recalled, and moved in 1914 to New York City, where he worked as a porter, stoker, bartender, and waiter. He even started his own restaurant before moving, around 1917, from black bohemia in the Tenderloin to a lodging house on West 131st Street, and he was soon well known at local clubs and cabarets like Leroy's. "Harlem was my first positive reaction to American life," he recalled. "It was like entering a paradise of my own people." McKay moved to Harlem just as he began rejecting dialect poetry in favor of verse in standard English and using strict, traditional poetic structures, which makes it ironic—or racist—that his writing found its way into downtown, left-wing magazines that focused on experimental literature. McKay was also approached by Harlem's movers and shakers. He found Du Bois too cold and formal but he hit it off with James Weldon Johnson. Harlem's black Reds, especially Hubert Harrison, welcomed him unreservedly, especially after July of 1919 when, working as a waiter on the Pennsylvania Railroad, McKay published his poem "If We Must Die" in a downtown left-wing magazine called the *Liberator.* The poem was a response to yet another nationwide outbreak of racial violence, called "Red Summer," in which riots in thirty cities resulted in seventy-seven lynchings, including the murder of ten black veterans of World War I, some of whom were strung up in their uniforms. Like the Silent Protest Parade, "If We Must Die" temporarily unified Harlem's squabbling factions. The reaction elsewhere was less enthusiastic, and the poem was read into the *Congressional Record* as evidence of a trend among African-Americans toward subversion.

Red Summer galvanized Harlem. Du Bois realized he had been wrong to think that blacks should close ranks with the rest of the country to support the war. His conflicts with the mainstream race organizations grew until he quit the NAACP, disillusioned by its seeming lack of accomplishment, though he did stay on at the *Crisis*. The events of the summer of 1919 had a different effect on A. Philip Randolph, who had overcome his distaste for Garvey, joining the International League of Darker Peoples and helping to plan a UNIA meeting of five thousand people at the Palace Casino. Randolph even got the backing of Garvey to represent the UNIA at Versailles, but the U.S. State Department refused to issue him a passport. Eventually, though, Randolph grew disgusted with Garvey's obsessive focus on race. His affair with socialism didn't last either. The Russian revolution was celebrated by the *Messenger,* and interest in socialism was peaking in Harlem. The election of November 1917, when New York's socialists put one city judge, seven aldermen, and ten state assemblymen into office, had inspired a mass celebration at "Trotsky Square," as the corner of Fifth Avenue and 110th Street was known. But Red Summer challenged the viability of radical labor politics. Randolph ran for New York State comptroller in 1920 on a ticket crowded with uptown socialists, but they all lost, and Randolph began moving toward more conventional left-wing politics, just as Richard Moore and Cyril Briggs were going over to the communists. Even longtime Republicans like James Weldon Johnson saw a future for Democrats, at least the anti-Tammany kind, in Harlem.

In less than two decades, Harlem had been transformed from a Jewish and Italian neighborhood with pockets of blacks living near the Harlem and Hudson rivers to the navel of the black universe; the black population had risen from four thousand in 1905 and fifteen thousand in 1915 to eighty-four thousand in 1920. A critical mass of newly arrived black writers, artists, and intellectuals were now out to change themselves and their world, and the rest of the world, too. They resurrected from the cold ashes of Red Summer a hot, syncopated way of life that seemed less appropriate to an American ghetto than to one of Paris's arrondissements—the whorehouses, gambling dens, and speakeasies of the Prohibition era were making Harlem synonymous around the world with racial, sexual, and artistic freedom. The New Negro was growing up.

8

"THE KINGDOM OF CULTURE"

Harlem's Renaissance Comes of Age

On October 14, 1919, a Harlemite named George Tyler burst into the Universal Negro Improvement Society offices at 56 West 135th Street and overpowered Marcus Garvey's secretary. Shouting that the UNIA owed him $25, Tyler pulled a pistol and shot Garvey. The Harlem Renaissance might have died then and there had Tyler's aim been better, but Garvey was only slightly injured. Bleeding from his leg and forehead, he helped police pursue Tyler in a madcap chase through Harlem. Garvey, whose moment had arrived two and a half months earlier, when he began holding nightly meetings of the Universal Negro Improvement Society at Liberty Hall—a squat, dilapidated basement with room for six thousand at 114 West 138th Street—portrayed the assassination attempt in portentous terms. His survival was proof of his divine mission, he claimed, as was the fact that the assailant, who had supposedly been hired by the U.S. district attorney at the behest of the UNIA's enemies, killed himself while awaiting trial. Given what we now know about the scale of public and private efforts to bring down Garvey, the accusations don't seem so preposterous. Then again, maybe Garvey planned it all himself.

Historians may argue about when the New Negro movement became the Harlem Renaissance, but they all agree that by the end of World War I something new was happening uptown, and it wasn't just Prohibition, which was an economic godsend, at least in the short run. The seeds of political and economic change that Garvey, Booker T. Washington, W.E.B. Du Bois, A. Philip Randolph, and so many others had sown were resulting in a cultural harvest that would include the poems of Langston Hughes, the songs of Duke Ellington, the vocal recitals of Paul Robeson, the films of Oscar Micheaux, and the photographs of James Van Der Zee. However dire economic conditions might have been in the tenements along the side streets, Harlem was becoming the "joy spot of America," according to *Billboard* magazine. The godfather of the New Negro movement, Alain Locke, boasted that Seventh Avenue was home to "more style, life, variety and novelty than can be observed in any single length of thorofare in the country." All of the strutting and striving, Locke announced, was the "renewed race spirit" at work, a joyful reinvestment in an ancient, African inheritance that suddenly seemed both totally modern and absolutely American.

The name "Harlem Renaissance" was slow to come into common usage, perhaps because uptown Manhattan took such a long time to become the mecca of the New Negro. The weeklong celebration— the *Times* noted that "they don't do things by halves in Harlem"— marking the extension of West 125th Street to the Hudson River in late 1920 was all but closed to uptown's blacks. For years to come, Negroes were denied service as customers on 125th Street, and kept out of stores by Irish bouncers. It wasn't until the mid-1920s that black Harlem reached the once fancy neighborhoods above West 145th Street and below West 125th Street. Even then, most of the African-Americans, some newly arrived from the American South or the West Indies, some uptowners for generations, who occupied those brownstone blocks were anything but rich. Long before the stock market crash, black Harlem had become a community in crisis, leading the nation in poverty, crime, overcrowding, unemployment, juvenile delinquency, malnutrition, and infant and maternal mortality. Such conditions provoked a variety of impassioned political responses. A new generation of leaders was out every day on the stepladders and editorial pages, but their struggle with the ironies and contradictions of being men and women who happened to be black often descended into crude, essentialist thinking about race. How could the questions posed by the integrationist *Crisis,* the secular bible of black America, or by mainstream figures such as the forbidding Adam Clayton Powell, whipsawed by the competing demands of economic advance and moral uplift, compare with Garvey's bold answers and boisterous parades? Many Harlemites believed that culture could redeem conditions, but in practice this meant white slummers prowling the neighborhood's hundreds of nightclubs—many of them closed to blacks—looking for gin and genius, as Hubert Harrison put it. White publishers haunting rent parties looking for New Negro authors were more earnest, but the man and woman on the street were working too hard to pay much attention to the latest developments in black literary modernism. They did make the time for the stage shows that came to Harlem's theaters, where performers were still wrestling with the distressingly fertile conventions of blackface minstrelsy that had ruled black culture in America for generations. Even as Albert Einstein came to Morningside Heights in 1921 to announce that time was the fourth dimension, down in the Harlem Valley jazz musicians were turning ragtime into blues and jazz, to the joy and alarm of the culture at large. Was Harlem in the 1920s a "foretaste of paradise," as the novelist Arna Bontemps put it, or was it what Claude McKay called a "cultured hell"? Perhaps it was both.

The popular image of Harlem in the Jazz Age is that of a racial Eden. The truth was very different. In 1920 fewer than 6 percent of black males in New York City worked as professionals, and even then opportunities were restricted, with black doctors, lawyers, and dentists limited to uptown work. Race ruled even there. It was only in 1920 that Harlem Hospital, a dreary, substandard institution that had not long before moved from East 120th Street to 506 Lenox Avenue, hired its first black doctor, Louis T. Wright, a twenty-nine-year-old Georgia native who was awarded a Purple Heart in World War I before moving to West 138th Street and setting up a private practice. Wright began protesting the poor treatment of black patients at Harlem Hospital and agitating for an end to racist hiring policies. It wasn't until 1923 that the first black nurses were hired. Three years later May Edward Chinn, who came from Massachusetts to Harlem at the age of twenty-one and accompanied Paul Robeson on piano to help pay tuition at Columbia University, became Harlem Hospital's first black female intern. By then Wright had organized Harlem's first black hospital, the Edgecombe Sanatorium, though his signal achievement may have been his daughter, Barbara, who became a surgeon at Harlem Hospital, where she pioneered the use of antibiotics, and chaired the NAACP.

W.E.B. Du Bois believed that "Talented Tenthers" like the Wrights would lead all of Negro America into a better future. But the divide between the tiny black upper class and the enormous black working class seemed just as insurmountable as the "color line" that Du Bois so accurately identified as the key problem of the era. Labor demand remained strong in New York City after World War I because of a roaring economy and continuing restrictions on "nonwhite" immigration, but Harlemites didn't fully share in the boom, typically finding work only at the lowest rungs of the economy. Getting a job as a postal clerk, Pullman porter, or elevator operator was a stroke of fortune. White employers refused to hire blacks for any jobs that involved customer service. Meanwhile, difficulty in securing business loans and finding landlords who would rent commercial space to Negroes meant that Harlem's Colored Merchants Association counted only seventeen affiliated stores by the end of the decade. This was not a matter of simple antiblack sentiment, however, since American-born blacks were considered by employers, black and white, to be less desirable as employees than West Indians. Job ads often specified "West Indian preferred," which made for tensions among blacks, who already had plenty of problems with their Irish, Italian, and Jewish neighbors.

A more complex set of rules governed relations between blacks and Puerto Ricans, who were mostly white and Catholic but often less than welcome at Catholic churches. Stickball games at Young Devil's Field, on East 115th Street between Madison and Park avenues, saw the Irish and Italians for once on the same team when they faced the "Spanish," as the Puerto Ricans were called. Encounters between these groups weren't always so civilized. In the summer of 1926 police got a tip that a group of Puerto Rican teenagers was planning to invade Lenox Avenue and West 115th Street as a defensive measure against harassment. Sure enough, on the evening of July 26, two dozen Puerto Rican youths armed with big sticks showed up on Lenox Avenue in parade formation. The police scattered the group and all but three sixteen-year-olds escaped. Retaliation wasn't long in coming. Two days later, an armed West Harlem mob, apparently Negro and Irish thugs hired by Jewish merchants, descended on Puerto Rican East Harlem, resulting in fifty injuries. The new racial realities predicted by the prophets of the uptown renaissance weren't going to be much of an improvement on the old ones, it seemed.

The Great Migration generation had come from the American South, the West Indies, and the Spanish-speaking Caribbean to take advantage of Harlem's modern housing stock, wide and pleasant boulevards, plentiful parks, and better schools, not to mention improved economic conditions. Both Adam Clayton Powell of the Abyssinian Baptist Church and W. W. Brown of the Metropolitan Baptist Church made "Buy Property" a central theme of their sermons, a strategy drawn straight from the gospel of Booker T. Washington. But racial segregation in the housing market still stood in the way. Striver's Row, which had gotten off to a poor start back in 1893, when the slowdown in the housing market caught the developers with only 9 of 149 units filled, and forced the sale of the rest of the complex at bargain prices, but only to whites, was desegregated only after the end of World War I, attracting the likes of the singer Ethel Waters, the architect Vertner Tandy, the boxer Harry "The Black Panther" Wills, and the alderman Charles H. Roberts. But Striver's Row was also home to Harlemites who "strived like hell to pay the rent and taxes," in the words of James P. Johnson. Astor Row, as West 130th Street between Lenox and Fifth avenues was known, was desegregated around the same time, but it was limited to the tiny Negro aristocracy. As the black belt spread north of West 145th Street, west of Seventh Avenue, east of Fifth Avenue, and south of 125th Street, more and more buildings bore signs that read "Just Opened for Colored." All too often, that meant "Only for Colored," which white residents interpreted as "run for your lives."

But even after the Harlem Renaissance had arrived, blacks were still barred from buildings in Sugar Hill—the neighborhood overlooking the Harlem Valley, including the old Harlem Heights (now called Hamilton Heights) and Washington Heights (which then referred to everything north of West 145th Street)—with their uniformed doormen, expensive mahogany fixtures, modern plumbing, and electric refrigerators.

One of the few classy uptown addresses open to moneyed black strivers was the brand-new Paul Laurence Dunbar complex, the earliest experiment in planned social housing uptown. Located between Seventh Avenue and Eighth Avenue, along West 149th and West 150th streets, this cooperative complex consisted of six six-story buildings built in 1926 by John D. Rockefeller and included a day-care center and Harlem's first and only black bank—this at a time when Chicago had several black financial institutions. The Dunbar complex, which refused to accept members of "the sporting fraternity, daughters of joy, [or] the criminal elements," quickly sold out, but the Dunbar apartments were an exception. As a result of continuing racial restrictions, most blacks packed themselves into squalid tenements or fast-deteriorating single-family row houses subdivided into a dozen or more apartments. On many blocks, stoops were removed from row houses to make room for churches, barbershops, beauty parlors, offices, and funeral homes. As early as 1920 the New York *Herald and Sun* was complaining that "among these people the limit has been reached— both as to their financial ability to pay and as to the number of people that may be packed into a given space." Five years later, Manhattan's population density of 223 people per acre was dwarfed by Harlem's 336 people per acre, which made it one of the most densely populated places on earth, five times as crowded as black Chicago.

New Negroes had been paying more for less when it came to housing since before the turn of the century, and during the 1920s things got even worse. The average rent for Negroes in Harlem was $56 a month, about half of their take-home pay, while whites paid about $32 per month for nicer apartments on better blocks, even as they brought home higher salaries, according to the Urban League.

The New York *Age* reported that it wasn't just white landlords but black ones as well who, in a time-honored tradition, took advantage of low vacancy rates. More than one in four black families took in lodgers to meet rising rents, compared to about one in nine white families. Still, demand for housing remained so strong that Harlemites rented out their beds, floors, bathtubs, coal bins, and basements. Acquaintances working different shifts even rented a single bed together and took turns, a practice known as "hot bedding" or "hot sheeting."

Faced with such economic problems as high rents, Harlemites turned to cultural solutions, inventing a new genre of music at all-night rent parties, where tenants charged as many as a hundred revelers 10 cents to come in—25 cents or more on Thursdays, known as Kitchen Mechanics night because domestics customarily took Fridays off. Those who were serious about making money this way even printed up announcements on cards that they would leave in apartment lobbies or elevators. These invitations, which had a pride of place in Langston Hughes's collection of Harlemiana, offer priceless insights into life uptown in the 1920s.

Shake it and break it. Hang it on the
Wall, sling it out the window, and
Catch it before it falls at
A SOCIAL WHIST PARTY
Given by
Jane Doe
2 E. 133rd St. Apt. I
Saturday Evening
March 16, 1929
Music by Texas Slim   Refreshments

These gatherings, also known as struts, shouts, jumps, or parlor socials, featured fried chicken, pigs' feet, chitlins, and greens—food so delicious, the saying went, "it could make you slap your mama." Even more persuasive was the gin made in the bathtub or the quarter pints of corn liquor known as "shorties" that were on offer. Some hostesses replaced the regular lightbulbs with red ones and brought in prostitutes. But it was the music that made rent parties popular. The piano "ticklers" who had developed the style known as Harlem stride in the years before World War I at uptown clubs and cabarets now found themselves in demand in private homes, where a looser, more individualistic style emerged. The pianist Willie "The Lion" Smith, a staple of the earliest clubs of black Harlem, became the most popular of the rent party performers, even as he packed crowds into the Garden of Joy, an outdoor club located on an empty lot at Seventh Avenue near West 139th Street, and then at the recently opened Capitol Palace, a block away at 575 Lenox Avenue. The most virtuosic of the rent party pianists was James P. Johnson, who was born in New Jersey in 1891 and settled in New York in 1919, where he quickly became one of the most celebrated exponents of the uptown stride style—his piano roll recording of "The Harlem Strut" quickly became a classic. Ticklers such as Luckey Roberts, Richard "Abba-Labba" McLean, Corky Williams, Beetle Henderson, and Thad "Snowball" Wilson, who could play only in the key of B-natural, were also rent party regulars. They all started the evening with warm-up chords and arpeggios and spent the rest of the night moving through a variety of black and white tunes—"Thou Swell" by Rodgers and Hart was a favorite—showing off a roiling, pumping left hand that strummed the rhythm and an agile, darting right hand that tickled out the melody, climaxing just before sunrise with a hot rag. As day broke the music coasted into a slow drag, and revelers did the Monkey Hunch, a dance that showed how exhausted they were. Not all of the guests were black, and not all of them were even adults: it was only years later that the hosts of one party realized that the wide-eyed youth from the neighborhood sitting cross-legged by the piano had been a local named George Gershwin.

None of the rent party ticklers swung harder than Thomas "Fats" Waller, who was born in 1904 at 107 West 134th Street, which makes him one of the very first New Negroes who was also a native Harlemite. Waller's risqué musical humor made him a national star, but in the

years before World War I he was most well known for his size. At a time
when many of his neighbors weren't getting enough food, the Waller
family ate too well. Waller's bed-ridden mother, who considered her
children's extra girth a point of pride, was indulgent at meal times,
but she was otherwise protective, letting them out of the house only
to go to school or work. Waller saw another Harlem as a delivery boy
for a fancy Jewish delicatessen on 125th Street. His mother wanted
him to become a preacher, but the boy was more attracted to music,
and as soon as he was old enough he used to sneak out to shows at
the Lafayette Theatre. Eventually, the Wallers got a piano, bought by
Waller's brother, Lawrence, who served in the Harlem Hellfighters.
Waller's first professional work as a musician consisted of Saturday
afternoon concerts for schoolchildren at the Crescent Theatre. Just
across the street, the organist who accompanied films at the Lincoln
Theatre let Waller perform during intermissions, and eventually he
was hired to play the Wurlitzer there full-time. It was at the Lincoln
that Waller developed his unique musical alchemy, which turned saccharine material into art by imbuing it with the by turns cheeky and
introspective flavors of Harlem stride. Getting paid $23 a week for
it was Waller's dream come true, but it gave his mother, who reviled
jazz as "devil music," a fatal heart attack. Constantly at odds with his
increasingly religious father, Waller struck out on his own, dropping
out of high school. Only sixteen years old and still in short pants, he
studied with James P. Johnson and Willie "The Lion" Smith, even as
he mentored younger pianists.

Waller's raucous way with popular tunes of the day, in which tears
and laughter engaged in a never-ending slapstick tussle, made him a
fixture on the rent party circuit, though other pianists tempered their
admiration with envy—he was able to "cut" them in the song of their
choice in all twelve keys. He also began leading his own ensembles
and composing pop classics such as "Honeysuckle Rose," "I'm Gonna
Sit Right Down and Write Myself a Letter," "Dinah," and "The Joint
Is Jumpin'," as well as writing for nightclub revues. But Waller was
notoriously unreliable. The "Hot Man of Harlem" started the day with
two double shots, which he called "my liquid ham and eggs," and he

polished off a fifth of whiskey before gigs. His contracts stipulated a good piano and even better liquor. If by the end of the evening he was in no shape to go home, he would stay at Mother Shepherd's speakeasy and boardinghouse, at 107 West 133rd Street, or he might sneak into the Abyssinian Baptist Church to play spirituals on the organ.

Although live music was the most common form of entertainment at rent parties, the piano ticklers were being replaced by a new kind of technology called the phonograph and another kind of music called blues. The earliest examples, crude yet wise, simple in form and yet infinitely open to variation, were written by a college-educated Alabaman named W. C. Handy who was based in Memphis. During his travels through the rural South as a minstrel show cornetist in the years after the turn of the century, Handy had been impressed by the way that amateur black musicians improvised "stop-time" breaks and flattened the third and seventh tones of the musical scale in order to produce "blue" notes. Neither technique was well known outside the deepest South, and Handy's use of both in an electioneering ditty named "Memphis Blues" attracted the attention of a black insurance executive from Georgia named Harry Pace. Handy and Pace decided to start a music publishing company, and on a business trip to New York City in 1914 they convinced Sophie Tucker to add Handy's "St. Louis Blues" to her routine. Music historians have identified it as the very first crossover success. But it wasn't until 1920, with the release of a record called "Crazy Blues," that a national craze for blues music helped the phonograph become the country's primary musical medium. The tune was written by an Alabaman named Perry Bradford who hung out at the Colored Vaudeville Benevolent Association's offices at 424 Lenox Avenue and who dreamed up the idea of recording black singers backed by black bands playing black material. Mamie Smith, a singer from Cincinnati who had been singing the tune under the name "Harlem Blues" for more than a year in Bradford's show *Maid in Harlem* at the Lincoln Theatre, recorded a version that, despite the ridiculously expensive price of $1 and suspicions among the black middle classes about the morally problematic nature of the music—being a blues musician, the saying went, was like being black twice—became a massive hit. "Crazy Blues" sold more than seventy-five thousand copies in a few weeks in Harlem alone and 1.5 million nationwide within a few months, inaugurating a new era in American music and turning the phonograph record from a novelty into an industry.

The blues craze of the early 1920s was dominated by white-owned record labels, but there was plenty of room for Negroes with initiative, starting with none other than Harry Pace, who formed a recording label called Black Swan in the basement of his Striver's Row home. He set the tone for the company, which was not at first a blues and jazz label but a "cultural" endeavor featuring largely classical recordings. With the backing of W.E.B. Du Bois and John Nail, Pace was able to hire the classical composer William Grant Still as house arranger. Lester Walton, who had been a member of the Frogs, the manager of the Lafayette Theatre, and the drama critic for the New York *Age,* became business manager. In its first year Black Swan sold $100,000 worth of records through the mail and in variety shops, dry goods merchants, and furniture stores, enough to move the company into proper quarters at 2289 Seventh Avenue.

Pace was an excellent talent scout. He regretted rejecting Bessie Smith as "too nitty gritty," but he did sign Ethel Waters, whose earthy versions of "Down Home Blues" and "Oh, Daddy" sold five hundred thousand copies in six months, and he made stars out of Alberta Hunter, Lucille Hegamin, and Trixie Smith. The blues soon replaced rags, parlor songs, marches, and waltzes on American phonographs—"jazz" was at this point less a musical genre than a lifestyle—and *Metronome* magazine observed that "every phonograph company has a colored girl recording." The light-skinned Pace, accused of passing for white for business reasons, had a complicated notion of racial uplift. Black Swan advertised itself as a "race music" label, with Pace trumpeting: "All other colored records are by artists only passing for colored," and "Every Singer and Musician Used in All Our Records Is Colored." The truth is that he more than once recorded white singers and marketed them as black. Nor was he above a lowest-common-denominator approach to material. In 1921 Mamie Smith recorded a naughty number called "Mama Whip! Mama Spank! (If Her Daddy Don't Come Home)." Was

Pace a race traitor or was he, like Philip Payton, a businessman whose notion of racial uplift happened to be profitable?

Black Swan was only one of many recording companies, black and white, to turn a generation of blues divas into national celebrities, but there was one singer who got away. The most beloved entertainer in Harlem during its glory years was not a down-and-dirty blues queen but a diminutive, spritely pop princess named Florence Mills. Born in 1895 in Washington, D.C., Mills performed in her hometown starting as a young child under the stage name Baby Florence. She didn't make it uptown until 1921 when she joined a show called *Shuffle Along*, which was the first black show on segregated Broadway in more than a decade. The production was a big step forward for everyone involved, especially the composers Noble Sissle and Eubie Blake, and the librettists Flournoy Miller and Aubrey Lyles, but it made the career of Mills, who stunned and delighted audiences with her renditions of "I'm Just Wild About Harry" and "Love Will Find a Way." Still, some New Negroes had their doubts about this turning point in the Harlem Renaissance. The New York *Age*'s Theophilus Lewis called the show "trash" because of its embrace of many of the cruder conventions of blackface minstrelsy.

Mills didn't have the best voice or the best moves. Rather, the devotion she inspired was due to her loyalty to her core audience—she turned down a lucrative offer from Ziegfeld's Follies in order to stay in the black theater. She was uptown's everywoman, a down-to-earth star who greeted her neighbors on West 135th Street by name and rode the subway. After *Shuffle Along* she had her pick of work, starring in Harlem shows that made it to Broadway, such as *Plantation Revue, Dover Street to Dixie, From Dixie to Broadway.* She took the leading role in *Blackbirds of 1926,* which ran for six weeks at the newly opened, racially segregated Alhambra Theatre, at Seventh Avenue and West 126th Street—it had previously been the Keith Vaudeville House—before moving to London, where the prince of Wales was so impressed that he saw the show two dozen times. When Mills returned to the United States in September of 1927 thousands of fans showed up to greet her, but just a few weeks later she was rushed to the hospital, where she died at the age of thirty-two of the side effects of appendicitis, never having made a record or a film. Harlem gave Mills an extravagant sendoff, with nine thousand people coming to the viewing at Howell's Mortuary and well over one hundred thousand watching the funeral procession. Another three thousand people crowded the service at Mother Zion AME Church before a plane released a flock of blackbirds above Seventh Avenue in memory of her song "I'm a Little Blackbird Looking for a Bluebird." Not since the death of James Reese Europe had Harlem mourned one of its own so deeply, but tastes were changing, and they didn't take long to find another favorite.

The only veteran of *Shuffle Along* to challenge Mills in talent, popularity, and critical acclaim was Paul Robeson, born in segregated Princeton, New Jersey, in 1898, the son of a North Carolina slave who escaped at the age of fifteen to serve in the Union army in the Civil War before becoming a preacher. Robeson distinguished himself both in the classroom and on the playing field, in addition to being a prize-winning public speaker who as a boy filled in for his father in church. Teammates at Rutgers University broke Robeson's nose on the first day of football, while opposing squads—they often met at the Polo Grounds, one of uptown's few unsegregated recreational facilities— targeted him for special brutality. Despite the demands of playing semiprofessional basketball at Harlem's Manhattan Casino, singing solo recitals—"I only have an octave," he joked, "but it's the right octave"—and working as a porter at Grand Central Station, Robeson graduated as valedictorian in 1919. After watching the combustive passions of the Harlem Hellfighters parade being doused by news of Red Summer, he became determined to do something for the race. He starred in the groundbreaking production of the white dramatist Ridgely Torrence's play *Simon the Cyrenian* at the Harlem YMCA, which had only recently relocated from midtown's black bohemia to West 135th Street, before starting law school. He earned tuition money by coaching and playing football, singing, tutoring Latin, and working at the post office. He also spent some time at a white law firm but he quit because his secretary refused to work with a Negro. Robeson somehow found time to enjoy Harlem to the fullest, often in the company of the novelist and doctor Rudolph Fisher. Along with days in the law library and nights on the town, the tireless Robeson played in a number of groundbreaking shows, including *Shuffle Along,* before graduating from Columbia Law School in 1923. But he gave up a career as an attorney to star in the Provincetown Players' versions of two Eugene O'Neill plays. The first was a revival of *The Emperor Jones,* the story of a Harlem pullman porter who escapes jail in the United States to set himself up as a Caribbean dictator. The role originally belonged to Charles Gilpin, a Virginian who came to New York before World War I and worked as an elevator operator rather than stoop to blackface minstrelsy. When he heard that O'Neill wanted to use a Negro instead of a white actor in blackface in *The Emperor Jones,* Gilpin brought his elevator to the first floor and walked away. His performance won him fame and honor, but he was unable to accept an award from the Drama League of New York because the event was whites-only, one of many humiliations that turned Gilpin to drink. Gilpin's uncompromising racial attitudes also worked against him. He objected to O'Neill's advice to his Negro actors to "Be yourselves!" and, when O'Neill decided against Gilpin for the new version of *The Emperor Jones* three years later, America's most distinguished black actor went back to working as an elevator operator. Of course, it was not just Gilpin's intransigence but Robeson's onstage incandescence that convinced O'Neill to choose him for the new version of *The Emperor Jones,* as well as for his latest drama, a tragic race romance called *All God's Chillun Got Wings.*

Robeson soon became one of the most popular figures uptown, with so many admirers that it took the "Black Colossus" an entire afternoon to walk down Seventh Avenue from West 143rd Street to West 133rd Street. After dark, Robeson partied with downtown whites such as Eugene O'Neill, Sherwood Anderson, Louise Brooks, and Alfred Knopf, as well as with Harlem royalty including James Weldon Johnson and Roland Hayes. He even escorted the Dahomeyan prince Kojo Touvalou Houenou on a tour of the Negro Mecca. One typical summer night in 1925 Robeson led his companions on a drinking binge that started at his home on West 127th Street and then moved

to dinner at Craig's restaurant, a show at the Lincoln Theatre, back
to West 127th Street for more drinks, a show at the Lafayette, music
and dancing at Smalls Paradise, a visit to the Vaudeville Club, and
then back home again. But Robeson remained an artist above all. He
studied spirituals with the singer Harry Burleigh, who had helped
elevate "sorrow songs," as Du Bois called them, from crude folk material only a notch above the blues to the level of art songs, and he
began performing all-spirituals concerts. Although not particularly
religious, Robeson had been raised in the church, so the raw emotional-
ity of Robeson's performances of "Go Down, Moses," "Joshua Fit the
Battle of Jericho," and "Steal Away" wasn't an act. Harlem had become
even more segregated since World War I, especially when it came to
nightlife. Even Robeson wasn't allowed into many restaurants, clubs,
and theaters. He was also increasingly unable to find good roles. He
turned down the lead in at least one Broadway show that would have
required him to black up. So Robeson got into the movies, accepting
the unheard-of sum of $100,000 to appear in *Body and Soul,* by the black
filmmaker Oscar Micheaux, a South Dakota rancher turned novelist
who had moved to Harlem and made a name for himself by making
the very first all-black, full-length feature film.

While New Negroes were turning their blues into *the* blues, Harlem's
Latinos Nuevos were creating their own cultural renaissance. "South
of the Border" flavors had permeated American popular music since
the nineteenth century. W. C. Handy, who had performed with local
musicians in Cuba as early as 1900, inserted a full-blown *habanera* into
his landmark 1917 composition "St. Louis Blues," James Reese Europe
recorded a song called "Darky Tango," and there wasn't a major big
band or uptown show that didn't use Latino musicians. But what the
pianist Jelly Roll Morton called "the Latin tinge" was little more than
a fad, hence the tango and rumba lessons, contests, teas, picnics, and
balls that took place at venues like the Palace Casino and the Manhattan Casino. That didn't start to change until 1917, when the Puerto
Rican singer María Teresa Vera played the old Apollo Theater. The

Club Cívico Puertorriqueno had a dance hall and a house band to play in it on East 125th Street as early as 1923, but more often social clubs simply rented facilities like the vast Park Palace and the more intimate Park Plaza, two clubs in the same building at the corner of West 110th Street and Fifth Avenue. But Harlemites couldn't hear authentic Latin music regularly until 1926, when the old Apollo, which could no longer attract Jewish audiences to see vaudeville, began featuring music from Mexico, Puerto Rico, and Cuba on Sunday nights. Soon East Harlemites could frequent the Golden Casino, the Toreador, the Kubanacan, the Teatro Triboro, the Star Casino, the San José, and the Mount Morris Theatre, at Fifth Avenue and West 116th Street, also known as the Campoamor, after the Havana theater of the same name. These venues offered not just concerts and dances but a rich variety of Spanish-language film, serious drama, vaudeville, and benefits. Puerto Ricans dominated these events, although Cubans, Mexicans, and Dominicans were also part of the mix. As in Negro Harlem, there were usually a handful of slummers as well. Ethnic and national tensions erupted from time to time, especially when Cuban bands faced off against those from Puerto Rico. But as far as the music was concerned, the racial caste system that operated west of Fifth Avenue and downtown, where many functions involving Latin music were *"para raza blanca,"* was unheard of in East Harlem, which soon boasted its own constellation of star performers. At the same time, black jazz musicians continued to raid the Latin music repertoire, performing tunes like Moises Simons's "El Manicero" or "The Peanut Vendor" after the song became a hit for a Cuban named Don Azpiazu and his Havana Casino Orchestra.

The first bona fide uptown Latin music icon was Manuel "Canario" Jiménez, who came to East Harlem in 1914 and joined the Merchant Marines, where he got his nickname for singing as beautifully as a canary. Canario was to the East Harlem *plena* as W. C. Handy was to the blues: not the inventor but the popularizer. Like the blues, the *plena* was a tightly structured, African-derived musical form that could be endlessly adapted, resulting in romantic songs such as "Cuando Las Mujeres Quieren a los Hombres" ("When Women Love Men") and the current-events tune "La Prohibición Nos Tiene" ("Prohibition's Got Us"). It was particularly well suited to the subject of immigrant dislocation, and *plenas* like "Los Misterios de Lenox" ("The Mysteries of Lenox Avenue") and "En la Ciento Diez y Seis" ("On 116th Street") confronted the joys and sorrows of Puerto Ricans uptown.

The blues would never have become popular had it not been for the sound businessmen like instincts of W. C. Handy and Harry Pace, and the same was true for Latin music. A white Puerto Rican dentist named Julio Roqué, who excelled as a pianist and violinist in addition to conducting, composing, and arranging, used his office as a booking agency for his own groups, and others as well, and he often worked on the teeth of musicians for free. Roqué even started the "Revista Roqué," the first Spanish-language radio program in New York, which featured Roqué's own recordings on the Victor label, as well as guests from Cuba, Puerto Rico, Mexico, and of course El Barrio in between advertisements for Roqué's own brand of toothpaste and mouthwash.

Commerce and art also went hand in hand in the combined music and grocery store on Madison Avenue near East 115th Street run by two black Puerto Rican siblings named Victoria and Rafael Hernández. A veteran of James Reese Europe's Harlem Hellfighters, Rafael took care of the music while Victoria took care of the money—she was known by her friends as La Madrina ("The Godmother") and by her enemies as La Judía ("The Jewess"), the latter a term of derision, not necessarily an indication that she was Jewish. Either way, she made her brother a star by convincing him to give up the faux-Latin stage costumes for proper American suits. As in the Negro Mecca, the search for an authentic identity required a fearless experimentation in combination with centuries-old traditions. But Harlemites, whatever their skin color or language, didn't live by culture alone.

The quest for dignity being pursued by Negro and Latino entertainers in the 1920s seemed quixotic at a time when living conditions in Harlem were already bad and deteriorating rapidly. An exploding population and no new housing construction meant ever stronger demand, which gave landlords small incentive to maintain buildings properly. This created conditions that ranged from deplorable to dangerous. One city commission found that most uptown housing was unfit even for animals. This wasn't only a problem in Negro and Latino Harlem, but in the remaining Italian and Jewish neighborhoods as well. Tuberculosis rates in black neighborhoods, already twice that of white areas at the end of World War I, doubled during the 1920s, while epidemics of poliomyelitis and influenza proved too much for Italian casket makers to handle. The five-piece band and painted backdrop of a pastoral scene that immigrants favored at funerals ceased to become the rule, since most funeral homes had only one of each.

The irrelevance of mainstream politics in the face of these kinds of realities was one reason that Marcus Garvey attracted so many followers. It wasn't only "chronic Republicanism" but gerrymandering that kept blacks from dominating any single district. That didn't mean politicians were totally ineffective. Uptown's most beloved public servant was neither black nor a Harlemite. The Republican Jimmy Walker, known as the jazz mayor because he frequented speakeasies with a Ziegfeld girl on his arm, won uptown easily in both 1925 and 1929 and returned the favor by acting decisively on racial issues such as the desegregation of Harlem Hospital. Another favorite was Abraham Grenthal, a Jewish Republican state legislator who out-Tammanied Tammany Hall, working for more playgrounds and bathhouses, better housing conditions, and restrictions on rent increases. Despite his popularity, Grenthal was opposed by the New York *Age*'s Fred Moore, who helped Grenthal's black rival for the assembly seat, Charles W. Fillmore—a New York State tax auditor and yet another veteran of the Harlem Hellfighters—unseat Grenthal in an election that saw Moore become one of Harlem's aldermen.

The rise of the movement known as "Black Tammany" promised change, especially in the form of the United Colored Democracy, the Negro wing of the Democratic Party, which flourished under the leadership of Ferdinand Q. Morton. After becoming Civil Service Commission chairman in 1922—payback for years of delivering votes—Morton exercised real power, helping put an end to years of blacks being frozen out of jobs as firemen or policemen or as anything beyond menial laborers at public agencies. Harlemites paid a price for the success of Morton, who ran Democratic Harlem like a fiefdom, controlling patronage and determining who ran for office. He demanded that suitors for a place on the Democratic ticket kick back 10 percent of their earnings. As if that weren't enough power, he also bought the New York *Age*.

Latino politics was slower to develop across town, where political clubs based on national origin impeded East Harlemites from speaking with a single voice. It wasn't until late July 1926, when Harlem's Jews, Irish, and blacks joined forces against the "invasion" of what the *New York Times* called a "Porto Rican army," that uptown's Latinos came together for the first time as a community. Led by the Porto Rican Brotherhood of New York, they complained to the police commissioner about frequent assaults by blacks and called a protest meeting early the next month at the Harlem Casino to discuss the situation. The idea was not simply to respond to the recent crisis but to work on more fundamental problems, including the lack of a Puerto Rican community center uptown. This self-defining moment promised to become the Latino equivalent of the Silent Protest Parade. But the overtures these groups made to black, Jewish, and Italian Harlemites were mostly futile, and they realized that change would come only from within. Whereas outsiders had been lumping together all Spanish-speakers as "Spanish" (hence the misleading and, to some, insulting term "Spanish Harlem") East Harlem now became known as El Barrio, or "the Neighborhood." The political unity of Latinos was easily accomplished, at least in comparison to the situation in Negro Harlem, as the coming together of Spanish-speakers uptown was made all the easier because most Latinos reflexively supported Democrats and rejected socialism and nationalism. It wasn't a matter of ideological affinity. This was after all the same party that split up Harlem into four assembly districts with the goal of dividing Jewish, black, Italian, and Latino votes. Rather they supported Tammany Hall because, despite the growing Republican presence, that's where the political power in New York City was. Tammany Hall could count on votes in El Barrio without offering much in return.

Another result of the events of 1926 was the founding of El Barrio's first newspaper by a group of writers, theater workers, and *tabaqueros*. The slogan of *El Gráfico,* which was Semanario Defensor de la Raza Hispana, or "Defender of the Hispanic Race," neatly captured how ideologically portable the Garveyesque investment in race could be in the 1920s. The leading figure behind *El Gráfico,* the actor and writer Alberto O'Farrill, couldn't avoid being inspired by the UNIA, up to a point. Born in 1899 in Cuba, he arrived in East Harlem in the early 1920s. He spent much of the decade onstage, where he specialized in "negrito" (Spanish-language blackface), comic musical sketches, and operetta. When it came to journalism, O'Farrill could be deadly serious, and *El Gráfico* offered an uncompromising pan-Hispanic vision that included not just news and editorials critical of United States policy in Puerto Rico but fiction, advice columns, movie reviews, and cartoons. There was also a first-person column called "Ofa," about a black Puerto Rican immigrant adjusting to life in the Big Apple. But the kind of racial diversity that dominated El Barrio seemed incompatible with the increasingly strict racial polarization favored by both blacks and whites across town in the Negro Mecca.

While the mainstream politicians conducted business as usual, Garvey was busy getting things done, or so it seemed. "Up, you mighty race," the UNIA's slogan said. "You can accomplish what you will." Garvey willed much, but his accomplishments are still subject to dispute. After the end of World War I the UNIA grew quickly, as much because of Garvey's magnetic personality as increasing black poverty and a rising tide of racism. Still, his pronouncements on the organization's size were notoriously unreliable. He eventually claimed two million followers in thirty branch offices across the Americas, when in fact the UNIA's membership never topped twenty thousand. They paid dues of 35 cents a month in return for illness and death benefits, but few ever saw anything concrete in return. That didn't seem to matter, as long as Garvey articulated clear and direct solutions to the problems that plagued black Harlemites. This wasn't only a matter of loyalty.

Some Garveyites had fled socialism in the wake of Red Summer and were simply looking for an ideological home. Others with less radical leanings felt unrepresented by the philanthropists and academics in charge of the Urban League and the NAACP. Garvey had even attracted some conservative black Republicans who worshipped Booker T. Washington, read the New York *Age*, and responded to the common sense of Garvey's question "How can a Negro be conservative? What has he to conserve?"

Garvey started UNIA restaurants, grocery stores, laundries, a publishing house, a textile factory, a hat shop, a hotel, and a tailor. Garvey's UNIA shipping line and cruise company, the Black Star Line—contrary to popular opinion, it never focused on sending African-Americans back to Africa—was financed by selling shares at $5 each, but only to Negroes. In the depths of Red Summer the idea seemed foolish. But he was soon showing off the S.S. *Yarmouth*, a decades-old cotton and coal barge on the Hudson River at West 135th Street. In fact, the ship didn't even belong to the Black Star Line yet, which, as the New York State district attorney's office notified Garvey, constituted legal fraud. Garvey wrote off the warning as nothing more than the work of jealous enemies.

Garvey was a genius at raising money but a disaster at running things. He promised poor Harlemites that "the Black Star Line will turn over large profits and dividends to stockholders and operate to their interest even whilst they sleep." But Garvey failed to make the first payment of $6,500 on the newly rechristened S.S. *Frederick Douglass*. The maiden voyage was delayed until October 1919 when, cheered on by the UNIA band and thousands of spectators, many of whom had paid a dollar to tour the ship, the vessel made its way down the Hudson River from West 135th Street to West 23rd Street, captained by whites hired by the white owners—without insurance they couldn't put Garvey's people at the wheel. Garvey eventually solved that problem and the next month the vessel sailed to the West Indies and Central America, returning in January bearing two hundred passengers and eight hundred thousand pounds of firewood. A month later a second voyage started from Harlem bound for the West Indies, where it picked up coconuts and delivered them to New York. Garvey was suddenly the owner of what looked to become a successful business. He recapitalized the venture, bought two more boats, and began dreaming about a Black Star navy.

Garvey's broader goals were also coming into focus. He held the UNIA's first annual convention, the International Convention of Negro Peoples of the World. More than twenty-five thousand delegates from dozens of countries paraded from Harlem to the old Madison Square Garden, shouting along with Garvey as he exhorted: "One God! One Aim! One Destiny!" Although Garvey was a strict anticolonialist, he loved the trappings of Old World grandeur. He wore a gold, green, and purple gown and a feathered helmet and assumed the position of provisional president of the African Republic, despite never having even visited the continent. Garvey gave the UNIA's leadership outrageous and fanciful titles: *Negro World* contributing editor John E. Bruce was named Knight of the Nile, while others received titles such as Overlord of Uganda and Duke of the Niger. During the monthlong convention, Garvey unveiled the tricolor UNIA flag: red for blood, black for race, and green for Africa. Marcus Garvey cigars, lapel buttons, and medals, as well as stock in UNIA businesses, were all for sale.

Marcus Garvey's movement was driven by imagery—skin color, flags, uniforms, and pictures taken by the UNIA's official photographer, a Massachusetts native named James Van Der Zee who came to Harlem at the age of twenty-two in 1908. He settled at Lenox Avenue and West 138th Street and worked as an elevator operator, waiter, and violinist before opening Guarantee Photo in 1916 at 109 West 135th Street. With the help of his second wife, a white woman who passed as black, he specialized in commercial portrait photography, capturing school and church groups, social clubs, athletic teams, weddings, funerals, and families. "The Rembrandt of Harlem" also snapped Mamie Smith, Bojangles Robinson, Florence Mills, and Jack Johnson, the world heavyweight champion prizefighter who was now making a career for himself as a musician, actor, nightclub impresario, stockbroker, and lecturer. Van Der Zee's images often ended up on posters and calendars, as well as in Garvey's *Negro World,* but he considered himself an artist, and one who rebelled against the realist strain that then prevailed in photography. In contrast, Van Der Zee's work was dramatically stylized, with far-fetched poses and extensive backdrops, costumes, and makeup. In the darkroom Van Der Zee went even further, using retouching to lighten skin color or straighten hair; he called it "beautifying."

Uplifting the race clearly meant different things to different Harlemites. Even as the fame of the provisional president of Africa grew, opposition was building. At first, the radicals mostly left Garvey alone, nor did he draw much comment from the mainstream figures W.E.B. Du Bois, Charles Anderson, and Adam Clayton Powell, who even let his son march with the UNIA. Eventually, however, Harlem's Talented Tenth began to change their minds, starting with Garvey's fellow Jamaican Claude McKay, who made it respectable to remain distant from the UNIA when, in 1919, he declined to read "If We Must Die" at Liberty Hall.

Part of the opposition was due to the questionable nature of Garvey's business operations. He overpaid for ships and then mismanaged them, though he never enriched himself at the expense of stockholders or customers. Then again, the Black Star Line did buy his home at 235 West 131st Street, and it also paid the bills of UNIA businesses. The UNIA even bought Black Star Line shares. Such transactions were irregular, and in some cases illegal, but then again no Garvey enterprise kept proper records. The S.S. *Frederick Douglass* sailed to the Caribbean three times, the last time piloted by a white man, but it never exceeded seven knots and it couldn't fight even the mild currents of the Straits of Florida. One of Garvey's boats making day trips up the Hudson River, again piloted by a white captain, never made money, and it sank in late 1920. There was a deadly explosion on board another Black Star Line vessel. Nor were Garvey efforts at "Liberian Construction" successful. He raised more than $137,000 and in 1921 sent representatives to the country in West Africa in order to found a new African capital, but the delegation ran out of money. Harlemites were willing to give money to Garvey, but uprooting themselves once again in search of a better life in Africa, of all places—the actor Charles Gilpin wondered publically how he could go back to a country he'd never been to—was beyond most of them, especially after they learned that Liberia's politicians had confiscated construction materials and deported the delegation.

Garvey's commitment to race pride was impressive but skin deep. *Negro World* promoted the very first colored dolls, manufactured in Harlem in "mulatto," "light brown," and "high brown." As time went on, it became clear that Garvey's obsession with race and racial purity would never be politically viable. He started denying UNIA membership to blacks who married whites. He called Du Bois a cross-bred tool of white puppeteers. He swore that the light-skinned Cyril Briggs of the African Blood Brotherhood was only passing for black. Hubert Harrison drove the circulation of *Negro World* to more than two hundred thousand but he quit because of Garvey's mania for racial purity. A. Philip Randolph formed an anti-Garvey group called Friends of Negro Freedom, which held meetings attacking Garvey's brand of black capitalism on Sunday nights at the Lafayette Theatre, where the cruel joke that UNIA stood for "Ugliest Negroes in America" got plenty of laughs. Garvey countered his critics by appealing to a higher authority. He founded an African Orthodox Church, led by George Alexander McGuire, an Episcopalian priest from Boston who preached that God, Mary, and Jesus were all black, and that the devil was white. McGuire argued, "When Europe was inhabited by a race of cannibals, a race of savages, naked men, heathens and pagans, Africa was peopled with a race of cultured black men, who were masters in art, science, and literature."

In addition to founding a UNIA church, Garvey maintained close links to Harlem's tiny group of black Hebrews, who traced their lineage to the ancient Jewish community in Ethiopia. In Harlem they followed a professional wrestler turned rabbi—his formal religious credentials were questionable—from Lagos, Nigeria, named Wentworth Arthur Matthew. Along with Arnold Josiah Ford, a Barbados-born musician and "rabbi" who composed the UNIA anthem and served as Garvey's musical director, Matthew founded Beth B'nai Abraham Synagogue at 29 West 131st Street. The congregation followed many

traditional practices but remained unacceptable to mainstream Jewish
organizations because of its embrace of everything from Ethiopian
Orthodox Christian traditions to Garveyite racial pseudoscience to
mental telepathy. A split between Ford and Matthew resulted in the
founding of Congregation Beth Ha-Tefilah, also known as the Com-
mandment Keepers of the Living God, which bought the 1890 mansion
of John Dwight, the heir to the Arm and Hammer baking soda fortune,
at 1 West 123rd Street. Within a few years the movement had grown
to include nearly two thousand followers, most of them West Indian
Garveyites, in three black synagogues in Harlem, according to the
New York *Sun*. One of them, the Royal Order of Ethiopian Hebrews,
founded by elder Warren Robinson at West 128th Street and Lenox
Avenue, featured gospel-style music and lots of Yiddish before it closed
amid charges of child abuse and financial misconduct.

Garvey knew the risks of associating with such characters, but he
knew the benefits, too, and the UNIA became a platform for all manner
of extremism and eccentricity. One of the UNIA's most outrageous
figures was the Trinidadian "Gentleman Flyer," Hubert Fauntleroy
Julian, who often put an "M.D." after his name—it stood for "mechanical designer." In mid-April of 1923 Harlemites began to notice posters
announcing: "WATCH THE CLOUDS—JULIAN IS ARRIVING FROM THE SKY."
Sure enough, within a week he had donned a scarlet bodysuit and
jumped out of a plane trailing a flag that read "Hoenig's Optical Is
Open Today." He drifted down onto the roof of a nearby post office,
disappointing the Harlem funeral home that had paid for the right
to exhibit his corpse. Eventually, the man dubbed the Black Eagle by
the New York *Telegram* began thinking bigger. In 1924 he donned a
sky-blue flight suit, climbed into the cockpit of a plane called the *Abys-
sinia,* and took off from the Hudson River at West 139th Street bound
for Ethiopia. It would have been the first solo transatlantic flight had
Julian not crashed in Flushing Bay minutes after takeoff.

UNIA clowns like Hubert Julian got lots of laughs, but many
Harlemites had serious concerns about Garvey, not so much because of
his racial agenda as his opposition to the international labor socialism
that still dominated the left in Harlem. When Garvey wasn't mocking

the light skin color of the leaders and adherents of the NAACP or the African Blood Brotherhood, he was doing J. Edgar Hoover's work and calling them communists—even as he proposed nationalizing industries. The federal government, which had black operatives inside the UNIA, finally arrested Garvey in January 1922 on mail fraud charges. Then it came out that Garvey, who had long bragged of his status as "a full-blooded black man" of "pure African" stock, and who banned anyone of mixed race from holding office, had traveled to Atlanta and met secretly with the KKK in order to gain the Klan's support for a Back to Africa movement. Harlem's establishment exploded in anger. Du Bois wrote in the *Crisis* that Garvey was "the most dangerous enemy of the Negro race in America and the world" and that he was "either a lunatic or a traitor." A. Philip Randolph, who held mass meetings demanding that the United States deport Garvey, wasn't wholly surprised when he opened a package in the mail and found a human hand with a note ordering the *Messenger* to back off on its criticism of Garvey. Such tactics led a group of race leaders, including Robert Bagnall of the NAACP, John E. Nail, Chandler Owen, and Harry Pace, to ask the United States attorney general's office, which had long labored to silence the *Messenger,* to "completely disband and extirpate this vicious movement." Garvey struck back with his favorite weapon, calling the group, which purposely did not include Du Bois or Randolph, "nearly all Octoroons and Quadroons." Eventually Garvey was indicted and brought to trial, where he fired his lawyer and took charge of his own defense. The proceedings at times resembled a legal circus, until Garvey was convicted, fined $1,000, and sentenced to five years in prison. There was time for one last speech to followers. "My work is just begun," Garvey told the crowd at Liberty Hall. Out on bail pending an appeal, he tried to stave off disaster by hiring as *Negro World*'s new assistant managing editor the legendary T. Thomas Fortune, by then a much diminished figure, weakened by decades of alcoholism and constant changes in political allegiance. Garvey started a new shipping line but the government blocked the deal. He even made overtures toward Tammany Hall, but seeing Garvey genuflecting before white Democrats was too much for many UNIA supporters, who abandoned the movement in droves, especially after Garvey was convicted on new tax evasion and perjury charges. Nonetheless, a popular song from 1924 has a West Indian New Yorker fantasizing about returning to the islands and planning a Garvey-inspired comeback.

Done give up de bestest job
A'runnin' elevator
I told my boss "Mon" I'd be back
Sometime sooner or later.

When I git back to this great land
You better watch me Harvey
'Cause I'm gonna be a great big "Mon"
Like my frien' Marcus Garvey.

With core support like that, Garvey was undeterred, insisting that his work, like that of Jesus Christ himself, wasn't yet finished. "Look for me in the whirlwind," he wrote. Had the barely literate Garvey read his Bible more closely, he might have refrained from quoting such a self-incriminating passage from the prophet Hosea, the full version of which warns: "They sow the wind and shall reap the whirlwind." With Garvey out of the way, the political interests that had joined to attack him broke apart. W. A. Domingo, appalled by the anti–West Indian rhetoric of the *Messenger* during the first Garvey trial, kept his distance from A. Philip Randolph, as did James Weldon Johnson and the NAACP, which was as always leery of anything that smacked of radical labor. Even Chandler Owen, who became a bitter opponent of the socialists after his brother was denied admission to one of New York's all-white socialist unions, gave up on Randolph. But new coalitions were in the making. Randolph, an ideologically agile survivor, started inviting a variety of race radicals and left-wingers to his house on West 142nd Street for Sunday morning brunch and conversation. Among the new faces was a young socialist from Rhode Island, George Schuyler, who was soon doing everything at the *Messenger* from editing copy to mopping the floor of the newspaper's two messy rooms at 2305 Seventh Avenue.

Randolph needed all the help he could get when he was asked in 1925 to help organize workers at the Pullman Company, the country's biggest private employer of blacks. Jobs as Pullman porters were at the time very desirable, ranking just below doctors, engineers, and lawyers in the black economy. It was steady work, and even though employees had to provide their own uniforms, tools, supplies, and food, porters were relatively well compensated, earning about $70 a month. Randolph worried about fixing something that wasn't broken, but after five hundred porters turned up to an organizing meeting at the Elks Imperial Lodge #127 on West 129th Street, he knew that the numbers were on the side of the Brotherhood of Sleeping Car Porters. Ironically, it wasn't the antiunion intransigence of the Pullman Company—which had broken many unionization efforts, harassed and fired brotherhood members, and portrayed Randolph as a traitorous bolshevik while presenting itself as a blessing to the race—that made the struggle so difficult but the intense racism of the labor movement as a whole. Most unions still refused membership to blacks. Labor organizations that did accept them, including the American Federation of Labor, did so only in principle, not in practice. Nor could Randolph always count on local support. The Abyssinian Baptist Church, Salem Methodist Church, and St. James Presbyterian all stood behind him, but uptown preachers regularly gave over their pulpits to antiunion speakers, and the New York *Age* refused to help an enterprise so opposed to the antimilitant ideals of Booker T. Washington. As the struggle dragged on, the brotherhood saw its membership rolls dwindle, and because it refused donations from whites money was always short. Randolph himself, who rarely saw a paycheck, was living in poverty because the wives of his many enemies shunned his wife's hair salon. In the midst of a much-celebrated Negro Renaissance, the most optimistic man in Harlem was losing hope.

The politics of the New Negro movement was long in the making, yet its literature seemed to come out of nowhere. There were no publishing

houses or journals devoted to Negro literature before World War I, and
none of the very few novels published in the United States after the
turn of the century by blacks such as Paul Laurence Dunbar, Charles
Chesnutt, or James Weldon Johnson were set in Harlem—they didn't
even mention uptown's growing black community. Nor was drama
central to the articulation of the new racial sensibility, since even
productions at black theaters often smacked of Old Negro traditions.
Downtown dramas by white writers provided most of the legitimate
acting opportunities for blacks throughout the period. It was only in
1923 that Willis Richardson's *The Chip Woman's Fortune* became the
first legitimate drama by a Negro to make it to Broadway. Starting the
next year, W.E.B. Du Bois founded the Krigwa Players (an acronym
for Crisis Guild of Writers and Artists), but the group focused on
black versions of the traditional classics. It wasn't until 1929 that the
National Colored Players, the first theater troupe allied with the new
racial aesthetics, began working out of the West End Theatre.

While African-American novelists and dramatists struggled to
imagine an art worthy of the Negro Mecca, poetry got the job done.
Once again, a Jamaican led the way, rejecting both the now embarrassing dialect verse and the stilted imitations of formal English verse that
still dominated black poetry. After Claude McKay broke through to
wider recognition with his 1919 poem "If We Must Die," he became
a communist and spent most of his time with the Greenwich Village
bohemian crowd. He hadn't given up on race, and though he didn't
have much use for the skin games so often played by what he derisively
termed "that NAACP crowd," his poetry combined traditional formal
rigor with political militancy, harnessing delicate rhythms to daring
and defiant racial ideas. His collection *Harlem Shadows,* often considered the first book of the Harlem Renaissance, was published in 1922
to wildly enthusiastic reviews in both black and white newspapers.
McKay still wasn't satisfied. His notions about the artistic and political
significance of skin color helped define the New Negro movement,
but he despised being known as a black writer. Longing to escape
from what he called the "suffocating ghetto of color consciousness,"
McKay became the first New Negro to reject the movement, shock-

ing his friends, uptown and downtown, by taking off for Russia. He never again lived in Harlem, though in his imagination he never lived anywhere else.

McKay's departure came just as the mainstream black institutions were getting into the arts, what W.E.B. Du Bois called "the kingdom of culture." If Du Bois was for a time the reigning monarch of that nation, his queen was the literary editor of the *Crisis*. Jessie Fauset was born in the early 1880s and raised in Philadelphia in a well-educated, ambitious, and politically aware family that sent her to Cornell, where she majored in Latin and Greek and became the first black woman to make Phi Beta Kappa there or anywhere. She supported herself as a teacher in Washington, D.C., until 1918 when, at an age when the few black women in America who had careers could consider changing them, she accepted Du Bois's job offer and moved in with her sister at Seventh Avenue and West 117th Street. Fauset became one of the first New Negresses, an audaciously modern woman who smoked, danced, wore short skirts, and hosted a tony Sunday afternoon salon where guests were expected to speak French.

As literary editor of Du Bois's *Crisis*, Fauset was always on the lookout for home-grown talent. Her signal discovery was Langston Hughes, who always said he was in love with Harlem long before he ever got there. Born in 1902 in Missouri and raised in Kansas, Ohio, and Mexico, Hughes learned to read from the Old Testament and the New Testament, and from the New Negro Testament: Du Bois's *Crisis*. Hughes was nineteen years old and still in high school when he sent Fauset a poem called "The Negro Speaks of Rivers." Her response to this confident manifesto of solidarity with the black race and the human race as a whole encouraged Hughes to come to New York, having promised his father that he would study something practical at Columbia. He never kept his promise, having found more inspiration in the morning rush hour scene on West 135th Street, with its rainbow of skin colors and ideologies, than in his textbooks. After being assigned a broom closet near the dormitory exit, far away from his white peers, he moved into the Harlem YMCA, which was becoming the first destination for many newcomers, and started drinking in the atmosphere. He listened to the street corner speakers and went almost daily to the theater. He haunted the 135th Street public library, which a white librarian named Ernestine Rose was turning into the unofficial staging area of the Harlem Renaissance—she hired black assistants, sponsored concerts and art shows, and opened the building up to meetings of the NAACP, the Liberty League, the Anti-lynching Crusade, the Mozart Choral Society, the Mayor's Committee on Rent Profiteering, and the Book Lovers Club. Hughes stayed up for nights on end making the nightclub scene. When Bert Williams died, Hughes attended the funeral rather than take an exam. In the spring of 1922 he came out from under the protective wings of Jessie Fauset and W.E.B. Du Bois and joined a Merchant Marine vessel bound for Africa, becoming the first New Negro to visit the continent. He left convinced that however lost, obscured, or incomprehensible Africa might be to Negroes in America, it could still provide an endlessly relevant source of artistic inspiration. It was the blues, though, which Hughes had been hearing in uptown cabarets, that instigated the breakthrough poetry published in his first book, *The Weary Blues,* in 1926. Not everyone loved the book, whose very title advertised allegiance with a musical genre that was still a source of shame and scandal.

Soon after discovering the Harlem Renaissance's poet laureate Jessie Fauset found a novelist to match. Jean Toomer was born in 1894 into Washington, D.C.'s byzantine mulatto aristocracy, where he was sometimes white and sometimes black, depending on the family finances. After attending M Street High School, where Fauset was a teacher, Toomer came to Harlem around 1917. He took classes at City College before drifting around the South, where he first heard the blues. He returned to Harlem and with Fauset's encouragement published *Cane,* a masterpiece regardless of time, place, or race, in part because the book was, like Toomer himself, uncategorizable. Its mingling of high modernist form and rural African-American folk content stunned the critics, but before the year was out he was denying his race, exploding angrily after his publisher called him "a promising Negro writer," and planning his escape.

Jesse Fauset kept scouring the regional black press for new voices, but she found the poet Countee Cullen right in her own backyard. Cullen's origins are, like that of so many Harlemites, a mystery, but it is clear that he was living uptown by 1917, when he was taken in by the Reverend Frederick Ashbury Cullen of Harlem's Salem Methodist Episcopal Church and given a home at 234 West 131st Street. By the time he graduated from DeWitt Clinton High School and was headed to New York University he knew he was a writer. But he hesitated before the blackness that so many Harlem writers were embracing. "Yet I do marvel at this curious thing," Cullen wrote in one of his best-known poems. "To make a poet black, and bid him sing!" While still in college Cullen had won a slew of national poetry contests, among them those sponsored by the NAACP and the Urban League, and he had published in the premier Negro journals of the day, including Fauset's *Crisis*. He was living in Salem Methodist's church parsonage, a grand, fourteen-room row house at 2190 Seventh Avenue, and keeping his homosexuality only partly in the closet, when he published his first book, *Color*. The title was perhaps misleading, since he insisted that he was "a POET and not a NEGRO Poet." Cullen refused money from the white philanthropists who seemed determined to finance a certain kind of blackness.

Even as she groomed the careers of others Fauset had plans for a book of her own. That was not an unusual situation in the NAACP, whose top brass, starting with Du Bois and James Weldon Johnson, published novels. Even more successful was Walter White, an Atlantan whose light skin color—he called himself a "voluntary Negro"—proved useful in investigating southern lynchings on behalf of the NAACP, and whose home at 90 Edgecombe Avenue in Sugar Hill attracted some of the most important figures, white and black, in music, literature, philosophy, and politics. White's 1924 book *The Fire in the Flint* almost became the first Harlem Renaissance novel—by that time, Jean Toomer was denying that *Cane* was even a black novel—but Fauset beat him to it with *There Is Confusion*, a roman à clef about a poor but hardworking striver and the terminally classy daughter of a prominent Harlem family. Whatever the artistic faults of *There Is Confusion*—Fauset counted herself among those race-preoccupied Negroes who were "so persistently persecuted and harassed that we can think, breathe, do nothing but consider our great obsession"—it was the start of something big.

It was a bespectacled sociologist named Charles S. Johnson who realized that *There Is Confusion* was more than a mere book, and the banquet he held to celebrate its publication is yet another of the moments that is said to have kicked off the Harlem Renaissance. Johnson, whose attitudes about resisting racism were inspired by having watched his father, a Baptist preacher, face down a Virginia lynch mob, was among the masses of Negroes who signed up for service in World War I, working his way up from private to sergeant major with the 103rd Pioneer Infantry unit in France. He returned from Europe a week after the Chicago riot that left thirty-eight people dead and joined the National Urban League before moving to New York City in 1923 to become the organization's director of research. The next year he founded *Opportunity: A Journal of Negro Life*, but it was only after Johnson began attending the nonstop salon his secretary Ethel Ray Nance hosted at 580 St. Nicholas Avenue that he became aware of a burgeoning literary scene that promised more change than a library full of sociological studies.

Johnson's belief in the uplifting powers of culture was according to many accounts the Copernican shift that made the Harlem Renaissance viable, and the March 21, 1924, party that *Opportunity* sponsored to celebrate Fauset's novel—ironically, the gathering took place not in Harlem but at downtown's Civic Club because no other banquet hall in the city was open to both women and blacks—was not merely a book party but a celebration of the "Debut of the Younger School of Negro Writers." What had been planned as a quiet dinner turned into a major cultural event, attended not only by mandarins of New Negro culture such as Walter White, James Weldon Johnson, and W.E.B. Du Bois, but by white tastemakers the likes of H. L. Mencken, Carl Van Doren, and Eugene O'Neill. What they ate and wore was soon forgotten, but hearing Langston Hughes's "The Weary Blues" read by James Weldon Johnson had an indelible impact. Within a week the publisher Alfred Knopf was begging Hughes for a book.

The success of the Civic Club affair was due largely to Alain Locke, who was born in 1885 into the same kind of old black Philadelphia family that had produced Jessie Fauset. After graduating from Harvard, Locke became the first black Rhodes scholar and joined the faculty of Howard University, where he taught his students that the African arts might serve as a source of cultural renewal for Negroes and for all Americans, even if for most blacks Africa was, in Countee Cullen's ironic words, "a book one thumbs." Still, it wasn't a terribly risky gesture for Locke, who owed much to Arthur Schomburg's claim that "the American Negro must remake his past in order to remake his future." Nor could Locke fail to acknowledge Europeans such as Sigmund Freud, Pablo Picasso, and André Breton, who had looked to "the dark continent" as a beacon of modernism. He was surely aware that the black writer William Stanley Brathwaite had written as early as 1901: "We are at the commencement of a 'negroid' renaissance." So this diminutive, gay, snobbish, squeaky-voiced philosopher who never lived uptown—but who knew Harlem from the Black Bottom to Sugar Hill—seemed an unlikely godfather for the Harlem Renaissance, especially since he was responsible for as much conflict as cooperation. The *Messenger* and Claude McKay despised the Du Boisian elitism that Locke personified, and Jean Toomer declined to attend the Civic Club dinner on the grounds that he was no longer a Negro. At the same time, the increasingly political dimension of Langston Hughes's poetry was alienating Jessie Fauset and Countee Cullen.

These rumblings of discontent couldn't stop the momentum of the Civic Club dinner, which so impressed the white editor of the *Survey Graphic*, an illustrated magazine that appealed to a broad white readership, that he hired Locke to edit the March 1925 issue, which was to be devoted to the New Negro movement. *Harlem: Mecca of the New Negro*, included works by the usual suspects, with articles by James Weldon Johnson, Arthur Schomburg, Walter White, and Locke himself, whose "Enter the New Negro" became the unofficial manifesto of the

Harlem Renaissance. There was also poetry by the familiar figures
Claude McKay, Langston Hughes, Countee Cullen, and Jean Toomer.
Harlemites were more excited by the newcomers. The most prominent
was a Kansan named Aaron Douglas who arrived in Harlem in 1924
at the age of twenty-six and embarked on a modernist reimagining of
African visual aesthetics. Another new talent was Rudolph Fisher, a
doctor from Washington, D.C., who moved to Harlem in 1925 at the
age of twenty-eight and divided his time between taking medical and
artistic X-rays of his neighbors. The commercial success of *Harlem:
Mecca of the New Negro*—it sold forty-four thousand copies in a matter
of weeks—inspired Locke to reach for an even wider audience. Six
months later he convinced the publishers Albert and Charles Boni to
expand the collection into a book called *The New Negro.*

Charles Johnson upped the stakes by holding a literary competition. The first *Opportunity* honors, awarded by a biracial panel of
literary bigwigs, were handed out in May 1925 at a downtown dinner. Within days of the awards ceremony, which was clearly meant to
recall the Civic Club dinner of a year earlier, a Negro Renaissance
was being heralded on the front pages of the newspapers, uptown and
downtown. W.E.B. Du Bois was so impressed that he arranged for a
similar contest to be sponsored by the *Crisis,* with the winners announced at a banquet at the Renaissance Casino. The *Opportunity* and
Crisis awards honored Langston Hughes and Countee Cullen as well
as a number of new discoveries such as Dorothy West and her cousin,
Helene Johnson. The real find that year was a new arrival named Zora
Neale Hurston. As with so many New Negroes, the facts surrounding
her early years were lost to government institutions that didn't offer
the dignity of a birth certificate to Negroes, but also to what Hurston
herself would later call the Negro "will to adorn." She seems to have
been born around 1901 in Eatonville, Florida, a voluntarily black town
where everyone from the prostitutes to the politicians were black, and
where black pride was the order of the day. She studied at Howard
University with Alain Locke and supported herself by working as
a manicurist and maid. When *Opportunity* knocked, Hurston moved
to New York with $1.50 in her pocket. She slept on the couch at

580 St. Nicholas Avenue, attended Barnard College, and worked as the novelist Fannie Hurst's private secretary.

The age of cooperation and mutual congratulation that the *Opportunity* and *Crisis* awards represented came to an end in 1926 with the publication of a novel that few Harlemites seem to have read. The title made sure of that. *Nigger Heaven* was the fourth novel published by Carl Van Vechten, a forty-six-year-old, rich, white Iowa native who had an unerring sense for the new. He had recently discovered Harlem and become the most prominent of the white slummers—the popular song "Go Harlem" referred to people who "Go inspectin' / Like Van Vechten." Carlo, as his friend Langston Hughes called him, squired William Faulkner, F. Scott Fitzgerald, and other celebrities on all-night odysseys to rent parties, restaurants, nightclubs, speakeasies, gambling halls, and dance palaces. But Van Vechten, who was so well known and so well liked uptown that he could always count on his wayward hip flask being returned to him by night's end, was more than yet another interloper. He freely invited Harlemites, high and low, to his midtown home, where they met everyone from Tallulah Bankhead to Rudolph Valentino to Theodore Dreiser. A porter at Grand Central Station is said to have recognized an otherwise anonymous old lady as Mrs. Astor, and when she asked how he knew her name, he replied, "I met you Saturday when we shared bootleg gin at Carl Van Vechten's." Countee Cullen told Hughes that Van Vechten was "coining money out of the niggers," but Van Vechten's assistance to Harlem's artists and intellectuals was undeniable. He set up Paul Robeson's breakthrough concert at Town Hall and helped convince Alfred Knopf to publish James Weldon Johnson, Langston Hughes, and Rudolph Fisher. His photography and reporting on Harlem and black culture in *Vanity Fair,* the *Smart Set,* and *Harper's* were crucial efforts in bringing the accomplishments of the Harlem Renaissance to a wider public

Nigger Heaven put an end to the fun, at least as far as Van Vechten's nights uptown were concerned. Many observers have gone so far as to claim that this roman à clef about a young black writer whose descent into lowlife is hastened when he forsakes his librarian girlfriend for an infamous heiress was the beginning of the end of the

Harlem Renaissance. Published in the midst of a surge in the number of southern lynchings, even as Jazz Age whites celebrated blacks and black culture, *Nigger Heaven* became a cultural litmus test, beginning with the title, which referred to the blacks-only balcony section of segregated theaters uptown. Van Vechten was hardly the first person, or even the first white person, to write a serious novel about black people, nor was Van Vechten alone among white American writers in exploring the complex resonances of "the n-word." Harlemites nonetheless complained that Van Vechten had repaid their generosity with a scorn that was making a rich man even richer. The novel quickly sold a hundred thousand copies and went through thirteen reprintings in two years. Van Vechten was from the start sensitive to the possible responses. He included a footnote at the first use of the word "nigger" that recognized its problematic history and usage, and before publication he showed the manuscript to his closest friends uptown, including Langston Hughes, James Weldon Johnson, and Rudolph Fisher, in order to test its offensiveness. None found a problem with the book's title or its contents. Hughes even wrote the blues lyrics that appear at the beginning of every chapter. Nonetheless, Van Vechten was lynched in effigy at the corner of Seventh Avenue and West 135th Street, and his book was burned. Du Bois wrote that *Nigger Heaven* was "an affront to the hospitality of black folk and the intelligence of white," while Hubert Harrison considered the novel nothing more than an updated minstrel show. Had Van Vechten robbed Harlem of its renaissance? Or had it existed only in the pages of a few downtown literary magazines?

The controversy over *Nigger Heaven* took place in a rarefied atmosphere that was foreign to most Harlemites. Indeed, what was most significant about the book was not the controversial title but the way it intensified long-standing cultural divisions between old New Negroes who demanded that black art uplift the race and new New Negroes who proposed that racial progress would be fatally compromised by taking race too seriously. As it turned out, there was a third way, pioneered by Wallace Thurman, the most terrible of a generation of enfants terribles. Born in Salt Lake City, Utah, Thurman worked as a journalist in Los Angeles before moving to Harlem in 1925 "with nothing but his nerve," according to legend. By early the next year the twenty-four-year-old Thurman was using his position as managing editor of the *Messenger* to promote the new generation of Harlem writers. Thurman soon gained a reputation as a brilliant artist with a complicated personal life, at once cynical about race and ashamed of his dark skin color. To make things even more complicated, Thurman was freethinking when it came to the sexuality of others but unable to come to terms with his own. He never got over the shame of having been arrested during a gay assignation in a public bathroom shortly after his arrival in New York, even though homosexuality was hardly a scandal uptown, not when gay nightclubs were so popular and when lesbian blues singers were hit makers. Heavy drinking helped Thurman survive—it certainly made him the life of the nonstop party at the rooming house where the next phase of the Harlem Renaissance was born. "Niggerati Manor," as 267 West 136th Street was known, was home not only to Thurman but to Aaron Douglas and Richard Bruce Nugent, a twenty-year-old writer and artist from Washington, D.C., who was as far out of the closet as Wallace Thurman was in it. Nugent, who wrote some of the earliest gay fiction in American literature, decorated the walls of the house with images of African jungle dwellers in drag.

This hothouse atmosphere attracted Langston Hughes, who spent the summer of 1926 on West 136th Street basking in the success of his first book. Hughes was now America's Negro poet laureate, and when he talked about racial art, friends and enemies listened. After the ever unpredictable George Schuyler claimed in an article called "The Negro Art Hokum" that race was irrelevant to artists who happened to be black, Hughes responded with "The Negro Artist and the Racial Mountain," an essay arguing that both race fetishists and propagandists on the one hand and subjectivists and aesthetes on the other had it wrong. People were more than their skin color but they denied race at their peril. "No great poet has ever been afraid of being himself," Hughes wrote. "We know we are beautiful. And ugly too."

The increasing ideological and artistic independence exercised by the residents of Niggerati Manor demanded an outlet, and in that magical summer of 1926 Thurman and his roommates started their own literary magazine. *FIRE!!: A Quarterly Devoted to Younger Negro Artists* went on sale later that year and went nowhere. Its outrageous one-dollar cover price was bad enough, but its frank and even prurient embrace of a working-class black bohemian vision was shocking to many readers. Its bold rejection of the political and racial norms of the Talented Tenth led the literary establishment to savage the publication in print and snub its contributors in person. Thurman lost what little money he had on *FIRE!!* and, after unsold copies were destroyed in, irony of ironies, a warehouse blaze, he had no way to put together a second issue. Yet even before *FIRE!!* went up in flames its influence was spreading.

In 1927 Harlem saw the opening of a salon called the Dark Tower, with interiors by Richard Bruce Nugent and Aaron Douglas, and copies of Langston Hughes's poem "The Weary Blues" and Countee Cullen's "The Dark Tower" hanging on opposite walls. It was located above the hair parlor and beauty college at 108-10 West 136th Street, which as every Harlemite knew was the mansion that had belonged to America's "Mahogany Millionairess," Madame C. J. Walker. After she died in 1919 her daughter, A'Lelia Walker, had become a fixture of Harlem's boisterous nightlife in a silver turban and harem pants. She turned her surprisingly modest one-bedroom apartment at 80 Edgecombe Avenue into the place where the coffee-colored cream of Harlem's Talented Tenth, white slummers from downtown, Hollywood stars, and European nobility, as well as her own informal court, mingled with uptown crooks and cads. The Dark Tower was the fulfillment of A'Lelia's ambitions to become a matron of the arts, which according to the woman whom Langston Hughes called the "Joy Princess of Harlem's 1920s" meant serving caviar sandwiches and woodcock salad to tuxedoed white folks willing and able to pay.

The vast majority of Harlemites never heard of the Dark Tower, most of those who knew about it couldn't afford the prices, and many of those who could afford it wouldn't be caught dead there. Instead, Harlemites patronized the theaters, ballrooms, dance halls, and nightclubs where a parallel Harlem Renaissance was happening, fueled by bootleg liquor and jazz and subsidized by a new generation of white investors. In 1925 an Austrian immigrant named Leo Brecher and a Jewish graduate of City College named Frank Schiffman followed up on their success in turning the Lincoln Theatre into a movie house by taking over Harlem's "Cradle of Stars," the famed Lafayette Theatre, and transforming it into an all-black vaudeville house. It was there that a young trumpeter from New Orleans named Louis Armstrong was first introduced to Harlem audiences. The Lafayette's only real competition at that point was the Renaissance Theatre, at 2341 Seventh Avenue, which was built in 1920 as part of the old Garden of Joy site by William C. Roach, a UNIA-tithing immigrant from Montserrat. In addition to concerts and dances with the best talent that the Negro Mecca had on hand, the Renaissance featured floor shows, gambling, and even basketball—it was the home court of the New York Renaissance Big Five, or the "Rennies," the first black professional basketball team.

That kind of imaginative programming was key to the success of Harlem's theaters and dance halls in the 1920s, especially as Latinos began to create their own renaissance. At first, audiences looking for Spanish-language entertainment had to leave El Barrio to find it. The "Teatro Alhambra" produced René Borgia's *En La Calle 116,* a play about life in El Barrio, but it was that landmark of Negro Harlem the Apollo Theater that became the most important venue for Spanish-language drama and musical theater uptown, from the classics to out-and-out farces featuring actors in *negrito.* At first, the Apollo hosted one-shot works in Spanish, but later the management instituted all-day Sunday shows that might include Ramón Reynado's company performing comedies or even operas with the great Mexican baritone Rodolfo de Hoyos, Cristino Inclán's Companía de Bufos Cubanos, starring none other than *El Gráfico* editor Alberto O'Farrill in blackface, or G. Pando's *El Negro Que Tenía El Alma Blanca,* "The Negro Who Had a White Soul." Inspired by the success of Spanish-language works at the Apollo, the East Harlem venues the Jewell

Theatre, the Verona, Clairmont Hall, the Teatro San José, and the
Teatro Triboro began programming similar works, often featuring
the *negritos* O'Farrill or Jesús Solís as well as other stars such as Juan
Rivera or Fortunato Bonanova. A revue at the East Harlem's Teatro
Variedades called *Harlem Arrabalero,* again starring Alberto O'Farrill,
was the definitive Spanish-language version of nocturnal life uptown
complete with poverty, violence, and sex.

Less respectable forms of entertainment became even more popular during the 1920s. The Manhattan Casino changed its name to the
Rockland Palace and began hosting the annual dances of the Hamilton
Lodge of Odd Fellows, which featured not just both whites and blacks
but gays and straights cross-dressed every which way. Harlem was
distinctly unoffended. Female and male impersonators had long found
underground performance opportunities uptown, and in the 1920s
Harlem's "pansy shows" and striptease acts were a few degrees hotter
than those available downtown. The most prominent examples of such
entertainment were the specialty of a journalist named Billy Minsky,
who was descended from a famous eastern European rabbi. Raised on
the Lower East Side, Minsky got into the burlesque business with his
brothers after the stories he wrote for the New York *World* about the
Becker and Rosenthal case led to an attempt on his life. "Girls, gags, and
music" kept seats in the space above the Harlem Opera House called
the Little Apollo filled, especially when the shows cost only 75 cents,
compared to $4.40 for Ziegfeld's Follies. One of the most popular acts
was Isabelle Van, known as "the sex seeker," who started her act fully
clothed and exited after removing each piece of clothing, reappearing
and leaving again, until the patient audience was finally rewarded with
a glimpse of one of her breasts. Then there were the relatively mild
comic skits, like the one in which a female patient asks a doctor, "What
did you do before you were a doctor?" The doctor pats her posterior
and answers, "I was a rear admiral." Eventually audiences demanded
racier material. Robert Alda, the father of the actor Alan Alda, became
one of Harlem's "tit serenaders," so called because they sang between
striptease acts. The Minsky brothers began pushing decency boundaries far beyond—or below, in this case—what was allowed anywhere

else. "Try to Get In!" the advertisements leered. The dancer Mae Dix had an act in which she appeared before a topless chorus line and stripped away everything but a banana placed strategically between her legs. Even the banana came off as she exited. This was the type of act that led to a police raid in 1925, but when charges were dismissed the Minsky brothers decided to do away with the comedy sketches and focus on the strippers, known as the "Minsky Rosebuds," which resulted in four sold-out shows a day. It also convinced Hurtig and Seamon's, next door to the Harlem Opera House, to start presenting risqué acts with talent as young as fifteen years old, and soon other theaters followed suit.

Despite the strong demand for burlesque acts, lavish floor shows set to the music now known as jazz dominated a new generation of nightclubs that opened in the wake of Prohibition. One of the most sophisticated nightspots was a basement space called Connie's Inn, on Seventh Avenue near West 131st Street, next to the Lafayette Theatre and close to the legendary Tree of Hope, Harlem's Blarney Stone, where so many black Harlemites in the entertainment business gathered to gossip and trade tips. The owners were a pair of German-Jewish brothers from Harlem, Connie and George Immerman, with an unerring sense of Harlem's future. Connie's Inn, which opened in 1923, was one of the first new Harlem jazz clubs with a whites-only policy, and not just any whites but an international array of the rich and famous. The New York *Age* was skeptical: "Immerman's is opened to Slummers; sports; 'coke' addicts, and high rollers of the white race who come to Harlem to indulge in illicit and illegal recreations." Later the club became a "black and tan" establishment, letting in light-skinned colored customers after hours. Harlemites were willing to bear such indignities because the entertainment was worth it, especially the club's floor shows. Fats Waller, who had once worked for the Immermans as a delivery boy when they were the humble owners of a delicatessen, wrote four shows each year with his lyricist, Andy Razaf, a native of Washington, D.C., who preached from a 135th Street stepladder against the use of the terms "nigger," "darky," and "coon" before joining up with Waller and writing the songs like "Honeysuckle Rose" and "What

Did I Do to Be So Black and Blue?" They also worked on a larger scale. Their most successful effort was the show *Hot Chocolates*, which featured Edith Wilson and Louis Armstrong and did so well that it calved a Broadway version with an onstage imitation of Connie's Inn, complete with guests and waiters onstage and a version of the club's "Sun-Tanned Beauty Chorus," which included men in drag.

The splendors of Connie's Inn are remembered today only by aficionados of jazz history, but almost anyone who knows anything about the history of New York City is familiar with the unique synthesis of racism and art achieved at the Cotton Club. The space had been a dance club called Douglas Hall before being taken over by Jack Johnson in 1920 and then by the gangster Owney "The Killer" Madden and his secret backer, Al Capone. At the Cotton Club, which officially opened in 1923 at the northeast corner of Lenox Avenue and West 142nd Street, the music had to compete with the decor, which was the work of the modernist designer Joseph Urban, who outfitted the space to resemble an old-time plantation, from the log cabin–themed stairs outside to the murals that depicted slave shacks and cotton fields, while the stage itself was modeled after the veranda of a slave owner's mansion. The Cotton Club revues, which were written by white Broadway and Tin Pan Alley composers, featured twenty café-au-lait-colored girl singers and dancers. There were even white women who passed for colored in order to earn a princely $50 per week. The most famous member of the chorus was Lena Horne, who was so young when she first started that her mother came along and made sure she did her homework between shows. The Cotton Club inspired imitators like the Catagonia Club, also known as Pod and Jerry's, a one-room speakeasy that opened in 1925 at 166 West 133rd Street—the entire block was known as Jungle Alley—and featured more reasonable prices than the Cotton Club. The owners also introduced a more progressive racial policy, attracting celebrities who had gone to high school in Harlem just a few blocks away, such as Tallulah Bankhead and many musicians, including Billie Holiday, who failed her audition as a dancer in 1927 but wowed the owners with her singing.

Despite the talent onstage and the bootleg alcohol at the tables, things at the Cotton Club didn't really begin to swing until the arrival of an ambitious young pianist and bandleader from Washington, D.C., named Duke Ellington. Born in 1899 into a family of middle-class strivers—his father was a servant at the White House—Ellington came to New York City in 1923. At the Lafayette, "America's Leading Colored Theatre," Ellington worked with Wilbur Sweatman's orchestra as part of a vaudeville show, complete with dancers, comics, and acrobats before breaking out to lead his own group. White audiences looking for "sweet" sounds and blacks hungry for "hot" tunes loved the way Ellington orchestrated the piano gestures of the uptown ticklers, turning a midsized ragtime ensemble into an jazz orchestra capable of frantic grace in "East St. Louis Toodle-o" and languorous sophistication in "Mood Indigo." It was Ellington's gig at the Cotton Club starting in December of 1927—"Be big or you'll be dead," Owney Madden told him—that turned the Jazz Age into the Swing Era and put Harlem permanently on the map of American music. Ellington's pioneering balance between song and solo, between the composer's vision and the instrumentalist's touch, mirrored the productive oppositions and tensions of the American experiment itself. It was largely due to Ellington that the Cotton Club became the most exclusive club in the city. There was a "royal box" kept at the ready for Mayor Jimmy Walker—his uptown constituents, whose skin color was too dark and whose pocketbooks were too light to get past the bouncers, had to make do with radio broadcasts from the club sponsored by Moe Levy's West 149th Street clothing shop.

If Connie's Inn was known for its floor shows, and the Cotton Club was known for its music, the place for dancing was the Savoy Ballroom, a massive hall at 596 Lenox Avenue that gave rise to one of the key songs of the Swing Era, "Stompin' at the Savoy," by Andy Razaf and Edgar Sampson. A black real estate speculator named Charles Buchanan, backed by a Jewish luggage manufacturer turned talent scout named Moe Gale, opened the club in 1926 to enormous fanfare. Named after London's famed Savoy Hotel, it didn't look like much from the outside but the inside was spectacular. Taking up a full city block, it held up to five thousand people and allowed most of them to dance at the same time on its 250- by 50-foot polished maple dance floor. The Savoy was alone among the big clubs uptown in racially integrating both its dance floor and its twin bandstands. The 50-cent admission charge was low enough to allow elevator operators and domestics to mingle with celebrities the likes of George Gershwin, Marlene Dietrich, Greta Garbo, Sergei Eisenstein, Le Corbusier, and the Prince of Wales.

The Track, as the Savoy's dance floor was known, became the premier dance hall in the country—Lana Turner famously dubbed the club "the home of happy feet." A dozen hostesses offered 10-cent dances, but more often than not the customers would be the ones offering instruction in the gravity-defying Lindy Hop, a dance that got its name after Charles Lindbergh's transatlantic crossing, as well as in the moves called the Camelback, the Shimmy, the Stomp, and the Jitterbug Jive. Nowhere else in Harlem was the connection between dancers and musicians as symbiotic, and every major orchestra based in or passing through New York played there. But no Savoy headliner was more beloved than Fletcher Henderson. Born in 1897 in Georgia into a middle-class black family that steered him toward both art and science, Henderson graduated from Atlanta University and came to New York in 1920 to study chemistry, but racial discrimination made finding work as a pharmacist impossible. He supported himself by working as a song plugger, producer, and featured artist for Harry Pace and W. C. Handy. By mid-1924 he was gigging in midtown and helping to move jazz beyond ragtime and dixieland styles and into big band swing. Henderson's songs—among them, "Christopher Columbus," "Clarinet Marmalade," and "Prince of Wails"—rejected the sweet style favored by white bands in favor of a hot style that provided a precise and sophisticated but hard-swinging context for thrilling soloists like Louis Armstrong and Coleman Hawkins. It all came together in the musical confrontations—rent party cutting contests writ large—known as battles of the bands, events that became so emotionally charged that the Savoy's owners more than once had to call in the city's riot squad.

The only other major racially integrated venue uptown was Smalls Paradise, which opened in late 1925 at Seventh Avenue and West 135th Street under the ownership of Ed Smalls, the South Carolina-born grandson of the Civil War hero Robert Smalls. He came north and worked as an elevator operator before opening the Sugar Cane Club, a basement space at Fifth Avenue and 135th Street that had been one of the first Harlem nightspots to court whites from downtown. His next venture, Smalls Paradise, could hold up to fifteen hundred people and usually did, partly because there was no door charge and patrons didn't pay champagne prices for seltzer. While a typical night for four at Connie's Inn cost $50, the equivalent of a week's paycheck for lucky Harlemites, revelers who came to Smalls to see the bands of Charlie Johnson, Fletcher Henderson, Willie "The Lion" Smith, or James P. Johnson spent less than half of that.

Harlem nightlife in the 1920s was by no means dominated by huge, swanky clubs filled with champagne-swigging, tuxedoed downtowners. Duke Ellington's sidemen drank with white celebrities like Mae West and Paul Whiteman at the Nest Club, only one of a number of smaller, affordable, mixed-race all-night spots on West 133rd Street. None was more popular than the Lenox Club, which opened in 1925 next to the Cotton Club. A 7 a.m. whistle meant that patrons, including the actor Harold Lloyd and the writer Walter Winchell, who had grown up in Harlem, needed to finish breakfast and go to work. Then there were clubs that were just a few notches above rent parties. The Cellar Café, run by an ex-boxer named Edmond Johnson and later known as Edmond's Cellar, was a basement dive at Fifth Avenue and 132nd Street that opened around the end of World War I and featured the young Ethel Waters, who later remembered the dirty, dangerous, and disreputable club as "the last stop on the way down." Many of Harlem's least reputable clubs featured transvestite acts known as "pansy parades." While the Ubangi Club attracted crowds of gays and lesbians, "Queeriosities" ruled the Clam House, a West 133rd Street dive owned by a lesbian named Gladys Bentley, who dressed up as a man and performed double entendre numbers while she flirted with women in the audience. One male performer even dressed up as Gloria Swanson and wowed audiences with the risqué song "Hot Nuts."

No matter how fancy the decor, no matter how exclusive the clientele, no matter how good the music and dancing, all of Harlem's nightclubs counted on the thirst for alcohol that gripped the nation during Prohibition. In addition to the nightclubs, which marked up booze by a thousand percent or more, much of which went to paying off cops and judges, hundreds of bakeries, cigar stores, and delis sold liquor under the counter. Parts of Harlem had been known as vice districts since the nineteenth century, but now uptown Manhattan became synonymous with all manner of crime. A *New York Times* article from 1926 called "Strange Crimes of Little Africa" claimed that most of Harlem's 250,000 residents found their neighborhoods safe and orderly before going on to chronicle uptown's never-ending epidemic of blood-soaked crimes of passion.

Prohibition helped passion of another sort remain profitable. The notorious West 141st Street whorehouse called the Daisy Chain was only one of some sixty bordellos uptown, more than in any other city neighborhood. In addition to their "daughters of joy," whorehouses and after-hours clubs were also prime places to score illegal drugs, especially marijuana, though "vipers" could also buy joints right out in the open under the Tree of Hope. Such activity was possible, of course, only with the assistance of the police, many of whom got rich by ignoring petty dealers such as Mezz Mezzrow, Louis Armstrong's connection, and by looking the other way at Kaiser's, a "tea pad" in the basement of 212 West 133rd Street.

Of course, the real money was in organized crime, and everyone knew it. The Cotton Club's owner Owney Madden rode around Harlem in a bullet-proof Dusenberg and arranged for the curbside murder of his competition Barron Wilkins, who had moved on to run the Executive Club. The biggest bootlegger of them all, Arnold Rothstein, kept a lower profile, investing in Harlem real estate as a way to launder money and backing the shows *Keep Shufflin'* and *Hot*

Chocolates. Rothstein was also responsible for turning an Italian-born juvenile delinquent named Francesco Castiglia into the archetypal Jazz Age gangster. Born in Calabria in 1891, he followed his father to America several years later. "Sell everything," the old man had written back to the old country. "Don't forget the red peppers. Bring a lot of them." Castiglia's mother heeded the advice, and the family was even able to open a food store in East Harlem. Francesco Castiglia was renamed Frank Costello and grew up at 234 East 108th Street, in the heart of the Italian ghetto. This enterprising youth got a job delivering telegraphs and was soon gambling and shooting craps. He was barely into his teens when Rothstein took him under his wing, and soon Costello was splitting his winnings with cops in return for protection. From there it was a short step to helping politicians buy votes and becoming the biggest bootlegger in the country.

While white gangsters concentrated on bootlegging, black criminals got into illegal gambling. Casper Holstein, a native of Saint Croix, owned the Lenox Club, the Saratoga Club, and the Turf Club, but most of his profits came from an informal West Indian gambling scam called *bolito,* which he expanded into the numbers, also known as policy gambling. Harlemites would bet their hard-earned nickels and dimes on a lucky number and hope it matched the figure that represented the daily volume at the New York Stock Exchange. The odds of winning were 900 to 1, even as Holstein paid off at a rate of 600 to 1. The difference—up to $15,000 a day—paid the salaries of an army of employees who would take bets, transport cash, and count and launder money. It made Holstein one of the first African-American millionaires, known to blow up to $35,000 in a single afternoon at the track. Sometimes he put his money to better use, investing in real estate and donating large sums to Fisk and Howard universities, as well as to Democratic politicians. He funded homes for destitute girls in Liberia and India and helped relief efforts after hurricanes in the West Indies. Closer to home, Holstein founded Harlem's Elks Lodge #45, built a private sanatorium, and backed *Opportunity'*s prize competitions for literature. After the fall of Marcus Garvey, Holstein even bought Liberty Hall and gave it back to the UNIA. But Holstein's dominance didn't last. Dozens of Harlem gangsters were soon copying his business model, among them a Puerto Rican immigrant named Henry Miro who arrived in El Barrio in 1916 at the age of fourteen and became the neighborhood "banker," giving his employees buttons bearing the letter M, I, R, or O as a way of tipping off the cops. There was enough to go around until Arnold Rothstein's protégé, Dutch Schultz, left to form his own gang. He looked to his stomping grounds of Jewish Harlem and recruited Luke Rosenkranz and Bo Weinberg to be his gunmen and Abbadabba Berman to do the books. They used coffins to smuggle whiskey and gin into the Harlem funeral home he owned and then sold it at Connie's Inn, where he was a secret investor. In 1928 he kidnapped Holstein in broad daylight on West 146th Street and held him for $50,000 ransom. Five days later Holstein was released, having turned over the bulk of his operations to Schultz. The rest of Harlem's black numbers kingpins got the message, with the exception of "Madame" Stephanie St. Clair, the so-called Queen of Policy, a native of Martinique who spoke fluent French as she continued to direct dozens of numbers runners from her apartment at 409 Edgecombe Avenue.

Harlem's churches led the fight against "drink, drugs, dice, and dance," and leading the leaders was the legendary Reverend Adam Clayton Powell, who was born in Virginia in 1865 to a black and Native American ex-slave and a white German slaveholder and grew up in a one-room shack. After he got saved at the age of twenty he went to college, law school, and theological seminary, and in 1908 he took over the Abyssinian Baptist Church, which had been founded downtown a century earlier by visiting Ethiopians who had rebelled against the racial segregation enforced in New York's churches and moved uptown. He was distressed to learn that his son, Adam Clayton Powell Jr., kept getting kicked off the informal baseball field occupied by an Italian farmer who raised goats at 136 West 138th Street—it had been part of a whites-only outdoor nightclub called Mamie Smith's Garden of Joy that Vertner Tandy built on a large rocky outcropping—but the reverend was overjoyed to have discovered at last the perfect place to build a new church. Powell oversaw the completion in 1923 of a massive neo-Gothic church that immediately attracted some of the wealthiest and lightest-skinned Negro Baptists in the city. The church grew so quickly that Powell, a towering, dashing man with a famously energetic and distinctive preaching style—unlike most of his colleagues, he did not improvise—publicly burned its mortgage after just four years. By the end of the decade the Abyssinian Baptist Church was the biggest and most influential black religious institution in the country, because Powell saw religion not as a matter of private spirituality but as a public calling. A disciple of Booker T. Washington, Powell had helped organize the NAACP and the Urban League, and he made sure the church focused on community service, offering everything from financial assistance to clothing and food banks to sports and education. There was even a summer camp and a missionary operation in Africa.

Many preachers tried to imitate Powell's success. Just a year after the Abyssinian Baptist Church moved uptown, the Mother AME Zion Church's Reverend George W. Fraser outdid Powell by hiring the black architect George W. Foster to build a neo-Gothic building on West 137th Street, while the King's Chapel Pentecostal Assembly hired Vertner Tandy to build a modernist home on Fifth Avenue. But taking advantage of white flight was more common. Salem Methodist Episcopal Church took over the all-white Metropolitan Methodist Episcopal Church, while Temple Israel became Mount Olivet Baptist Church. Even the old Harlem Casino got religion and was transformed into the Refuge Temple of the Church of Our Lord Jesus Christ. Meanwhile, the storefront churches and basement salvation temples, such as the Live-Ever-Die-Never Church and the Metaphysical Church of the Divine Investigation, were more popular than ever, even though many of them seemed to specialize in relieving congregants of any money they had left over after playing the numbers. Just down the food chain from the storefront churches were itinerant preachers, for example, Elder Clayhorn Martin, known as the "Barefoot Prophet," a one-man religion who wandered in long white robes from rent party to pool hall calculating the wages of sin uptown. Then there were the "obi men" who sold herbs, roots, powders, charms, and conjurations that promised to heal everything from teething pain to broken hearts.

Since the established Harlem Catholic houses of worship considered Latin Americans even more suspect—which is to say less white—than Italians, Latino churches were slow to take root and located mostly in West Harlem. The first Spanish-language church uptown, Iglesia Luterana Sion, was founded in 1873 in the old St. Johannes Kirche, but it wasn't until the 1920s that the residents of El Barrio started building their own Spanish-language Catholic churches, including St. Cecilia, Our Lady of the Miraculous Medal, and Holy Agony. Like their Italian neighbors, Puerto Ricans made up for the lack of their own churches by bringing their religion into the streets, marking Good Friday with a parade that reenacted the stations of the cross.

To many Harlemites, black and Latino, it seemed as if a new era was just getting under way, with the rise of a new generation of religious and political leaders, the reinvention of American popular music and dance in the clubs of Jungle Alley and the dance palaces of Lenox Avenue, and the arrival of a new crop of black novelists, playwrights, and poets. Events proved otherwise. After Marcus Garvey went to jail in 1925, the UNIA was increasingly focused on expanding into other cities and even overseas. Garvey's link to Harlem was permanently severed in 1927, when he was expelled from the United States and began a journey that took him back to Jamaica and then to England, where he died at the age of fifty-three, never having stepped foot on African soil. Garvey left a complicated legacy. Doubters claimed he was nothing more than a lucky man, in the right place at the right time with the right message. Many Harlemites still revere this poorly educated and coal-black West Indian immigrant who became an international apostle of racial pride by reinventing the black past, translating that ideology into practice by standing up to Harlem's café au lait establishment, and building from scratch a political machine that offered an alternative to the two-party political system that held back Negroes. "Tragic," like "genius," was a much-abused word in Harlem in the 1920s. Garvey, whose downfall was J. Edgar Hoover's first success, was both.

Garvey's departure was only the first in a string of losses that Harlem suffered starting in the mid-1920s. His unruly disciple Hubert Harrison, one of the most brilliant and charismatic of the stepladder speakers at the outdoor university along Lenox Avenue, who insisted that there never was such a thing as a Harlem Renaissance, died in 1927 at the age of forty-four of appendicitis. Another blow came the next year, when Claude McKay, who had encountered an enthusiastic welcome in the Soviet Union, realized that communism would always put class before race and published a novel to put both in disturbing perspective. *Home to Harlem* pulled no punches when it came to the downside of living uptown, which helped it become one of the first black best sellers. White critics loved the book but, with the exception of James Weldon Johnson, the Negro Mecca's literati gave it a ferocious reception. After the *Inter-State Tattler* claimed the novel "out-niggered Mr. Van Vechten," McKay left Harlem for good. The fuss over *Home to Harlem* almost eclipsed the appearance of Nella Larsen's *Quicksand,* a mixed-race melodrama that came out that same year to enthusiastic reviews. Larsen, a mysteriously secretive nurse and librarian who had been discovered by Jessie Fauset, followed that achievement a year later with *Passing,* still considered the definitive fictional treatment of the moral and psychological perils of crossing the color line, but by the end of the decade Larsen was anxious to get away from Harlem. A Guggenheim award in 1930—she was the first black fellow in the institution's history—allowed Larsen to spend two years in Europe, but accusations of plagiarism followed her, and though she returned to Harlem her literary career was over. A similar fate awaited Jean Toomer, whose obsessive search for racelessness was traceable not just to a childhood spent on the color line but to a growing inter-est in the arcane philosophy of George Ivanovich Gurdjieff, whose insistence on inner and outer transcendence was attracting converts among America's bohemian classes. Toomer was struggling to bring

Gurdjieff uptown when, in 1926, he experienced a spiritual awakening
while standing on a midtown subway platform. It marked the end of
his commitment to Harlem and to race in general.

Claude McKay, Nella Larsen, and Jean Toomer had personal
reasons for staying away. Many of their old friends and colleagues
had professional reasons for leaving, answering the call of Fisk University, which decimated the ranks of the Negro Mecca's Talented
Tenth. Located in Nashville, Tennessee, Fisk was a small, out-of-
the-way school, but the prospect of regular paychecks was a powerful
attraction. Over the next decade the school cherry-picked Harlem's
finest, including Charles Johnson, whose program of cultural uplift
at *Opportunity* was no longer supported by the Urban League. James
Weldon Johnson followed up the publication in 1930 of *Black Manhattan,* a groundbreaking work of African-American history, by moving
to Nashville, though he came back each fall to his home at 187 West
135th Street. His death in a 1938 car crash robbed black America of its
most authoritative voice. Fisk also claimed Arna Bontemps, a Seventh
Day Adventist who came from Los Angeles to Harlem after being discovered by Jessie Fauset. Aaron Douglas managed to complete murals
at New York's Ebony Club, the 135th Street branch of the New York
Public Library, and the Harlem YMCA before moving to Nashville.

Harlem lost some of its most distinctive remaining talents to
tragically early deaths. The actor Charles Gilpin died drunk and impoverished in 1930 at the age of fifty-two. He was hardly the first
New Negro undone by booze and bigotry. After the disaster of *FIRE!!,*
Wallace Thurman was undeterred, writing a hit Broadway play and
publishing two novels, *The Blacker the Berry,* which was the first black
novel to take skin color as its subject, and *Infants of the Spring,* a roman à clef that was the first novel ever written expressly for a black
readership. It came as no surprise to Thurman to see that the latter
was unenthusiastically received. How could a novel whose opening
scene includes a gay, interracial pickup scene reach a large readership? Always a heavy drinker, Thurman's health declined, and the
wild, racially mixed rent parties he threw at his home on West 139th
Street were more than once broken up by his drunken suicide attempts.

Just a few days after Thurman succumbed to tuberculosis in 1934, Harlemites learned of the death of another of their most distinctive literary voices. For much of the decade Rudolph Fisher spent his days in a white medical coat and his nights in a tuxedo, taking in the club and cabaret scene. In between, he also published two novels, *The Walls of Jericho*, a dauntingly cynical look at skin color and real estate uptown, and *The Conjure Man Dies*, the first black detective novel. But his career as a doctor and a writer was cut short when he died at the age of thirty-seven from intestinal cancer, apparently caused by years of exposure to X-rays.

The glory days weren't quite over. In 1928 Countee Cullen shocked everyone by taking a wife, and not just any wife. In a sundown ceremony at his father's Salem Methodist Church, Cullen married Nina Yolande Du Bois, the only surviving child of the father of them all. It had all the trappings of a royal union, but the marriage was disastrous: Cullen was gay and Yolande was in love with the bandleader Jimmy Lunceford. A divorce was inevitable, and Cullen's writing suffered. His one and only novel, *One Way to Heaven*, was brushed aside. Du Bois didn't even commission a review in the *Crisis*. It was payback, no doubt, to a wayward son-in-law. Cullen took a job teaching French and English at P.S. 139, also known as Frederick Douglass Junior High School, at 140th Street near Lenox Avenue, and moved to the suburbs.

Cullen's onetime best friend Langston Hughes was one of the few who stayed in Harlem and went on to greater things. The crown prince of the Harlem Renaissance published his second volume of poetry, *Fine Clothes to the Jew*, in 1927. Many critics and readers were put off, not just by the title but by the way in which these new poems frankly confronted the realities of Negro life in Harlem. Reviews in the Negro periodicals were unforgiving—one called uptown's poet laureate a sewer-dwelling "poet low-rate"—but that was the least of his problems. Hughes was now being seen on the arm of Charlotte Osgood Mason, a wealthy, elderly white widow infatuated with all things Negro, who believed that only the primitive "child races" could save Western civilization from the catastrophes of white reason and order. The rhetoric made Harlemites cringe, but Mason's belief in the regenerative function of the arts of Africa and its diaspora was shared by many distinguished minds, black and white. Her cash handouts to her "little boys and girls" were also convincing, for a time. Although Paul Robeson and Jean Toomer resisted her invitations, Hughes, Alain Locke, Claude McKay, Richmond Barthé, Aaron Douglas, and Zora Neale Hurston all sat at her feet while she held forth from on high. Eventually Hughes got fed up with Mason's suggestions about the kind of poetry he should write and what kind of music he should listen to and what kind of politicians he should vote for. He broke with her in the summer of 1930, realizing that of all the white negrophiles of the Harlem Renaissance Mason had been the most dangerous, because she was the most generous.

Slightly depressed by the break with his mother figure, Hughes became positively ill after he lost his sister figure, having clashed with Zora Neale Hurston over a play they tried to write together. What little writing Hughes did during the period he called his "personal crash" found little support. Even as the *Crisis* was handing out awards for literature, Du Bois, like Charles Johnson, was having doubts about the role that the arts should play in improving the lot of America's Negroes. Du Bois began to turn the *Crisis* from an effete journal of rhymed, introspective racial musings alongside lynching statistics, news about baby contests, and advertisements for skin lighteners into a serious forum for discussions of economics and politics. By 1929 the journal had phased out its cultural project altogether. Unable to get a job in publishing—who wanted to hire a single, black woman in her forties?—Jessie Fauset had to take a job teaching French at DeWitt Clinton High School. Eventually, like so many of her peers, she left Harlem altogether, moving to New Jersey and giving up on writing.

Despite all the death, defection, and dissension, the Harlem Renaissance took years to fade away. As late as 1934 the socialite slummer Nancy Cunard brought out *The Negro Anthology*, which introduced a new generation to the cultural pluralism of Alain Locke's *New Negro*, but by then it was clear that philanthropy, politics, and gin had done poisonous work. Most of those Harlem Renaissance writers with the discipline to make a career out of literature—Jessie Fauset, Wallace

Thurman, Nella Larsen, Arna Bontemps, Rudolph Fisher, Claude McKay, Walter White, and W.E.B. Du Bois—lacked a first-rate imagination, or died too young, or gave up too soon. Superior talents such as Jean Toomer or Eric Walrond failed to create a substantial body of work, while the geniuses Langston Hughes, Zora Neale Hurston, and Duke Ellington had yet to reach their peak. Was this really a bona fide artistic movement or was it simply a fortuitous gathering of individual talent with little more in common than the color of their skin and the neighborhood in which they were more or less forced to live for a time?

If there really was a Harlem Renaissance, determining its time of death is as difficult as discovering its moment of birth. Pessimists thought the party was over as early as 1925, even as the New York *Herald Tribune* announced that the country was "on the edge, if not already in the midst, of what might not improperly be called a Negro renaissance." Claude McKay, who coined the term "Negro metropolis," believed that even before the mid-1920s Harlem had turned into "an all white picnic ground with no apparent gain to the blacks." In 1927 Rudolph Fisher wrote an article called "The Caucasian Storms Harlem," arguing that the New Negro Renaissance was nothing more than a blackface revolution, a rage for exotica and primitivism. That opinion was confirmed the next year by a study showing that eighty-one of eighty-five uptown speakeasies were owned by whites. Alain Locke claimed that the Harlem Renaissance had been "scuttled from within," but the continued dominance of "vice, dice, and lice" uptown made the question of beginnings and endings of less interest to Langston Hughes. All talk about racial art and racial assertion aside, he knew that Harlemites were still prisoners of segregation. Central Harlem's population was more than two hundred thousand in 1929, an increase of as much as 500 percent in just three decades. Almost 97 percent of the neighborhood was now black, its residents largely unable to live, work, shop, or play anywhere else. What came in between was for the most part irrelevant since, as Hughes avowed, "Ordinary Negroes hadn't heard of the Negro Renaissance."

9

"MOON OVER HARLEM"
The Great Depression Uptown, 1929–1943

"I don't know nothin' 'bout no Depression," the housekeeper of the eminent sociologist E. Franklin Frazier used to say. "I ain't seen nuthin' but hard times all my life." Indeed, in February of 1930, four months after the stock market crash but well before the arrival of the national economic crisis, the New York *Herald Tribune* found that Harlem was "the poorest, the unhealthiest, the unhappiest and the most crowded single large section of New York City." Yet as bad as things got during the 1930s, when Harlem was "on the verge of starvation," as a writer for the Federal Writers Project put it, the Negro mecca continued to attract masses of blacks from the American South and the West Indies in search of jobs and justice. Granted, charities mitigated some of the suffering, and the implementation of the New Deal brought a level of government assistance that blacks had never dreamed possible. Demonstrations and boycotts convinced the store owners of 125th Street to welcome blacks as both employees and customers, though disposable income was starting to vanish and unemployment was rising. Negroes could finally join previously all-white unions and even start labor organizations of their own, though neither process was easy. Laundry workers seeking to unionize in the 1920s had been asked by labor organizers, "Have you a backbone or a wishbone?" In the 1930s, Harlemites would need both.

In the 1920s Harlem became the biggest black city in the world, having grown from a population of eighty-four thousand in 1920 to more than two hundred thousand in 1930, which was of course possible only because of the departure of 120,000 Jews, Irish, and Italians. By 1940 that number had grown to more than 250,000, and central and lower Harlem were almost 100 percent black, while East Harlem was increasingly a destination for Puerto Ricans, many of whom also claimed African origins. Between the West Indians and the Puerto Ricans, almost half of all blacks uptown between the wars were foreign-born, and very few of them had it easy.

To be sure, there were plenty of rich people in Harlem during the Great Depression. The New York *Age* snobbishly monitored the border between Harlem high society and everyone else, and in the late 1930s there was even a magazine, called the *Vanguard*, that put together a list of "The Elite of African Descent." These were the residents of Sugar Hill or Hamilton Heights or Striver's Row, the members of fraternities and sororities that held formal balls, threw coming-out parties for their daughters, and showed off their furs and automobiles and European vacations. But the number of people who could spend $150 in a single night at the Savoy Ballroom or Smalls Paradise was tiny. In the early 1930s, well before the uptown economy hit bottom, only 15 percent of Harlemites could be considered middle class, and the number of upper-class Harlemites was a small proportion of that.

It was a lucky Harlemite who managed to find a job as an elevator operator or sales clerk, and messengers, porters, dishwashers, and factory laborers considered themselves blessed, but this was a relative matter. The average Harlemite made under $18 per sixty-six-hour week, compared to whites, who were paid about $23 for a sixty-hour week for similar work during the early years of the Depression, according to the New York *Herald Tribune*. For women things were even more bleak, with domestic servants making $15 per week and laundresses making less than half of that, while whites in those positions brought home nearly twice as much. The cost of living declined as the Depression deepened, but so did family incomes. In the early 1930s a quarter of all Harlemites were out of work. College graduates were unable to get work even as manual laborers, and after 1933, when Prohibition was repealed and the uptown entertainment industry began its long, agonizing decline, overall unemployment reached 50 percent. Langston

Hughes commented, "The depression brought everybody down a peg or two. And the Negroes had but few pegs to fall."

Continued population growth—the number of black arrivals far surpassed the number of suburban-bound whites—and little new housing construction meant that population densities in Harlem rose above levels that had been described as unmanageable decades before. The block bounded by Lenox and Eighth avenues, between West 138th and West 139th streets, was the most tightly packed in the city, with 820 people per acre, or about three times the Manhattan average. Overcrowding was only part of the problem. Along Fifth Avenue from West 135th Street to West 138th Street, central heating was rare, and the few residents of tenements with indoor bathrooms often had to share each floor's single toilet with four or five extended families— most Harlemites still used outhouses located in backyards and alleys. One study from the mid-1930s found that 60 percent of all Harlemites lived in apartments in desperate need of repair, partly because superintendents were given free basement apartments but no salaries, which meant that they had to work full-time jobs that left no time to maintain the buildings. Even then, rents remained higher than economically comparable white neighborhoods. Evicted families out on the street with their pitiful heaps of belongings—much of which would end up for sale in East Harlem's twenty-six junkyards—were a common sight in the 1930s, becoming a flashpoint for political demonstrations. Many evicted families joined masses of homeless newcomers from the South in spending the night in St. Nicholas Park.

Harlem still attracted the great and the good, and those looking for traces of the sweet life had only to follow Duke Ellington's advice and "Take the A Train" to Sugar Hill—it was one man's guide to the city's underground transportation system. Observant subway riders could see the porters and domestics get off at West 125th Street, the clerks and secretaries depart at West 135th Street, and the doctors and lawyers leave at West 145th Street. Many professionals still aspired to the Paul Laurence Dunbar houses, even after residents defaulting on their mortgages starting in 1929 convinced the sponsor, John D. Rockefeller, to turn the whole complex into rentals. Another magnet

for Talented Tenthers on Sugar Hill was the Colonial Parkway Apartments, at 409 Edgecombe Avenue overlooking the Polo Grounds. Built
in 1917 for whites—baseball's homerun king Babe Ruth was among the
first tenants—the building was desegregated in the late 1920s and was
almost completely black by the end of the 1930s. The famed "Triple
Nickel," as 555 Edgecombe Avenue was known, began welcoming
blacks only in 1939, and even then only a "better" class that included
W.E.B. Du Bois, Paul Robeson, and Cab Calloway. Such transitions
weren't always friendly. In 1937 the first black residents of Hamilton
Terrace were greeted with a shower of stones thrown by local white
children. But even Harlem's toniest black neighborhoods were beginning to deteriorate, as grand, single-family homes built before the turn
of the century were broken up into multiple apartments or rooming
houses, especially in the old Jewish neighborhoods bordering Central
and Morningside parks. The area from West 110th Street to West 125th
Street was only 30 percent black in 1930, but by World War II it was
90 percent black and almost 100 percent poor.

If housing is a reliable indicator of the condition of a community,
health care is even more telling. The mortality rate in central Harlem
was 40 percent higher than the city average during the early years of
the Depression, while the infant mortality rate was twice the city average, as was the percentage of Harlemites with pneumonia, typhoid,
and tuberculosis—in the "lung blocks" of the Harlem Valley, rates
of infection were up to nine times the city average. Uptowners joked
that the definition of a Harlem tenement was a hundred sharecrop-
per cabins from the Mississippi Delta plus tuberculosis. Harlemites
who could afford it could choose from the private Community and
Sydenham hospitals. The rest—more than two hundred thousand
people—had to settle for the 273 beds (many in closets and hallways),
52 cribs, and 3 ambulances of the Harlem Hospital, with its virtually
all-white staff. With a death rate twice that of other city hospitals, it
was known as the "Butcher Shop."

Things were hardest on children, 60 percent of whom—more
than three times the city average—were malnourished, and black Harlem's public schools themselves were in scandalous condition, largely

unrenovated since their construction decades earlier, most without libraries or gymnasiums, and some without indoor bathrooms; Harlemites quipped that P.S. stood for "public sewer." These schools were also dangerously overcrowded, some holding five times the legal capacity. Moreover, it was the policy of the New York City Board of Education to punish troublesome or underperforming teachers by placing them uptown, which meant that Harlem's children received the worst education that the city had to offer.

Despite the fact that families were on average smaller than their white counterparts downtown, black mothers were more likely to work outside the home in order to pay uptown's higher rents. New York City Family Court saw rising rates of nonsupport and desertion cases. About 20 percent of all minors in Harlem were living in households with no father, a number that reached 50 percent on the poorest blocks. Many children worked, which wasn't always as bad as it sounds. Many of the kids who got jobs waving towels to fan away the cigar smoke at East Harlem's boxing clubs could train at the Boys' Club on Lexington Avenue and East 126th Street for only 10 cents a month. Some of them—for instance, the Italian Lenny Del Genio and the Jewish Benny Leonard—made it big in the world of professional prizefighting. Children were usually left to their own devices, which led to high rates of truancy and juvenile delinquency. Before World War I, black children represented 2 percent of all children in New York City and 2 percent of all juvenile cases heard in court. By 1929 black children represented 3 percent of all city minors, but 11 percent of all cases heard in children's court. That figure rose to 25 percent by 1938, a situation portrayed with heartbreaking realism in Ann Petry's 1946 novel *The Street,* which tells the story of a single mother struggling to raise a son on West 116th Street between Seventh and Eighth avenues—the story was inspired by Petry's own experience working at an after-school program at P.S. 10. Not all of Harlem's children were doomed by such conditions. The jazz saxophonist Sonny Rollins, the son of socialist immigrants from Saint Thomas who settled into a tenement on West 137th Street between Lenox and Seventh avenues, attended P.S. 89—Fats Waller's alma mater—which was located next door to

Barron's nightclub. Attending mostly white Benjamin Franklin High School required riding a crosstown bus that was regularly pelted by local Italian kids. His free time was spent taking 20-cent saxophone lessons at the West 131st Street branch of the YMCA, practicing on rooftops, or hanging around the Kinghaven Apartments in Sugar Hill, where his musical idol, Coleman Hawkins, lived.

If the early years of the Depression hit Harlemites harder than other black New Yorkers, that was in part because they had remained so politically marginal. That changed when the most beloved scion of Italian East Harlem, Fiorello La Guardia, realized that the political system that had more or less controlled New York since before the Civil War was unsuited to the modern metropolis. The Irishmen who still dominated Tammany Hall were not natural political allies of Harlem's Italians, Jews, blacks, West Indians, and Puerto Ricans. The man who more than any other single figure was responsible for the making of modern New York City, not only its roads, bridges, parks, playgrounds, and housing projects but the indomitable spirit that allowed it to survive the Great Depression and fight World War II, was not, strictly speaking, a local boy. Born downtown in 1882 to an Apulian immigrant and a Jewish mother from Trieste, La Guardia grew up in Arizona, the southwest territories, the Midwest, and Florida. After college, he entered the diplomatic service and worked in Hungary and Italy before returning to the United States in 1907 to work as a translator at Ellis Island. He graduated from New York University Law School in 1910 and got involved in Republican politics, representing Greenwich Village on the city's Board of Aldermen and then in the House of Representatives. When the United States entered World War I, La Guardia signed up with the air force. He was wounded twice while flying bombing missions, which earned him valuable credibility when he came home and ran as a Republican for the congressional seat representing mostly Jewish and Italian parts of the Bronx and East Harlem. The incumbent, Henry Frank, was not only Jewish but Tammany's candidate. He called La Guardia an anti-Semitic carpetbagger from downtown. La Guardia responded by playing up his Jewish heritage and challenging Frank to a debate in Yiddish, knowing perfectly well that the assimilated Frank couldn't speak the language. "Is he looking for a job as a *shames*?" La Guardia said of Frank, using the Yiddish term for the janitor of a synagogue—it can also mean a sycophant or even a stool pigeon—"or does he want to be elected congressman?" La Guardia won by only 168 votes, but East Harlemites were clearly taken with him. He returned the affection, turning his headquarters at 247 East 116th Street into a de facto walk-in social services center. It wasn't until 1929 that La Guardia became a Harlemite for real, moving into a modest, four-room apartment in a tenement at 23 East 109th Street. Here he ran for mayor, unsuccessfully in 1929 and then successfully in 1933 on a fusion ticket that brought together Democrats who had no loyalty to the perennially corrupt Tammany machine and Republicans tired of losing. Together they broke Tammany Hall's grip on city politics, at least for a while.

By the time La Guardia became mayor, Italian East Harlem was already in the grip of the Depression and changing fast. Block after block still resembled Rome or Naples, from the *corso* of Doctors and Lawyers Row to the staggering poverty of the blocks just to the south, which provided settings for the novels of Leonard Covello's friend Garibaldi Lapolla, who taught at Thomas Jefferson High School and wrote three novels—*The Fire in the Flesh* (1931), *Miss Rollins in Love* (1932), and *The Grand Gennaro* (1935)—that chronicled life in Italian East Harlem.

Lapolla found few readers in his own neighborhood, not only because of low literacy rates among adults but because those who read fiction seemed to prefer an alternative to their own harrowing experiences. Even before the Depression reached its nadir, unemployment was 45 percent. Many East Harlemites stayed off relief by farming tiny plots in Jefferson Park rather than submit to the humiliating inspections of relief workers whose visits brought shame on the whole family. Somewhat more dignity was forthcoming at settlement houses like Haarlem House or Casa del Popolo, which sponsored clubs, job training, services for immigrants, and activities for four hundred children, though most local kids were expected to help the family make ends meet, not have fun. That was necessary because of the pittance earned by their parents in East Harlem's rail yards, gas- and icehouses, masonry and lumberyards, blacksmith shops, cigar factories, sweatshops, and piano builders—when jobs were even available. In contrast, the vice business flourished, with Lexington Avenue from East 117th to East 122nd streets filled with brothels and 50-cent Polish streetwalkers. Above 125th Street on the east side was the territory of Swedish and Finnish prostitutes. The numbers racket in the 1930s was almost as popular among Italians and Puerto Ricans in East Harlem as it was among Negroes to the west and north, as was gambling on sports.

Becoming New York City's ninety-ninth mayor was one thing. Guiding what was now the world's biggest city through the depths of the Great Depression, when more than 140,000 families in New York City were on government relief and the city's debt amounted to almost $2 billion, was something else altogether. La Guardia made sure the city survived by putting idea over ideology and embracing Franklin D. Roosevelt's plan to keep the country afloat with an unprecedented government investment in job creation through public works projects. Harlem got housing projects, a Music and Art High School at Convent Avenue and West 135th Street, pools in Colonial (now known as Jackie Robinson) Park and Thomas Jefferson Park, and infrastructure such as the Triboro Bridge, the West Side Highway, the East River Drive, the Lincoln and Holland tunnels, and the airport that would later bear the mayor's name.

La Guardia maintained support in East Harlem by keeping his Italian heritage in the foreground. That meant both chatting in Italian with constituents in the streets as well as putting Italian-Americans in positions of power. He selected Edward Corsi, a native of Capistrano who grew up in East Harlem, as his commissioner of public welfare, a position he left only to serve as Roosevelt's commissioner of immigration. La Guardia's reputation as a racial progressive got him 90 percent of the city's black vote in 1933. He had to work even harder to keep the allegiance of Negro Harlemites, who wanted more than token representation in government. La Guardia banned racial discrimination in city hiring. By the end of his tenure there were some five thousand black civil servants, who became the core of the city's black middle class. He named many African-Americans to prominent public offices. La Guardia ended the use of police clubs and made police brutality a special concern, though change wasn't coming fast enough, it seems. Complaints persisted that La Guardia cared more about Italians and Jews, that he seemed to pay attention to what was going on in Negro Harlem only when blacks got into trouble with their white neighbors. In fact, most of La Guardia's initiatives transcended race and ethnicity. Housing had long been a priority for La Guardia, whose first term saw the demolition of more than four hundred substandard buildings uptown, and he created the New York City Public Housing Authority with the purpose of transforming tenement neighborhoods. The arrival of the first housing projects in the 1930s signaled a major change. Slum clearance sounded good, but the projects destroyed much of what made Harlem home. This was especially true in El Barrio, where housing projects undermined the extended family arrangements that characterized the homes of so many *Boricuas*—Puerto Rican nationalists referred to themselves that way to recall the aboriginal name of the island. East Harlemites were also concerned by La Guardia's decision to face the growing problem caused by thousands of unlicensed pushcart vendors working the streets of East Harlem, turning First Avenue from East 104th to East 116th streets into an open-air market. La Guardia evicted 250 of these pushcart peddlers, most of them Italians, Latinos, and Jews, and relocated many of them to the space beneath the viaduct of the New York Central Railroad, along Park Avenue from East 111th to East 116th streets. It became the best place in the city for Italians to shop for fruit, vegetables, fish, meat, olive oil, wine, and cheese. Soon the market was attracting twenty-five thousand shoppers per day, many of whom came extra early to capitalize on superstitious Jewish vendors who would rather lose money than lose the first customer of the day. As the Latino presence in the neighborhood grew, vendors began offering tamarind, guava, avocado, and plantains, as well as hog maws, pig ears, and tripe.

La Marqueta, as it was rechristened, was the kind of infrastructure project that convinced Italian, Jewish, Latino, and Negro Harlemites alike to keep their local boy in City Hall.

While Mayor La Guardia was building a mighty nonpartisan coalition out of the city's mainstream political discontents, many Negro Harlemites were becoming convinced that nothing would really change uptown until they made peace with Tammany Hall. The movement was spearheaded by J. Raymond Jones, a native of the Danish West Indies who arrived in Harlem at the age of eighteen in 1919. Like so many members of Harlem's great migration generation he found himself marching with the UNIA. Marcus Garvey hired Jones to turn around the UNIA restaurants, grocery stores, and laundry, but Jones chafed under the ideological control that the UNIA demanded, so in 1921 he joined the white-led United Colored Democracy. Jones soon mastered New York State's arcane election rules and got a black municipal judge elected in a mostly black neighborhood, not an insignificant step forward, since these judges ruled on issues such as evictions, which were becoming a major issue as the Depression deepened. Ironically, Jones's mastery of the subtleties of Harlem's relationship with Tammany Hall—he became known as the "Harlem Fox"—coincided with the temporary decline of the Democrats in New York City that occurred after the fall of Mayor Jimmy Walker and the rise of La Guardia. With only 29 percent of uptowners casting ballots, Jones saw an opportunity. Democrats at the national level had never had much success with Negro voters, and now Tammany Hall Democrats could not even count on Negro Harlem at the local level. When Jones demanded the installation of black political appointees he got them.

Political change came more slowly to El Barrio. Those exhilarating months in 1926 when Puerto Ricans, Cubans, Mexicans, Panamanians, and Dominicans closed ranks to present a unified political force led to few concrete changes. After *El Gráfico* closed in 1931 there wasn't even a Spanish-language newspaper for a community that numbered sixty thousand and was growing faster than ever. Half of them were

Puerto Ricans, who as American citizens could travel to the mainland without much trouble. If poor economic conditions weren't enough incentive, there was the 1932 hurricane that devastated the island, sending a wave of refugees north. Among them was the young Rosa Delores Alverío, who grew up to become the actress Rita Moreno. There were also more than six thousand Cubans in El Barrio in the early 1930s, a community that was far more influential than its size suggests. The Puerto Rican arrivals were generally uneducated and unskilled, but many of the Cubans had an education, a profession, and a strong political consciousness. Tammany Hall began paying real attention to the Latino vote starting only in the mid-1930s, when Republicans decided to court Latinos. El Barrio's José Negrón Cesteros, who arrived in the United States in 1913, was named the Puerto Rican division chair of the Democratic National Committee in 1936. By that time many Puerto Ricans had sided with the Republicans, though it wasn't until a decade later that voters in El Barrio, outraged by a police massacre at a nationalist rally in Ponce, Puerto Rico, put a Puerto Rican Republican in office. Oscar Garcia Rivera's election to the state assembly made him the first Puerto Rican elected to public office in the United States. If there was one cause that united Puerto Ricans in El Barrio, it was the struggle for the island's independence. Gonzalo O'Neill's play *Bajo Una Sola Bandera* ("Under Just One Flag"), a politically charged drama endorsing Puerto Rican nationalism, wowed audiences from across the political spectrum at the Park Palace.

No matter which party controlled City Hall, deepening poverty and skyrocketing crime—the homicide rate in central Harlem, which was almost twice the city average in 1925, rose to more than six times the city average a decade later—weren't always La Guardia's highest priority. His first term made a priority out of fighting policy gambling, which by some accounts had become uptown's biggest industry since white gangsters, searching for a way to replace the income lost when Prohibition was repealed, had taken over. Dutch Schultz crowded out the Italians, pacifying them by giving a quarter of the Harlem policy business to Ciro Terranova, though the Artichoke King was soon targeted by La Guardia on antitrust grounds and banned from New York City—he nonetheless continued to live at 338 East 116th Street. Schultz knew how to handle the mafia, but things were more complicated when it came to maintaining dominance over Negro organized crime. In 1931 he had invited Harlem's top black numbers bankers to a secret meeting, put a pistol on the table, and announced, "I'm your partner." So far, so good, but Schultz then eliminated numbers runners, all of whom were black, and he made betting available only in his uptown candy shops. Negro Harlemites were outraged at the number of family men being put out of business and began a boycott, supported somewhat improbably by the NAACP, that convinced Schultz to reinstate the runners, who were, not coincidentally, his first line of defense against the law. By the end of La Guardia's first term, a third of all arrests uptown were on numbers-related charges, almost all of them black runners. Meanwhile, white gangsters increasingly followed the money, which was not in 10-cent bets but in dollar bags of heroin. Throughout the 1930s the corner of Lenox Avenue and West 135th Street was a public market for marijuana, cocaine, opium, morphine, and heroin. Harlemites could openly smoke marijuana without fear of arrest, as long as their dealers made sure police and prosecutors were kept satisfied. Much the same was true of prostitution uptown, which accounted for almost a third of all prostitution charges citywide. Streetwalkers worked Seventh Avenue between West 110th and West 115th streets, which was known as the Market, but most of the action was in bordellos, some of which featured girls as young as fourteen. Still, La Guardia's campaigns against such "disorderly houses" seemed to focus at times not on morality but on public health. Most of the "expensive girls" arrested in that summer at the whorehouse at 32 West 112th Street had syphilis or gonorrhea, while the overall incidence of venereal disease uptown was a shocking seven times the city average. The Harlem judge who heard the case ordered the very embarrassing testing of sixteen patrons, all of them white. Such high-profile cases made for good publicity but little more.

La Guardia was more successful in cracking down on Harlem's burlesque and striptease houses, which had only grown in popularity

after the stock market crash. Nowhere else in the city could audiences
pay so little to see so much. In the early 1930s the Minsky brothers
brought "the living art" to their newly opened New Gotham Theatre
at 167 East 125th Street. This low-budget operation did away with
any pretense and became renowned for the raciest acts in the country,
including "Julius Teaser" and "Panties Inferno." Mae Dix's new act,
called "Let's Take a Trip," called for her to come out dressed for a
journey and slowly strip until only three parts of her body remained
covered by signs reading "Stop," "Go," and "Detour." La Guardia ordered the theater closed in 1933, but a state court bought the manager's argument that any nudity at the New Gotham was simulated.
One of the dancers had a G-string with fake pubic hair just to show
inspectors. At the Apollo, which the newly emboldened Minsky brothers now controlled, a chorus line of no fewer than twenty-eight girls
went topless. La Guardia was outraged, demanding stricter decency
guidelines for the licensing of theaters, which led to a two-year court
battle, itself quite a show when three of the accused strippers were
called upon by the defense to demonstrate their routines. The judge
stopped them just in time. The New Gotham's license was revoked
for six months, along with those of fourteen other burlesque venues,
though within weeks the Harlem Uproar House, which was a nightclub
and therefore not subject to theatrical licensing, featured a naughty
act called "The Funeral of Striptease."

Many Harlemites believed La Guardia's energetic pursuit of gamblers,
vipers, and strippers distracted him from dealing with race problems,
which inspired the mainstream civil rights organizations to step up.
The Urban League helped with food, clothing, and housing, and they
even offered a job placement service, but there were simply too few
jobs to be had. The NAACP couldn't do much better, at least in terms
of day-to-day survival, because the organization was in such turmoil.
Still reeling from the decline in membership from ninety-thousand to
twenty thousand during the 1920s, the organization, which depended
on both the checks of white philanthropists and the pennies of its

members, halved its budget after the stock market crash. Du Bois stopped getting a paycheck from the *Crisis,* forcing him to default on his mortgage. He was unable to pay the legal bills for his daughter Yolande's divorce from Countee Cullen. He was soon to be forced out of the NAACP altogether after he published an article exploring the advantages of racial segregation.

The incoming executive director of the NAACP, Walter White, tried to keep the Harlem office relevant, which meant not just clothes, food, and jobs but new blood. Among White's new recruits was a young lawyer from Baltimore named Thurgood Marshall, who had spent much of his childhood in Harlem while his father was a waiter on the New York Central Railroad. Marshall learned early on to confront racism. "If someone calls you a 'Nigger,'" his father told him, "take it up right then and there—either win or lose right then and there." In 1936 White convinced the twenty-eight-year-old Marshall, by then a graduate of Lincoln and Howard, the Yale and Harvard of black America, to shut down his Baltimore law office and move to New York. There he helped the national office move beyond often-abstract legal issues such as equal protection and due process and start taking on discrimination in the workplace, school desegregation, and lynching. This tall, rumpled man took his pleasure seriously, regularly taking his wife, Buster, for drinking and gambling at Happy Rhone's Club, which was the NAACP's unofficial headquarters. After closing time, they would head to the after-hours places along West 125th Street for more down-to-earth pleasures, and then a sunrise breakfast at Dicky Wells's Club, before going back home to 409 Edgecombe Avenue.

Harlemites may have had mixed feelings about the Urban League and the NAACP, but there weren't many alternatives. Black Americans couldn't look to organized labor for jobs or political direction because most unions were still all-white. Despite decades of attempts to integrate labor, by the start of the 1930s fewer than 10 percent of blacks nationwide working in the most heavily unionized sectors—for example, industry and manufacturing—were represented by a labor organization. Even the *Amsterdam News* resisted the organizing efforts of the American Newspaper Guild. Things were different for Latinos, who were considered white enough for organized labor, it seems, especially after a major strike by the International Ladies Garment Workers Union in 1933 drew in masses of picketers along East 125th Street and resulted in the unionization of dozens of East Harlem sweatshops where Boricuas toiled. What finally changed the way organized labor looked at race was the 1935 National Labor Relations Act, which outlawed the company unions that management had traditionally used to undermine organizing. Among the earliest beneficiaries of the new law was A. Philip Randolph's Brotherhood of Sleeping Car Porters, which in 1937, twelve years to the day after its first meeting, finally signed a contract with the Pullman Company, the first collective bargaining agreement ever achieved by a black union.

Another reason that it took so long for a black labor movement to grow uptown was the continuing appeal of socialism. The movement had struggled for relevance in black Harlem even before the Red Scare of 1919, in part because of government persecution and in part because socialism was largely the province of West Indian race radicals whose program seemed downright deranged to the teeming masses of the great migration just looking for work. The crash was good news for the communists, whose offices at 306 Lenox Avenue were filled with newly relevant discussions about capitalism terminable and interminable. Events closer to home also helped. In 1930 a black party member with the somewhat improbable name of Alfred Levy was killed by police during a Lenox Avenue demonstration, and a few days later a Mexican communist named Gonzalo Gonzalez was killed by officers while on his way to a party gathering at the Harlem Casino, events that gained the party much sympathy uptown. But there were self-inflicted wounds. A 1931 "trial" at the Harlem Casino saw party members "convict" a Finnish Harlemite and a party member named August Yokinen of racism. Then came that landmark event in the history of American politics called the Scottsboro Boys trial, which for a time looked as if it would finally make communism a genuine political option. The case stemmed from a 1931 incident in which nine black youths were accused of raping two white women on an Alabama train, convicted by an all-white jury, and sentenced to death. They would have gotten it, had not the Communist Party made what was obviously a miscarriage of justice a national issue, and an uptown one, too. While the NAACP and the *Amsterdam News* dithered, at least at first, the communists held rallies, dances, and meetings to raise money and consciousness. They enlisted a constellation of famous Harlemites, not just politically engaged figures like Langston Hughes, who dedicated an entire book of poems to the cause, but Cab Calloway, a radical in nothing but the cut of his zoot suit, who provided the music for a 1932 benefit at the Rockland Palace.

The most visible and committed voice of communism uptown was Paul Robeson, who by the time of the Depression was not only the most famous Negro in America but one of the most famous Americans in the world, despite a chronic inability to find work that was up to his talents. The uptown press attacked him relentlessly for appearing in plays that called on him to use the word "nigger," though in 1934 Robeson replaced the word "nigger" with "darky" in the film version of *Showboat,* a substitution that irked lyricist Oscar Hammerstein II. Despite Robeson and other high-profile supporters, as well as the righteous momentum of the Scottsboro Boys case, which dragged on for more than a decade, the Communist Party counted only three hundred or so members uptown in the mid-1930s.

The only group that embraced communism en masse were the Jews of City College, still a hotbed of radical politics. One professor, Morris Schappes, was fired and tried and sentenced to two years in prison for alleged activities as a communist spy, and Julius Rosenberg, a Harlem native, joined CCNY's Young Communist League before being exposed as a Soviet spy. More typical was the political journey of figures such as Alfred Kazin, Sidney Hook, Irving Howe, Irving Kristol, Nathan Glazer, Gertrude Himmelfarb, Leslie Fiedler, Isaac Rosenfeld, and Daniel Bell, who traded in the faith of their ancestors for communism—each of the alcoves in the City College library was claimed by a different sect—before graduating to form the conservative core of the anticommunist group referred to as the New York Intellectuals.

*   *   *

Another reason for communism's failure to attract the masses was the domination of uptown cultural life by religion. Half of all Harlemites claimed membership in one of dozens of established churches, and most of the rest attended one of hundreds of smaller, storefront operations. It was ironic, then, that the most significant ally that the Communist Party made uptown in the 1930s was Adam Clayton Powell Jr., who was the public face of Harlem from the Jazz Age to the Black Power era. He was born in 1908 to the son of the seventeenth leader of the already venerable Abyssinian Baptist Church, which was still located in the Tenderloin, though the Powells lived uptown. A blond-haired, blued eyed, light-skinned child, Powell was spoiled rotten by his mother, his sister, and their maid, who dressed him in girlish outfits of velvet and patent leather. Eventually, Powell escaped the ten-room penthouse at 227 West 136th Street and discovered the rest of Harlem.

Powell's childhood stomping grounds were flanked by Jews to the south, Irish to the west, and Italians to the east, so racial, ethnic, and religious conflicts were frequent. As boundaries shifted to accommodate Harlem's growing Negro population, the interactions grew more violent. In order to attend P.S. 5, Powell would join a dozen black children each morning and afternoon to make the perilous crossing of white-dominated Eighth Avenue. Things weren't always so simple. Powell's extremely light skin color—he bragged he was neither fish nor fowl—made him vulnerable to the assaults of whites who thought he was black and of blacks who thought he was white. After graduating from the prestigious Townsend Harris High School he entered City College, but he was distracted by girls and basketball and flunked out in his second year. In 1926 Powell enrolled in the otherwise all-white Colgate college, in upstate New York, where his taste for good times and his encyclopedic knowledge of night life in New York City—he was one of the very few blacks who managed to gain entry to the Cotton Club—made him many friends.

That all changed late one night in 1930, when Powell heard a divine voice calling him to the ministry. The next morning he telephoned his parents and switched his major from premed to religion. Powell's father asked him to choose between the ministry and his girlfriend, the Cotton Club chorine Isabel Washington. The church membership was more forgiving, and Washington was baptized by her boyfriend one Sunday as the Cotton Club chorus line watched in astonishment from the pews. When his father had a nervous breakdown due to overwork Powell all but took over. The younger Powell somehow found a way to combine eternal life in heaven with the good life uptown, tooling around in his father's Pierce Arrow and strolling Seventh Avenue every Sunday afternoon after church in an ascot, tails, top hat, cane, and spats. He announced, "I am not a full-Bible Christian," which meant that he was free to drink, smoke, and consort with his adoring female parishioners. Still, Powell considered economic justice and racial integration fundamental to the Christian mission, and his church was as concerned with the minds and bodies of its eight thousand members as with their souls. He turned his home over to community center activities, ran literacy classes, job training and referral programs, and organized a soup kitchen that fed a thousand people every day.

What turned Powell from a local hero into a national leader was a string of street campaigns he led to confront the racial discrimination that still dominated life uptown. First on the list was challenging prejudiced hiring practices at Harlem Hospital, which under the economic pressure of the Depression had fired five Negro doctors in 1931. Powell led community meetings, picketed the hospital, and brought thousands of people to City Hall to demonstrate, resulting in the reinstatement of the doctors and the elimination of racial discrimination in hiring altogether. It was a stunning victory for the twenty-two-year-old Powell, and it inspired him to take on many problems that his savior had otherwise left to Caesar. Powell helped found the Harlem Cooperating Committee on Relief and Unemployment, which offered housing, clothing, job services, and health care. He assisted in the formation of the Consolidated Tenants League, which held protests and withheld rent from landlords who failed to maintain their buildings properly or who unfairly evicted tenants. Economic discrimination was even higher on Powell's agenda. In the 1930s fewer than four hundred of uptown's twelve thousand businesses were owned by blacks, including only four of Harlem's 172 grocery stores, and only one of dozens of uptown theaters. The fact that saloons and funeral parlors were better represented was hardly something to celebrate.

Powell wasn't alone in seeking to end the racial status quo on 125th Street. A group called the Harlem Housewives League targeted the big chain stores like Woolworth's and A&P, both of which refused to hire Negroes in anything but menial positions. At the same time, more than a hundred black shopkeepers joined the Colored Merchants Association, an organization that was soon taken over by extremists more interested in publicity than in helping struggling store owners. The most prominent of these race radicals was the Afro-eccentric charlatan born Eugene Brown in Philadelphia and raised in Massachusetts before becoming a Harlem gangster of some renown. He reinvented himself as a Buddhist named Bishop Conshankin, but it was as a Muslim named Amirin Al-Minin Sufi Abdul Hamid that he set up a booth on Lenox Avenue, exhorting Harlem's white merchants to "Share the jobs!" He also collected money from black Harlemites who seem to have contributed primarily in order to shut him up. In 1932 he encroached once too often on the ideological and geographical territory of the UNIA, leading to a violent clash, after which police banned public activities by both groups. That only encouraged Hamid, who bragged of his Egyptian genealogy and took to wearing an "African" costume that included a turban, cape, and riding crop, to boycott a white-owned five-and-dime, butcher, and grocer in what still looked less like a racial protest than a shakedown.

Powell was able to keep his distance from the extremists until he got involved in the renowned "Don't Buy Where You Can't Work" campaign against Harlem's fanciest and largest retailer, Blumstein's department store. After the death of the founder, Louis Blumstein, in 1920, his sons had torn down the old building and spent more than $1 million to build the so-called uptown Saks Fifth Avenue, whose limestone and copper exterior and massive vertical sign dominated West 125th Street between Sixth and Seventh avenues well into the next century. Blumstein's began hiring blacks in 1929, but only as porters and elevator operators, never in sales. Even though that policy was more progressive than that of its neighbors, Harlemites weren't mollified. In 1932 the New York *Age* published the names of blacks who shopped at Blumstein's as a way to shame them. When that didn't work, a thirty-four-year-old Philadelphia native named Effa Manley who worked in the garment industry convinced *Age* publisher Fred Moore and the Reverend John Johnson of St. Martin's Episcopal Church to form a coalition of more than sixty groups to fight racism on Harlem's main commercial thoroughfare. The greatest strength of the Citizens League for Fair Play was its diversity: it included Harlem's fanciest churches and social clubs, Democratic and Republican organizations, and even communist and Garveyite race separatist groups, as well as independent voices like Powell's. Starting in July of 1934, Citizens League members manned picket lines every day in front of Blumstein's, holding signs that read "Don't Buy Where You Can't Work." The Citizens League's more extreme affiliates went even further, insulting, harassing, and even assaulting shoppers. Despite such distractions, the Blumstein's boycott was bound to succeed—no store uptown could survive the one-two punch of a boycott and the Great Depression both. After more than a month of demonstrations, an offer was made to hire a dozen black clerks right away and bring in even more by the end of the year. Eventually, Blumstein's become a model for doing business in black communities, introducing the country's first black Santa Claus and the first black display mannequins.

The battle against racism on 125th Street had been successful, and the Citizens League disbanded, but the outcome of the broader war remained in doubt. Indeed, the more extreme members of the Citizens League were just getting started. Two Garveyites named Arthur Reid and Ira Kemp kept on picketing Blumstein's under the sign of something called the Harlem Labor Union, actually a small-scale labor racketeering organization specializing in convincing businesses to fire unaffiliated black employees in order to hire black Harlem Labor

Union members. Hamid, whose anti-Semitic rallies and parades earned him the title the "Black Hitler," not only rejected Blumstein's offer and set up his own parallel picket but broadened his protest to other stores on 125th Street. Give us $3 up front and 25 cents each week, Hamid suggested, and replace light-skinned black workers with my darker-skinned friends, or we will shut you down. He didn't admit that his "friends" also kicked back a percentage of their salaries to him and paid monthly dues to belong to his organization. But the race radicals riding on Adam Clayton Powell Jr.'s coattails weren't in it for the long run, especially not after a series of court decisions—one handed down in 1935 by State Supreme Court judge Salvatore Cotillo, himself a resident of Italian East Harlem—found that Hamid's demonstrations weren't protected by the First Amendment in absence of a bona fide labor issue. Hamid found new interests, marrying Madame Stephanie St. Clair, the Policy Queen of Harlem, and starting an automobile repair shop and a green grocer that avoided taxes by calling itself the Universal Temple of Tranquillity, but before the end of the decade St. Clair shot and killed Hamid in a fit of jealousy.

Harlemites overjoyed by the success of Powell's boycotts soon came back to reality. Despite the victory at Blumstein's, fewer than one hundred of the four thousand people working on 125th Street were black, according to one survey, all in menial positions, and four out of five Harlem businesses refused to hire blacks at all. Negroes still weren't allowed to try on clothes at Koch's and Blumstein's, and more than one 125th Street movie theater still restricted blacks to the upper balconies. Neither the Theresa Hotel nor the Triboro Hotel, at Fifth Avenue and 125th Street, welcomed blacks. Finally, many newly integrated shops and recently opened black-owned businesses simply couldn't survive the depths of the Great Depression, and all employees, black and white, lost their jobs. The bigger picture was even more troubling. In the Harlem Valley, 40 percent of families relied on government support to survive, though that meant only $22 per month, even as the federal government estimated that more than $90 was necessary for the typical family to avoid poverty. It is hard to believe that the events of March 19, 1935, took many people by surprise.

* * *

What many historians believe ended the Harlem Renaissance and marked the beginning of Harlem's descent into semipermanent status as America's representative black ghetto started late in the afternoon at the S. H. Kress five-and-ten, a notoriously racist department store at 256 West 125th Street. After a sixteen-year-old Puerto Rican boy named Lino Rivera was caught stealing a 10-cent penknife, the manager intervened, and Rivera bit him. The struggle ended with Rivera being dragged down to the store basement to wait for the police, who let him go out the store's back exit on West 124th Street. The crowd that gathered in the front of the store saw an ambulance arriving to treat the manager's bite wound and the coincidental presence of a hearse parked at the store's back entrance as evidence that police had beaten Rivera to death. Things became so agitated that the store had to close. By early evening the Communist Party, ever ready to take advantage of unrest, had issued handbills claiming that Rivera had been beaten in a "Lynch Attack." Someone broke one of Kress's plate-glass windows, sparking an outbreak of violence that soon drew in several thousand Harlemites who looted white businesses. Not even some stores with signs that read "This shop is run by COLORED people" were safe from the mayhem.

White shopkeepers represented by the Merchants Association of Harlem insisted that Governor Herbert Lehman send in troops, but as long as Harlem's rage was directed at property and not at people, Lehman reasoned, it was best to let the five hundred cops that the city had called in handle things. Mayor La Guardia also acted with restraint, calling for peace and order and circulating photos of Rivera with Harlem's famed first black cop, Samuel Battle. It wasn't until the next evening that things were quiet enough for a dozen glaziers under police protection to start fixing the 626 store windows that had been broken. Other damage was irreparable. Three blacks had been killed, more than two hundred people were injured—including eight police officers—and more than one hundred were arrested. The relatively small number of casualties belies how great a trauma it was to the entire community.

The difficult and disappointing truth is that La Guardia was a gradualist when it came to race. It took months for him to appoint a commission to look into the causes of the riot. The group included Countee Cullen, Hubert Delaney, E. Franklin Frazier, and A. Philip Randolph, but it was led by whites and did most of its work behind closed doors. It wasn't until more than a year later that the commission presented its findings, and Harlemites were outraged when the mayor refused to make the report public. The *Amsterdam News* printed a copy, but Harlemites learned little they didn't already know. The commissioners found the root causes of the riot in racism and discrimination, pointing to Harlem's numerous all-white institutions, including seven political clubs, nine lodges, twelve hospitals and health care facilities, eleven schools and libraries, thirteen social service agencies, and sixty-six adult recreational facilities. "So long as these conditions persist," the report concluded, "no one knows when they will lead to recurrence, with possibly greater violence." La Guardia tried to turn things around by increasing support for public housing, integrating the city Hospital Department, pushing for new school construction, and promoting more black civil service workers, but these were isolated gestures. When nothing more than a simple case of boyhood shoplifting could spark a riot, nothing less than a social restructuring that took into account labor, housing, schools, and health care could prevent one.

At least as far as Harlem was concerned, Mussolini could not have picked a worse time than October 1935 to invade and occupy Ethiopia, a country as close to the hearts of many Negroes as Italy was to Italian East Harlemites. A handful of uptown blacks had actually traveled to East Africa to offer assistance following Ethiopia's independence from Italy in 1896, and the saxophone-playing aviator Hubert Julian had later been in charge of Ethiopia's minuscule air force. Long-standing tensions between Negroes and Italians, ready to snap after the riot of

March 1935, now rose to intolerable levels. Uptown Italians celebrated Mussolini's bid at empire building, donating rings and wristwatches to the effort. Black Harlemites, many of whom still waved the red, gold, black, and green, and who could still hear the stepladder preachers of 125th Street maintain that "Africa is the black man's home," reacted angrily. Graffiti reading "Italians Keep Out" began appearing and Mayor La Guardia, an Italian-American who counted on the black vote, was so concerned that he instructed the police to activate the city's emergency reserve system. At P.S. 178, which was one-third black and one-third Italian, a fight between two twelve-year-olds escalated into a school-yard race riot that drew in parents and spread to Lenox Avenue near West 118th Street, where the Italian owners of the King Julius Market became alarmed at a crowd of more than two hundred angry African-Americans that had gathered. One man in the crowd exhorted: "Harlem is for the Negro. Drive the Italians out of Harlem. Drive the white man out of Harlem." Eventually they stormed the store, which was defended by five Italian and ten black employees, before forty cops, plus the emergency unit, drove away the mob. Meanwhile, radical race groups like the Black Legion and the Nationalist Negro Movement began holding protests, and a group of black nurses raised money for medicine and supplies for the Ethiopian victims of Mussolini's misadventure. Harlem's International Council of Friends of Ethiopia sent Willis Huggins to address the League of Nations on the issue. Uptown's Ethiopian World Federation published a newspaper, *Voice of Ethiopia*, while the newly formed Ethiopian Pacific Movement held protests meetings at the Rockland Palace. Harlemites even set up recruiting stations for those who wanted to help fight Mussolini. More than a thousand signed up, among them an airplane pilot from Chicago named John C. Robinson, who went by the nickname the "Brown Condor."

East Harlem's Puerto Rican community was also in turmoil in the wake of the riot of 1935. The residents of El Barrio had long been manning the stepladders to call for an independent Puerto Rico, but they couldn't ignore what they saw all around them, especially after the release of a study that found that Puerto Rican children were far more likely to be mentally defective than other New York kids. Then while en route to a concert at Lewisohn Stadium in July of 1936, Mayor La Guardia tuned in to his police scanner and heard about the shooting of a Puerto Rican named Raymond Lopez outside a West 116th Street florist by a local boxer named Bernel Saunders, who was known as the "Bully of Harlem." More than a hundred cops managed to pacify the crowd of Puerto Ricans that had gathered, but the situation remained volatile. Things threatened to explode again after an associate of Joey Rao, a high-ranking mafioso, was murdered execution-style in his East 107th Street apartment, presumably by Puerto Rican drug dealers. The expected gang war never happened, but the two groups remained wary of each other.

If Mayor La Guardia was looking for easy answers to the question of how to turn Harlem around, the unrest that followed the Ethiopian invasion was proof that it was going to be a complicated task. Adam Clayton Powell Jr. already knew that, writing in the liberal New York *Post* that the disturbance of March 1935 "was not a riot. It was an open, unorganized protest against empty stomachs, overcrowded tenements, filthy sanitation, rotten foodstuffs, chiselling landlords and merchants, discrimination on relief, disenfranchisement, and against a disinterested administration." Powell stepped up the use of demonstrations and boycotts that had been so successful against Harlem Hospital and Blumstein's. He formed the Greater New York Coordinating Committee on Employment, a coalition of more than two hundred organizations representing more than 170,000 members who aimed at national chains like Grant's, Woolworth's, Liggett's, and Chock Full O' Nuts, all of which backed down and began hiring blacks. The committee also broke Consolidated Gas and New York Edison's discriminatory hiring practices with a "Black-Out Boycott" on Tuesday nights, and it successfully targeted the notoriously racist New York Telephone by leading a Bill Payers Parade in which Harlemites all but paralyzed the company's operations by settling their bills with pennies. Even the all-white uptown chamber of commerce agreed to make changes in hiring policies on 125th Street.

Success made Powell begin to think bigger. In November 1937, the American Labor Party and the Republican Party both supported his campaign for City Council, and with a "People's Committee" of almost two thousand volunteers in eight campaign headquarters, it was no surprise to see Powell win easily, becoming the first Negro to hold that position. Powell had once boasted of being an "outsider to power," beholden to no political party, but he was now becoming an insider—at least as inside as a Negro, even a light-skinned one, could get at the time. It wasn't just Powell who represented Harlem's growing political power. J. Raymond Jones's friend Daniel Burrows became the leader of the last white political district uptown, and Hulan Jack, a native of British Guyana who came to New York in 1923, won election to the state assembly with the support of Tammany Hall.

Powell would have been considerably less influential without the twelve thousand members of the Abyssinian Baptist Church, which he had finally inherited from his father. Right away he issued a challenge to his peers: "Harlem has sixty-eight churches, excluding the fly-by-nighters. You can count on your fingers all of them that are worth keeping open." Powell wasn't afraid to criticize the established churches, but he was really talking about places like the tiny Holy Star Spiritual Church, which stayed in the black by selling something called Prosperity Oil at 10 cents a flask. A broader audience sought out Sweet Daddy Grace, who was born in 1884 on the Cape Verde Islands and founded churches in Massachusetts and Washington, D.C., before moving to Harlem and starting the United House of Prayer for All People. Daddy Grace practiced a typically uptown form of spiritual capitalism, charging a dollar for firehose baptisms and selling a line of products that included toothpaste, soap, ice cream, and cookies. He even branched out into real estate, buying 555 Edgecombe Avenue, the famed Triple Nickle of Sugar Hill. Even more flamboyant was the Reverend Dr. George W. Becton, the "Dancing Evangelist," who presided over a church called the World's Gospel Feast. He got rich by having his followers contribute "A Dime a Day for God." The money went into Becton's pocket, a fact he never hid. "God ain't broke," he explained. The most famous of all of Harlem's religious sects was the one ran by Father Divine. Born George Baker in 1870 in Georgia, he arrived in Harlem around 1933 and opened the first of more than a dozen "Heavens," as his churches were known. This dapper and diminutive character forbade sex, drugs, smoking, swearing, racism, slovenliness, and violence. No one was allowed to get the chemical hair-straightening known as a conk, which was becoming the rage after having been invented by a West 153rd Street barber. Even the word "Negro" was banned. Father Divine refused to allow his congregants to buy on the installment plan, nor were they allowed to go on relief. Followers, whom he referred to as "angels," took names like Holy Shinelight, Happy Sweets, or Pleasing Joy and gave him their life savings. That was in addition to the profits raked in by his restaurants, dry cleaners, barbershops, grocery stores, coal yards, shoeshine stands, and newspaper kiosks that prominently displayed his newspaper, called the *New Day*. Not all of it went into his pocket. Anyone who walked into one of his Heavens got a meal of grits, collard greens, hog maws, and chitterlings—personally blessed by Father Divine himself—for 25 cents or less. The truly destitute didn't have to pay anything at all, and they might even get to meet Mayor La Guardia or First Lady Eleanor Roosevelt when they dropped in. Perhaps Harlemites clung to such questionable forms of assistance because of the racism of many city charities. The Salvation Army sent its black clients from all over the city to its Harlem shelter rather than have them share facilities with whites elsewhere. The Children's Aid Society, which had an all-white board of directors, ran separate summer camps for black and white children. More dignified conditions ruled at black-owned private philanthropies such as Utopia Children's House, which offered free medical care, meals, clothing, and pre- and after-school programs. The severity of the Depression, which meant fewer donations, taxed private philanthropies beyond their abilities. But help was on the way.

*   *   *

Harlemites viewed the collection of legislation and executive developments known as the New Deal with skepticism. Social Security, the Federal Deposit Insurance Corporation, minimum wage laws, and labor union protections were welcome arrivals, but Harlemites never got their fair share of the rest. The Home Owners Loan Corporation rejected a disproportionate number of applicants from Harlem by listing any apartment with a boarder as a boardinghouse. The Federal Nursery Project blanketed New York City with day-care programs, except in Harlem. More than half of all Harlemites who applied for relief in the mid-1930s were turned away, so only one in four eligible uptown families actually received cash assistance, compared to half of eligible white families. Blame fell on racist relief inspectors, who were notoriously intrusive, looking into closets and refrigerators as they searched for reasons to deny payments to Negroes. Such treatment was tolerated by higher-ups because of the White House's insistence on putting national recovery ahead of fighting intolerance. And those who got relief didn't get enough. The Emergency Relief Board offered a four-person family with no working adults a maximum of $70 per month, while the federal government itself admitted that the minimum for survival in the city was $83.31, even more uptown, where landlords still charged more than in working-class white neighborhoods elsewhere. Works Progress Administration staff in skilled positions might make as much as $95 per month, but few of those jobs went to Negroes.

Protests against a New Deal that at times resembled the old deal prompted Washington and City Hall to take action, with limited success. The WPA added more relief offices uptown, in addition to nine summer and after-school recreation centers, and the federal government finally decided to start offering payments to support illegitimate minors. The Public Works Administration enlarged Harlem Hospital, and WPA money and laborers supported many medical clinics, but still Harlemites remained underserved. Even though the WPA funded for educational programs, from academic programs in traditional subjects to job training programs, slots to train dictaphone transcribers remained suspiciously full when Negroes applied. The Public Works Administration did build two schools in Harlem, the first new public educational facilities that Harlemites had seen in decades—the rest remained dangerously overcrowded and dilapidated. Of the 255 new playgrounds built during this period, only one was in Harlem, and though uptowners did get two public swimming pools, the one in Colonial Park was far north of black Harlem's core and the other one was far to the east, in the Italian neighborhood of Jefferson Park.

Housing did get more serious attention in this period, starting with the construction of the $4.5 million Harlem River Houses project, which was built in 1937 on nine acres between Seventh Avenue and Macomb's Place north of West 151st Street, on land donated by the Rockefeller family. One of the first city housing projects to be built with federal money, it was a striking success. More than twenty thousand families applied for fewer than six hundred units, some of which cost as little as $20 per month. The three four-story buildings, designed in part by John Louis Wilson Jr., one of the few Negroes licensed to practice architecture in New York, included lounges and courtyards for socializing, a nursery school, playrooms, a health clinic, and laundry rooms. The project attracted criticism because it disrupted the street grid and turned its focus away from the street and toward protected inner spaces, but that design had advantages: for the first two years there was not a single reported crime.

The residents of the Harlem River Houses took special pride in the artwork that adorned the complex, in particular the massive friezes of Richmond Barthé, a St. Louis native who was a latecomer to the Harlem Renaissance and whose career bloomed under the New Deal's commitment to the arts. For all the shortcomings of the Works Progress Administration—Negroes were given no significant managerial roles and work that addressed racial discrimination too frontally was subject to censorship—the agency subsidized the work of hundreds of uptown painters, sculptors, writers, musicians, and entertainers through new federal agencies devoted to art, theater, writing, and music. Aaron Douglas, a fixture of the younger generation of New Negroes in the 1920s, became the president of the Harlem Artists Guild, a Federal

Arts Project–backed group that funded the murals he painted at the 135th Street Public Library. Federal Arts Project funding was vital to the painter Palmer Hayden, a native Virginian who served in World War I—the name was given to him by a white officer who had trouble pronouncing his birth name, Peyton Hedgeman—before landing in Harlem, where his paintings depicted the lives of ordinary Harlemites struggling to stay afloat in the Great Depression.

No one blossomed under the Federal Arts Project's initiatives like Augusta Savage. Still a teenager when she moved during World War I from Florida to New York City, she founded the Salon of Contemporary Negro Art, the city's first black art gallery. By the early 1930s she was also teaching, at first in storefronts that she rented and then at the Uptown Art Laboratory, later renamed the Harlem Community Art Center, where WPA money helped create some of the most accomplished artists to come out of Harlem in the 1930s. Figures such as Georgette Seabrooke and William Artis studied painting, drawing, sculpture, and weaving there with teachers Norman Lewis and William Henry Johnson, among others. All the while Savage was making her own sculptures. Her 1937 work *The Harp*, inspired by James Weldon Johnson's black national anthem, also known as "Lift Ev'ry Voice and Sing," was prominently exhibited at the 1939 World's Fair in New York.

The rising star of the younger generation of artists was Romare Bearden, who was born in 1911 in North Carolina and grew up in Harlem, where his mother, Bessye, was the New York editor of the Chicago *Defender*. Guests at the Bearden home, across the street from the Lafayette Theatre, included everyone from W.E.B. Du Bois and Paul Robeson to Duke Ellington and Langston Hughes. After attending Frederick Douglass Junior High School and DeWitt Clinton's annex on West 116th Street, Bearden began hanging around the artists at 306 West 141st Street, the second floor of an old stable that drew so many artists and writers, including Hughes, Claude McKay, and the sculptor Henry Bannarn, that they became known as the 306 Group. Bearden could also be found at the Harlem Artists Guild, although he also took a job as a New York City social worker in order to support himself.

The only member of this new generation of painters to rival Bearden was Jacob Lawrence, a New Jersey native who first came to New York City in 1927 at the age of ten. After a period spent in foster homes and settlement houses, he moved with his mother to 142 West 143rd Street and attended P.S. 68 and P.S. 139. He also spent time at the after-school program at Utopia Children's House, where he studied art with Charles Alston, whose WPA-sponsored murals from 1936 at Harlem Hospital, called *Magic and Medicine*, were executed in the social realist style that he had helped make the lingua franca of uptown art at the time. Lawrence was also a fixture at Alston's studio at 306 West 141st Street. The sixty Lawrence paintings from 1941 known as *The Migration of the Negro*, which have been called the finest artwork of the Great Depression, were followed by a group of paintings called the *Harlem* series, which captured the quiet dignity of humble institutions like the barbershop and the health clinic at Harlem Hospital. Works like *They Live in Fire Traps* show that Lawrence, who lived on Striver's Row before moving to Hamilton Terrace, was also capable of outrage. Not all visual artists during the Depression benefited from New Deal largesse, especially those who worked outside the boundaries of what was then considered fine art. The cartoonist Oliver Harrington, born to a black mother and a Jewish-Hungarian father in 1912 in upstate New York, came to Harlem in 1929 and worked in the NAACP's public relations department before he began drawing for the *Amsterdam News*, creating a chubby, melancholy character named Bootsie, who observed life in Harlem with its frequent ups and even more frequent downs.

The Depression is considered the golden age of American photography, but though the WPA supported work by white photographers such as Helen Levitt and Aaron Siskind, who memorably recorded conditions uptown during the most difficult years of the 1930s, black picture takers were almost always on their own. James Van Der Zee, who had so diligently documented the rise of the New Negro, fell on hard times after the stock market crash. He moved his studio from West 135th Street to a former automobile showroom on Seventh Avenue in 1930, where he continued to strike a masterfully manipulative balance between realism and the dream of something better. The representa-

It was a tweedy, spectacled sociologist from Chicago named Charles Johnson who kicked off the Harlem Renaissance's cultural program by inviting writers and artists to contribute to *Opportunity*, the journal of the National Urban League.

MISS JESSIE REDMON FAUSET

Some of Harlem's newest cultural aristocracy at a 1924 party celebrating Langston Hughes literary accomplishments. From left: Hughes, Charles S. Johnson, E. Franklin Frazier, Rudolph Fisher, and Hubert T. Delaney, gather on the rooftop of 580 St. Nicholas Avenue.

The author of the first novel of the Harlem Renaissance, Jessie Fauset also discovered and published a whole generation of New Negro writers, among them Countee Cullen, Langston Hughes, Zora Neale Hurston, Claude McKay, and Jean Toomer.

James Reese Europe (at left conducting the Harlem Hellfighters military band in France) essentially invented the jazz idiom before leading his legendary ensemble into battle in World War I. Europe survived both German mustard gas and the racism of the American military only to die at the hands of his own drummer at age thirty-eight.

Like so many stalwarts of the New Negro Movement, the pianist and composer Duke Ellington was raised in a middle-class home in Washington, D.C., but once he saw Harlem in 1923, he was hooked for life, spending much of the next five decades capturing its spirit.

The best-known African-American in the world in the 1920s and 1930s, Paul Robeson was also Harlem's most beloved entertainer, especially after he became the target of government surveillance and harassment. He is pictured here in 1943 or 1944 playing softball in Central Park with the cast of *Othello*.

Madam C. J. Walker was one of Harlem's best-known figures, and America's first black millionairess, having made a fortune on products that straightened hair and lightened skin color.

Racism at the Cotton Club, from its plantation décor to its whites-only door policy to its menu, never held back headliners like Duke Ellington, Cab Calloway, or Fletcher Henderson.

Musicians of all kinds flourished uptown, including the writer George Schuyler's daughter, Philippa, a classical musical prodigy, shown here leading a children's choir.

Small's Paradise, at Seventh Avenue and West 135th Street, was as well known for its big band music as for its "café au lait chorines."

Marcus Garvey's 1919 wedding photograph identifies him not only as the founder and president general of the Universal Negro Improvement Association but as "First Provisional President of Africa," a sign of the ambition and looseness with facts that helped cause his downfall.

Marcus Garvey — signature

First Provisional President of Africa

FOUNDER and PRESIDENT GENERAL of
THE
UNIVERSAL NEGRO IMPROVEMENT
ASSOCIATION

Far and away the most talented pianist of his generation, James P. Johnson dominated Harlem's ragtime, stride, and barrelhouse piano scene—he also mentored Fats Waller and George Gershwin—before trying his hand at classical composition.

Built in 1915 on the City College campus, Lewisohn Stadium attracted up to eighteen thousand spectators to its sporting and theatrical events before it was torn down in 1973 to make way for the unlovely North Academic Center building.

Even as Harlem's traditional Jewish community left in droves, uptown's "Royal Order of Ethiopian Hebrews" (pictured here in a 1940 service) was growing steadily.

During World War II, 125th Street remained a stage for freelance preachers, stepladder professors, and book salesmen from Lewis Micheaux's National Memorial Bookstore.

Adam Clayton Powell, Jr. turned the Abyssinian Baptist Church into a formidable force against racism and poverty, but by the 1960s he was living the life of a matinee idol, with the headshot to prove it.

Since shortly after the first Italians settled uptown in the late-nineteenth century, a "Festa" honoring the patron saint of East Harlem has been the highlight of each summer.

In the 1930s and 1940s, Minton's Playhouse was the birthplace of a new kind of jazz called bebop, whose leading exponent on piano, Thelonious Monk, is pictured here with colleagues Howard McGhee, Roy Eldridge, and Teddy Hill.

Long before Billie Holiday (pictured in 1947 with her dog, Mister) became one of the most acclaimed of jazz singers, she was popular with audiences at the Apollo Theatre.

Harlem was the cradle of Latin music in America, with figures like Augusto Coen, Arsenio Rodriguez, Perez Prado, Rafael Hernández, Alberto Socarrás, and Machito, pictured here with the singer Graciela, pioneering the genre's unique instrumentation and performance style.

Of the many boxers who captured the hearts of Harlemites, the most driven was Sugar Ray Robinson, shown here in 1954 demonstrating his post-retirement fitness on the awning of his Harlem tavern.

Many Harlemites point to the Riot of 1943 as the point of no return for Harlem.

Willie Mays, who lived near the Polo Grounds when he played for the New York Giants, often joined in the local childrens' stickball game.

No one epitomized Harlem style like James Brown, whose over-the-top stage show made "The Hardest Working Man in Show Business" a favorite of crowds at the Apollo Theatre.

Known as "Mr. Untouchable," Nicky Barnes was the undisputed boss of the Harlem heroin trade for much of the 1970s.

In the 1960s, as entire Harlem blocks passed a predictable cycle of decay, arson, and abandonment, life went on as usual.

Harlemites were shocked when Malcolm Little, the hoodlum, drug dealer, numbers runner, and pimp they had known as "Detroit Red," returned uptown as Malcolm X, the presumed successor to the Black Muslim leader Elijah Muhammad.

For decades, Harlem politics was dominated by David Dinkins, Percy Sutton, and Charles Rangel, who along with Basil Paterson were often blamed for the poor city services, shameful school conditions, and a crippling lack of economic opportunity that remained facts of life uptown.

While the world focused on Martin Luther King, Jr.'s struggles against racism and poverty in the south, Harlemites, shown here during a 1965 march, remained a vital source of inspiration and support for the Civil Rights movement.

Pacifism was the primary weapon used against racism by Bayard Rustin, known as the Socrates of the Civil Rights movement, pictured here preparing some of his younger allies for a 1964 demonstration.

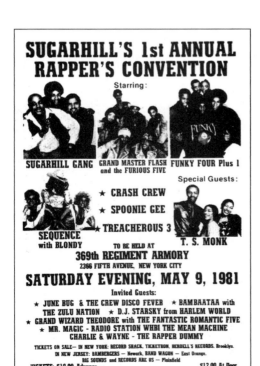

SUGARHILL'S 1st ANNUAL
RAPPER'S CONVENTION
Starring:

SUGARHILL GANG   GRAND MASTER FLASH   FUNKY FOUR Plus 1
and the FURIOUS FIVE

Special Guests:

★ CRASH CREW
★ SPOONIE GEE
★ TREACHEROUS 3
SEQUENCE
with BLONDY   TO BE HELD AT   T. S. MONK
369th REGIMENT ARMORY
2366 FIFTH AVENUE, NEW YORK CITY

SATURDAY EVENING, MAY 9, 1981
Invited Guests:
★ JUNE BUG & THE CREW DISCO FEVER   ★ BAMBAATAA with
THE ZULU NATION   ★ D.J. STARSKY from HARLEM WORLD
★ GRAND WIZARD THEODORE with THE FANTASTIC ROMANTIC FIVE
★ MR. MAGIC - RADIO STATION WHBI THE MEAN MACHINE
CHARLIE & WAYNE - THE RAPPER DUMMY
TICKETS ON SALE— IN NEW YORK: RECORD SHACK, TICKETRON, BENDELL'S RECORDS, Brooklyn.
IN NEW JERSEY: BAMBERGERS — Newark, BAND WAGON — East Orange.
BIG SOUNDS and RECORDS ARE US — Plainfield
TICKETS: $10.00 Advance — $12.00 At Door

Many of rap music's pioneers grew up in Harlem and had their first professional gigs in uptown's community centers, crumbling Jazz Age dance halls, or simply in playgrounds or at "park jams."

A resurgence of free-market initiatives encouraged by Washington, Albany, and city hall helped figures like Geoffrey Canada, founder of the Harlem Children's Zone, offer hope to families left behind by a well-meaning but sclerotic public school system.

Columbia University's bold plan to expand its campus into the decaying industrial neighborhood between Morningside and Harlem Heights aroused strong opposition among locals who feared losing their homes and businesses to gentrification.

In a development symbolic of the way in which Harlem's future is being literally constructed out of its past, West 148th Street's P.S. 90, built in 1906 by the famed school architect Charles B.J. Snyder but vacant since the 1970s, has been converted into condominiums.

Bill Clinton's decision upon leaving the White House to locate his foundation's offices on 125th Street was seen by many Harlemites as an important vote of confidence in the future of the neighborhood.

tive photograph of Harlemites during the Jazz Age, *Couple in Raccoon Coats,* was actually made in 1932, three years after the crash supposedly brought down the curtain on the utopian fervor of the race capital of the world. Austin Hansen, a Virgin Islander, worked as a freelancer for the *Amsterdam News* before opening his own studio on West 135th Street. Then there were the twin brothers from Kentucky, Morgan and Marvin Smith, who came to Harlem in 1933 at the age of twenty-three—Morgan studied sculpture with Augusta Savage at the Harlem Community Art Center, while Marvin worked as a WPA gardener at Mount Morris Park—before starting a photo service providing Harlem newspapers with everything from news shots of politicians and entertainers to impressionistic street scenes, especially those involving soapbox orators.

The Depression devastated the theater world uptown. The closure of most drama companies in the early 1930s put hundreds of actors, dancers, and musicians out of work, so the creation of a WPA division supporting drama was a godsend, making possible a variety of productions ranging from children's plays and experimental theater to "ethnic" productions—the Harlem-born film director Jules Dassin got his first drama experience as a child actor in Yiddish theater sponsored by the Federal Theater Project. There was even a Federal Theater Project circus, which performed at East Harlem's Star Casino. Of course, the best-remembered of the theater project's efforts was the Negro Theater Unit, which had its origins in the actress Rose McClendon's call for a national black theater that would not only nurture the next Charles Gilpin or Paul Robeson but develop new black audiences. The appointment of a young director named John Houseman to organize the Negro unit at first met some resistance. Houseman was half Jewish, born in Romania and raised in patrician England, but Harlemites remembered that he had directed Virgil Thomson's groundbreaking all-black opera *Four Saints in Three Acts,* in which McClendon had performed. With duties that included supervising a Negro Youth Theater, a vaudeville and variety group, and a dance company focusing on African material, Houseman quickly gained the confidence of his players by defying the threats of the all-white theater unions. He hired more than eight hundred black writers, actors, musicians, directors, technicians, stagehands, and administrators, making him the biggest employer of blacks in New York City.

The work that put Houseman's Negro unit on the map was an all-black version of *Macbeth* directed by a virtually unknown young man with almost no stage experience named Orson Welles. It was another controversial choice, but Welles's decision to set the play in a Haitian jungle and model the title role after a legendary Negro king of Haiti was a winning gesture. Welles hired only five professional actors to perform in what became known as the "Voodoo Macbeth." The rest were amateurs, including a group of drummers from Sierra Leone who upon arriving at the theater sacrificed fifteen black goats and then used the skins to make drums. After four months of rehearsals led by the early jazz pioneer Joe Jordan, the play finally opened on April 14, 1936, in all of its "barbaric splendor," according to the *New York Times*. The show received ecstatic reviews and ran for almost three months, reaching more than a hundred thousand people, most of whom were locals who paid 45 cents per ticket—among them the young James Baldwin, then a student of Countee Cullen at Frederick Douglass Junior High School. Not since *Shuffle Along* had Harlem captured the attention of the New York theater world. Unfortunately, the "Voodoo Macbeth" was the last gasp of the New Negro Movement, not the growth pains of the Harlem Renaissance.

The Federal Theater Project claimed to offer "a frontier against disease, dirt, poverty, illiteracy, unemployment, and despair" by offering "free, adult, uncensored" drama. That never pleased higher-ups at the WPA or their superiors in Congress, which slashed the program's budget in 1938. The example of the Negro unit did inspire Langston Hughes to launch his own amateur company, the Communist Party–backed Harlem Suitcase Theater. To Hughes's disappointment, the group's politically controversial material, such as *From Slavery Through the Blues to Now—and Then Some!*, which included scenes representing the "Don't Buy Where You Can't Work" boycotts and the riot of 1935, limited its popularity. It shut down after only two seasons, but many of its participants got work in Frederick O'Neal and Abram Hill's newly opened American Negro Theater, which was based at the 135th Street New York Public Library and which was where Ossie Davis, Ruby Dee, Sidney Poitier, and Harry Belafonte all got their starts.

Harlem's writers tended to have more radical political baggage, but the New Deal had something for them, too. In 1935 the Federal Writers Project began handing out weekly $20 checks to established talents such as Arna Bontemps, Zora Neale Hurston, and Claude McKay as well as to the young Ralph Ellison, a trumpeter from Oklahoma who arrived in Harlem on Independence Day of 1936 at the age of twenty-three. His plan was to study at the Community Art Center and find a job that would allow him to return to Tuskegee in the fall. After stumbling on Langston Hughes and Alain Locke in the lobby of the 135th Street YMCA, Ellison never considered living anywhere else but Harlem, even if that meant nights in St. Nicholas Park, along with other new arrivals from the South with nowhere else to go. Hughes hired Ellison as an amanuensis and brought him to shows at the Apollo Theater, to Charles Alston's gallery, and to the Ethiopian Art School at 313 West 137th Street, run by Charles Seifert. That was one way for Ellison, who had given up on the trumpet, to learn that he would never make a great sculptor either. Ellison got a position with the Federal Writers Project for $21.67 a week researching the history of Negro New York, interviewing Harlemites as part of the project's Living Lore unit. This involved recording the word games children played at the playground at P.S. 89, at Lenox Avenue and West 135th Street. He also transcribed the songs of street vendors like the Sorrel Woman and De Sweet Pertater Man as they struggled to make it through another day. Ellison's WPA-sponsored immersion in folklore ended up being crucial to his development as a novelist, inspiring him to leaven his high modernist style with a dose of the black folk experience. Ellison was also spending much of his time with Hughes's old friend Dorothy Thompson, discussing radical politics and literature at her Convent Avenue apartment.

Thompson brought Ellison to meetings at the communists' uptown headquarters, where he observed the push for mainstream acceptance that would result in alliances with the Urban League and

Father Divine and even bring in party leaders to speak in the pulpits of the Abyssinian Baptist Church and other mainstream houses of worship. Like most participants in the Federal Writers Project, and like most socialists and communists uptown, Ellison never formally joined the Communist Party, but its promise to fight racism and nominate a black candidate for vice president won him over. Harlem was the place where the communists were going to win or lose national black support, according to the party strategists, which is why they focused their efforts there. They formed the Young Communists League and founded the Harlem Workers Center, a school that enrolled thousands of members agitating for better schools and drew huge crowds to chant "Black and White, Unite and Fight" at outdoor mass meetings. Of course, communism in the mid-1930s wasn't only about labor theory, or even about work. The party was by this time well known for its parties, where interracial romance was the order of the day, so much so at one point that there was an effort to crack down on marriages between black and white members. That kind of thinking, and the Moscow trials of 1936, disillusioned many left-wingers. By 1938 only a few hundred Harlemites identified themselves as Communist Party members, and that number was shrinking fast. After the short-lived Hitler-Stalin Pact of 1939, even sympathizers like A. Philip Randolph and Langston Hughes distanced themselves.

Pressure on the United States to get involved in the growing conflict in Europe and the Communist Party's refusal to oppose segregation in the American military—as in the previous world war, a united front trumped such supposedly secondary concerns—convinced most remaining members to leave. But socialist ideals still attracted considerable support, especially when voiced by Vito Marcantonio, a native of Italian Harlem who went on to earn a reputation as the most radical and uncompromising politician of his generation, a diminutive figure whose ferocious sense of justice made him an international political legend. Marc, as his constituents called him, was born in 1902 in a tenement at the corner of First Avenue and East 112th Street into a family that was poor but proud—Marc's grandmother had once received a comradely kiss from Garibaldi. Marc was an excellent student at P.S. 85, where he was pals with Thomas Luchese, with whom he remained friends even after Luchese joined the mafia. An outspoken, risk-taking leader even then, Marc was one of the few Catholic children who refused to heed warnings about the Presbyterian water fountain at Neighborhood House, and the only boy among his friends to go on to high school, which brought a measure of shame in a neighborhood where manhood meant going out and earning a living. Most of his friends had dropped out after sixth grade and become entrepreneurs, buying chewing gum for 5 cents a pack and selling it on the subway for 10 cents, which might net a dollar a day, though it was important to learn to evade the tough Irish truant officers. Marc went to DeWitt Clinton High School but his interests were extracurricular. He was only a seventeen-year-old high school student when he took over the East Harlem Tenants League. Marc was also beginning to think more globally, telling his classmates that World War I was international capital's war, a notion he got from the East Harlem socialist leader Morris Hillquit, who lost a congressional campaign by a heartbreakingly small margin; for years afterward, the district was known among left-wingers as "Hillquit's District."

Marc graduated from DeWitt Clinton and entered college, but most of his time was spent coaching basketball at Haarlem House and managing Fiorello La Guardia's successful congressional campaign against Tammany Hall's Jewish candidate Henry Frank. Marc eventually joined La Guardia's law firm as a ten-dollar-a-week clerk and successfully ran three of his congressional campaigns. A gallant, old-fashioned gentleman, Marc never took off his jacket in the presence of women in public, though he wasn't above jumping off the back of a campaign truck and plunging into a roiling brawl against La Guardia's opponents at an evening rally. All the while, Marc was preparing for a career of his own. He successfully ran as a Republican for the congressional seat left empty when La Guardia became mayor. Marc was a charismatic, even spellbinding speaker, especially when his preelection speeches at the Lucky Corner, as the intersection of Lexington Avenue and East 116th Street was known, were accompanied by hymns associated with Garibaldi or by live performances by Paul Robeson.

Once Marc came out from La Guardia's shadow he proved to be a master politician, at least on his home turf. His headquarters on Doctors and Lawyers Row were open seven days a week, twenty-four hours a day to locals with problems. He saw each one of them personally, listening to their troubles with their landlords, their bosses, or their government. With that kind of attitude, it is no wonder that Marc, who lived at 229 East 116th Street, next door to Leonard Covello, was as popular among Jews, Negroes, and Puerto Ricans as he was among Italians. As a member of the House Territories Committee, he knew what Nuyorican cared about and was unafraid to speak his mind, making plenty of enemies when he spoke out forcefully against Puerto Rico's governor Blanton Winship. The president of the island's Senate even called Marc a stooge of the communists and the "Harlem nationalists," by which he meant Puerto Ricans in Harlem working for an independent Puerto Rico.

A master of *personalismo*, the art and science of local political contacts, he spoke not only English and Italian but Spanish and Yiddish, and he kept Negroes, Italians, Puerto Ricans, and Jews on his staff. A very serious neighborhood joke went: "Did anyone in East Harlem vote against Marc? Didn't people oppose Christ when he walked the earth?" Marc was somewhat less successful in Washington, D.C. Part of the problem was that he was a party of one—far to the left of the Tammany Democrats yet a declared Republican because of his loyalty to La Guardia. Nonetheless, Marc was unafraid of challenging his mentor when it came to Ethiopia in 1935, speaking forcefully against Mussolini and fascism at a time when many Italians, including La Guardia, remained guarded. Marc also issued stinging criticisms of Roosevelt, suggesting that his New Deal did not reach far enough. Marc suggested "reopening and operating shut-down factories by and for the benefit of the unemployed." Eventually, Marc found himself without the reliable support of any major political party, so he got by on temporary alliances not only with Democrats and Republicans but with the American Labor Party, the communist-affiliated American People's Party, and even with Communist Party members themselves. His neighbors called it a *fritto misto*, or mixed dish of fried food.

As accurately as he read East Harlem's needs, Marc found himself tacking against local opinion when it came to international relations. Although an uptown fascist group called the Circolo Mario Morgantini had about a thousand members in the late 1930s, most uptown Italians had lost their enthusiasm for Mussolini and couldn't agree with Marc that Roosevelt should stay focused on the domestic situation. It was only after Hitler invaded Russia in mid-1941 that Marc went from being the most committed noninterventionist in Congress to its biggest hawk. East Harlemites were glad to have him back, but Marc's enemies in Washington, D.C., mistrusted his change of heart and began planning his downfall.

If Marc's commitment to communism was ill-considered, the position of Paul Robeson seemed like out-and-out folly or worse. America's most prominent Soviet apologist was living back in Harlem for the first time in more than a decade, but he found himself out of step with his neighbors when it came to politics. He hung on to his illusions about communism's role in keeping the peace in Europe even after the Nazi-Soviet pact. Convinced that Robeson was a communist agent, the FBI monitored his activities, recorded his telephone calls, and bugged his apartment. Worst of all, the agency pressured its contacts on Broadway and in Hollywood to make sure stage and screen work failed to materialize for Robeson.

A happier balance between art and politics was struck by Richard Wright. Born in Mississippi in 1908, Wright made his way from Chicago to Harlem in 1937, where he took a job as bureau chief of the newly opened uptown offices of the communist *Daily Worker.* Wright often had to swallow his tongue and go along with the party line, which as usual considered fighting racism less important than building an international labor movement. Wright quit to join the Federal Writers Project and work on *Uncle Tom's Children,* a short story collection hailed upon its publication in 1938 as a milestone in the use of literary naturalism to treat the lives of black Americans. The book earned Wright a place in the Writers Project's Creative Work Program, which allowed him to complete his novel *Native Son* two years later. The story of a Mississippi boy named Bigger Thomas who moves north and descends into an inferno of poverty and violence made Wright one of America's best-selling authors. But some uptown readers, recalling Carl Van Vechten's *Nigger Heaven* and Claude McKay's *Home to Harlem*, thought that Wright had given white people what they desired in a novel: just another crazy nigger. Wright left Harlem, though the "Sepia Steinbeck," who finally broke with the communists in 1942, would often come back, if for nothing else than to get his hair cut properly. Anticommunists believed Wright was proof that the WPA programs for arts were at best a New Deal boondoggle and at worst a "red nest." But even blacks stung by the racism of the WPA arts initiatives had to acknowledge that in *Native Son* the much-touted "New Deal for the Arts" had produced a masterpiece.

Many Harlemites considered the Great Depression to be divine retribution for the good times of the Jazz Age. The economic crisis cut into the amount of money both downtown and uptown revelers could spend in nightclubs, many of which could no longer afford lavish stage productions. Connie's Inn survived the onset of the Depression, with court lyricist Andy Razaf still celebrating uptown life in shows such as *Hot Harlem* and *Harlem Hotcha*. Then in 1932 the gangster Vincent "Mad Dog" Coll kidnapped one of the club's owners, George Immerman, and held him for three days, until his mother came up with $45,000 in ransom money. A shoot-out at the club the next year convinced the Immermans to close down the business. The Band Box, Barron's, Pod and Jerry's, the Nest Club, and the Lafayette Theatre hung on longer, but the widespread legal availability of alcohol after the end of Prohibition in 1933 bankrupted many of the 125 established nightclubs that survived the crash. A few came back under new management. The Capitol Palace reopened as the Saratoga Club and Barron's became Clark Monroe's Uptown, while the Rhythm Club space beneath the Lafayette Theatre became the Hoofer's Club, a showcase for dancers Bojangles Robinson, Baby Lawrence, and Honi Coles. Tallulah Bankhead and Artie Shaw continued to come uptown to party long after Harlem was no longer in vogue, making a name for Fat Man's Bar and Grill, on West 155th

Street. The gangsters also kept coming. Dutch Schultz would show up on a Friday night, give the owner enough money to shut down for the evening, and have an all-weekend party, with the female staff stripping to their underwear to put on a show just for him. No wonder *Theatre Arts Monthly* still considered a night uptown "an emotional holiday." But during the depths of the Depression the crowds who couldn't afford any holiday, emotional or otherwise, stopped coming.

Ironically, the Cotton Club didn't come into its own until several years after the crash, when Duke Ellington's orchestra gave up its steady gig. Cab Calloway, born in 1907 in Baltimore where he was a high school classmate of Thurgood Marshall, came to Harlem in the late 1920s, took over the Cotton Club bandstand, and became even more popular than Ellington on the strength of his hit record "Minnie the Moocher," which recounted the life and times of a Harlem hipster. Even as the Depression demanded austerity, Calloway dressed in zoot suits, outrageously colored, high-waisted outfits with huge cuffs and deep pleats, a padded jacket that almost swept the floor, a long watch chain, a rakishly angled fedora, pointed, shiny shoes, and a trend-setting conked hairstyle that reached almost to his shoulders. Calloway also popularized the sometimes cryptic Harlem slang that swept across America in the swing era. The right zoot suit meant that a "cat" (guy) was "togged to the bricks" (well dressed) for an "early black" (evening) of "gum beating" (talking), drinking "scrap iron" (whiskey) or even "blowing his wig" (becoming enthusiastic) with a "fine dinner" (beautiful woman) with lovely "glams" (eyes)—smoking some "bush" (marijuana) helped, too. They might go to a "clam bake" (jam session), and when it was all over they would "cop a nod" (sleep) before starting all over again. Despite Calloway's popularity, the Cotton Club's days were numbered after its owner Owney Madden went away to Sing Sing prison in March of 1933. There were valiant efforts to hang on, with the club continuing to distribute Christmastime food packages. The famed chorus line started accepting male dancers in 1934, and the club even started admitting Negroes, though only a few, and only at tables near the kitchen. After the 1935 riot the Cotton Club shut its doors for good and moved downtown.

While Connie's Inn and the Cotton Club were closing their doors, many smaller, less expensive clubs sprang up, including the Coal Bed, the Air Raid Shelter, and the Glory Hole. Even in the mid-1930s *Collier's* magazine could still call Harlem a "national synonym for naughtiness." Whites from downtown looking for interracial homosexual action could still find it at a cheap, seedy nightclub called Chez Clinton. Anyone spending time in these sorts of places in the early 1930s was bound to run into a young singer named Billie Holiday. Born Eleanora Fagan Gough in Philadelphia in 1915 and raised in Baltimore by her mother, a maid who moonlighted as a prostitute, she came to New York with her family around 1929 and settled at 151 West 140th Street, a luxury building that housed a well-known bordello. Before long Holiday was turning twenty-dollar tricks and singing with the house bands at Harlem dives like the Clam House, Tillie's Chicken Shack, Basement Brownie's, Pod and Jerry's, and Mexico's. Then in 1933 a young white dropout from Yale named John Hammond came uptown in search of swinging music and progressive politics. He discovered Holiday, who was performing at Monette Moore's Supper Club, going from table to table singing risqué numbers like "Hot Nuts." Hammond introduced Holiday to Benny Goodman, who invited her to participate in the first racially integrated recording session in jazz history.

It was only in the mid-1930s that Holiday became a favorite at the Apollo, and word soon spread about the fresh-faced, chubby girl who could move in a heartbeat from a purr to a shout, from naughty humor to moral outrage. Then in early 1937 John Hammond introduced her to his latest discovery, Count Basie, a New Jersey native who learned to play the organ literally at Fats Waller's feet and had then gone west to imbibe the rough and ready sound of the territory bands, as the orchestras of Jay McShann, Bennie Moten, Andy Kirk, and Mary Lou Williams were known. The pairing of Billie and Basie was a musical match made in heaven, and the Apollo's patrons were more than glad to be witnesses at this musical nuptials.

By this time the Apollo Theater was already both sacred and sleazy. Throughout the 1930s blackface and blackface-style comedy routines by the likes of Butterbeans and Susie, Moms Mabley, Pigmeat Markham, Kingfish Moore, and Dusty Fletcher, who were popular with audiences of every race, were the theater's biggest draws. Then one of the owners, Frank Schiffman, who had owned the Lafayette Theatre and also had a stake in the Roosevelt and Douglass theaters, inaugurated amateur night at the Apollo. These events, in which inexperienced performers competed before the most demanding audiences in the world, and which were originally put on at the Lafayette, were a way for Schiffman, a notorious skinflint, to get fresh acts for free.

While the all-white Connie's Inn and the Cotton Club were on their way down, the racially integrated Smalls Paradise became an even more popular spot, with waiters who sang and danced their way between the tables, all night, every night. Harlem's other major integrated club, the Savoy Ballroom, now entered its golden age, led by the Chick Webb Orchestra. A native of Baltimore, Webb was crippled by spinal tuberculosis, but his musical skills on the drums survived intact, and after his arrival in Harlem in 1926 at the age of seventeen he appropriated the driving, blues-fueled swing of the territory bands and melded it with big-city sophistication. Webb didn't hit the big time until 1935, when he introduced a gangly, seventeen-year-old singer with an impossibly athletic voice named Ella Fitzgerald, who had won an amateur contest at the Harlem Opera House. Webb, who lived on Striver's Row, never lost a battle of the bands, not even on the night in 1937 when five thousand spectators—another five thousand gathered in the streets outside—witnessed him take on Benny Goodman. Webb also established an uncanny connection with the Savoy dancers. With their airborne styles and sexually suggestive moves, Savoy dancers like Frankie "Musclehead" Manning, Dawn Hampton, Freddie Rios, and Buster Brown were as comfortable with the Lindy Hop as with the newer dances the Suzie-Q, the Hucklebuck, and the Camel Walk.

In the late 1930s the Savoy Ballroom and Smalls Paradise competed with the massive Golden Gate Ballroom, located in the old Douglas Theatre. Despite bringing in talent the likes of Count Basie, Coleman Hawkins, Teddy Wilson, and Hot Lips Page, the Golden Gate didn't last. That surprised no one. Big band music and swing dancing were falling out of fashion in favor of the new styles of bebop and rhythm and blues. Moreover, fewer whites were coming uptown because of fears about their safety, and those numbers dwindled even further after police banned military personnel from visiting Harlem in the summer of 1942. The city actually closed the Savoy Ballroom— "syncopation addicts" were outraged—after 164 sailors and soldiers were said to have contracted venereal diseases from women they met there. The club was able to reopen only after the owners promised to stop advertising in white newspapers. In the 1920s Harlem's good and great had looked forward to a time when the color line might fade away. To be sure, whenever Adam Clayton Powell or A. Philip Randolph or Paul Robeson or Duke Ellington stood up, America noticed. But as Depression gave way to wartime, race was more real than ever.

Deteriorating social conditions in El Barrio in the 1930s made for better music, just like across town. Cuban dance music could be heard nightly at the Park Palace and other Latin music clubs springing up all over East Harlem. It became hard to avoid the rumba, an Afro-Cuban musical and dance form that became popular among jazz musicians. The b-side of Cab Calloway's immortal 1931 hit "Minnie the Moocher" was a song called "Doin' the Rumba," and there was even a nightclub called the Rhumba Palace, at Lenox Avenue and West 125th Street. Music stores that also served as informal booking agencies and record labels began popping up, among them Casa Latino and the Spanish Music Center. The inventor of that business model, Rafael Hernández, remained influential as a musician, with his Trio Borinquen performing at the White House. Of course, his core audience was uptown, and the most powerful of Hernández's three thousand or so compositions was "Lamento Borincano," which articulated the sense of loss that every Nuyorican felt. The song became the unofficial anthem of El Barrio, though it was Federico Pagani who became widely known as the godfather of Latin music in East Harlem. Eventually the craze for the *plena* was replaced by *boleros, guarachas, son,* and *merengue,* and even jazz shrines like the Renaissance Casino began programming more

Latin music. The Harlem Opera House hired a Cuban ensemble led by Nilo Melendez, the composer of the hit tune "Green Eyes," while the Savoy Ballroom signed the San Domingo Serenaders, a mixed-race group that included two Cubans, a handful of Panamanians, and many Americans.

One of the brightest stars in the uptown Latin music constellation during the Great Depression was Alberto Socarrás, a Cuban flutist and bandleader who played with jazz pioneers Benny Carter and Erskine Hawkins and is credited with having invented Latin jazz. Socarrás's main rival was a Puerto Rican trumpeter named Augusto Coen, who served in World War I before moving to East Harlem. Coen got work in the pit orchestras of Broadway shows, including *Rhapsody in Black* and *Blackbirds of 1928,* and he played with Duke Ellington and Fletcher Henderson before striking out on his own with his own groups, which, like the ensembles of Socarrás, gave up Latin instruments in an attempt to find a place in the swing era. More than once Coen was pitted against Socarrás in a battle of the bands at the Park Palace, a meeting that was advertised at an East Harlem movie house in between features—"FLASH! FLASH! FLASH! WAR! WAR! WAR! ... BETWEEN CUBA AND PUERTO RICO." It led to fistfights in the theater. But there were moments of pan-Hispanic solidarity, too. When the new Mount Morris theater reopened at Fifth Avenue and East 116th Street as the Teatro Campoamor, after the Spanish writer Ramón de Campoamor, the featured performer was the Argentinean tango singer Carlos Gardel, who attracted an audience of fifteen hundred inside the hall and more than three thousand people outside on the streets. But it was as the Teatro Hispano that the building became known as the music home of El Rey del Pregón Borincano, where the percussionist Johnny Rodriguez—he was the brother of the singer Tito Rodriguez—held court with a house band including Noro Morales, the composer of a tribute to El Barrio called "110th Street and Fifth Avenue." If the Puerto Rican music of El Barrio—a national music invented and developed in another country—taught America nothing else, it was that the country's future, as much as its past, was a multiracial one that treated matters like skin color and national origin with equal parts respect and skepticism. It was a tension that played itself out very differently across town in Negro Harlem, especially as the conflict in Europe loomed.

Langston Hughes observed, "Theories of Nordic supremacy and economic suppression have long been realities to us. In America, Negroes do not need to be told what fascism is in action. We know." That knowledge inspired more than one hundred thousand jubilant fans of the boxer Joe Louis to take to the streets to celebrate his 1938 victory over Germany's Max Schmeling. It was as if the "Brown Bomber," the son of Alabama sharecroppers, had defeated Hitler himself. But their enthusiasm for the war that drew in the United States several years later was decidedly mixed, and the atmosphere in Harlem in the early 1940s was a curious mix of euphoria and despair. As they were during World War I many Harlemites were proud patriots. Six days after the Japanese attack on Pearl Harbor, the New York *Age* ran a headline that screamed: "Harlemites Rush to Aid Country at War." The relatively conservative newspaper may not have spoken for all Harlemites, but they did buy enough war bonds to outfit a navy vessel called the *Bert Williams,* even as their husbands and sons—one in seven enlisted men was black—were serving in the racially segregated units that were still the rule in the American armed forces. Not every Harlemite who received a letter from the local draft offices on Lenox Avenue was so enthusiastic. The fledgling jazz trumpeter Dizzy Gillespie evaded service by convincing his draft officer that, although Germans had never wronged him, he might be unreliable with a gun around American white men.

The legendary labor leader A. Philip Randolph saw an opportunity to make broader changes. He knew that African-Americans put up with a Jim Crow military because the larger goal of winning the war promised to lift the country out of the Depression. But he also knew that black civilians were being denied the opportunity, despite domestic labor shortages, to reap the economic benefits of the war boom at home. Harlemites were largely shut out of the defense industries: on the eve of American entry into the conflict, there were only 142 blacks working in the thirty thousand war-related jobs in the city. Having finally succeeded in organizing the Brotherhood of Sleeping Car Porters, and now president of the National Negro Congress, Randolph was in a position to make the White House listen. He threatened President Franklin Roosevelt: desegregate the military and the industries supporting the war or we will march on Washington. Roosevelt, anxious at the prospect of a black army advancing on the nation's capital during wartime, became the first president since Lincoln to take a decisive stance against racism. Executive Order 8802, which outlawed discrimination in the armed forces and the defense industry, promised to be a godsend to Harlem, not just in terms of the number of blacks who now got jobs but in the kinds of jobs they could get. Though Roosevelt hadn't addressed racism in the labor market more broadly—seven American Federation of Labor unions were still segregated, and five others accepted no blacks at all—the war years saw rising numbers of Harlemites in skilled and semiskilled jobs, which more than any other factor was responsible for the creation of a black middle class. Adam Clayton Powell nonetheless warned Harlemites against the dubious benefits of "artificial prosperity." Indeed, Executive Order 8802 did too little, too late: unemployment eased but a third of central Harlemites were still jobless or on relief. Things were especially bad for black women, more than 60 percent of whom worked as domestics, when they could get work at all.

Mayor La Guardia, who maintained a residence at Fifth Avenue and East 109th Street and who had won 70 percent of the black vote when he was reelected to a third term in 1941, had promised Harlemites to stand against intolerance, but the war in Europe made racism at home a low priority, a situation that caused immense frustration uptown. Adam Clayton Powell Jr.'s 1941 boycott of the city's private bus lines, which had refused to hire black drivers, was deemed unpatriotic. Indeed, any talk of living conditions uptown, which were improving so slowly as to convince many Harlemites that the war was nothing but a white man's boom, was seen as hindering the war effort. Meanwhile, the infant mortality rate had declined only slightly

since the early 1930s, and although the city had made great strides
in fighting tuberculosis the disease still struck the residents of the
worst blocks of central Harlem four times more frequently than it
did elsewhere in Manhattan. Public nursing and convalescent homes
were now accepting blacks, and almost a thousand children in central
Harlem attended nineteen new, city-funded day-care centers, but
these facilities met only a tiny fraction of the need. After three decades
in which almost no new educational facilities had been built uptown,
the city had opened five new public schools in Harlem. Among them
was the mostly white Benjamin Franklin High School, which was the
result of Leonard Covello's efforts to bring to Harlem a general high
school, as opposed to the trade or industrial school favored by the
city, which could serve as a testing ground for the ideals of progressive education. That meant nonpunitive discipline, high standards for
immigrants, bilingual education, the involvement of community and
family, and keeping the school open year-round, twenty-four hours
per day. But overcrowding and poor conditions remained the rule at
black schools. As for higher education, the percentage of members
of the tony Abyssinian Baptist Church that had college degrees had
gone from 3 percent in the early 1930s to 13 percent a decade later,
but a college degree was no guarantee of success, not when New
York's economy remained shot through with racial discrimination.

The few Harlemites who attended college graduated to discover
little opportunity in the workplace. Those with less education had
known that all along. Domestics were paid 10 cents per hour, even while
the cost of living uptown remained higher than downtown: bacon cost
42 cents per pound in uptown chain grocery stores that refused to hire
blacks, compared to only 34 cents on the Lower East Side, and rents
remained higher than in white, working-class neighborhoods, even as
housing conditions deteriorated. A 1941 survey of West Harlem found
that 1,979 of 2,191 buildings studied had few working windows, lacked
heat or hot water, or were overrun by vermin. Still, attention to conditions uptown took second place to the war effort, and when in early
1943 newspapers warned of a "Crime Wave in Harlem" La Guardia
forgot about his own commission's findings of police brutality during

the riot of 1935. He advised a group of rookie cops, "Shoot first and be quick on the trigger." Malcolm X, who moved to Harlem during this period, sensed that it was on the verge of violence that would make the riot of 1935 look like a pacifist rally. "One could almost smell trouble ready to break out," he later remembered.

As bad as things were during the Depression, Harlem was reaching what looked like a point of no return. On the evening of Sunday, August 1, 1943, a twenty-six-year-old Negro soldier came to the aid of a prostitute arrested by a white police officer at the Braddock Hotel, a once fancy establishment at 272 West 126th Street that now had a reputation for trouble. The soldier struck the cop in the head and tried to flee but was shot in the shoulder and arrested. Within an hour thousands of angry Harlemites had taken to the streets. Someone threw a bottle and, within minutes, the flames were spreading across 125th Street and up Eighth Avenue to cries of "Get the white man!"

These events shouldn't have taken the city by surprise. In late June, Detroit had been engulfed in a racial disturbance that left seventeen blacks and nine whites dead, along with hundreds of people of both races injured and millions of dollars in property damage. Rallies and meetings in Harlem had warned of the possibility of such events uptown, but La Guardia wrote off these activities as the work of agitators. Langston Hughes had seen more clearly what was headed Harlem's way, having published in July a blues of warning in Adam Clayton Powell's newspaper the *People's Voice:* "Looky here, America, / What you done done / Let things drift / Until the riots come." Clearly, it wasn't a single racial incident but years of hopeless anger that inspired the riot of 1943.

It is difficult to reconstruct a scene of such intense mayhem, partly because it was two disturbances. The first was a chaotic protest in which "normal Harlemites" rioted against generations of poverty and discrimination. It was only around one a.m. that another element— "criminal subhuman savages," according to Adam Clayton Powell Sr.—began looting and vandalizing. Unlike in 1935, they left black

stores and black cops alone, and they even avoided Chinese laundries—more than two thousand Asians called Harlem home in the
1940s—some of which famously posted signs that read "Me Colored
Too." The sounds of shouting, breaking glass, fire alarms, sirens, and
gunfire were overwhelming, especially on 125th, 135th, and 145th
streets, where mobs numbering in the thousands moved in waves. Milk
and whiskey ran in the streets, with crowds trampling bread and broken
glass underfoot. These events made an unforgettable impression on
a six-year-old named Claude Brown—he grew up to write the stunning memoir *Manchild in the Promised Land*—who listened from his
apartment at Eighth Avenue and West 145th Street and thought the
Germans were bombing Harlem. They also inspired William Johnson's series of paintings *Moon Over Harlem*, which drew from notorious
news photos of children in stolen tuxedos and top hats. Ralph Ellison
ventured out from behind his desk at the *Negro Quarterly* to witness
some of the worst rioting, on West 117th and West 118th streets between Lenox and Eighth avenues, hoarding the details for his fictional
account of the riot in *Invisible Man*. Richard Wright raced to Harlem
from his home in Brooklyn and paced up and down Eighth Avenue.

La Guardia, who "had his Italian up," the civil rights leader Roy
Wilkins later recalled, quickly sped uptown and deployed more than
six thousand police officers, setting up a command post at the West
123rd Street police precinct, where he met with the hostile crowd
gathered there. La Guardia, who had recently lost much goodwill
among blacks for not insisting on an antidiscrimination clause at downtown's Stuyvesant Town housing project, fearlessly scolded looters and
pleaded with them to go home. He made radio broadcasts intended
to calm New Yorkers and reached out to prominent Negro leaders.
When it became clear that the violence wasn't diminishing, La Guardia ordered Harlem sealed off—only milk trucks and food deliveries
were allowed through—issued a curfew, and closed all bars and liquor
stores. The riot raged through the night. By the time the police restored order on Thursday, fifteen hundred stores had been looted and
firemen had battled thirty-two blazes. There were nearly a thousand
arrests, so many that Harlem's jails couldn't hold them. Almost seven

hundred people were injured, including forty-five policemen, taxing the capacity of Harlem Hospital, whose emergency room floor was slick with blood. Six people were killed, all black, five of them shot by police. The Braddock Hotel opened the next day, but it took some twelve hundred sanitation workers three days to clean up the worst riot in Harlem's history.

The *Amsterdam News* called the riot a tragedy for which Harlemites were themselves responsible: "Harlem has sung and danced when it should have been working and praying." But blaming the victims wasn't a popular typical view. The relationship between Adam Clayton Powell Jr., who was out of town when the riot occurred, and Mayor La Guardia had deteriorated seriously, but Powell praised the mayor's restraint during the disturbance. If La Guardia had learned one lesson from the riot of 1935, it was to respond swiftly and decisively. Before the end of the summer his commissioner of markets and the Office of Price Administration had cited more than one hundred Harlem stores for ignoring price restrictions, and he pushed for ending racial discrimination and inadequate funding for public housing. He funneled more city money into programs to fight juvenile delinquency, and New York City caught up with every other major American city and passed rent control laws. But could La Guardia have prevented the riot of 1943? Not according to James Baldwin, who grew up at Park Avenue and East 132nd Street and lost his father to natural causes on August 2. The ride to the graveyard through the devastation left him with one thought: "Harlem needed something to smash."

Langston Hughes was out of town for the riot, but he raced back only to learn that his watch, which was being cleaned at Hubert's Jewelers, at Lenox Avenue and West 125th Street, was lost when the shop was overrun. Still, Hughes announced his sympathy with the rioters. "All the best colored people declare they have been set back fifty years," he wrote. "I don't know from what." Hughes was optimistic enough to turn down an offer from Fisk University, even after he was knifed uptown in early 1944. Hughes had something to be optimistic about. A year earlier he had been lounging at his favorite pub, Patsy's Bar and Grill, at 2623 Eighth Avenue, when he overheard a man explaining to a woman that he worked making cranks in a defense plant, for what purpose he didn't inquire. "I don't crank those cranks," the man said. "I just make 'em." Hughes, impressed by the laconic, vernacular power of the man's way of speaking, had found a new muse: it was, he said, like "myself talking to me. Or else me talking to myself." Hughes created a character, Jesse B. Semple, based on the man, for his column in the Chicago *Defender*. "Simple," as he was known, might have been an uneducated southern-born Negro, but he took on the most pressing issues of the day—the war, Jim Crow, politics, education, women's rights—with an intelligence, passion, and humor that made the column a national favorite. This character, who distrusted all whites except Eleanor Roosevelt, became Hughes's bread and butter, the material for hundreds of columns over the next two decades. No matter how true to life Hughes's creation was, however, actual Harlemites had it worse.

The Great Depression turned Harlem into a black ghetto, 80 percent of whose businesses were owned by whites. Perhaps Harlemites could have saved themselves had not the twin tragic follies of communism, which sacrificed racism on the altar of the international class struggle, and race nationalism, which offered short-term psychological benefits but few significant long-term returns in terms of material conditions uptown, remained so seductive. Then again, improvements, however small, in economic status, housing, health, and education, the integration of 125th Street, and the elimination of racial discrimination in war industries were made all but irrelevant by the riot of 1943, in which a few decisive hours of violence uptown undid years of righteous struggle. Many of the apartments and businesses struck by the riot remained empty. The continued arrival of immigrants from Puerto Rico, Cuba, the Dominican Republic, Panama, Mexico, and many other Latin American countries had made El Barrio the capital of the Spanish-speaking Caribbean, but when they weren't listening to "Lamento Borincano" they turned to a *plena* called "El Home Relief." More than 150,000 Italian East Harlemites had followed their Jewish neighbors to the Upper West Side, the outer boroughs, or the suburbs in the 1930s, and the social turmoil of the war years convinced many of those who had chosen to remain that Harlem was no longer *bella* or *nostra*. It wasn't only whites who were leaving. Now middle-class blacks found that Sugar Hill had become "vinegar sour," as Claude McKay put it, and were moving to the Bronx or Queens, the first signs of an implosion uptown that wouldn't reverse itself for more than half a century. Demographics were still destiny uptown.

10

"TEMPUS FUGUE-IT"
Harlem in the Civil Rights Era, 1943–1965

The riot of 1943 was supposed to be a wake-up call. Harlemites hoped that the rest of the city, and maybe even the rest of the country, would finally notice that after decades of boom and bust, self-help and philanthropy, tribal assertion and racial integration, conditions uptown were worse than ever. When Harlem's soldiers came home from World War II, they found their neighborhoods in ruins, with heroin stalking the avenues and most of their heroes dead or in exile. By any measure—poverty, racism, joblessness, health, education, or simply the sight of block after block of burned-out, boarded-up buildings—the Negro Mecca increasingly seemed beyond redemption.

No one exemplifies the complex social harmonies of the postwar years better than the swinging sinner named Malcolm Little, who as Malcolm X became uptown's unofficial patron saint. Born in 1925 in Nebraska, Little grew up in Wisconsin and Michigan, where his father, an itinerant Baptist minister and UNIA organizer, was killed in 1932 by white supremacists. His mother was left to raise eight children alone, though after she had a nervous breakdown in 1937 the children went to foster homes. Little first saw Harlem around 1941, when he was a cook on a Pullman railroad car running between Boston and Washington, D.C. One Thursday night he got off at Pennsylvania Station and took a taxi uptown, where his outrageous attire—his orange shoes matched his hair—gave sophisticated Harlemites a laugh. Malcolm X liked to say that most American Negroes were fatally confused. To be sure, the zoot-suited hepcat named Malcolm Little was more confused than most when he first settled in Harlem.

Like generations of outsiders who fell in love with uptown Manhattan at first sight, Little was astounded by the endless varieties of racial, ethnic, and religious energy he found among its four hundred thousand residents. Among the neighborhood's white holdouts were the notoriously reclusive Collyer brothers, who in 1947 were found buried in their overstuffed row house at 2078 Fifth Avenue under two lifetimes' worth of old newspapers, books, lampshades, beds, bowling balls, jars of pickled human organs, broken baby carriages, collapsed umbrellas, defunct pianos, and rusty bicycles. Their Jewish neighbors were gone, but just to the south Italian Harlem was still a city unto itself, though not for long. In the 1940s three-quarters of East Harlem's residents were Italian, enough to support four Roman Catholic parishes and four Protestant churches, as well as more than a hundred benevolent and mutual societies that sponsored concerts and debates, offered health and death benefits, or simply provided a place to play bocce and drink espresso. Nonetheless, more and more uptown Italians were just a step behind the Jews of lower Harlem in leaving for the Bronx and Queens. The decline of Italian East Harlem was perhaps most visible in the *festa* of the Madonna of Mount Carmel, which was becoming less and less spiritual and more and more commercial. The church took over the event, going so far as to remove an altar fresco showing members of the congregation with connections to organized crime, and at its peak in the 1940s almost three hundred thousand people jammed the streets of East Harlem to catch a glimpse of the Madonna. Later, the procession route was truncated, men and women began marching together, and gunfire was replaced by fireworks.

It was only after World War II that East Harlem got the nickname Spanish Harlem, as generations of immigrants—it might well be called the Latino great migration—achieved a critical cultural mass. Rumor had it that Vito Marcantonio invited Puerto Ricans to East Harlem to get their votes, but there were plenty of other motives for making the journey. Wages on the islands remained half of what workers in the United States were earning, and making the move was faster and easier than ever. A boat called the *Marine Tiger* carried more than twenty-five thousand migrants a year from San Juan to New York City before the late 1940s, when tens of thousands of Puerto Ricans started making the journey by airplane each year, a development described by *Life* magazine as history's first diaspora via airplane. Those numbers increased in the early 1950s, as Puerto Ricans were not only exempt from the McCarran-Walter Act—immigration legislation that favored northern European immigrants over those from Latin America, Asia, the Middle East, and Africa—but actively recruited as part of an American program called Operation Bootstrap. More than half a million Puerto Ricans had arrived by the 1960s.

Not all of the newcomers lived out their dreams. Work in defense plants dried up after 1945, and there was less factory work as the city's industrial base began to wither. The number of union garment factories in East Harlem had shrunk considerably by the 1950s. The rest paid only half the union minimum wage, and without union protection working conditions could be dangerous. The situation didn't hit Boricuas as hard as it did Negro Harlemites, since a strong entrepreneurial streak among Puerto Ricans meant there were more locally owned small businesses in East Harlem—most of the neighborhood's hundreds of candy stores and bodegas were family-owned—which provided the kind of economic stability that was missing across town. Especially beloved were hundreds of modest shops called *botánicas*, which sold specially blessed candles, herbs, incense, icons, medals, statuettes, and even hair restorers and books containing the secrets needed to hit the numbers. More than 80 percent of all Puerto Rican Harlemites were born Catholic, but only half of all Boricuas attended Mass regularly. Like their Italian predecessors, Puerto Ricans had a complicated relationship with the church, which frowned on a spiritual life that combined Catholic Mass, baptism, marriage, and last rites with island animism and African-influences. Many Puerto Ricans heeded the call of Protestant churches that offered services and pastoral guidance in Spanish, the most successful of which was the East Harlem Protestant Parish. Organized by the Union Theological Seminary in the late 1940s in Norman Thomas's old stomping grounds, within a decade the Parish consisted of fifteen ministers running a drug treatment center, job training programs, and soup kitchens. More typical of the spiritual life of El Barrio were the dozens of storefront operations whose charismatic preachers led jam-packed services that went on for most of every day and into the evening.

Of course, when Malcolm X referred to Malcolm Little's Harlem as "a technicolor bazaar," it was the diversity of black people that he had in mind. This wasn't only a matter of skin color. Whole neighborhoods were being taken over by West Indians—Little's own mother was from Grenada—and their benevolent societies were central to the social scene, providing not only life insurance and death benefits for members but sponsoring the annual West Indian Day street carnival. Had Little only been more interested in Africa, he might have encountered Kwame Nkrumah, who would go on to become Ghana's first president, and Nnamdi Azikiwe, later Nigeria's first president, at meetings of Harlem's Blyden Society for the Study of African History. But Little was too busy dancing. He became a regular at Smalls Paradise, where patrons still packed the dance floor so tightly they joked they could get only a dime's worth of space for their $1.25 admission fee. Little also haunted the Savoy Ballroom and the Apollo Theater, frequented the bars of the Theresa and Braddock hotels, and drank at La Marr-Cherie Bar and the Lenox Lounge before retiring to his rented room at the Harlem Y. After he lost his railroad job in 1942 due to customer complaints, he got a job as a bathroom attendant and waiter at Smalls and moved from the Y to a less than reputable boardinghouse on St. Nicholas Avenue. He was now a Harlemite for life, or so he hoped.

After being fired from Smalls Paradise in mid-1943—he was caught in a sting operation targeting pimps, though his worst offense seems to have been selling joints to johns—he got work as a waiter at Jimmy's Chicken Shack, at 763 St. Nicholas Avenue, evaded the draft by faking mental illness and claiming he wanted to kill crackers down

Harlem

South, and got his first apartment, a street-front cellar near Convent Avenue and West 147th Street. It wasn't difficult for someone with Little's brains and ambitions to land on his feet. He had learned a lot at Smalls, where he had also hustled condoms and alcohol to patrons and watched over the gambling room in the back of the club. Now he began running craps games in back of the Apollo and eventually graduated to dealing marijuana or "gage" to musicians at 50 cents per joint. Little became the main connection for the "teaheads" from the bands of Duke Ellington and Lionel Hampton. He was known across Harlem as "Detroit Red," to distinguish him from a young funnyman called "Chicago Red," with whom he had worked in the kitchen of Jimmy's and who would later come to fame as the comedian Redd Foxx.

Little had gotten into dealing marijuana precisely when it became popular uptown, but he never stuck with one racket for long and soon he started to sell bootleg whiskey. He also worked as a "steerer," picking up white men in Times Square and bringing them to uptown prostitutes who kicked back a percentage. Little never became as successful as locally famous procurers Sammy the Pimp, Cadillac Drake, or Dollar Bill but, then again, he didn't seem to want to. Instead, he pinned his hopes on hitting the numbers, where $20 could win $12,000. In 1949 the New York *Age* reported that "nobody comes to Harlem anymore" and as the nightlife dwindled, Little began to work as a numbers runner himself, picking up bets in the morning, keeping 10 percent for himself, and delivering the rest to the controller, who would take another 5 percent for himself and give the rest to the "banker," almost inevitably a white gangster. Virtually the only exception to the rigid segregation of the numbers industry was Bumpy Johnson, a native of South Carolina who loved fine, flashy clothing. More than once he rose from the floor in front of the bar of the Alhambra Theatre after having beaten some underling into submission and asked, "Is my tie straight?" The fact that he had been shot more than a dozen times and arrested too many times to count on his way to the top only added to Johnson's reputation as the Robin Hood of Harlem, who saved families from eviction and took lonely waitresses at the Theresa Hotel to the after-hours action at Wells's Supper Club.

Bumpy Johnson may have been the only black man to stand up to the mob, but in the years after the war Harlem was virtually overrun with dozens of Negro gangs, like the Royal Knights, the Mutineers, and the Comanches. When they weren't fighting each other with daggers, ice picks, or zip guns these gangs concentrated on burglary. A group called the Forty Thieves would plant a member in a store before closing time and then spend the night cleaning the place out. Children and teenaged members were crucial to the survival of these gangs because of their clean records. They even had their own gangs—Claude Brown was a member of the Buccaneers. Malcolm Little was too proud to submit to anyone else's discipline, and eventually he formed his own gang, though he had to snort cocaine to get his courage up before jobs. Did Harlem have nothing better to offer?

During his "lost" years uptown, Malcolm Little would sneer at a politician such as J. Raymond Jones, but the Harlem Fox was making the kinds of changes that Little and his running buddies never bothered to dream about. Jones had realized that because political clubs decided who ran for public office, they often wielded more power than the politicians who got elected. So in 1943 Jones started the George Washington Carver Political Club, a multiracial but black-controlled Democratic organization that came to exercise an unchallenged dominance over East Harlem. The Tammany mayor William O'Dwyer, who succeeded Fiorello La Guardia in part because he looked to Jones as "my eyes and ears in Harlem," made Jones his deputy commissioner of housing and building, the highest appointed city post held by a Negro. Still, Jones remained rooted in Harlem, frequenting both the Renaissance Ballroom, a favorite of local elites, and Smalls Paradise, which attracted a less respectable clientele. But Jones's success in putting black Harlemites into elected office, as well as onto various commissions and judicial positions, began to work against him. Tammany Hall feared the black vote and began a campaign of undermining uptown leaders by accusing them of communist sympathies. After 1950, when O'Dwyer resigned amid corruption charges, Jones was left even more vulnerable. He gave up politics in 1953, walking away from his position as district leader and stepping down as boss of the Carver Club to open up room for new blood. The job of doing Tammany's bidding went to Hulan Jack, a native of Saint Lucia who served in the state assembly before becoming the first African American Manhattan borough president.

Tammany Hall also helped bring down Vito Marcantonio by redrawing the boundaries of his congressional district to include the mostly white and conservative Upper East Side. But what really finished Marc was the change in public attitudes toward communism. Although he had never been a party member, Marc embraced socialists and socialism without shame and was unafraid to take up unpopular positions—he was the only member of Congress to cast a vote against the Korean War. After Democrats, Republicans, and Liberals ganged up to defeat him in the congressional election in 1950, Marc kept his offices on East 116th Street open and went back to his law practice, but he collapsed from a heart attack and died on his way to work in 1954 at the age of fifty-one. More than ten thousand Italians, Puerto Ricans, Jews, communists, and more gathered at the corner of First Avenue and East 115th Street to pay their respects; there was even a large Negro contingent, led by W.E.B. Du Bois. The only bitter note was sounded by the Catholic Church, which denied Marc a resting place in a Catholic cemetery because he had lapsed long ago. In the end, Marc was laid to rest a few feet away from La Guardia in Woodlawn Cemetery in the Bronx. Marcantonio's unapologetic sympathies with communism when it was most unspeakable may have made him an isolated loner in Washington, D.C., but in East Harlem he had the backing of communists and liberal Republicans and Democrats, Italians, Negroes, Puerto Ricans, and Jews. It was a mix that could be found nowhere else on earth, he liked to say. Marcantonio even managed to avoid the hostility of the Garveyite splinter groups, who still attended UNIA conferences every August in Harlem, just like the old days, and even started celebrating August 1 as Marcus Garvey Day—a 1953 rally attracted two thousand supporters and featured a beauty contest that crowned a "Miss Africa."

Adam Clayton Powell Jr. survived the kind of opposition Raymond Jones and Vito Marcantonio struggled with. After only three years on the City Council, Powell ran for Congress as an independent, turning his Coordinating Committee for Employment into an election machine called the People's Committee. Until this time, gerrymandering made sure that Harlem was represented in Congress by whites. It was Powell who helped black voters realize that in 1944 a new era was upon them. Under the Garveyesque banner "One People, One Fight, One Victory," Powell convinced the Republicans and the American Labor Party to support him. With a campaign war chest filled by liberal Jews who were impressed by his opposition to British rule in Palestine, Powell's victory made him only the fourth African-American in history to serve in Congress, and the first from the Northeast. Powell joked to Dizzy Gillespie about being "Head Nigger in Charge," but it was as "Mr. Civil Rights" that Powell personally desegregated the congressional barbershop and dining room. He even put an end to the use of the word "nigger" on the floor of the House of Representatives. He fought successfully against the poll tax, lynching, and discrimination in defense industries and immigration, and he helped to establish the nation's first minimum wage law. The price of Powell's success was estrangement from many of the left-wing figures with whom he had achieved so much in the past. For a time, Paul Robeson and almost anyone else tainted by communism or race nationalism were no longer welcome at the Abyssinian Baptist Church, where Powell still delivered two sermons every Sunday morning.

Powell had now reached movie star status, with the cars, clothes, and women that went along with it. In 1955 he helped make Bessie Allison Buchanan, who had danced on the Cotton Club's famed chorus line and married Savoy Ballroom owner Charles Buchanan, the first black female member of the New York State Assembly. But it was constituent services that kept Powell in Harlem's good graces. Up to seven thousand people came to see him each year to complain about their landlords or bosses, and following up was work that he considered more important than whatever he accomplished in Congress. That attitude often put Powell, who had been monitored by the FBI since 1943, at political risk. After cops killed a uniformed soldier on Eighth Avenue in December of 1950, Powell learned that the New York Police Department had a secret agreement with the FBI to let the city handle its own problems with police brutality, a discovery that won him few friends downtown. Then, in 1956, Powell crossed party lines to vote for Eisenhower. The Democrats, who had long worried that Powell was too far to the left, declared he was now too far to the right. It wasn't long before several Washington, D.C., journalists were calling Powell the least effective member of Congress.

When Powell left for Washington, his City Council seat had gone to Benjamin Davis Jr., a black communist from Georgia who had come to Harlem in the 1930s to edit the party's uptown newspaper, the *Harlem Liberator*. Davis's election represented the party's most remarkable coup in decades of organizing uptown. It couldn't have happened without the help of the membership of the otherwise conservative Abyssinian Baptist Church and of celebrities, too, such as Bumpy Johnson, Count Basie, Billie Holiday, and Paul Robeson, though it was mostly the work of Powell, who hadn't yet turned anticommunist, and whose local power was so uncontested that elections were but a formality. However, once in office the Communist Party affiliation that had made Davis into a Harlem hero hindered his ability to work with mainstream politicians. He joined the Democrats in 1947 but it was already too late. Two years later he was convicted of conspiring to overthrow the government and kicked off the City Council.

Davis's fate was a warning to Harlem's few remaining communists. The most prominent exception was, as usual, Paul Robeson. In August of 1949 his uptown protest against the jailing of a black member of the party almost turned into an anticommunist lynching, complete with a violent mob, a cross burning, and shouts of "Dirty commie!" Few were surprised the next year when the State Department voided Robeson's passport. He was only fifty-two years old and at the peak of his creative powers, but he would never recapture his artistic prominence or his unique moral standing. In 1951 the *Crisis* attacked Robeson as 'a Kremlin stooge,' and the next year he got into a fight at the Red Rooster tavern, at West 138th Street and Seventh Avenue, with Brooklyn Dodgers baseball star Don Newcombe, who told Robeson, "I'm joining the army to fight people like you." Members of Robeson's college fraternity, Alpha Phi Alpha, lambasted him at a meeting at their St. Nicholas Avenue headquarters. Even that bastion of left-wing politics, City College, banned him from campus appearances. Lonely, exhausted, depressed, and suicidal, Robeson remained unrepentant in his support for the Soviet Union until the very end. The greatest Othello of the era died in 1976 in Philadelphia, having loved his own people well, to be sure, but not wisely.

Long-standing rumors that the NAACP "neutralized" Robeson are unproven, but the organization certainly had a motive. The mainstream civil rights group was in a full-blown ideological crisis in the years after the war, its members' dedication to legal action and scholarly research having accomplished little more than the street protests of the race radicals. These years in the wilderness came to an end in 1954, when the NAACP's Thurgood Marshall convinced the United States Supreme Court to outlaw segregation in the Topeka, Kansas, public schools. Even Du Bois, who had broken with the NAACP and moved to Brooklyn—he bought Arthur Miller's house—was shocked, declaring, "I have seen the impossible happen." As it turns out, the promised land was in sight, but the black Moses would never enter. That was to be the job of a black Joshua named Bayard Rustin.

The victories of the civil rights movement in the wake of *Brown v. Board of Education* are most often associated with the rise of a generation of activists and protesters from the black church. In fact, the figure who finally united the race radicals and the mainstream groups, the communists and the capitalists, the separatists and the integrationists, the figure who focused the movement on the rural, unreconstructed South was not Du Bois or Adam Clayton Powell Jr. or A. Philip Randolph or even Martin Luther King Jr., but Rustin, a gay, illegitimate, Quaker socialist from Pennsylvania. With a grandmother who had helped found the NAACP—James Weldon Johnson and Du Bois stayed with the Rustins whenever business brought him to town—Rustin was certainly poised to make an impact when he arrived in Harlem in 1937 at the age of twenty-two. But he was a

complicated man whose interest in music and theater—he worked
for a time as a WPA dance instructor—vied for his attention with
night classes at City College, where he became liaison to the Young
Communists League. That didn't last long, mostly because the communists aggressively recruited blacks but then forbade them from
addressing racism in America, at the time a Soviet ally. Rustin came
to realize that, since before World War I, the wide variety of political
choices available to African-Americans, once thought to be evidence
of political maturity, had in fact stifled progress by pitting them against
one another. It was perhaps natural that Rustin gravitated toward
Randolph, another CCNY dropout and political firebrand who had
been burned by the communists. Rustin had joined Randolph in trying to convince President Roosevelt to address racism in the armed
services, but he broke with Randolph after his old mentor accepted
Roosevelt's decision to focus on discrimination in war industries and
leave the military itself alone. Rustin joined Norman Thomas's Fellowship of Reconciliation, a pacifist group that ran an ashram at Fifth
Avenue and West 125th Street. As unlikely as a meditation center next
door to a nightclub called the Bucket of Blood may sound, it inspired
a growing number of Harlemites interested in disciplined reflection
on what Mahatma Gandhi called "truth force."

Rustin taught Harlem a new kind of pacifism, one in which opposing the Korean War, South African apartheid, and segregation in
the military were all part of the same struggle. In Rustin's mind, bold
resistance against segregation and discrimination went hand-in-hand
with concerts of classical songs and spirituals. He served a three-year
prison term for resisting the draft and joined with the NAACP to organize the interracial effort to end segregation on interstate travel—it
was the very first Freedom Ride. Then in 1953 Rustin was arrested in
California after being caught having sex with two men in a parked car.
Rustin had always been open about his homosexuality, and since his
earliest days in Harlem he had moved effortlessly between uptown's
gay and straight communities, but his allies in the civil rights movement
didn't consider gay rights to be a part of their agenda. Convinced that
Rustin's homosexuality endangered their credibility they deserted him.

But the influence of the "Uptown Gandhi" was unstoppable. Rustin had shown Harlem and all of America that the movement for racial justice could no longer be defined by the terms—W.E.B. Du Bois versus Booker T. Washington, legal action versus street protest, communist versus nationalist, even black versus white—that for more than a half century had kept uptown down.

While scientists at a Columbia University facility at an old dairy plant on West 125th Street were splitting the atom as part of the Manhattan Project, a few blocks away a new generation of musicians was fracturing the elemental swing rhythms that had dominated jazz for decades. They called it bebop, an onomatopoeic term that reproduced the music's playfully precise approach to musical time, although Langston Hughes's character Simple claimed the genre as a social statement: the word itself, he insisted, came from "the police beating Negroes' heads. Every time a cop hits a Negro with a billy club, that old club says, 'BOP! BOP! . . . BEBOP! . . . MOP! . . . BOP!'"

Bebop got its start around 1938, when a saxophonist named Henry Minton, who was the first black delegate of the local musicians union, took over the Hotel Cecil, at 206 West 118th Street, and started a jazz club. Minton's was advertised as the "Showplace of Harlem," but the modest basement wasn't much of a place at all, at least compared to the grand dance palaces of Lenox and Seventh avenues. Around 1940, the club's jam sessions each Monday night, the regular night off for most musicians, proved so popular that they were soon going every night from 10 p.m. until the legal closing time of 4 a.m. These jams, featuring a young and mostly unknown rhythm section of piano, bass, and drums backing visiting soloists, were serious business. Any club hosting jam sessions became a de facto hiring hall, with more experienced players in effect auditioning new recruits on the spot. Playing obscure songs in unusual or difficult keys was one sure way to weed out the amateurs and the old-timers, and at Minton's things could move from competitive to aggressive in the course of a chorus. Many young musicians were humiliated this way as teenagers in the 1930s, and in some respects bebop, with its bracingly modern rhythms and exotic harmonies, was their revenge.

Virtually alone among the older generation of Harlem entertainers who could keep up was the swing era composer Mary Lou Williams, who turned her apartment at the Dewey Square Hotel, just up the street from Minton's, into an after-hours gathering place for everyone from white swing musicians to younger beboppers. Both rooms pulsed with a new form of iconoclastic timekeeping invented by Kenny Clarke, a drummer from Philadelphia who overturned jazz dogma by using the cymbal to maintain the pulse. He effectively redefined jazz time so that it was no longer a steadily thumping, danceable four-four beat but a more flexible kind of rhythm that urged soloists both forward and inward. The big bass drum was for accents—"dropping bombs," unfriendly witnesses called it.

Of course, inventing modern jazz was more than a matter of unmasking the venerable percussion tradition of the four-on-the-floor bass drum as a corny cliché, and Clarke didn't really hit his stride until he met a quirky and brilliant pianist named Thelonious Monk. Born in North Carolina in 1923, Monk grew up in Manhattan, in the old Negro neighborhood called San Juan Hill. By the early 1940s he was showing up at Minton's, where he sometimes puzzled but always impressed his peers and his audiences with blunt, loping solos and angular, rough-hewn compositions. Clarke and Monk found a perfect complement in Dizzy Gillespie, a trumpeter with a wicked sense of humor and a blazing fluidity on his instrument. Born John Birks Gillespie in 1917 in South Carolina, he acquired the nickname Dizzy because of his good-natured love of troublemaking fun on and off the bandstand. He came to Harlem in 1937 and started haunting the after-hours jam sessions. Within two years he was playing in the trumpet section of Cab Calloway's band, which soon became a bebop incubator. After Calloway's Cotton Club gig ended at 3 a.m. Gillespie, who was developing the look that would signal membership in the newly emerging bebop subculture—goatee, beret, and sunglasses, indoors and out—would head to Minton's. There he encountered a guitarist named Charlie Christian, who had started out in Oklahoma

City, playing an early precursor of rhythm and blues and rock and roll known as the jump blues. Every night Christian would race from his gig as a straight-ahead swing strummer with Benny Goodman up to Minton's, where he kept a spare amplifier. If Clarke ensured his place in jazz history by breaking up time, Christian's immortal contribution was to put it back together, with long strings of rapid-fire, minimally accented eighth notes that embody bebop improvisation.

Minton's wasn't the only bebop laboratory. Dizzy Gillespie's nocturnal perambulations through Harlem took him to a dozen clubs, as much in search of ever hotter jams as in an effort to evade the musicians union's "walking representative," who was in charge of catching members playing without a contract. One of Gillespie's favorites was Clark Monroe's Uptown House, which is less well remembered by music historians than Minton's but of equal importance; one of the very first bebop recordings was an amateur disc cut there in 1941 and named "Kerouac," after a white jazz enthusiast who went to school up the hill at Columbia and who would later claim that bop birthed the beats. The Uptown House was located in the unmarked cellar—the Hollywood matinee idol John Garfield still found his way in—once occupied by Barron Wilkins's club. Jam sessions started after Minton's closed and went on until the next afternoon, powered by the drumming of a Brooklynite named Max Roach. Monroe's greatest discovery was an alto saxophonist named Charlie Parker, who was born in 1920 in Kansas City and who played with local bands before taking off on his own in 1939 for Harlem. It was at Dan Wall's Chili House, on Seventh Avenue near West 139th Street, that Parker underwent the musical conversion experience that marks the formal beginning of the bebop revolution. Jamming on the Ray Noble tune "Cherokee," Parker discovered that using the upper tones of standard chords opened up a new harmonic frontier. It was not a new discovery—Bach and Beethoven knew all about it—but it was the eureka moment that made jazz modern. By 1942 Parker was stunning the crowds at Minton's and Monroe's night after night with aggressive, headlong solos that seemed to stake out new harmonic territory with every breath. Bebop music, fashion, argot, even their preferred drug, heroin—Parker's addiction was nearly as much a part of his legend as his musical skills—were soon sweeping across Harlem. By changing the focus of jazz from the complex interplay of composer, big band, and dancers into providing space for heroic, self-made, freedom-seeking soloists the beboppers turned jazz from entertainment into art.

Bebop was born uptown but it came to maturity on West 52nd Street, where so much of New York's live jazz scene had relocated. Still, dozens of clubs offered live music in Harlem in the postwar years. The legendary stride pianist Lucky Roberts ran Lucky's Rendezvous, at 773 St. Nicholas Avenue, while Joe Wells's Upstairs Room, at 2249 Seventh Avenue, featured a wide variety of jazz, from the pre–World War I era duo of Noble Sissle and Eubie Blake to the swing and bebop sounds of Mary Lou Williams, as well as famous fried chicken. Next door was a lounge run by Count Basie himself, primarily to give his own music a platform, though the club was soon best known for attracting gamblers, gangsters, and politicians. A more respectable crowd gathered at the Red Rooster, on Seventh Avenue near West 137th Street. The most exclusive clientele, including the boxer Joe Louis and white actresses such as Lana Turner and Tallulah Bankhead, headed for music, drinking, and gambling to an unnamed after-hours club at St. Nicholas Avenue and West 148th Street. Meanwhile, the large Harlem venues continued to get by. The Rockland Palace and the Audubon Ballroom stayed afloat by hosting political meetings, while the Renaissance Ballroom, Smalls Paradise, Savoy Ballroom, and Apollo Theater offered a new kind of dance music called rhythm and blues.

Much has been made of the way bebop divided New Negroes from Newer Negroes. Richard Wright was no fan of bebop, walking out of a club to which he brought the French philosopher Simone de Beauvoir. To be sure, many old-timers devoted to the thrilling public interplay between the sounds on the bandstand and the moves on the dance floor didn't appreciate being part of an audience of seated nightclub listeners, many of whom seemed to be young musicians themselves, intent on decoding an intellectual puzzle. But figures from both schools appeared together at live gigs and on recordings, and many Harlemites caught on right away. Paul Robeson loved Thelonious Monk's music, saw Dizzy Gillespie at the Apollo, and caught a Charlie Parker gig at the Manhattan Casino.

Langston Hughes was even more enthusiastic about bebop, perhaps because he saw how deeply rooted in Harlem the music was. Indeed, Hughes earned his authority when it came to bebop partly because, unlike most of the writers and artists of his generation, he had remained in Harlem, once insisting, "I would rather have a kitchenette in Harlem than a mansion in Westchester." He would do better than that. In 1947 he used the proceeds from *Street Scene,* his successful Broadway collaboration with Kurt Weill, to pay a Finnish couple $12,500 for the row house at 20 East 127th Street. Hughes's spartan, two-room bachelor's suite on the third floor was his first and only real home uptown, and he never lived anywhere else. The crown prince of the Harlem Renaissance, who had been under surveillance by the FBI since 1940, became an avuncular neighborhood fixture, sitting with neighbors on stoops and sending their children on errands, for which he tipped them lavishly. During the afternoon he read in the children's sections of the 135th Street New York Public Library; the writer Toni Cade Bambara remembers seeing him there when she was a child. At night he would visit the Baby Grand, at 319 West 125th Street—it was the young comedian Nipsey Russell's regular gig—or the Palm Café, which faced the Theresa Hotel, where he could be seen mingling with everyone from Harry Belafonte and Sidney Poitier to Adam Clayton Powell Jr. Hughes could also be seen at the bar at Seventh Avenue near West 124th Street owned by Sugar Ray Robinson, whose forty straight victories before he was brought down by Jake LaMotta made him one of Harlem's best-loved celebrities, and where Hughes might play chess with Dizzy Gillespie or chat with celebrities Frank Sinatra or Elizabeth Taylor.

This routine resulted in an extraordinary third act for Hughes, "the O. Henry of Harlem." Liberated from the aesthetic battles of the 1920s and the political conflicts of the 1930s, black America's poet laureate produced *Montage of a Dream Deferred* in 1951, a bebop epic that better than any other work of art revealed the contradictions of life in Harlem at midcentury, famously asking, in a poem rarely referred to by its proper title, "Harlem": "What happens to a dream deferred?"

* * *

While Hughes was making his nightly rounds during the war years, he couldn't have missed the tall, skinny hustler with flaming red hair and a white girl on his arm. But when things got too hot in Harlem, Malcolm Little returned to Boston, where he was arrested on larceny and firearms charges and convicted in 1946. He was sentenced to ten years in prison, where he became an adherent of the group popularly known as the Nation of Islam or the Black Muslims, though the official name was the Lost Found Nation of Islam in the Wilderness of North America. It was founded in Detroit in 1930 by a mysterious peddler who called himself Wallace D. Fard, or W. Fard Muhammad, apparently the newest identity of Arnold Josiah Ford, the Garveyite rabbi who helped found Harlem's first Ethiopian synagogue before traveling to Africa and embracing Islam. The unknowability of Fard's history didn't pose a problem, given the other leaps of faith he asked his followers to make. The Nation of Islam shared much with conventional Muslim sects, such as forbidding pork and alcohol, but it also preached very un-Islamic notions: "original man" was black, according to Fard, but somewhere in prehistory he had been seduced by a white devil concocted in a laboratory by an evil scientist. By 1934 Fard was gone and the Nation of Islam was being run by Elijah Muhammad. Born Elijah Poole in 1897 to Georgia sharecroppers, he nevertheless convinced followers that he was the human incarnation of Allah. Jail was a primary recruiting ground for the Nation of Islam, and it still is. After Little, who had changed his name to Malcolm X—the "X" represented the slaves who were his ancestors—was released on parole in 1952, he returned to Detroit and, under the protection of the Nation of Islam and with the encouragement of Elijah Muhammad, was able to begin a new life. In 1953 he became the assistant minister of Detroit's Temple #1, though he was constantly on the road, founding temples in Boston and Philadelphia. The next year he was sent by Elijah Muhammad to New York City to work out of Harlem's Temple #7, located in a tiny storefront at 106 West 127th Street.

There were many race extremists still mounting the stepladders of Seventh Avenue in the postwar years, such as Charles Kenyatta, Josef ben Jochannan, Eddie "Pork Chop" Davis-Forman, Arthur Reid, and Sister Lucille, known as the "Firebrand." The difference was that the Nation of Islam had not only passion but a plan. They wanted to exempt African-Americans from all taxes and send their children to all-black schools with all-black curricula. They turned whites away from their mosques, forbade miscegenation, and sought a separate state or territory in the United States to be reserved for blacks only. It may have shocked people elsewhere but Harlemites had heard most of it before and passed by. Mainstream civil rights leaders, disturbed in particular by the Nation of Islam's anti-Semitic edge—recall that the NAACP was founded and funded mostly by Jews—shunned them. Nonetheless, the Nation of Islam did offer an alternative, however troubling, to the cycle of street and jail that drew in so many young Harlemites. The group embraced strict rules about hygiene and personal conduct: tobacco, alcohol, and drugs were strictly forbidden, sexual relations were carefully regulated, and modesty in appearance, especially among women, was closely monitored.

The NAACP's Supreme Court victory in *Brown v. Board of Education* in 1954 brought little comfort to the Nation of Islam or other race radicals, who scorned the decision for its implication that all-black schools were necessarily inferior, and who insisted that the court's order to schools to carry out the decision "with all due deliberate speed" was a ruse to maintain the status quo. Frustration with the slow pace of change led W.E.B. Du Bois to join the Communist Party, renounce his American citizenship, and move to Ghana. The NAACP's Thurgood Marshall, for once in agreement with the Nation of Islam, took "all due deliberate speed" to mean "as slowly as possible."

Malcolm X now spent most of his working hours, and most of his leisure time as well, spreading the word of Elijah Muhammad among Harlem's junkies, hustlers, alcoholics, whores, pimps, and homeless. He planted himself on Sunday afternoons in front of churches that were just ending their services and even chided old ladies for straightening

352 Harlem

eir hair. Then there was his weekly column in the *Amsterdam News* and the highly charged street protests, where he made the most of the reluctance of mainstream civil rights leaders to show up. Although he had moved to Queens to raise a family, he became minister of Temple #7 in Harlem and began promoting the neighborhood as a seedbed for a new American revolution. More than eight thousand people went to the 369th Armory for a two-hour speech by Elijah Muhammad that summer, but it was clear that Malcolm X was becoming the public face of the Nation of Islam.

One of the key events that turned Malcolm X from a disturbing curiosity into a legitimate power broker was his half hour conversation with Fidel Castro in 1960 at the Theresa Hotel, when the Cuban leader was in New York for the opening of the United Nations General Assembly. Owned since the 1930s by the black businessman Lovie B. Woods, who had a string of uptown flophouses, the 'Waldorf of Harlem' was a favored spot for celebrities, including Joe Louis, Lena Horne, and Lester Young. The hotel, which was already starting to show signs of decline, flew the Cuban flag and welcomed Castro and his entourage of eighty people. Castro reciprocated, mingling with the staff and sitting down with maintenance workers to dinner, his treat. Castro met Malcolm X again—though he declined to dine at Mosque #7—and arranged for him to meet the premier of the Soviet Union, an event that drew hundreds of cops to keep an eye on thousands of adoring Harlemites. Elijah Muhammad, the man who had plucked Malcolm Little from prison and turned him into Malcolm X, started to worry that his disciple had grown too influential.

Despite his rise to international prominence, Malcolm X still "fished" for converts and spoke at mass meetings in front of Lewis Michaux's bookstore against Jim Crow terror down South. He also found inspiration in Harlem itself, which had become a national symbol of poverty and injustice. The federal government was now disqualifying families with an unemployed father from receiving assistance, a decision accelerating the fission of the black nuclear family. Half of all senior citizens and children in Harlem were living in poverty, and the numbers were worsening fast. Public education, which in decades past had provided a way out for at least some Harlem children, was worse than ever, a situation brought to wider public recognition by the novel *Blackboard Jungle,* by Evan Hunter, who had been born Salvatore Lombino in Italian East Harlem. In the 1960s, Harlem's more than thirty thousand schoolchildren were crammed into far too few schools. Not even a delinquency rate twice the city average was enough to ease overcrowding. Those children who showed up were still often taught by the system's worst teachers. New York City had outlawed racial segregation in the public schools in 1902, and the Supreme Court confirmed that vision in 1954, but only two of Harlem's schools were less than 90 percent black during this period, and the gap between white and black school performance was scandalous. After outraged parents, led by a firebrand named Carrie Haynes, set up their own school in 1958 in the Emmanuel Sunday School, at East 126th Street and Third Avenue, and sued the city for using race to determine the boundaries of school districts, parents for the first time were allowed to transfer children in poorly performing schools to better schools out of district, often out of Harlem. Ironically, that left the worst schools even more impoverished. Even parents of students from the relatively fancy P.S. 197, the local school for the solidly middle-class Lenox Terrace and Riverton housing projects, started asking for transfers, and test scores across Harlem plummeted. By the mid-1960s, 75 percent of junior high schoolers weren't reading at grade level. The majority of those few who graduated from high school earned only the "general" diplomas that did not fulfill college admissions requirements.

Things were even more dire in El Barrio, where overcrowding meant that many students had to attend school in shifts. What went on in the classrooms was also disquieting. Historically, the city schools simply immersed non-English-speaking children in American language and culture; it wasn't until 1948 that the first bilingual teachers were hired by the school system, and, even then, not as full-timers. A decade later there were only eighty bilingual teachers city-wide for almost a hundred thousand Puerto Rican schoolchildren. The size and density of the Puerto Rican community uptown and their sense that the Spanish language and an American passport were not mutually exclusive meant that Puerto Ricans were slower than Italians or Jews to give up their native language, though they had their own English-language poet laureate in the public school teacher Julia de Burgos. Despite the challenges, in the postwar years East Harlem's schools helped turn many immigrant children into distinguished Americans, including Richard Carmona, who went on to become the surgeon general of the United States, Erik Estrada, who became a television star in the 1970s, and Oscar Hijuelos, the first Latino writer to win the Pulitzer Prize for fiction, for his 1989 novel *The Mambo Kings Play Songs of Love*, which memorialized the golden age of Latin music uptown.

Although theories for Harlem's decline in the years after World War II abound, the most convincing explanation places the blame largely on changes in the structure of New York City's economy. Between 1952 and 1965 the city lost almost ninety-thousand manufacturing jobs, which had been a key source of economic stability uptown. At the same time, the service jobs that blacks were finally eligible for after New York outlawed workplace discrimination tended to come with smaller paychecks and no union protection. In fact, the labor movement remained a racist stronghold and an impediment to change. In 1963 the Brotherhood of Locomotive Firemen and Engineers became the last major union to stop barring blacks from membership, but in the mid-1960s there were almost no blacks in positions of power in the major labor organizations, not even in supposedly progressive unions like the International Ladies Garment Workers Union. Things weren't much easier for business owners uptown. In the decade after its founding in 1954, the federal Small Business Agency made only seven loans to blacks. Two decades after the founding of the Carver Federal Savings Bank, it was still the only black-owned financial institution uptown—this at a time when Chicago had many. Meanwhile, the only major department store left in Harlem, Blumstein's, was white-owned. In 1962 the New York City Commission on Human Rights charged that 125th Street landlords had a gentleman's agreement not to allow any black-owned shops at all between Seventh and Eighth avenues. Black-owned barbershops, beauty parlors, and laundromats were common uptown, but businesses relating to death and destruction, the most dependable and profitable ventures, were in the hands of outsiders. In the early 1960s a quarter of all businesses were bars and liquor stores, almost all of them white-owned. Harlem had ninety-three funeral homes but no museums.

The best business opportunity was dealing heroin, which swept Harlem like a plague in the years after the war. It would have been impossible without the cooperation of police, who for decades had been working hand-in-hand with East Harlem's mafiosi. That relationship became even closer after Thomas Gaetano Luchese, who grew up in East Harlem and joined the Morello-Terranova mob, ascended in 1953 to become boss of the crime family that bore his name, and Fat Tony Salerno, who also rose from East Harlem's streets, became boss of the Genovese crime family. Both organizations hired smugglers who bought heroin for five dollars an ounce in Lebanon, cut it with cornstarch or confectioners sugar, divided it up into $4 fixes, and sold it for almost $9,000 on the streets of Harlem. On West 117th Street between Fifth and Lenox avenues heroin, which was known among blacks as "duji" or "horse," was always available, day or night. Rates of narcotics use in Harlem, then the center of the national drug trade, was ten times that of the rest of the city. Even children weren't spared addiction, a phenomenon recounted in heartbreaking detail by Piri Thomas in his memoir *Down These Mean Streets*. As a member of a local Puerto Rican gang called the TNTs, Thomas was expected to participate in petty theft, and though scarcely more than a child he found himself trying cigarettes, then marijuana, cocaine, and alcohol. Eventually he became a heroin and pot dealer and a junkie himself, "hustling, whoring, hating" his way through the day.

There were seven major gangs during this period in El Barrio, all of which included members ranging in age from under ten to "seniors" over twenty years old. These gangs, such as the Viceroys, who operated between East 109th and East 114th streets, and the Dragons, who claimed Lexington Avenue between East 102nd and East 105th streets, defended their territory and their women—many gangs also had female affiliates—by any means necessary. In the 1950s the rising number of teen gangs in El Barrio brought conflicts with the Italian mobsters who still operated in the neighborhood as well as with nearby Negro gangs. A brawl between black and Puerto Rican gang members in 1955 at Broadway and West 129th Street, well out of Boricua territory, resulted in the stabbing of a fifteen-year-old, though police congratulated themselves on preventing an escalation into a full-fledged gang war. Around the same time, a Puerto Rican youth was knifed by a gang of Italian teens outside of Benjamin Franklin High School, which administrators had hoped would be a bulwark against intolerance. Such events spurred the city into action, and by the late 1950s the gang scene was changing. The opening of the Board of Education's Robert E. Wagner Senior Youth and Adult Center on East 120th Street between First and Second avenues—where a pair of Puerto Rican immigrants named Mickey and Negra Rosario trained generations of fleet, smart, hands-high Nuyorican prizefighters, including Hector Camacho—gave would-be gangsters something legal to do and a place to do it, and the organizations simply faded away. Other gangs in El Barrio "went social." The Enchanters became the Conservatives, while the Senecas became the Manhattan Seneca Social Club.

One of the things that helped Piri Thomas kick drugs was a prison conversion to the Nation of Islam, but Elijah Muhammad's spiritual army wasn't alone in redeeming addicts. Starting in 1951 the Reverend Norman C. Eddy of the East Harlem Protestant Parish began a Narcotics Committee that began working with young addicts, the Metropolitan Community Methodist Church and the Church of the Master. There were also nonspiritual options. An immigrant from Trinidad, Dr. Muriel Petioni, pioneered the modern medical treatment of drug addiction at a clinic at 114 West 131st Street. But the handful of programs that treated addicts couldn't turn around the plague. Harlem in the early 1960s drew in twenty thousand uptown dealers, couriers, and users. Junkies looking to raise money for four fixes of heroin to make it through the day drove the crime rate in Harlem to six times the city average. In 1961 thirteen people were murdered on the notorious blocks from Fifth to Lenox avenues between West 126th and West 140th streets, almost all of them in drug-related incidents.

The notion that drug addiction was not just a moral issue but a public health problem was slow to arrive uptown, no doubt because the level of basic health care lagged so far behind the rest of the city. In the years after the war, some major indicators such as tuberculosis slowly showed signs of improvement, but infant mortality was still twice the city average, and the rate of venereal disease infection was still more than six times the city average. In the wake of the 1954 United States Supreme Court ruling outlawing school segregation, which so eloquently decried the psychological effects of poverty and racism on mental health, physicians, too, began to worry about mental health. The self-perpetuating pathologies of life uptown—Harlemites were being committed to New York's appalling mental institutions at three times the rate of the city as a whole—were most thoroughly documented by the sociologist Kenneth Clark, who contended that hopelessness and hate were as destructive as the conditions that bred them: bad schools, poor health care, substandard housing, broken families, domestic violence, substance abuse, and unemployment. Clark did more than just study the psychological effects of racism. Confronting, reversing, and preventing the damage that racism did to self-esteem in children was the impetus behind an "experiment in community psychiatry" that Clark founded in 1962. Though it existed for only two years, Harlem Youth Opportunities Unlimited became a famous example of a different way of doing things, offering everything from job training to art lessons. The book that grew out of Clark's experiment, *Dark Ghetto: Dilemmas of Social Power,* documented in searing detail the challenges of life due to the racism of the period. More than one out of every seven Harlemites was jobless, which was twice the figure for New York City as a whole, and the statistics were even worse for young women. Only 7 percent of men worked as professionals, less than a third the city average, and even that didn't guarantee a good living. Doctors who made house calls for patients on public assistance received only three dollars from the city for each visit, and that was more money than they made on private visits, which sometimes didn't pay at all. More than two-thirds of men and almost three-quarters of Harlem's women worked in menial positions, and not because they were unprepared for more challenging work but simply because so many careers were still effectively closed to Negroes. Only education and jobs, Clark found, could offer alternatives to the economic immobility that imprisoned them and threatened to disable them psychologically.

Instead, the city focused on housing, long a catastrophe in over-crowded Harlem. Older housing stock had deteriorated to the point that a 1960 federal study found 11 percent of buildings dilapidated and another 33 percent failing fast, even as rents remained higher than in working-class white communities elsewhere in the city. Things were especially bad in East Harlem. The block between First and Second avenues on East 100th Street, which had been a mixed neighborhood of working-class Jews, blacks, and Italians in the 1920s and '30s, was notorious. By the 1940s, when Puerto Ricans began to arrive in large numbers, the area was already declining. By 1962 only 411 of the block's 1,440 apartments were considered habitable.

Tearing down the city's worst neighborhoods was simple. Building them up again proved more complicated. The housing projects that now symbolize the failure of mid-twentieth-century urban planning sounded good at first to Harlemites long used to a highly discriminatory private real estate market. One of the earliest public housing developments in the city, the low-rise Harlem River Houses, was internationally lauded for its humane scale and civilized amenities. But the massive and forbidding East River Houses, completed during the war years along First Avenue from East 102nd to East 105th streets, proved more influential, and more damaging.

The scale of postwar public housing construction seems impossibly large half a century later. Despite cuts in New York City's capital improvements programs after the war, the Housing Authority teamed up with the state and federal slum clearance and urban renewal funds to construct thousands of cheap, modern, airy apartments surrounded by grass and trees in more than a dozen projects, most in the poorest tenement neighborhoods of the Harlem Valley and East Harlem. These towering monoliths, which were part of a master plan envisioned by Robert Moses, the controversial power broker who was so responsible for the look and feel of New York City in the postwar years, came in for criticism even before they were completed. Families and businesses displaced by construction had to pay moving expenses themselves, and residents who wished to return had to reapply for space in the new buildings. But many of those displaced couldn't qualify for apartments in the projects because they were single, lived in an extended family, counted "undesirables" such as convicted felons in the household, or exceeded income limits, and left the neighborhood. The housing projects were intended to ease crushing population densities—according to some estimates, Harlem was home to five times as many people as its real estate was meant to house—and therefore contained only two-thirds the number of occupants as the tenements they replaced. Some of those evicted became "site migrants" who moved into city-owned tenements slated for later demolition. Urban renewal, the saying went, meant Negro removal, though things were more complicated than that: the city actually steered black applicants toward projects in Harlem and white applicants elsewhere. Even within Harlem, the housing projects became a vehicle for segregation, albeit economic: the residents of the upper-middle-class Riverton Houses were shielded from the lower-class slum dwellers of East 132nd Street by the lower-middle-class residents of the Abraham Lincoln Houses in between.

The housing projects reduced population densities, but only by destroying the complex, unpredictable, flexible spaces for social interactions that made Harlem what it was: the stoop, the open window, the bench, the playground, the small business, the back garden. The projects also introduced tens of thousands of Harlemites into a dependent relation on a city that was drifting into bankruptcy. By the time the construction of public housing slowed down in the 1960s, more than 20 percent of all Harlemites were living in projects, and one-third of East Harlem had been razed and resurrected. These complexes, which had swallowed up so many neighborhood treasures including the Cotton Club, the Polo Grounds, and the Savoy Ballroom, soon began deteriorating. The wide lawns that constituted the only patches of green for blocks were fenced off.

Robert Moses didn't limit his "improvements" to housing. In Riverside Park, he spent $8 million per mile below West 110th Street and only $1.7 million per mile above it. Harlemites got only one football field out of five that Moses built in the park and one playground out of seventeen. They got none of the wide walkways, broad fields, exquisite landscaping, tennis courts, roller skating and bicycle paths, horseshoe courts, and harbors that Moses built farther south. He decided not to cover the New York Central Railroad tracks running through Harlem with a grand promenade, as he did farther south. Manhattanville got a concrete and steel viaduct that plunged a stretch of the magnificent Hudson River shoreline into shadow.

With the city doing so little for the neighborhood in the way of parks and recreation, Harlem did for itself. In 1946 a City College student and part-time Parks Department employee named Holcombe Rucker started an amateur basketball tournament at the West 155th Street courts. But the real action came during more informal moments, when professionals such as Wilt Chamberlain and, later, Julius Erving might meet and get beat by inspired amateurs, Harlem legends Earl "The Goat" Manigault—who could clear forty-two inches when he jumped—Richard "Pee Wee" Kirkland, Herman "Helicopter" Knowings, and Joe "The Destroyer" Hammond. They all inspired a boy named Ferdinand Lewis Alcindor Jr., who moved from a Harlem tenement to the Dyckman housing projects in 1950. He reached six-feet-nine while still in high school and made a career out of the game, which he eventually dominated under the name Kareem Abdul-Jabbar.

When Holcombe Rucker began his tournament, basketball wasn't popular among African-Americans, who weren't even allowed on professional courts with whites. City College helped change that. In the years after the war, the school's basketball coach, Nat Holman, molded a group of mostly black and Jewish college students into a national powerhouse, in the process all but inventing the modern game. The thrilling speed, timing, and give-and-go offenses—was this a bebop sport?—were all pioneered under Holman's direction by a group of full-time students, not athletes on scholarship, who showed the country what interracial cooperation could achieve. Things peaked in 1950, when City College won both the National Invitational Tournament and the NCAA titles. But their glory was short-lived. The next year several players admitted to point shaving, a scandal that drew in college teams across the country.

Basketball was just about the only sport that Harlemites didn't see in the years after World War II at the Polo Grounds, which was the fourth arena to bear that name, and which hosted everything from ice skating to rodeos and even midget auto racing. It was there in 1941 that Joe Louis fought the fight of his career—probably the most thrilling fight in all of boxing history—coming back from twelve rounds of Billy Conn's humiliation to hang on to his title. After the war the arena was a holy ground for fans of Sugar Ray Robinson, who reclaimed his crown from Randy Turpin in 1951 in front of more than sixty thousand spectators. It was also at the Polo Grounds that Floyd Patterson was knocked to the canvas seven times in the third round before losing the heavyweight title to Ingemar Johansson in 1959, although the next year Patterson regained the title, knocking out Johansson in the fifth round.

Of course, for many New Yorkers, the Polo Grounds meant football, in particular the New York Giants, who played there from 1925 to 1955. They were followed by the New York Titans, a founding franchise of the American Football League—they changed their name to the Jets before following so many of their uptown fans to Queens. Baseball was even more popular at the Polo Grounds, home field of the all-black New York Cubans, owned by the former numbers king-pin Alejandro Pompez. Fans also came to Harlem to watch all-white teams play under the famous Longines clock and Chesterfield cigarette advertisements that loomed over the clubhouse. And although part of the appeal of the stadium for black fans was its racially integrated seating, it says much about the racism that marred professional baseball that the record books ignore the very first person to hit a ball over the notorious center-field fence: Luke Easter of the Negro Leagues. Indeed, during Jackie Robinson's harrowing first season with the Brooklyn Dodgers, the Polo Grounds hosted the 1947 Negro Leagues All Star game for a crowd of thirty-eight thousand spectators, only about seven hundred of whom were white. By 1951 things had changed, and the New York Giants boasted a black center fielder named Willie Mays, who took the team from fifth place to a pennant victory and became a local hero—he lived on the ground floor of an apartment building near the stadium and local children would wake him up by knocking on his window and asking him to play stickball on 155th Street, which he did. But in 1957 the Giants left, and though the Mets played at the Polo Grounds in 1962 and 1963, the next year the stadium, where fans had seen Mel Ott's five hundredth home run, Bobby Thomson's shot heard around the world, and Willie Mays's famous World Series catch, was demolished to make way for yet another monstrously large public housing project.

The open spaces of upper Harlem were home to several tennis clubs. The sport had been popular among uptown whites going back to the late nineteenth century, and by the 1920s the American Tennis Association, the Ideal Tennis Club, and the Turf Tennis Club were holding tournaments. But the finest tennis player Harlem ever produced was a Negro named Althea Gibson, who was born in 1927 to South Carolina sharecroppers and grew up on West 143rd Street between Lenox and Seventh avenues, where the Police Athletic League set up a paddleball court. Formal lessons at the Harlem River Tennis Courts and at the Cosmopolitan Tennis Club led to prizes at all-Negro youth tournaments and then at racially mixed events. Eventually "the Jackie Robinson of tennis" became the first African-American woman to win at Wimbledon, followed by the U.S. Open's women's singles prize at Forest Hills, the first time a Negro, male or female, had won a United States championship tournament.

* * *

By the time Gibson ascended to the peak of the tennis world, she had left Harlem far behind, living in North Carolina, Florida, and Missouri before settling in New Jersey. It was a trend that dated back almost to the start of the Harlem Renaissance. In 1947 *Ebony* magazine still found so many distinguished faces on Sugar Hill that it announced that dropping a bomb on 409 Edgecombe "would wipe out Negro leadership for the next 40 years." But middle-class blacks were leaving Harlem, just as middle-class Jews had done decades earlier. Zora Neale Hurston left for Florida after being falsely charged in 1948 with sexually abusing a ten-year-old neighbor. By 1955 Queens was home to Louis Armstrong, Count Basie, Joe Louis, Ella Fitzgerald, and Dizzy Gillespie and the borough's St. Albans neighborhood was being called the "suburban Sugar Hill." Charlie Parker moved to the East Village, though he would come uptown every night to score heroin. Meanwhile, the Upper West Side drew Billie Holiday, Max Roach, and Miles Davis. Even Duke Ellington left 935 St. Nicholas Avenue, where he had lived since 1939, though Harlem nonetheless remained his primary source of inspiration for the longer, more ambitious works *Harlem Air Shaft* and *Black, Brown and Beige*. As a result of all of the departures, the well-known 1958 photo of fifty-seven jazz greats known as "A Great Day in Harlem," taken in front of 17 East 126th Street, was an anachronism. Hardly any of the musicians who showed up lived in the neighborhood, and most of those who did soon left.

Mass transportation, which had made Harlem a century earlier, helped unmake it. New subway lines and suburban trains put the outer boroughs, Westchester County, Connecticut, Long Island, and New Jersey, with their safer and cleaner streets, better schools, and affordable single-family homes, within closer reach. Even a high birth rate and another great migration—more than 1.5 million blacks left the South and settled in northern cities in the 1950s—couldn't stop Harlem from losing almost a third of its black population from 1947 to 1952. That was just the start: from 1952 to 1957 blacks, most of them civil servants, teachers, and nurses from Harlem, bought some eleven thousand homes in Queens.

Like his old friend Langston Hughes, Ralph Ellison stayed uptown. Ellison's first novel (and the only novel published during his lifetime), *Invisible Man,* which came out in 1952, was inspired by the memory of a blackface comedy act that he had seen at the Apollo back in 1937. It's a loosely autobiographical tale of a hapless young black man from the South who ruins his opportunities at a black college before coming to Harlem, where finds himself swept up in a Communist Party–like movement called the Brotherhood. He leaves it all behind during the climax of the book, a shattering depiction of the 1943 Harlem riot. The novel became a best seller and made Ellison the first black fiction writer to win the National Book Award. This merciless examination of Negro America and its discontents wasn't totally without hope: Harlem had after all turned a fairly talented sculptor and middling trumpet player into a novelist of genius. "If Harlem is the scene of the Negro's death agony," Ellison wrote, "it is also the setting of his transcendence."

Ralph Ellison's intimations of a new Harlem Renaissance were shared by John Henrik Clarke, an Alabama native who came to Harlem in 1933 on the top of a freight train and founded the Harlem Writers Guild after the war. His home became a breeding ground for a new generation of writers, including John Oliver Killens, Rosa Guy, Douglas Turner Ward, Audre Lorde, Maya Angelou, and Walter Mosley. Ironically, the definitive portrait of Harlem at mid-century came from a writer who never lived there but who like so many African-Americans claimed it as his own. Chester Himes grew up in Ohio and fell into a life of crime and punishment—robbery, drugs, prostitution, bootlegging, and passing bad checks, followed by prison—before becoming a writer. He first saw Harlem in 1941 and he visited frequently to gather material for a series of crime novels about two black detectives, Coffin Ed and Gravedigger Jones, who rule the streets with an idiosyncratic but ultimately admirable sense of justice.

With the closure of so many performance spaces in the war years, drama no longer played the central cultural role that it had in the 1920s, when Harlem had attracted such a wealth of new writing talent, or in the 1930s, when the Federal Theater Project supported so much important work. Nonetheless, the Little Theatre of the Harlem YMCA was a key source of new talent in the 1940s and '50s, nurturing such figures as Esther Rolle, Eartha Kitt, Roscoe Lee Brown, Sidney Poitier, and Cicely Tyson. Also vital to the small but influential uptown theater scene was the Elks Community Theatre, which introduced Ossie Davis, whose partnership with an actress named Ruby Dee would last more than half a century, as they grew from local celebrities to national folk heroes, combining independent and commercial work in theater and film with a dedication to racial justice that Harlemites always rewarded.

The ever harsher realities of life uptown inspired a new generation of musicians pushing the bebop revolution even further. Dizzy Gillespie turned the aesthetic mongrel known as Latin jazz from a novelty into a distinct musical genre, with its own audiences and record labels, when he hired a Cuban percussionist named Chano Pozo. "Dizzy no peaky pani and I no peaky engly," Pozo joked. "But boff peaki African." The collaboration ended prematurely after Pozo was killed at the Rio Bar, on Lenox Avenue near West 111th Street, over a drug deal gone wrong. Violence and drugs were all too central a feature for the second generation of beboppers, most of whom were Harlem natives and all of whom were Parker fanatics. Perhaps the most talented was Bud Powell, the son of a stride pianist who earned his living as a building superintendent. Born in 1924 just a few blocks away from the musical maelstrom of Jungle Alley, Powell was a child prodigy with a future as a classical performer, but he was more excited by jazz, and he was performing in nightclubs before he was in his teens, earning a reputation as a fluent, thoughtful improviser and composer of such ambitious works as "Tempus Fugue-It" before alcoholism and mental illness undermined his career and ended his life at the age of forty-one. Another Parker acolyte was a skinny, reticent trumpeter from the Midwest named Miles Davis, who arrived in New York in

1944 to attend Juilliard, the most prestigious music conservatory in the country, then located at Broadway and West 122nd Street. But classical music wasn't for Davis. Before exams, he would slip outside with his only friend at the school, Larry Rivers, who would later become a painter of some renown, and smoke marijuana. The two passed every time. Not surprisingly, Davis dropped out of school and joined Charlie Parker's quintet. As soon as he could afford it he also joined the exodus to Queens. When he performed in Manhattan in the late 1940s and early 1950s, it was not to the dwindling uptown club scene but to 52nd Street, where so much of the jazz world had relocated.

Even before bebop entered its silver age, it was being eclipsed in popularity by new kinds of black dance music that would all later be called rhythm and blues. The first star of this new genre was an alto saxophonist and singer from Arkansas named Louis Jordan, who played with Chick Webb at the Savoy Ballroom before forming his own group. Jordan's Tympani Five went from standing ovations at the Apollo Theater to two dozen hit recordings in the 1940s, including novelty "jump blues" numbers titled "Five Guys Named Moe," "Is You Is or Is You Ain't My Baby," and "Open the Door, Richard." The Apollo was Jordan's home away from home and a prime breeding ground for the new music. When a young and unknown Elvis Presley came to New York for the first time, his top priority was seeing "Harlem's High Spot for Colored Shows." Presley was wowed by Bo Diddley, but nothing spread the name of the Apollo like Amateur Night, which was still the single most important incubator of talent in American entertainment, not only in music but in dance and stand-up comedy—Flip Wilson, a veteran of Amateur Night, actually lived in one of the theater's storage rooms while struggling for wider recognition. Things came more easily to Ruth Brown, Pearl Bailey, King Curtis, Wilson Pickett, and Screamin' Jay Hawkins, who were all heard across the country via the theater's syndicated radio program. In the late 1940s the Schiffmans brought in the singer Sister Rosetta Tharpe, who moved effortlessly between jazz, blues, and gospel. Sacred music went over so well at the Apollo that Harlemites could soon see all-gospel shows. The same crowds also applauded secular vocal groups such as the Orioles, the

Platters, and Clyde McPhatter and the Drifters, all of whom specialized in close-harmony romantic ballads. Doo-wop, as it was called, drew much of its best talent from Harlem, including the Ravens, who were organized by Jimmy Ricks, a waiter at the Four Hundred Tavern and the L Bar, and Frankie Lymon and the Teenagers. The first female doo-wop group with a number-one single was the Bobbettes, five girls from P.S. 109 who first appeared at Apollo Amateur Night in 1956. That was also the year that a twenty-three-year-old from Georgia who melded the funky danceability of rhythm and blues, the emotional delivery of gospel, and the precision timing of the doo-woppers, won Amateur Night in borrowed shoes and a suit. His name was James Brown.

Rhythm and blues wasn't alone in reinfusing the Harlem music scene with dance energies that had dwindled during bebop's prime years. It was also in the late 1940s and early 1950s that Latin music came to artistic maturity. It would have been impossible without the Cuban-born trumpeter Mario Bauza, who had known Dizzy Gillespie from Cab Calloway's brass section and who had introduced Gillespie to Chano Pozo. Actually, Bauza was less important as an instrumentalist than as an informal, one-man booking agent. He introduced Harlemites to his brother-in-law, the Cuban singer, percussionist, and bandleader Frank Grillo, better known as Machito, whose kinetic performances with his Afro-Cubans at the Park Plaza—they were the country's first racially integrated orchestra—became the stuff of legend. One of the few Latin musicians who could compete with Machito in terms of inspiring dancers was the Cuban-born guitarist Arsenio "The Blind Marvel" Rodriguez. In fact, Rodriguez's most important contribution was putting the conga drum, an instrument that for generations had been banned in Cuba because of its supposedly backward, "African" implications—its arrival uptown was celebrated by the song "La Conga Llegó A Park Avenue," or "The Conga Came to Park Avenue"—into the heart of the music's pulse.

Rodriguez played frequently at the Golden Casino, as well as at the two other uptown dance halls, the Rockland Palace and the Audubon Ballroom, that began programming Latin music in addition to jazz and rhythm and blues. But it was the Park Palace that drew

the biggest crowds and the hottest acts; the hottest of them all was
Tito Puente, who was born in Harlem Hospital in 1923 and grew up
on East 110th Street between Madison and Park avenues. He studied
piano and trap drums with the legendary Victoria Hernández at the
New York School of Music, at Lenox Avenue and West 125th Street.
After a stint with his idol Machito, Puente served in the navy and
studied at Juilliard just as Miles Davis was dropping out. Like the jazz
trumpeter, Puente found the wider world more interesting than the
ivory tower, and he started a band called the Picadilly Boys. Within
a few years Puente was Latin music's most popular figure, inspiring
talented younger locals like Hector La Voé, Willie Colon, Johnny
Pacheco, Celia Cruz, Joe Cuba, Johnny Colon, who founded the East
Harlem Music School on Lexington Avenue, and Eddie Palmieri, who
memorialized the old neighborhood with his song "Harlem River
Drive." Midtown venues were becoming the place to hear live Latin
music but its inspiration was still uptown.

Things were more difficult for visual artists uptown, where painters and sculptors were weaning themselves from the largesse of the
WPA. After serving in World War II, Romare Bearden, who lived in an
apartment above the Apollo and then at the Monterrey, a West 114th
Street residence hotel for black actors, turned from painting to song
writing. He composed for Billy Eckstine and Tito Puente, who made
his "Seabreeze" into a hit—and a popular cocktail. Bearden didn't really come back to art until the mid-1950s, when he moved downtown.
Jacob Lawrence, who had lived on Striver's Row and Hamilton Terrace,
also left Harlem, returning only for visits.

　　Things were somewhat different for uptown photographers who
had from the start supported themselves with journalism, portraiture,
and commercial work, but after the war many Harlemites lost the
means or the motive for celebrating themselves. James Van Der Zee
had to downsize, moving into smaller quarters at 272 Lenox Avenue,
where he worked taking passport photos and restoring old photographs,
and he fell into poverty and obscurity. Morgan and Marvin Smith, who

worked in a studio next door to the Apollo, could still sell pictures of Nat King Cole and Adam Clayton Powell Jr. at their weddings, as well as Joe Louis and Josephine Baker in their private moments. Fashion also paid the bills of a new generation of uptown photographers for a time. Gordon Parks, a native of Kansas came to prominence at *Vogue* and *Glamour* before being hired as the first black staff photographer at *Life*, where he focused on capturing deteriorating conditions uptown. That was also the emphasis of the work of Helen Levitt, a white photographer from Brooklyn who documented Harlem's difficult truths at midcentury by capturing chalk drawings left by children on Harlem's poverty-stricken streets and walls. Roy De Carava, a Harlem-based native New Yorker born in 1919, also managed to stake out a position somewhere between art and journalism, contributing to Edward Steichen's celebrated 1955 exhibit at the Museum of Modern Art called *The Family of Man* and even starting an exhibition space called A Photographer's Gallery.

Harlem's writers, musicians, and artists all maintained close contacts, and not just socially. The common experience of poverty and discrimination, as well as a shared sense of racial or ethnic pride, was a powerful source of cohesion when it came to collaborations between musicians and dancers, architects and sculptors, and novelists and the painters who designed their book jackets. The same could not be said of Harlem's always contentious political scene, in which Republicans and Democrats, capitalists and communists, and integrationists and race nationalists fought one another more fiercely than they did their common adversaries. The arrival of a new generation of church-oriented activists from the South led by Martin Luther King Jr. made things even more complicated. In September 1958 King published *Stride Toward Freedom: The Montgomery Story*, an account of the bus boycott that led to the desegregation of Montgomery, Alabama's public transportation system, and he came to New York to drum up publicity for the book. It seemed like a perfectly natural strategy, at least from a sales point of view. New York had not only the largest concentration of

African-Americans in the nation, it was also a town in which Democrats and Republicans both considered themselves liberals when it
came to race matters. But King got a lot more than he bargained for.
He was walking into a gubernatorial race between the Democratic
New York State governor Averell Harriman and his challenger, the
Republican Nelson Rockefeller, both of whom had identified Harlem as a crucial element in the November election. King would also
have to face down the grand old men of the NAACP, who frowned
upon his supposedly undignified antics down South. In fact, King's
media-friendly program of civil disobedience was competing with the
organization for hearts, minds, and dollars and was winning—no less
an authority than Thurgood Marshall called King a "first-rate rabble
rouser." Moreover, concerns that the leftists who gravitated toward
King might taint the NAACP led some of the organization's officials,
including Marshall, to keep the FBI informed about the communists
in King's camp. By staying in a midtown hotel in September of 1958
King was simply avoiding the perils of uptown politics.

There was another reason for King to avoid the Theresa. The
hotel had begun accepting black guests only in the late 1930s, and then
only out of necessity. The change, signaled by stationing the hotel's
only black bartender, Big Steve, behind a plate-glass window and letting passersby make their own assumptions, was seen by some as the
cause of the hotel's decline. In fact, guests had long been complaining about poor service and dilapidated furnishings, but management
simply ignored the cracked mirrors that lined the lobby, the chipped
black-and-white tiled floor, and the peeling beige and green wallpaper.
Despite such neglect, the Theresa remained a popular spot with both
diplomats and honeymooners. After all, there wasn't much choice.
Many Harlemites lived there year-round, with students from Columbia
University and Harlem Hospital's unmarried nurses mingling with
socialites such as Grace Nail Johnson and the *Negro Yearbook* editor
Florence Murray as well as entertainers Cab Calloway, Jimmie Lunceford, Billy Eckstine, Lucky Millinder, and Moms Mabley. The dancer
Bojangles Robinson could often be seen at the red leather banquettes
or at the fifty-one-foot-long, J-shaped bar, drinking Southern Comfort,

telling coon jokes, and begging someone to get into an argument with him, just for fun. Joe Louis ate his mushroom omelet every morning at the Theresa's coffee shop when he was in Harlem, often sharing the place with Thurgood Marshall and Bumpy Johnson. Later in the day guests might spot cartoonist Ollie Harrington hard at work on his next drawing for the Pittsburgh *Courier*.

With that kind of action, the hotel's three hundred rooms were fully booked two or three months in advance, everything from the two-dollar rooms to the eight-dollar suites, especially if it was the night of a Joe Louis fight. The Black National Newspaper Publishing Association had offices on the second floor, so the hotel was a natural for press conferences. Radio stations WLIB and WWRL, broadcasting from the Theresa, didn't have to go far for celebrity interviews. Publication parties for Richard Wright's *Native Son* and Ann Petry's *The Street* were held in the orchid-themed dining room. One flight up was the mezzanine lounge, the club room, and the fashion boutique of Etienne Johnson. Lena Horne, Sarah Vaughan, and Josephine Baker all shopped there. There was even a barbershop that offered the best conk in Harlem. It cost twelve dollars and the most uppity pimps came in twice a month.

Oddly enough, the most important room at the Theresa was the humble Pittsburgh *Courier* office across Seventh Avenue, where the gossip columnist Billy Rowe could find material just by looking out his window. Rowe, a native of South Carolina who had grown up in Harlem, was known as the black Walter Winchell, not only because of his arch, saccharine writing style but because of the Winchellesque system of cash payments he accepted in return for mentions in the column. As with Winchell, who grew up in Harlem—woe to those who didn't play along. Using information gleaned from the hotel's "sidewalk captains"— most prominently the diminutive, foul-mouthed, possibly female Pee Wee Marquette, also Willie Bryant, an actor, radio announcer, and the unofficial mayor of Harlem—Rowe gave the inside story on celebrity sex, money, drugs, fame, arrests, and anything else newsworthy.

Lovie B. Woods tried to clean up the Theresa's reputation by firing the manager, William Harmon Brown, a thirty-two-year-old

Pennsylvania native who lived with his family—his son Ronald later
became the first black secretary of commerce—in a spacious three-
bedroom apartment on the top floor of the hotel, next to the singer
Dinah Washington. Brown, a dashing figure with a well-known taste
for cards and women, had managed to attract Harlem's surviving Talented Tenth, but he had also welcomed too many guests who came to
drink and gamble. The new manager was the bandleader Andy Kirk,
a Jehovah's Witness who drove away the kind of society that kept the
hotel afloat. Brown was back in 1958, running what the New York *Age*
was calling "a maudlin burlesque of her former greatness."

Clearly, the Theresa was no place for Martin Luther King Jr. But
how would the rest of Harlem welcome him? For that, King reached
out to A. Philip Randolph, whose ability to make unlikely alliances
made him the most brilliant, powerful, and successful political strategist in Harlem's history. In the 1950s Randolph ascended to the highest
ranks of the labor movement, becoming vice president of the executive
council of the newly formed, 1.5-million-member-strong AFL-CIO.
Though Randolph was at heart less of a race activist than a labor activist, he turned his newly acquired power and influence toward the
civil rights movement. Randolph helped organize the 1957 Prayer
Pilgrimage to Washington, D.C., where a crowd of thirty thousand
gathered to watch Martin Luther King Jr. speak. The next year Randolph participated in youth marches for school integration, and he
even became a member of the Bethel AME Chapel, though he never
attended. If King could rely on anyone to calm the uptown waters and
then get them ready for walking it was Randolph.

On Thursday, September 18, 1958, King came uptown for a book
signing at the Baptist-affiliated Empire State bookstore and then attended an evening meeting of some eight hundred people at the Williams Institutional CMA Church to raise money for the Southern
Christian Leadership Council's Crusade for Citizenship. The Empire
State bookstore was in some respects a surprising choice of venue,
since King had already been invited to hold the event at the notorious National Memorial African bookstore, at 101 West 125th Street,
whose regular customers included Adam Clayton Powell Jr., W.E.B.

Du Bois, Langston Hughes, Malcolm X, and Louis Armstrong, as well as generations of less prominent readers interested in all things racial. King had good reasons for avoiding Lewis Michaux, the store's owner. Micheaux was born in 1884 into a Virginia family that was destined for distinction: his little brother was Elder Solomon "Lightfoot" Micheaux, a charismatic radio preacher, and there is also evidence that he was related to the groundbreaking black filmmaker and novelist Oscar Micheaux. Lewis arrived in Harlem shortly after World War I and began selling books from a pushcart. In 1930 he opened a bookstore at the corner of Seventh Avenue and West 125th Street, though he had to live in the store and take a side job as a window washer to keep afloat. Micheaux combined his passion for books with his love of his race, remaining a Garveyite long after the movement had dwindled. Micheaux's "House of Common Sense and Proper Propaganda," as he dubbed it, was the most politically radical bookstore in Harlem. At one point he featured a book called *The Goddamn White Man* in his front window, refusing to obey police orders to take down the display; Micheaux successfully defended himself in court and the display stayed. When he heard that King was coming to Harlem to sign books, Micheaux offered to turn over his bookstore for the day, but King's aides didn't even respond and it's hard to blame them. King may have been relatively cavalier about the communists in his midst at this point, but he knew that the last thing he needed was to be associated with a black nationalist like Lewis Michaux. As it turned out, King was unable to avoid a confrontation, not after Micheaux heard that King would be coming back uptown on Saturday to sign books at the white-owned Blumstein's department store, which didn't even sell books.

On Friday, September 19, King held a rally in front of the Theresa Hotel, an event that attracted Governor Harriman and Nelson Rockefeller, as well as some of the most important black figures in the country, including A. Philip Randolph, Jackie Robinson, and Hulan Jack. Duke Ellington and his orchestra provided the entertainment. Conspicuously missing was the most prominent race leader in the United States, Congressman Adam Clayton Powell Jr., who no longer felt welcome after having thumbed his nose at Tammany Hall by endorsing the Republican Eisenhower in the 1956 presidential election. Harlemites showed up in such numbers that police closed off the street in front of the hotel. Crowds gathered again the next afternoon, when King returned to Blumstein's for the book signing. The management made sure there was an extra police presence to monitor the "Buy Black" demonstration that Micheaux had set up, but no one was ready for what happened next. A woman named Izola Ware Curry, who had tried to disrupt the previous day's rally by heckling King, walked in the store's front door, cut to the front of the line of autograph seekers next to the shoe department, approached the young black man sitting at a table behind a pile of books, and asked "Is this Martin Luther King?" Curry had been born in 1916 to Georgia sharecroppers, and like so many Negroes of her time she ended up in Harlem, where she worked as a part-time domestic and full-time anticommunist. By the time of King's visit in September 1958, Curry had become convinced that the party was using the black church in general and King in particular to persecute her.

When King answered "yes," Curry reached under her coat, took out a letter opener, and stabbed King deep in the chest—why she didn't use the gun she had in her purse is a mystery. She started shouting, "I've been after him for six years! I'm glad I done it!" and ran away. Curry was pursued by a group of ladies who had been waiting in line and was finally stopped by an *Amsterdam News* adman. All the while she raved, "Dr. King has ruined my life! He's no good! The NAACP is no good, it's communistic!" In the midst of all the chaos, King remained calm, even though he had a blade lodged between his heart and his lungs. Any sudden movement might have killed him, but King comforted the crowd around him, promising, "Everything is going to be all right." Within a half hour of the attack, he was in an ambulance on his way to Harlem Hospital, a decision that later came under a great deal of scrutiny. Why, wondered many people, wasn't he brought to a better— meaning white—hospital? In fact, the black and white doctors who cared for King knew very well how to deal with stab wounds, which were part of the normal routine on uptown Saturday nights. This is not to say that Harlem Hospital was up to the standards of New York

City's other hospitals. Patients were cared for in open wards or in beds lining the halls, and mortality rates were so disturbing that Harlemites called their only public hospital "the morgue." The situation alarmed A. Philip Randolph, who waited outside the emergency room, but his fears were unfounded: the chief of surgery, Aubré Maynard, who had been among Harlem Hospital's first group of black doctors back in 1925, handled King's wound without incident.

After King identified Izola Curry from his hospital bed she was brought to the West 123rd Street precinct in Harlem, where the "deranged Negro domestic," as the newspapers called her, was charged with felonious assault. Found to be mentally unstable and incapable of standing trial she was sent away to an insane asylum. Harlem seems never to have heard from her again. As for King, he stayed two more weeks at Harlem Hospital and then recuperated further in Brooklyn, left with only a cross-shaped scar on his chest—he loved the symbolism. King, who was only twenty-nine at the time, was marked by his experience in other ways as well. Whatever else his later assertion that "I've been to the mountaintop" meant, it also referred to the moment at Blumstein's when a sneeze or a cough could have killed him.

Once it was clear that King would survive, Harlemites turned their attention back to the governor's race. Nelson Rockefeller got the endorsement of Count Basie and Cab Calloway but lost to Harriman, who had been able to convince Adam Clayton Powell Jr. to support him. In fact, it was a deal in which Powell got Tammany support for his bid to chair the House Committee on Education and Labor, the first Negro to chair that or any other congressional body. The year 1958 was crucial for Harlem politics for another reason. Five years after retiring from public service, Raymond Jones, the Harlem Fox, came back, determined to make peace between the regulars at Tammany Hall and the reformers, between the unholy and the holier than thou, as he put it. After helping to return the marginalized Adam Clayton Powell Jr. to Congress, Jones made a deal in the presidential primary of 1960 to support Lyndon Johnson for president if Powell would become the chair of the powerful House Education and Labor Committee. Johnson lost the nomination to John F. Kennedy, but Powell was awarded his committee chairmanship anyway, and he was soon strutting the halls of Congress with as much power and panache as he had on Seventh Avenue. Harlemites had their doubts. Powell came out strongly on civil rights issues, at least in speeches. "I'm not going to watch the parade pass me by," he said. "I'm gonna lead it." But he denounced the NAACP as a "white-controlled" organization. Powell and Jones returned to power just as the campaign for civil rights was peaking in the South and energizing voters uptown, but neither man had a significant role in what is now seen as the zenith of the entire movement; Powell even opposed the civil rights bill of 1963.

The familiar story of how Martin Luther King Jr.'s 1963 March on Washington fixed his place forever as an American hero has never properly acknowledged the essential role that Harlemites including A. Philip Randolph and Bayard Rustin played. History associates the movement with the southern black church, but it was just as much the work of Harlem ex-socialists, albeit with a strong dose of Gandhian truth force. In this respect, King's experiences uptown in 1958 were a wake-up call. He realized that he would have to protect himself personally from those who wished to harm him. Audience members threw only eggs at King during a later appearance at Harlem's Salem Methodist Episcopal Church, but he would have to be ready for something worse. King also realized he would have to walk the line between a movement run by personal charisma and one that depended on compromise as much as on confrontation. And he knew now that he might not have much time to accomplish his goals. "I am different from my father," he said in 1961. "I feel the need of being free now."

In February 1963 King realized that a civil rights march he was planning for July would have to compete for media attention with a demonstration that Randolph was planning for October. King and Randolph decided to combine forces, a prospect that convinced President John F. Kennedy to invite both of them, along with John Lewis of the Student Nonviolent Coordinating Committee, Whitney Young of the Urban League, Roy Wilkins of the NAACP, and James Farmer of CORE, to the White House in June to try and persuade them to cancel the march. A mass demonstration, Kennedy said to his guests, would only jeopardize the White House's pending civil rights bill. No one in the room was convinced. Although Kennedy is today popularly associated with the rising tide of racial progressivism in civil rights era, he was in fact no friend of the movement; he was unwilling to bear the political costs of associating himself with a movement that was at the time still far outside the mainstream. Things would be very different by the time President Lyndon Johnson elevated Thurgood Marshall to solicitor general and then to Supreme Court justice. Randolph once again led the way in refusing to accommodate a sitting president's request to back down and let time heal the country's racial wounds.

Credit also belongs to Bayard Rustin, who came up with the notion that the 1963 march should address not just labor and economic issues but freedom itself, hence the little recognized formal name of the event: the March on Washington for Jobs and Freedom. Rustin had fallen on hard times after being kicked out of the Fellowship of Reconciliation in 1953 for being a homosexual. He made money buying and selling antiques and repairing musical instruments before being offered the position of executive secretary of the War Resisters League. In 1956 he began working closely with Martin Luther King Jr., and two months after the start of the Montgomery bus boycott Rustin traveled to Alabama to school King, who had bought a gun with which to defend himself and his family, and his supporters, who were forming armed militias to patrol the homes of local civil rights leaders, in using nonviolent techniques to resist Jim Crow. They took to each other right away, and Rustin became a crucial strategist for King, introducing him to Gandhian principles for peaceably achieving social change. Rustin also convinced King that the civil rights movement needed a new institution to spread change across the south: the Southern Christian Leadership Conference. He worked closely with King on the next year's Prayer Pilgrimage in Washington, D.C.; Rustin's signature is all over King's famous speech from that event. From a desk and a telephone at the Harlem Labor Center on 125th Street, Rustin began raising money for King and basically functioned as the brains of his movement. It was in Harlem that Rustin engineered the 1958 and 1959 Youth Marches for Integrated Schools in Washington, D.C., recruiting a number of young people who would go on to become civil rights leaders themselves, including John Lewis, Stokely Carmichael, Eleanor Holmes Norton, Maya Angelou, and Bob Moses.

Rustin began planning the SCLC's actions during the presidential conventions to be held in Chicago and Los Angeles in the summer of 1960, but he was stymied by Adam Clayton Powell Jr. who in late June became concerned that Rustin's activities threatened to alienate southern Democrats, whose support Powell desperately needed if he was to gain real power in Washington. Powell was also concerned that the campaign of John F. Kennedy, whom he fawningly admired, might be derailed by the demonstrations that Rustin specialized in. In a betrayal that shocked only those people who didn't known him very well, Powell went on a public offensive against Rustin and Randolph, smearing them as irresponsible radicals who were controlling King like a puppet. At the same time, Powell sent a secret ultimatum to King, threatening to tell the world that King and Rustin were lovers unless Randolph called off the convention protests and banished Rustin from the civil rights movement. Although Powell's claims were laughable, Rustin, on the advice of Randolph, stepped down. Once again, he feared his personal life had endangered his political goals, and he was devastated by the failure of Randolph and King to stand up to the scurrilous blackmail attempt. Now purged, at least temporarily, from the civil rights movement, Rustin disbanded his group of volunteers on 125th Street (Stokely Carmichael and Bob Moses went on to found the Student Nonviolent Coordinating Committee). But the man who claimed "I believe in social dislocation and creative trouble" didn't disappear altogether from the political scene. In 1963 Randolph, who had never been quite comfortable with his decision to distance himself from Rustin, asked him to develop a march on the nation's capital to mark the centenary of the Emancipation Proclamation. Rustin convinced SNCC, CORE, and the SCLC to join. The NAACP and the Urban League, both of which balked even at nonviolent demonstrations, were a harder sell. Randolph promised that there would be no acts of civil disobedience, a compromise that was unacceptable to the younger generation of civil rights activists; it was the beginning of a fatal split in the movement.

Working out of an office at the Reverend Thomas Kilgore's Baptist church on West 130th Street, the tireless Rustin brought all of his organizing experience toward realizing a peaceful gathering of a hundred thousand people in the nation's capital. It would be, Rustin seemed to sense, a unique focal point in American history. And it couldn't happen without someone like Rustin to provide the vision, not to mention the toilets, transportation, water, food, doctors, and security. But once again Rustin found himself under fire on personal grounds. Roy Wilkins of the NAACP objected to the high profile Rustin was taking in the organizing efforts. Randolph responded by suggesting that Rustin operate more anonymously. By 6 a.m. on August 28, just hours after the death in Ghana of W.E.B. Du Bois, the press was already querying Randolph about low turnout. Pretending to read from a blank sheet of paper, Randolph assured reporters that everything was on schedule. Within hours more than two hundred thousand had arrived, double the expected number. Many Harlemites had bought six-dollar round-trip tickets on "Sally's Special Freedom Bus," available at Sally's restaurant, at 2067 Seventh Avenue. Randolph, the elder statesman of the civil rights movement and the prime architect of mass black politics of twentieth-century America, the only figure on the left who could get everyone and anyone on the telephone and convince them to show up, had the place of honor on the steps of the Lincoln Memorial. King's "I Have a Dream" speech became the signal moment of the civil rights movement, a victory that was no less important for being rhetorical. After it was all over, Rustin and Randolph made the cover of *Life* magazine and Rustin was hailed from coast to coast as the Socrates of the civil rights movement. But two weeks later a church bombing in Birmingham, Alabama—where for months King and his followers had been the target of attack dogs and fire hoses—killed four black girls and ended the golden age of nonviolent social change that King and the other speakers had hoped for.

* * *

Not everyone uptown celebrated nonviolence. It was also in 1963 that Elijah Muhammad made Malcolm X his first national minister. That was less a reward than an effort to take a rising star off the streets of Harlem, where he had so much influence. Although rumors about Elijah Muhammad's marital infidelities were widespread, it was only when Malcolm X heard them from the comedian Dick Gregory backstage at the Apollo that he began to take them seriously. Then, on December 1, 1963, he remarked to the press that the assassination of President Kennedy a week earlier might have been expected and even deserved—it was just a matter of "chickens coming home to roost." The callous remark outraged a nation in mourning and Elijah Muhammad punished Malcolm X with a three-month period of isolation. Elijah Muhammad was right to fear his underling's growing influence. In twelve years with the Nation of Islam Malcolm X had increased membership from hundreds to tens of thousands and opened more than a hundred mosques in all fifty states. However, for Malcolm X the Nation of Islam had come to represent another ghetto, another gang, another prison. He broke out once again. In April he left for the Middle East to perform the pilgrimage to Mecca that is required of all Muslims. It was on this journey, which included stops in nine countries in Africa and the Mideast, that Malcolm X, overwhelmed by the multiracial nature of an Islam that he was for the first time experiencing, came to realize how distorted the Nation of Islam's version of the religion was, especially when it came to skin color. The Islam he witnessed emphasized the equality of all humans, not the racial antagonism that Elijah Muhammad preached. Malcolm X converted and returned home determined to do things differently. He was only thirty-nine but he knew he might not have much time.

While Malcolm X was away, his many enemies had been busy. Police blamed him for inspiring a group of Harlemites to start a riflery club. His name also came up after a Black Muslim–linked gang called the Blood Brothers killed the elderly white owner of an uptown clothing store. But upon his arrival everyone seemed to forget about those things. El-Hajj Malik El-Shabazz landed on May 21, 1964, at the newly renamed John F. Kennedy Airport and that evening gave a press conference at the Theresa Hotel's Skyline Ballroom. Reporters surprised by his new name, his long hair, and his beard were even more shocked by his new way of thinking about the old issues. Shabazz was now backing away from the extreme positions he had espoused as a member of the Nation of Islam, including black nationalism, racial separatism, and anti-Semitism. He found himself reaching out to colleagues and partners he had always scorned. He wasn't always successful. Thurgood Marshall for one had always considered him a dangerous troublemaker and a "lowlife," and he rebuffed his overtures, refusing to talk to him when they passed each other on Seventh Avenue. Shabazz began holding meetings on Sunday afternoons and called the organization that emerged the Organization of Afro-American Unity. He took over the balcony-level dining hall of the Theresa as a headquarters, though he spent most of his time at the back table or in the telephone booth of a Muslim-owned coffee shop at 22 West 135th Street, where he enjoyed the ice cream. Shabazz was back in the Middle East in July when he heard the news that more than four hundred people had been arrested and dozens wounded during a week in which thousands of Harlemites rioted after a white cop had killed a Negro boy on the Upper East Side. There was once again chaos on the streets, with more than 118 injuries, 465 arrests, and some six hundred fires and burglaries. Concerns that Mayor Robert Wagner Jr. had failed to restrain the police in the manner of Fiorello La Guardia a generation earlier were widespread, but it must be remembered that there were similar riots that summer in Rochester, Chicago, San Francisco, and Atlanta. That kind of violence convinced many observers that the end of the civil rights movement was at hand, at least uptown—Adam Clayton Powell Jr. told Martin Luther King Jr. to "Get the hell out of Harlem, this is my territory."

Malcolm Shabazz wasn't surprised to hear about the riots. He was only at a loss as to why they had not been much worse. For all of his crimes as a young man, for all of the stridency of his racial militancy in the Nation of Islam, he had never been the violent type. But as a mainstream Muslim who now embraced more explicitly peaceful ways of social change, Malcolm Shabazz was haunted by the violence of others, especially since he still spent so much time "fishing" for converts along Harlem's less-traveled streets. He had been getting anonymous death threats for years, and he was convinced the more recent ones were coming from the Nation of Islam, which had been trying to evict him from his home in Queens. He went public with his situation in early February of 1965, claiming that there had been two recent attempts on his life, both ordered by the Nation of Islam, though it could have been any one of two dozen black nationalist groups. Either way, Shabazz sensed danger. "It's time for martyrs now," he told the photographer Gordon Parks. On February 14, 1965, his home was firebombed while Shabazz, his pregnant wife, and four daughters were asleep. As the next meeting of the Organization of Afro-American Unity approached, scheduled for Harlem's Audubon Ballroom at two o'clock on Sunday, February 21, 1965, he became more concerned about his security. Still, he refused offers of personal police protection, as he had sixteen times before, and he insisted that he didn't want arrivals at the Audubon to be frisked: "If I can't be safe among my own kind, where can I be?"

The Audubon Ballroom, built by the Hollywood pioneer William Fox at Broadway and West 165th Street in 1912, was already one of Harlem's sacred sites. The gorgeous Thomas Lamb building, its terra-cotta facade decorated with images of court jesters, the voyage of Jason's *Argo*, and fox motifs in honor of the owner, had been an important venue for vaudeville, and under the names the Beverly Hills Theatre and the San Juan Theatre it hosted big band dances in the 1930s in its second-floor ballroom. In the 1940s the Audubon changed with the times again, presenting the new music known as bebop—Sonny Rollins's very first composition was titled "Audubon." The Audubon was also an important place for community events. Rooms below street level were rented out to local businesses and organizations and even a synagogue. In the 1950s the king and queen of Harlem were crowned at the Audubon every year at Mardi Gras.

When Malcolm Shabazz came to the Audubon's stage and greeted the crowd with his usual "Asalaikum, brothers and sisters!" a fight broke out near the front row. "Hold it! Hold it!" he shouted. "Don't get excited! Let's cool it, brothers." These were his last words. Three men stood up in the first row and shot him in the chest, hand, and chin. Shabazz was dead even before the gunmen fled into the chaos of hundreds of screaming, shouting, weeping supporters, including many children and at least three undercover police officers. Within six hours police had arrested twenty-two-year-old Thomas Hagan, also known as Talmadge Hayer, who tried to flee but was assaulted by the crowd and shot in the leg by one of Shabazz's bodyguards. The other gunmen got away, almost running over the bookseller Lewis Michaux, who had arrived late. Shabazz was brought across the street, to Columbia Presbyterian Hospital, where the staff unsuccessfully tried to resuscitate him. After the recent disturbances that had rocked Harlem, city officials worried that the assassination of one of Harlem's most beloved heroes would spark yet another riot. The police closed down Mosque #7 and sent out extra officers, but this was a community in mourning, not rebellion. Harlem's days of rage were over, it seems. Shabazz's body was taken to the Unity Funeral Home, at Eighth Avenue near West 126th Street, where it was cleaned, prepared, and dressed neatly in a conservative suit and tie, laid on a bed of cream-colored velvet, and sealed under a sheet of glass in an open bronze casket. Viewing was scheduled to begin the next day but was delayed due to bomb threats and to an explosion that burned down Mosque #7. Shabazz's widow, Betty, arrived at 6:15 and an hour later the public was admitted, some two thousand people of all races shuffling past the coffin until the funeral home shut its doors at 11 p.m. This went on for three more days, while Shabazz's closest friends and associates tried frantically to find a house of worship that would host the funeral service the following Saturday. There were no takers, certainly not among the biggest mainstream churches including the Abyssinian Baptist Church—Malcolm X had burned those bridges long ago—until Bishop Alvin Childs of the Faith Temple Church of God in Christ stepped up and offered his building, an old movie palace at Amsterdam Avenue near West 147th Street that could hold about seventeen hundred people. As the day of the funeral approached things heated up. Childs received death threats, and callers promised to burn down the church. Then police arrested two more suspects in the murder, both members of the Nation of Islam, raising more fears

of a riot. Still, twenty-two thousand managed to file past the body in
peace. At 11 p.m. on Friday, a Sudanese sheikh who had met Shabazz
in Mecca prepared the body for an orthodox Muslim burial, anoint-
ing it and wrapping it in a shroud. Harlem shut down that Saturday,
February 27, 1965, with six thousand people in the streets and cops
everywhere. Inside the church, Shabazz's body rested in an open coffin before a gigantic floral Muslim star and crescent. The actor Ossie
Davis read greetings and messages of condolences from the likes of
Martin Luther King Jr. and Kwame Nkrumah before beginning a eu-
logy whose climax is now famous. "In honoring him, we honor the
best in ourselves," Davis preached. "And we will know him then for
what he was and is—a Prince—our black shining Prince!—who didn't
hesitate to die, because he loved us so."

After the three-hour service was over, there was a final viewing
by the family. Betty Shabazz, who was pregnant with twins, could
barely support herself as the coffin that held her husband's body was
loaded into the hearse and driven to an upstate cemetery. As for the
suspects in the murder, the next year saw three members of the Nation
of Islam—Talmadge Hayer, Norman 3X Butler, and Thomas 15X Johnson—convicted and sentenced to life. By that time, *The Autobiography
of Malcolm X* had been published, and Elijah Muhammad's misdeeds
were public knowledge. The Nation of Islam denied any involvement
in the crime, though its leaders and members, especially Shabazz's
rival Louis Farrakhan, had long walked the line between warning and
threat when it came to Shabazz. The Nation of Islam survived, coming
under the leadership of Farrakhan after Elijah Muhammad's death.

Shabazz's own family never enjoyed the peace that Islam preaches
and prophecies. Betty Shabazz left the NOI, turned to conventional
Islam, and grew into a dignified matron of the civil rights movement.
She even mended fences with Farrakhan, but in 1995 her daughter
Qubilah was charged with conspiracy to murder Farrakhan, and two
years later Betty Shabazz died after her twelve-year-old grandson
set fire to her house. No one dared suggest that this was a matter of
chickens coming home to roost, but all were surprised at how far one
of Harlem's royal families had fallen.

11

HARLEM NIGHTMARE
1965–1990

In 1970 Bishop William L. Bonner of Harlem's Greater Refuge Temple asked a group of uptown ministers to plead with their congregants, many of whom drove into the city only on Sunday mornings, to come back to Harlem the rest of the week, too. The Negro Mecca, the capital of black America, the cradle of the Negro renaissance, a key node in the civil rights movement now needed to beg its residents to return. Unrest and urban renewal had reduced the population to half of what it was in the 1920s. Those who remained were used to hard times, but they were unprepared for the unemployment, crime, drugs, corruption, deteriorating schools and housing, simultaneous overcrowding and further population loss that would make the Depression seem mild. The clubs and theaters that incubated ragtime, early jazz, swing, bebop, and rhythm and blues were torn down or left to rot—the legendary Monroe's Uptown House became a liquor store owned by the baseball player Roy Campanella. Fun City, as one observer put it, had become Run City. Moments of national racial triumph, such as Alex Haley's *Roots*, the Supreme Court's decision to uphold the constitutionality of affirmative action, Jesse Jackson's historic presidential campaign, and Vanessa Williams's crowning as the first black Miss America only confirmed the sense that Harlem had been left behind, especially after New York City's fiscal crisis led to cuts in essential services. New York was now a majority-nonwhite city, but the living legacy of prejudice meant that power's face still wasn't colored.

Adam Clayton Powell Jr. was already the most important black politician in the country when he became chair of the House Committee on Education and Labor in 1961. In his new position he was a crucial figure in the implementation of the war on poverty, and he rightfully took much credit for the shower of food stamps, health programs, educational initiatives, and jobs that rained down. It was unlike anything seen since the 1930s, but as in the Depression it didn't seem to make much of a difference. Harlemites genuflected before Powell, but in time his flamboyant lifestyle seemed less fitting for a preacher and politician than a pimp, many voters thought. It wasn't just a matter of image. An outstanding arrest warrant for failure to pay damages in a libel suit meant that he returned to Harlem only when Congress was in session, when he was protected by official immunity, or to preach at the Abyssinian Baptist Church on Sundays, when by long-standing local custom no warrants were served. Then, in 1967, Powell was forced to relinquish his prestigious committee chairmanship due to accusations of personal indiscretions, including misuse of congressional funds. Powell claimed he was the victim of racial persecution, but few people believed him: there was hardly a political bridge he hadn't burned over the past half century. The House stripped Powell of his office, and though he soon won the seat back, his ability to work in Washington, D.C., had been fatally damaged by his humiliating expulsion and he all but gave up on the job. In 1969 the United States Supreme Court restored him to office, but by then he was barely functioning. He missed votes on student loans, Social Security, voting rights, and milk programs for children. Much of the time he was holding court at his unofficial headquarters, the Red Rooster tavern. He praised the Black Panthers and scorned Harlem's "bourgeois Negroes," but his political instincts had all but abandoned him. He lost his 1970 reelection campaign by 150 votes and retreated to the Bahamas, where a bad heart and a degrading tax evasion proceeding reduced him to a shadow of his former self by the time of his death in 1972. The year after Powell's death, the northeast corner of Seventh Avenue and West 125th Street was crowned—some say defaced—by the Adam Clayton Powell Jr. State Office building, the only building in Harlem taller than the Theresa Hotel. Ironically, when the structure was still in the planning stages, Powell had showed up on the spot, where generations of Harlemites had listened to him harness the spiritual energies of his father's generation in the service of secular change, to insist that Harlem needed more affordable housing—rents averaged a third more than in poor white neighborhoods—not an office building.

While Powell self-destructed, J. Raymond Jones scored his biggest victories. In 1964, after he won a seat on the City Council over the opposition of both Powell and Hulan Jack, the Democrats made Jones the first black chief of Tammany Hall and charged him with unifying the party. Not even the Harlem Fox could do the impossible, and in 1965 almost 40 percent of black Democrats in New York City, including many Harlemites, voted for a white, liberal Republican candidate for mayor named John Lindsay. There were plenty of black winners that day, including a whole new generation of Harlem politicians known to friends as the Group and to enemies as the Gang of Four. Charles Rangel, whose grandfather had been an elevator operator in the Criminal Court building downtown, was born in 1930 in Harlem and worked his way through college and law school as a desk clerk at the Theresa Hotel. He was destined for greater things, but it wasn't until 1966, when he became one of Harlem's representatives in the state assembly, that his name became well known uptown. Rangel went on to win Adam Clayton Powell Jr.'s seat in Congress, where he founded the Congressional Black Caucus and became the first African-American to sit on the powerful House Ways and Means Committee, his gravelly voice becoming one of the most insistently recognizable in Washington, D.C., especially when it came to minorities, women, and veterans. On civil rights issues, Rangel often reached out for advice to Basil Paterson, who was born in Harlem in 1926 to West Indian immigrants and became a state senator in 1966. He served two terms before going into private practice in 1970, though he remained as influential as ever; in 1978 he returned to politics as Ed Koch's deputy mayor, and the next year Governor Hugh Carey made him New York's first black secretary of state. Another member of the class of 1966 was a forty-one-year-old lawyer from New Jersey named David Dinkins, whose membership in J. Raymond Jones's Carver Democratic Club led to a seat in the assembly. Like Rangel and Paterson, the state legislature was only a stepping-stone for Dinkins, who in 1975 became city clerk, an important patronage position that he occupied for a decade before being elected borough president of Manhattan. The least well known of Harlem's Gang of Four may have been its most accomplished. Percy Sutton was born in Texas in 1920 and served in World War II with the Tuskegee airmen before law school and a stint in a Harlem firm that represented the NAACP. Sutton eventually became the president of the organization's New York City chapter, and in 1965 he entered the assembly. There he helped form the black and Puerto Rican legislative caucus before stepping down to become Manhattan borough president in 1966—he replaced Constance Baker Motley, a former NAACP litigator who was becoming a federal judge. But Sutton found himself stymied by politics as usual, and after leaving the Democratic Party in 1969 along with Adam Clayton Powell Jr. in order to back the Republican-Liberal-Independent incumbent mayor John Lindsay, he got more involved in the business world, teaming up in 1971 with Wilbur Tatum, David Dinkins, Clarence Jones, and Carl McCall to buy the *Amsterdam News*. He also set up Inner City Broadcasting, which was soon Harlem's largest business.

While Harlem's Gang of Four was consolidating its power by advancing a compromise between the Du Boisian agenda of racial uplift and Booker T. Washington's bootstrap capitalism, a new generation of activists was resurrecting race nationalism for the postcolonial age. The followers of Marcus Garvey were still active as the United African Nationalist Movement, still celebrating Marcus Garvey Day each August with demonstrations featuring signs reading "Are You Working?" and "What Happened to Your Job?" Now a new organization, convinced that the Civil Rights Acts of 1964 and 1968 and the Voting Rights Act of 1965 were largely powerless to combat southern racism and terror, excised the red and green of the UNIA's banner and kept only the black. The Black Power movement offered the kind of race nationalism that most Harlemites had been rejecting since before World War I, but like the UNIA it was the most seductive agenda setter uptown in the late 1960s and early 1970s, appealing, at least superficially, to a wider public than the organization's membership figures suggest. The man most associated with the term "Black Power," Stokely Carmichael, was born in Trinidad in 1941 and arrived with his family in Harlem in 1952. At first the civil rights movement left him cold, but galvanized by the Greensboro, North Carolina, lunch counter sit-ins of 1960 Carmichael joined the Congress of Racial Equality for numerous Freedom Rides. When he became a Student Nonviolent Coordinating Committee (SNCC) organizer in Alabama, he chose to represent the struggle with a black panther—a fateful choice. In 1966 Carmichael was made chair of SNCC, which was still closely linked with mainstream civil rights organizations and their methods. But the violence that peaceful civil rights workers met in the South turned many integrationists into revolutionaries. Carmichael began moving the organization from peaceful confrontation to more forceful means. The change led many civil rights figures, including Martin Luther King Jr., to wonder whether a political agenda obsessed with the empowerment of one race shared too much with the Jim Crow agenda. But Carmichael, who was becoming enamored with communist regimes in Cuba, North Vietnam, and China, was not as far removed from mainstream black opinion as it initially may seem. Around the same time he began using the term "Black Power"—it was actually Richard Wright's coinage—the National Committee of Negro Churchmen took out a full-page advertisement in the *New York Times* to come to the defense of this new generation of uptown race radicals. Even the stodgy *Amsterdam News* had started using the terms "black" and "African-American," a change that had been for decades the personal crusade of the legendary black communist Audley "Queen Mother" Moore.

Carmichael became a guiding voice for the Black Panthers, the militant Black Power group founded by Sam E. Anderson and Max

Stanford in Harlem in 1966, several months before the better-known
and better-armed West Coast branch. The Harlem Black Panthers
were numerous or intimidating enough to take over a September
1966 SNCC fund-raiser at the Mount Morris Presbyterian Church.
Originally hired to provide security, uniformed Panthers ejected white
journalists and made sure that no one interrupted Carmichael while
he excoriated the United States for its involvement in Vietnam and
presented a visionary global program of nonwhite self-determination.
Carmichael, at the time still the leader of a multiracial civil rights
organization, only suggested that violence might have a role in such a
project. In contrast, Stanford, who was close to Malcolm X, offered the
audience the recipe for molotov cocktails and claimed that with such
weapons the United States "could be brought down to its knees." Stanford also announced a plan to boycott the opening of two new schools
in East Harlem that the Board of Education was planning to run by
the old rules, meaning the school would be all black and Latino, even
while the curriculum ignored black and Latino history and culture.

The Panthers, most of whom lived on West 125th Street near
Lenox Avenue and at Eighth Avenue and West 155th Street, were
increasingly determined to distance themselves from the civil rights
movement, which they scornfully identified with an older generation
of polite accommodationists. The election in 1966 of the Republican
Edward Brooke of Massachusetts as the first black member of the
U.S. Senate since Reconstruction, the legalization of interracial marriage by the Supreme Court in 1967, and the elevation of Thurgood
Marshall to that bench the same year were too little, too late for the
Panthers, though they disagreed fiercely on questions of how much
and how soon. After Eldridge Cleaver took over the group in 1968 and
broadened its scope from oppressed black Americans to oppressed
groups everywhere, the Panthers almost fell apart. Many insisted that
counterintelligence efforts by the FBI were to blame. New leadership
that focused on race to the point of obsession now came to power,
with a new head, Dhoruba bin Wahad, setting up new offices at 2026
Seventh Avenue. He also organized residences for members, among
them Lumumba (Zayd) and Afeni Shakur, whose young son, Tupac,

acted in Harlem theater groups—later he would rap his way to fame. Stokely Carmichael, who was moving with Cleaver away from an exceptionalist vision of American racism and toward a more international point of view that looked beyond skin color, was finally expelled from the SNCC in 1968, but he never found an ideological home with bin Wahad's Panthers. Eventually he moved to Guinea, West Africa, and began his last battle, against terminal prostate cancer. Carmichael claimed that "the forces of American imperialism" gave it to him, and he had mixed feelings about being treated at Columbia Presbyterian Hospital, where Malcolm X had met his end.

The Harlem heyday of the Black Panthers was brief. Many members were deeply disturbed to learn that one of their own had been tortured during the course of an internal "trial" on "charges" that he was a police informer, "sentenced" to death, and then murdered. Even more troubling was the indictment of twenty-one Panthers in 1969 on charges of conspiring to bomb stores, subway stations, and police precincts. All of the accused won acquittals—ironically, their legal assistance came from the very group they despised above all, the NAACP. But the support that the blackface nationalism of the Panthers attracted uptown, where race messiahs whose plans were as monochromatic as that of their enemies, were nothing new, was broad and shallow. The tunnel vision of these race radicals led not to some imagined Sun Kingdom in a resurrected Africa that they had never even visited, but into a black hole of violence, nationalism, anti-Semitism, and misogyny. The revolution never took the A train.

"Politics can be the graveyard of the poet," Langston Hughes wrote in 1964, "and only poetry can be his resurrection." Hughes, who knew that every generation of Harlem artists needed to learn that, was addressing himself to the central figure of the black arts movement, LeRoi Jones, who was born in New Jersey into the kind of stable, middle-class household that produced so many uptown race rebels. After flunking out of Howard University, he served in the air force before moving to Greenwich Village in 1957 at the age of twenty-three. His poems

indulged in a beatnik surrealism that made a splash among the white
bohemians but it was his skill as a dramatist, in often shocking and
bold plays such as *Dutchman, The Toilet,* and *The Slave,* that made Jones
the unofficial Negro of the Beat Generation. Jones was at a party in
Greenwich Village when he heard that Malcolm X had been murdered. He raced uptown and, as far as his white friends and wife were
concerned, never returned. Jones had already joined with a group of
Harlemites, including Larry Neal, Rolland Snellings (later known as
Askia Touré), and Clarence Reed. All of them took inspiration from
Addison Gayle, a Virginian who went to City College before inventing
the aesthetic wing of the Black Power movement. Together they took
over the building at 146 West 130th Street and founded the Black Arts
Repertory Theatre/ School (BART/S) as an experiment in race-based
stagecraft. They weren't inventing things from scratch. Even before the
rise of the Black Arts movement, efforts were under way to re-create
the stage traditions that were so important to the rise of Harlem as
the Negro Mecca, including the Harlem School of the Arts, founded
in 1963 by the opera singer Dorothy Maynor, and the New Heritage
Repertory Theatre Company, founded the next year by Roger Thurman, a veteran of the American Negro Theatre. BART/S distinguished
itself by offering some of the ugliest, most disturbing explorations of
race that Harlem had ever seen, including one Jones play that featured
blacks in whiteface. There were also lectures by Harold Cruse, whose
scathing critique of integration formed the basis for his groundbreaking book *The Crisis of the Negro Intellectual.* Despite its antiestablishment
flavor, and an official ideology that even many Harlemites found eccentric at best, BART/S actually received federal funding for a time,
and it inspired a new generation of Harlem arts institutions, among
them the New Lafayette Theatre, the Boys Choir of Harlem, and the
National Black Theatre, which was an offshoot of the Harlem School
of the Arts. Even Harlem's Latinos took inspiration from Jones's vision of a radical theater. The East Harlem Gut Theater was formed
in 1966 by the poet Victor Hernandez Cruz, who was born in Puerto
Rico in 1949 and who grew up on the Lower East Side before making

the same physical and ideological journey to Harlem that LeRoi Jones made around the same time.

Perhaps the most successful group that grew out of the Harlem School of the Arts was the Dance Theatre of Harlem, which tacked against the prevailing trend toward racial art. The company, the first black troupe in the world to focus on classical ballet, was conceived in a garage at 466 West 152nd Street in 1968 by a white West Coaster named Karel Shook and Arthur Mitchell, a Harlemite, who, unlike so many Black Power figures who preached the cleansing power of violence, had experienced it firsthand during the riot of 1943. The son of a janitor who spent most of his time in prison for a variety of petty offenses, Mitchell worked as a shoeshine boy to help support his family. He studied tap dancing at the local Police Athletic League, and at New York City's renowned High School for the Performing Arts he gravitated toward ballet. In 1955 he became the first African-American to join the New York City Ballet, where he became known as the Jackie Robinson of classical dance. Because the dance company that Mitchell eventually founded with Shook was resolutely "nonpolitical and unethnic" it outlasted uptown radicals then calling for followers to "Think Black, Talk Black, Act Black, Create Black, Buy Black, Vote Black, and Live Black."

The Black Arts movement had mixed dealings with the old guard. A number of established writers from an earlier generation, including Gwendolyn Brooks, were enthusiastic supporters. Others, like Ralph Ellison and Albert Murray, rejected LeRoi Jones and his circle unequivocally, considering their paradoxical reinvestment in race as cultural suicide and plain bad taste. How could anyone reject the blues as an "invalid" art form that preached resignation in the face of injustice? Relations between the Black Arts figures and Langston Hughes were more complicated. Hughes, who had almost single-handedly elevated the blues and vernacular black culture to the level of high art back in the 1920s, was an early fan of Jones. But as skin color increasingly dominated Jones's agenda, Hughes began having second thoughts. Hughes chose to miss a BART/S fund-raiser in 1965, even as he declined to march down South with Martin Luther King Jr. Hughes's character Simple, who had once insisted, "As long as what is is, I will take Harlem for mine," finally left in 1967 and moved to the suburbs, ominously warning, "Life to me is where peoples is at." Hughes himself remained in Harlem, even as his neighborhood turned into a slum, ravaged by decades of poverty, racism, and now heroin, but he died before the year was out. There was no preacher at the funeral but plenty of blues, and Arna Bontemps read Hughes's "Night Funeral in Harlem" and "Dear Lovely Death" before the remains of the crown prince of the Harlem Renaissance, who remained a vital force in American culture for three generations, was taken out to the tune of Duke Ellington's "Do Nothing Till You Hear from Me.

The yoking of politics and art uptown resulted in some dubious literature and drama, but the music made by the race radicals was never less than compelling. A 1969 fund-raiser for Harlem's United Block Association managed to attract Jimi Hendrix, who as a youth from the West Coast had appeared at the Apollo with Ike Turner. More representative of where music was heading was a proto rap group called the Last Poets, who came together in the spring of 1968, just a few months after the murder of Martin Luther King Jr., to celebrate the birthday of Malcolm X, in Mount Morris Park, soon to be renamed after Marcus Garvey. Formed by three Harlemites named David Nelson, Gylan Kain, and Abiodun Oyewole, the Last Poets worked out of a loft on East 125th Street near Madison Avenue. There they invested the hybrid of speech and song that uptowners Cab Calloway and Louis Jordan and others had playfully invented with a political thrust that responded forcefully to the poverty, racism, unemployment, drugs, and deteriorating infrastructure in which the performers lived. The rhythmically charged form of performance protest in songs such as "Run Nigger" and "Niggers Are Scared of Revolution" seemed provocative to outsiders. The group had links to political extremists, and they indulged in the racism and anti-Semitism long popular among uptown fringe groups. But the Last Poets, who referred to Lenox Avenue as Malcolm X Boulevard two decades before the city made the change official, were simply trying to manifest the Harlem tradition of speaking what they thought was the truth to power, no matter how difficult or ugly.

It took years for Harlemites to turn the innovations of the Last Poets into rap and hip-hop. In the meantime, the popularity of jazz dwindled, despite the efforts of longtime Harlemites including the godmother of the beboppers Mary Lou Williams, who had turned her new home at 63 Hamilton Terrace into a twenty-four-hour jazz academy that attracted Cedar Walton, Horace Parlan, Hilton Ruiz, and Andrew Hill, among other students. Jazz venues, including the smaller clubs like Monroe's Uptown House, Club Baron, La Famille, and Joe Wells's, as well as theaters and dance halls such as the Audubon, the Lincoln, the Renaissance Casino, and Smalls Paradise, which was purchased by the basketball star Wilt Chamberlain, survived by bringing in rhythm and blues acts, for example, Arthur Prysock and Ray Charles. The greatest of them all, the Apollo, could still fill seats with the ever relevant James Brown, whose "Say It Loud (I'm Black and I'm Proud)" signaled his allegiance with a movement he had helped invent. Even so, the theater survived from day to day by accepting the fact that in the 1970s it was not jazz or rhythm and blues but a new kind of black dance music, both slick and funky, coming out of Detroit, Philadelphia, and Memphis that was dominating radios, record players, and jukeboxes. It was soul music that kept the Apollo's Amateur Night a must-see, with crowds cheering on the likes of Stephanie Mills, the Jackson Five, the Spinners, and Gladys Knight. For the first time since the turn of the century Harlem was no longer the center of the black musical universe, but black musicians still considered the Apollo sacred artistic territory, worthy of pilgrimage. When Aretha Franklin, who came from Detroit, first saw her name on the Apollo's marquee in the mid-1960s she wept and exclaimed, "I am home!"

Despite their reputation as wild-eyed revolutionaries, the Black Panthers shared at least one important focus with mainstream civil rights groups: education. The NAACP had helped persuade the Supreme Court to end school segregation in 1954, but the struggle was far from over, and not just in the Jim Crow South. Harlem schools, which were accommodating waves of poor black and Puerto Rican newcomers even as the neighborhood's last upwardly mobile whites left for the suburbs, were the worst in the city. Not surprisingly, efforts to change broad demographic patterns reinforced by the economics of racism were doomed. Two integration plans in the early 1960s, when New York had the biggest school system in the country, with almost a million students (nearly 40 percent of them black or Puerto Rican), almost a hundred thousand teachers (only 8 percent of whom were black), and over forty thousand administrators (only 3 percent of whom were black), accomplished little. Fewer than 10 percent of diplomas accepted by college admissions offices went to black or Puerto Rican students.

School conditions got so bad that Harlem parents organized a boycott of the schools in February of 1964, which inspired the city to build a new kind of school in East Harlem. Located at the corner of Madison Avenue and East 128th Street, Intermediate School 201 was the most expensive in the city's history, but as construction neared completion parents who were at the leading edge of the movement for local control of education were disturbed to see that it looked more like a prison than a school. Worse, the inability of the school to attract whites from nearby districts meant that I.S. 201 would effectively be segregated. Parents were further stung when they learned that black and Puerto Rican children would attend a school named after someone named Arthur Schomburg—not only a white man but a Jew, they thought.

It was at this point that one of the most venerable voices of progressive politics got involved. The meeting that A. Philip Randolph held at his home with leaders of the largely white teachers union made him few friends among I.S. 201 parents, especially the firebrands who mistook his respect for opposing views as weakness—they labeled him an Uncle Tom. Randolph's protégé Bayard Rustin also tried to help, but parents mistrusted his insistence on moving beyond race-based activism. Rustin's prescient warning to the Black Power crowd so influential among I.S. 201 parents that their emphasis on separatism would devastate their movement—"being black is not a program," he insisted—went unheard.

The parents who finally decided that they would rather have no school than the one the Board of Education was planning saw themselves as civil rights activists, though their rhetoric was inspired by the most fanatical of the Black Panthers. Parents called the Board of Education the "Board of Genocide" and claimed that the teachers' union was out to "miseducate and destroy black and Puerto Rican children." Soon it became clear that the most extreme parents were asking not just for racial balance at the school but demanding full control. They demanded the right to choose teachers and staff—all black, of course—and envisioned hallways lined with images of Marcus Garvey and Muhammad Ali, with background recordings by LeRoi Jones, Aretha Franklin, and Malcolm X. Most parents had gone along so far, but they began to have doubts when they heard that their children would be considered third-world revolutionaries, pledging allegiance to the flag of Africa, using Yoruba and Swahili as the languages of instruction, and immersing themselves in a "black survival curriculum," with courses in black history and gun handling that prepared them for the rigors of the coming racial apocalypse.

Mayor Lindsay, fearful of yet another riot—the most radical of the parents promised that "blood would flow in the streets of Harlem" if I.S. 201 opened as planned in September of 1966—gave in and delayed the official opening of the school while negotiations continued. Still, several dozen protesters were jailed when they tried to prevent the white principal from going to work—Roy Innis of the Harlem branch of the Congress of Racial Equality called it "a prelude to war." When I.S. 201 and the primary schools that fed it became a single experimental school district that parents and local residents would run via an elected community school board, the white principal quit, followed by most of the teachers and staff. Replacements were found and the school was opened, but it quickly declined into what the Ford Foundation, which had helped fund the school, called "an armed camp." One black teacher who had to clear a path through the chaotic, garbage-strewn hallways that were the dominion of students armed with knives, commented, "This isn't a school, this is a jungle."

Less vocal parents—most of them Puerto Ricans who felt that blacks had hijacked the struggle—requested that their children be transferred out of I.S. 201, and as time went on there were fewer and fewer voices to restrain the extremists. One uptown radical, Charles Kenyatta, told the New York *Post*, "I'm all for seizing the schools right now and holding them at gunpoint." A memorial program for Malcolm X that was closed to police and white reporters quickly devolved into a call for racial vengeance. The crowd heckled James Baldwin so forcefully when he talked about building bridges between the races that he was unable to finish his speech. They thunderously applauded a LeRoi Jones play that revived the worst of the pseudo-scientific racism of the stepladder speakers on 125th Street: once upon a time, the play insisted, whites crawled on all fours before stealing from blacks the knowledge of standing upright. Next came a speech by Herman Ferguson, a low-level I.S. 201 administrator and the brains behind the proposed revolutionary curriculum. Out on bail on weapons charges related to a conspiracy to murder Urban League and NAACP officials, Ferguson insulted the school superintendent as a "honkie Irishman" and claimed that the conflict in Vietnam was a secret war on American blacks, who needed to arm themselves against the assault. But when the event was over everyone went home. Ferguson, who was eventually chosen as principal of I.S. 55, had to admit that the revolution still wasn't at hand.

Race riots rolled across forty-three American cities in the summer of 1966 in a frenzied and frustrated protest against poverty and racism, but uptown Manhattan, where Mayor Lindsay, who had been active in the passage of the civil rights bill of 1964, won 40 percent of the vote the year before, remained relatively quiet. He had his detractors. That summer Lindsay was threatened during a visit to West 135th Street by crowds chanting "Get that cracker." But he was determined to keep the peace. He appointed one of his aides, Barry Gottehrer, to help prevent unrest by monitoring everything from street repairs to unemployment. Gottehrer took the pulse of the community by hanging out at the Glamour Inn, at Seventh Avenue and West 127th Street. He maintained especially close links with a group of uptown race radicals called the Five Percenters, a Nation of Islam splinter group that took its name from their belief that 5 percent of humanity was destined to fight the 10 percent who were devils and therefore liberate the remaining 85 percent. The group was led by a Virginian named Clarence "Pudding" Smith who served in the Korean War before joining Malcolm X's Mosque #7 in Harlem and changing his name to Clarence 13X. He soon quit the Nation of Islam and renamed himself Allah the Father, starting his own organization on Seventh Avenue and preaching a pseudo-African and Islamic numerology he called "Supreme Mathematics." The Five Percenters never numbered more than a few hundred members, but they were a significant voice of protest, and not a totally benign one. Like many radical groups throughout the decades, they sustained themselves by squeezing protection money out of storekeepers. They also held incendiary rallies in Mount Morris Park, where Allah the Father announced, "If we don't get some of the poverty money to build our own Mosque we're going to kill all light-skinned babies, bomb the houses of Negro policemen, and riot."

The summer of love, 1967, wasn't color-blind. The year that saw Aretha Franklin's "Respect" and Jimi Hendrix's "Are You Experienced?" again brought race riots to dozens of cities by African-Americans who realized that such protests wouldn't pay for diapers. Harlem wasn't totally spared, though this time it looked like the revolution would be in Spanish. The residents of El Barrio had long found themselves in a better position than uptown blacks when it came to racial discrimination. Nonetheless, for decades they had been active in civil rights groups, especially when it came to education. During the 1964 school boycott, only 350 of 2,300 students at the largely Puerto Rican Benjamin Franklin High School showed up. As time passed, however, many Boricuas became frustrated with nonviolent protest, in particular in the face of police misconduct.

Their moment came in the early hours of Sunday, July 23, 1967, when two white off-duty cops intervened in a fight at the corner of

Third Avenue and East 111th Street and shot a twenty-seven-year-old Harlemite named Renaldo Rodriquez. When the news spread, crowds began massing on Third Avenue and destroying whatever they could lay their hands on. Police arrived, followed shortly by Mayor Lindsay, and by sunrise it was over, at least temporarily. A handful of civilians and police were hospitalized but none died, and Lindsay was relieved to be able to call it not a riot but a disturbance. Later that night, though, more "disturbances" broke out near the site of the shooting. Residents set fires in the street, threw bottles and cans, broke windows, and looted two dozen stores. A mob moved north on Third Avenue to East 126th Street, where they clashed with a wall of 250 policemen. Things quieted down by the early hours of Monday, July 24, but the next night brought more chaos, as more than a thousand East Harlemites overran a gas station on East 109th Street, attacked a television journalist, and burned his car. Early Tuesday morning, residents drew a line in chalk across East 110th Street and claimed the blocks north of that border as Puerto Rican territory. By the time order had been restored later on Tuesday morning, four people had been killed and 103 were injured, but Harlemites took little comfort from the fact that it was a mere "disturbance" compared to Newark's twenty-six deaths or Detroit's forty-three fatalities that summer.

Lindsay's credibility among urban minorities got a boost when the National Advisory Commission on Civil Disorders, on which he served, called the plight of the urban poor the country's worst domestic problem and warned of increasing violence if the country as a whole didn't immediately take decisive action against racism and poverty. Even immediately would have been too late to prevent the unrest that took place following the assassination of Martin Luther King Jr. in Memphis, Tennessee, on April 4, 1968. King had appeared uptown infrequently after the attempt on his life at Blumstein's, most recently coming to the Convent Avenue Baptist Church in late March of 1968, and the day before his assassination he publicly recalled his close call in Harlem. Many Harlemites had not always agreed with King; Bayard Rustin, for one, believed that it was a "suicidal" mistake for the civil rights movement to focus on ending the Vietnam

War, though he had to agree with King's assertion that "the bombs that we drop in Vietnam will explode in Harlem." But like so many Americans of so many races they were devastated by the news of his murder. President Johnson ordered Rustin's plane to Memphis rerouted to Washington, D.C., to work with the White House to help contain black reaction, but it was too late because it wasn't just about King anymore, not in Harlem. A cold snap in January 1968 had sent hundreds of residents whose landlords weren't providing heat to the temporary safety of armories or hotels. Then in February a weeklong strike by sanitation workers left streets piled waist-high with garbage. So Harlemites were on the verge of exploding even before they heard the news from Memphis. Within minutes, crowds began gathering on 125th Street. Mayor Lindsay arrived around 10:30 p.m., protected by Allah the Father's Five Percenters, and he gave a speech at the corner of Eighth Avenue and West 125th Street. He met with local race leaders on 125th Street and then decided to go for a walk, but he soon found himself in the middle of an angry mob at the corner of Seventh Avenue and West 127th Street and managed to get himself into Percy Sutton's limousine just in time. By midnight there was a riot going on. The sound of King's speeches, broadcast over loudspeakers set up in front of music stores, was jarringly accompanied by the shouts of looters, the crash of bottles and broken glass, and the thud of rocks. Lindsay returned around 1 a.m. but he stayed for only an hour. Things had simply gotten too dangerous. Stores along 125th Street and Lenox Avenue were emptied by the rioters and over the next four days there were 373 arrests, dozens of injured policemen, and almost six hundred burglaries and fires—firemen were actually targeted by snipers shooting from buildings at the corner of Lenox Avenue and West 126th Street. It wasn't until April 7, when a parade moved up Seventh Avenue in remembrance of King, that things quieted down. Lindsay's order to the police to let Harlemites get their anger out of their system as long as it was directed at property and not against human lives was opposed by landlords and storekeepers of all races. Indeed, for those who seek to identify the moment when Harlem truly became a lost cause, the riot of 1968 is the likeliest suspect: most of the few businesses that survived the riots of 1935, 1943, 1963, and 1968 left forever.

Then things got even worse. Just three weeks after the riots came yet another violent uprising that all but paralyzed the downtown power structure and delivered another blow to Harlem's future. The conflict began with Columbia University's plans to take over part of Morningside Park for a school gym. After seven decades in Morningside Heights, the university was pressed for space, and the overgrown strip of park that separated the Ivory Tower from the Black Bottom seemed like a logical place to grow. But Columbia's gymnasium, first proposed back in 1958, would be open to Harlemites only through a back entrance on the Harlem side. The proposal struck many as frighteningly reminiscent of southern-style segregation—they called the plan "Gym Crow."

Columbia officials hoped that the further deterioration of Morningside Park, considered the most dangerous park in the country, "a raw no-man's-land between a ghetto and affluence," in the words of one observer, would build support for the gym, but things had changed since the late 1950s. Columbia had embarked on a controversial expansion plan, buying more than one hundred residential buildings and emptying them of seventy-five hundred people, most of them black and Puerto Rican. In addition, Columbia students were now talking back to the university about its activities, especially its involvement in Vietnam War industries and research. Finally, the very nature of political activism had changed, with radical groups once again flourishing and inspiring public officials to more extreme positions. Whereas the Harlem state senator James Watson had approved the old Columbia gym plan several years earlier, now uptown politicians tried to kill it. As for ordinary Harlemites, a 1967 poll found that most people were unaware of the proposal, and among those who had heard about it half were in favor.

Once the race radicals heard about the proposal, however, the tone of the protests became more heated. The announcement that Columbia was planning to commit $3 million in aid to Harlem struck many as nothing more than a bribe. In December 1967 the Black Power leader

H. Rap Brown told the virtually all-white Columbia student body that they were morally obliged to stop construction by blowing up the project. Four months later, on April 23, hundreds of students and their allies gathered at the center of campus and denounced Columbia as a "white citadel of hypocrisy" and its leadership as "war criminals." They stormed the gym construction site and took one of the deans hostage, occupying five buildings and decorating them with images of Che Guevara, Vladimir Lenin, Stokely Carmichael, and Malcolm X as well as the official flag of the Vietcong. The takeover may have seemed like a grotesquely naive, adolescent outbreak of spring fever but the students attracted the support of assemblyman Charles Rangel, state senator Basil Paterson, and borough president Percy Sutton, who told the students, "Whatever you do, we're with you." Dozens of Harlemites joined the forty or so black Columbia students who had occupied Hamilton Hall and declared it an all-black zone, to be defended, it was rumored, by grenades and guns. The police abided by the Columbia administration's intentions to let what the *Village Voice* called "the Groovy Revolution" die down by itself. It didn't. A week after the start of the protest, Columbia officials finally called in the police. In a middle-of-the-night invasion, police forcibly cleared students from the buildings they had occupied. The fact that the city called in more than fourteen hundred police officers to arrest some seven hundred protesters led observers to call it a police riot, but of the 103 people injured that night, 14 were cops, and only 3 of 174 charges of excessive force heard by the Police Civilian Complaint Review Board were approved.

As the cops and the radicals nursed their wounds, plans for the gym faded away, and Morningside Park slipped deeper into decay and danger, leaving most Harlemites worse off than ever. Nonetheless, the events of April 1968 were heard around the world, inspiring student uprisings from California to Paris. It took a bit more time for the rest of Harlem to get into the spirit. In 1969 forty black and Puerto Rican students from City College objecting to the unrepresentative number of minorities at the school briefly took over several campus buildings and renamed the school Harlem University. Unlike at Columbia, the handling of the incident by CCNY administration and the police was circumspect, and the aftermath was far more productive. Starting in the summer of 1970, for the first time in its history, New York City's premier public institution of higher education guaranteed a place for any student with a high school degree. It seemed like an excellent idea, but the execution proved problematic, because the city's public school system was failing. If only one in ten students at the CUNY schools granting bachelor degrees were black or Puerto Rican, that was in part because so few minorities were graduating from high school with the necessary qualifications. Within a year of the change the number of minority students doubled. City College and the rest of the CUNY schools had benefited from years of increased spending on education—from 1966 to 1973 city spending on post-secondary education soared, from $35 million to $200 million—but they were unprepared for the era of open admissions. Nor were many of these new students ready for college-level study. They required costly special classes in reading and math, especially at CCNY, within walking distance of the city's poorest, most overcrowded high schools.

The spirit of protest extended to the visual arts. In early 1969 the Metropolitan Museum of Art opened an exhibit called *Harlem on My Mind: Cultural Capital of Black America, 1900–1968*. With more than twelve hundred photographs and other images on display, as well as musical recordings, the show celebrated black Harlem's incredibly rich and varied cultural history with respect and enthusiasm. But what seemed like a brilliant if long overdue idea became a lightning rod for conflict, and yet another formidable citadel of high culture came under attack. Harlemites were outraged that the museum had hired a Jewish curator with no special expertise in black culture to organize a show whose very name came from a song by the Russian-Jewish composer Irving Berlin, who knew the uptown scene only as a slummer. Harlemites also objected to the fact that four of the seven museum staff members who worked on the show were white, and none of the rest were from Harlem. Even before the opening, a group called the Harlem Cultural

Council, led by the writer Ed Taylor, protested loudly that the museum had denied Harlemites the opportunity to represent themselves.

The Metropolitan Museum show was hugely successful, drawing record crowds over three months—in the end, the protesters accomplished little, aside from persuading the city to appoint the much underrated black painter Charles Alston to the City Art Commission. A more direct beneficiary of the show was James Van Der Zee, who had been documenting Harlem since the 1920s but had slipped into poverty and obscurity. In 1968 he had a tiny studio on Lenox Avenue and could barely afford to eat. It was sheer chance that one of the show's curators happened to pass by one day. Inside, he found a lifetime's worth of art that rejected the overtly political tradition represented in the show by the white photographers Aaron Siskind and Bruce Davidson, who captured the many faces of Harlem, especially the victims of poverty and racism. *Harlem on My Mind* jump-started Van Der Zee's career, but not right away. The day after the exhibit ended, Van Der Zee and his wife, Gaynella, were thrown out of their home, a sad, ugly scene documented in detail by the *New York Times*. Gaynella was so hysterical that she went after the officials evicting them with an aerosol can of insecticide and had to be anesthetized and taken away. But Van Der Zee was soon in demand for his portrait work again, and for the rest of his life he was acknowledged as one of the most important artists that Harlem had produced. The Metropolitan Museum show may not have pleased some Harlemites, but its influence was decisive in the movement to give minority artists their own institutions. By the end of the decade art institutions closer to home such as the Museo del Barrio and the Studio Museum in Harlem were thriving.

There would be several more bouts of unrest before Harlem bid goodbye to a decade that had brought to national consciousness both the seriousness of conditions and the paucity of easy solutions. It was not despair but optimism that, in 1968, inspired two college students named Mickey Melendez and Pablo Guzman to form an East Harlem branch of the downtown gang called the Young Lords. They began canvassing the neighborhood to find out what their neighbors really needed. As it turned out, East Harlemites weren't just worried about police brutality and education but about garbage—and not just the 1968 strike by sanitation workers but the general failure of the city to keep streets uptown clean. In 1969 Melendez and Guzman initiated a "Garbage Offensive" in which they recruited East Harlemites to sweep the trash littering their sidewalks into five-foot-high barricades at more than a dozen key intersections and burn it. Then the Young Lords, operating from their headquarters at the corner of Madison Avenue and East 111th Street, stole a mobile X-ray unit to protest high rates of tuberculosis in East Harlem. They occupied the First Spanish United Methodist Church, at Lexington Avenue and East 111th Street, which stood empty every day of the week but Sunday, and renamed it the People's Church, turning it into a community center, complete with medical clinic, soup kitchen, and classrooms. Like the Nation of Islam, East Harlem's Young Lords formulated a strict code of personal conduct, one that forbade the use of heroin and speed and banned any form of intoxication while on duty, though they seem to have raised most of their money by selling marijuana. Such rules gained them much local goodwill.

In 1971 the Young Lords found themselves at odds over the use of violence, the possibility of an allegiance with the Black Panthers, and the importance of supporting Puerto Rican independence as opposed to focusing on conditions in East Harlem. In the chaos that ensued, the group was reorganized and it eventually became the Maoist-influenced Puerto Rican Revolutionary Workers Party. They continued to be active in issues of poverty and racism but their focus turned to anti-colonial activities—their last hurrah came when they seized and oc-cupied the Statue of Liberty in 1977—and they never regained the grassroots credibility or national publicity that the Young Lords had in their two years on the streets of El Barrio.

By the 1970s the era of mass violence in Harlem was over, but friction with the police often led to smaller-scale incidents. The worst was a clash between cops and members of the Nation of Islam's Mosque #7 in April 1972. Following the death of Malcolm X the Nation of Islam lost much of its credibility, with many of the sect's followers turning to traditional Sunni Islam. Still, the organization continued to grow, fed by a constant stream of prison converts attracted to the race pride, strict standards of personal hygiene and conduct, and the promise of a new identity. The Nation of Islam was always notorious about inflating its membership numbers, so there is much doubt about whether national membership ever reached the hundreds of thousands, as they claimed, and whether the sect's assets, in the form of real estate, schools, shops, factories, and newspapers, reached $75 million. Whatever the correct figures, Malcolm X's old kingdom was flourishing. After 1965 the Nation of Islam, now being led by Louis Farrakhan, turned the burnt-out shell of the old Lenox Casino, at 102 West 116th Street, into the domed Mohammed Temple of Islam, with a bookstore, restaurant, clothing shop, and a school called the University of Islam.

Malcolm X had led Nation of Islam members in many public protests, but things had never turned violent, and police tended to see the Black Muslims as a basically harmless group of fanatically neat crazies who would just as soon have nothing to do with anything white, especially the police. It took only a single incident to change that relationship forever. On Friday, April 14, 1972, close to the end of the Muslim sabbath, police received a call reporting a "10-13"—meaning that a police officer was down—at 102 West 116th Street, the old Lenox Dancing Academy. Two officers rushed to the scene, where despite a long-standing unwritten agreement that the police would give special treatment to Harlem's mosques and never enter without warning, they burst in through the front door and found themselves trapped. Reinforcements arrived but they were unable to help three officers who still remained inside. One was killed by a point-blank shot to the chest, though the authorities didn't find that out until they drove seventeen members of the mosque down a set of stairs and trapped them in the cellar. Word spread quickly, and within a few minutes both Charles Rangel and Louis Farrakhan were on the scene, imploring the police to let all of the suspects go, lest a riot begin. The top police brass then arrived and halted the investigation, apparently because of the circumstances under which the cops had entered the building. Nonetheless, within minutes more than a thousand people massed outside the mosque, attacking police and white journalists and setting fire to a patrol car. There the conflict seems to have ended, and though the work of the police had just begun no one was ever convicted. The police actually prevented a proper investigation of the murder scene or questioning of witnesses, all in the name of avoiding large-scale violence. Worse, the mayor and the police commissioner broke a decades-old custom by failing to attend the murdered cop's funeral. City Hall had once again avoided mass violence but at what price?

Harlemites who claimed that the Great Depression had little impact on a community with little to lose couldn't shrug off the fiscal crisis that engulfed New York City in the mid-1970s. Like most American cities, New York in the 1960s saw huge increases in spending, with budgets for police, fire, hospitals, and health care doubling and money spent on welfare-related programs exploding by 300 percent, but poverty levels remained far higher uptown than the rest of the city. Throughout the 1960s the average annual family income in Harlem was under $4,000, well below the official poverty line of $6,000. Welfare had been intended to provide temporary support to these families but during this period it became a permanent fact of life. By 1981 a third of all families in central Harlem were on government assistance. Mayor Lindsay should have seen as early as the recession of 1969 that inflation and decreasing tax revenues were forcing the city to borrow to meet expenses. By 1975 the budget deficit had reached $13 billion, and there was no way to fund this crushing debt, except by cutting services, laying off workers, and raising taxes. Fourteen percent of the police force was let go, and uptown, where Harlemites had long felt both harassed and underprotected, crime soared, with a near tripling in the number of youth arrests in central Harlem. More than fifteen thousand teachers and public school employees citywide lost their jobs. The impact was felt most strongly in Harlem, where schools were understaffed to begin with. At the same time, transit fares and taxes rose. Harlem's unemployment rate, always a problem, reached almost 40 percent, and many of those who had jobs could barely pay their bills. Few of the thousand or so East Harlem businesses displaced by housing projects ever returned. The number of manufacturing jobs uptown, which had declined by two-thirds in the 1960s, practically disappeared in the 1970s. When East Harlem's biggest remaining industrial employer, the Washburn Wire Factory, closed in 1976, nearly eight hundred spring and hanger makers lost their jobs.

As a hundred thousand Harlemites fled to the outer boroughs, to the suburbs, or back to the South in the 1960s and '70s, central Harlem lost a third of its residents, El Barrio saw "urban renewal" halve the number of housing units, and two-thirds of the residents of lower Harlem vanished. Pockets of relative stability survived along Striver's Row, on Hamilton Heights and Sugar Hill, and around Mount Morris Park. Along Broadway, the population actually increased, no doubt due to immigration from the West Indies, Central America, and West Africa. But depopulation had terrible consequences for everyone who remained. Many venerable, even sacred institutions were failing. The Theresa Hotel closed in the early 1970s, only to reopen as an office building. The sign for Blumstein's department store remained but the store itself shut down and was divided and subleased to a number of smaller businesses. The 135th Street YMCA, the first refuge for generations of new arrivals and a nerve center of so much cultural activity, shut its doors in 1975. The dozens of places to hear live music in the years before World War II, from grand ballrooms to cellar cubicles that operated only after hours, disappeared almost entirely. The closing of Filmway Studios on East 127th Street, where *Midnight Cowboy, Klute, The Taking of Pelham, One, Two, Three,* and *The Godfather* were filmed—major organized crime activity in Italian East Harlem had essentially ended with a crackdown on the heroin trade, but many of the actors who had roles in *The Godfather,* including the boxer Lenny Del Genio, were recruited from the streets of East Harlem, and the film's star Al Pacino was a local boy—effectively marked the end of studio filmmaking in Manhattan. The Apollo Theater had survived by keeping up with the latest trends in music, from rhythm and blues to soul and funk, but the Schiffmans found it increasingly difficult to make a profit, given the extortionate demands of the Five Percenters. After a local teen was shot and killed during a Smokey Robinson performance in December of 1975 the Apollo closed its doors. In early 1978 the theater came under the control of a group whose silent partner was the heroin kingpin Nicky Barnes, and the theater was renovated and reopened in May of that year, with live programming that included Latin music, disco, and funk. Once again the Apollo was swinging, with Parliament Funkadelic and Bob Marley appearing on the marquee. But mismanagement and the difficulty in convincing audiences to brave the trip uptown drove the theater into bankruptcy. When the Apollo's newest savior, the veteran politician and businessman Percy Sutton, came on the scene in 1981, the theater was in such bad condition that even a four-year, $14 million renovation—including $3.5 million in state money—couldn't put the business on sound footing.

Experts in urban studies call such developments as the rise in poverty, population loss, and deteriorating health statistics "quiet riots," because the economic effects of such slow changes attract less attention than mass uprisings but have similar effects. In the 1970s many Harlem politicians congratulated themselves on the fact that there had been no violent public disturbances in years. But things didn't remain calm. On July 13, 1977, a blackout swept across the city and for two days pandemonium ruled Harlem's streets. A reduced police force kept calm in business districts downtown and in most white neighborhoods across the city, but in Harlem there were two days of chaos, with armed clashes on the streets and looting of the few stores that remained open. The blackout of 1977, coming so soon after the fiscal crisis, had major repercussions. A congressman named Ed Koch used the events to unseat Mayor Abe Beame and to usher in an era of fiscal responsibility that got the city back on its feet financially, but Harlemites were hard hit. Despite fierce community opposition, Koch invoked financial necessity in closing Sydenham Hospital—it was later turned into housing for low-income senior citizens—and five uptown health clinics run by the city, which not only forced even more patients into the already notoriously overcrowded Harlem Hospital but took away more than a thousand jobs.

Following the 1977 blackout, huge swathes of the neighborhood began to resemble the bombed-out European cities of World War II. Longtime landlords found themselves in a business with fewer and fewer takers, so they sold to unscrupulous newcomers who saved money by skimping on maintenance and renovation. In the 1960s and 1970s it was estimated that one half of uptown's 216,000 buildings were substandard, and the city's Department of Buildings was getting some five hundred complaints per day about housing conditions. At a certain point—especially if tenants withheld rent or couldn't pay—it became more profitable for landlords to set fire to their buildings and take the insurance payout or to abandon them altogether as a tax loss. That was the way almost two-thirds of Harlem's private property came into the city's hands. City control of property made redevelopment plans easier, but there was precious little money for that, especially after 1972, when President Nixon ordered a freeze on all new federally funded housing developments. Public projects that did go forward, such as the Lionel Hampton Apartments, at West 130th Street and St. Nicholas Avenue, or the twin thirty-five-story high-rises named for Arthur Schomburg that went up in 1975 at the northeast corner of Central Park, met resistance from locals who believed the new developments were hastening the departure of Harlem's blacks and Puerto Ricans. The mantra of the protesters, "urban renewal means Negro removal," wasn't so far-fetched. Koch had ended the practice of allowing neighbors the first opportunity to buy abandoned property that the city had taken over, which attracted outsiders looking merely for a good real estate investment.

The rising crime rates that scared so many people away from even New York's fanciest neighborhoods actually hit Harlem harder, with residents complaining bitterly that the police were too busy collecting from drug dealers, numbers runners, and prostitutes to pay much attention to the mostly black victims of muggings, purse snatchings, petty thefts, and robberies. In the 1970s, the number of youth arrests in central Harlem almost tripled. Many of these crimes were committed by members of gangs, for example, the Savage Samurais, whose initiation rites included russian roulette and line beatings and who recruited through offshoots called the Young Samurais and even the Baby Samurais. Some Harlemites had clearly decided to trade in "We Shall Overcome" for "We Shall Overrun." More and more business owners decided that Harlem simply wasn't worth the risk, and those that remained installed steel gates that gave the neighborhood the look of a ghost town after dark. Even that didn't stop robberies or break-ins: in the first nine months of 1968 robbers targeted thirty-four of forty-seven stores on West 116th Street between Seventh and Eighth avenues, and, as if in sympathy, the Tree of Hope had died. Then the stump was smashed during a car crash. Not only were businesses affected by what the NAACP called a "reign of criminal terror." Harlem murders, robberies, assaults, and rapes were reported in such breathless headlines that it all but ensured Harlem's status as a national synonym for urban danger.

If a case can be made for tolerating gambling and prostitution as "victimless" crimes, the same cannot be said of the flourishing heroin trade. Between 1972 and 1978 the number of drug-related complaints in central Harlem doubled. Most of them came from the neighborhood along Lenox Avenue from West 130th to West 135th streets, known in the 1920s as the Hollow and now renamed Junkie's Hollow. After Bumpy Johnson was released from prison he tried to make a go of it again in the drug trade, but the man who had once extracted protection money from virtually every store on 125th Street was under constant police surveillance—meaning that he wasn't "cooperating"—and he died at Wells's restaurant in 1968 in the arms of his protégé Frank Lucas. Only fourteen when he came to Harlem in 1946 from his native North Carolina, where he already had a long prison record, Lucas quickly got a reputation as a stickup man. He met Johnson at Lump's Pool Hall and soon the two were inseparable. Johnson bought Lucas new clothes and let him stay for months at his penthouse facing Mount Morris Park. In return, Lucas served as Johnson's go-between with mob boss Fat Tony Salerno, delivering drugs and picking up cash. There was also bloody work to be done, including making sure rivals disappeared. After murdering a fearsome competitor named Tango in front of the Canaan Baptist Church, Lucas was considered untouchable, accountable only to himself and to Johnson, a living link to the gory, glory days of the Harlem Renaissance.

After Johnson died, Lucas was determined to make some changes in the old man's crime empire. For starters, his drug dealings with the mafia had taught Lucas the downside of depending on outside suppliers. He traveled to Vietnam and found a source for heroin at one-tenth the price of what the mob charged. Looking for a way to ship the drugs back to the United States, he borrowed a trick from the Jazz Age gangster Dutch Schultz and started packing the drugs into America-bound coffins fitted with false bottoms. Lucas called it his "cadaver connection." Back in Harlem, he had a dozen women wearing nothing but surgical masks as they processed and packed the product around the clock. The result of Lucas's "womb-to-tomb" operation was a brand of heroin known as Blue Magic, which became the most popular fix in Harlem because of its purity.

More than a third of the country's addicts lived uptown by the early 1970s, and they could buy more than seventy kinds of heroin in plastic baggies labeled with names that say much about the black experience in America: Harlem Hijack, Past Due, Tragic Magic, and even KKK. Lucas's product was the best, hitting the open-air drug market on the corner of Eighth Avenue and West 116th Street every day at 4 p.m., when cops changed shifts and were less likely to be out on patrol, and selling out five hours later for a profit of $300,000 per kilo. The crowds got so large—Lucas recalled without remorse that "we had enough niggers in the street to make a Tarzan movie"—that the Transit Authority had to reroute its Eighth Avenue bus. Lucas counted on a battalion of five hundred armed employees, the core of which was a group of Lucas family members, brought up from North Carolina and dubbed the Country Boys. That kind of power ensured him an entrée into uptown's aristocracy, and he counted among his close friends Sugar Ray Robinson, Wilt Chamberlain, and Joe Louis, who once borrowed $50,000 from Lucas to pay off a tax bill. Despite his success, Lucas began to think about getting out of the business. Eventually he got his wish. After years of being protected by New York's famously corrupt Special Investigations Unit, Lucas was busted in 1975, tried—Joe Louis attended every trial session in protest—and sentenced to forty years in prison. There he became a Catholic and a Baptist both, just to be on the safe side, though he was able to have drugs and prostitutes delivered to his cell at any time.

The arrest of Lucas made room for a new boss, Leroy "Nicky" Barnes, who grew up near Lucas's drug bazaar at Eighth Avenue and West 116th Street. Barnes became a junkie and a dealer early on, but it was only after West 116th Street met East 116th Street in the form of the gangster Crazy Joey Gallo, a longtime mob fixture in Italian East Harlem, that Barnes's career was made. Frank Lucas boasted of his independence from mafia suppliers, but Barnes looked at his mob sources as an asset, and he soon made Lucas seem like a wallflower. With his wide lapeled, boldly colored suits, huge collars, and grotesquely large sunglasses, Barnes helped define what became known as the "Superfly" look on display in so many blaxploitation movies of the 1970s. Barnes lived the life to go with the fashion, buying a mansion in Riverdale and driving around town in a Maserati, though he is also remembered as having served as a church deacon who handed out turkeys at Thanksgiving and distributed toys to Harlem kids at Christmas. The feds attempted three times to try "Mr. Untouchable" on charges ranging from bribery to drug dealing to murder before they finally convicted him of heroin trafficking in 1977. It was the first federal trial to be held before an anonymous jury. Barnes got life without parole, a sentence that was reduced when he began cooperating with the authorities in an undercover operation that put dozens of former friends and family members behind bars.

There were pockets of resistance to heroin's invasion. Many churches and community centers ran addict treatment programs. None was more inspiring than the efforts of Clara McBride Hale, who worked with drug addicted mothers and their children in a West 122nd Street brownstone called Hale House. But in the mid-1980s Harlem was unprepared to fight a new, smokable form of cocaine called crack. Crack was better business than heroin, because it was produced not half a world away, like heroin, but just a short boat or plane ride from the Gulf Coast. Best of all, a small, inexpensive amount of crack cocaine could, after just a single use, hook a customer, who would then be highly motivated to do whatever it took, from mugging to murder, to get the next fix. Blocks of East Harlem and Washington Heights were all but controlled by gangs: the Wild Cowboys, the Young Talented Children, and the Jheri Curls, a multimillion-dollar business headquartered on West 157th Street that hired legions of teenaged dealers who paid for cars, guns, ammunition, and wages for their own employees and still managed to clear thousands of dollars each week. It was a story begging to be transmuted into art.

Rap music was invented by the sons of welfare families living in housing projects and tenements in Harlem and the Bronx, and although boasting about romantic conquests or the verbal skill and ingenuity of the rapper was central to the incipient aesthetic, racism, poverty, hunger, disease, drugs, violence, joblessness, war, and police corruption were just as important. After the heyday of the Last Poets, the music that would develop into rap could be heard at "park jams," outdoor parties in parks, empty lots, in the streets, or in playgrounds in the early 1970s. A disc jockey operating a double turntable powered by an illegal connection to a lamppost often overlapped the beginning and ending of songs, a technique known as "cutting." Some played entire records simultaneously or scratched the records back and forth under the needle of the turntable, which effectively introduced a new instrument, part percussion, part electronic effect, into the repertoire of American music. Running the party was an MC, or master of ceremonies, who greeted revelers, challenged competitors, or "rapped" about everything from his love life to politics.

Music historians have emphasized the importance of the South Bronx in the development of hip-hop, but the earliest rappers seem to have been two Harlemites called DJ Baron and DJ Breakout, who performed at parties in the mid-1970s at the Minisink Community Center. By the late 1970s Harlem rappers Disco King Mario, Eddie Cheever (also known as Cheba, slang for marijuana), DJ Lovebug Starski, and DJ Hollywood were poised to become more commercial, in part because their easygoing, humorous raps were simply more fun than the harsher, more politically confrontational style that developed around the same time across the Harlem River. It also didn't hurt that Harlem abounded in long-shuttered performance venues, including the medium-sized spaces Studio 125, Harlem World, the C and C Disco, and the Phipps Police Athletic League, as well as the eminent theaters Smalls Paradise, the Renaissance Ballroom, the Audubon Ballroom, the 369th Regiment Armory, and the Apollo. These shows were dominated by rappers such as Dancin' Doug from the Polo Grounds Houses, the Disco 4 from the Drew Hamilton projects, the Magnificent 7 from the Eastside Houses, and the Cold Crush Brothers' JDL—the son of a fervent Five Percenter—from the St. Nicholas Houses. Audiences also applauded Bronx residents Afrika Bambaataa (who grew up in Harlem), DJ Pete Jones, Grand Wizard Theodore, and a Jamaican named Clive "Kool Herc" Campbell, who introduced to the rap repertoire the highly kinetic, jagged, limb-twisting style of street choreography known as break dancing. Many of these characters were recruited from a dingy second-story drug den in the South Bronx called Disco Fever and brought to Harlem by two Columbia students named Ovid Santoro and José Alfano—just like John Hammond, another young Ivy Leaguer who discovered the future of music uptown back in the 1930s.

Rap's watershed moment came in 1977 at a 125th Street performance space called the Charles Gallery, when a City College sophomore named Russell Simmons met Kurtis Blow, a fellow student who was spending most of his time rapping at anyone who would listen. Simmons saw the commercial potential of this new art form and started booking Blow and a second generation of rap pioneers. Also in his stable of talent was Run DMC, the group that Simmons's brother Joseph "DJ Run" Simmons started with two friends named

Jason "Jam Master Jay" Mizell and Darryl "DMC" McDaniels. They used to raise lunch money at Harlem's Rice High School by selling bootleg cassettes of rap shows. Simmons and Blow's first record, 1979's "Christmas Rapping," quickly moved from 125th Street's Record Shack to the national chains and made Blow rap's first star. The record also turned Simmons from a struggling promoter of a motley crew of street kids into the head of what would soon become the largest black music company in the world. But back in 1979 Simmons still had competition in the form of Sugar Hill Records, a New Jersey company that scoured uptown's streets looking for talent and came up with the high-speed rapper Kool Moe Dee, the Crash Crew from the Lincoln Projects, as well as the Treacherous Three and the Fearless Four, both from the St. Nicholas Terrace Projects. It was the Sugar Hill Gang's "Rapper's Delight" that became the first rap hit, selling two million copies in the United States in 1980 and another six million internationally. Rap had moved from a local, folk phenomenon to mass entertainment, and Sugar Hill soon had a full roster of hit makers, including Grand Master Flash and the Furious Five, whose 1982 hit "The Message" ushered in a new, more politically aware style known as "conscious rap." It was hard for many outsiders to believe that rap was just starting, or that within a few years it would become the number-one-selling genre of popular music in the world. Harlemites weren't surprised—they'd done it before.

Ironically, one of the most important figures behind the popularization of rap and hip-hop was Mayor Ed Koch, a City College graduate and longtime political liberal who was an especially despised figure uptown because of his often cavalier approach to race relations. In the late 1970s interactions between blacks and whites in New York City were more complicated than they had been since the 1950s, especially with regard to law enforcement. A poll found that more than half of all black New Yorkers believed police brutality was standard police practice, even as only 13 percent of the city's Negroes had actually witnessed or been the victim of some form of police brutality, but the issue was no less urgent because of its largely symbolic status. In 1980 the New York Police Department was ordered to address a racial imbalance that resulted in a 90 percent white police force. Things continued to improve when, in 1984, Mayor Koch hired Benjamin Ward as the city's first black police commissioner. Ward had been tarnished by his handling of the 1972 murder of the police officer at the Nation of Islam's Harlem mosque, but in his five-year term he restored much confidence in the Police Department, which had for years been plagued by corruption and racism. Ward presided over a decline in violent crime, but that may have had less to do with his management than with a rising economic tide downtown that had lifted all boats, even in Harlem. Yet Ward found he could do little to fight Harlem's drug trade, especially when it came to crack, which by the mid-1980s was less a drug enforcement problem than a public health crisis.

Koch was also considered a villain uptown because of his role in making the budget cuts that helped the city recover from bankruptcy. The fiscal crisis was over but Harlem wasn't bouncing back. The percentage of New Yorkers living under the poverty line increased from 29 percent in 1979 to 33 percent in 1990, and as always things were even worse uptown, where by the end of Koch's reign the median income was just over $14,000 per year. The majority of Harlem children were born out of wedlock, and from 1985 to 1990 the number of children in foster care in the city, 56 percent of whom were black, doubled. Koch appointed Richard Green in 1988 as the city's first black school chancellor, but the situation he inherited was too much for any one administrator, black or white. With only $5,590 being spent each year per Harlem child, half of what kids on Long Island pulled in, it is no surprise that test scores scraped the bottom. Despite the opening of a new Harlem Hospital building in 1969, infant mortality figures in the 1970s remained almost double the city average. The numbers were also considerably higher than the figure in Mississippi, a stinging rebuke to the sacrifices of the generation of the great migration that had come north for a better way of life. Harlem Hospital at one point actually ran out of penicillin.

By the end of Koch's term in office in 1989 Harlem had been virtually emptied out of its upper and middle classes, and the cultural and even racial diversity that also characterized the glory years was gone. The Schomburg branch of the New York Public Library had become the premier scholarly resource for African-American history and culture, especially since moving out of the old McKim, Mead, and White library at 103 West 135th Street and into a $3.8 million modern facility, but the vigorous and diverse local black press that had thrived since before World War I was dying on the vine. CCNY, which had expanded by buying the old Manhattanville College property in the 1940s, kept growing, with the administration undertaking a construction boom that resulted in the North Academic Center in 1983, which included a new school library named after Morris Raphael Cohen. A new stadium went up in 1990, but that meant tearing down the old Lewisohn Stadium, and no amount of new construction could hide the fact that it had been years since a CCNY degree signified academic excellence. Despite being represented by blacks in Washington, D.C., Albany, and downtown, Harlem had lost its most beloved and effective leaders. A. Philip Randolph, the stern but civilized figure once known as "the most dangerous black man in America," who more than any other single person was responsible for shattering the color line, moved downtown in 1968 after being mugged at the Dunbar Apartments. The man who inherited Randolph's style of aggressive pacifism, Bayard Rustin, was also gone, having long before moved downtown. Even the black church, which had for so many decades rooted Harlemites to their neighborhoods, suffered the loss of many generous and motivated members to the suburbs. Some churches did prosper. After the grandest of all uptown movie palaces, the thirty-five-hundred-seat Loew's 175th Street, closed in 1967, the Moorish-Oriental-Aztec structure was taken over by the Christ United Church of Dr. Frederick Eikerenkoetter, also known as Reverend Ike, who called himself "the success and prosperity preacher": he sold Christian tchotchkes on cable television and counseled his congregants: "The best thing you can do for the poor is not be one of them."

Not all of Harlem's abandoned real estate was put to such good use. The one-two punch of abandonment and arson meant that by 1990 the city had been forced to take control of some one thousand buildings in central Harlem, and conditions in these units scarcely improved under Koch. While Brooklyn boomed, especially the newly black neighborhoods Williamsburg, Fort Greene, and Bedford Stuyvesant, the disinvestment, redlining, and deteriorating municipal services of the Koch years led to a further population decline uptown of 35 percent, and much of central Harlem resembled an active war zone. The popular 1984 film *Brother from Another Planet* had a character on the uptown A Train that was pulling into the West 59th Street station at Columbus Circle, the last stop before 125th Street, tell an all-too revealing joke: "Want to see all the white people disappear?"

12

OLD AND NEW DREAMS
Reviving the Renaissance

After decades of poverty, racism, crime, drugs, disinvestment, and unemployment, few people remembered the days when Duke Ellington, A. Philip Randolph, Langston Hughes, Adam Clayton Powell Jr., Joe Louis, Richard Wright, or Malcolm X could make all of Harlem and much of the rest of the world sit down and pay attention or stand up and cheer. So it was a glorious moment when, on November 7, 1989, David Dinkins was elected New York City's first African-American mayor. Was everything finally about to change? In the 1980s, New York City had begun to recover from the economic troubles of the previous decade but Harlem was slower to share in the good news. It was only in the Dinkins era that the pattern of population loss that went back to the Great Depression came to a halt. By the end of the decade the population had actually grown by 20 percent, to about 340,000 people. This wasn't good news for everyone. Those who deplored the deterioration of race relations in the city under Mayor Ed Koch criticized the way he opened up the uptown real estate market to white outsiders, putting thousands of city-owned properties back on the private market, where the highest bid, and not deepest commitment to the neighborhood, counted most. Then again, many longtime residents didn't quite know what to think about the gentler wave of gentrification that was being led by middle-class African-Americans whose parents had fled decades earlier. Once again, race wasn't the problem uptown, nor was it the solution.

David Dinkins wasn't the only Harlemite to reach national prominence. After managing Jesse Jackson's historic 1989 presidential campaign, Ron Brown became the first black leader of the Democratic
National Committee. That same year Colin Powell, who as a child lived
on Morningside Avenue, became the first black chair of the United
States Armed Forces. More troubling was the rise to prominence of
the Nation of Islam's Louis Farrakhan, who was still suspected uptown
of having masterminded the murder of Malcolm X. The local news on
race matters also wasn't always good. Conflicts between longtime Harlemites and Korean shop owners on 125th Street and two high-profile
racial murders in Brooklyn—was this more evidence that Harlem might
no longer be the focal point of the nation's African-American community?—showed how combustible things still were. Many observers
wondered whether the trickle of government and nonprofit initiatives
attempting to transform neighborhoods like West 129th Street between
Fifth and Lenox avenues, which the *New York Times* famously called
"Another America" in 1994, did as much harm than good, since both
the criminals and their victims were being forced out. Either way, at
some point in the late 1990s that trickle turned into a river, as a billion
dollars in city, state, federal, and private economic development funds
began flowing into Harlem. Whites began arriving, attracted by housing that remained undervalued even after quintupling in price over the
past decade—even as apartments averaging about $300 per month in
notorious public housing projects drew tenants from a long waiting list.
That was just the start. The largest burst of commercial development
and new housing construction in a century was only starting, although
money for huge, showy projects and tourism gobbled up most of the
funds. Only 16 percent went to small businesses, and less than a percent
supported social initiatives.

David Dinkins was not the first African-American from Harlem to
run for mayor. Percy Sutton, Basil Paterson, and Denny Farrell had
all aspired to the office, but each was undone by a failure to capture
broad support outside the city's black community. Dinkins avoided

that problem by resurrecting John Lindsay's old constituency of mainstream minority voters and white liberals. Even J. Raymond Jones, who had for more than half a century been making sure African-American New Yorkers won elections, came out of his retirement on the Virgin Islands to lend his support.

Over his decades of service Dinkins had earned a reputation as a gallant, somewhat phlegmatic figure, but he energetically set about attempting to heal New York's racial divisions, something that had eluded every mayor in the city's modern history. That was made all the more difficult by a City College professor of black studies named Leonard Jeffries Jr. who had long espoused views—and a wardrobe— that smacked more of the Black Panthers than the faculty club, and who had long used his position to advance perspectives on history and culture that crossed the line into a racism that was bizarre even by the serendipitous standards of Afro-centrism. White people, and especially Jews, Jeffries claimed in a 1991 academic conference, were biologically and philosophically members of a cold and soulless "ice culture" that had somehow managed to dominate the supposedly superior African "sun people." As offensive and absurd as his ideas were, Jeffries had strong support uptown, where homegrown, quasi-scientific theories about race that came distressingly close to mirroring white supremacy were nothing new. Though he was forced to step down as the chair of the Department of African American Studies, Jeffries remained a tenured professor and a popular figure uptown, while CCNY quietly tried to restore its credibility.

As in the glory years of the Harlem Renaissance, economic conditions were partly responsible for racial extremism. During the 1980s median income was half the city average, and the number of Harlemites on public assistance had grown from a third to nearly half. Harlem had made some measure of economic recovery in terms of its unemployment rate, but in some neighborhoods, especially East Harlem, joblessness reached four times the national average. The stock market climbed to dizzying heights, but upper Manhattan had become an economic wasteland. What development that did occur was controversial. Harlem was home to the city's main garbage transfer stations, Manhattan's biggest sewage treatment facility, and almost three-quarters of all of Manhattan's bus depots, which led to dangerously high rates of asthma, especially among children, although smoking, substance abuse, poor diet, and lack of exercise all contributed. Indeed, the physical condition of Harlemites was worse than ever. The incidence of cancer in the 1990s was 300 per 100,000 residents, more than twice the national figure, and childhood obesity—once a sign of wealth—was becoming a major public health problem, with more than half of all Harlem children classified as overweight. Among adults the incidence of a new disease called AIDS was 179 per 100,000 residents, more than fourteen times the national statistic. By the end of the 1990s AIDS was the number one cause of death for Harlemites in the twenty-five to forty-four-year-old age group, and the disease was killing twenty babies each day at Harlem Hospital. The overall mortality rate was double that of the city's white communities, while life expectancy in central Harlem, according to a famous statistic, was worse than in Bangladesh. Only 37 percent of fifteen-year-old boys in Harlem could expect to reach the age of sixty-five. Solving those kinds of problems was beyond the power of any mayor, whatever his race.

Dinkins's mixed record when it came to tackling the racially inflected issues of unemployment, public dependency, and crime helped his Republican opponent in 1994, Rudolph Giuliani, win by a landslide. But Giuliani struggled to turn Harlem around. Median income did rise slightly and the number of Harlemites on welfare dropped by 50 percent, but these advances were the result primarily of federal initiatives and a roaring economy. Meanwhile, joblessness uptown increased to almost 20 percent by the end of his first term, and three-quarters of all children in central Harlem still lived in poverty. Giuliani, who had accused Dinkins of being soft on crime, took credit for a huge reduction in crime in the city. In fact, it was Dinkins who had increased the size of the police force and deployed officers on neighborhood beats, an approach to public safety that took cops out of their locked, bulletproof patrol cars and back in the faces of New York's criminals. The number of offenses in some areas uptown dropped by almost a third. The number of burglaries below 125th Street fell by 84 percent and rape incidence dropped by 54 percent, while the murder rate dropped 80 percent. Drug dealing was still a major problem. Heroin remained a particular challenge, especially because of the crimes committed by addicts, and because of the rising incidence of AIDS among users of intravenous drugs. But the drug of choice for both dealer and user was still crack, and the money to be made in Harlem, where 90 percent of all cocaine coming into the city was processed, was astonishing. On what the *Daily News* called "Harlem's worst block," West 140th Street between Seventh and Eighth avenues, eight out of thirty-six tenements were given over to the drug trade. The city was eventually able to shut down the Dominican-dominated narcotics market there, but the dealers simply moved to surrounding blocks, which soon became known as "Cocaine City."

Crime was falling but in the process many law-abiding Harlemites felt terrorized by the very public servants who were supposed to protect them. In addition to ongoing problems with police brutality, uptown precincts had become notoriously corrupt, with police officers stealing and dealing drugs. A 1994 sting operation by the NYPD Internal Affairs Unit caught on videotape three cops from the 30th Precinct breaking into an apartment on West 139th Street, stealing drugs and cash, and thrashing the occupant. Dozens of officers from "The Dirty Thirty" were eventually arrested, leading to more than a hundred convictions being overturned.

Giuliani's unwavering support for the police also meant rejecting the strategy of accommodation that generations of mayors had taken when it came to public disturbances. In early 1994, police once again received a "10-13" from 102 West 116th Street, precisely the circumstance that had led to the death of a police officer at the same spot twenty-two years earlier. Now things were different. The Nation of Islam's Mosque #7 had severed ties with the Nation of Islam, taken the name Masjid Malcolm Shabazz Mosque, and embraced traditional Islam, but Giuliani had ended a three-decade-old policy of special treatment for mosques. The police charged in, and after a confrontation in which eight cops were wounded, Giuliani backed the cops unequivocally and snubbed the self-appointed "community leaders"

Al Sharpton and C. Vernon Mason. The mayor had upheld the law but wounded the sensibilities of many Harlemites.

By that time Muslims—many of them immigrants from the Middle East and South Asia—were no longer represented solely by the Nation of Islam but by mainstream sects that, starting in 1991, considered the Islamic Center of New York, on the southernmost boundary of East Harlem, to be their flagship mosque. Within a decade there were six hundred thousand Muslims in New York City. Harlem alone counted three major traditional mosques, as well as dozens of smaller ones that resembled the old storefront churches that had for a century dotted the uptown landscape, as well as a handful of Islamic schools. There was even a mosque for Latinos, the Alianza Islamica, at Lexington Avenue and East 106th Street—the flag that waved in front featured images of a Moorish warrior and the Puerto Rican native known as a Taino—which offered sermons in English, Spanish, and Arabic as well as a wide variety of social programs, including drug treatment, AIDS prevention, and a soup kitchen. The institution nonetheless got a chilly reception both from neighborhood Christians concerned about losing their own parishioners and from Harlem Muslims concerned that this Latino mosque wasn't quite traditional enough.

It didn't take long for Giuliani to borrow a page from nineteenth-century Tammany Hall and start considering this growing minority group as potential voters. The Nation of Islam was still the public face of Islam in America, which was rarely a good thing, especially after the NOI's Million Youth March of September 1998 ended in public unrest on what was now officially known as Malcolm X Boulevard. But Giuliani knew that the group no longer represented most Muslims in the United States, and he began reaching out to mainstream Islamic leaders, who tended to be more conservative than non-Muslim blacks and therefore possible Republicans. In 1999 he appointed as the city's first Muslim police chaplain Izak-El M. Pasha, a former member of the Nation of Islam who had embraced Sunni Islam and taken over the Masjid Malcolm Shabazz Mosque, attracting more than eight thousand worshippers, most from West Africa but also from Pakistan, Saudi Arabia, and even Russia. The prominence of this African-American

Muslim Republican who drew support from a new generation of immigrants from Africa made it clear that the political rules of Harlem were changing.

In the 1960s the Black Power movement reinvented Africanness from scratch, largely ignoring the many Africans who lived uptown, and who regarded their black neighbors with a mixture of curiosity and disappointment. Africans had lived in Harlem since the earliest period of transatlantic exploration, but it wasn't until the twentieth century that Somali, Moroccan, and West African sailors or stowaways began to put their stamp on the Negro Mecca. A number of educated Africans had also spent time uptown, including the first president of Nigeria, Nnamdi Azikiwe, and K. W. Aggrey of Ghana, who married an American woman and had a daughter who became an American ambassador. A Nigerian named Kingsley Azumba Mbadiwe ran the African Academy of Arts and Research, which sponsored concerts at which Dizzy Gillespie, Charlie Parker, and Max Roach had early contacts with Afro-Cuban music in the 1940s. Emperor Haile Selassie of Ethiopia, a country that was such an important symbol to Harlemites in the 1920s and '30s, came uptown in 1954 to meet with Adam Clayton Powell Jr., giving a Coptic cross to the Abyssinian Baptist Church. In 1958 the motorcade of the Ghanaian prime minister Kwame Nkrumah, who had worked as a fishmonger in Harlem and slept on the subway in the 1940s, was cheered on by twenty thousand Harlemites and received by ten thousand at the 369th Armory, at Fifth Avenue and 142nd Street. Nkrumah was back in Harlem two years later, speechifying at the corner of Lenox Avenue and West 125th Street, and it was at Nkrumah's invitation that W.E.B. Du Bois finally decided to give up on the United States and relocate to Ghana. Another pioneer of African independence, President Sekou Touré of the newly founded republic of Guinea, came to Harlem in late 1959, and the first democratically elected prime minister of the Congo, Patrice Lumumba, spoke at a Nation of Islam rally in Harlem in 1960. In the early 1960s, Harlemites became especially interested in South Africa.

The coleader of the African National Congress, Oliver Tambo, came to Harlem in 1963, and the next year marked the first annual African Day parade in Harlem.

The best-known African uptown in the postwar decades was a Nigerian named Babatunde Olatunji, who more than any other figure was responsible for introducing authentic West African culture not only to Harlem but to the entire country. He came to the United States in 1950 on a Rotary scholarship intended to turn him into a diplomat, but he ended up becoming a musical emissary, appearing at civil rights events and recording *Drums of Passion,* which became a pop hit and led to appearances across the country, from the Apollo Theater to the *Ed Sullivan Show.* Education became an increasingly important part of Olatunji's program, and in 1964 he organized the Center of African Culture at 43 East 125th Street, which for the next quarter century offered music and dance lessons, workshops, lectures, exhibits, and concerts. It was there, in 1967, that the jazz saxophonist John Coltrane played his penultimate concert, just a few blocks away from where the composers of his signature tune "My Favorite Things," Richard Rodgers and Oscar Hammerstein II, had grown up.

Most African immigrants uptown were not looking for fame but fortune. After the successful colonial independence movements of the post–World War II period, many ambitious Africans looked to England and France for educational or economic advancement, but more stringent immigration laws in western Europe in the 1960s and '70s reoriented African immigration toward the United States, and to Harlem in particular. More than eighty thousand Africans immigrated to the United States in the 1980s from Nigeria, Liberia, Ethiopia, and Ghana and, later, Mali, Senegal, Niger, Guinea, and the Ivory Coast. Most ended up living uptown, though they worked downtown as illegal street vendors, selling wristwatches, umbrellas, luggage, sunglasses, pirated music and movies, T-shirts, and caps, as well as African textiles and sculpture. Meanwhile, their wives and female relatives opened shops on West 116th Street—after a century, Harlem once again had its own "Little Africa"—featuring hair braiding ($50 for corn rows) and extensions ($10 per synthetic plait). Eventually, French, Wolof,

Hausa, Malinke, Bamana, and Songhay drowned out English on West 116th Street, where diners could choose from a variety of restaurants specializing in not just West African food but the cuisines of individual geographical regions. The Keursokhna restaurant, at 225 West 116th Street, was a favorite of the Senegalese, among them the singer Youssou N'Dour, who made sure to visit whenever he was in New York City.

In the 1990s the relaxation of restrictions on immigration from West Africa, and the determination of the World Bank to force West African countries to crack down on deficit spending, inspiring the 1994 devaluation of local currencies and the halving of incomes, meant even more Africans looked to the United States. The number of Africans in New York City about doubled, from some forty thousand to more than eighty thousand, with most of them making their homes around West 116th Street. As with earlier generations of immigrants from southern and eastern Europe life wasn't easy. The newcomers were frequently poor and uneducated, though in some respects Africans were better off than native-born black Americans. In 1990, 47 percent of African immigrants claimed a college education, compared to 13 percent of African-Americans, and average income for Africans was a third higher than that of native-born blacks. There were also cultural differences. Most African immigrants adhered to the strict behavioral practices of Islam and therefore avoided alcohol, cigarettes, and extramarital sex, while working hard at any job they could find and living abstemiously in order to send as much money as possible back home. It was a strong contrast to the substance abuse, extramarital sex, and chronic unemployment they saw around them. Such differences were the source of tensions, just like those between West Indian immigrants and native-born blacks back in the 1920s. Some native-born blacks in Harlem called the West Africans carpetbaggers whose ancestors had sold their neighbors into slavery hundreds of years before. Some Africans replied that more than a century after the end of slavery American blacks were too lazy and irresponsible to improve themselves. The truth was of course more complicated.

Many Africans came on their own, but most were subsidized by their families or by local businessmen back home. The Hausa of

Nigeria and Niger—distinguishable by their long, white robes, their
attachment to Islamic scholarship, and their centuries-long tradition
of restless wandering in hostile territories as they sold kola nuts—
sponsored dozens of peddlers on 125th Street. Also prominent were
immigrants belonging to the Mouridi, a Sufi sect founded in Senegal in
1898 by Ahamadu Bamba, whose descendant Cheikh Amadou Bamba
saw peanut farmers losing land to the ever encroaching Sahara in the
1970s and counseled his followers: "Go forth and work." Though some
left their families behind for good, most sent money back regularly
and worked toward bringing them to the United States. By the turn of
the twenty-first century the uptown Mouridi, most of them married
men, with wives and children back in Africa, were sending more than
$4 million back home from Harlem each year, according to some es-
timates. But it would take years of work—often illegal—as cabdriver,
security guard, grocery store clerk, or delivery boy to make enough
money to bring their families over. It was a challenge that generations
of Harlem immigrants had overcome. These Africans lived in the very
same slums that had housed new arrivals a century earlier. Like those
immigrants, they often shared living quarters and even beds with those
from the same family or region. Home for many francophone Africans
was the Park View Hotel, at 55 West 110th Street, nicknamed Le Cent
Dix. In the 1990s it was a dilapidated single room occupancy hotel, its
two hundred units filthy with vermin and overflowing with housing
violations but home to five hundred or more Africans, almost all of
whom worked as street vendors. Conditions at the hotel may have been
less than ideal, but it provided a relatively cheap and commitment-
free place to live, not to mention the chance for people from the same
region to live together. Since most of these immigrants were illegal,
fearing any contact with banks, police, or hospitals, sticking together
was imperative. Just like Harlem's Jews and Italians a century before,
and uptown's West Indians after World War I, these Africans formed
cooperative organizations to help with personal crises or offer low-
interest loans.

      By the early 1990s many African street vendors had moved their
operations closer to what was now home, with West 125th Street be-

tween Sixth and Seventh avenues becoming a collegial and chaotic postcolonial bazaar. At the corner of Lenox Avenue, presided over by the spirit and image of the father of black capitalism, Marcus Garvey, Gambians and Senegalese sold incense, beads, leather goods, and jewelery made of leather and shells, while merchants from Mali specialized in textiles. The most popular fabrics were crudely woven cotton bedspreads and tablecloths from Mali graced by bold geometric patterns in black and white, known as mud cloth. Another big seller was kente cloth, a brightly striped yellow, green, blue, and red silk item from Ghana worn only on ceremonial occasions, though Harlem's newest entrepreneurs favored a cheaper version made of cotton— ironically, this potent symbol of African civilization was now made by Korean manufacturers in New Jersey—and stitched it into everything from baseball caps and T-shirts to watchbands and neckties. Farther west were merchants from Niger and Kenya selling watches, videos, sunglasses, T-shirts, and baseball caps from China as well as leather and straw hats, baskets, and bags from Turkey. Also popular was anything decorated with the X that signified Malcolm X, a connection that many of the peddlers were unaware of, even though some of them worshipped at the Masjid Malcolm Shabbaz Mosque. Next were African-Americans selling the Qur'an as well as Afro-centric books, music, and videos, most of which were, incongruously, bought from Israelis, Arabs, or Dominicans. Near Adam Clayton Powell Jr. Boulevard, Ugandans sold posters and Senegalese sold earrings and eyeglasses, while Jamaicans capitalized on the demand for blackness by selling "African"-style sculptures that aesthetically were closer to the negrophilia of the 1920s than the glorious past of the mother continent. Closer to Eighth Avenue, the market petered out until it was just a few stands with rap and hip-hop mix tapes.

The situation on West 125th Street was clearly unlawful. Most of the hundreds of peddlers were unlicensed, paid no taxes, and sold pirated or even stolen goods. Social Security cards were available for $500. They blocked streets and sidewalks during the day and left behind piles of trash at night. But not too many people were complaining, so Harlem's cops were ordered to focus on violent crime, not on these

quiet, respectful, dapper Africans who might gross up to $700 on a typi-
cal Saturday night in good weather. Eventually, though, the established
merchants on 125th Street grouped together as the Harlem Business
Alliance and complained to the mayor. The vendors also had a group,
the 125th Street Vendors Association, which was soon unmasked as
a vehicle for some of the most unsavory political elements uptown:
the association was less a cooperative than a shakedown operation,
one that resembled the dubious organizations that sprang up in the
same place half a century earlier in the name of economic justice. Its
leader, a Florida native named Morris Powell, who had compiled a
lengthy police record that included ten arrests and four convictions
on weapons charges in his years of selling aromatic oils and bean pies
on 125th Street, collected $20 per month from each vendor in return
for "protection." It was a small price to pay since, as illegal immigrants,
many of the vendors could hardly go to the police.

   After the vendors announced plans to hold a march that would
shut down West 125th Street, the Dinkins administration, ever eager
to avoid the kind of confrontation that the previous mayor thrived on,
chose not to shut them down. The march did proceed and Harlem's
main artery did indeed come to a standstill for several hours, but
there were no major incidents. Still, many merchants deplored the
decision as an act of accommodation to racial extremists, and they
looked forward to more decisive action from a new mayor. Once in
office, Rudolph Giuliani worked out a plan in which four hundred
vendors could relocate to a vacant lot on West 116th Street on a site
owned by the Masjid Malcolm Shabazz Mosque. For a $100 registra-
tion fee and $7 per day rent—the mosque also promised to give the
city 30 percent of revenues in lieu of taxes—the peddlers from 125th
Street could set up shop in a new space that would be clean, safe, and
comfortable, with electricity and bathrooms. The Vendors Association refused the offer, while the Nation of Islam called for a boycott
of non-black shops on 125th Street, and a shadowy group of race
agitators called Concerned People for the Development of Harlem
began issuing threats about retaliation against a white government
supposedly invading black territory and putting black people out of

work. On the morning of October 17, 1994, police set up barricades on West 125th street between Lenox Avenue and Adam Clayton Powell Jr. Boulevard and prevented peddlers from setting up. A small protest resulted in the arrest of twenty-two people, including Powell, who was charged with illegal use of a bullhorn. Several dozen vendors dressed in army surplus gear gathered behind a UNIA flag and marched down to the new market, but many of the Africans declined to participate, fearing arrest and deportation. Within a few days things were quiet again. City Hall had won, and the Malcolm Shabazz Harlem Market, a $1.3 million project on a 22,000-square-foot lot on the south side of West 116th Street, just east of Adam Clayton Powell Jr. Boulevard, opened two months later, with room for 115 stores and booths, just in time for the Kwanzaa and Christmas shopping season. Soon the market had become the best place in the city to buy African and Africanesque textiles and art, attracting tour buses whose operators, naturally, got kickbacks from the merchants. This negrophilic mall, where the global economy met the universal fascination with blackness, showed that Harlem was no longer just the capital of black America but a focal point of the global black diaspora.

The struggle over West 125th Street was amicably resolved, especially since the African vendors were soon back on 125th Street, but the broader battle against racially motivated economic injustice was not over. Sometimes it wasn't even clear who the enemy was. Not long after the eviction of the illegal merchants from West 125th Street, Sikhulu Shange, a former dancer from South Africa who had for decades sublet a music shop in the Blumstein's building from a Jewish businessman named Fred Harari, received an eviction notice. Miles Davis, James Brown, and Michael Jackson had all shopped at Shange's store, located in a complex called Freddy's, but the star of the protest that followed was none other than Morris Powell, assisted by the professional race agitator and secret FBI informant Al Sharpton. The battle to desegregate 125th Street had supposedly been won decades earlier on that very spot, but a study by the Harlem Business Improvement District found that only

158 of 322 businesses on 125th Street were black-owned. Still, it was hard to believe that the protesters were, as they claimed, acting in the spirit of Adam Clayton Powell Jr.'s "Don't Buy Where You Can't Work" actions after the protests degenerated into anti-Semitic death threats. Picketers shouted that Harari was a "bloodsucking Jew" and called black shoppers who refused to honor the boycott race traitors. Protesters pantomimed lighting matches and throwing them at the store.

On the morning of December 8, 1995, one of the protesters, a fifty-one-year-old Harlem-born ex-con turned black nationalist street vendor named Roland J. Smith Jr., who also went by Abugunde Mulocko, entered Freddy's brandishing a gun. He told all the African-Americans to leave and took seven hostages—including Latinos, Guyanese immigrants, and one black Harlemite—before shooting four white people, dousing stacks of clothing with paint thinner, lighting them on fire, and shooting himself in the chest. When the smoke cleared, Smith's hostages had died—the store's sprinkler system hadn't worked and the only emergency exit had been bricked up. Despite the ferocious rhetoric of the boycott, Powell and Sharpton denied any link to Smith or his actions and dismissed the claim that the boycott had inspired Smith's actions. Powell was out on 125th Street the very next day urging shoppers to pass by a neighboring Jewish-owned store, Bargain World. Powell and Sharpton had less to say when it became clear that it was not Harari who was behind Shange's eviction but a Washington, D.C.–based, black Baptist congregation that was planning to renovate and expand. Powell and Sharpton were eventually cleared of any responsibility for the arson and murder, and Freddy's eventually reopened, as did Shange's record store, but the episode had made many Harlemites pessimistic about the future of a 125th Street in which skin color was still the biggest seller.

Fears that incidents like the fire at Freddy's would restrain Harlem's comeback were unfounded. From 1994 to 2001, more than $1.2 billion from a variety of public and private sources, buoyed by a strong national and local economy, poured into Harlem. Much of that money went into business development. Storefronts that had been vacant for decades were suddenly occupied by national retailers, and downtown developers attracted public and private development money for shopping malls and hotels. The rest went into housing. Half of the thousands of buildings that had been abandoned and taken over by the city, representing more than half of all of Harlem, began coming back on the market. Indeed, it was the upward creep in the mid-1980s in housing prices in the loveliest of the old neighborhoods, such as Striver's Row, Hamilton Heights, Mount Morris, and Sugar Hill, and those near Central Park, that told most Harlemites that a revival was in the works. A huge, unsightly condominium complex called Towers on the Park appeared in 1987 at the northwest corner of Central Park, but the real action was in the renovation of Harlem's older housing stock. Many brownstone blocks had been preserved through the nightmare years largely because of what Harlem's premier architectural historian Michael Henry Adams calls "fortuitous neglect." Hard times kept away the wrecking balls. So did City Hall: between 1999 and 2004 a wave of landmark designations resulted in five hundred buildings, about 16 percent of all Harlem's structures, receiving official protection. Among the grand old apartment buildings that remained intact was Graham Court, where Zora Neale Hurston once lived. Fifty percent vacant in the 1980s, the building stood in for a run-down and dangerous drug warehouse in the 1990 film *New Jack City.* Just ten years later prices there were rising, and rumor had it that celebrities—for instance, the actor Danny Glover—were among the building's new residents. A downturn in the New York City real estate market in the mid-1990s did slow things down, but it also brought in speculators. In 1996 the average price for a brownstone in Harlem was less than $200,000, but not for long. The row house at 4 West 122nd Street, built for $15,000 in 1889, and sold for only $7,500 in the 1940s, found a buyer willing to pay almost $1 million in 2000, though that situation was hardly representative. At that time, anyone with $400,000 could still buy a run-down, four-story, 4,500-square-foot carriage house with six fireplaces. By 2002, brownstones in good condition in less distinguished areas were going for up to $1 million. Those in need of major renovation were still available for as little as $200,000, but within two years row houses in move-in condition on Hamilton Terrace were going for $2 million or more, and houses in need of major renovation were becoming scarce at any price. In 2004 the market began to take off, starting with a wave of speculation in Hamilton Heights. The house at 20 Hamilton Terrace that sold for $600,000 in mid-2004 was flipped for more than $1 million before the end of the year. Soon owners of houses on the street were getting daily, hand-written million-dollar offers slipped under their front doors, a practice seen as predatory even by the empress of uptown real estate Willie Kathryn Suggs, who had long worked Harlem almost without competition. Now she was facing off against giants like Corcoran, which opened an office on Frederick Douglass Boulevard and brought in seventeen full-time real estate agents to start pushing uptown real estate, which still cost a third less than elsewhere in Manhattan. Particularly popular was the practice of splitting up row houses and brownstones into three or four condominiums that could sell for up to $1 million each. In 2005 the sale of a town house on West 138th Street for $2.6 million was a new record, but it was smashed the next year when a Yale economics professor agreed to pay $3.89 million for an eight-bedroom row house on Convent Avenue, which had been purchased in 1993 for under $300,000.

After a decade of steeply rising real estate prices—10 percent or more each year—a second wave of speculation began, as developers put up luxury co-ops and condominiums, many with a balcony, wood-burning stove, parking garage, gym, and concierge and valet service. That was what the developers envisioned for the Lenox, a seventy-seven-unit luxury high-rise that began rising in 2005 at the corner of Central Park North and Lenox Avenue. The advertisements referred to "The New Harlem," and with two-bedroom apartments going for almost $700,000 it was clear that few residents of the old Harlem would be among the buyers. Mixed-income developments were also part of the picture, in part because they could use tax breaks and other forms of public funding to subsidize construction, when in fact it was the market-rate portion of the building that was supposed to help finance the low-income apartments. The Kalahari, a $100 million project started in 2006 on West 116th Street between Fifth Avenue and Malcolm X Boulevard, was financed through an agreement in which half of the 249 condos would go to middle- and lower-income families. These units would be subsidized by the other half, which were sold at market rate to buyers attracted to amenities like indoor parking, squash courts, and a movie theater showing "culturally specific" films—uptown code for "black." The fact that any racial code at all was necessary was telling. More altruistic, at least in principle, were ventures sponsored by nongovernmental but nonprofit development organizations. The Harlem Community Development Corporation was organized in 1995 by the Empire State Development Corporation from the remains of the Harlem Urban Development Corporation, which had been conspicuously unsuccessful at stimulating Harlem's economy, despite having attracted almost $90 million in state money. The HCDC took over 1-10 Mount Morris Park West, which had started out a century earlier as row houses for upper-middle-class Jewish families but which had become a burned out and abandoned block known as the "Ruins"—the city and state had been unable to overcome neighborhood opposition to its plans for a drug addiction treatment facility there in the 1960s or plans for a minimum security prison for women there in the 1990s. HCDC ran into no such opposition a decade later in renovating the Ruins and selling them as town houses at market rates. There was of course a flip side to all the change. The overheated market led to rising rates of harassment and eviction, and since the city typically took little interest in landlords who stopped providing heat and hot water, failed to maintain front-door locks, or fight rodent problems, Harlemites once again took it upon themselves to fight back. The Harlem Tenants Council, run by the indefatigable Nellie Bailey, was one of many grassroots groups formed to help uptowners fight for their housing rights.

Some Harlemites were kept out of the booming real estate market not by their incomes but by racism. The banking industry had long openly discriminated against blacks, denying loans on the basis of both race and neighborhood, a process known as red-lining. Only 6 percent of Harlemites were home owners in the 1990s, the

lowest figure for any major black community in the country, though
the numbers were creeping upward, thanks to federal housing money
aimed at more than eight hundred city-owned abandoned structures
in Harlem. By 2003 the city was in charge of half that many buildings.
Most of the buildings were renovated, but the city also built thousands of new units aimed at low- and middle-income families, most
in partnership with nonprofit organizations. The Malcolm Shabazz
Gardens, a $16.5 million development of more than forty three-unit
town houses on West 117th Street, was a joint venture between J. P.
Morgan Chase Community Development; the city's Department of
Housing, Preservation, and Development; and Imam Pasha's Malcolm
Shabazz Mosque. City officials bragged that they had sponsored housing for ten thousand people in Harlem from 1994 to 2000, but one
of the city's signature housing renovation programs uptown, called
Homeworks, which targeted vacant city-owned brownstones starting
in 1995, set financial requirements that put most Harlemites out of
the running and then allowed the new owners to divide the buildings
up into two or three units that could be rented out at market rates.
Whatever the long-term goals, the city was effectively subsidizing the
profits of well-to-do landlords and helping to drive up the rents in the
surrounding neighborhood.

The trend that tripled the price of residential real estate in Harlem in the 1990s also had its effects on commercial real estate development. The creation in 1993 of a Business Improvement District on West
125th Street from Fifth to Morningside avenues, resulting in improved
sanitation, lighting, landscaping, and maintenance, was certainly a
factor. By the time Michael Bloomberg, a lifelong Democrat who was
elected as a Republican, came to occupy the mayor's office in 2002,
Harlem was attracting businesses such as H&M, Marshalls, Staples,
Krispy Kreme, the Body Shop, Starbucks, and Modell's on the west
side and Seaman's furniture, a Duane Reade drugstore, a Payless shoe
store, and Fleet Bank on the east side. But many Harlemites would
date the revitalization of the uptown economy to 1994, when President
Clinton's Department of Housing and Urban Development identified
Harlem as one of six Empowerment Zones nationwide, meaning that

over the next decade the area would be eligible for more than $100 million in federal development funds and $250 million in tax credits, as well as help in running programs devoted to job training and creation, small business assistance, and support for cultural organizations. Immediately, the Upper Manhattan Empowerment Zone, as it was officially called, became a major player. More than two dozen Harlem churches received reconstruction funds from UMEZ, including the Abyssinian Baptist Church, which got a new roof and windows. UMEZ funding—along with the support of Bill Clinton's Small Business Initiative and a grant from the philanthropist Eugene Lang, who had grown up in Harlem and attended P.S. 121—helped a native of Sugar Hill, Sharon Lawrence, transform the old Alhambra Ballroom into the Harlem Lanes bowling alley. But UMEZ tended to be drawn toward more ambitious, flashier ventures. The most successful was the $11.2 million investment in a 275,000-square-foot project called Harlem USA, which in 2001 filled most of the block between West 124th and West 125th streets from Frederick Douglass Boulevard to St. Nicholas Avenue, with businesses including a Disney Store, Old Navy, and HMV. The Harlem USA project also included a film multiplex named after the former basketball star Magic Johnson, who was also personally involved in its development. Not all of the Harlem USA project consisted of huge businesses. When the radical Liberation Books closed in 2003, unable to afford a 700 percent increase in rent, a Denverite named Clara Villarosa stepped into the gap, getting a $425,000 loan to open the Hue-Man Bookstore, specializing in African-American culture, the first bookstore to open in Harlem in decades, followed just two years later by Kurt Thometz's Jumel Terrace Books, at 426 West 160th Street, which also specialized in black culture and Africana. UMEZ also gave a $575,000 loan to Alvin Reed, the owner of the Lenox Lounge, the last remaining jazz club from Harlem's glory days, at 288 Lenox Avenue, just south of West 125th Street. Reed, who had come to Harlem from Virginia in 1945 and bought the club in 1988, made sure to preserve Billie Holiday's favorite seat from the days when the owners exempted her from the racial segregation that otherwise prevailed.

UMEZ's most ambitious plan was to tear down the six buildings
of the old Washburn Wire Factory in East Harlem and build a million-
square-foot commercial development called East River Plaza, to be
anchored by a massive Target discount department store. Commit-
ments from commercial tenants and the state Department of Motor
Vehicles also guaranteed the viability of Gotham Plaza, a $23 million
initiative of the New York City Economic Development Authority
and UMEZ consisting of a three-story building with 120,000 square
feet of commercial space on East 125th Street between Third and
Lexington avenues. Virtually next door were plans for another UMEZ
initiative called Harlem Center, a 300,000-square-foot, twelve-story
project undertaken by the developer Bruce Ratner's Forest City corporation. Yet another high-profile UMEZ initiative, though the most
questionable, was called Harlem Park, a 660,000-square-foot, $236
million project at Park Avenue and East 125th Street, on a vacant lot
owned by the ailing New York College of Podiatric Medicine. The
development was to be anchored by a fifty-one-story-tall, 222-room
Marriott Courtyard Hotel designed by the much in demand Mexican
architect Enrique Norten, which included a promise to offer a quarter
of its 2,800 construction and permanent jobs to locals. Harlem Park
would also feature 160,000 square feet of office and 57,000 square feet
of commercial space, as well as one hundred units of luxury condominiums and include a health club and a parking garage. The 2002
deal was celebrated by the usual contingent of politicians, and even
the *Amsterdam News* hailed the project. Troublingly, the developer of
what was to be the first major hotel in Harlem since the Theresa shut
down in 1966 had no experience in such a project. Instead, his major
qualification seems to have been a close relationship with the head
of the State Economic Development Agency, which allowed him to
qualify for an extra state loan at well below market interest rates. The
plans were also able to satisfy the cash-hungry college, which had seen
its enrollment dwindle to fewer than three hundred students. Work on
the project, which broke ground in 2005, went ahead slowly, impeded
by the discovery that the site was contaminated by toxic waste. The
developer was then indicted for allegedly defrauding the U.S. Depart-

ment of Housing and Urban Development by underpaying workers at a public housing development in Rockland County. By 2008, two years after the project was scheduled to have been opened, with potential tenants, among them Major League Baseball, were fleeing.

Harlem Park was for most uptowners yet more evidence that outsiders were putting uptown development dollars into their pockets, all the while advancing their own careers. One of UMEZ's attorneys, a former employee of the city Department of Housing, Preservation, and Development, went on to become the CEO of Harlem Congregations for Community Improvement, a nonprofit foundation founded in 1986 and including representatives from most of Harlem's churches, mosques, and synagogues. Another executive used UMEZ as a stepping-stone between HPD, the New York City Housing Partnership, and the Carver Bank. Even worse, in 2001 UMEZ was implicated in a massive scandal involving unscrupulous developers attracted by federal financing. So hasty was the greed that at one point contractors began the demolition of 58 Edgecombe Avenue while residents were still in their beds. Another scandal broke when the public learned that more than five hundred buildings in Harlem and Brooklyn were used as part of a conspiracy of appraisers, engineers, and mortgage brokers to get federally guaranteed mortgages for properties bought from non-profit organizations for purposefully inflated prices. The conspirators, who charged unusually high fees, would then default on the loans— $60 million in total—take the money, and abandon the properties, many of which were still occupied. UMEZ's indirect involvement in many of these properties couldn't help but leave many Harlemites doubtful about its commitment to change. It came as no surprise to these critics that by 2002 the organization had distributed only about a third of its funds, much of it to the already profitable conglomerates Disney and Chase Manhattan Bank, with very little to show for it as far as the big developments went.

Yet, there were some successes. Among the very first signs of positive change in East Harlem was the arrival in 2000 of a 45,000-square-foot Pathmark on East 125th Street between Lexington and Third avenues, achieved through the cooperation of a number of organizations, including Randy Daniels's Metropolitan Economic Revitalization Fund and Harlem Congregations for Community Improvement which would be neighbors with a Hyatt Hotel, Whole Foods market planned by football Hall of Famer Emmitt Smith. On East 117th Street's East river Plaza, on the site of the old Washburn Wire Factory, shoppers began crowding into a Costco that opened in 2009, though the store refused to honor food stamps and two months after opening laid off 160 employees. The Target store that opened in the same complex in 2010 got off to a better start, and the city was determined to renovate and expand La Marqueta. On the other side of town, the Aloft Hotel opened at West 124th Street and Frederick Doublass Boulevard, the first hotel to open in Harlem in decades. The opening of such basic neighborhood amenities may seem a meager indicator of progress, but Harlemites had long complained about the lack of full-service, affordable food stores.

Harlem's churches had been major forces in the development of housing since the 1920s, and in the 1970s they formed nonprofit organizations that built thousands of apartments. Although the most visible effort of HCCI was the Pathmark in East Harlem, the organization quietly built or renovated thousands of units of housing, including thirteen hundred apartments on Fifth Avenue between 110th and 115th streets, as well as Bradhurst Court, a $52 million development at Frederick Douglass Boulevard and West 145th Street that included six thousand square feet of retail space, a soul food restaurant, and room for 118 cars in an underground garage. Such a development may have seemed out of character for the neighborhood. After all, in 1990 fewer than 1 percent of families in the immediate area had incomes over $50,000. But HCCI knew which way the entire neighborhood was developing. By 2000 more than 10 percent of the families there were making over $75,000 per year. In addition to housing, HCCI also branched out into health care services for people with AIDS, literacy initiatives, and job programs. One of HCCI's most prominent affiliates, the Abyssinian Baptist Church, spun off a community-based, nonprofit development organization in 1989. Backed by the very considerable moral, political, and financial power of the Reverend Calvin Butts and his four-thousand-plus-member-strong congregation, the Abyssinian Development Corporation attracted and invested more than $300 million in housing and developments.

Realizing such ambitious goals didn't come easily, and sometimes they didn't come at all. Around 2001 word got out about a proposal called Uptown New York, which would take up most of the block between Second and Third avenues along East 125th Street. The billion-dollar plan called for fifteen hundred apartments and 700,000 square feet of commercial space. Residents of East Harlem, already disturbed by the opening of Manhattan's largest automobile mall just to the north, weren't bought off by the promise that Uptown New York would include a complex devoted to Latino entertainment. They were relieved when Mayor Bloomberg withdrew support for the project in 2006: The plaqns were soon replaced by a proposed $700 million East Harlem Media, Entertainment, and cultural Center, with a hotel, office and retail space, and 800 housing units. But even before the national financial crisis that began in 2008, the boom in construction was turning into a glut that resembled the speculative wave of construction that had swept over Harlem a century earlier, with similarly mixed results.

New York magazine famously claimed as early as 1998 that Harlem's revival was largely nonexistent, because the neighborhood still had no big supermarket, no video store, and nowhere to buy a television. In fact, the revival of small business activity outside the 125th Street corridor had already meant large food shops, video stores, and plenty of places to buy consumer electronics, many of them admittedly gray market. There were also some interesting surprises, especially in the culture business. In 2005 the fashion designer Malcolm Harris debuted his new collection in a show at his Convent Avenue town house, and Harlem fashions were also on display at the Brownstone, a fashion showcase and café at 2032 Fifth Avenue. That same year, the Jumel Terrace neighborhood became home to the Museum of Art and Origins, started by

George Preston, a Harlem native and professor at City College, at 430
West 162nd Street. Also in 2005, the white filmmaker Albert Maysles
moved to Harlem and founded an all-documentary movie theater that
included a program to teach underprivileged youngsters how to make
movies. There were even two new theater companies, the Faison Firehouse Theatre, on West 124th Street, founded by George Faison, who
was the original choreographer of the Broadway show *The Wiz,* and
the Classical Theatre of Harlem, founded at the Harlem School of the
Arts by two white dramatists in 1999. The company was soon being
lauded internationally for programs that included classic works in the
European tradition by Shakespeare and Bertolt Brecht as well as by
the esteemed black writers Derek Walcott and August Wilson, with a
budget that grew fast enough to allow them in 2003 to move into two
attached row houses at 645 St. Nicholas Avenue, near West 141st Street.
Even the Romanesque Revival stone gatehouse at West 135th Street and
Convent Avenue, built in the nineteenth century as a pumping station
for the Croton water project and vacant since 1984, opened in 2006 as
a venue for music, dance, and theater. By that time the racially mixed
Bill T. Jones / Arnie Zane Dance Company had moved uptown.

Literature uptown was also making a comeback. Harlem mourned
the 1994 death of Ralph Ellison, who lived at 730 Riverside Drive—
Harlemites still recall Ellison strolling around the neighborhood, with
his dapper suits and pencil mustache, greeting his neighbors in his
kind baritone—and was buried in nearby Trinity Cemetery. But his
close friend Albert Murray, a man Duke Ellington once called "the
most unsquarest man in the world," was just reaching the peak of his
influence, still making his home at the Lenox Terrace Complex. The
Harlem Writers Guild, which had helped introduce new voices like
Maya Angelou—who now lived part-time uptown—kept turning out
writers, among them the bona fide star Terry McMillan but also newer
voices such as Grace Edwards, who sets her mysteries in Harlem.

Less surprising than the emergence of a new generation of independent clothing designers or bookstores or art galleries was the continued success of restaurants. Old favorites, especially those specializing
in soul food, despite the cuisine's appalling effects on the health of

diners, continued to draw both locals and visitors willing to step off the tour bus—much resented as "drive-through safaris"—and experience Harlem at ground level. These included Showman's, on West 125th Street, which opened in 1942, and Perk's Fine Cuisine, which under the management of the former "mayor of Harlem" Henry Perkins, specialized in soul food and live jazz at Manhattan Avenue and West 123rd Street. The undisputed success in the hamhocks, smothered chicken, pigs' feet, and chitterlings business was Sylvia's, which remained not only Harlem's most beloved restaurant but the epicenter of a $20 million soul food empire. Wells Chicken and Waffles, which originated that typically Harlem dish to satisfy nightclubbers who stopped by in the 1930s sometime between dinner and breakfast, and where Nat King Cole celebrated his wedding, reopened in 2020 at Adam Clayton Powell, Jr. Boulevard and West 143rd Street. Despite soaring commercial rents, which doubled in the early and mid-2000s, entrepreneurs also began blanketing Harlem with other kinds of restaurants. Celebrity Chef Marcus Samuelsson, a resident of Harlem since 2004, resurrected the old Red Rooster Restaurant in a new location at Lenox Avenue and West 125th Street. The neighborhood under the viaduct along the Hudson River north of West 125th Street, now home to the West Harlem Piers Park, saw so many new popular new places that it was being referred to as the harlem Meatpacking District. Seats were often hard to come by at the International House of Pancakes located in Thurgood Marshall Academy, on the site of the old Smalls Paradise. In lower Harlem, fancy restaurants and food shops showed off everything from French-Mexican fusion to neo-Chinese cuisine, a caviar and champagne bar, and a wine store featuring the products of black-owned vineyards. Some of these restaurants didn't survive the latest financial crisis but a proposal to build a Harlem Culinary Institute in the long abandoned Corn Exchange building at East 125th Street and Madison Avenue kept hopes high until the building burned down and was demolished.

Things in East Harlem also changed, especially in the old Italian blocks. In the 1960s there were only five thousand Italian families left in East

Harlem, supporting just a few churches, undertakers, wine shops, and food stores. The *festa* of the Madonna of East 115th Street attracted only a few thousand people, most of them tourists, and by the 1980s it was abandoned altogether for a time. The doors of Our Lady of Mount Carmel church, which had always been kept open around the clock regardless of the weather, in order to keep the Madonna visible, were now usually locked tight to keep away the junkies, the hoodlums, and the vandals. By 1990 there were fewer than a thousand Italians left in East Harlem, most of them elderly residents of public housing, and a decade later that number had fallen to only some four hundred. As the Latino community in East Harlem grew, the *festa* was overshadowed by the Three Kings Parade each January. The longtime neighborhood favorite Andy's Colonial restaurant closed in 2003, as did the unnamed breakfast spot at the corner of First Avenue and East 116th Street, which had opened in 1922 and served generations of local children, as well as the actors Al Pacino and Anthony Quinn, the mob boss Fat Tony Salerno, and the rapper Ice-T. Still, some of the favorite old restaurants flourished. Rao's, which dated to the nineteenth century, and remained at East 114th Street and Pleasant Avenue, was a favored gathering spot for celebrities including Martin Scorsese, Billy Joel, Tony Bennett, Billy Crystal, Woody Allen, and Robert De Niro, though an infamous shooting in 2004 scared away many patrons. That didn't bother the organized crime figures who kept coming; FBI wiretaps picked up mob bosses feuding not about hits and percentages but about rights to the different tables. Above the restaurant, and totally aboveboard after a 2005 renovation, were twenty-two units of high-priced rental apartments, with one-bedrooms going for $2,000 per month and a two-bedroom penthouse available for $5,400 per month. Slightly less colorful than Rao's was Patsy's Pizza, which opened in 1933 at First Avenue and East 118th Street and once took a takeout order of three hundred pies from Frank Sinatra, for delivery to California. Also going strong were Louie and Ernie's pizzeria, which opened in the 1940s, and Morrone's bakery, which when it opened in 1958 on East 116th Street between First and Second avenues competed with more than two dozen other Italian bakeries nearby. By the turn of the century it was the only one. Median income in El Barrio went up

10 percent during the Giuliani years, while the number of owner-occupied housing units was up by almost a fifth, and the number of college-educated residents increased by 45 percent.

Another surprise in the new century was the rebirth of the up-town art scene. The Studio Museum in Harlem thrived under the leadership of Thelma Golden, whose 2004 show *Harlemworld: Metropolis as Metaphor* introduced to the wider culture the term "post-black," but the most exciting developments were to be seen in the dozens of smaller, independent spaces that built relationships with the artists who started moving back to Harlem. The best known of the new gal-leries was Triple Candie, on West 126th Street, which dazzled visitors with a 2006 show of found art and multimedia and conceptual works by David Hammond. As impressive as the art scene became, some of the most vital cultural energies came from music, as they always had. The movable musical feast known as the Jazzmobile survived, attracting huge crowds each summer to Grant's Tomb. Long-standing institu-tions including the Lenox Lounge, Showman's Café, and St. Nick's Pub remained popular. New clubs also sprung up—Jimmy's Uptown, the Lickety Split, the Robin's Nest, and Striver's Lounge. Even Minton's, the birthplace of bebop, reopened in 2006 after decades of standing vacant.

Of course, by the time of Harlem's New Renaissance, the music to be reckoned with was hip-hop. But popularity came at a price. A 1991 charity basketball game with rap entertainment at City College turned disastrous when more than five thousand people showed up, far more than the facility could accommodate. With seven security guards sharing two walkie-talkies and nine of the gym's eleven exits locked, a mob scene ensued that killed nine people. As for the music most associated with Harlem, on the fortieth anniversary of Art Kane's famous 1958 photograph of the greatest figures of the jazz world, only eleven survivors of the original could be found, and the building they stood before on East 126th Street was a boarded-up ruin. It was nonetheless a fitting backdrop for the more than two hundred rappers gathered for an updated version of the old photograph by an eighty-four-year-old Gordon Parks, including hip-hop pioneers Kool Herc, Grand Master Flash, DJ Hollywood, and Kurtis Blow, who had become a born-again Christian and host of a "Hip Hop Church." By that time, rap had produced its second generation of artists, among them Andre Harrell of the duo Jekyll and Hyde, who went on to head up Motown Records, an East Harlemite named Damon Dash, whose Roc-A-Fella Records recorded Jay Z and Kanye West, and Dash's boyhood buddy Cam'ron, who in turn recruited the rapper known as Ma$e.

Many older Harlemites had trouble making the leap from jazz to rhythm and blues to soul to rap, but not the Apollo Theater, although Harlem's most hallowed hall did have its troubles. There had been more than a decade of sporadic openings and closings, with numerous aborted attempts at revitalization, all trumpeted with great fanfare before descending into infighting, incompetence, and greed. Percy Sutton's vision of the Apollo regaining its old splendor was sound, but his timing was off, and by 1992 he had ceded control of the theater to the nonprofit Apollo Theater Foundation, chaired by Congressman Charles Rangel. It wasn't until 1995, when the Apollo Foundation was taken over by Grace Blake, that the theater began its comeback. That year, Malcolm X's widow Betty Shabazz chose the Apollo to come to a public reconciliation with Farrakhan. The old guard still played an important role in running the theater and in deciding its future. In 1998 the foundation's board of directors rejected a million-dollar bid to redevelop the theater, instead accepting a $400,000 offer by none other than Percy Sutton. The New York State attorney general, frowning on the deal, dissolved the board, but Sutton's Inner City Broadcasting was able to get a four-year contract for exclusive rights to broadcast from the Apollo for only $200,000, while eventually netting $26 million in proceeds. Meanwhile, the Apollo was building up its reputation yet again, now led by Harlemite and former AOL/Time Warner executive Derek Q. Johnson, who envisioned it as the centerpiece of a large-scale cultural complex on West 125th Street. That seemed like a long shot. In 2000 only one act per week was appearing at the theater; with fewer than two thousand seats, the theater was too big for small acts and too small for big acts, and ticket buyers still complained about that famous first balcony obscuring the view. The precipitous fall in donations from nonprofit foundations, corporations, and individuals that followed the terrorist attacks of September 11, 2001, threatened the Apollo's fund-raising, but the 2002 musical *Harlem Song*, produced by George Wolfe of the Public Theater, helped keep the theater afloat, though many Harlemites scorned the show as a nostalgic journey through a past that was as distant as it was glorious.

Despite the success of *Harlem Song*, the foundation's board soon put an end to Johnson's grand vision for the Apollo and kept the theater focused on what it had always done best. By 2004 the annual budget reached $10 million, with three hundred acts per year. It was at that point that the foundation's board authorized yet another renovation, this time including a new marquee, fixing the seats, installing new carpeting, and updating the audio and lighting systems. After seven decades Amateur Night remained popular, reaching a nationwide audience via a syndicated cable television show. Each week seventy-five people were auditioning, spending ninety seconds trying to gain a coveted spot before the most fearsomely honest audiences in the world the following Wednesday. After the 2006 death of James Brown, who in his final years had taken to stopping by unannounced to play the theater's piano in private, was there any alternative but to hold his memorial service at the Apollo?

The Apollo was certainly poised to survive Harlem's future. The same could not be said of its neighbor, the old Loew's Victoria Theatre, at 235-37 West 125th Street, which was built in 1917. In 2005 developers announced a plan to tear down the theater and build a twenty-five-story tower that would include a luxury hotel and 160,000 square feet of commercial space, as well as a Black Sports and Entertainment Hall of Fame. There was also talk of making the new complex the permanent home of the Classical Theater of Harlem and the Harlem Arts Alliance. Even the financial turmoil of 2008 didn't stop the city council from turning the seemingly cursed Uptown New York site on East 125th Street between Second and Third Avenues into a $700 million development featuring 800 apartments—600 of them for low- and moderate-income families—and a media and entertainment complex with an attached hotel. A Museum of African Art broke ground in the condominum tower at 1280 and Fifth Avenue, and the National Jazz

Museum in harlem, along with a movie theater, café, shops, and a city tourism center, were poised to move into a space across the street from the Apollo Theater and occupied from 1986 to 2001 by Mart 125.

The most controversial project facing Harlem in the first decade of the new century, but the one with the best chance of happening, involved Columbia University, which historically had had unproductive relations with its neighbors to the north and east. After the "Gym Crow" debacle of 1968, Columbia kept a low profile, though it did quietly buy dozens of properties near the campus. Its efforts to buy the famed Audubon Theatre were impossible to keep quiet. The old dance hall had closed its doors shortly after Malcolm Shabazz's murder in February of 1965 and was taken over by the city two years later, after the owner had failed to pay taxes. For a time it housed an automobile dealership before being used by the city's Department of Housing, Preservation, and Development, the Office of Neighborhood Services, and Community Board 12—it was known as "Little City Hall." In the 1980s, Columbia acquired the property and planned to demolish the entire building and put up a biomedical research center, but the university ran into strong neighborhood opposition. In one of the few instances when community opposition against grand plans succeeded, the two sides reached a compromise. A brand-new, five-building complex would go up on the site, including space for community organizations. The original polychromed terra-cotta facade would be preserved, and amenities would include a bank, a bookstore, a barbecue restaurant, a coffeehouse called the X Café, and a club called the Audubon Bar and Grill, featuring jazz on Monday nights. In 1997 a sixty-three-foot-long mural commemorating Malcolm X was installed and in 2003 a museum devoted to Malcolm X went up on the site, which now included shops, a theater, meeting halls, a restaurant, a bank, a worship center, and the Harlem–Washington Heights Historical Society.

Columbia's efforts to reshape eighteen blighted acres north of Morningside Heights proved more problematic. Manhattanville, where George Washington won his first significant victory of the Revolutionary War, and later a nineteenth-century hub of trade and manufacturing, had by the 1990s become what one observer called "an industrial slum." Less circumspect Harlemites called it "Murderville." Hemmed in between the subway viaduct and the elevated West Side Highway were only a few dozen residential buildings and businesses, including a massive and busy Fairway grocery store that opened in 1989 among the vacant lots, tire recappers, self-storage locations, bait shacks, and meatpackers. Columbia looked toward Manhattanville as a way to ease crowding on its campus, hiring the Italian architect Renzo Piano to come up with a master plan. The result was a striking vision of a $7 billion, seven-million-square-foot satellite campus with glass-fronted buildings as high as twenty-five stories containing housing, offices, Columbia's School of the Arts, and a brain science center, all surrounding a central piazza highlighted by cafés and shops, in addition to a convention center, a hotel, and an Amtrak stop. Columbia promised Harlem two thousand construction jobs over two decades and permanent employment for another nine thousand workers. Still, neighborhood opposition to the plan was vociferous. Harlemites admitted that the existing Columbia campus was overcrowded, but they believed that displacing Manhattanville's admittedly small number of residents and businesses while putting a new campus between West Harlem and a $20 million Harlem Piers park along the river was hardly a solution.

Another local concern was the environment and its impact on health care, which had been an issue in Manhattanville since 1986, when the city built the North River Water Pollution Control Plant, a twenty-two-acre facility that handled sewage treatment for more than one million residents of Manhattan's West Side. Some Harlemites bitterly opposed the project, considering the city's promise to build Riverbank State Park on top of the plant an insulting bribe. A $45 million health care center named for Ron Brown opened on Lenox Avenue near West 135th Street in the late 1990s and was welcome, but the benefits were, many Harlemites believed, offset by hundreds of job cuts at health clinics and at Harlem Hospital, which went from twelve full-time cardiologists to five, the result being that more than 7,000 heart t5ests were seriously mishandled. North General Hospital on Madison Avenue closed altogether, though it ws schueduled to be replaced with a walk-in clinic and rehabilitation center. Even the opening of a $40 million Harlem Health Center at Morningside Drive and West 125th Street, built by the hotel workers union for its more than thirty-six thousand affiliates, promised little in terms of overall health conditions. Uptowners expected more from Harlem Hospital's five-year, $226 million program of renovation and expansion, but no single hospital could do much to change an appallingly high mortality rate, an explosion of obesity among children, a deplorably high number of AIDS-infected babies dying every day, asthma rates double those of the city average, drug addiction rates twice those of other New York neighborhoods, and triple the incidence of childhood mental illness—all in a neighborhood in which one-third of all residents had no health insurance.

Columbia asserted that its Manhattanville campus would provide enough jobs to help lift the entire surrounding neighborhood out of the poverty behind the health problems. As for environmental concerns about the hazards of biotech research, Columbia countered that the university already operated a number of such facilities with a perfect safety record, and that such a laboratory posed a far smaller health risk than the continued underdevelopment of the neighborhood or even the radically conservative plan proposed by the anti-Columbia forces, a stubbornly low-density design that would preserve all of Manhattanville's current industry and housing. In the end, Columbia was able to move forward by acquiring or agreeing to lease about two-thirds of Manhattanville. A promise from the city to use its power of eminent domain if the owners remained recalcitrant was confirmed by the state's highest court in 2010. Hunter college anticipated no such problems in the building of its new school of social work on Third Avenue near East 118th Street.

Conspicuously absent from the negotiations surrounding Columbia's plans for Manhattanville was the effective involvement of Harlem's political class. The Gang of Four wielded less political power uptown than it ever had, partly out of choice. David Dinkins devoted his energies to teaching at Columbia University, and Percy Sutton, who dies in 2009, and Basil Paterson had largely retreated to business matters. The only one still active in politics was Charles Rangel, who reached new heights of power and influence during the Clinton years. During the presidency of George W. Bush, Rangel assumed the chairmanship of the House Ways and Means Committee, which set the nation's agenda on taxes, trade, and health care—"chairman of the money," they now called him. However, political infighting and accusations of impropriety and corruption resulted in his losing considerable authority, not only in Washington, D.C., but among voters in Harlem. First, Rangel refused to endorse the Democrat Eliot Spitzer for governor in 2006 because Spitzer had neglected to seek Rangel's advice in choosing the Harlem state senator David Paterson, the son of Basil Paterson, as running mate and candidate for lieutenant governor. After Spitzer stepped down two years later in a marital infidelity scandal and handed over the governor's mansion to Paterson, it was revealed that Rangel maintained not one but four rent-regulated apartments in the relatively posh Lenox Terrace apartment complex, even as he failed to pay taxes on income he derived from a home he owned in the Dominican Republic. Finally, many Harlemites looked askance at the wink-and-nod techniques that Rangel was using to raise funds for a Harlem school that would bear his name. The eighty-year-old man who inherited Adam Clayton Powell Jr.'s seat in Congress gave up his chairmanship of the House Ways and Means Committee in early 2010 but managed to win the Democratic nomination in September—against Powell's grandson, who had recently been convicted of driving while impaired—even while facing House Ethics Subcommittee charges, had failed to learn how easily the appearence of personal impropriety could outweigh decades of public service. As for Governor David Paterson, he decided not to run for re-election after a furor over his behind-the-scenes intervention in a domestic abuse case involving one of his aides.

Meanwhile, a newer generation of politicians struggled with very personal versions of uptown history, among them Assemblyman Keith Wright, the son of the legendary judge Bruce "Let 'Em

Loose" Wright, and State Senator Jose M. Serrano, the son of Congressman Jose Serrano. Adam Clayton Powell IV served in the New
York City Council and in the state's assembly, though his career was
tarnished by accusations of sexual misconduct in 2004. Of course,
the most prominent new Harlemite of the twenty-first century was
former president Bill Clinton, who after leaving the White House
began working out of a nondescript office building at 55 West 125th
Street. Many looked askance at Clinton's arrival, claiming that he was
yet another white carpetbagger. An organization called the New Black
Panthers organized protests that included banners reading "CLINTON=
GENTRIFICATION." But it was impossible to ignore how the former president, a lifelong striver and a risk taker, a lawmaker and rule breaker, as
well as a competent jazz saxophonist and an Arkansas-bred aficionado
of soul food—Toni Morrison famously called him America's first black
president—had more in common with his new neighbors than at first
seemed obvious. Popular, brilliant, determined, haunted by possibility, Clinton quickly won over his neighbors by joining the Harlem
YMCA, starting an organization called the Harlem Small Business
Initiative, bringing his foundation Operation Hope to Harlem, and
starting public school programs in music and economics.

One of the most inspiring of the new breed of uptowners was, like
most of uptown's heroes through the ages, not from Harlem. Geoffrey
Canada, a native of the South Bronx, organized the Harlem Children's
Zone, a social services agency that blanketed ninety-seven square
blocks around Lexington Avenue and East 125th Street, including
nine thousand children, with cradle to college programs, including
arts, education, sports, job counselling, legal services, health care, and
housing. As with the efforts of Kenneth Clark's HARYOU program
from the 1960s, it seemed like an impossible task. Some neighborhoods
began to recover in the 1990s, but a decade later average annual income uptown was only $26,000, which was just under half the national
average, and only a small increase over the situation under Ed Koch's
last days. Only half of all Harlemites had a high school diploma. East
Harlem lagged even further behind, with more than 50 percent of its
residents living in poverty and more children in foster care than in

any other area in the entire country Canada, who envisioned a "no-excuses culture of high expectations, marketplace accountability, and tightly structured schedules," told parents: "Nobody's coming to save your children. You have to save your own children."

Canada realized that making changes would depend on making the most of Harlem's overcrowded, understaffed, dilapidated public schools. The old Benjamin Franklin High School, at Pleasant Avenue and East 116th Street, had been reinvented as the Manhattan Center for Mathematics and Science, but by the time students were ready for high school the damage was already done. In El Barrio three-quarters of all fourth graders were failing to read at grade level, and during the Bloomberg years most Harlem schoolchildren still weren't earning a high school degree. Canada founded Promise Academy, a privately funded charter school—meaning that it was exempt from normal union regulations governing hiring and firing—at Madison Avenue and East 125th Street that, starting in 2004, attempted to offer children from kindergarten through high school not only a "dawn to dusk" school day but a longer school year that would help the youngest and neediest make the most of a summer break that would otherwise be spent in front of the television or on the streets. Canada saw that almost half of the students were overweight because of poor eating habits at home. An informal poll showed him that most of the students had never even eaten a fresh peach. Canada decided that meals served at the school, including breakfast, would consist of locally grown, organic food. Every child would also have a sports period otherwise unavailable in inner-city schools. By the end of the first school year, the number of five- and six-year-olds learning at the appropriate grade level rose from 11 percent to 80 percent, though older students were still struggling. But not everything Canada touched turned to gold. Bespite the enthusiastic support of no less than president Obama, the harlem Childrens Zone's attempts to build a Promise Academy at the St. Nicholas Houses, displacing playgrounds and gardens, ran into fierce local opposition, much of it directed at the charter schools movement in a general for its supposedly anti-union approach and its tendency to keep out special education and English as a Second language students.

Although Promise Academy received the lion's share of the publicity, a number of schools were posting extraordinary results. In 2009 East Harlem's Amber Charter School outperformed every other charter school in the city, and the Harlem Science and Arts Center, Leadership Village Charter School, and Harlem Village Academy all had more than 85 percent of their student bodies reading at grade level. In fact, the entire neighborhood was already benefiting from Harlem's revival.

The kind of innovative, local solutions that Geoffrey Canada introduced were also offered by a Jamaican immigrant and City College graduate named Maurice Ashley, the first black grandmaster in the world of competitive chess. He started a team called the Raging Rooks at Junior High School 43 and another one called the Dark Knights at Mott Hall Intermediate School. Ashley built these teams, which represented families who had lived uptown for generations, as well as immigrants from Albania, China, Colombia, the Dominican Republic, Ecuador, Mexico, and Poland, into nationally known powerhouses, despite the access to private teachers and camps that was commonplace among their competitors. In 1997 the Dark Nights were taken over by a native Harlemite named Jerald Times, who came from a poor, broken home and lived for years in the Langston Hughes house. Times, who hustled chess at the Elegance Barber Shop, on Lenox Avenue, led the Dark Knights to several national championships by preaching an uptown gospel—he calls it "the sacred hierarchy"—of God, family, school, and chess and by exposing his students to a variety of inspirations, including visits by a tai chi master and a traditional Latino storyteller. Victory in the face of similar odds has also been the story of another group of young Harlemites who made up the Harlem All-Stars Little League team. In 2002 they made it to the league World Series. Funded by a Harlem couple named Dwight and Iris Raiford, the All-Stars did it without the expensive equipment and private coaches that their opponents had access to, instead holding practices in a vacant lot and playing games in run-down Marcus Garvey Park. The same kind of improvisatory approach was also on display at the "Castle," a 1913 Catholic School called St. Walburgas Academy, at Riverside Drive and West 140th Street, which had been abandoned in the 1970s and was in 1998 renovated as a group home for fifty-nine former convicts by the Fortune Society, a social services organization specializing in reintegrating prisoners back into society. Similarly, Bobby Robinson's Happy House Records made it into the new century and its sixth decade, at new quarters on Frederick Douglass Boulevard.

Among the most prominent of the newer generation of Harlem leadership was the Reverend Calvin O. Butts III, the head of the Abyssinian Baptist Church. Born on the Lower East Side in 1949, he studied philosophy at Morehouse College before returning to New York to take a degree at Union Theological Seminary, making sure that the church remained in the forefront of the religious and secular revival. The old description of the Negro mecca, with "a bar on every corner and a church on every block," seemed truer than ever, with more than four hundred Christian institutions—from storefront, charismatic sects to established and flourishing congregations—which was almost twice the number of half a century ago. But there was nothing like the Abyssinian Baptist Church, America's best-known church, which remained a major force in community development. In 2003 the Abyssinian Baptist Church spent $36 million to renovate the old Smalls Paradise building, at Adam Clayton Powell Jr. Boulevard and West 135th Street, to house the Thurgood Marshall Academy, a combined middle and high school that the church founded in 1993. Of course, the Abyssinian Baptist Church had no monopoly on the good news uptown. When Nelson Mandela visited New York in 1994 for the first time as the president of South Africa, he appeared at the Canaan Baptist Church, led by the Reverend Wyatt Tee Walker, who had known Martin Luther King Jr. in seminary school and who went on to become the first executive director of the SCLC. Mother Zion AME Church still boasted a sign on the outside of the building reading "We love you, and there's nothing you can do about it." Even the Elmendorf Reformed Church, at 171 East 121st Street, which traced its roots back to Harlem's very first church, was flourishing. Harlem's biggest black synagogue, the Commandment Keepers, in the old Dwight Mansion just off Marcus

Garvey Park, was undermined by a battle over rabbinical succession and sold to the writers Darryl Pinckney and James Fenton.

Even as Harlem seemed to rise from the dead, some of its most beloved institutions were in trouble. St. Thomas the Apostle Church, the gorgeous 1907 Roman Catholic institution at West 118th Street and St. Nicholas Avenue, was closed by the Archdiocese on New York, as was our Lady Queen of Angels in East Harlem, and the Church of St. Charles Borromeo's Monsignor Wallace A. Harris resigned in 2010 amid allegations of sex abuse. Even the National Catholic Museum on east 115th Street shut its doors permanently. the Little Flower Baptist church on Fredrick Douglass Boulevard closed its doors, and the Mount Morris Ascension Presbyterian Church fell on hard times, as did the Rescue Baptist Church. Even after All Souls Church closed its upstate summer camp, its Alchoholics Anonymous program, it couldn't afford a full-time preacher. The Boys Choir of Harlem, founded in 1968 by Walter Turnbull in the basement of Ephesus Church at Lenox Avenue and West 123rd Street, also fell on hard times. For more than three decades the Boys Choir was one of the most visible signs of life uptown, with numerous concert performances and recordings, international tours, and the formation of the Girls Choir of Harlem in 1997 and a Choir Academy of Harlem. Although three-quarters of the school's students came from poor homes with single parents, they outperformed many of the city's upper-middle-class communities, with a graduation rate of 98 percent, compared to 30 percent in the rest of Harlem. Then in 2003 the organization was rocked by allegations of sexual abuse by one of the school's counselors. Turnbull, the head of the choir, not only failed to report the accusation to the authorities, as required by law, or to fire the counselor, but he bailed him out with $2,000 of the school's money and, with the support of Congressman Charles Rangel and the choir board, publicly denied the claims all way to trial, where the counselor was found guilty on two dozen counts of sexual abuse. The difficulties only deepened in early 2006, when the New York City Board of Education, which had had enough of Turnbull, ordered the choir out

of its city-owned building at Madison Avenue and East 127th Street.
Turnbull managed to reach a compromise in which he would step down
as chief executive but remain as artistic director. Meanwhile, funders
fled the situation and the school's staff of coaches, accompanists, and
choreographers shrunk from twenty-five to eight and then to none.
After Turnbull's death in 2007, the choir also met its demise.

Well before the global economic turmoil started in 2008 that
ended up threatening the future of Riverbank State Park and East
Harlem's Wagner Pool and drive up Harlem unemployment to 18 percent—four times the national average—uptown Manhattan remained
a financial question mark for both philanthropists and investors. Money
problems dogged the Dance Theater of Harlem, one of New York's
premier dance institutions. In 2004, the thirty-five-year-old organization, faced with a $2.4 million debt that it attributed to declining
contributions since the terrorist attacks of 2001, closed its school after
failing to pay its liability insurance, laid off dozens of dancers, and
canceled its coming season, though a flurry of donations allowed the
school to open early the next year and the organization even attracted
million-dollar grants from the Ford and Catherine Steinberg foundations in 2006. Hard times also struck the Opus 118 Harlem Center for
Strings, which was celebrated in the 1999 film *Music of the Heart* for
reintroducing music education in East Harlem public schools, but it
turned out much of the problem was self-inflicted. In 2004 the director of the program, Katherine Gooney, admitted to having defrauded
the program of more than $45,000. A similar betrayal was uncovered
in 2001 when Lorraine Hale, who had taken over Hale House, which
her mother had founded in 1969 to assist drug-addicted mothers, was
charged by the state with seventy-two counts of mismanagement and
fraud. She pleaded guilty the next year to overseeing abusive child care
practices—her husband allegedly called their charges "cash cows"—as
well as a complex scheme in which she had helped steal more than $1
million from her own charity, in part by charging market rate rents for
apartments that she told the city would go to poor families.

City College also struggled. The school announced a $250 million
expansion plan that would put a new dormitory, academic buildings,

and research units at the southern end of the campus, yet the black-
est sheep at what should be one of the country's premier institutions
of black scholarship, Leonard Jeffries, continued to attract publicity
that undermined City College's reputation, broadcasting the racialist
philosophy that had so damaged the school's reputation.

The role of race in Harlem's future will surely be complicated. In 1997
Wilbert A. Tatum turned over the *Amsterdam News,* whose circulation
had fallen from more than a hundred thousand in the 1960s to under
thirty thousand three decades later, to his half-Jewish daughter, Elinor.
It was distressing news for those devoted to promoting one race only,
a sign that the new Harlem wouldn't be that different from the old
Harlem. To be sure, in part because of the focus on big projects and
national franchises, fewer than half of the business on 125th Street
were owned by blacks, though this was less a question of race than
of local ownership, a pattern that applied to the city as a whole. The
same was true in Harlem's residential real estate, which after a decade
of surging activity saw prices grind to a halt and start falling back in
2009. It was in part due to a glut of new apartments— shades of a
century ago?—which caused prices to fall by a third. the real estate
giant Cocoran went so far as to close its uptown offices in 2010. Even
venerable real estate like the Riverton Houses was vulnerable, its owners foreclosing in 2010. A black middle class was on the march, and
black celebrities such as the actor Samuel L. Jackson, the singer Alicia
Keys, NBA Hall of Famer Walt Frazier, the writer Maya Angelou, and
the basketball legend Kareem Abdul-Jabbar were all rumored to have
bought homes uptown, but Harlem was less black than it had been in
almost a century, and the continuing influx of Africans, Latinos, Asians,
and whites promised to make it a more diverse community. By 2005
the area's racial balance had changed so drastically that for the first
time in decades a Harlem neighborhood was represented by a white
City Council member. Then again, new attitudes about race—was
"post-black" the right word?—were sweeping across Harlem. In 2005
a charming little family-owned thrift shop on West 125th Street spe-

cializing in black memorabilia began selling mementos from the Jim Crow era, from ashtrays and cookie jars featuring corpulent, coal-black Jemimas and grinning Uncle Toms to an actual KKK hood. Harlemites rejoiced in November 2008 over the election of Barack Obama as the first black president, but not all of them—the *Amsterdam News* had backed Hillary Clinton in the Democratic primary, remembering that picking politicians by skin color hadn't always been good for Harlem.

Although the arrival of an African community was the most visible development in recent decades, the continuing Latinization of uptown Manhattan may prove more significant. The percentage of African-Americans in Harlem dropped from 88 percent in 1990 to 80 percent in 2000 to 40 percent in 2010, but as much as a third of that figure consisted of Latinos of partially African descent who did not claim black racial status on census forms. Meanwhile, the number of whites increased to about 8 percent, or some twenty-three thousand, although again Latinos—mostly Dominicans, Puerto Ricans, and Mexicans—posed a particular statistical challenge, since many of those who were racially white tended to identify by ethnicity when it came to the census. In East Harlem, the number of non-Hispanics was growing so fast that by the turn of the century non–Spanish speakers made up 45 percent of the population. Such figures were closely watched by Julián Zugazagoitia, the Mexican director of the Museo del Barrio, which since 1977 has operated from a former orphanage at Fifth Avenue and East 104th Street. Tougher national attitudes toward illegal immigration—such as proposals to deny public services including education and food stamps to the children of illegals—and more restrictions on legal immigration may slow the "whiting up" of Harlem. But how reliable an indicator of economic status will skin color remain? James Weldon Johnson asked back in 1930: "Will the Negroes of Harlem be able to hold it?" He thought not, though the process is taking longer than he'd imagined.

If the transformation from a multiracial if segregated community into a black monolith coincided with the decline of Harlem, changing demographics since the 1990s that promised more diversity in the capital of blackness are also bringing new challenges. A rising middle class seemed to inspire a new wave of muggings and robberies of tourists, new residents, and commuters at the 125th Street Metro North station in 2006—cops warned outsiders and newcomers not be lured into vulnerability by what the newspapers said about falling crime rates. The fact that Frank Lucas's story could be filmed, as *American Gangster,* on location in Harlem in 2006 was one sign of how slowly things were changing—it took little cosmetic work to make some blocks resemble the burned-out ghetto of the 1970s. But this wasn't a simple matter of aesthetics. Crime continued to be an all-too-common fact of life and death, especially after the economic boom ended and the uptown housing bubble burst. Drugs were still for sale out on Lexington Avenue and East 125th Street, and while the number of shootings was virtually unchanged citywide from 2009 to 2010, in East Harlem the figure was up by 243 percent, and other uptown precincts weren't far behind. In 2007 the Reverend Philip Mann, who for almost three decades had served as the leader of the Blessed Sacrament Baptist Church, was stabbed to death in his home on Fifth Avenue. Such events led Harlemites to ask, What enabled the Dutch, the Germans, the Irish, the Italians, the Jews, and to a lesser extent the Latinos to live out the American dream, while the Negroes, who arrived with more or less equivalent levels of poverty and education, have not? To be sure, the nature of community life in Jewish, Italian, and Latino East Harlem, protected from the incursions of outsiders by language barriers, was very different from that of African-Americans. Single or married men who temporarily left their wives and children behind constituted the bulk of the first waves of Jewish, Italian, and Latino immigrants, but eventually intact and even extended families became bastions of stability that provided for a better chance at psychological and economic well-being and advancement. Meanwhile the black family unit, under attack for centuries, became less stable as time went on. Also, the deplorable and yet somehow deeply American discrimination experienced by minority immigrants uptown did not compare to the suffering experienced by African-Americans who had fled the legal terror of Jim Crow in the South to find conditions that were only marginally better in Harlem.

It is a time-honored uptown tradition to misread Harlem's changes. The notion that this time is the fire next time has echoed from the stepladders of the Seventh Avenue speechifiers for more than a century. After all, change is Harlem's defining characteristic, as much as improvisation is the watchword of its music, from jazz to rap, bred by the people who live on what the Indians call the River that Runs Both Ways. At the same time, some things have not changed over the centuries, such as the tensions between natives and new arrivals—between Indians and European settlers in the seventeenth century, between Protestants and Catholics, between western and eastern European Jews, between Jews and blacks, between native-born Negroes and West Indians, between Puerto Ricans and Dominicans, and between African-Americans and African immigrants. Such tensions have always reflected and inspired both conflict and more progressive ways of understanding social identity and its relation to economic class. The line that Harlemites have always walked between secular pleasures and the demands of religion has resulted in a popular culture—from blues to hip-hop—deeply informed by the quest for justice. Strains between the desire for self-determination uptown and the inevitability of downtown authority have always given rise to Harlem politicians with an often fatal streak of independence. Collisions between the quest for economic self-sufficience and dependence on outsiders with grand plans, from the Randel plan to the Manhattanville project, have always allowed Harlemites to define themselves not just as apart from all other New Yorkers but as the divided soul of the city itself.

Nonetheless, this time around, Harlemites are witnessing the most important transformation of the community in six decades. For the first time since the 1920s Harlem is attracting wealth. The rich are once again preceded by a group of related strivers—American-Africans this time, instead of African-Americans—seeking to take advantage of what is still the most undervalued real estate on the island. The distant approach of the long-awaited Second Avenue subway and the development of the Hudson and Harlem waterfronts promise to turn the uptown economy away from real estate speculation and toward a more sustainable mix of residential and business activity, an echo of the events a century ago that brought so much promise. In 2006 the Department of City Planning began a project that analyzed the zoning patterns along 125th Street from river to river to allow higher buildings containing housing, office space, and shops at the major intersections, particularly those with subway stations, while retaining the low-rise, neighborhood feel of the surrounding residential blocks. How could that be bad, especially if it protects Harlem's sacred places, from the Apollo, where performers still rub the last remaining stump of Seventh Avenue's Tree of Hope before taking the stage, to the Theresa Hotel, which was scheduled to become a satellite location of Columbia University's Teachers College, and from the newly swinging Minton's to the Harlem YMCA, which after remaining closed altogether from 1975 to 1992 completed a $2.5 million renovation in 2004, and the West 135th Street's Schomburg Center of the New York Public Library, which underwent an extensive expansion and renovation in 1990, topped off by a ceremony in which Langston Hughes's ashes were reinterred under the lobby? The old Blumstein's sign is no longer visible on 125th Street, but it is not gone—only obscured by a banner from Touro College of Osteopathic Medicine, which was founded as a Jewish educational institution in 1970 but now courts students of every religion, even while serving only kosher food and shutting down on the Sabbath.

The same combination of hard work, good luck, and faith allowed the Hamilton Grange to be lifted carefully from its spot on Convent Avenue and West 141st Street and inched down the block and around the corner to the more bucolic and historically authentic setting of St. Nicholas Park. The wild turkey that was recently spotted at the Riverton Houses reminded Harlemites of the transformative power of their recorded past and their imagined future, both always in the making.

ILLUSTRATION CREDITS

Manatus Map: Library of Congress

Indian Woman and Child: W.L. Calver/Reginald Pelham Bolton, *Indian Paths in the Great Metropolis*

Signature of Jan de la Montagne: James Riker, *Revised History of Harlem*

Pieter Stuyvesant: Hendrick Coutourier/New-York Historical Society

New Harlem Village Plots: James Riker, *Revised History of Harlem*

Map of Harlem: James Riker, *Revised History of Harlem*

Morris-Jumel Mansion: Detroit Publishing Company/Library of Congress

View of Harlem from Morrisania: Emmet Collection/New York Public Library

The Battle of Harlem Heights: *Harper's Weekly*

Hamilton Grange: Jamison Stoltz

Harlem Plains: George Hayward/New York Public Library

Eliza Jumel: William Henry Shelton, *The Jumel Mansion*

View of the Hudson at Manhattanville: Museum of the City of New York, Gift of Miss Alice Lawrence

Fast Trotters on Harlem Lane: John Cameron/Library of Congress

Lenox Avenue North from West 110th Street: *Valentine's Manual*

Jacob Cantor: *Notable New Yorkers*

"Who Stole the People's Money?": *Harper's Weekly*

West 133rd Street: Silas A. Holmes/New-York Historical Society

The Hebrew Orphan Asylum: New York Public Library

Manhattanville Shore: Wallace Bruce, *Panorama of the Hudson*

Richard Croker: *Notable New Yorkers*

Oscar Hammerstein I: *Notable New Yorkers*

The Harlem Opera House: Museum of the City of New York, Byron Company, Museum Purchase, 1941

Harlem's Little Italy: Museum of the City of New York, Byron Company Collection

Boat Parade on the Harlem River: Library of Congress/B.J. Falk

Fifth Avenue between116th and 117th Streets: Museum of the City of New York, Photo Archives

"Lefty Louie" Rosenberg and "Gyp the Blood" Horowitz: Bain News Service/Library of Congress

George Gershwin: Bain News Service/Library of Congress

Groucho and Harpo Marx: British Film Institute

Harry Houdini: Library of Congress

Bert Williams and George Walker: Robinson Locke Collection/New York Public Library

Sheet Music for "The Luckiest Coon in Town": New York Public Library

Silent Protest Parade: Schomburg Center for Research in Black Culture/ New York Public Library

Charles Johnson: Gordon Parks/Farm Security Administration/Office of War Information/Library of Congress

Langston Hughes, Charles S. Johnson, E. Franklin Frazier, Rudolph Fisher, and Hubert T. Delaney: Regina Andrews Photo Collection/New York Public Library

Jessie Fauset: *Negro Poets and Their Poems*/New York Public Library

James Reese Europe and the Harlem Hellfighters: New York Public Library

Duke Ellington: William P. Gottlieb/Library of Congress

Paul Robeson: Farm Security Administration/Office of War Information/ Library of Congress

Madame C.J. Walker: Schomburg Center for Research in Black Culture/ New York Public Library

Cotton Club Menu: Public Domain

Philippa Schuyler: Library of Congress/U.S. Farm Security Administration/Office of War Information.

Small's Paradise: Bettmann/Corbis

Marcus Garvey: Schomburg Center for Research in Black Culture/ New York Public Library

James P. Johnson: William P. Gottlieb/Library of Congress

Lewisohn Stadium: Empire Photographers/New York Public Library

Ethiopian Hebrews: Alexander Alland/New York Public Library

Bookseller on 125th Street: Roger Smith/Farm Security Administration/ Office of War Information/Library of Congress

Adam Clayton Powell, Jr.: James J. Kriegsman/Library of Congress

The Feast of Our Lady of Mount Carmel: Percy Loomis Sperr/New York Public Library

Beboppers at Minton's: William P. Gottlieb/Library of Congress

Billie Holiday: William P. Gottlieb/Library of Congress

Machito and Graciela: William P. Gottlieb/Library of Congress

Bettmann/Corbis: Sugar Ray Robinson

The Riot of 1943: Associated Press

Willie Mays: Bettmann/Corbis

James Brown: Michael Ochs Archives/Corbis

Nicky Barnes: New York Times/Redux Pictures

Basketball While Harlem Burns: New York Times/Redux Pictures

Malcolm X: Marion S. Trikosko /Library of Congress

Harlem Politicians: New York Times/Redux Pictures

"We March With Selma!": Stanley Wolfson/New York World Telegram and Sun/Library of Congress

Bayard Rustin and A. Philip Randolph: Ed Ford/World Telegram and Sun/ Library of Congress

Hip Hop Poster: Charlie Ahearn/Pow Wow Productions

Geoffrey Canada: Harlem Children's Zone

Manhattanville in 2010: Jamison Stoltz

P.S. 90: Curtis + Ginsberg Architects LLP

Bill Clinton in Harlem: Associated Press

SOURCES AND
FURTHER READING

In lieu of a traditional scholarly apparatus documenting my sources, which would be irrelevant to most readers, quadruple the size of this book, and dominated by references to obscure texts available to only the most perspicacious of researchers, what follows is a guide to the most significant and accessible sources regarding more than four centuries of Harlem history. A more detailed list of sources, an extensive bibliography, and a brief guide to musical and film resources is available on the author's Web site.

Abdullah, Zain. *Black Mecca: The African Muslims of Harlem.* New York: Oxford University Press, 2010.

Ackerman, Kenneth D. *Boss Tweed: The Rise and Fall of the Corrupt Pol Who Conceived the Soul of Modern New York.* New York: Carroll and Graf, 2006.

Adams, Michael Henry. *Harlem: Lost and Found.* New York: Monicelli, 2002.

Anderson, Jervis. *A. Philip Randolph: A Biographical Portrait.* Berkeley: University of California Press, 1972.

———. *This Was Harlem: A Cultural Portrait, 1900–1950.* New York: Farrar, Straus, Giroux, 1981.

———. *Bayard Rustin: Troubles I've Seen.* New York: HarperCollins, 1997.

Attie, Alice. *Harlem on the Verge.* New York: Quantuck Lane Press, 2003.

Audubon, John James. *Writings and Drawings.* New York: Library of America, 1999.

Badger, Reid. *A Life in Ragtime: A Biography of James Reese Europe.* New York: Oxford University Press, 1995.

Baldwin, James. *The Price of the Ticket: Collected Nonfiction, 1948–1985.* New York: St. Martin's, 1985.

Bayor, R. H. and T. J. Meagher. *The New York Irish.* Baltimore: Johns Hopkins University Press, 1996.

Bell, Christopher. *East Harlem.* Charleston: Images of America/Arcadia, 2003.

———. *East Harlem Revisited.* Charleston: Images of America/Arcadia, 2010.

Berlin, Edward A. *Ragtime: A Musical and Cultural History.* Berkeley: University of California Press, 1980.

Binder, Frederick M. and David Reimers. *All the Nations Under Heaven: An Ethnic and Racial History of New York City.* New York: Columbia University Press, 1995.

Birmingham, Frederic. *It Was Fun While It Lasted.* Philadelphia: Lippincott, 1960.

Birmingham, Stephen. *"Our Crowd": The Great Jewish Families of New York.* New York: Harper and Row, 1967.

Bloom, Alexander. *Prodigal Sons: The New York Intellectuals and Their World.* New York: Oxford University Press, 1986.

Bolton, Reginald Pelham. *Washington Heights Manhattan: Its Eventful Past.* New York: Dyckman Institute, 1924.

Bontemps, Arna, ed. *The Harlem Renaissance Remembered.* New York: Dodd, Mead, 1972.

——— and Jack Conroy. *They Seek a City.* Garden City: Doubleday, Doran, 1945.

Bourgois, Philippe. *In Search of Respect: Selling Crack in El Barrio.* New York: Cambridge University Press, 1995.

Brandt, Nat. *Harlem at War: The Black Experience in World War II.* Syracuse: Syracuse University Press, 1996.

Brodhead, John Romeyn. *History of the State of New York, 1609–1664.* New York: Harper and Brothers, 1853; repr. 1871.

Brodsky, Alyn. *The Great Mayor: Fiorello La Guardia and the Making of the City of New York.* New York: St. Martin's, 2003.

Brown, Claude. *Manchild in the Promised Land.* New York: Macmillan, 1965.

Burrows, Edwin G. and Mike Wallace. *Gotham: A History of New York City to 1898.* New York: Oxford University Press, 1999.

Bustard, Bruce I. *A New Deal for the Arts.* Seattle: University of Washington Press, 1997.

Cannato, Vincent. *The Ungovernable City: John Lindsay and His Struggle to Save New York.* New York: Basic Books, 2001.

Caro, Robert. *The Power Broker: Robert Moses and the Fall of New York.* New York: Knopf/Vintage, 1974.

Chang, Jeff. *Can't Stop Won't Stop: A History of the Hip-Hop Generation.* New York: Picador, 2005.

Charters, Samuel, and Leonard Kunstadt. *Jazz: A History of the New York Scene.* New York: Da Capo, 1962.

Chenault, Lawrence Royce. *The Puerto Rican Migrant in New York City.* New York: Columbia, 1938; repr. New York: Russell and Russell, 1970.

Chepesiuk, Ron. *Gangsters of Harlem.* Fort Lee: Barricade/National Book Network, 2007.

Chernow, Ron. *Alexander Hamilton.* New York: Penguin, 2004.

Clark, Kenneth. *Dark Ghetto: Dilemmas of Social Power.* Middletown: Wesleyan University Press, 1955; repr. New York: Harper and Row, 1965.

Cohen, Harvey G. *Duke Ellington's America.* Chicago: University of Chicago Press, 2010.

Cronon, E. David. *Black Moses: The Story of Marcus Garvey and the Universal Negro Improvement Association.* Madison: University of Wisconsin Press, 1955.

Crowder, Ralph. *Street Scholars and Stepladder Radicals: Self-Trained Black Historians and the Harlem Experience.* New York: New York University Press, 2007.

Cruse, Harold. *The Crisis of the Negro Intellectual.* New York: Morrow, 1967.

Cunard, Nancy, ed. *Negro: An Anthology.* New York: Negro Universities Press, 1969.

Dance, Stanley. *The World of Swing.* New York: Scribner's, 1974.

De Forest, Emily Johnston. *A Walloon Family in America: Lockwood de Forest and His Forbears, 1500–1848*, two vols. Boston: Houghton Mifflin, 1914.

DeVeaux, Scott. *The Birth of Bebop: A Social and Musical History.* Berkeley: University of California Press, 1997.

Diner, Hasia. *A Time for Gathering: The Second Migration, 1820–1880.* Baltimore: Johns Hopkins University Press, 1992.

Dodson, Howard, Christopher Moore, and Roberta Yancy, eds. *The Black New Yorkers: 400 Years of African American History, The Schomburg Illustrated Chronology.* New York: Wiley and Sons, 2000.

Douglas, Ann. *Terrible Honesty: Mongrel Manhattan in the 1920s.* New York: Farrar, Straus, Giroux, 1995.

Ellington, Edward Kennedy. *Duke Ellington: Music Is My Mistress.* New York: Da Capo, 1976.

Ellison, Ralph. *Going to the Territory.* New York: Vintage, 1995.

———. *Shadow and Act.* New York: Random House, 1964.

Erenberg, Lewis. *Steppin' Out: New York Nightlife and the Transformation of American Culture, 1890–1930.* Chicago: University of Chicago Press, 1981.

Falkner, Leonard. *Painted Lady: Eliza Jumel: Her Life and Times.* New York: Dutton, 1962.

Federal Writers Project of the Works Progress Administration of the City of New York. *The Italians of New York: A Survey.* New York: Random House, 1938.

Fernow, Berthold, ed. *Records of New Amsterdam From 1653 to 1674*, seven volumes. New York: Knickerbocker Press, 1897.

Fields, Armond and L. Marc Fields. *From the Bowery to Broadway: Lew Fields and the Roots of American Popular Theatre.* New York: Oxford University Press, 1993. Hopkins University Press, 1992.

Fricke, Jim and Charlie Ahearn. *Yes Yes Y'all: The Experience Music Project Oral History of Hip Hop's First Decade.* New York: Da Capo, 2002.

Gehring, Charles T. *A Guide to Dutch Manuscripts Relating to New Netherland in United States Repositories.* Albany: State University of New York Press, 1978.

Gilpin, Patrick J. and Marybeth Gasman. *Charles Johnson: Leadership Beyond the Veil in the Age of Jim Crow.* Albany: SUNY Press, 2003.

Glazer, Nathan and Daniel Patrick Moynihan. *Beyond the Melting Pot: The Negroes, Puerto Ricans, Jews, Italians, and Irish of New York City.* Cambridge: MIT Press, 1963.

Golden, Thelma. *Harlem: A Century in Images.* New York: Rizzoli, 2010.

Goodfriend, Joyce D. *Before the Melting Pot: Society and Culture in Colonial New York, 1664–1730.* Princeton: Princeton University Press, 1992.

Green, Charles, and Basil Wilson. *The Struggle for Black Empowerment in New York City: Beyond the Politics of Pigmentation.* New York: Praeger, 1989.

Greenberg, Cheryl Lynn. *"Or Does It Explode?": Black Harlem in the Great Depression.* New York: Oxford University Press, 1991.

Gurock, Jeffrey. *When Harlem Was Jewish, 1870–1930.* New York: Columbia University Press, 1979.

Hamilton, Charles and Stokely Carmichael. *Black Power: The Politics of Liberation.* New York: Vintage, 1967.

Hapgood, Hutchins. *The Spirit of the Ghetto: Studies of the Jewish Ghetto of New York.* New York: Funk and Wagnalls, 1902.

Harris, Leslie M. *In the Shadow of Slavery: African Americans in New York City, 1626–1863.* Chicago: University of Chicago Press, 2003.

Harrison, Daphne Duval. *Black Pearls: Blues Queens of the 1920s.* New Brunswick: Rutgers University Press, 1988.

Haskins, Jim. *The Cotton Club.* New York: Random House, 1977.

———. *James Van DerZee: The Picture Takin' Man.* Trenton: Africa World Press, 1991.

Haygood, Wil. *King of the Cats: The Life and Times of Adam Clayton Powell, Jr.* Boston: Houghton Mifflin, 1993.

A History of Real Estate, Building, and Architecture in New York City During the Last Quarter of a Century. New York: Real Estate Record and Guide, 1898; repr. New York: Arno, 1967.

Hodges, Graham Russell. *Root and Branch: African Americans in New York and East Jersey, 1613–1863.* Chapel Hill, University of North Carolina Press, 1999.

Hood, Clifton. *722 Miles: The Building of the Subways and How They Transformed New York.* New York: Simon and Schuster, 1993.

Howe, Irving. *World of Our Fathers.* New York: Harcourt Brace Jovanovich, 1976.

Huggins, Nathan. *Harlem Renaissance.* New York: Oxford University Press, 1971.

Hughes, Langston. *The Best of Simple.* New York: HarperCollins, 2000.

Innes, J .H. *New Amsterdam and Its People: Studies, Social and Topographical, of the Town Under Dutch and Early English Rule,* two volumes. New York: Scribner's, 1902; repr. Port Washington: Ira J. Friedman, 1969.

Jablonski, Edward. *Gershwin.* Garden City: Doubleday, 1987.

Jackson, G. John. *Hubert Henry Harrison: The Black Socrates.* Austin: American Aetheist Press, 1987.

Jackson, John L. *Harlemworld: Doing Race and Class in Contemporary Black America.* Chicago: University of Chicago Press, 2001.

Jackson, Lawrence. *Ralph Ellison: Emergence of Genius.* New York: Wiley, 2002.

Jacobs, Jaap. *New Netherland: A Dutch Colony in Seventeenth-Century America.* Boston: Brill, 2005.

James, Winston. *Holding Aloft the Banner of Ethiopia: Caribbean Radicalism in Early Twentieth Century America.* New York: Verso, 1991.

Jameson, J. Franklin, ed. *Narratives of New Netherland, 1609–1664.* New York: Scribner's, 1909.

Johnson, James Weldon. *Along This Way: The Autobiography of James Weldon Johnson.* New York: Viking, 1933.

———. *Black Manhattan.* New York: Knopf, 1930.

Kasinitz, Philip. *Caribbean New York: Black Immigrants and the Politics of Race.* Ithaca: Cornell, 1992.

Kellogg, Charles Flint. *The NAACP: A History of the National Association for the Advancement of Colored People.* Baltimore: Johns Hopkins University Press, 1967.

Kessner, Thomas. *The Golden Door: Italian and Jewish Immigrant Mobility in New York City, 1880–1915.* New York: Oxford University Press, 1977.

Lemann, Nicholas. *The Promised Land: The Great Black Migration and How It Changed America.* New York: Knopf, 1991.

Lewis, Alfred Henry. *Richard Croker.* New York: Life Publishing, 1901.

Lewis, David Levering. *W.E.B. Du Bois, 1868–1919: Biography of a Race.* New York: Holt, 1993.

———. *When Harlem Was in Vogue.* New York: Knopf, 1981.

Locke, Alain, ed. *The New Negro.* New York: Boni, 1925.

Lomask, Milton. *Aaron Burr,* two vols. New York: Farrar Straus Giroux, 1979–1982.

Loza, Steven. *Tito Puente and the Making of Latin Music.* Urbana: University of Illinois Press, 1999.

Malcolm X and Alex Haley. *The Autobiography of Malcom X.* New York: Ballantine, 1965.

Marberry, Craig and Michael Cunningham. *Spirit of Harlem: A Portrait of America's Most Exciting Neighborhood.* New York: Doubleday, 2003.

Matos-Rodriguez, Felix V. and Pedro Juan Hernandez. *Pioneros: Puerto Ricans in New York City, 1892–1948.* Charleston: Arcadia Press, 2001.

McKissach, Patricia and Frederick. *A Long, Hard Journey: The Story of the Pullman Porter.* New York: Walker, 1989.

McLeod, Christian (Anna C. Ruddy). *The Heart of a Stranger: A Story of Little Italy.* New York: Revell, 1908.

Melendez, Miguel "Mickey". *We Took the Streets: Fighting for Latino Rights with the Young Lords.* New York: St. Martin, 2003.

Meyer, Gerald. *Vito Marcantonio: Radical Politician, 1902–1954.* Albany: State University of New York Press, 1989.

Mills, C. Wright, Clarence Senior, and Rose Goldsen. *The Puerto Rican Journey: New York's Newest Immigrants.* New York: Harper, 1950.

Minsky, Morton and Milt Machlin. *Minsky's Burlesque: A Fast and Funny Look at America's Bawdiest Era.* New York: Arbor House, 1968.

Morgan, Thomas L. and William Barlow. *From Cakewalks to Concert Halls: An Illustrated History of African American Popular Music From 1895 to 1930.* Washington, D.C.: Elliot and Clarke, 1992.

Morris, Aldon. *The Origins of the Civil Rights Movement.* New York: Free Press, 1984.

Naison, Mark. *Communists in Harlem During the Depression.* Urbana: University of Illinois Press, 1983.

Nelson, Havelock and Gonzalez, Michael A. *Bring the Noise: A Guide to Rap Music and Hip-Hop Culture.* New York: Harmony, 1991.

Nelson, Peter N. *A More Unbending Battle: The Harlem Hellfighters' Struggle for Freedom in World War I and Equality at Home.* New York: Basic Books/Civitas, 2009.

O'Callaghan, Edmund B. *History of New Netherland; or New York Under the Dutch*, two volumes. New York: Appleton, 1846–1848.

————. and Berthold Fernouw, ed. and trans. *Documents Related to the Colonial History of the State of New York*, 15 vols. Albany: Weed, Parsons, 1856–1887.

Orsi, Robert. *The Madonna of 115th Street: Faith and Community in Italian Harlem, 1880–1950*. New Haven: Yale University Press, 1985.

Osofsky, Gilbert. *Harlem: The Making of a Ghetto: Negro New York, 1890–1930*. New York: Harper and Row, 1963.

Phelps-Stokes, I.N. *The Iconography of Manhattan Island, 1498–1909, Compiled from Original Sources*. New York: Dodd, 1909–1928.

Pierce, Carl Horton. *New Harlem Past and Present: The Story of an Amazing Civic Wrong, Now at Last to be Righted*. New York: New Harlem Publishing, 1903.

Pirsson, John W. *The Dutch Grants, Harlem Patents and Tidal Creeks*. New York: L.K. Strouse, 1889.

Powell, Adam Clayton, Jr. *Adam by Adam: The Autobiography of Adam Clayton Powell, Jr*. Secaucus: Carol Publishing, 1994.

Powell, Adam Clayton, Sr. *Against the Tide: An Autobiography*. New York: R.R. Smith, 1938.

Rampersad, Arnold. *The Life of Langston Hughes*, two vols. New York: Oxford, 1986–1988.

Rangel, Charles. *And I Haven't Had a Bad Day Since: From the Streets of Harlem to the Halls of Congress*. New York: St. Martin's, 2007.

Rhodes, Richard. *John James Audubon: The Making of an American*. New York: Knopf, 2004.

Rhodes-Pitts, Sharifa. *Harlem Is Nowhere: A Journey to the Mecca of Black America*. New York: Little, Brown, 2011.

Riis, Jacob. *How the Other Half Lives*. New York: Scribner's, 1890; repr. Boston: Bedford, 1996.

Riis, Thomas L. *Just Before Jazz: Black Musical Theater in New York, 1890–1915*. Washington, D.C.: Smithsonian Institute Press, 1989.

Riker, James. *Revised History of Harlem: Its Origin and Early Annals*. New York: Self-published, 1881; rev. ed. New York: New Harlem Publishing, 1904.

Rink, Oliver. *Holland on the Hudson: An Economic and Social History of Dutch New York.* Ithaca: Cornell University Press, 1986.

Rosenzweig, Roy and Elizabeth Blackmar. *The Park and the People: A History of Central Park.* Ithaca: Cornell University Press, 1992.

Rudy, Willis. *The College of the City of New York: A History, 1847–1947.* New York: City College Press, 1949.

Sachar, Howard. *A History of the Jews in America.* New York: Knopf, 1992.

Salazar, Max. *Mambo Kingdom: Latin Music in New York.* New York: Schirmer, 2003.

Sampson, Henry T. *Blacks in Blackface: A Source Book on Early Black Musical Shows.* Metuchen: Scarecrow, 1980.

Sánchez-Korrol, Virginia. *From Colonia to Community: The History of Puerto Ricans in New York City, 1917–1948.* Westport: Greenwood Press, 1983.

Sanderson, Eric and Markley Boyer. *Mannahatta: A Natural History of New York City.* New York: Abrams, 2009.

Schama, Simon. *The Embarassment of Riches.* New York: Knopf, 1988.

Schecter, Barnet. *The Battle for New York: The City at the Heart of the American Revolution.* New York: Walker, 2002.

———. *The Devil's Own Work: The Civil WarDraft Riots and the Fight to Reconstruct America.* New York: Walker, 2005.

Scheiner, Seth. *Negro Mecca: A History of the Negro in New York City, 1865–1920.* New York: New York University Press, 1965.

Schiffman, Jack. *Uptown: The Story of Harlem's Apollo Theatre.* New York: Cowles, 1971.

Schoener, Allon, ed. *Harlem on My Mind: Cultural Capital of Black America, 1900–1968.* New York: Random House, 1968; repr. New York: New Press, 1995.

Schuller, Gunther. *Early Jazz: Its Roots and Develeopment.* New York: Oxford University Press, 1986.

Selvaggi, Giuseppi. *The Rise of the Mafia in New York: From 1896 Through World War II,* trans. William A. Packer. New York: Bobbs-Merrill, 1978.

Sexton, Patricia Cayo. *Spanish Harlem: Anatomy of Poverty.* New York: Harper, 1966.

Sheean, Vincent. *Oscar Hammerstein I: The Life and Exploits of an Impressario.* New York: Simon and Schuster, 1956.

Shepherd, William R. *The Battle of Harlem Heights.* New York: Putnam, 1989.

Sherman, Russell Leigh. *The Tenants of East Harlem.* Berkeley: University of California Press, 2006.

Singer, Barry. *Black and Blue: The Life and Lyrics of Andy Razaf.* New York: Schirmer, 1992.

Smith, Eric Ledell. *Bert Williams: A Biography of the Pioneer Black Comedian.* Jefferson, NC: Macfarland, 1992.

Smith, Morgan and Marvin. *Harlem: The Vision of Morgan and Marvin Smith.* Lexington: University of Kentucky Press, 1997.

Smith, Willie the Lion. *Music on My Mind.* Garden City: Doubleday, 1964.

Stearns, Marshall. *Jazz Dance.* New York: Macmillan, 1968.

Stern, Robert A.M., Thomas Mellins, and David Fishman. *New York 1880: Architecture and Urbanism in the Gilded Age.* New York: Monacelli Press, 1999.

————, Gregory Gilmartin, and John Montague Massengale. *New York 1900: Metropolitan Architecture and Urbanism, 1890–1915.* New York: Rizzoli, 1983.

————. *New York 1930: Architecture and Urbanism Between the Two World Wars.* New York: Rizzoli, 1987.

Stern, Robert A.M., Thomas Mellins, and David Fishman. *New York 1960: Architecture and Urbanism Between the Second World War and the Bicentennial.* New York: Monacelli Press, 1995.

Stoddard, Lotthrop. *Master of Manhattan: The Life of Richard Croker.* New York: Longmans, Green, 1931.

Stoller, Paul. *Money Has No Smell: The Africanization of New York City.* Chicago: University of Chicago Press, 2002.

Thomas, Piri. *Down These Mean Streets.* New York: Knopf, 1967.

Thornbrough, Emma Lou. *T. Thomas Fortune: Militant Journalist.* Chicago: University of Chicago Press, 1972.

Toler, Henry Pennington. *The New Harlem Register: A Genealogy of the Descendants of the Twenty-Three Original Patentees.* New York: New Harlem Publishing, 1903.

Tough, Paul. *Whatever It Takes: Geoffrey Canada's Quest to Change Harlem and America.* Boston: Houghton Mifflin, 2008.

Van DerZee, James. *The Harlem Book of the Dead.* Dobbs Ferry: Morgan and Morgan, 1978.

Vergara, Camilo Jose. *The Unmaking of a Ghetto: Harlem, 1970–2009.* Chicago: University of Chicago Press, 2011.

Wald, Alan. *The New York Intellectuals: The Rise and Decline of the Anti-Stalinist Left from the 1930s to the 1980s.* Chapel Hill: University of North Carolina Press, 1987.

Wall, Cheryl. *Women of the Harlem Renaissance.* Bloomington: Indiana University Press, 1995.

Ward, Geoffrey. *Unforgiveable Blackness: The Rise and Fall of Jack Johnson.* New York: Knopf, 2004.

Watkins-Owens, Irma. *Blood Relations: Caribbean Immigrants and the Harlem Community, 1900–1930.* Bloomington: Indiana University Press, 1996.

Watson, Steven. *The Harlem Renaissance: Hub of African-American Culture, 1920–1930.* New York: Pantheon, 1995.

Watts, Jill. *God, Harlem, USA: The Father Divine Story.* Berkeley: University of California Press, 1992.

Weissman, Joselit, Jenna. *Our Gang: Jewish Crime and the New York Jewish Community.* Bloomington: Indiana University Press, 1983.

White, Shane, Stephen Garton, Stephen Robertson, and Graham White. *Playing the Numbers: Gambling in Harlem Between the Wars.* Cambridge: Harvard University Press, 2010.

Wilkerson, Isabel. *The Warmth of Other Suns: The Epic Story of America's Great Migration.* New York: Random House, 2010.

Williams, Oscar. *George S. Schuyler: Portrait of a Black Conservative.* Knoxville, University of Tennessee Press, 2007.

INDEX

Frogs, 186
fur, 10
fur trade, 13

Gallo, Crazy Joe, 414
Galluci, Don Giosuele, 151–52
gambling, 151–52, 154–55, 273, 348
Gang of Four, 387, 388, 452
gangs, 153, 339, 355–56, 405–6, 412, 415
"Garbage Offensive," 406
Garcia Rivera, Oscar, 292
Gardel, Carlos, 325
Garden of Joy, 233
Garfield, John, 347
Garner, James C., 176
Garvey, Andrew ("Prince of Plasters"), 106
Garvey, Marcus, 212, 215, 246–51, 431
  Age and, 246
  black conservatives and, 246
  Booker T. Washington and, 212, 246
  Claude McKay and, 223
  criminal conviction, 251, 252
  Du Bois and, 212–13, 248, 249, 251
  expelled from United States, 276
  fall of, 273, 276, 277
  followers, 243, 246, 388
  George Tyler's attempted assassination of, 226
  Harlem and, 276, 277
  Hubert Harrison and, 277
  jailed, 276
  KKK and, 251
  legacy, 276–77, 340
  Negro World (newspaper) and, 215

overview, 211–12
personality, 245
Philip Randolph and, 212, 224, 249, 251
political and economic change and, 226–27
racial purity and, 249
radicals and, 248
Raymond Jones and, 291
song about, 252
UNIA and, 212, 215, 224, 226, 245–47, 249
gas lighting, 103
Genet, Henry, 106, 108, 132
gentrification, 421, 453
George Washington Carver Political Club, 339, 340
German Harlem, 129–30
German immigration, 100–101
German Jews, 114–16, 119, 125–26, 135, 136
  sweatshops owned by, 146
  Tammany Hall and, 129
  in West Harlem, 147–48
Gerritsen, Lubbert, 48, 49
Gershowitz, Israel, 164
Gershowitz, Jacob, 164
Gershwin, George, 164–65, 169, 191, 216, 233
Gershwin, Ira, 164, 216
Ghana, 427
ghettos, 140
Gibson, Althea, 362–63
Gillespie, Dizzy, 346, 347, 365, 367, 427
Gilmore, Buddy, 192
Gilpin, Charles, 239, 249, 278
Gilroy, Thomas, 127
Girls Choir of Harlem, 457

Ohlkert Candy Shop, 133
Olatunji, Babtunde, 428
Old Broadway Synagogue, 457
Olga Hotel, 207
Olmsted, Frederick Law, 117
omnibuses, 85
125th Street, 113, 119, 124, 196,
    412. *See also* Hollow Way
  battle to integrate/desegregate,
    282, 300–302, 332, 432–34
  black-owned businesses on, 355,
    434, 460
  demonstrations and boycotts on,
    282, 296, 302, 401, 432–34
  discrimination and segregation
    on, 184, 227, 282, 302, 307,
    355
  extension to Hudson River, 227
  Korean shop owners on, 422
  landlords on, 355, 401
  stepladder preachers on, 305, 398
  street peddlers/illegal merchants
    on, 146, 430–33
125th Street Theatre, 125, 163, 164
125th Street Vendors Association,
    432
O'Neill, Eugene, 239
opera, all-black, 313
Operation Hope, 454
Opportunity (journal), 206, 260, 278
Opus 118 Harlem Center for
    Strings, 459
orchestra(s), 78, 122, 192, 197, 270,
    321, 322, 373
  first racially integrated, 367
  jazz, 191, 269. *See also* Memphis
    Students
  ragtime, 186, 221, 269. *See also*
    Memphis Students

Organization of Afro-American
    Unity, 381, 382
organized crime, 151–56, 272–74,
    292–93, 355. *See also* drugs
Oriental America (Broadway show),
    188
"Oriental Israelites," 114
Orpheum Music Hall, 160, 161
Oscar Hammerstein's Columbus
    Theatre. *See* Columbus
    Theatre
Otterspoor (Otter Track), 19, 24
Our Lady of Mount Carmel
    church, 445
Out Ward, 50, 52
Owen, Chandler, 207–8, 213,
    221–22, 251, 252

Pabst Harlem Restaurant, 132
Pace, Harry, 235–37, 242, 251, 270
pacifism, 344
Pagani, Federico, 324
Palace Casino, 194, 215, 224, 240
"pansy parades," 271
"pansy shows," 266
Park Palace, 241, 324, 325, 367–68
Park Plaza, 241
Park View Hotel, 430
Parker, Charlie "Bird," 347–48, 363,
    427
Parker, Henry C., 178, 179. *See also*
    Nail and Parker
parks, public, 120–21
Pasha, Izak-El M., 426
Paterson, Basil, 387–88, 403, 422,
    453
Paterson, David, 453
Pathmark, 442
Patsy's Bar and Grill, 332

Powell, Adam Clayton, Sr., 180,
197, 198, 227, 230, 248, 274,
275, 329
Powell, Adam Clayton, IV, 454
Powell, Bud, 365
Powell, Colin, 422
Powell, Morris, 432, 433
Pozo, Chano, 365
preachers
stepladder, 277, 305, 398, 461
storefront, 337
street corner, 208
Presley, Elvis, 366
Preston, George, 444
Proctor, F. F., 125
Proctor's 125th Street Theater, 125.
See also 125th Street Theatre
Prohibition, 272, 283
Promise Academy, 455
Property Owners Improvement
Association of Harlem, 182,
183
property ownership, 11–13, 34
by blacks, 180–81, 230
required for suffrage, 173, 201
property rights, 38
prosecutor, public, 36
Prosperity Oil, 307
prostitution, 272, 293, 329
Protective Association for 130th to
132nd Streets, 182
Protestants and Catholics, 101, 143,
336
Puente, Tito, 368
Puerto Rican East Harlem, 230, 335
Puerto Rican Harlem, 219. *See also*
El Barrio
Puerto Rican immigrants, 336

Puerto Rican nationalism, 292,
305–6. *See also* Boricuas
Puerto Rican Revolutionary
Workers Party, 406
Puerto Ricans, 169, 210, 211, 217,
218
blacks' relations with, 229–30,
356
opposition to the "invasion" of,
244
Pullman Company, 253, 296

Quaker community, 96, 173
"quiet riots," 410

race extremists, 351
race riots. *See* Harlem Riot of 1935;
riots
racial boundaries, informal, 175
racial discrimination, 133, 181–84,
228–29, 302. *See also specific
topics*
racial segregation, 34, 90, 181, 184.
See also specific topics
racial supremacy, theories of, 326
racial taxonomy, 101
racial violence, 97, 176, 214. *See also*
riots
Raging Rooks, 455
ragtime, 186–88. *See also* Memphis
Students
railroads, 85–87, 104–5
Randel, John, Jr., 76, 79, 80, 93
Randel plan, 79–80
Randolph, A. Philip, 212, 213, 224,
324, 396
Bayard Rustin and, 344, 378–79,
396, 419

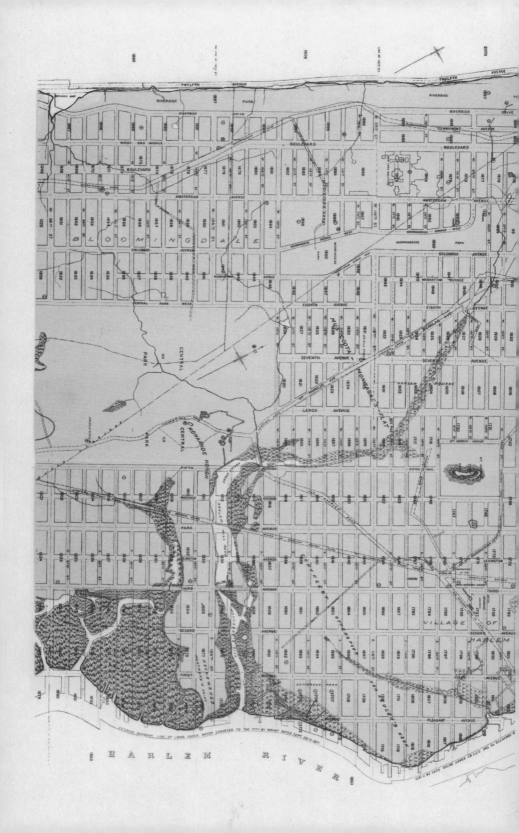